LONDON

The Virago Woman's Travel Guides

Series Editor: Ros Belford

Amsterdam
London
New York
Paris
Rome
San Francisco

forthcoming:

Athens and The Greek Islands
Great Britain

The Virago Woman's Travel Guide to

LONDON

JOSIE BARNARD

BOOK PASSAGE PRESS a division of RDR BOOKS

Berkeley, California

Published by BOOK PASSAGE PRESS, a division of RDR Books
P.O. Box 5212, Berkeley, California 94705

Printed in Hong Kong by Twin Age Limited

First published in the United Kingdom by Virago Press LTD. 1994

ISBN 1-57143-017-2
Library of Congress Catalog Card Number: 94-70038

Virago Cover Design: The Senate
U.S. Cover Design: Bonnie Smetts Design
U.S. Editor: Wendy Ann Logsdon
Editorial Associate: Deborah Dunn

CONTENTS

ACKNOWLEDGEMENTS

For Kate, Mike and Jason.

With many thanks to: Ian Anderson at Delsey Luggage and David MacDonald at the Back Shop; to Lindsay Hunt for hotels. Special thanks to (alphabetically): John Barnard, Tim Brotherton, Lisa Darnell, Kate Hibbert, Cat Ledger, Hermione Lee and Judith Murray. And thanks to Arabella Boxer, Ros Belford, Nick Campailer, Sophia Chaucard-Smith, Dodie Clarke, Tim and Tiff, Maria Glot, David Grunberg, Stephen Masterson, Ben Mathews, Jane Miles, Gay Mill, Maureen Mills, Bob Richards, Simon Rowland-Jones, Susan Schulman.

This book does not aim to be comprehensive but intends to mix sound advice, information, and considerations of a selection of women through history who have helped make London what it is today.

LONDON

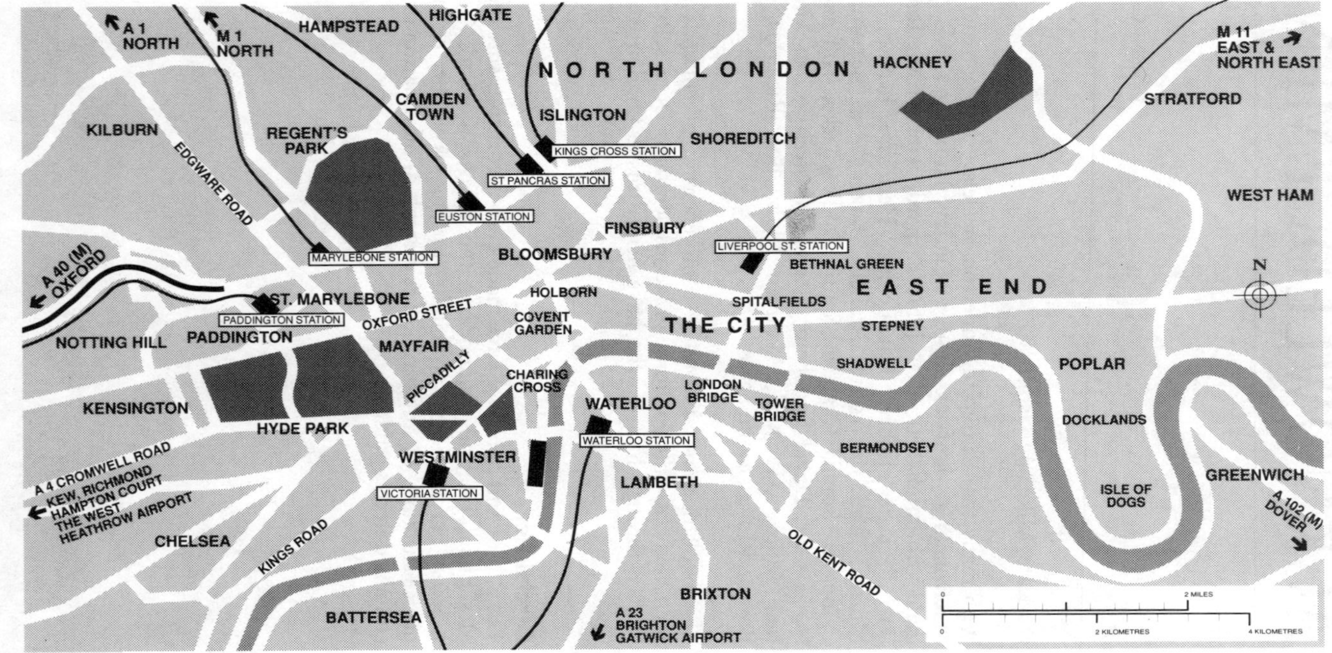

A 1 NORTH
M 1 NORTH
HAMPSTEAD
HIGHGATE
NORTH LONDON
HACKNEY
M 11 EAST & NORTH EAST
KILBURN
EDGWARE ROAD
CAMDEN TOWN
REGENT'S PARK
ISLINGTON
KINGS CROSS STATION
ST PANCRAS STATION
EUSTON STATION
SHOREDITCH
STRATFORD
WEST HAM
FINSBURY
MARYLEBONE STATION
BLOOMSBURY
LIVERPOOL ST. STATION
BETHNAL GREEN
A 40 (M) OXFORD
ST. MARYLEBONE
HOLBORN
EAST END
N
PADDINGTON STATION
OXFORD STREET
SPITALFIELDS
COVENT GARDEN
THE CITY
STEPNEY
NOTTING HILL
PADDINGTON
MAYFAIR
SHADWELL
POPLAR
PICCADILLY
CHARING CROSS
LONDON BRIDGE
KENSINGTON
WATERLOO
TOWER BRIDGE
DOCKLANDS
HYDE PARK
WATERLOO STATION
BERMONDSEY
WESTMINSTER
A 4 CROMWELL ROAD
KEW, RICHMOND
HAMPTON COURT
THE WEST
HEATHROW AIRPORT
VICTORIA STATION
LAMBETH
GREENWICH
ISLE OF DOGS
A 102 (M) DOVER
CHELSEA
KINGS ROAD
OLD KENT ROAD
BRIXTON
BATTERSEA
A 23
BRIGHTON
GATWICK AIRPORT
0
2 MILES
0
2 KILOMETRES
4 KILOMETRES

INTRODUCTION

London's a feast – indeed, there's *so* much to see and do that you might have to restrain your appetite. Just scan the skyline, and already you're spoilt for choice. In the City the grey-ribbed dome of St Paul's Cathedral encases the haunting Whispering Gallery. Nearby, the spire of St Brides rises in wedding-cake tiers above basement Roman ruins. Nelson on his column in Trafalgar Square presides over one of the finest art galleries in the world.

Whatever you choose in whatever order, make sure to give yourself enough time really to savour not only the major sights but also the joys of simple things, such as standing on Tower Bridge at dusk watching the red-glinting waters of the eddying Thames, or picnicking amidst the trees and grassland of Hampstead Heath, or eating roasted chestnuts on a crisp winter's day at the gates of the British Museum. People-watch in a Soho espresso bar and again while travelling on the Underground. There you'll see a cross-section of Londoners – from paint-spattered art student to bowler-hatted City gent to Chinatown storekeeper reading a Cantonese paper flown in from Hong Kong – all swaying in unison as the tube train hurtles on, maybe taking you to boating in Hyde Park, or perhaps to the vibrant markets of Portobello, Camden and Carnaby Street. Later, as daylight fades, Shaftesbury Avenue theatreland lights up amber, ruby and jade, and the arcing road shimmers with slow-moving black cabs and red double-decker buses of a dated curving design that gives credence to actress Bette Midler's declaration 'When it's three o'clock in New York, it's still 1938 in London'. Yet while the brollies and Burberry macs, scone cream teas and 'Gor Blimey Guv!' dialect of cabbies and market traders can conjure scenes from crackly Ealing film reels, today the Burberry macs are accessorised with Day-glo knapsacks and the market traders carry mobile phones.

In most places an old-fashioned sense of safety prevails. Your biggest day to day worry is likely to be a scattering of pickpockets who are easily deterred (see p.17). Most visitors find that London is easy to negotiate by public transport and has an overwhelmingly friendly, honest feel – although there are detractors. Points of complaint are the legendary British reserve, which can be mistaken for coolness, and the weather, which is a national talking point for two reasons. It's a neutral topic you can break the ice with; and no one knows what it's going to do next: you might see, at a bus-stop, an optimist dressed in shorts next to a pessimist with overcoat and umbrella. Use rainy days as the perfect excuse to go to the museums; make the most of outdoors London on sunny days.

London is filled with people who love their city and its history. For Bloomsbury novelist Virginia Woolf, seeking out obscure parts of London and retreading favourite paths almost amounted to an obsession. Her 5 May 1924 diary entry reads:

> London is enchanting. I step out upon a tawny coloured magic carpet, it seems, & [*sic*] get carried into beauty without raising a finger. The nights are amazing, with all the white porticoes & broad silent avenues. And people pop in & out, lightly, divertingly like rabbits; & I look down Southampton Row, wet as a seal's back or red & yellow with sunshine, & watch the omnibus going & coming, & hear the old crazy organs. One of these days I will write about London, & how it takes up the private life & carries it on, without any effort.

LONDON'S WOMEN'S HISTORY

Each era is explored in the area that best illustrates their period through a building or museum; here's how to pick a roughly chronological route through London's women's history:

Roman London, see p.131 (The City)
Medieval London, see p.133 (The City)
Tudor and Elizabethan London, see p.184 (South London)
Stuart London, see p.156 (West London)
Georgian London, see p.47 (Soho)
Victorian London, see p.210 (East End)
Wartime London, see pp.122 and 192 (Bloomsbury; Imperial War Museum)
1960s and 1970s, see p.159 (West London)
Thatcher Years, see p.90 (Westminster)

THINGS TO DO

Outdoors: take a boat ride down **The Thames** (see p.199); picnic in **Kew Gardens** (see p.204).
Free: get quite lost in the small **Sir John Soane's Museum** (see p.74) and thoroughly lost in the **British Museum** (see p.126); be careful not to overdo it at the wonderful **National** and **Tate Galleries** (see pp.82, 103).
Atmosphere: sit in a **Soho** bar on a Friday or Saturday night (see pp.267, 273); eat dim sum in **Chinatown** on a Sunday (see p.263); take a stroll in **Hyde Park** (see p.164); take a pint in a **river pub** on a sunny evening (see p.303).
For children: feed the pigeons in **Trafalgar Square** (see p.81); chat with Beefeaters at the **Tower of London** (see p.151); journey to the **Horniman Museum** (see p.359).

PRACTICALITIES

When to Go

Temperatures are generally mild, averaging the mid-60s in summer and the mid-40s in winter. May and June are the freshest, sunniest months, and they are off-season; July and August are the warmest, but thronging with tourists; September can be the best time to visit because there are fewer tourists and the weather is still mainly good; October and November are the rainiest, with occasional stunning crisp autumn days; and December and January are coldest, cloudy and, with the fortnight exception of mainly home-based Christmas cheer, they can be grim.

Women travelling with children should consider braving the London peak season for the comprehensive children's programmes that go with Easter, summer and Christmas holidays; women on a budget should, however, *avoid* peak seasons; businesswomen keen to maximise working hours should be aware that on bank holidays, over Christmas, New Year and Easter, most of London really *does* close down; and everyone should, when packing, remember some common complaints about London (by North Americans in particular): that in winter central heating tends to be inadequate (pack thermal underwear); that in summer air-conditioning is practically nonexistent (prepare to strip down to bare essentials); and that all year round weather is erratic (pack a mix-&-match selection of woollies and T-shirts plus a sturdy mac or brolly). When packing, make sure that your **luggage** leaves you independent, as a woman struggling with awkward suitcases and baggage at airports and stations is easy prey. Invest in a knapsack that converts into a carry-on, a suitcase with wheels incorporated, or – at the very least – buy a pair of strap-on wheels. Of the knapsack/carry-on manufacturers, Lowe and Karrimoor have good back systems, but Eagle Creek comes out best for making luggage that is comfortable, convertible and smart enough for metropolitan business trips. As for suitcases with wheels, the two top makes are Delsey and Samsonite, with Delsey in the lead for its extensive research into customers' needs: the Delsey handles are so comfortable they patented them; handles, wheels and structure survive test-drops from great heights and airport luggage handlers. When buying luggage bear in mind that you pay for what you get. Expect price tags of around $150 for quality that will last.

British **time** changes twice annually: at the end of March the clocks go forward by one hour to give British Summer Time (BST), and at the end of October they go back one hour to Greenwich Mean Time (GMT).

BANK HOLIDAYS

On many public holidays a lot of shops and tourist attractions stay open, but little is open for Christmas Eve, Christmas Day or New Year's Day. On all bank holidays London Transport runs a reduced bus and Underground service.
May Day Holiday, first Monday in May;
Spring Bank Holiday, last Monday in May;
Summer Bank Holiday, last Monday in August;
Christmas Day, 25 December;
Boxing Day, 26 December;
New Year's Day, 1 January;
Good Friday and Easter Monday, around beginning of April (variable).

FESTIVALS AND EVENTS

Two bizarre daily/alternate day events unique to London are: the **Ceremony of the Keys** at the Tower of London (Tower Hill Underground), a ritualised scripted locking up of the Tower beginning at 9.35 p.m. every night except Christmas and lasting half an hour (*to book, send a stamped addressed envelope to The Resident Governor, Queen's House, HM Tower of London, EC3*); and **Changing the Guard** at Buckingham Palace (St James's Park or Victoria Underground), which was once a practical shift-changing of the guards who protected the royals but is now a scarlet tunic and bearskin hat ceremony hemmed in by coach parties that is best seen from the palace gates (*times are May–July 11.30 a.m. daily and Aug–Apr 11.30 a.m. alternate days, but you should arrive early to secure a good vantage point*). For additional information or details of one-off events, contact the **London Tourist Board** at *Victoria Station Forecourt, London SW1, tel. 071 730 3488*. And below is a selection of annual dates for your diary:

January

The **January Sales** are legendary and consequently as violent as rugby scrums and often without featuring any real bargains, but nevertheless worth visiting – celebrated store sales are **Harrods** (*Knightsbridge, SW7, tel. 071 730 1234*) and **Liberty's** (*Regent Street, W1, tel. 071 734 1234*), and look in the weekly listings magazine *Time Out* for a round-up of the best of the rest.

The **Holiday on Ice** spectacular of professional ice-skaters lavishly costumed according to an annual theme at Wembley Arena has become a traditional New Year's family treat since it started in 1955 (*starts at end of Jan and runs through Feb, tickets from £6–£13, tel. 081 900 1234*).

February

For the **Chinese New Year** celebrations, giant dragons undulate through lantern-strung Gerrard and Lisle Streets (WC2) 'eating' cabbages and coins donated by local restaurants (*celebrations on the first Sunday after the Chinese New Year 11 a.m.–5 p.m., tel. Chinatown Chinese Association to confirm on 071 437 5256*) – children love it; watch out for pickpockets.

March

The highly acclaimed **London Lesbian and Gay Film Festival** at the National Film Theatre and selected venues, which programmes a wide range of films from low-budget avant-garde video art to nearly mainstream, is the largest festival of its kind in the world, so it can get booked up – phone ahead for programme details and ticket availability (*tel. 071 928 3232 or 071 633 0274 for recorded information*).

The **Soho Pancake Day Race** is an eggy-floury mess of people fighting down Carnaby Street with flailing frying pans from noon on Shrove Tuesday (*last day before Lent; tel. 071 287 0907 if you want to join in*).

The rather more serious **Ideal Home Exhibition** (mid-March to April) is a massive, several-floored display of the latest interior design ideas and energy-saving gadgets that costs £6 for adults, £3 for children and the price of an energy-building lunch from the pleasant, if institutionalised, piazza (*at the Earls Court Exhibition Centre, SW5, tel. 071 222 9341*).

April

Every **April Fool's Day** (*first day of April*) practical jokers are, by tradition, given free rein to 'April Fool' until noon: national papers and TV news programmes run apparently serious joke items, perhaps most famously the convincing 'spaghetti tree harvest' story; children in playgrounds give each other a 'pinch and a punch for the first of the month', then a retaliatory 'nip and a kick for being so quick'.

At the **London Marathon** you'll see celebrities running beside Londoners in jogging shorts and crazy outfits to raise money for charity before collapsing into health-restoring silver foil bags with a Mars bar at the end of the 26.2-mile race from Greenwich Park to Westminster Bridge via Victoria Embankment and St James's Park (*takes place mid-April starting 9.30 a.m., tel. 081 948 7935 to confirm*).

May

The celebrated four-day Horticultural Society plant and garden accessories extravaganza called the **Chelsea Flower Show** features an Advice Bureau for anyone with genuine gardening questions and a lot of society ladies on exclusive members-only days (*held in the Royal Hospital Grounds, tel. 071 828 1744 to check which days are open to the public, tickets £10, children under five and dogs not admitted*).

June

See *Time Out* magazine listings for details of the medley of London-based **Gay Pride** events through the last two weeks in June, culminating in a march on Saturday and attracting thousands from all over the country.

Epsom Racecourse's **Derby Day** (*first Wednesday in June*), which was made infamous when suffragette Emily Wilding Davison threw herself in front of the king's horse and died as a result of her wounds, is advertised as one of the world's greatest horse races of three-year-old colts and fillies, but you must book well in advance (*tickets £7–£24, available from January from The Secretary, Racecourse Paddock, Epsom, Surrey, tel. 0372 726311, funfair on Epsom Downs*).

The **Royal Academy Summer Exhibition** gives amateurs a first chance to have their works hung beside those of celebrated living artists – there's often criticism that the judges select only mediocre still-lifes and wishy-washy watercolour landscapes; the title 'RA' beside Academy graduates' names establishes instant kudos: judge for yourself and enjoy overhearing society gossip as you meander mellowly with a glass of wine (*at the Royal Academy, Burlington House, Piccadilly, for about two and a half months, tel. 071 439 7438, admission £3.60 adults to £1.80 children*).

Royal Ascot at Ascot Racecourse for three days is more about the attendees than the race: for months beforehand high-society ladies panic about getting the right *hat* for the occasion; every day the Queen and her family drive over from Windsor in open-top carriages (*don't expect to get near the Royal Enclosure and book well in advance by writing to The Secretary, Grand Stand, Ascot, Berkshire, tel. 0344 22211*).

Wimbledon Lawn Tennis Championships is another terribly English champagne-and-strawberries plus fancy-straw-hats occasion and not much more accessible, but you can queue for returns on the day of the match you want to see, or you can watch it on telly (*otherwise send an SAE the previous Sept–Dec for a ticket by ballot to All England Club, PO Box 98, Church Road, SW19, tel. 081 944 1066*).

July

The four-day **Hampton Court Palace International Flower Show** is more easily enjoyable than the Chelsea Flower Show and in a more exciting location (*aquatics section and musical entertainment; Hampton Court Palace, East Molesey; tel. the Organiser's Office on 081 977 0050 for details*).

August

The **Notting Hill Carnival** is difficult to travel to and from, as roads and nearby Underground stations get jammed with the thousands of revellers who enjoy colourful carnival floats in the day and dance to reggae music till the small hours despite heavy police presence sparked by some carnival violence in the early 1980s (*last Sunday and Monday in August around North Kensington between Ladbroke Grove, Notting Hill and Westbourne Grove Undergrounds, tel. 081 964 0544*).

At the **Hampstead Heath Fair** on the August Bank Holiday weekend, eat candyfloss and hot dogs then wish you hadn't on dodgems, big wheels and Wurlitzers.

September

The **Great River Race** is a perfect excuse to drink early-morning Pimms by the Thames while watching Chinese dragonboats, Hawaiian war canoes and Viking longboats compete in the UK Traditional Boat Championships and then go to Richmond Park with your children for a picnic afterwards – or if you haven't the stomach for Pimms in the morning, catch the end of the race and go to Greenwich Palace (*beginning of September; race starts 9.30 a.m. below Ham House, Richmond and finishes at Greenwich Pier at around 1 p.m.*).

October

While infant schools all over England sell cans of baked beans and pineapple rings from wheatsheaf-laden tables to celebrate, tradition has it, the summer harvest, London's famed cockney Pearly Kings and Queens – complete with eccentric button-covered outfits – have their own special **Costermongers' Pearly Harvest Festival** at St Martin-in-the-Fields (*Trafalgar Square, first Sunday of October*), where you can buy fresh veg from costermongers shouting cockney rhyming slang in yer 'boat race' (face).

November

Bonfire Night celebrates the failure of Catholic Guy Fawkes's 1605 attempt to blow up James I in his Protestant Parliament with bonfires burning second-hand-overcoat-cloaked newspaper and wood effigies of Fawkes, fireworks displays, lurid red toffee-apples and gingerbread men either on 5 November or on the nearest weekend in parks and private gardens all over London (*check the Evening Standard that day, Time Out magazine that week, or phone the LTB for public venue details*).

Only pre-1905 cars can enter the Benson and Hedges–RAC London to Brighton **Veteran Car Run** (*on the first Sunday of November*), which was established in 1896 when the law stating that cars must be heralded by a flag-bearing running man was abolished – 8–9 a.m. start from Hyde Park Corner (W1) for the glinting spectacle of vintage radiator caps and bewhiskered drivers (*tel. 0753 681736*).

Pomp and ceremony surrounds **The Lord Mayor's Show** on the second Saturday in November, when the new Lord Mayor rides in a gilded coach with colourful floats and military bands through the City of London to be sworn in at the Law Courts at 11.50 a.m. (*arrive 30 minutes early for a good view; tel. 071 606 3030 for information*).

See a mixture of new films, premières, young film-makers' first breaks and avant-garde films gathered under theme banners at the fêted **London Film Festival** (*National Film Theatre, tel. 071 928 3232 or 071 633 0274 for recorded information*).

December

Bond Street (W1), Oxford Street (W1), Jermyn Street (SW1) and Regent Street (W1) are strung with **Christmas Lights** from mid-November, and the annual gift of a towering **Christmas Tree** in thanks for British help in World War II from Norway goes up in Trafalgar Square on 3 December.

Cost of Living

Note that hotel accommodation and alcohol take big whacks out of budgets, especially with the exchange rate (at the time of writing) at .66 pence (sterling) to the dollar. It is easy to mistake the numerical value of British pounds for dollars while travelling, so use caution when dealing with currency.

A budget day = £46

Night in a hostel, or in a cheap hotel, £20.
Tea and toast café breakfast £1, and £5 for lunch.
One bus, one taxi, £8.
Dinner in a cheap restaurant, £10.
A couple of drinks in a basic bar, £3.

An average day = £111

Room with bath, £60.
Breakfast in café, £5.
One day's public transport (3 tube/bus journeys and one cab), £10.
Lunch in café, £8.
Dinner in mid-priced restaurant, £20.
Drinks in a pleasant café or bar, £8.

A luxury day = £322
Room in a 4* hotel, £200.
Breakfast in hotel or upmarket café, £10.
Day's public transport (2 tube/bus journeys, 2 cabs), £17.
Lunch in a grill, £15.
Dinner in upmarket restaurant, £60.
Drinks in classy café or bar, £20.

Entertainment
Art galleries/museums average £6.
Clubs start at £3.50 but average £10.
Entertainment, including theatre and concerts, starts at £5 for alternative events and can go up to over £100 for exclusive mainstream tickets.

Information

Get the ***A–Z***, which has been Londoners' Bible since one Phyllis Pearsall personally delivered copies of the first books on borrowed handbarrows in 1936 (see Recommended Books). The ***A–Z*** – or, in full, the *London A–Z Street Atlas* (pub. Geographers' A–Z Map Company) – is available in fold-out-map or book form priced around £4 from decent bookshops, train station bookstalls and most newsagents (the book versions are best if you're walking around the streets, as they're easy to dip in and out of inconspicuously; the fold out maps give a sense of perspective). Free maps of London are generally inadequate. London's specialist map and travel shop is **Stanfords** (*12–14 Long Acre, WC2*) or, for beautiful surroundings and travel guides cleverly stacked next to relevant fiction, go to **Daunts** (*83 Marylebone High Street, W1*). The **London Tourist Board** can help you with all aspects of your stay, from accommodation through restaurants to sightseeing (*tel. 071 730 3488*); for lots of leaflets plus bus and tube maps, go in person (five main LTB centres are: in **Harrods,** *Basement Banking Hall, Harrods, Knightsbridge, SW7, tel. 071 730 1234, open 9 a.m.–6 p.m. Mon–Sat*; **Heathrow Terminals 1, 2, 3,** *Underground Station Concourse, Heathrow Airport, open 8 a.m.–4.30 p.m. daily;* **Liverpool Street,** *Underground Station, EC2, open 9 a.m.–4 p.m. Mon–Sat, 8.30 a.m.–3.30 p.m. Sun*; **Selfridges,** *Basement Services Arcade, Selfridges, Oxford Street, W1, tel. 071 629 1234, open 9.30 a.m.–6 p.m. Mon–Wed, Fri, Sat, 10 a.m.–8 p.m. Thur*; **Victoria Station Forecourt,** *Victoria Station, tel. 071 730 3488, open 8 a.m.–7 p.m. Mon–Sat, 8 a.m.–4 p.m. Sun*).

The Press

The daily ***Evening Standard*** does have snippets of national and international news, but it's really about **London** – buy it early on in your stay to find out where to eat, what to see and who's doing what with whom at which glitterati events, and on Fridays buy it for the free accompanying glossy magazine. As for the national tabloids, if you want tiny amounts of heavily anti-Labour Party news with astoundingly unbelievable SHOCK HORROR headlines, buy the nation's bestselling paper, the extremely right-wing *Sun*, which is most famous for its coy, busty pin-up 'Page Three' girls. Some say the *Sun*'s nearest rival, the tabloid ***Daily Mirror***, risks losing its identity since trying to shake off its leftish-wing image. The ***Daily Express*** and the ***Daily Mail*** manage to be neither tabloid (downmarket) nor 'quality' but in-between, decently informed, fairly easy reads. The only left-of-centre quality broadsheet is the ***Guardian***, which boasts good news coverage and, every Monday, Tuesday, Wednesday and Friday, a 'Women's Page'. The ***Independent*** produces some smart young journalists; the Saturday edition is especially full of sharp writing and meaty articles. Despite several revamps, ***The Times*** loses out on several readerships for being perceived as either duller than the popular *Daily Mail* or less challenging than the *Guardian* and the *Independent*, although the ability to complete the Cryptic Crossword remains, oddly, accepted proof of high intelligence. The right-wing ***Daily Telegraph*** launched a 1980s spirited fight to attract a younger audience. The pink ***Financial Times*** is not just an essential buy for anyone working in the finance world, but covers general news and has good arts pages.

A long Sunday breakfast over the papers and colour supplements is a British tradition, and many people buy a selection. Of the Sunday tabloids, the biggest seller is the ***News of the World***, but the most extraordinary is the ***Sunday Sport***, which is famous for social-crisis headlines such as 'My Wife's Boobs Are So Big She Can't Do The Ironing'. The ***Sunday Express*** is a respected and very readable tabloid, as is the ***Mail on Sunday***, which is popular with readers of quality broadsheets for the accompanying gossipy *You* magazine. The quality Sunday broadsheets continue to dither over the balance appropriate for relaxing weekend readers: war gore, glitzy media star features, serious arts reviews and escapist glossy travel sections. The issue-based ***Sunday Times*** champions right-wing views, constructs elaborate exclusive special offers designed for an upmarket readership (such as five-star chef masterclasses), and recently relaunched the accompanying magazine, 'The Culture'. Meanwhile the ***Observer***, after a 1993 takeover by the *Guardian*, remains a solid mix of news and arts coverage. The ***Sunday Telegraph*** is better than the weekday version and good on arts. The biggest strength of the ***Independent on Sunday*** is that it has headhunted lots of other papers' best writers; the news is adequate – the real effort goes into the arts section.

Of the weekly magazines, the one that will give you a couple of pages of local newsy editorial plus comprehensive listings of London's culture, entertainment, nightlife and events – featuring special 'Children' and 'Gay' sections (although information specifically for lesbians is often skimpy) – is ***Time Out***. The free ***Where London*** (available at most mid- to high-priced hotels) caters mainly for tourists and business travellers, offering listings and features. The satirical and often anti-women, anti-gay ***Private Eye*** cocks snooks at the news, the Establishment and members of London's glitterati (read the *Evening Standard* for a few days and you'll be able to match up real people with the *Eye*'s thinly disguised versions). ***i-D*** is a proudly pretentious purveyor of street culture; here, along with eccentric fashion shoots, you'll find high-trend club and shop information. ***Hello!*** magazine is treated by swish 'Sloanes' as a snapshot album of our friends the royal family, and a coolly ironical media set buy it out of an odd mixture of wry humour and reverent voyeurism. The self-proclaimed 'Britain's Best Black Newspaper' is ***The Voice***, available in most big newsagents and almost all newsagents in Brixton, where it is printed.

Free weeklies such as ***Ms London*** and ***Girl About Town*** (distributed from Monday at most big Underground stations) feature lots of job ads plus occasionally interesting features aimed at late-teen trainees and temps. Matt colour magazines with titles like ***Woman's Own*** and ***Woman*** aim articles and features plus knitting/sewing patterns at thirty-to-forty-year-old professional family women. Glossies like ***Company, She, Elle, Marie Claire*** and ***Cosmopolitan*** present politics/issues, fashion spreads, interviews and reviews.

Glossies along the lines of ***Tatler, Harpers and Queen*** and, to a lesser extent, ***Vogue*** target high society with fashion spreads and lots of gossip, and appeal to a range of readers from students splashing out to women who enjoy the escapist voyeurism of the Deb Balls and Ascot party photos. ***The Lady***, as the title suggests, is an ancient institution – women from all walks of life turn to the back for reliable babysitting services, and the genteel publication still advises women and Ladies from the Counties on tricky topics such as shopping in London. Some over-fifties, it's said, use *The Lady* as an unofficial Lonely Hearts column – turn to carefully worded ads for housekeepers, etc.

In November 1992 the American feminist magazine ***Ms.*** was launched in Britain. The number of male pin-up and feature magazines for 'sensual, intelligent' women such as ***For Her*** increases. British mothers may strive in vain to keep young teenage daughters away from the cosmetics tips mixed in with green consciousness of magazines with titles like *Mizz* and *Shout*.

The lesbian community is served by newspapers such as *Gay*

Times, Capital Gay and ***Pink Paper*** (available free at cafés including First Out and the Angel Café, see Eating and Drinking). A welcome recent addition that may or may not stay the course is the by-lesbians-for-lesbians ***Shebang*** magazine, which is glam dyke with political features and a 'listings and lines' section at the back. Feminist and lesbian comic strip lovers rejoice in ***Fanny***, which – funds permitting – publishes one or two Fanny comic books a year with titles including 'Immaculate Deception' and 'Voyeuse' (available at **Gosh!**, Museum Street WC1).

Women's and Lesbian Information

London's key lesbian information sources are the bars and cafés including **First Out, Angel Café, Village Bar** and, on a Monday night, the **Drill Hall Arts Centre** (see Eating and Drinking), where you can pick up flyers, lesbian and gay publications, and chat to the staff if they're not too busy. The **Lesbian Line** (*071 251 6911*) operates 7 p.m.–10 p.m. Mon–Thur and 2 p.m.–10 p.m. Fri, and offers information, advice and counselling. If you can get through, the volunteer staff on the always busy 24-hour **Gay and Lesbian Switchboard** (*071 837 7324*) will do their utmost to help with a wide range of questions and information requests, including where's trendy to go on a Friday night, appropriate political resource organisations, services from tattooing to bookshops and sympathetic doctors – or if you just want to talk, they'll listen.

For lesbian and feminist information, go to the bookshops **Silver Moon** and **Gay's the Word** (see Shopping) and to resource centres including the Wesley House **London Women's Centre** (listed under Women and Feminism in Practicalities).

Foreign Publications

For a good selection of foreign newspapers, go to the two newsagents on Old Compton Street (W1) in Soho. For a smaller selection that's often more recent, go to the main Piccadilly Circus branch of Tower Records (W1). For all the Irish papers, go to the newsagent at the Camden Town Underground end of Parkway, NW1.

Communications

Post Most post offices are open Mon–Fri 9 a.m.–5.30 p.m. and Sat 9 a.m.–1 p.m. The Trafalgar Square Post Office is open Mon–Sat 8 a.m.–8 p.m., and it's here that you should have Poste Restante mail sent: envelopes should be addressed to you 'Poste Restante, Trafalgar Square Post Office, 24–28 King William IV St,

London WC2N 4DL (*tel. 071 930 9580*); poste restante mail will be kept for one month if it comes from abroad. Buy stamps at post offices and at newsagents or shops displaying the red Post Office logo. Stamps for postcards and letters sent within the EC cost around 20 pence. Second-class post can take up to four days; and first-class should take no more than two days and may arrive within twenty-four hours). International airmail postcards and aerograms (prestamped airmail letters destined anywhere in the world) cost around 40 pence. Airmail takes four to seven days to get to, for example, Australia, and although surface mail is cheaper, it can take up to three months to arrive. For parcel charges and regulations, pick up a free pamphlet at any post office.

Faxing Almost all hotels offer faxing services, usually limited to Mon–Fri 9.30 a.m.–5.30 p.m. office hours. Look under 'Facsimile Bureaux' in the Yellow Pages, or choose from one of these three well-located fax offices: **1, 2, 3 Express Fax Service,** *67 Chancery Lane, WC2, tel. 071 404 5464;* **Chesham Executive Centre,** *150 Regent Street, W1, tel. 071 439 6288;* **Covent Garden Fax and Telex Bureau,** *1 Russell Chambers, The Plaza, WC2, tel. 071 379 4368.*

Telephones You realise that the old-fashioned red telephone box is nearly extinct when you see it wistfully celebrated on postcards. The replacement blue-and-grey cabins display a dancing figure tooting a horn on the door. This is the British Telecom motif. You'll also see snazzy blue Mercury booths, which won't take money, only Mercury phonecards (available at newsagents carrying the blue lightning Mercury motif); however, Mercury calls work out about 20 per cent cheaper than British Telecom calls. British Telecom, or 'BT' have new booths with digital instruction panels which tell you when to put your money in and how much; in the old-fashioned phone boxes, don't put any money in until your call has been answered, then feed in your 10ps like crazy, especially if you're interrupted by a *beep beep*, which means if you don't you'll be cut off any minute; finally, try always to keep a BT phonecard handy (available at newsagents including John Menzies and WH Smith) so you can use the phones on Underground stations. The noises to listen for are *brrrr brrrr* when the phone you're calling is ringing, a squeakier, broken *beep-beep–beep-beep* if it's engaged, and a depressing continuous *boop-boop-boop* if the number is unobtainable.

Now for the numbers themselves. London numbers have either an 071 prefix for Central London or 081 for beyond Central London plus the suburbs (phone users have been known to pay thousands of pounds to change an 081 number to 071). If you're calling an 071 number within an 071 area, omit the 071. If you're calling from outside England, omit the first '0' and start with just 71 or 81. Hotel phones are the most expensive, phone booths are cheaper, and domestic phones slightly cheaper again, but none is fixed price for local calls – the cost is per unit used (that is, the more you speak, the more you pay). Calls are most expensive weekday mornings; so-called 'cheap rate' operates evenings and all day Saturday and Sunday. For international calls, dial the international code (010), then the country code, then the city code. BT publishes a free pamphlet with instructions, code and price details (available at tourist offices and most hotels).

Media

Television

There are four television channels: BBC1, BBC2, ITV and Channel 4. Satellite TV, for which users must have a satellite dish and pay subscription, features MTV (non-stop pop music) and is dominated by Sky, which has a news, sport and movie channel.

The three main British soap operas give an idea of the programming differences between the four TV channels: BBC1's *EastEnders*, starring wide boys, wide girls, an out homosexual and occasional race issues, is mass-market with a conscience; the once downmarket, now cult classic Manchester-based *Coronation Street* – featuring the indomitable Rover's Return barmaid Bet Lynch – is on the largely populist, occasionally seriously journalistic ITV; the soap that serves a Molotov cocktail of social issues including rape and domestic violence in Liverpool, *Brookside*, is on the relatively new 'alternative' Channel 4; and finally, BBC2 is the 'cultural channel', so no soaps here but lots of Open University courses, news programmes including the well-worth-watching *Newsnight* and the widely respected arts *Late Show*.

The introduction of satellite and cable television, plus the auctioning of ITV franchises and a major shake-up at the BBC, threaten the long-prized quality of British television. Satellite channel Sky shows mainstream films and sport in most hotels, and the pop music MTV cable station is shown in bars that are or aspire to be trendy; the mainly admirable London Weekend Television takes over ITV on weekends; through the week you get Carlton, which has been accused of Machiavellian tactics and ruthless ratings-counting. The licence fees paid by television owners ensure – at least for the time being – the luxury of no adverts on BBC1 or BBC2.

To find out what's on for a week, either buy the *Radio Times* and the *TV Times* or economy-buy *Time Out*. National and local papers detail each day's viewing.

Children are served by early-evening weekday programmes which also satisfy adults, partly because they've been running so long that they inspire dewy-eyed reminiscences – for example, *Blue Peter* (BBC1), a national institution famous for DIY gift demonstrations that end with the instruction 'cover in sticky-backed plastic', and the always fascinatingly unfashionable music show *Top of the Pops* (BBC1). There's usually a hyped new 'youth' programme (i.e. *The Word*) characterised by fast cuts and lots of pop interviews by dynamically trendy 'youth' presenters. Violent or sexually explicit programmes are banned before 9 p.m.

Breakfast television on BBC1 and ITV is an easy-viewing mixture of fashion, lycra exercise slots and light news. Women comedians who regularly have their own shows on BBC2 include politically incisive and often off-the-wall Dawn French and Jennifer Saunders (known together as French and Saunders), wry social commentator Victoria Wood and fast one-liner Josie Lawrence.

For local news, tune in early evenings to tabloidy programmes with names like *London Tonight* (ITV) and later in the evening for more serious versions, such as the *London Programme* (ITV). For national news, tune into BBC1 at 1 p.m., 6 p.m. and 9 p.m.

Radio

London's BBC radio stations share the advantages of BBC TV: the licence fee makes no ads necessary and allows a certain amount of freedom from commercial pressures, although Conservative Party accusations of left-wing bias have resulted in incidences of censorship. The station that best satisfies 'the Beeb's' historic educate, entertain, inform remit is Radio 4.

For comprehensive radio listings see the *Radio Times* and the daily newspapers; the back of *Time Out* has only selected reviews.

BBC Radio 1 (*275m/1089kHz, MW; 98.8mHz, FM*) plays mainstream chart pop music mixed with some indie music, human-interest phone-ins and competitions with pop-related prizes. **BBC Radio 2** (*89.2mHz, FM*) plays middle-of-the-road music for an over-forty-five market, then broadcasts quizzes for evenings. **BBC Radio 3** (*247m/1215kHz, MW; 91.3mHz, FM*) is a classical music station that's praised for achieving quality over listening figures. A short route to discovering a variety of British obsessions is to listen to **Radio 4**, which starts predawn with the hypnotic 'Shipping Forecast', features the legendary 'Woman's Hour', the fascinating 'Gardeners' Question Time', plus 'The Archers' – the soap drama that was founded in the 1950s to inform Britain's farmers about agricultural problems and solutions and is now much more about adultery, housing shortages and *in vitro* fertilisation in not-so-rural

Ambridge – and, through each day, you'll hear news, story readings, comic talk-shows and plays. From March 1994 there will be a BBC 24 hour news and sport station (*433m/693kHz, 330m/909kHz, MW*), but for local news, community programmes and entertainment listings, tune into GLR (*94.9FM*), the local BBC station for London, who pride themselves on providing programming for an 'intelligent' audience.

Pirate stations appear and disappear rapidly (just twiddle the dial to find current ones) and as licences are handed out, pirates become mainstream – notably **Kiss FM** (*100mHz, FM*), which churns out dance music and pop interviews. Other independents include **Jazz FM** (*102.2mHz, MW*), which plays mainly easy-listening jazz, the popular populist **Classic FM** (*100.9 FM*), **Capital FM** (*95.8mHz, FM*), which mixes current pop hits with local London news twenty-four hours a day and runs a Flatshare line plus the Capital Help Line, and **Virgin 1215 FM** (*1197, 1215, MW*), a grown-ups' rock music station.

Language

It could be said that London literally has a language of its own: cockney rhyming slang. But while you can simply ask the teasing cabbie or East End market trader for translations of 'take a butcher's' (look), 'trouble and strife' (wife), 'pork pies' (lies) and 'Rosie Lee' (tea), in all sorts of situations you'll encounter subtleties of accent, nuance and pronunciation that can get you into trouble whether you're from Toronto, Toowoomba, Texas or Taunton. 'Beauchamp', for example, is pronounced 'Beecham', 'Berkeley' is 'Bark-lee' and if you see 'Cholmondley' or 'Featherstonehaugh' you risk getting a pitying glance or even outright laughter if you say anything other than 'Chumley' and 'Fanshaw' respectively. As for regional accents, Londoners will declare complete lack of prejudice, then ask a Mancunian (someone from Manchester) if they are from Scotland and say they hear it's lovely up there but of course they could never themselves live north of the Watford Gap (just north of London). Other than 'proper' English accents, only upper-class Scottish and Irish accents are acceptable in, for example, the upper echelons of the City, but amongst the traders on the Stock Exchange floor broad accents from cockney to Liverpool's 'Scouse' are positively promotion-enhancing. With a foreign accent you can get away with more in the workplace because colleagues can't so easily make class assumptions; tourist Canadians and Americans, New Zealanders and Australians can assume stereotypical Yankee/Aussie brashness and (1) be forgiven, (2) achieve desired advantages including, for example, queue-jumping. Below are listed some commonly confusing terms:

bobby	local policeman, traditionally on a bike
to book	to reserve
the box	TV
brolly	umbrella
cheerio	goodbye
cheers	thanks and 'here's to you'
coppers	pennies
court shoes	women's pumps
dosh	cash
fiver	five-pound note
flat	apartment
ground floor	first floor (and so on up the building)
Hoover	vacuum cleaner
jam	jelly
jelly	Jell–O
kip/forty winks	brief sleep
lavatory/toilet/loo	restroom
mad	crazy (not angry)
nick	steal
pavement	sidewalk
pissed/plastered	drunk
pumps/plimsolls	trainers
queue	line
quid	pound
rubber	eraser (not contraceptive)
tube/Underground	London Subway
Sloane/Sloane Ranger	someone given to saying 'ya' and wearing a Barbour who probably lives near Sloane Street
snogging/necking	sucking face, or kissing
sorry	substitute for 'excuse me' (& apology)
to take the piss out of	to poke fun at
tosh/rubbish	nonsense
wellies	rubber boots

Police and Crime

What *do* British policemen keep in their helmets? One rush-hour morning at Goodge Street Underground station, a young woman was stung by a bee and surprised to see a policeman dash over and produce from his helmet … a basic first-aid kit. Not all policemen and women carry such handy emergency measures, but most will do their very best to help with problems from getting lost to having bags snatched.

London's crime figures are not the highest in the country. Nottingham and Newcastle came top in the 1991 official league table, while the Metropolitan area came only seventh. Reported rapes in the Metropolitan area April 1991 to March 1992 totalled 1,176, a figure that is substantially less than half the number of rapes reported in New York. Of 'violence against the person' crimes in 1991, only 17 per cent in the Metropolitan area involved a weapon. The crimes Londoners and visitors alike should watch out for are **bag-snatching** and **pickpocketing**, both of which are generally non-violent but highly professional rackets. The in-vogue scams change frequently, but some constants include: in cafés, kicking a bag that has been left on the floor over to an accomplice who casually picks it up and walks away (hold your bag or hook it over your knee); slicing a Stanley blade through the bottom of bag/knapsack and removing desired items (carry your bag where you can see it); and thirdly, on the streets in gangs, one does the three-card trick, one 'stooges' (i.e. puts money on the winning card to attract the punters) while two or three 'dippers' (pickpockets) take their pick of wallets and purses from the curious crowd. If 'dippers' are trawling a particular Underground station, staff will usually chalk a warning on to the blackboard by the escalators.

There's no need to become overworried and spoil your holiday, but do take **sensible precautions**. Metropolitan Police Crime Prevention Officer Gill Smith suggests that bum-bags are better than knapsacks because they can be hidden under clothes; she suggests that handbags should be held in the crook of your arm or hung over your shoulder under your coat but *never* across your body, as the bag-snatcher may then pull you down and injure you as they try to take the bag. Flashy handbags attract attention. If you have expensive things to carry round, perhaps try a grubby plastic carrier bag instead. Better still, Gill Smith suggests that you never keep anything in your bag that you'd fight for – objects of sentimental value, for example. She advises that you hand over your bag immediately (especially in the unlikely event of a weapon being involved). She suggests that if you keep your keys and some loose change in your pocket, then at least you might not have to hand these over too, but she says *don't* keep a separate wad of 'mugger's money' – if your assailant discovers you've kept money back, he or she could become violent.

All sorts of alarms and sprays are on the market, each with problems. The sprays can be taken from you and used against you (note – Mace is illegal in Britain). The alarms are more often than not mistaken for car alarms and ignored, so although the alarm is still useful (it might surprise the potential attacker long enough for you to get away), Gill Smith advises shouting as a good alternative. 'Help' is generally less effective than 'Fire', but shout anything at all that might attract attention. Ideally, of course, try not to get into a threatening situation in the first place. Keep to well-lit roads, preferably the middle of them (that's assuming there's not much traffic, of course). If the route from the Underground station looks unnerving, get the station master to help you order a cab. To avoid fumbling in your bag on the street, and so becoming an easy target, get your keys out while you're on the train. Always be aware of what's going on around you (personal stereos while jogging or on trains, for example, are a very bad idea if you're alone); trust your instincts (if you don't like the look of someone, don't worry about offending them – change carriages). Finally – and perhaps most important, Gill Smith says – be confident. Interviews with offenders in prison show clearly that those who look like victims are more likely to be chosen as victims. Stride out, for example, in flat shoes with trousers, or in a skirt that allows for easy movement. Gill Smith thinks self-defence classes are probably a bad idea (they may encourage a false sense of security, given that in the event you might forget the appropriate moves and simply freeze), but she encourages any activity that will enhance self-esteem. A soft martial art like t'ai chi will improve co-ordination and alertness, but if the thought of doing anything sporty fills you with horror, Gill Smith says – believe it or not – take up gardening or the flower-arranging course you've been putting off – if it makes you feel better about yourself, she says, then do it. The extra confidence will be evident on the streets.

If something is lost or stolen, report it to the police immediately. This is important for insurance purposes (companies will want a police statement as proof), in case someone does return it, and so that the police can monitor trends. Phone **directory inquiries** on **142** to find out your nearest station, which will be marked by a blue light. In the case of **emergency**, dial **999**.

It is illegal to smoke anywhere on the Underground, and if you are under sixteen. Anyone under eighteen cannot drive or be sold alcohol in pubs or off-licences. For advice on civil law – for example, consumer problems or traffic offences – contact the **Mary Ward Legal Centre** (*42 Queen Square, WC1, tel. Legal 071 881 7009, Financial 071 831 7079*). If the Mary Ward Legal Centre cannot deal with your query, they will refer you to an organisation that can. The **Citizen's Advice Bureau** (*contact Greater London Office for local branch details, 136–144 City Road, EC1, tel. 071 251 2000; open 9.30 a.m.–5 p.m. Mon–Fri*) is overworked and underfunded but will give free advice on legal, financial and personal matters.

If you are the victim of a **sex crime**, phone 999 or go to the nearest police station if you decide to report it to the police (see on), and/or contact the London Rape Crisis Centre for support, advice and counselling.

Women Against Rape (*King's Cross Women's Centre, 71 Tonbridge Street, WC1H 9DZ, tel. 071 837 7509*) offers counselling, legal advice and support for women who have been raped or sexually assaulted, and it is a campaigning organisation. If the answering machine is on, staff will do their best to get back to you as soon as possible.

London Rape Crisis Centre (*PO Box 69, London WC1X 9NJ, tel. 071 837 1600 24 hours or 071 278 3956 office hours*) will accompany you to the police, courts, doctors and abortion/VD clinics. Below is some of the centre's advice:

WHAT TO DO IF YOU ARE SEXUALLY ASSAULTED OR RAPED

If you decide to report to the police –

- Report to the police as soon as possible – delay may go against your case.
- If at all possible, tell someone what has happened as soon as you can – a witness to your distress and an early complaint will help.
- Do not wash, tidy yourself or change clothing because you may destroy valuable evidence.
- Do not take any drugs or alcohol.
- Call a friend or the Rape Crisis Centre so that someone can give you support during police and medical procedures.
- Take a change of warm clothing with you – the police may keep some of your original clothing for tests and evidence.
- Making notes about the rape may help you when you give your statement, but don't worry if you can't do this. Important things to remember are the sequence of events, details, and what was said. There is no reason why you should talk to any police officer except the one in charge of your case.

Medical examination, internal and external

- You can ask for your own GP or a woman doctor, if you prefer. The sole purpose of this examination is to collect medical evidence of rape or sexual assault.
- You may be asked to look at mug shots, accompany the police to the scene of the crime, or identify your assailant/s.
- You can ask for your name not to be read out in court.
- If you feel you are not being treated well, ask to see the officer in charge of the station.
- Whether or not you report to the police – talk to someone about what has happened – you need a friend at this time.
- See a doctor to check for: VD, AIDS, pregnancy and possible injury.

Sexual Harassment

'Cor! I'd like to be *your* bicycle seat' is the archetypal building-site worker's comment yelled from scaffolding, but public harassment of this sort is infrequent and usually affable. There may be a few unnecessary graspings of your hand as change is passed to you by leering men in takeaway sandwich cafés. Avoid King's Cross on your own at night, when you may be kerb-crawled by someone mistaking you for a prostitute. In Mayfair, if you're alone in a bar, the management may try to hustle you out under the assumption that you are a high-class prostitute. Two women publicly demonstrating the affection of lovers will be dealt with sharply in many pubs and restaurants, with either ejection or foul looks; on the streets, the obvious embarrassment of passers-by is almost inevitable – perhaps with the exception of the centre of Brixton and on the Hackney–Islington border. Businesswomen used to being treated with the utmost respect might be surprised how many men think it's OK to call women 'dear' and 'love', unaware that they are raising hackles.

Health and Sex

Former Prime Minister Margaret Thatcher put the thumbscrews on the once globally envied NHS (National Health Service) in the 1980s, and today – although free health care, including contraception, is still available, and the public NHS compares favourably in terms of expertise and service with the private health sector – doctors' waiting lists can be long, and if you have to go to casualty, take a flask, sandwiches and a good book.

If you have a **minor illness**, note that the staff behind the prescriptions counters are generally better informed than, say, their counterparts in Canada, and may be able to give you advice and sell you appropriate medication on the spot.

LATE-NIGHT CHEMISTS

Bliss Chemist
5 Marble Arch, W1, tel. 071 723 6116; open 9 a.m.–midnight daily.

Boots
44–46 Regent Street, W1, tel. 081 734 6126; open 8.30 a.m.–8.30 p.m. Mon–Sat; noon–6 p.m. Sun.

Boots
75 Queensway, W2, tel. 071 229 9266; open 9 a.m.– 10 p.m. Mon–Sat.

To call an ambulance in an **emergency, dial 999. Emergency NHS medical treatment** is available **free** to everyone, resident or visiting (go direct to a hospital casualty department); Australians, Canadians, EC members and students/trainees on at least a twelve-week course are entitled to further free treatment; Americans on vacation who are referred for further treatment will have to foot the bill unless they are covered by insurance (check exactly what your insurance covers before you leave). A twenty-four-hour private casualty clinic is **Medical Express** (*171A Harley Street, W1, tel. 071 499 1991; consultation within 30 minutes guaranteed at base-cost of £65*). Even if you're entitled to free NHS treatment it can be cheaper to go straight to the chemist, as there is a basic NHS **prescription charge** unless you are unemployed, an OAP (senior citizen), a child, a student and/or pregnant, in which case you are exempt from payment.

24-HOUR CASUALTY DEPARTMENTS

Always phone ahead to check against closure.

Charing Cross Hospital
Fulham Palace Road (entrance in St Dunstan's Road), W6, tel. 081 846 1234.

Guy's Hospital
St Thomas Street (entrance in Weston Street), SE1, tel. 071 955 5000.

Hammersmith Hospital
150 Du Cane Road, W12, tel. 081 743 2030.

London Hospital
Whitechapel Road, E1, tel. 071 377 7000.

Royal Free Hospital
Pond Street, NW3, tel. 071 794 0500.

St Thomas' Hospital
Lambeth Palace Road, SE1, tel. 071 928 9292.

University College Hospital
Gower Street (entrance in Grafton Way), WC1, tel. 071 387 9300.

Tampons and sanitary towels are widely available, although the British don't go in much for the perfumed variety, so if you're brand-loyal, it's best to bring your own. Of the British varieties, Tampax have applicators; Lil-lets are conveniently smaller than pocket size; Boots do an environment-friendly tampon; Vespré is one of the best of the range of towels with securing 'wings'. All chemists stock a good variety of brands; toilets in many pubs, restaurants, hotels, major sights, etc., have one-brand wall vendors; most corner shops have a limited range of high-priced stock (in some small/suburban corner shops sanitary towels are still surreptitiously slipped across sweet counters in brown paper bags by red-faced proprietors).

Mothers, if you want diapers, ask for nappies; pacifiers are known as dummies; a Tylonol substitute is paracetamol; and Junior Disprin is the same as Calpol. If your child's illness warrants a visit to the doctor, be assured that GPs (general practitioners), as their name implies, have a general knowledge that incorporates paediatrics; if the GP refers your child to a hospital, you need not be alarmed – it may simply be that the GP wants your child to see a specialist.

Some **alternative health** therapies are available on the NHS (mainly osteopathy). If you haven't got time to go on an NHS waiting list or you're interested in therapies not offered on the NHS, an organisation that can give you information on complementary medicine and refer you to the nearest practitioner is the **Institute for Complementary Medicine** (*Unit 4, Tavern Quay, SE16, tel. 071 237 5165*). If you have even a vague idea of what you want (i.e. acupuncture, reflexology, homeopathy, hypnotherapy, osteopathy, massage), go direct to one of the following natural health centres (they'll all give you informed and helpful advice if the Institute has proved inadequate): the **City Health Centre** (*36–37 Featherstone Street, EC1, tel. 071 251 4429*) is large and handy for anyone working in the City; west London's **London Natural Health Clinic** (*Arnica House, 170 Campden Hill Road, W8, tel. 071 938 3788*) boasts, in addition to the expected list of therapies, Kirlian photographic diagnosis and spiritual healing; the convenient West End location of the **Neal's Yard Therapy Rooms** (*2 Neals Yard, WC2, tel. 071 379 7662*) is reflected in the prices; for mind-boggling variety including reiki, energy balancing and polarity therapy go to **Primrose Healing Centre** (*9 St George's Mews, NW1, tel. 071 586 0148*); and last but definitely not least is cosy Clapham's admirable **South London Natural Health Centre** (*7a Clapham Common Southside, SW4, tel. 071 720 8817*), which has one of London's few floatation tanks and the unusual offer of fifteen minutes free with any practitioner to see if they offer what you want.

If you think **prevention** is better than cure, you may want to take up a martial art (t'ai chi is recommended for anyone whose work puts strain on their neck and/or back – writing, typing, knitting and driving are notorious aggravators), or perhaps you'd prefer meditation (which can be used to combat stress). Martial arts can also be applied for use in self-defence (see Police and Crime in Practicalities for relevant advice). The **Martial Arts Commission** (*tel. 0891 111314*) will give you recorded information on the nature of different martial arts and local learning venues; *Time Out* magazine's 'classifieds' section is also a good starting point. For meditation, try the **East West Centre, Self Care Classes** (*188 Old Street, EC1, tel. 071 251 4076*) or the **West London Buddhist Centre** (*tel. 071 727 9382 for details of W2 and Ealing six-week courses*). If you have a back problem or want to avoid one, you'll be grateful for the **Back Shop** (see Shopping).

Contraception

You shouldn't have much – if any – trouble persuading men in London to use condoms. AIDS has not reached epidemic proportions, as it has in New York, but you should still take precautions. Contraceptives – including condoms, the Pill, the cap and the coil – are all available free at short notice on the National Health from family planning clinics, as is the morning-after pill – see box for addresses. Staff in family planning clinics are in the main friendly, supportive and non-judgemental. The vaginal sponge is available and the female condom widely available from chemists, but the reliability of both in terms of protection against pregnancy and venereal disease has been questioned by experts. Many public women's toilets have condom vending machines, and new colourful condom dispensers with youth appeal are gradually appearing on streets over the city.

FAMILY PLANNING

Unless specified, the following operate Mon–Fri 9 a.m.–5 p.m. working hours. For panic advice, call your local GP.

British Pregnancy Advisory Service, *7 Belgrave Road, SW1, tel. 071 222 0985.* Everything here costs, so if you want contraception you might prefer to go to an NHS Family Planning Clinic or the Margaret Pyke Centre (see below): the Pill from BPAS will come to around £2, pregnancy tests £5. Counselling and fast referrals to nursing homes for private BPAS abortions are available.

Brook Advisory Centres, *233 Tottenham Court Road, W1, tel. 071 323 1522 for information on your nearest of the 13 Brook Advisory Centres.* Brook specialises in offering young people free, confidential birth control advice and supplies; anyone over twenty-one must pay. This is the place to come if you can't discuss contraception with your parents and/or your GP has been unhelpful.

Family Planning Association, *27–35 Mortimer Street, W1, tel. 071 636 7866.* Britain has 1,800 NHS-run family planning clinics – phone this central number to find your nearest.

Margaret Pyke, *15 Bateman Buildings, Soho Square, W1, tel. 071 734 9351.* A friendly, free, Central London family planning clinic.

Marie Stopes Clinics, *108 & 114 Whitfield Street, W1, tel. 071 388 0662 for Family Planning or 071 388 5554 for Sterilisation; open 9.30 a.m.–1 p.m. Sat.* High costs (£25 for a family planning consultation) but a wide range of services (including sterilisation and counselling on sexual problems). The main advantage is speed.

Pregnancy Advisory Service, *11–13 Charlotte Street, W1, tel. 071 637 8962; open 9.30 a.m.–12.30 p.m. Sat.* The morning-after pill, pregnancy tests and abortions are available at cost from or through the Pregnancy Advisory Service, which is a registered charity, but PAS does not supply contraceptives.

Women's Health, *52 Featherstone Street, EC1, tel. 071 251 6580.* This is an information and resource centre. Phone or write (enclosing a stamped addressed envelope) with questions on any aspect of women's health, or if you want to be put in touch with a support group.

Abortion

Until the mid-nineteenth century, a widely used method of birth control was abortion induced 'by hot baths, heavy purges, jumping off tables and galloping on horse-back', writes Lawrence Stone in *The Family, Sex and Marriage in England 1500–1800*; he goes on to refer to the case of a 'pious Victorian lady', Mary, wife of the second Lord Alderley, who, when she found herself pregnant yet again, conclued that her husband's resources were already strained, so took what she felt to be appropriate action, writing to Lord Alderley in 1847: 'A hot bath, a tremendous walk, and a great dose have succeeded'. In 1861 such actions were made illegal under the Offences Against the Person Act, and not until the 1960s was abortion law reform considered.

The 1967 Abortion Act 'made it legal for a doctor to perform an abortion if two other registered medical practitioners agreed that the continuation of the pregnancy would be a greater risk to the life or health of the woman or her existing children, than an abortion would be, or if there was a serious risk that the child would be physically or mentally handicapped' (Lesley Doyal and Mary Ann Elston in *Women in Britain Today*, OUP). However, the NHS was given no extra resources to carry out abortions, and by the 1970s feminist health activists had formed the National Abortion Campaign (NAC) to argue that the women concerned, not their doctors, should have the right to choose. Today – largely as a result of still limited NHS resources and the attitudes of some doctors – less than half of abortions in Britain are performed within the NHS.

If you want **to have an abortion** on the National Health or privately, seek advice quickly from one of the family planning clinics listed in the box, as NHS waiting lists are long and even private abortions can take time to arrange – the later the abortion is carried out, the greater the risk of physical and psychological complications. The legal limit for abortion is twenty-eight weeks, but most doctors are reluctant to authorise late abortions. If the NHS cannot perform the abortion before you are ten weeks pregnant, it might be better to go private.

AIDS and VD

These NHS clinics affiliated to major hospitals specialise in genito-urinary conditions, treating both sexually transmitted diseases and conditions including thrush and cystitis:

Burnard Clinic, *Charing Cross Hospital, Fulham Palace Road (entrance in St Dunstan's Road, W6, tel. 081 846 1577; open Wed 2–5 p.m.* This STD clinic is specifically for lesbian and bisexual women. By appointment only.

St Mary's Hospital Special Clinic, *Praed Street, W2, tel. 071 725 1697; open 9 a.m.–6 p.m. Mon, Tue, Thur, Fri and 10 a.m.–6 p.m. Wed.* No appointment necessary. Free and confidential.

University College Hospital Special Clinic, *Gower Street, WC1, tel. 071 388 9625; open 9 a.m.–11.30 a.m., 1–5 p.m. Mon–Fri.* Appointment necessary.

West London Hospital Special Clinic, *Charing Cross Hospital, Fulham Palace Road, W6, tel. 081 846 7834; open 9.30 a.m.–12.30 p.m., 2–5 p.m. Mon–Tues, Thur–Fri.* No appointment necessary.

AIDS tests are available at all the euphemistically named 'Special' sexually transmitted diseases (VD) clinics listed above. For information on AIDS, you can collect three government pamphlets (*AIDS: The Facts, Safer Sex and the Condom*, and *AIDS: The Test*) either from the clinics above or by post with a stamped addressed envelope from Health Education Authority, Hamilton House, Mabledon

Place, W1; or if you want support, information and/or advice, contact one of the following:

AIDS Telephone Helpline, *0800 567 123; open 24 hours daily.* Free and confidential help and information service for anyone concerned about HIV/AIDS and safer sex.

Body Positive, *51B Philbeach Gardens, SW5, tel. 071 835 1045; open 11 a.m.–5 p.m. Mon–Fri.* This is a drop-in centre for and run by people who are HIV positive.

Health Line, *081 681 3311; open 4–8 p.m. Mon–Fri; 0392 59191; open 24 hours.* Of the 300 tapes, 16 give advice on AIDS with contact names of appropriate groups.

Positively Women, *5 Sebastian Street, EC1V OHE, tel. 071 490 5501 (admin), 071 490 5515 (client services) and 071 490 2327 (Helpline, Mon–Fri 12–2 p.m.).* Positively Women provides a range of support and counselling services to women who are HIV positive, and to children directly affected by HIV.

Terrence Higgins Trust, *52–54 Gray's Inn Road, WC1, Helpline 071 242 1010, Legal Line 071 405 2381; open 3–10 p.m. daily for general advice.* Advice and counselling for those with AIDS/HIV and their families, lovers and friends. The Terrence Higgins Trust is also a political campaigning organisation.

Women and Feminism

London has a vast number of women's support groups, organisations and pressure groups. For more information than there's room for here, use the **Everywoman Directory** (£5.95 from Everywoman Sales, 34 Islington Green, London N1 8DU) as an unfortunately rather dated resource; also try the **King's Cross Women's Centre** and the **London Women's Centre** (LWC) – both are understaffed and overworked umbrella organisations, but will do their best to help. With the London Lesbian and Gay Centre on Cowcross Street sadly gone bust, the focus of the lesbian and gay scene has dispersed. To find out about it, look back to Information and target LWC as well as the **Drill Hall Arts Centre** (see box). Feminists should also head for LWC, and although you'll have to pay to get in, a visit to the **Fawcett Library** is a must.

WOMEN'S ORGANISATIONS

Drill Hall Arts Centre, *16 Chenies Street, WC1E 7ET, tel. 071 631 1253.* Every Monday night there's a women-only bar at the Centre; performances in the theatre are more often than not by and for lesbians and gay men. Drop into the foyer for flyers and ask at reception about current events.

Fawcett Library, *London Guildhall University, Calcutta House, Old Castle Street, E1 7NT, tel. 071 247 5826 or 071 320 1000 ext. 570; open during term time Mon 11 a.m.–8.30 p.m., Wed–Fri 10 a.m.–5 p.m. (during Christmas, Easter and July–Sept summer vacations opening times are erratic); day membership is £2 per day waged and £1 unwaged or for a year £10/£5.* Hidden way down in a long basement room is Britain's largest archive of suffragist and feminist literature and ephemera, including letters on the 'woman question' by Queen Victoria, Florence Nightingale, William Gladstone and Thomas Hardy. Now a riveting research resource, in its original incarnation as home to the campaigning feminist group the Fawcett Society, the library (which was rehoused in the London Guildhall University to avoid disbandment in 1977) was a key venue for lectures and talks by women including Dame Ethel Smyth and Virginia Woolf, whose Fawcett Library address became her feminist essay *Three Guineas*. The one qualified librarian and a part-time archivist have continued to gather feminist material, including some of the provocative 1970s tin badges.

Feminist Library, *5 Westminster Bridge Road, SE1 7XW, tel. 071 928 7789. Open Tues 11 a.m.–8 p.m., Sat and Sun 2–5 p.m.*. Phone ahead to check that the threatened closure hasn't happened. Established in 1975 by Dale Spender, Zoë Fairbairns, Leonora Davidoff and Wendy Davies, the library is currently the largest lending and reference library of contemporary feminist material in the UK. It also provides information on women's studies and quarterly events. The building is functional. The library is run on a collective basis.

Kings Cross Women's Centre, *71 Tonbridge Street, WC1, tel. 071 837 7509 (minicom/voice). Open Tues–Thur 11 a.m.–5 p.m. Phone Mon–Fri 11 a.m.–5 p.m.* A multiracial drop-in, resource, advice and survival information women's centre. Organisations housed at the centre include the English Collective of Prostitutes (PO Box 287, London NW6 5QU), Black Women for Wages for Housework (PO Box 287, London NW6 5QU), WinVisible (see Women with Disabilities) and Campaign Against the Child Support Act.

Lesbian Archive and Information Centre (LAIC), *BCM 7005, London WC1N 3XX, tel. 071 405 6475; phone to check that you can go in 6.30–8.30 p.m. Thursdays and 3–6 p.m. Saturdays.* The collection of information by and about lesbians includes a collection of 800 books and pamphlets (Radclyffe Hall's *Well of Loneliness* to 1960s lesbian 'pulp' such as *The Dark Side of Venus*). Ephemera includes postcards (of the Afro-American late poet Audre Lorde), a 'Pint Drinking Lesbians' badge as well as posters, conference papers and a gravy-stained T-shirt.

London Women's Centre, *Wesley House, 4 Wild Court (off Kingsway), Holborn, WC2B 5AU, tel. 071 831 6946); full access for people with disabilities.* LWC is an amazing resource centre in a maze-like back-alley building with an appropriate history: in 1912 it housed the charitable 'Methodist Sisters' and England's first purpose-built crèche, which still exists today as the Kingsway Children's Centre upstairs. Saved by the now defunct Greater London Council (GLC) in 1985, LWC is now an independent umbrella organisation housing thirteen separate groups that empower women and facilitate action. You can also come here for gym, jacuzzi and sauna at the plush, amicable **Wild Court Fitness Suite** (*tel. 071 831 6946; £8 per day membership; open Mon, Wed, Fri 7.30 a.m.–9 p.m., Tues and Thur noon–9 p.m., Sat 10 a.m.–4 p.m.; phone ahead if it's your first time for a fitness assessment*). For a friendly atmosphere and a varied, nutritious menu, come to the bright-orange women-only **Wild Wesleys** café (*open Tues–Fri 11.30 a.m.–2.30 p.m., 6 p.m.–8.30 p.m.; Mon and Sat 11.30 a.m.–2 p.m.;*

children welcome). Call in to pick up flyers and the LWC bimonthly *Update*, which will include details of events in the theatre, meetings in the conference room and one-off women-only parties, which are billed as 'wicked and wild' and swing till the early hours.

The **Women's Resource Centre**, which is now housed at LWC (tel. 071 405 4045), is an advice, information, and referal centre that runs a telephone directory line called Wire (Wire (Wire open Mon, Tues, Thurs, Fri 11 a.m.–4 p.m.; drop into WRC Tues 10 a.m.–noon and Thurs 4 p.m.–6 p.m.).

Organisations housed in LWC include: the support/campaigning group for African women **Akina Mama Wa Afrika** (*tel. 071 405 0678*); for childminding facilities, the **Fleet Street Nursery** (*tel. 071 831 9179*) and the **Kingsway Children's Centre** (*tel. 071 831 7460*); and the **Lesbian Archives** (*phone 071 405 6475 for current opening times*).

Positively Women, *5 Sebastian Street, EC1V 0HE, tel. 071 490 5501 (admin), 071 490 5515 (client services) and 071 490 2327 (Helpline, Mon–Fri 12–2 p.m.)*. Positively Women provides a range of support and counselling services to women who are HIV positive and to children affected by HIV. Essays by positive women on their fears and hopes are collected together in *Positively Women* (Sheba).

Women Artists' Slide Library, *Fulham Palace, Bishops Avenue, SW6 6EA, tel. 071 731 7618; open to the public for £1 door charge Tues–Fri 10 a.m.–5 p.m.*. WASL, the UK's largest reference source on women in the visual arts, houses over 20,000 slides of women artists' works from all over the world throughout history. Supplementary material includes videos and magazines. You can write with an annual subscription of £15 if you want to receive WASL's bimonthly *Women's Art Magazine*.

Feminism in London: a brief history

Through the lifetimes of Mary Wollstonecraft, Emmeline Pankhurst and Germaine Greer, London has been the seat of government, a hotbed of intellectual debate and the heart of the national print (and in this century, broadcast) media network, and therefore key to British feminism. Here are some highlights.

Mary Wollstonecraft (1759–97; see p.128) is generally cited as the first British – indeed, European – feminist for taking French Enlightenment ideas of social justice and applying them to her sex in *A Vindication of the Rights of Woman* (1792). The passion of her writing and the courage and drama of her personal life made her a pioneering feminist heroine. Her bold cry that women should have equal rights with men was taken up again six decades later by the Langham Place Group, and in particular by the nineteenth-century feminist reformer **Barbara Bodichon** (see p.110), who urged a sympathetic young MP, John Stuart Mill, to write as a man on man's injustices in the now classic feminist text *The Subjection of Women* (1869). Another early member of the Langham Place Group, political activist **Josephine Butler**, led a purity crusade to save individual prostitutes and expose the institutionalised hypocrisy of Victorian men who, she argued, effectively legalised prostitution by using prostitutes, then outlawed them as sources of disease with the 1870s Contagious Diseases Acts.

Conflicting factions in the British feminist movement had united at the turn of the century over the question of suffrage – 'Votes for Women!', declared **Christabel Pankhurst** – but even members of the famous Pankhurst family (see pp.95, 220) split over methods: the charismatic **Mrs Emmeline Pankhurst**, impatient with Keir Hardie's Independent Labour Party's cautious approach to women's suffrage, founded the rival Women's Social and Political Union (WSPU) in 1903 and, with her elder daughter Christabel, advocated revolutionary tactics including loud heckling at by-elections, smashing government and shop windows, and hunger-striking once in prison. Emmeline's younger daughter, **Sylvia Pankhurst**, was ousted from the WSPU for continuing to support both mass rallies and the involvement of working-class women. With the outbreak of World War I she in turn denounced Emmeline's growing evangelical patriotism and taste for dictatorial leadership.

When World War I brought the vote in 1918 only to women of privilege, equal rights feminists and socialist women were confirmed in their belief that the issue of class was paramount. By the time the vote was won for all women in 1928, feminism was well on its way to becoming many feminisms. But first there was a lull, or even a backlash. Women members of the Labour Party who had helped to found the Women's Birth Control Group in 1924 faced Labour men's vehement opposition and voted in 1928 to end support for the increased availability of contraception in favour of Party loyalty.

World War II caused a resurgence. Women began to realise, wrote wartime politician **Edith Summerskill**, that 'the war is being prosecuted by both sexes but directed only by one'. Single-issue pressure groups formed and began lobbying Parliament – for equal pay, homosexual law reform, and abortion. On the issue of abortion, feminists were supported by eugenics campaigners keen to limit the number of births to inadequate mothers who might become burdens on the state. In 1967 feminist abortion campaigners were able to celebrate a partial victory when the Abortion Act allowed women to have an abortion, but only with the agreement of two doctors.

The Pill and the liberated 1960s had left many women confused. Was the rejection of monogamy and celebration of promiscuity really the answer? Consciousness-raising groups started up in women's front rooms. At rallies in parks women bore banners bearing slogans like 'The personal is the political'. In the 1970s socialist feminists, including Juliet Mitchell (who wrote *Women: The Longest Revolution*, Virago) and Sheila Rowbotham (*Hidden from History*, Pluto) were rewriting history from a feminist perspective, and Germaine Greer's survey of women's subordination, *The Female Eunuch* (1970, MacGibbon & Kee) was earning her national notoriety and, at the same time, went some way towards popularising feminism.

Women in publishing were organising and writing, but still at the mercy of commissioning editors. Marsha Rowe and Rosie Boycott founded the radical feminist magazine *Spare Rib*, and in 1973 Carmen Callil, with Ursula Owen and Harriet Spicer, founded Virago – the best-known, with its distinctive green-back reissues of women's classics, of the women's presses, including The Women's Press, Pandora and Sheba, founded in the 1970s and 1980s.

In the 1980s, feminists including Juliet Mitchell and Lynne Segal began to find the Marxist analysis of women's position wanting, and turned to psychoanalysis in an attempt to establish why women continued to fall into set roles. During the 1980s the Prime Ministership of Margaret Thatcher signalled to many the end of feminism. Some hailed the advent of post-feminism – 'It means', says youth TV presenter Katie Puckrick, 'we can achieve our ambitions guided by our own standards of excellence.' But Germaine Greer, still contentious, countered: 'The term "post-feminism" suggests that feminism is a fashion (by analogy with modernism) and has been superseded by something more up to date – which is bullshit.'

WOMEN AND CULTURE

'London is one of the most culturally tolerant cities in Europe,' says Bisi Adeleye-Fayemi of Akina Mama wa Afrika, explaining that although 'any woman who looks *different*' is likely to be hassled at Customs ('Irish and black women are commonly strip-searched as a result of IRA fears and the new stereotype of African women as drug couriers'), 'Britain at least has race laws which may be inadequate but can be used as tools'; and on a day-to-day level in shops and on the streets, stares and harassment are rare.

Since Tudor times, influxes of foreigners have been at once invited and rejected, being viewed with favour by the Crown/government/employers for bringing new skills/cheap labour and envied by residents for their prosperity and/or resented as competition. In 1517, during anti-alien riots, Spitalfields apprentices and watermen sacked the merchant homes of wealthy Flemings, French and Italians. By the end of the sixteenth century the black population had soared because – says Folarin Shyllon in *Black People in Britain 1555–1833* (OUP) – black servants had become fashionable as well as exploitable: in 1662 Pepys recorded that when Lord Sandwich brought Catherine of Braganza from Portugal to be Charles II's queen, he brought as a gift 'a little Turke and a negroe'; seven years later he wrote: '5th April 1669. For a cookmaid we have ever since Bridget went, used a black-a-moor of Mr. Batelier's Doll, who dresses our meat mightily well'; it was common for slaves to be maltreated and required to wear collars like dogs, as is shown in a 'Hue and Cry' advertisement in *The London Gazette* of 1688: 'A black boy, and Indian, about 13 years old, run away the 8th inst. from Putney, with a collar about his neck with this inscription: "The Lady Bromfield's black, in Lincoln's Inn Fields".'

Recurring main reasons for groups leaving their homeland over the centuries with hopes of settling in Britain have been religious persecution and high unemployment, the last often combined with civil unrest: Spanish and Portuguese Sephardic Jews fled the Inquisition in the seventeenth century, and since 1984 Kurdish refugees seeking asylum from Turkey have joined relatives in Haringey; job prospects and salaries were low in West India in the 1950s and in Columbia and the Philippines in the 1970s – one interviewee in *Undocumented Lives* (Runnymede Trust), 'Lolita', explains to Ardill and Cross: 'Now my salary [as a housemaid] compared with the Philippines is already the same as a manager or a doctor.' Britain's reasons for encouraging migrants also reveal a pattern: Elyse Dodgson notes in *Motherland* (Heinemann) that 'In the nineteenth century the building of the canals and railways alone caused the arrival of over 700,000 Irish immigrants'; the post-World War II economic boom in Britain and the number of workers killed led to advertisements in Commonwealth countries, including the West Indies – where 'The mother country needs you!' posters went up, the National Health Service established job centres in order to attract nursing staff to British hospitals, and London Transport appointed bus crews – and in *Point of Arrival* (Methuen), Chaim Bermant comments, on the same period: 'The Pakistanis were needed in a way that no previous immigrant group had been. The war had depleted the population of the East End, but not the job opportunities in the engineering workshops, chemical concerns, vehicle maintenance plants, and above all, the garment trade.' The number of women from the Commonwealth entering Britain independently for work or studies has been higher than that of most migrant groups, but Nancy Foner's statement in her 1981 study of Jamaicans in London – that 'Men seemed to receive preference as the expected family providers in amassing funds to pay for the passage' – has applied to most immigrant groups, and for many it is simply culturally unacceptable for women to act alone. During the 1950s, all-male Pakistani dormitories sprung up in the East End; wives and children followed later.

Unfamiliarity and, more often than not, 'illegal alien' status make new arrivals targets for exploitation. Elyse Dodgson reports how spivs, wide boys, extortionate landlords and 'sharks' of both races pounced on disorientated West Indians as they disembarked, shocked by the cold and burdened with suitcases, in the 1950s. 'There's the problem with language and adapting to the weather and that sort of thing…I still feel completely lost,' 'Elisabeth' told Ardill and Cross, and went on to describe life in her overpriced lodgings:

> 'if we have the lights on, they complain because we've had them on too long, and the same applies now in winter with the heating. I don't know, but I have the idea that he might know we are not legal here, because otherwise he knows that he would be troubled with things – because if you have any problem you can just call to the police or any authority to complain about this.'

Pain at separation from families is almost inevitable. 'My son, I left him with my mother,' says 'Therese' in *Undocumented Lives*: 'I miss my son, but I've got to work [illegally as a nanny] to give him a life. There are no jobs in the Seychelles.' Until the 1968 Race Relations Act, the 'colour bar' operated – that is, boarding-houses could display signs such as 'Sorry – no coloureds' without fear of reprisal. One of Elyse Dodgson's interviewees in *Motherland* recalls: 'I went to Peak Freans that used to have loads of part-time jobs and this woman said to me, "We've got jobs yes, but we can't give it to all your people." I was surprised but I didn't take it as racist then…I thought it was reasonable for her to say that.'

The few jobs open to migrants have long been mainly unskilled and badly paid. At the end of the eighteenth century the Metropolitan Magistrate Patrick Colquhoun commented on some who had turned to the money-forging industry that thrived around Whitechapel:

> 'The Jews confine themselves principally to the coinage and circulation of copper; while the Irish women are the chief utterers and colourers of base silver. A vast number of these low females have acquired the mischievous art of colouring bad shillings and sixpences which they purchase from the employers of Jew-boys who cry *bad shillings*.'

A repeated source of distress and confusion has been governments' changing policies. Couples with children have been separated as a result of the recent introduction of the 'primary purpose' law, which means that an individual can be deported if the primary purpose of their marriage is judged to be residency. Ardill and Cross comment that the British promotion of educational opportunities for overseas students was not accompanied by grants, and relevant laws allowed husbands to bring wives but not wives to bring husbands. They also point out that 'For nationals of Commonwealth countries, Britain is an obvious destination', yet 'Home Office statistics show that Ghana led the league table of deportation orders'.

In the past, laws alone made expulsion targets plain. Bermant reports that Jews were expelled from England on All Saints' Day 1290, and 'as early as 1413 there was a statute ordering "that all Irishmen and Irish clerics and beggars called chamberdykins be voided out of the realm".' In April 1993, the first survey of runaway migrant workers in the UK (*Britain's Secret Slaves*, Anti-Slavery International) showed that in the first eight months of 1992, 8,613 entry clearances were issued under the concession that allows foreign visitors to bring domestic staff on condition that they do not change employer. The report found that 89.1 per cent of domestic servants interviewed were subject to psychological abuse; most have their passports confiscated when they arrive, are regularly denied food and are made to sleep in the hall, the kitchen or even the toilet.

Trevor Jones's recent study of *Britain's Ethnic Minorities* showed that Afro-Caribbean women have similar job levels to those of white women and a higher level of qualifications than women of other ethnic minorities; while high proportions of Bangladeshi and Pakistani women do not work outside the home.

The problem of domestic violence within the Turkish and Asian communities was highlighted by the case of Kiranjit Ahluwalia, the battered wife who killed her husband and was freed on appeal from a life sentence (having served three years in prison) in summer 1992, championed by Southall Black Sisters (SBS), who blame a combination of the marriage laws, which can force women to stay with violent husbands for fear of deportation, and inbred cultural rules. SBS member Hannana Siddiqui refers to the Asian *izzat*, an unspoken traditional law which forbids any act that dishonours the community from being reported to the authorities; breaking this law renders the informer an outcast.

But campaigning groups, including SBS, go from strength to strength – Southall Black Sisters, formed in 1979, received the Liberty Award 'in recognition of their outstanding contribution towards the furtherance of civil liberties and human rights in the United Kingdom in 1992' – and grass-roots organisations such as the Union of Turkish Women form to provide translators, counselling and legal and health information.

For comprehensive listings of women's networks and organisations, get the *Everywoman Directory* (£6.50 from Everywoman Sales, 34 Islington Green, London N1 8DU) or contact one of the women's centres listed on pp. 25–7.

Women with Disabilities

London is a nightmare for anyone with disabilities – wheelchair users can't get to the deep-level sections of the Underground; even major galleries and sights that advertise 'wheelchair access' are often referring only to a service lift filled with mops and pails in the darkest corner of the building – but the city is slowly getting better, largely due to the work of campaigning groups such as **RADAR** (Royal Association for Disability and Rehabilitation), which was formed in 1977 to 'remove architectural, economic and attitudinal/social barriers which impose restrictions on disabled people'. Before you set off for London, send for the list of RADAR's publications (see on for contact address), which include free or very cheap leaflets and factsheets on all sorts of topics from education to housing to employment to holidays as well as booklets costing from £1 to £5 on access, getting the best from your wheelchair, and sports centres. RADAR can also supply you with an **NKS** (National Key Scheme key), the key that gets you into the locked disabled access toilets in London and throughout Britain. An NKS key costs £2.50 (to cover administration and postage).

Another leaflet worth sending for in advance is the London Tourist Board and Convention Bureau's leaflet **London For All** (write to *LTB, Victoria Station Forecourt, London SW1* or tel. *071 730 3488*), which details a number of suitable hotels with the recommendation that you always phone the hotel manager beforehand to discuss your particular access requirements.

Since 1984 **London Transport's Unit for Disabled Passengers** has been developing a range of services, including: 'Mobility Buses', which have lift mechanisms at the middle exit door and special seating space (the buses currently operate on eight networks); 'Carelink', a wheelchair-accessible minibus service connecting the main BR stations with the 'Airbus' routes to Heathrow; and 'Dial-a-Ride', a fleet of 200 minibuses for elderly and disabled visitors who can't travel by bus or train. For more information contact the LRT Disability Unit at *55 Broadway, London SW1H 0BD, tel. 071 222 5600*.

Even armed with the Access Guide (see on), before you go out and about *always* phone ahead to check details of accessibility. If a gallery, historic building, restaurant or bar you want to visit isn't mentioned in the Access Guide or by Artsline, then phone ahead and ask the staff for help.

Information

Access in London 1989 *(published by Pauline Hephaistos Survey and available for £4.10 inc. post and packing from RADAR, 25 Mortimer Street, London W1N 8AB, tel. 071 637 5400)*. The information on entertainment, travel in and around London, sporting facilities, pubs and restaurants, shopping, and open-air events are not 100 per cent reliable (an update is overdue), but the accommodation section was revised in 1991, and the publication is still an *extremely* useful starting point. RADAR can also send you *Access to the Underground 1990* for £1.75 inc. post and packing.

Artsline *(5 Crowndale Road, London NW1 1TU, tel. 071 388 2227)*. Artsline provides access details and information about entertainments from theatres, cinemas, exhibitions and concerts to workshops and festivals throughout Greater London.

GLAD *(336 Brixton Road, London SW9 7AA, tel. 071 274 0107)*. GLAD, the Greater London Association for Disabled People, will give you information on transport.

Restaurant Switchboard *(tel. 081 888 8080; 9 a.m.–8 p.m. Mon–Sat)*. The switchboard gives information on restaurants that suit your particular needs, and will make a booking for you.

Where to Stay in London *(published by LTB at £3.40 inc. p&p, write to LTB, Victoria Station Forecourt, London SW1; tel. 071 730 3488)*. This gives you more accommodation information than the small, free LTB leaflet (mentioned above).

Support Groups and Services

Feminist Audio Books *(52–54 Featherstone Street, London EC1, tel. 071 251 0713)*. This organisation can supply feminist books on tape for women who are partially sighted or blind. Volunteers to read on to tape are welcome.

Gemma *(BM Box 5700, London WC1N 3XX)*. Gemma's leaflet describes the organisation as 'a friendship circle' for 'lesbian and bisexual women, with or without a disability/illness, and over 16 years old'. It is not 'a dating agency', but 'lasting relationships and rewarding friendships have resulted from membership of Gemma' which, for a year's subscription to the quarterly Newsletter (available on cassette and in print), costs £2–£5 depending on income (personal ads in the listings are free). The London group runs a monthly social in Camden, and Gemma will try to put you in touch with other groups relevant to your needs. Contact Gemma by letter, tape or braille with a stamped addressed envelope.

Network for the Handicapped (*16 Princeton Street, London WC1, tel. 071 831 8031/7740*). Advice and information, mainly legal, for disabled persons and their families. Will represent people living in Greater London area before tribunals, for example in employment or social security cases.

WinVisible (*King's Cross Women's Centre, 71 Tonbridge Street, London WC1, tel. 071 837 7509. Wheelchair accessible*). WinVisible (Women with Visible and Invisible Disabilities) is principally a campaigning organisation – for economic independence, mobility, access and housing and against racism, welfare cuts, rape and military–industrial pollution. It's best to phone ahead and make an appointment if you want to see members of WinVisible.

Directory

AMBULANCE
Dial 999.

BABYSITTING
See p.358 (Children).

BUS/UNDERGROUND INFORMATION
Twenty-four-hour information line: 071 222 1234.

CAR BREAKDOWN/SERVICING
The AA (Automobile Association, tel. 0800 887766 freefone breakdown service) allows you to join on the spot for roughly the same amount of money as other organisations' call-out fees, and gives priority to lone women drivers.

CAR HIRE
A big, reliable agency with lots of branches is Hertz, 081 679 1799; for cheaper rental try Holiday Autos, 071 491 1111.

CASUALTY DEPARTMENTS
See p.21 (Health and Sex).

CHEMIST (LATE OPENING)
See p.20 (Health and Sex).

CRÈCHES AND PLAYGROUPS
See p.358 (Children).

DENTAL CARE
Phone the 24-hour Dental Emergency Care Service on 071 937 3951 for referral to your nearest operating private or NHS dentist; for cut-price treatment go to Guy's Hospital Dental School at St Thomas' Street, SE1, tel. 071 955 5000.

DRY CLEANERS
Danish Express Laundry (tel. 071 435 6131) is one of few dry cleaners that will promise a regular collection and delivery service to most parts of London.

Embassies, Consulates and High Commissions
Look in the Yellow Pages under Embassies or tel. 142 for those not listed here: America, 071 499 9000; Australia, 071 379 4334; Canada, 071 629 9492; New Zealand, 071 930 8422.

Emergency
Lesbian and Gay Bereavement Project, 081 200 0511, staffed 3 p.m.–6 p.m. weekdays, will offer counselling and practical help with funeral arrangements.

Family planning
See p.23 (Health and Sex).

Feminist organisations
See p.25 (Women and Feminism)

Finding a job
Cash-in-hand bar/restaurant work is getting hard to find – just pluck up courage and go into one you like the look of; for a wide range of jobs, look in the job pages of the *Evening Standard*; for secretarial and temporary work, look in the freebie women's magazines distributed at Underground stations and try agencies such as Brook Street Agency (071 493 8531) (look under Employment Agencies in the Yellow Pages); scour local newsagents' noticeboards and community noticeboards in cafés, for example in Food for Thought (See Eating and Drinking) for New Age/alternative jobs.

Finding a flat
Word of mouth is the best way, so ask everyone you know; arm yourself with *Time Out, Loot* and the *Evening Standard*; listen to the Capital Radio 'Midweek' flatshare list; if you go through an agency, be sure it's reputable and prepare to pay a commission; scour local newsagents' noticeboards and community noticeboards. When you inspect flats, try to avoid going after dark and *always* tell someone where you're going and how long you expect to be – or, better still, don't go alone.

Helplines
Alcoholics Anonymous, 071 352 3001; Capital Helpline (advice on anything, if you can get through), 071 388 7575; Car Clamp Recovery Club (expensive but quick), 071 235 9901; Healthline (for taped information on a variety of health issues), 081 681 3311; Samaritans (phone with any problems including suicidal depression), 071 734 2800; Timeline, 123; Weathercall, 0898 500401.

Launderettes
Hotels have laundry services, or you can go to a launderette. You'll find plenty in the Yellow Pages.

Left luggage
Most main stations have left luggage offices, although some people prefer to make quiet use of a public gallery's free left luggage offices (backpacks and excessively large suitcases may be rejected). Well-located offices are at Euston Station (071 928 5151) and Victoria Station (071 928 5151).

Legal Help
See p.16 (Police and Crime).

Lesbian organisations
See p.25 (Women's Organisations) and p.313 (Club Lesbian Section).

Locksmith
GK Locksmith, 45 Stoke Newington Church Street, N16, tel. 071 254 4617. Call-out service available for

any emergency lock situation, like getting locked out of your flat; and GK's is one of the few locksmiths that will, instead of automatically bunging in a new lock, actually repair an old lock (for example, on a beloved heirloom trunk).

Lost property

Inform the police if you have lost something, and if it was lost on a bus or Underground train tel. 071 486 2496.

Parking Information

Phone National Car Parks (071 499 7050) to get hold of their free map showing key car parks, and bear in mind that if you park illegally you may be towed away or clamped, in which case call Hyde Park Police Car Pound and Payment Centre on 071 252 2222. To find out what constitutes legal parking, get a copy of the *Highway Code* from most newsagents (costs under £1).

Police

Tel. 999 for emergency.

Rape Crisis

Twenty-four-hour phoneline, 071 837 1600; and see p.18 (Police and Crime).

Sport and Leisure

See p.329 (Entertainment).

Tipping

Some cafés and restaurants automatically include a tip in the bill (you can refuse to pay it), and this approach gives an idea of how bad the British are thought to be at tipping. Unless you're in an expensive restaurant, tips are gratefully received rather than expected. Reckon on an extra 15 per cent in restaurants and taxis, and say 'One for yourself' in bars/pubs (the bartender will take one or two pounds out of your change at their discretion).

Toilets

Nice public toilets in London are few and far between. If you are in a hotel, restaurant, gallery or museum, make use of the toilets. If you are caught short, have a coffee in a café to make yourself a customer or just ignore the 'For customers only' sign and stride boldly in. Hotels are good places to go (again, stride purposefully). Good central toilets that won't cost include those in Harrods (Knightsbridge, SW1), National Gallery (Trafalgar Square, WC2), Selfridges (Oxford Street, W1), South Bank Centre (SE1; late-opening), Swiss Centre (Wardour Street, W1; go downstairs).

Train information

Euston (071 387 7070); King's Cross (071 278 2477); Paddington (071 262 6767); Victoria (071 922 6216); Waterloo (071 928 5100); Charing Cross (071 928 5100).

Arrival

Arriving in London is a mainly safe but gloomy experience: getting from plane to Underground ticket machine to tube train at Heathrow is a demoralising, shin-bashing obstacle course of pillars and metal barriers; the road and overground rail routes into the city offer views of traffic jams, decrepit suburbia, industrial works and run-down backs of Victorian terraces; and at Victoria Coach Station the rugby scrum of backpackers and pensioners is as stress-making as the long trudge to the Underground station is weary-making. With the exception of King's Cross train station, safety's not such a big consideration, but still make sure you're independent with your luggage (see When to Go), because at airports and train stations free yellow trolleys are available but hard to find, porters are elusive, and whether you arrive by train, plane or bus you're likely to have to walk long distances that are unbearable if your baggage is awkward and heavy. If you've a choice, aim to arrive during the day, because London is *not* a twenty-four-hour city: public transport stops after hours so if you can't afford a cab from Heathrow, you'll have a safe and clean but long, boring and uncomfortable wait in an airport lounge.

Plane London has two main airports, Heathrow and Gatwick, **Heathrow** is linked to London by the Piccadilly line of the **Underground**, or subway system, and the Heathrow–Central London trip will take 50–60 minutes and cost around £3 (if you intend to make more than one journey before midnight, buy a travelcard – see on). Alternatively, take a **cab** for around £25 (the trip's less than 60 minutes unless it's the rush hour, in which case it can be *much* more), or use the **Airbus**, which takes 60–80 minutes and costs £5 single/£8 return and for under-sixteens £3 single/£5 return (*tel. 071 222 1234*). Despite the luggage-laden-passenger-unfriendly design of the Heathrow Underground station, tube train is the cheapest, fastest option. When you're leaving London, check *beforehand* if your plane leaves from terminal 1, 2, 3 or 4, as they are served by different Underground station stops.

Gatwick is served by the fast, efficient **Gatwick Express**, which departs from Victoria train station every 15 minutes during the day and every hour through the night, takes 35 minutes, costs around £8 adults, £4 children each way and has a buffet car on board (*tel. 071 928 2113*). You can also join the Gatwick train at King's Cross. **Taxi** is a needlessly expensive and, especially in the rush hour, slow way to travel; the **Flightline 777** bus to Victoria Station takes about 75 minutes and doesn't save much money on a single (£6 single, £8 return, half-price for children; *tel. 081 668 7261*). Many seasoned travellers find Gatwick preferable to Heathrow because of the Gatwick Express and also the well-stocked chemists, although the range of stationery available is limited and expensive.

Train London has three main train stations for fast intercity British Rail travel – **Euston, King's Cross** and **Victoria** – and five train stations that are used more for commuter/day-trip-sized journeys: **Charing Cross, St Pancras, Waterloo, Liverpool Street** and **Paddington.** King's Cross suffers from an overblown prostitution and drug-related crime reputation, but the worst you'll find inside the station itself is an occasional tired drunk curled up in a corner under a ragged overcoat trying to get some sleep. Don't wander the streets around King's Cross at night, though – stand in line for a black cab (ask a member of the station staff to direct you to the official rank). For **British Rail Travel Enquiries** tel. *071 928 5100*; for information and tickets go to the **British Rail Travel Centre** at 24 Grosvenor Gardens, SW1 (tel. *071 730 3488*), any good travel agent, or to the ticket office of one of the main train stations. Passes to ask about that might save you money include: if you're under twenty-four and/or a full-time student (with proof), the **Young Person's Railcard**; if you're over sixty, a **Senior Railcard**; if you're travelling in the Network South-East area of England, a **Network Card** for individuals, couples, or families. On some destinations you can make considerable savings by booking an Apex at least one week in advance.

Coach The part-implemented plans to spruce up Victoria Coach Station only highlight the horrors: it's hard to believe, for example, that the station entered the 1990s with neither glazed screens to separate passengers from exhaust fumes and recklessly reversing vehicles nor TV monitors displaying arrival/departure information (the VDUs are still few and far between and merely reduce passenger panic). Nevertheless, with the exception of the Gatwick Airport Flightline, the National Express company does operate a network of impressively far-reaching and money-saving, if time-consuming, coach routes. Some of the major ones even show movie videos and boast air-conditioning and 'hostesses' who brave the juddering aisles with tea in polystyrene cups and cellophane-suffocated sandwiches. A **Discount Coach Card** is available to students, disabled and senior citizens.

Getting Around

You get some of the best scenic routes round London from the top of a double-decker bus or a canal/Thames boat (see p.199); London black cabs are convenient, slow in the rush hour but safe and quick at night; and if you can avoid the rush-hour crush, the tube is a fast and efficient good value. That's 'good value', not 'cheap': London's bus and tube fares are some of the highest in Europe, and it's well worth investing in a **travelcard** (still available at the time of going to press), which allows unlimited travel on bus and tube for a day (around £3, not valid before 9.30 a.m.) or a week (over £10). There are usually several full-colour tube maps in every Underground station (near the ticket vending machines and on the platform), and bus maps for that area are sometimes available at the ticket office. Otherwise, phone the London Regional Transport twenty-four-hour, seven-day **inquiry service** on *071 222 1234*, or drop into an **LRT Travel Information Centre** (there's one at Euston train station, King's Cross train station, Victoria train station and Oxford Street Underground station). Costs of individual tickets depend on your location and destination. At night, if you've any worries, take a cab. Most women alone avoid the Underground at pub-chucking-out-time (11 to 11.30 p.m.), and after about midnight the Underground closes down completely till early morning; the night buses are irregular but ideal for anyone who's out on the town on a budget (especially on a Friday and Saturday night, the top decks are usually filled with drunken revellers more intent on rowdily joshing each other than giving anyone else trouble).

The Underground A limited commitment to supporting the arts, recent recognition of the tourist value of tradition and the 1987 King's Cross fire have benefited the London Underground system: most platforms are commendably colourful, anyway – film and theatre adverts are dotted over the theme-based décor (e.g. Egyptian mummies up the walls at Holborn for the British Museum) – and in addition LRT commissions artists' posters (popular examples include Howard Hodgkin's 1990 gouache-on-board *Highgate Ponds* and Jenny Tuffs's 1987 watercolour *The New Kew*), and strips of spare advertising space in tube-train carriages are filled with Poems on the Underground, dating from anonymous sixteenth century to 1990s London poet Maura Dooley; English Heritage awarded Mornington Crescent Station protected status and LRT's policy is no longer to rip out old stations and modernise but to renovate, as with the Bakerloo Line Edgware Road booking office, which is done out with replicas of the original 1907 fittings; and as a result of the King's Cross fire, safety and security measures have improved drastically, which can mean delays (an unattended bag or a whiff of smoke gets stations closed down instantly), but is a special relief for women travelling alone: video cameras and angled mirrors in passages have been introduced, every platform has a public telephone (for which you'll need a BT phonecard, available from most newsagents), and every platform has a white circular 'Help Point' with a green button in the middle that connects you with staff for information or emergency assistance (if it's not answered within ten seconds, your call is transferred automatically to the British Transport Police control room at St James's Park). London Underground is also patrolled by the British Transport division of the police, and less often by the controversial voluntary safety patrol organisation the Guardian Angels. Crime is low on the

THE LONDON UNDERGROUND

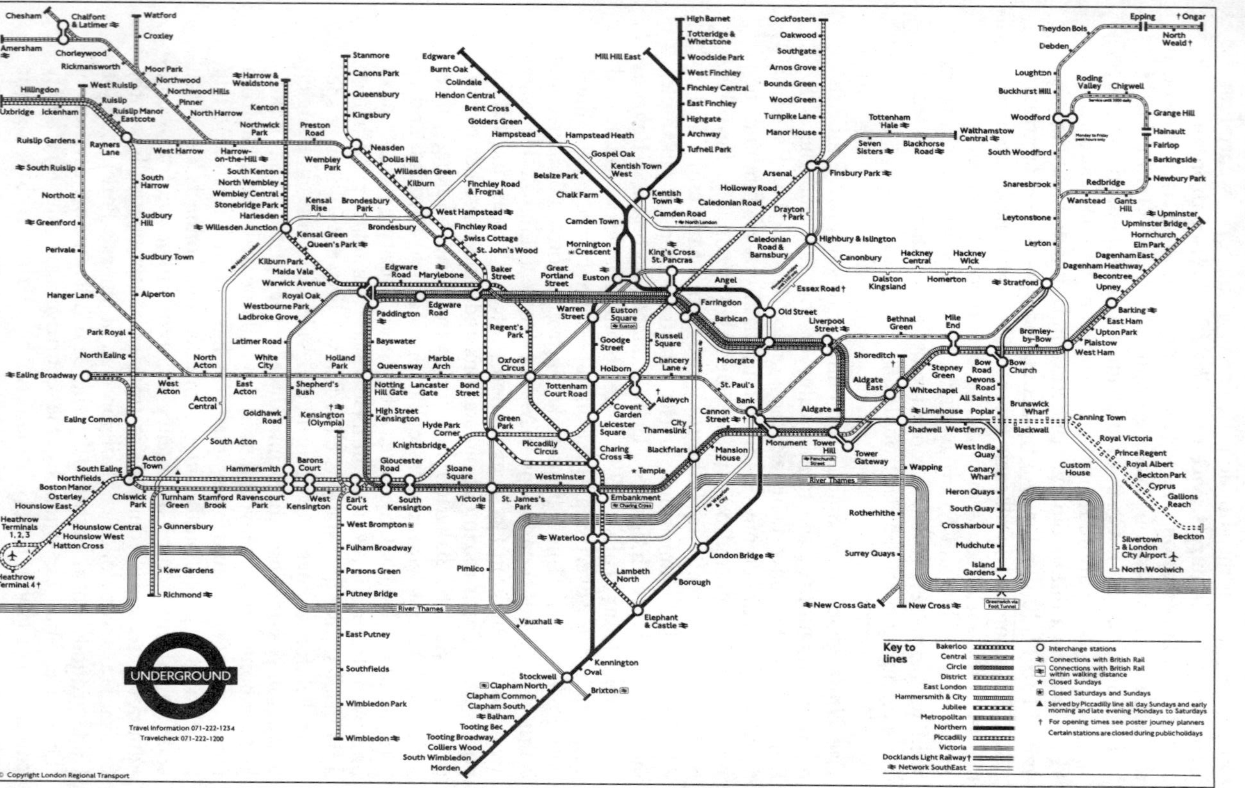

London Transport Underground Map Registered User Number 93/1959

Underground, but beware of pick pockets at busy Central London stations, including Oxford Circus, and expect to be approached by a few men and women begging. If you're travelling alone at night, it's wise to avoid carriages with no one in them – you'll probably find a cluster of women with books and don't-dare-come-near-me faces somewhere in the middle of the train.

Smoking is illegal anywhere on the Underground. Tubes run daily except Christmas Day from roughly 5.30 a.m. to 12.30 a.m. Mon–Sat, and 7 a.m. to 11.30 p.m. Sundays (details of last trains are often posted at the ticket barriers, or just ask a member of staff). If you haven't bought a travelcard (see above), use a coin-slot ticket machine or the ticket window. Show your ticket to the person in the booth on your way to the stairs/escalators or feed it through the automatic barriers – either way, hold on to it until the end of your journey in case a ticket inspector gets on. If you have anything cumbersome, such as a pushchair or suitcase, you'll have to get a member of staff to let you through the special gate in stations without the special luggage barrier. The eleven Underground lines all have names (Jubilee, Northern, Central, etc.) and the platforms tell you whether the train is going Eastbound or Westbound/Northbound or Southbound. It's an easy system once you're used to it, but if you're confused at first, ask fellow passengers for help. The Central Line (red on the maps) and the Circle Line (yellow on the map) will get you to most of the major Central London sights.

Buses There are fewer good old red double-decker buses with separate driver and conductor, but since they're a tourist attraction in themselves they probably won't be phased out completely. The new-style red London bus has automatic doors and the driver also takes the ticket money, and the 1984 London Regional Transport Act required LRT to offer routes for competitive tender, so you'll also see Grey-Green buses, bright yellow Capital buses and blue 'hoppa' buses: you can use your travelcard on any bus bearing a small red and white sign saying 'London Transport Service'. State your destination and the conductor/driver will tell you the price of the ticket (generally more than 50p and under £1.50); it helps if you have the right change, but it is not essential. Hang on to your ticket in case an inspector gets on. Night buses run from about 11 p.m. to 6 a.m. and have an 'N' in front of the number (for example, the 73 and N73 run the same route, but one's day and one's night). LRT bus maps show details of the night buses (look for the 'N'), and if in doubt head for Trafalgar Square, where all night buses leave from and return to. One-day travelcards are not valid on night buses, but period passes are.

Taxis 'Nothing can astonish a London taxi-driver,' says the narrator of Iris Murdoch's novel *Under the Net* while speeding away with a kidnapped caged film star dog that had been lowered through the fold-back roof, a facility which is no longer available, although the optional inscrutability of cabbies continues. Their vehicles are still generically called black cabs, but not all London's sturdy round-edged cabs with yellow lights on top are black – they come in different colours now, and even sometimes with editions of the *London Evening Standard* printed on them. If the yellow light is on you can hail them on the street; major train stations have black cab ranks outside; a central booking number is *071 727 7200* (you can ask for a cab that accommodates a wheelchair). The meter automatically starts at £1 plus 20p per person, 10p per piece of luggage and 40p if it's after midnight or a public holiday. A trip across Central London should cost between £5 and £8. All black cab drivers have an official badge number (on their lapel and in front of the passenger seat) and they have to prove they know every street in London and the shortest route to it to pass a rigorous test called 'the Knowledge'. They sometimes yell comic or infuriating diatribes back at you (jocular/appalling racist comments and well-meant/aggressive sexist remarks are common). If you are for any reason unhappy about your journey, take the cabbie's number and complain to the **Public Carriage Office** (*071 230 1631*). Sexual assault in a black cab is *extremely* unlikely (two cases of sexual assault by men posing as black cab drivers infuriated the black cab fraternity, who have a strict code of honour). You can, however, ensure an extra degree of security by paying £5 to open an account with the black cab Dial-a-Cab service (*tel. 071 251 0581*): when you order the cab the phone operator will give you the driver's pin number, which he will announce to you on his arrival; on reaching your destination, the driver will automatically wait until you're safely inside the door.

Minicabs, which you can order only by phone, not by hailing, are cheaper but the driver may not know the streets well or share the black cabbies' code of honour, so a woman alone might feel uneasy. The Metropolitan Police Crime Prevention Division advises women to avoid minicabs, unless it's from one of the women-driver women-only services, including **Women's Safe Transport** (*081 748 6036*), which operates within Hammersmith and Fulham; **Women's Safe Transport Lambeth** (*071 274 4641*), which operates within Lambeth; **Lady Cabs**, which operates Mon–Thur 7.45 a.m.–12.30 p.m., Fri till 1 a.m., Sat 9 a.m.–2 a.m. and Sun 10 a.m.–midnight in Archway and Holloway (*071 281 4803/272 3019*), in Islington and King's Cross (*071 383 3113*) and in Hackney and Stoke Newington (*071 254 3314/3501*); and **My Fair Lady** (*071 458 9200*). A new alternative that's much used by women who either don't like public transport or want to weave easily through rush-hour traffic jams to business meetings is **Taxibike** (*071 387 8888*), run by Addison Lee.

The motorbikes that are used for the taxi service are customised – there are extra luggage space, heated seats, a fitted apron to stop your skirt flying round your ears, and an intercom system so that you can converse with your driver – and cost around £2 a mile, with a minimum charge of £6.36.

Tours

London's streets date back to medieval and even Roman times – they can be a confusing maze, so you could consider orientating yourself with a tour early in your stay. There are a great many to choose from. For up-to-the-minute listings, phone the tourist board on 071 730 3489 or see *Time Out* magazine, and here are a handful of alternatives.

If you like a feet-on approach and the possibility of quizzing your guide, do a walking tour. Themes range from the London of historical figures such as Sherlock Holmes, Dickens or Jack the Ripper to thinly disguised pub crawls. Find out what the following have currently on offer: **The Original London Walks** (*071 624 3978*); **Streets of London** (*081 346 9255*); **City Walks of London** (*071 700 6931*); **Exciting Walks** *(071 624 9981)*; **The London Pub Walks** (*081 883 2656*).

For details of river tours, phone **River Boat Information Service** on *071 730 4812*.

Original London Transport Sightseeing Tour (*tel. 071 227 3456*) do tours that are about tradition – conducted in good old red double-decker buses. The only air-conditioning you're likely to get is in the open-topped versions; instead of the headphones some tour buses supply, here you'll get the personal touch: an informed and usually amusing tour guide whose patter is best heard if you sit near one of the speakers. You'll get to see all the major sights.

CENTRAL LONDON

Here you'll find London's shopping, historical, entertainment, business and eating centres – and some problems of definition. The 'square mile' is also known as 'the City' because in Roman and medieval times it was literally the whole city, but now the term 'the City' also means London's 'City chap'-peopled financial district. At the turn of the century a trip to 'the West End' for Edwardian ladies meant visits to tailors and bespoke hatters in the new 'boutiques' and department stores around Oxford Street; today Londoners still go shopping in 'the West End', but 'the West End' can also stand for theatreland and clubland, and the boundaries can stretch down to Westminster and even as far north as Belsize Park, where the Screen on the Green cinema is classified in some publications as 'West End first run'. Yet Belsize Park residents on their way towards Oxford Street might speak of 'going into town'. Definitions depend on contexts and who you're talking to: if you're confused at first, you'll soon be bandying the terms around as casually as everyone else.

Although it would be a hard slog to walk from the far east end of the City to the far west of the West End, everything in between is easily manageable if it's taken in chunks. London's big parks border Central London, so bear the squares in mind if you want a pleasant rest on a bench before pressing on (Russell Square and Golden Square tend to be less packed than Soho Square on sunny days). If you can, allow a couple of days or more to explore the City, for the square mile is crammed with major historical sights including the Tower of London, St Paul's Cathedral and the Museum of London (the City has few parks, so try churches for rests). Covent Garden has a good selection of child-friendly museums; older children love Baker Street's Madame Tussaud's. The royal residence, Buckingham Palace, is experimenting with opening its doors to the public; in Pimlico and Charing Cross you'll find London's national public art galleries (the Tate and the National); in St Marylebone and Holborn you'll find two of the capital's most enjoyably intimate museums, the Wallace Collection and the Sir John Soane Museum.

Decent public toilets are hard to find, so make use of café, restaurant and museum facilities as you patronise them, and remember that department store toilets are generally clean, free and equipped with baby-changing areas. For wining, dining, dancing and shopping, see the relevant chapters.

'OXFORD STREET TIDE'

The gleaming omnibuses and tortoises are gone, but the sales and bargains and shifty tricksters are still much as Virginia Woolf described them in her essay on Central London's central street in *The London Scene* (Hogarth Press):

> Oxford Street, it goes without saying, is not London's most distinguished thoroughfare. ... In Oxford Street there are too many bargains, too many sales, too many goods marked down to one and elevan three that only last week cost two and six. The buying and selling is too blatant and raucous. But as one saunters towards the sunset – and what with artificial light and mounds of silk and gleaming omnibuses, a perpetual sunset seems to brood over the Marble Arch – the garishness and gaudiness of the great rolling ribbon of Oxford Street has its fascination. It is like the pebbly bed of a river whose stones are for ever washed by a bright stream. Everything glitters and twinkles. The first spring day brings out barrows frilled with tulips, violets, daffodils in brilliant layers. The frail vessels eddy vaguely across the stream of the traffic. At one corner seedy magicians are making slips of coloured paper expand in magic tumblers into bristling forests of splendidly tinted flora – a subaqueous flower garden. At another, tortoises repose on litters of grass. ... One infers that the desire of man for the tortoise, like the desire of the moth for the star, is a constant element in human nature. Nevertheless, to see a woman stop and add a tortoise to her string of parcels is perhaps the rarest sight that human eyes can look upon. ... [Oxford Street] is a breeding ground, a forcing house of sensation. The pavement seems to sprout horrid tragedies; the divorces of actresses, the suicides of millionaires occur here with a frequency that is unknown in the more austere pavements of the residential districts. News changes quicker than in any other part of London. The press of people passing seems to lick the ink off the placards and to consume more of them and to demand fresh supplies of later editions faster than elsewhere. The mind becomes a glutinous slab that takes impressions and Oxford Street rolls off upon it a perpetual ribbon of changing sights, sounds and movement.

SOHO SEE MAP ON P.46

Named for the time when it was open fields ringing with seventeenth century aristocrats' hunting call of 'Soe Hoe', the area bounded by bookshop-lined Charing Cross Road, neon-lit Leicester Square, genteel Regent Street and shoppers' seedy bustling Oxford Street is now a mêlée of sleaze, high trend and media industry: pass the pinked-out windows of sex shops with names like Venus Emporium on your way to watch pop station MTV in a bar, and perhaps bump into Jerry Hall or Joanna Lumley on their way to a glitzy launch at the members' only Groucho Club or a voice-over recording studio near Wardour Street. Novelist Fay Weldon loves Wardour Street for its mixture of 'sin and film'; one street west

SOHO, PICCADILLY, MAYFAIR, MARYLEBONE

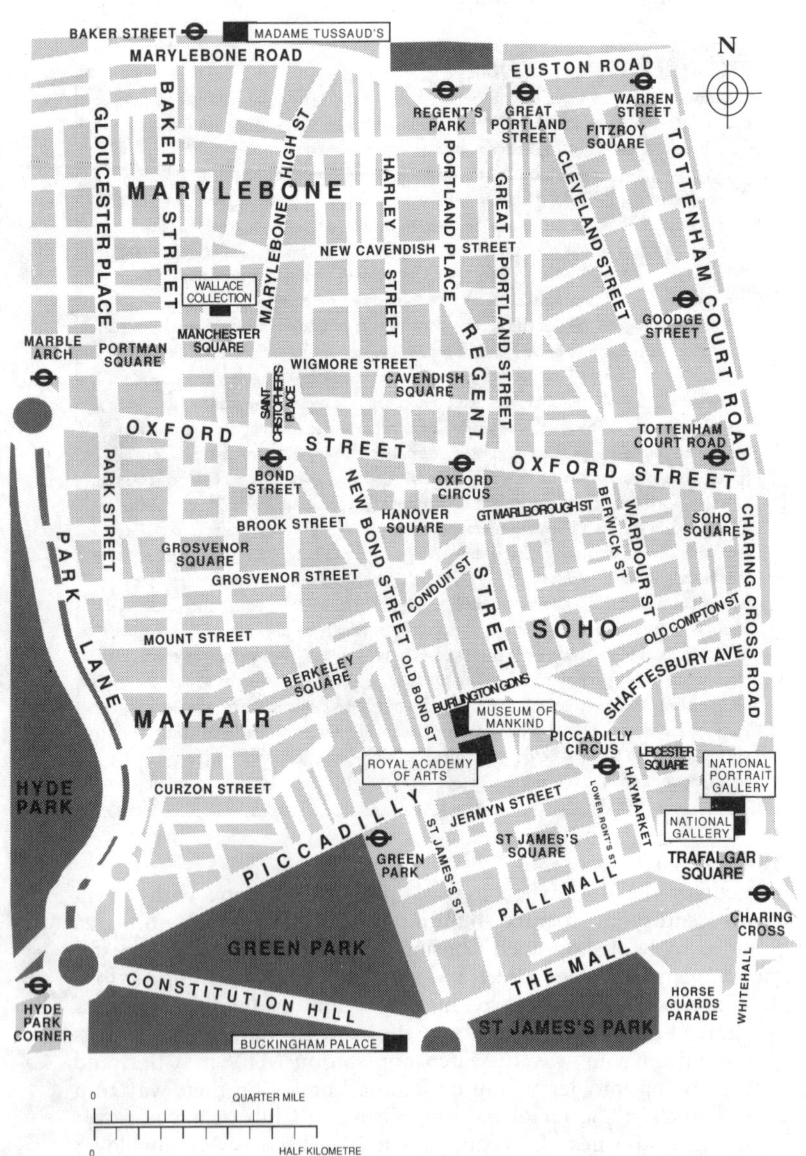

you'll find 'sin' above a vegetable market: Soho's street names have, historically, often commemorated the area's property owner/developers, such as Charles Gerard, Francis Compton and Richard Frith, and today's £1.5 billionaire Soho property owner/developer has his name on what has become an area landmark, the high-class strip joint Raymond Revuebar. The Revuebar's shows, featuring scanty sequin-lingerie-clad girls, are considered variously erotic, degrading and comic, and they are fixed in many a Japanese coach party's itinerary. If you choose not to join the audience of bemused tourist couples and lone businessmen, you could instead buy foreign newspapers, state-of-the-art Janet Fitch jewellery and Camisa's Italian delicacies in Old Compton Street – where silent speeding lycra-clad bike messengers can be a serious road safety hazard – and remember that Soho is perfect for people-watching and great if you're on your own: you can sit undisturbed for hours with coffee and papers at Maison Bertaux, Patisserie Valerie, Bar Italia or the Soho Brasserie (see Eating and Drinking); meander down Berwick Street market for cheap veg off barrows and the deafening 'ten fer a pound' bawl of their cockney proprietors; get Goth gear and Gaultier around pedestrian Carnaby Street before nipping into dark-wood-panelled Liberty's for hand-painted bowls and classic Liberty print scarves. Children will best enjoy the pocket that is Chinatown (around Gerrard Street), where telephone boxes are shaped like pagodas, shop fronts are lavished with jade figurines, dried salt fish and metal trays of fresh red bean buns, and child-friendly restaurants serve snack bowls of noodles or long, enjoyably chaotic dim sum (see pp.362–3). Night owls are served well, too, by the numerous bars and clubs, by Ronnie Scott's for early-morning jazz sets or Bar Italia for dawn coffee (despite all the sex shops, which some might find off-putting, Soho is one of the safest places in London at night because there are always lots of people about). And for those who love off-the-beaten-path sights, there's the House of St Barnabas and the Notre Dame de France.

Georgian London, from Jane Austen to wife-sales The eighteenth-century period known as 'Georgian' was named for the king Georges of the Hanoverian line who succeeded the childless Queen Anne. Their era is often caricatured as a comfortable secular time when men with lightly powdered curls lounged in coffee houses while 'accomplished' novel-reading, spinet-playing ladies decorated drawing-rooms. It was a time of steady growth that featured Hargreaves's invention of the spinning jenny (1764) and the spread of the ubiquitous solidly built, quietly stylish Georgian Square of which King's Square, later Soho Square, was typical and the House of Barnabas is a remnant you can tour today.

In his *Portrait of Jane Austen* (Penguin) David Cecil maintains that the novelist, whose conventionally sheltered upbringing required her to sign her works anonymously 'By a Lady', was a typical female member of the Georgian gentry. **Jane Austen** (1775–1817) moved in a rural circle of squires, well-bred parsons and naval and military officers whose wives and daughters delicately sipped afternoon tea from rose and gold Worcester in sunny sitting-rooms, wearing loose flowing dresses. Jane greatly enjoyed her occasional trips from the nearby countryside to London to visit her socially gifted favourite brother, Henry, who seems to have acted, presumably for the sake of discretion, as intermediary between Jane and her publisher, and gave her cherished experience of lively London society. Letters to her sister Cassandra excitedly describe the latest fashions and indulge in gossip – for example, of Mary Oxenden, who 'instead of dying, is going to marry William Hammond'; they tell of dinners, shopping and theatre-going, and of a visit to exhibitions of paintings, where, 'My preference for men and women always inclines me to attend more to the company than to the sight'.

Jane certainly approved of the values of the gentry. In *Romantics, Rebels and Reactionaries* (OUP), Marilyn Butler suggests that she was 'the gentry's greatest artist', arising 'at a time when they seem to be still at the height of their power, influence and prestige'. Butler says that Jane's 'reading in sermons and conduct-books, must have given her old-fashioned notions of social cohesion and obligation'. Although she was not uncritical, the plots of her novels condemn subversion. In *Sense and Sensibility*, says Butler, 'new, individualistic ideas (sensibility) encouraged by a specious stranger, Willoughby, bring [the central figure, Marianne] ... to the verge of death'. The kinds of subversions to which Austen was responding included the actions of women who decided that the fashion for secular 'good sense' meant rejecting arranged marriages. A flamboyant niece of Henry Fielding, **Lady Mary Wortley Montagu** (1689–1762), for example, eloped with a Whig MP to Turkey (where she learned of the smallpox inoculation and subsequently introduced it to England). A number of wealthy wives established their independence by running *salons* – some literary, such as that of the Bluestockings; others social, notably the Soho Square assembly rooms of Viennese opera singer **Theresa Cornelys** (1723–97), who was notorious – Casanova fathered one of her children – so that even though patrons of her pricey dances, card games and concerts included the respected Fanny Burney, Mrs Cornelys became known as the Circe of Soho. By contrast, the rise of 'affective individualism' (i.e. the value of individuals' will over religious fervour) allowed men a guilt- and judgement-free rein to satisfy their carnal desires, and one who recorded his escapades unashamedly was James Boswell.

When Boswell arrived in London in November 1762, aged twenty-two, what he described as his 'exceedingly amorous' constitution had already led to liaisons with several prostitutes, an actress, a young married woman of his own class, and a lower-class woman who became pregnant, and he had encountered 'Signore Gonorrhoea'. His pace didn't slow in London. Most nights of theatre and society engagements were concluded with a sexual exploit, sometimes for just a shilling and a glass of wine, and often he would add spice by varying the location, once taking a 'jolly young damsel' on the 'noble edifice' of Westminster Bridge. His enjoyment was a little checked by fear of venereal disease: in St James's Park with a whore 'for the first time I did engage in armour, which I found but dull satisfaction'. After his wedding to a slightly older and especially patient woman he only reduced his extra-marital affairs. Such behaviour was typical of some Georgian gentlemen. A 1786 caricature of the upper-class sexual scene by Rowlandson shows, as well as girls for sale, seven casks of the gonorrhoea cure 'Leake's Pills', pornographic publications with titles like *Fanny Hill* – 'For the Amusement of Military Gentlemen' – a bale of condoms marked 'Mrs Phillips (the original inventor)', and birch-rod bundles to be used for the then favourite gentlemen's sexual pastime, flagellation (see also the work of Hogarth in the Sir John Soane Museum).

The actress **Mrs Siddons** and the wilful **Hester Thrale** were but two wives who had to deal with the pox: Mrs Siddons caught it from her husband, and Mrs Thrale was obliged to spend hours on her knees in 1776 applying poultices to her husband's pox-enlarged testicle. In *The Family, Sex and Marriage 1500–1800* (Penguin) Lawrence Stone summarises the type of women most commonly used as mistresses and one-night stands before marriage: the *demi-monde* actresses tended to be more sexually permissive than other women of their class; milliners and shirt ruffle makers often threw in sexual services for the monthly retainer; and occasionally, well-educated women whose fathers had gone bankrupt and had no choice. If they were not mistresses of upper-class men, lower-class women commonly had bigamous husbands, for without a national police force it was easy for dissatisfied men simply to run away and start new families. If both parties wanted to separate, the couple could perform a 'wife-sale', a folk custom that served as divorce and involved the husband leading the wife with a symbolic halter to a market – for example Smithfield, where she was sold to the highest bidder 'as if she were a brood mare or a milch cow. A purchaser is generally provided beforehand' – that is, the new husband and price were usually agreed by the wife, but not always.

Whether they were lower- or upper-class, 'affective individualism' clearly did not apply to women, not least because from late afternoon onwards the streets were hazardous. Well-bred women had to be escorted or stay indoors. The roads were potholed, and the crude whale-oil lamps were few; men employed link-boys to walk in front with a flaring torch, and often found that the link-boys were in league with the gangs of robbers. Christopher Hibbert's *London, the Biography of a City* (Penguin) tells of a society called the Mohocks who, dedicated to 'doing all possible hurt to their fellow creatures', frequently forced prostitutes to 'stand on their heads in tar barrels so that they could prick their legs with their swords', and threw maidservants through the windows of their employers' houses.

By the middle of the eighteenth century Londoners were beginning to change their conviction that policing equalled a fearful threat to personal liberty, and came to realise that the practice of rewarding anyone who brought a criminal to justice had merely turned the most ruthless thieves into thief-catchers. Struggling-author-turned-magistrate Henry Fielding and his half-brother together trained the 'Bow Street Runners' to enforce the law – not for profit but for the good of society; by 1805 a permanent Horse Patrol was in operation, and as the Georgian period drew to a close the advent of a national law-and-order network heralded safety on the streets, although as late as the turn of the nineteenth century girls could not, Virginia Woolf complained retrospectively, go out on their own.

Once a botanist: Marie Stopes and her fight for birth control

Lawrence Stone notes that recorded incidences of birth control being practised to counteract poverty, paternity suits, and venereal disease date back to the sixteenth century: in 1590 the vicar of Weaverham in Cheshire was accused of instructing parishioners for whom more children would be a burden 'how to commit the sin of adultery or fornication and not beget or bring forth children'; a young man in Puritan Massachusetts denied paternity in 1771 claiming in court that he had practised *coitus interruptus* ('I fucked her once but I minded my pullbacks'); sponges were used by prostitutes as early as 1660, and by the eighteenth century respectable gentlemen were regularly using condoms for extra-marital affairs as 'preservatives from claps'. Then – for reasons including sex for pleasure, egotism and a Darwinian desire to purify the race – in early-twentieth-century Britain, birth control became the subject of fiery campaigning that is marked today in Soho and neighbouring Fitzrovia by the still operative Margaret Pyke family planning centre in Bateman's Buildings, Soho Square and the Marie Stopes house at 108 Whitfield Street.

Of the various women involved, **Helena Wright** (1888–1982) was a trained gynaecologist and a founder in 1930 of the National Birth Control Association; a member of the Association, **Margaret**

Pyke (1893–1966), was responsible for persuading local authorities finally to implement the 1931 Department of Health Circular that allowed married couples to be given contraception on health grounds; but the most famous campaigner was **Dr Marie Stopes** (1880–1958), even though many claimed that she had no authority to speak on birth control.

Stopes was a highly intelligent woman with ambitions for popular acclaim. After she had taken simultaneous degrees in geology, geography and botany at Edinburgh University, her trip to Japan in 1907 signified that she had gained an international reputation, but it was in the obscure field of Palaeobotany. Her initially poor sex life proved the making of her fame and small fortune. Frustrated by a cerebral romance with a Japanese professor and a marriage to Canadian botanist Reginald Ruggles Gate that was annulled on grounds of non-consummation, Stopes began, during the First World War, to apply scientific analysis in her journal to her sexual cycle. One section, entitled *Tabulation of Symptoms of Sexual Excitement in Solitude*, reads:

(a) Through constantly reverting in the midst of other business, to feelings of tenderness in kissing.

(b) Through the sensitiveness of breasts, so that one is conscious of their shape.

(c) Through a desire to be held closely round the waist, till corsets become tempting though normally they are abhorrent.

The journal became a manuscript which Marie showed to a medical man who found much to praise but suggested that she should supplement her self-knowledge with medical training. Marie refused, and even before the book was published as *Married Love*, she set herself up as an expert by presuming to criticise a leading London gynaecologist while lecturing a group of women doctors in 1916 on 'women's spontaneous and natural sex drive'. Undaunted by blackouts, bombing and wartime shortages, Stopes began a courtship with her 'flying man' Lieutenant Humphrey Roe, and personally scoured London for rationed paper to ensure publication eight months before the war ended. Sales of *Married Love* exceeded even Marie's wildest hopes, and the sexologist Havelock Ellis described her theory as 'the most notable advance made in recent years in the knowledge of women's psycho-physiological life'. In *Marie Stopes and the Sexual Revolution* (Faber), biographer June Rose suggests that the timing was propitious.

Marie's comprehensive, practical advice on sex appealed to women of all classes and political persuasions, including those who, like Marie herself, had been alienated by the law-breaking suffragette movement but could enjoy new freedoms precipitated by the war, including the right to vote, the opportunity to work in 'men's jobs' such as bus conducting and plumbing, and a relaxation of social mores that allowed women and men to mix more at a time when 'nice girls', Vera Brittain amongst them, learned the facts of life from books like *Adam Bede* and the Bible. However, *Married Love* was not just a sex manual; it was about enjoying sex within the context of married love, so it helped to ease the national moral panic caused by the high number of VD cases among British soldiers by promising to push Britain's young men into morally upright, disease-free and sexually satisfying unions. Lastly, Marie and her book gave added weight to the Eugenics Movement, which had gained credence when World War I recruitment drew attention to the large numbers of physically low-grade 'C3' people in the population. 'Like writers of the calibre of Shaw and HG Wells, Marie was inspired by the simplistic notion of human perfectibility', writes Rose. She 'believed passionately that if [the lower classes] could be persuaded not to breed, society would benefit.' In 1919 Marie was made a member of the National Birth-Rate Commission and at a meeting she declared, records Rose, that 'the simplest way of dealing with chronic cases of inherent disease, drunkenness or bad character would be to sterilise the parents'.

Eight years later, the continuing importance of Marie's contribution to the birth control movement was recognised when she was appointed to the Medical Committee of the National Birth-Rate Commission. But ultimately, Stopes was most important as a catalyst, limited in her ability to carry things through partly because few people could bear to work with her, or she with them. Her friendship with American birth control campaigner Margaret Sanger soured during the war, when Sanger thought about founding the first birth control clinic in Britain, which Stopes considered her prerogative and achieved with the Mother's Clinic in Holloway in 1921. In April 1930 Marie sent a letter to Pope Pius XI asking him to support contraception, saying that they were on the same side, both opposed to the 'evil practice of murderous abortion'; although he didn't reply, the Pope was rattled enough to make clear his opposition to birth control in a public published address and in an interview with a public health doctor enemy of Stopes's, Halliday Sutherland. In August 1930 Helena Wright managed to persuade the Lambeth Conference of Anglican Bishops, which ten years earlier had dismissed Stopes's 'divinely inspired' message, to express limited support for birth control. In 1933, after several years during which most members of the Medical Committee of the National Birth-Rate Commission resented Stopes's autocratic nature and she felt contempt for them, Stopes resigned. By the end of World War II, Marie Stopes's interests had shifted to literature. She took so many lovers that her long-suffering 'flying man' husband Humphrey Roe had to accept being an occasional guest on her sofa, and at sixty she published her second book of verse, *Love Songs for Young*

Lovers. June Rose comments that in the year of Stopes's death, the Lambeth Conference of Anglican Bishops vindicated her 'obscene' ideas by announcing: 'The procreation of children is not the sole purpose of Christian marriage ... the responsibility for deciding upon the number and frequency of children has been laid by God upon the conscience of the parents ...'

The House of St Barnabas

1 Greek Street, Soho Square. Open for viewing Wed 2.30–4.15 p.m., Thur 11 a.m.–12.30 p.m.; Holy Communion in the chapel at 7 p.m. Mon, Lunch Hour service 12.30 p.m. Wed. No charge; collection box for voluntary contributions at the door. Many unavoidable steps.

Boasting fine examples of original Georgian interior decorations and still operating as a refuge for destitute women, the charitable House of St Barnabas was founded in 1846 for 'deserving persons in distress' by a group of friends who, concerned about the destitute and homeless poor of London, enlisted the financial help of Queen Victoria, who gave £50, and the public support of Mrs Gladstone, who laid the cornerstone of the chapel.

Early inhabitants included butlers and ladies-in-waiting fallen on hard times, and young women waiting to emigrate to Australia where, it was rumoured, there were better job opportunities. The House was a Christian foundation, so inmates were required to 'attend Divine Service', and rules on cleanliness were strict: 'Every person on his admission into this House shall be thoroughly cleansed by using the Bath, after which clean linen will be given him, and he will go to bed and there remain until his own clothes are properly cleansed.' In 1939 admission was restricted to women and girls who today include women waiting to go into Mother and Baby Homes, homeless teenagers, battered wives and mentally handicapped women, most of the total thirty-five referred by the Social Services as short-stay residents. The residents' living quarters are not open to the public, although on the way to the garden and chapel you pass through the canteen dining area. A high point on the tour of Georgian décor is the clutch of pink-on-blue cherubs on the Council Chamber ceiling. It's said that Charles Dickens sat under the mulberry tree in the garden for the purpose of devising Dr Manette's London home in *A Tale of Two Cities*.

Notre Dame de France

5 Leicester Place, off Leicester Square. Some steps, helpful staff.

Hidden in an eerie alley between the bustle of cinema-filled Leicester Square and Chinatown is a haven of peace built by descendants of the Huguenots who sought refuge in London when Louis XIV revoked the seventeenth-century Edict of Nantes. It was completely rebuilt after World War II bombing, and the first thing you see on entering this circular Roman Catholic church is, above the altar, a large, almost kitsch, tapestry made by a Benedictine monk in Aubusson, France, in 1954, showing a white-robed woman symbolising Wisdom surrounded by a lamb, a deer and various fish and fowl representing the Creation. To your left, behind and around the side altar is a faint yet still imposing line-drawing mural by Jean Cocteau depicting, in three panels, Mary's annunciation and joy at becoming a mother; her sorrow at the crucifixion; and her triumph at the ascension. Opposite the Cocteau in the overlooking gallery is a white stone Virgin and Child, of which only the Virgin's head is the 1868 original. The rest, destroyed in the Blitz, was rebuilt in Paris after the head was parachuted into occupied France.

Covent Garden See map on p.55

Holy then whorish, Covent Garden is now a wholly enjoyable (or, for some, hateful) juggling act of trendy bars and 'greasy spoons', chic clothes boutiques and gritty organic-lifestyle centres, top-rate tourist sights and a community atmosphere that's unrivalled in Central London. The famed theatrical history is preserved in a museum and in street names (Garrick and Kemble), the old flower market has become the London Transport Museum, and the time when the area was a walled produce garden belonging to the Abbey of Westminster is recalled in the name, originally Garden of the Convent.

Covent Garden was laid out more or less as it is today in the 1630s, when the Earl of Bedford commissioned Inigo Jones to create a neighbourhood centred around an Italian-inspired piazza 'fitt for the habitacions of Gentlemen and men of ability' who were to be served by a few fruit and vegetable stalls along the walls of the Earl's own garden. But what began as a low-key domestic affair – families selling off surplus from their vegetable plots – grew into a sprawling commercial market, and the area's fate was sealed in 1660 when Charles II licensed two Theatre Royals. The influx of tone-lowering traders, whores and actresses caused high society to move out – West beyond Whitehall into the country – and Inigo Jones's ideal of a piazza lined with civilising Mediterranean coffee houses was subverted. The Swiss traveller César de Saussure noted that most of the coffee houses were also 'temples of Venus', not open till midnight and then filled with whores and rakes and noblemen and market women reeking of brandy and tobacco. Hogarth set his third plate of the *Rake's Progress* in the Rose Tavern on Russell Street, depicting a scene of debauchery in which a prostitute pickpockets the rake's watch with one hand and caresses him with

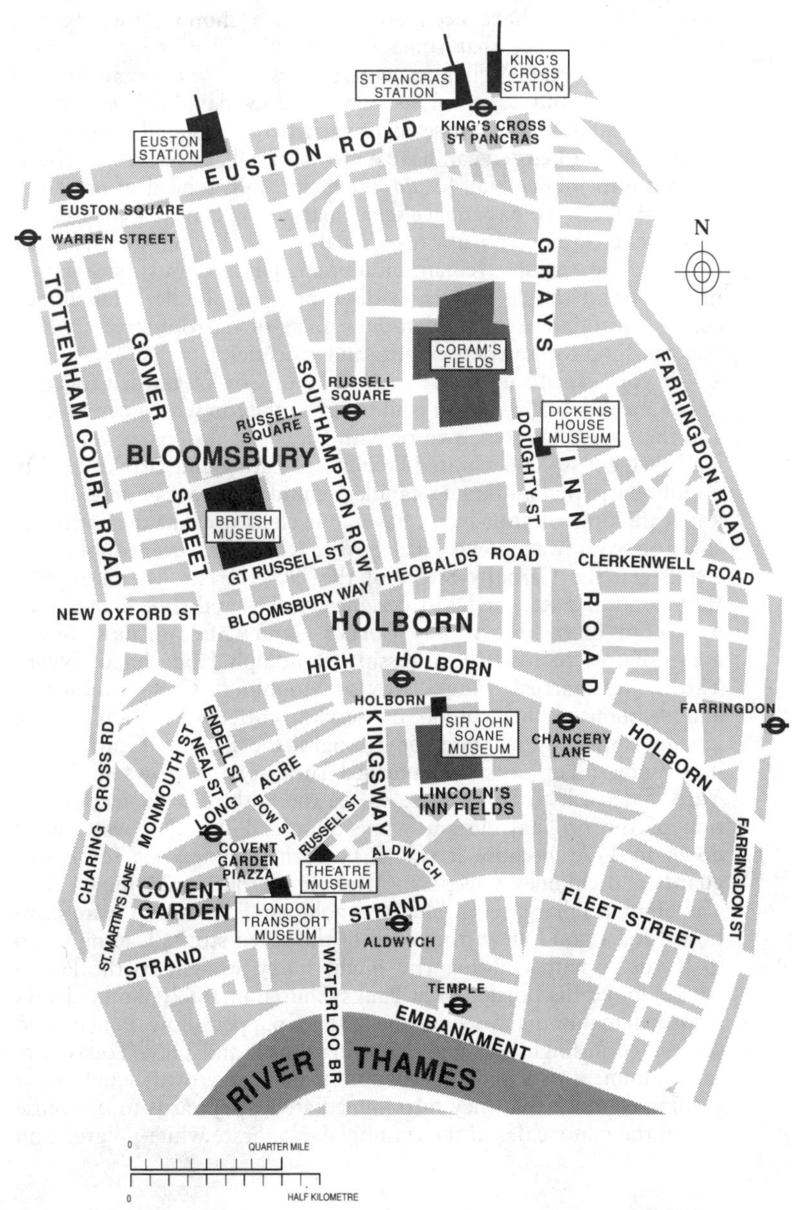

ST PANCRAS STATION
KING'S CROSS STATION
KING'S CROSS ST PANCRAS
EUSTON STATION
EUSTON ROAD
EUSTON SQUARE
WARREN STREET
N
GRAYS
TOTTENHAM COURT ROAD
GOWER STREET
SOUTHAMPTON ROW
CORAM'S FIELDS
RUSSELL SQUARE
RUSSELL SQUARE
DICKENS HOUSE MUSEUM
DOUGHTY ST
INN
FARRINGDON ROAD
BLOOMSBURY
BRITISH MUSEUM
GT RUSSELL ST
THEOBALDS ROAD
CLERKENWELL ROAD
NEW OXFORD ST
BLOOMSBURY WAY
HOLBORN
ROAD
HIGH HOLBORN
HOLBORN
KINGSWAY
SIR JOHN SOANE MUSEUM
CHANCERY LANE
FARRINGDON
HOLBORN
CHARING CROSS RD
MONMOUTH ST
NEAL ST
ENDELL ST
LONG ACRE
BOW ST
RUSSELL ST
LINCOLN'S INN FIELDS
COVENT GARDEN PIAZZA
THEATRE MUSEUM
ALDWYCH
FARRINGDON ST
COVENT GARDEN
ST. MARTIN'S LANE
LONDON TRANSPORT MUSEUM
STRAND
ALDWYCH
FLEET STREET
STRAND
WATERLOO BR
TEMPLE
EMBANKMENT
RIVER THAMES
0 QUARTER MILE
0 HALF KILOMETRE

the other while the house's dancer, or 'posture woman', takes a stocking off in the foreground (see the *Rake's Progress* at the Sir John Soane Museum).

The 1974 removal of the vegetable market to Nine Elms could have left Covent Garden bereft of vibrancy, but it did not: the old market buildings have been preserved as a shopping, eating and drinking experience that some find overly pretty-pretty but most enjoy for the regular juggling entertainers and select scattering of tarot readers and caricaturists. On a sunny day, with sounds of laughing children and glasses clinking where cafés spill on to pavements, Covent Garden can have a crowded, village fête atmosphere. Go south to Jubilee Hall for *ad hoc* tacky stalls typical of London's street markets. To experience what many now consider the essence of Covent Garden, go north to Neal Street. Expect to love it or detest it – few people remain indifferent. Find urban sophistication in high-trend shops, clubs and disco-pumping Jubilee Hall fitness classes; negotiate a pedestrian-only maze of narrow streets where you can shop for a variety of gifts and groceries.

If you want to mix your experience of Covent Garden together in one meandering day, you could start at the top with a cappuccino and the papers on your own or with friends at the sparse yet relaxing basement stone-decorated **Freuds** (see Eating and Drinking). Buy a clubbing hat, hand-made candles, chunky maraccas and, if you know the time of your birth, have your chart done at the astrology shop on your way down Neal Street, which has been dubbed by trendsters 'the Carnaby Street of the '90s' for its Michiko, John Richmond and Red or Dead designer clothes and shoe shops. Pick up a copy of *In and Around Covent Garden* (free in most of the area's shops) to read local gossip ('Randolph Hodgson of Neal's Yard Dairy married Anita LeRoy of Monmouth Coffee Rooms ... and symbolised their union by serving coffee ice cream') while lunching healthily in **Food for Thought**, the **Ecology Centre** or, if it's summer, outdoors on upturned rural-style barrows in **Neal's Yard**. Sidetrack to Seven Dials to see the faithful 1989 reconstruction of the original elegant white Sundial Pillar that was pulled down in 1773 because it was a favourite 'rendezvous for blackguards and chimney sweepers' (*Morning Chronicle*, 28 June 1773). The Sundial Pillar's seven blue and gold sundials on top were positioned for a good view from each of the seven streets leading up to it. If you're with children you might hurry straight to the Piazza where, under the portico of St Paul's Church in 1662, Samuel Pepys recorded in his diary seeing the Italian puppet show Punchinello performed in English as wife-battering Punch and Judy. Today fire-eaters, mime artists and sword-swallowers keep crowds laughing or gasping so much that they turn immediately afterwards to patronise one of the many cafés in the revamped, elaborate white-pillared and glass-roof-covered market, where stall-holders selling idiosyncrasies from boomerangs to juggling balls hum along to classical tunes played by music-student string quartets.

Events and activities on offer around the Piazza include: 'live' performances at the state-of-the-art puppet **Spitting Image Rubberworks**; art exhibitions at the **Africa Centre** (*38 King St, WC2, tel. 071 836 1973*); opera master classes and puppet shows at the **Theatre Museum**; and the chance to 'drive an 1890 Underground train' at the **London Transport Museum**. It's worth a quick walk past the no longer operative Bow Street Police Station (original home to the Bow Street Runners), if only for the sight – odd when you've become used to blue police lights – of lamps on either side of the main entrance that are white because Queen Victoria, on her way to the Royal Opera House, declared that blue was too dull. Come evening, if you're on your own, don't worry that all the bars and restaurants seem to be filling with couples and friends who've just left work or are on their way to the theatre – **Food for Thought** is a favourite healthy cheapie, and many London women who want a smart meal alone think immediately of **The Ivy** (see Eating and Drinking for more).

> 'For an actress to succeed,' said Ethel Barrymore, 'she must have the face of Venus, the Brains of Minerva, the grace of Terpsichore, the memory of Macaulay, the figure of Juno and the hide of a rhinoceros.'

From Orange-Selling to A Taste of Honey: Women in London's Theatre Since the 1660s, when Charles II patented two of the theatres on Drury Lane, the history of Covent Garden has been inextricably linked with that of the theatre, which is generally said to date back to 1587, when travelling players first performed on a stage at the Rose in Southwark. But for women the start-date is much later. Women were not allowed on stage at all until after the Restoration in 1660, and when they did begin to take the parts that had formerly been played by boys, critics declared that though they were attractive additions to the stage, theirs were second-rate portrayals of the 'Fair Sex'.

Contemporaries **Anne Bracegirdle** (1663–1748) and **Elizabeth Barry** (1658–1713) both became renowned leading ladies and, with Thomas Betterton, became co-managers of a new company in Lincoln's Inn Fields in 1695. But they were rare exceptions. Most women who appeared on stage were considered brazen and tarred with the same brush that had marred the reputations of their theatrical predecessors, the strolling players, or 'strollers'. Male strollers were thought to be 'rogues and vagabonds', and the women were notorious for their 'second business' of carnally coaxing the constable to turn a blind eye while they performed in a village barn or field. Women who trod the boards were thought to have loose morals at a price; even looser and cheaper were the women who sold oranges to the audience (most famously **Nell Gwyn**, later an actress, then Charles II's mistress). A hundred years later the upper galleries were still favourite haunts of prostitutes looking for business. As late as 1839 Thackeray wrote: 'A man that ... has been behind the scenes of an Opera, or has even been to the theatre and looked up to ... the second tier of boxes, must know that [Hogarth's] *Harlot's Progress* is still by no means concluded.'

Stagestruck youths would sometimes, to the horror of their families, run off with the raggle-taggle-strollers-O!, but mostly, new talent came in the form of actors' and actresses' children, who were used to the irregularities of stage life and could not hope to get a 'normal' job or be perceived as conventionally respectable – so some began to fight for respectability within their profession. **Sarah Siddons** (1755–1831) is famous as one of the first after Anne Bracegirdle to gain it (you can see an 1897 marble of her, dagger in hand, as the Tragic Muse by Léon-Joseph Chavalliaud on Paddington Green, W2). Young Sarah, the eldest of twelve children born into the Kemble family of touring players, was begged by her father not to marry an actor, William Siddons; she married him at the age of eighteen, began acting in provincial theatre, and caught the eye of a talent scout from London, appearing in triumph at Drury Lane in 1782 as Isabella in Garrick's version of *Fatal Marriage*. Described by Dr Johnson as 'a prodigious fine woman', she developed a grand, tragic style of acting that was well suited to the new large-scale theatres. William Hazlitt said: 'She was not less than a goddess, or than a prophetess inspired by the gods. Power was seated on her brow, passion emanated from her breast as from a shrine. She was tragedy personified.' It was said of her performance of the Lady Macbeth sleepwalking scene that one could 'smell the blood'. As she neared the end of her life, her style of acting came to be thought monotonous and outmoded, but Mrs Siddons had earned a level of respect that benefited those who came after her, including her niece, **Fanny Kemble** (1809–93).

Although she was not as beautiful as Mrs Siddons (smallpox had left her complexion muddied and only just passable under heavy stage make-up), Fanny had already been one of Drury Lane's favourite Shakespearian actresses for over a decade when, in 1843, a 'lower class' of people were at last allowed to perform and/or see Shakespeare's 'dangerous realism' in the taverns and Pleasure Gardens without fear of prosecution. But the protest marches with banners demanding 'Freedom for the People's Amusement' and 'Workers Want Theatres' also succeeded in widening the gulf between 'legitimate' Drury Lane theatre and lesser 'entertainments', for the 1843 Act allowed 'plays' to be performed whole only in places that did not serve food or drink. Queen Victoria greatly enjoyed the circus, but music hall, for example, was clearly branded a lesser art form. The Act did, however, give rise to experimental theatre, some of which was overtly political 'social drama': the plays of Shaw and Ibsen, exposing social ills, were performed as 'fringe' matinées, and from its founding in December 1908 the Actresses' Franchise League (AFL) produced suffrage plays that encapsulated the main current arguments of the women's movement and were staged anywhere from a church hall to a skating rink.

In *Innocent Flowers* (Virago), Julie Holledge reports that the first meeting of the AFL was held in the Criterion restaurant, Piccadilly, and attended by over 400 actresses including stars of the day such as Ellen Terry (whose first appearance had been at the age of nine yelling 'lustily' as the Spirit of the Mustard Pot in a Glasgow theatre). The purpose of the meeting was to pass a resolution demanding that the government extend the right to vote to women. Soon, actress Jane Comfort recalls, nearly every actress was a member of the AFL: 'The office was always open, but we had regular meetings there one day a week with tea and buns ... as a novelty, I used to charge them for their cups of tea. ... People didn't quite take to the idea, so we charged for the buns and let the tea be free.'

A certain attitude was still required for anyone who aspired to be a leading lady, when she might command a higher fee than male co-stars and boast greater audience-pulling power. It is perhaps not surprising, then, that so many actresses fought for the equal right to vote, but by the time it was won, the First World War had changed attitudes. Lena Ashwell organised concert parties to follow the troops to the front, where the only play that actresses had also performed to the suffragists was Barrie's *The Twelve Pound Look*, a domestic comedy in which a man finds out that his first wife left him for a typewriter. Serious acting was discouraged. Women's purpose on the front was to be, asserted Lena Ashwell, an 'unobtainable sex-object': 'it was an intense joy, as one man said to me, "to see a pair of slippers"; and the girl who at the beginning of the war always dressed in rather serviceable clothes, soon found out that the brightest colours and the prettiest frocks gave the greatest pleasure to the men'. Suffrage playwright Cicely Hamilton was still in France when she heard, in 1917, that her name was on the register of the Chelsea electorate, and she remembered 'all that suffrage had meant to us, a year or two before! How we had marched for the suffrage and held meetings and had been shouted at ... and that now, at this moment of achieved enfranchisement, what really interested me was ... the puff of smoke that the Archies sent after the escaping plane. Truth to tell, at that moment I didn't care a button for my vote.'

The carnage of war had been too awful. The Actresses' Franchise League disbanded and so too, in 1925, did the Pioneer Players, which had also produced plays by women on women's issues. But the AFL and the Pioneers perhaps led the way for women working in theatre during the lull between suffrage and the feminist movement of the late 1960s and 1970s. In *Carry On, Understudies* (Routledge), Michelene Wandor presents women who became not actresses but playwrights and tackled 'issues of sexual politics' in 'pre-feminist' plays of the 1950s and 1960s, notably Shelagh Delaney, whose *A Taste of Honey* was first produced by Joan Littlewood at the Theatre Royal, Stratford East, in 1958.

Today, women – including Caryl Churchill – have earned wide acclaim for plays that are not necessarily intended as feminist but are certainly informed by feminism. The impeccably respectable reputation of the late Dame Peggy Ashcroft represents a triumph for women in the history of British theatre. But the age-old divide between highbrow Shakespearian and 'lesser' entertainment continues. Although the 1843 Theatre Regulation Act broke the Covent Garden monopoly by allowing some forty new licensed playhouses to open, the Royal Opera House (formerly the Theatre Royal) still commands major media attention, attracts international stars and commands massive ticket prices; meanwhile, girls in Soho work as glorified strippers in Revue bars to get their Equity cards and so qualify for 'proper' acting jobs. The continued importance of 'reputation' and 'social standing' in the history of theatre is illustrated by two women – one who dared to create an entirely new role for herself and, two centuries later, one who dared to enjoy the low esteem in which her profession was held: Aphra Behn and Marie Lloyd.

Aphra Behn (1640–89) '... all women together ought to let flowers fall upon the tomb of Aphra Behn, for it was she who earned them the right to speak their minds,' wrote Virginia Woolf in *A Room of One's Own* of the woman who had seventeen plays produced in seventeen years at a time when there were only two theatres in London and 'respectable' women could only marry, 'teach children in a dark cellar, / Or work coifs for cracked groats and broken meats' (William Davenant, *The Wits*). Aphra Behn wrote several 'novels' before the novel had even been invented (Daniel Defoe is generally credited with producing the first novel, *Robinson Crusoe*, which was written some thirty years after Aphra's last).

Even in her first Drury Lane play, *The Forc'd Marriage*, (1670), Aphra Behn questioned society's values, and at Covent Garden's Will's Coffee House, where most women entered as prostitutes, she initiated political debates and loudly argued pro-Royalist. Of course, she had detractors. 'Mrs. Behn allow'd herself of writing loosely and giving some scandal to the modesty of her sex,' complained John Dryden (*c.* 1690). 'Intellectually, Mrs. Behn was qualified to lead the playwrights of her day through pure and bright ways,' declared one Dr Doran in 1888, 'but she was a mere harlot, who danced through uncleanness and dared them to follow. Remonstrance was useless with this wanton hussy.' Today Aphra Behn is lauded by feminists. 'The importance of Aphra Behn is that she was the first woman in England to earn her living by the pen,' wrote Vita Sackville-West in 1927. Aphra Behn herself said: 'All my life is nothing but extremes', which almost seems like understatement.

In *Reconstructing Aphra* (OUP) Angeline Goreau presents convincing evidence that Aphra was probably born with the surname Johnson near Canterbury, the 'illegitimate' or 'adopted' daughter of Lady Willoughby, wife of the founder and governor of the colony of Surinam (later Dutch Guiana) in South America, where she was travelling in her early twenties, when her father died. This event, Goreau argues, must have affected Aphra's life far beyond the immediate grief of bereavement: 'he could not now see to it that a dowry assured her a suitable marriage ... her economical survival, her future, her life, now depended on no one but herself. She was ultimately, as she later says, "forced to write for bread".' But before turning to the pen, Aphra became a spy for Charles II during the Anglo–Dutch war, even though, Bathusa Makin wrote at the time, 'Public employments in the field and courts are usually denied for women', for involvement in 'state-matters' was considered not naturally feminine (unless, of course, a woman was of royal birth – see p.156 for Queen Anne and Queen Mary). Aphra was introduced to the king by the unofficial jester, Killigrew; her brief was to find 'Mr. S' in Holland and convert him to the Royalist cause while also discovering any plans for invasion. In so doing, she met and married a Dutch merchant who soon died of fever. Back in England Aphra had trouble getting payment for her espionage and spent some time in a debtors' prison; Goreau surmises: 'Her instinct for independence must have been reinforced by the feeling that dependence on others could have dangerous consequences. She must also have begun to understand that real independence required a financial base.' Widowed, penniless and in her thirties, she moved to semi-slums like the proverbial Grub Street and made herself a playwright, maintaining a prodigious output of plays, 'novels' and translations to the end of her life.

Marie Lloyd (1870–1922) Queen of the music halls and original working-class hero famous for singing 'Oh Mr Porter' and 'My Old Man Said Follow the Van', Marie Lloyd was born Matilda Alice Victoria Wood in the East End of London to an artificial-flower maker who had aspirations to 'better' his family. But Marie was clear from the start that she liked entertaining: she and her sisters would 'do' several funerals in one day, enjoying the pageantry and spectacle of 'having a good cry'. And she formed a troupe, the Fairy Bell Minstrels. Her sister Alice wrote in the *Lloyds Sunday News* in 1922:

> Marie used to put us all into tights and, donning the same costume herself, padded with preposterous muscles, would lead what she called the Keleino Family of Acrobats, which set mother and father in roars of laughter – until one of us fell with a crash and laughter gave place to yells of pain.

She also prized working-class traditions. Marie loved Sunday tea and winkles so much that when the family moved to Lewisham she would go every week in her pony and trap up to the Old Kent Road to collect supplies. Her first theatrical break came when her father (who, forced by circumstance, had taken a second job as a music-hall waiter at the Eagle for £2 5s. a week) put her on the stage at Marie's insistence in 1885 at the age of fifteen. Her success came practically overnight. By the end of 1886 she was earning an astronomical £100 a week, enough to stop stealing other artists' songs (for which she had been severely reprimanded): she had her own material commissioned, and performed in the sharpest gowns London's seamstresses could provide.

Marie became known for the 'sauce' of her songs. Her performances were targeted by ardent anti-music-hall campaigners, including Frederick Charrington (who renounced a £1 million fortune because it came from brewing), who entitled his leaflets on music halls 'This Way to the Pit of Hell'. He and Mrs Ormiston Chant of the Purity Party fought to have music-hall licences revoked: in 1896 Mrs Chant had Marie up before the Licensing Authorities on charges of obscenity. With an absolutely straight face, Marie delivered the offending song, which was either the one about the girl 'who sits among the lettuce and the peas' or 'What's That For Eh?' by Lytton and LeBrunn, and she convinced the committee of her innocence – then, on her way out, she sang 'Come into the Garden, Maud' with all the *double entendre* that her audiences so loved in a stiflingly prurient age when 'nice' girls weren't supposed to enjoy sex, let alone sing about it.

At the turn of the century she was the unchallenged queen of the music halls and surprised colleagues by following a defiantly vulgar lifestyle. She preferred winkles, whelks and kippers off the coster's barrow and the company of jockeys, boxers, mates and music-hall colleagues to any ideas of 'bettering' herself. But in 1907 she joined picket lines to strike for better working conditions for chorus girls, and so began her fall from grace. By picketing she was offending music-hall managers, who were trying to inject respectability into their profession. Her peers were further outraged by her increasingly complicated love life. Having divorced Percy Courtney in 1904 and split with the Coster King, Alec Hurley, in 1910, she began an affair when she was forty with a dashing twenty-two-year-old jockey, the King of the Turf, Bernard Dillon, who was involved in a betting scam a year later, had his licence revoked, turned to drink, and began to drain Marie's financial resources. Even many of Marie's friends considered her dalliances an embarrassment.

The ultimate snub from the music-hall managers against whom she had picketed came in 1912, when Marie was not even selected as one of the 142 'walk-on' artists to represent her profession in the Royal Command Performance of Music Hall Artists at St Martin's Lane's Coliseum, which had been purpose-built without a bar by Oswald Stoll. King Edward VII, who had succeeded Victoria in 1902, enjoyed music hall (he had defiantly visited the Trocadero and Evans Supper Rooms against his mother's wishes). Stoll didn't want Marie's perceived vulgarity to jeopardise the chance afforded by the Royal Command Performance to make music hall art.

Marie's working-class following, however, did not waver, supporting her with roaring laughter till the last. When she collapsed on stage at the age of fifty-two, the audience thought it was a comic new way of ending her act. Three days later newsboys were shouting 'Marie Lloyd's Dead'; the bars of some pubs were wreathed in black; James Agate remembered in 1945 how 'a party of bookmakers fell to speaking of the dead artist. One said ... "She had a heart, had Marie". "The size of Waterloo Station," another rejoined.' Millions mourned and thousands lined the streets for her funeral. Floral tributes included a huge white horseshoe with whip, spurs and a blue cap 'From her Jockey Pals' and a vast presentation from 'The Costermongers of Farringdon Road'.

To chart women's history in the theatre with visual props, go to the absorbing Theatre Museum.

St Pauls, Covent Garden

Covent Garden Piazza, entrance off King Street.

Today it is easy to miss St Pauls, its biscuit-coloured Tuscan-inspired portico serving merely as a backdrop for street entertainers, but when the church was built (1631–8) under royal patronage it was considered an imposing monstrosity by most Londoners, who preferred the traditional gabled, mullioned Tudor and Jacobean structures to the new foreign architecture, which was 'like Bugbears or Gorgon heads'.

Round the back, skirt a raised and prettily formal garden, pass through the narthex – where benches are sometimes quiet beds for homeless people – and you are in a space that is at once plain and majestic, its relative simplicity dictated by the Earl of Bedford, who dismissed the planned church as a necessary appendage to his community, saying: 'I would not have it much better than a barn.' 'Well, then,' said Inigo Jones, 'you shall have the handsomest barn in England.' It does indeed feel like a grand barn, with delicately worked straw-gold mouldings edging the rectangular ceiling and gold candelabras hanging down almost to the plain wood pews.

St Pauls reflected the changing character of the neighbourhood, and soon became known as 'the actors' church': you'll see on the side and back walls memorial panels to – amongst many others – Boris Karloff, Dame Anna Neagle, Charlie Chaplin, Hattie Jacques and the 'King of Punch and Judy', Percy Press. Enjoy a surprise moment of peace before rejoining the Covent Garden madness, which you can hear faintly beyond the altar.

Spitting Image Rubberworks

Cubitts Yard, James Street, WC2, tel. 071 240 0393. Open Tues–Sun 11 a.m.–5.30 p.m. except summer, Easter and Christmas holidays when it is open till 6 p.m. Admission £3.95 adults, £2.95 children, OAPs, UB40s.

This is great for children, and adults will love it too: in a rough-hewn industrial space, everywhere you look there are caricature rubber puppet versions of famous people in different phases of completion. You can operate some of them yourself. You can also see the Queen come to life in a spoof TV nature programme that presents the Spitting Image tribe's 'birthing ritual'. If you know the satirical 'Spitting Image' television show, the Rubberworks offers a fascinating peek behind the scenes, and if you haven't seen the TV show it doesn't matter because in a dark back room puppets animated by computer and compressed air in sealed-off bits of firemen's hosepipe chat with children in the audience and perform a 'live' show.

Theatre Museum

Russell Street, Covent Garden, tel. 071 836 7891. Open 11 a.m.–7 p.m.; closed Mon and public holidays. Admission £3 adults, £1.50 concessions.

Children walk out with slashed faces and blood dripping from their hands, but don't worry – the clue to the source of the apparent pain comes when you see a little girl beaming with pleasure because her face has been done up like a leopard's for free in the Theatre Museum's **Slap!** exhibition, where trained make-up artists use a jelly-style product called 'wound-filler' and 'raw flesh' as well as sunny yellows and brown pencil for whiskers to make children, and occasional brave adults, chirrup with happiness. But that's not all. This packed branch of the Victoria and Albert Museum houses a huge collection of exhibits relating to the Performing Arts that started in 1924, when Mrs Gabrielle Enthoven donated a collection of theatrical memorabilia that was subsequently added to and has been housed since 1987 in this appropriately grand, theatrical building with frequent mirrors and maroon drapes.

One of the first things you see is a clumpy wooden Edwardian sound effects machine, which did the Giant's footsteps in *Jack and the Beanstalk*. Go down the walkway that displays handprints of famous theatre people, including Dame Peggy Ashcroft, and you come to the **Main Gallery**, which charts through posters, articles of clothing, props and supporting text the history of British theatre. There's a picture of Nell Gwyn, who 'excelled in racy comedy'; representing the next generation of actresses is Mrs Anne Oldfield, who was known in her comic roles from 1707 to 1728 for her silvery voice which, Voltaire declared, was the only English actress's he could follow without difficulty; see gloves and a mahogany dressing-table that reputedly belonged to Sarah Siddons and pictures – thought terribly saucy in the nineteenth century – of Lucy Eliza Vestris, who wore breeches showing a lot of leg; move on and you'll see the human skull given to Sarah Bernhardt by Victor Hugo, and as you come to the end of the exhibition, the current vogue for the 'rock musical' is acknowledged with the 1972 jumpsuit designed by Ossie Clarke for Mick Jagger. **The Wind in the Willows** exhibition, originally temporary but still here by popular demand, is designed to demystify the business of theatre by tracing how people move forward in jobs from carpentry to casting to stage management, using all sorts of visual aids from computer graphics to Alan Bennett's original manuscript for the play.

London Transport Museum

Covent Garden Piazza, WC2, tel. 071 379 6344. Open daily 10 a.m.–6 p.m. last admission 5.15 p.m. Admission £2 adults, £1.60 5–16-year-olds, OAPs, UB40s, £7.50 family ticket (two adults, two concessions). Café opening early 1994.

Perhaps surprisingly, a load of old trains and buses can be fascinating for anyone aged six to one hundred. Of course it's a PR exercise – loyal retired London Transport managers guide the tours (which are optional) – but the rhetoric, that London Transport is an integral part of London's history, rings true. Peer at a Georgian gentleman and lady perched genteelly on maroon seats in an old Shillibeer Horse omnibus; hear the coughing and hammering of workers digging the first Underground tunnel; see a photo of George Gibson with, hanging on a leather strap around his neck, the prototype of his mid-1940s invention, the Gibson bus ticket dispensing machine.

The museum is laid out well: the centre of the glass-topped flower market building displays dignified examples of 200 years of London Transport services from trams to trolley buses to motor buses, including the traditional red London bus and a driver's cab that visitors can operate. Around the sides of the vast building are thoroughly labelled exhibits of posters, plans and models, and there are special walled-off exhibitions, one featuring illustrative overhead projection with stereophonic sound; another using video game technology to let you try your hand at digging a tunnel. During the summer, Easter and Christmas holidays the museum runs popular treasure hunt programmes with seasonal themes – track down the Easter Bunny or Father Christmas – and a small treat for all participants at the end.

The Photographers Gallery

5 and 8 Great Newport Street, WC2, tel. 071 831 1772. Open Tues–Sat 11 a.m.–7 p.m. Admission free. Guided tours can be arranged for parties.

Opened in 1971 as the first independent gallery in Great Britain devoted entirely to professional photography, the Gallery presents twenty-one shows a year in three galleries. Sadly, it is often patronised more for the well-filled-sandwich-serving café, where seriously trendy St Martin's Art School students discuss photography instead of viewing the usually excellent shows ranging from selected work illustrating contemporary developments to historical surveys or individuals' shows offering new perspectives on key figures past and present. There is a good bookshop next door.

PICCADILLY SEE MAP ON P.46

Piccadilly Circus is not a circus but a triangle, and it is not at the centre, as you might think, but at the north-east corner of the area known today as Piccadilly, which you can experience as high-class and expensive – take tea at the Ritz, then buy baubled chic from **Salvatore Ferragamo** on Old Bond Street – or pop-culture hi-tech: croon with a wax Elvis at Rock Circus, and get the latest CDs or computer games at Tower Records. You can see paintings and exhibitions from the Establishment to the avant-garde at the **Royal Academy of Arts**, the **Museum of Mankind**, and the **Institute of Contemporary Arts (ICA)** (see Entertainment). You can buy very English gifts at Fortnum and Mason's or Burberry's in the Haymarket, and made-to-measure articles from bespoke shirtmakers and hatters around Jermyn Street. Christopher Wren's pollution-grey yet regal **St James's Church** has programmes of all sorts from Early Music festivals to New Age folk concerts, an art gallery in the basement and a good-quality café at the side, with outdoor seating for summertime.

You might find you're resident in the area, for as well as the famous Ritz, Piccadilly boasts one of the city's best hotels for businesspeople, the Meridien. Or you might be searching out a snack before a big-screen experience on Haymarket or a night at the theatre on Shaftesbury Avenue, in which case try the **New Piccadilly** if you're on a budget, and for indulgently glittering surroundings and reasonably priced food, the **Criterion Brasserie** alone or with friends (see Eating and Drinking). Whichever, take a minute to stand by the Piccadilly Circus **Statue of Eros**, which you may have to imagine rising out of a fountain Alfred Gilbert lavished in 1892 with 'fishes of all kinds, and every class of molluscous and crustacean life', for every time the council raises funds to replace it, vandals ruin the statue again. More often than not, tourists have to be satisfied with snapping each other next to a tarpaulin-covered mound that used to be Eros against backdrops of huge neon advertising boards and buskers who, at night, sometimes include punk fire-eaters. Piccadilly Circus and Leicester Square can become slightly seedy druggy places that are best avoided after dark, and at around 10.30 p.m., just after final curtains have fallen in the theatres, it can be impossible to get a taxi.

'Piccadilly' was named after an Elizabethan Somerset tailor who made his fortune stitching the frilled ruffs for collars and cuffs that were known as pickadils. Development in the area was caused by a courtier's ambition and Charles II's liking for a game similar to croquet. The craze for Italian *palla a maglio* (ball to mallet) was adopted by fashionable French people in the seventeenth century and by Charles II, who built a pall mall alley specially. At the same time he gave 40 acres of nearby land to his mother Henrietta Maria's favourite, Henry Jermyn, whose lack of conscience and principle gained him notoriety amongst his more scrupulous (and therefore poorer) peers, and won him positions of power. Henrietta Maria must have enjoyed his gambling and taste for intrigue, for she made him Vice Chamberlain in 1628 and seemed only to grow more fond of him after he seduced and refused to marry one of her maids of honour, making him Master of Horse in 1639. Described by one of many enemies, the poet Andrew Marvell, as a man with 'drayman's shoulders' and 'butcher's mien', Henry Jermyn intended that his graceful terraces and St James's Square should be inhabited by rich aristocrats. But the south side of Pall Mall proved appealing for its open views of St James's Park not only to aristocrats but also to royal mistresses, including Nell Gwyn, who kept hers the only freehold house on the south side of Pall Mall (No. 79). She teased her lover that she had 'always conveyed free under the crown and always would'. John Evelyn went walking in St James's Park with the king one day in 1671, and 'both saw and heard a very familiar discourse, [Nell Gwyn] looking out of her garden on a terrace at the top of her wall and [Charles] standing in the green sward under it'. Evelyn declared himself 'heartily sorry at this scene', and continued: 'Thence the King walked to the Duchess of Cleveland, another Lady of pleasure and curse of our nation'.

NELL GWYN, THE TOAST OF CHELSEA PENSIONERS

An acclaimed comic actress cheered especially for her role-reversal 'breeches parts' and a politically powerful mistress who remained King Charles's favourite for eighteen years, Nell Gwyn (1650–87) – also known as Eleanor/Ellen, Gwynne/Gwinn – began her career when she was barely into double figures serving pints at the salubrious Madame Ross's. Declaring that 'her heart broke' on seeing King Charles with his new bride, twelve-year-old Nell extended the range of services she offered to Madame Ross's clients. A 1752 memorialist wrote: 'She had now observed how gaily many ladies lived who had no other means of supporting their grandeur but by making such concessions to men of fortune, and stipulating such terms as both of them could afford to comply with.'

It seems that one Mr Duncan, a merchant, took a special fancy to her and kept her for two years in smarter lodgings at the Cock & Pie, where she kept a keen eye on Killigrew's plans to build the largest theatre in London, the King's Playhouse, on Brydges Street. Killigrew decided that the sale of 'strong waters' would encourage bawdy behaviour, so instead, on 10 February 1663, he granted a licence to Mary Megg, 'with full, free and sole liberty, license, power and authority to vend, utter and sell oranges, lemons, fruit, sweetmeats and all manner of fruiterers and confectioners wares'. Nell was employed with the instruction that she was to bring back 5d. for each orange, but could keep whatever else she earned from the ribald courtiers and merchants in the audience.

Since Nell was barely literate, her transfer from stalls to stage involved hours of having parts read to her until she knew the words by heart. Her rise to immense popularity was fast. Within two years of selling her first orange at the King's Playhouse, aged eighteen, she had been offered her own dressing-room. After retirement during the 1665 plague to the relatively healthy airs of Oxford, Nell's return to the stage was marked by the regular appearance in the audience of King Charles II, who soon wore round his neck a miniature of Nell that could have different mica overlays depicting various costumes inserted into the picture's frame. Charles and Nell shared a love of horse-racing, and Nell retained her passion for gambling and watching cockfighting and hangings. Her wit and vivacity were matched by her frankness: one courtier, William Fanshaw, was told, regarding his stinking periwig, to go 'straightways to Mr Gregorie and get a new one, so that [Nell] might not smelle him stinke two stories high'. Invitations to candlelit dinners at 79 Pall Mall were much sought after by foreign dignitaries, for it was here that much state business was discussed.

Nell was a people's hero, remaining loyal to her mother, who was known as a drunk, and her sister, who was married to a criminal, and she was probably instrumental in the founding of the Chelsea Hospital, where military pensioners toast her to this day.

Rock Circus

London Pavilion, Piccadilly Circus, W1, tel. 071 734 8025. Open 10 a.m.–9 p.m. every day except Fri and Sat when it stays open till 11 p.m. Admission £5.95 adults, £3.95 under-16s, £4.95 OAPs/students, free under-5s, family ticket £15.85.

Madam Tussaud's waxwork artistry combines with laser, robotic and audio technology to make Janis Joplin swing druggily into brief life and Beatles fans scream in your ears at the Cavern – but often the infrared signals between visitors' headphones and exhibits don't match up, so standing in front of George Michael you might incongruously hear Jimi Hendrix until you've jerked your head into the correct position for George's 'gotta have sex ...'

Young children might find Rock Circus dull, and teenagers may well deem it laughable.

Museum of Mankind

6 Burlington Gardens, W1, tel. 071 437 2224 or 071 323 8043 for information desk. Open Mon–Sat 10 a.m.–5 p.m., Sun 2.30–6 p.m., closed during the Christmas period, New Year's Day, Good Friday and the first Monday in May. Admission free. Wheelchair access by prior arrangement.

Completely unlike Rock Circus, this, the Ethnographic Department of the British Museum, is low-tech, absorbing and free. It is also low-budget and consequently mustily quiet, so you'll have plenty of time to explore the regularly changing exhibitions, which are constructed to illustrate lives in non-Western societies and cultures; exhibits including artefacts – domestic tools, clothes, housing – of indigenous peoples in the Americas, Oceania and Africa. Mystics love it; so do assistants from the nearby Bond Street shops and Cork Street art galleries, for its **Café de Colombia** is a haven filled with the aroma of fresh coffee and serving simple, delicious sandwiches and cakes.

Royal Academy of Arts

Burlington House, Piccadilly, W1, tel. 071 439 7438. Open daily 10 a.m.–6 p.m. Admission £3–£6 depending on exhibition and with concessions for children, students, UB40 and OAPs. Wheelchair access and toilets for the disabled.

The Royal Academy generally has two extensive exhibitions on at once, sometimes contemporary, and every year the venerable Burlington House – where Turner, Constable and Barbara Hepworth, amongst others, studied – fills with the famous **Summer Exhibition**, which gives little-known artists a chance to exhibit beside big names, and to sell their work. The upstairs Sackler Galleries have been revamped with sleek walls and glass lift by architect Norman Foster. Weekend queues can zigzag endlessly around the courtyard – early mornings midweek are best, and early Sunday mornings you can often get in cheaper. The airy and light restaurant is not cheap, but serves decent food. In the entrance hall, look up and you'll see idealised figures representing Design, Invention, Composition and Painting, modelled on the woman who painted them.

Angelica Kauffmann The hall ceiling of Burlington House features allegorical neo-classical figures painted by Angelica Kauffmann (1741–1807) when convention limited women artists to still lifes and society portraits. Kauffmann, despite being a founder member of the Royal Academy, was to be the Academy's only woman member until 1922. Her successful challenge to the male monopoly over history painting was all the more remarkable because nudes were essential components of the history painting genre, and women were barred from life classes. Indeed, the rule was so strict that when Johann Zoffany was asked to depict on canvas all 'The Academicians of the Royal Academy' (1772), he felt compelled by the presence of a nude male model to omit Angelica Kauffmann except in the form of a discreetly modest portrait on the wall. It was hardly surprising, then, that her execution of nudes left room for improvement, but this did not temper contemporaries' criticisms. Peter Pindar satirised Kauffmann in his 'Odes to the Royal Academicians':

> Angelica my plaudits gains,
> Her art so sweetly canvas stains
> Her dames so gracious, give me such delight
> But were she married to such gentle males
> As figured in her painted tales,
> I fear she'd find a stupid Wedding night.

Angelica Kauffmann was clearly exuberant – her flirtatious reputation generated scandal in connection with artist friends such as Dance, Fuseli and Reynolds – but high spirits and a resilient personality alone could not have ensured the popular success she came to enjoy in England (her works were even reproduced on a bestselling china service).

Angelica's father was a Swiss ecclesiastical painter, so she had access to paint, canvas and a tutor from an early age, and her father supported her unusual ambitions, giving up painting himself to become her agent. She later remembered herself as 'a brilliant young personage [who] sang beautifully, painted portraits as well as anyone, and was equipped with a brand of charm few could resist'. At the age of eleven she was commissioned to paint the Bishop of

Como's portrait, and by the age of twenty-two she was in Italy (first Rome, then Naples). Here she found and was able to develop her interest in neo-classicism through grandees she met, including Winckelmann, and through her election to the Accademia di San Luca.

It was in Venice in 1765 that she met the wife of the British Ambassador, Lady Wentworth, who persuaded her to come to England. Within a year she had earned enough money painting aristocrats' portraits to be able to buy security in the form of a house and time to pursue her commitment to grand-scale historical paintings. Helped by her time in Rome (a vital credential to being taken seriously in England), she sent *Venus Appearing to Aeneas, Penelope with the Bow of Ulysses* and *Hector Taking Leave of Andromache* to the Royal Academy in 1768. The works were not only exhibited – they confirmed her reputation (with Benjamin West) as the founder of the neo-classical style in England. Even when Kauffmann travelled abroad with the painter Zuchi, her second husband, she carried on sending works back to London. By the time of her death she had produced at least 500 paintings, of which only 200 are known. At Kenwood House (see North London), you can look at Kauffmann's *Gualtherius and Griselda* and *Rinaldo and Armida*.

TWO HOSTESSES: BEAUTIFUL BLESSINGTON AND FORTHRIGHT ASTOR

There was an art to throwing English dinners between the First and Second World Wars that *Nancy Astor* (1879–1964) was artfully able to abandon, declining to follow British aristocratic models of entertaining in favour of a freer style brought from her native America. 'She liked to mix her guests as she mixed flowers,' writes John Grigg in *Nancy Astor* (Sidgwick & Jackson):

> Though not free from snobbishness – whatever else she might think – about ancient and, more especially, royal families, and although always liable to be interested in celebrities for celebrity's sake, she did not confine her attention to the well-born, rich and famous, but asked many people … who would never otherwise have found themselves in such company.

Bought shortly after Nancy's 1906 marriage to Waldorf Astor, 4 St James's Square, with its dining-room designed to seat more than could easily be counted, was mainly satisfactory, although Nancy did complain to a friend in a letter that, being in a corner of the square, it created difficulties for the horses when people were arriving for a party. One guest who came more than once to No. 4 was Hitler's Foreign Minister, Joachim von Ribbentrop. Her son David recalled the first 1936 visit:

> My mother tried to treat [Ribbentrop] in her ordinary light way. Towards the end of the meal she said, 'Tell us a bit about your master, but I must warn you that anyone with a Charlie Chaplin moustache is never going to be taken seriously by the British public.' Ribbentrop, who had about as much humour as your left foot, sat there frozen and horrified and didn't make any reply. He left the lunch fairly early. … It was a magnificent failure.

It was perhaps in an attempt to make up that Nancy Astor staged a game of musical chairs after the next dinner at which, Dame Irene Ward remembered, Nancy whispered to all the guests to let Ribbentrop win.

Nancy Astor was educated and, not long after women had won the vote, it was possible for her to become Britain's first woman MP (see Westminster). A century earlier, the *Countess of Blessington* (1789–1849) had to rely on her looks plus a limited background of reading – done during a socially dubious relationship with a captain of the 11th Light Dragoons, Thomas Jenkins – from which, as a *salonnière* at 11 St James's Square, she could cull witty anecdotes.

Born Margaret Power in rural Tipperary, she was sold into marriage at fifteen to pay off her drunken squireen father's debts. After three months suffering violence from her military husband Maurice Farmer, she eloped to Hampshire with Thomas Jenkins, who thought: What a perfect countess! so he sold her for £10,000 to Lord Blessington. To make her happy, Blessington took her in autumn 1818 to London, where the excellent food and wine served by amiable hosts in the splendid rooms of 11 St James's Square made the Blessingtons' dinners a feature on the metropolitan scene – but not with the ladies. 'From the beginning it was evident that the Countess of Blessington had so gravely transgressed against the code of her kind that she was not to be "visited". Ladies of fashion were not necessarily averse to sexual irregularity,' wrote Michael Sadleir in his 1933 *Blessington-d'Orsay: A Masquerade* (Constable),

> But that an Irish nobody, who had lived in the country house of an ordinary commoner and then, by means unknown but certainly sinister, had snatched a titled and wealthy husband from under the very noses of matchmaking mammas, should now presume to act the smart London hostess was an outrage to morals and society.

It was agreed by male guests who discussed politics, literature and art at St James's Square that 'Miladi was a beauty', in possession of the ideal plump foot. After journalist P.G. Patmore saw Lady Blessington with her husband at the Royal Academy, where her portrait was shown in 1821, he wrote that he had 'seen no other so striking instance of the inferiority of art to nature as in this celebrated portrait of Lady Blessington. As the original stood before it, she fairly "killed" the copy.'

Sadleir asserts that Lord Blessington had a homosexual streak to his nature, and that Lady Blessington's first husband had instilled in her an aversion to sex that was at once her saving and her downfall. She had a look-don't-touch appeal for men that was to be soiled by her obsession with the dashing twenty-year-old Count d'Orsay, who conquered London society in 1821. Because, Sadleir suggests, d'Orsay was impotent, both Lord and Lady felt free to love him. But they rashly joined d'Orsay in France and moved with him to Genoa (where they met Lord Byron). By 1829 Blessington was dead, d'Orsay had married Harriet Gardiner, and the whole of London society was outraged. 'What a ménage is that of Lady Blessington!' wrote one journalist. 'This young gentleman, Lady Blessington, and the virgin-wife of 16 all live together.'

Having frittered away her fortune, the Countess of Blessington returned to England and took up writing for a living, publishing her journals and the acclaimed *Conversations of Lord Byron* (1834), and in 1846 she became a highly paid gossip writer for the *Daily News*. Nevertheless, in April 1849 she was forced by imminent arrest for debts to flee to Paris, where she died of heart disease within two months. Sadleir says that despite her wealth and title, behind a life story that has the style of the Regency and the raffishness of the Byronic world, Lady Blessington was deeply, incurably sad. 'There are so few', she wrote, 'before whom one would condescend to appear otherwise than happy.'

HOLBORN SEE MAP ON P.55

Despite weighty associations with the law, Holborn has a transient feel to it. In the Middle Ages it was the point at which routes out of the City split going north, west and to Oxford; today, Kingsway churns a noisily polluting river of traffic up from South to North London. Teenage children of eminent lawyers can't wait to fly the musty residential Inns of Court. Students at the London School of Economics have been known to skip lectures to check out Soho peepshows. Recession-hit bust businesses pass stock to used office furniture shops, and ski gear stores dress remaining well-paid workers for outward-bound skiing holidays. Yet in this space between Bloomsbury, Covent Garden and the City there are fascinating finds and still things that feel ancient: the gloomily grand original home of the British Broadcasting Corporation, which pinions Kingsway to Aldwych; the stodgy Government Bookshop and the **Public Record Office**, where in the small museum you can see the Domesday Book (*Chancery Lane, tel. 071 876 3444, open Mon–Fri 9.30 a.m.–5 p.m., free*); and the Wesley House Women's Centre (see Women and Feminism). Don't wander Holborn idly or expect to find many fun bars or restaurants, but don't miss it out. Target one of the following.

BEATRICE WEBB: 'MOULTING EAGLE'; 'AN EGO TORTURED'

The 'green rendered block' (Pevsner) of the London School of Economics (Houghton St, WC2) owes its existence largely to the spark and determination of one woman, Beatrice Webb (1858–1943), who was described by H.G. Wells as 'a tall commanding figure, splendid but a little untidy. … Her soul was bony, and at the base of her was a vanity gaunt and greedy'; George Bernard Shaw said: 'She was a great citizen, a great civiliser, and a great investigator'; Virginia Woolf called her 'a moulting eagle, with a bald neck and a bloodstained beak'; and biographer Carole Seymour Jones subtitles *Beatrice Webb* (Allison & Busby) 'Woman of Conflict'.

Webb has been caricatured as a puritanical Fabian social reformer who, with her husband Sidney, wrote 'unreadable books' and approved of Stalinist Russia because there was no 'spooning' in the parks. Seymour Jones says: 'In short, Beatrice's story is one of sexual repression, renunciation and sacrifice as, painfully, she reworked the Victorian feminine ideal of the "angel in the house" to follow her own original path as social investigator.'

Born to a wealthy railway magnate, Beatrice rejected her role as society lady, dismissed the stirrings of the movement for women's emancipation as a 'screeching sisterhood' and suppressed her sexual desire for the charismatic Joseph Chamberlain in order to enter a working married relationship with Sidney Webb – 'a man she found physically repulsive' – and so fight for the 'people of the abyss'. She was described variously as censorious, didactic and humourless; Leonard Woolf saw her 'neurotic turmoil of doubt and discontent … an ego tortured'; her private diaries voiced 'the Other Self'. Anorexia has been retrospectively diagnosed: 'Until I took to the rigid diet, the sensual side of my nature seemed to be growing at the expense of the intellectual,' she wrote in December 1901. In April of the same year she wrote: 'Are the books we [Sidney and Beatrice] have written together worth (to the community) the babies we might have had? Then again, I dream over the problem of whether one would marry the same man, in order to have babies, that one would select as a joint author?'

Above all, Beatrice was a doer. By the time she met Sidney Webb in 1891, aged thirty-three, she had already worked as her father's business associate and as a rent collector, helped Charles Booth with the survey *Life and Labour of the People of London* (1887), published her own research into East End dock life and given evidence to the House of Lords Committee on the Sweating System. With Sidney, she became one of the most influential researchers and propagandists of the new labour movement, publishing over a hundred books, pamphlets and articles and, amongst many other things, helping to found the London School of Economics in 1895.

When 'Old Hutch' Henry Hutchinson, a Fabian solicitor, committed suicide in July 1894, leaving £9,000 to the Fabian Society for socialist propaganda, an obvious use for the money – to make a 'political splash' by putting all the Fabian executives up for Parliament – was rejected by Beatrice, who decided that '*hard thinking*' was more important in the long run. She seized on the chance to set up a centre for original research which could realise her dream of 'a science of society' and attract 'clever men from the universities' who could, in the London School of Economics and Political Science, be converted to collectivism. The School soon became the centre of economic teaching, and Beatrice became confident that her books written with Sidney represented the only original work in economics. By the turn of the century she was vindicated when the Webbs 'packed' the University Commission and the School was awarded University status.

Beatrice considered suicide, or VWL – Voluntary Withdrawal from Life, as she called it – but in her eighty-fifth year she began to die of natural causes: her remaining kidney was failing her. In the last entry of her three-million-word diary she wrote: 'We shall all disappear. ... We shall not be frozen or hurt, but merely not exist.' The ashes of Beatrice and Sidney Webb now lie in Westminster Abbey, the only couple to be so honoured.

Sir John Soane's Museum

13 Lincoln's Inn Fields, WC2, tel. 071 430 0175. Open Tues–Sat 10 a.m.–5 p.m., closed Sun, Mon, Bank Holidays and Christmas Eve. Admission free. Lecture tours (also free) every Sat, 2.30 p.m. Unavoidable awkward steps.

There are hints as you approach that this house is not like the others in the square – two white statues keep guard from the second storey; the plain roof is crowned with a classical balustrade – but nothing can fully prepare you for what you'll find inside.

Born to a country builder, ambitious John Soane (1753–1837) became 'Sir', R.A., but could not be proud of his dilettante sons who, he decided, should not inherit his hard-earned fortune. When his wife died in 1815 Soane directed all his energies into his house, obtaining in 1833 a private Act of Parliament that would make it a museum preserved 'as nearly as possible in the state in which Sir John shall leave it'. He was an avid collector of antiquities and a distinguished architect – both these occupations are reflected in 13 Lincoln's Inn Fields – and he was an illusionist, whether aesthetic, humorous or sadistic it's hard to say. Recessed and angled mirrors, strangely bent stairways, murals of summer arbours, apparently accessible 'Gothic' subterranean rooms blocked off by stained glass give the illusion of extra space within this London house of standard dimensions, so causing you nearly or actually to bump into doors and walls.

With the exception of the main living areas – the darkly elegant ground-floor **Dining Room** and **Library** and the beautifully peaceful first-floor **Drawing Rooms** – no space is wasted. Not only are paintings in the **Picture Room** hung right up to the ceiling, but the north, south and west walls feature hinged planes with more pictures hung inside, and the south wall has two successive folding planes with a further recess beyond. The basement, which you might understandably imagine to consist of two or three rooms at most, has **Catacombs** within a crammed confusing catacomb that is divided into a **Crypt Ante-Room** starring a cast of a crouching Venus; **The Flaxman Recess** containing Flaxman's model 'Maternal Tenderness'; **The Sepulchral Chamber** boasting the famous Sarcophagus of Seti I; and **The Monks Parlour** built round an imaginary 'Padre Giovanni' whose 'tomb' (actually containing the remains of a favourite dog, Fanny) and the 'ruins' of whose 'cloister' (made up of miscellaneous fragments chiefly from the old fifteenth-century Palace of Westminster) are seen through a window.

The wondrous clutter of antiquities can be overwhelming. It is worth visiting the museum more than once and making sure not to miss two things. First, the sarcophagus, which was found in the tomb chamber of Seti I (1303–1290 BC) in the Valley of the Kings. This was turned down by the British Museum and bought by Soane for £2,000; it is now – sadly – in a glass case because the London smog was yellowing the white alabaster and causing the blue inlay to drop out. Second, in the Picture Room follow Tom Rakewell in Hogarth's cautionary *Rake's Progress* (1733–4) from young Heir to fashionable practitioner of music, fencing and dancing to enthusiastic participant of a prostitute-lavished Orgy in the Rose Tavern, Covent Garden to the Marriage (to a one-eyed but rich old woman) and then his inevitable decline in Prison and final demise in The Madhouse.

The museum has been lovingly and faithfully maintained almost exactly as Sir John wished. Notes around the house apologise for the need to install electricity.

Staple Inn

Holborn at Chancery Lane Underground.

Of all Holborn's time-honoured Inns of Court law institutions, this is the best one to visit.

The row of half-timbered houses with precarious-looking overhangs, jutting windows and pointed gables – London's only remaining sixteenth-century domestic architecture – is interesting enough to look at by itself, but there's more. Turn from the clashing street through an arched entrance in the centre of the block, and you're in a courtyard which 'imparts to the relieved pedestrian the sensation of having put cotton in his ears and velvet soles on his boots', wrote Charles Dickens in *Edwin Drood*. 'It is one of those nooks where a few smoky sparrows twitter in smoky trees, as though they called to one another, let us play at country.'

Once home to the woolmongers' export trade, and still bearing, above porches, their insignia (a bulging wool sack), Staple Inn was for most of its life an Inn of Chancery where law students passed their first year of studies, until it fell into disrepair and was bought in 1886 by the Prudential Assurance Company to house the Institute of Actuaries.

Today, join office workers and Insurers' Institute employees treasuring quiet moments with lunchtime sandwiches or coffee-break cigarettes.

The Dickens House Museum

48 Doughty Street, WC1, tel. 071 405 2127. Open Mon–Sat 10 a.m.–5 p.m. except Bank Holidays. Admission £3 adults.

This flat brown eighteenth-century house was Dickens's home from 1837 to 1839 and is now an enjoyable museum which, with the exception of a few pieces of very un-Victorian linoleum, is laid out much as it would have been when Charles Dickens (1812–70) lived here before his fast-growing family, including 'Mild Glo'ster' Mary (b. March 1838) and her sister 'Lucifer Box' Kate (b. October 1839), forced him to seek out larger premises. An impressive array of memorabilia has been added.

In the **Hall** you can see the rickety wood pantry window Oliver was supposed to have been pushed through by Bill Sykes on the occasion of the burglary in *Oliver Twist*. In the **Morning Room** the chocolate-box painting of a 'Nymph at the Waterfall' was modelled on Dickens's sister-in-law, Georgina Hogarth, whom he described as 'the best and truest friend man ever had', and who remained so loyal to him that she looked after his children and his house at Gad's Hill when he split with her sister, Catherine. Although the book-lined **Study** was the site of a large amount of Dickens's writing activity – here he penned most of *Oliver Twist, Nicholas Nickleby* and *Barnaby Rudge* – Dickens was fond of company, and his brother-in-law remembered how he

> came suddenly from his study into the room. 'What, you are here!' he exclaimed, 'I'll bring down my work.' It was his monthly portion of *Oliver Twist* ... he seated himself and recommenced his writing. We, at his bidding, went on talking 'our little nothings'; he, every now and then (the feather of his pen still moving rapidly from side to side), put in a cheerful interlude.

Upstairs is **Mary Hogarth's Room**, where Dickens's adored seventeen-year-old sister-in-law Mary Hogarth died of a heart seizure in Dickens's arms. Dickens wrote to Mary's grandfather that since his marriage to Catherine, her sister Mary had been 'the grace and life of our home – the admired of all, for her beauty and excellence – I could have better spared a much nearer relation or an older friend'. Dickens said that Mary's death was the model for the death of Little Nell in *The Old Curiosity Shop*. Perhaps Mary was in his mind two decades later when he appeared in one of his own amateur theatricals and so met Ellen Lawless Ternan, commonly known as Nelly. Despite extensive theatrical memorabilia in Mary Hogarth's Room and despite Ellen's key part in Dickens's life, she barely features here – just one portrait – presumably at least partly for these two reasons: her morally questionable relations with him were studiously ignored by contemporaries and even most future biographers; she herself worked hard to keep a low profile.

DICKENS'S 'N' FIGHTS BACK

In a way the story of Ellen Lawless Ternan is sad because it is told only for her association with Charles Dickens, with whom she had a relationship for almost thirteen years – from 1857 to his death in 1870 – when he was perhaps the most famous man in Britain. All the more impressive, then, that Ellen, known in his pocketbook as 'N', managed to remain almost invisible, keeping their affair secret even from her children during her lifetime, and ended her days a respectable schoolmaster's wife in Margate. This feat was remarkable not just because she had an affair with Dickens and was therefore a Fallen Woman: possibly worse, she was from *a theatrical family.*

Mrs Eleanor and Thomas Ternan were forging solid stage careers when Mr Ternan died in a Bethnal Green Lunatic Asylum of 'General Paralysis' (probably syphilis); Mrs Ternan was left alone to raise three daughters, the youngest of whom, Nelly, first dutifully trod the boards at the age of three. Unlike her gregarious sisters, she was reluctant, and in 1857 fate took her into an amateur melodramatic production called *The Frozen Deep*, co-written by and starring Charles Dickens. Although Claire Tomalin, Nelly's biographer, and Peter Ackroyd, Dickens's biographer, differ on the nature of the relationship that developed between Nelly and the great writer – Tomalin suggests that fear of pregnancy was a constant worry; Ackroyd concludes that the dead love-child was probably apocryphal and the affair unconsummated – neither doubts that Dickens was obsessed by Nelly from the start. Both cite her blond, blue-eyed look of innocence and her age, eighteen – the same as Dickens's daughter, Kate – as important factors: she seemed to embody Dickens's ideals of female heroines: virginal, says Ackroyd; 'a fresh, young, fair girl, living in poverty, earning her own bread, obliged to walk through the dark, corrupting streets and appear before sometimes ignoble audiences,' says Tomalin.

Dickens soon left, loudly and publicly, his uncharismatic, stoutly devoted wife of twenty-two years, Catherine. Fellow writer Thackeray announced to their club, the Garrick: 'It's with an actress'; 'All London,' declared *The New York Times*, 'had for some time been rife with legends concerning Dickens and an actress, with whom it was at last affirmed that the author of *David Copperfield* had eloped to Boulogne.' Nelly was not the only one who was keen to keep herself out of sight. Dickens denied all allegations in *The Times* and in his own paper, *Household Words*. Tomalin discusses a conspiracy of silence – between close friends, family doctors and most biographers – which was maintained to prevent a scandal; for Britain, not to say the world, worshipped Dickens 'as a man of unblemished character, the incarnation of broad Christian virtue and at the same time of domestic harmony'.

Dickens did occasionally tire of deceit, but friends pressed him to keep Nelly secret. Consequently, her biographical details are shady and often contradictory. Dickens's daughter Kate described her as 'small, fair-haired, rather pretty', with brains. Nelly described herself as having 'a figure like an oak tree and a complexion like a copper saucepan'. She reappears after spending time abroad in summer 1865, travelling first-class Paris to London by train with Dickens and probably her mother, 'beautifully dressed, wearing a gold watch and trinkets,' says Tomalin. 'She is by now an excellent French speaker; her hair is darker and no longer arranged in curls; she is thinner, more elegant, a little hollow-cheeked.' Some details of her life as Dickens's mistress in London can be gleaned from the annual pocketbook that escaped destruction by Dickens only because it was lost or stolen in 1867. 'N' pervades – her illness and recovery, their joint search for a house and move to Peckham, where, Tomalin suggests,

> on dark days she must have seen a long succession of years in Peckham stretching ahead, in which she was always ready for [Dickens], arriving in a hired carriage from the station, with his work, his cigars, his exact plans which allowed so much to her, so much to his public, so much to ... his official social world.

It may or may not have been with forethought, but Nelly maintained a dual life – secretly, a Fallen Woman; publicly, a delicate spinster accompanied by mother and sisters – which allowed her to construct a respectable life after Dickens's death, helped in no small part by money left her in his will. By the time she was settled into her new role as wife and mother, her closest friend's daughter, Helen Wickham, described her as sympathetic, charming, cultured, charitable and also someone quite able to 'victimise' her household, who allowed her husband to 'make a doormat of himself for her' and made extraordinary scenes 'when she didn't get her own way'. She could be 'rather a cruel tease' and 'quite a little spitfire'.

Both Claire Tomalin in *The Invisible Woman* (Penguin) and Peter Ackroyd in *Dickens* (Sinclair-Stevenson) are fascinating on Charles Dickens's unsettling views of and relations with women, whom, his daughter Kate once said, he did not understand at all.

Thomas Coram Foundation for Children

40 Brunswick Square, NW corner of Coram's Fields. Open Mon–Fri 9.30 a.m.–4 p.m., except public holidays and when special events are programmed (phone ahead to check), tel. 071 278 2424. Admission £1 adults, 50p children and OAPs.

This museum is an off-the-beaten-track quirky treat with a telling history.

The building itself is not old – a 1937 neo-Georgian square block – but inside, anciently ticking clocks accompany your trip round the **Courtroom**, which is rebuilt exactly like the original Foundling Hospital's, with dark-red walls and elaborate plaster mouldings. By the window, casements display, under protective blue felt converings, 'Tokens left with Children, 1741 to 1760' as means of identification, including jewellery and a small enamel sign saying 'ale'. In a case in the **Picture Gallery** there are dolls dressed in costumes formerly worn by foundling children; the extensive collection of pictures consists mainly of portraits of the Hospital's various governors, and of relevant scenes such as *Foundling Girls in the Chapel* and *The Admission of Children to the Hospital by Ballot*. Pictures continue down the staircase, which is the Hospital's original eighteenth-century oak staircase, its metal spike removed long ago because although it successfully prevented most children sliding down the banisters, one disobedient boy was killed in 1773.

Some History Thomas Coram was, by all accounts, an unlikely altruist. He was a blunt sea-captain who was born about 1668 in Lyme Regis and hard-headedly made a fortune in plantations in the new colonies of America, and it seems that he set about the difficult task of founding a Home for Foundling Children at least in part because he himself lost his mother at the age of seven and was sent to sea at eleven-and-a-half; he and his Bostonian wife Eunice never had children; and on trips between his retirement home in Rotherhithe and London he saw babies dying on dung heaps where they had been abandoned by 'profligate' mothers who, explained essayist Joseph Addison, were persuaded to forsake their natural tenderness by 'the fear of shame, or their inability to support those whom they gave life to'.

The reasons for so many women leaving their children to die were, of course, complex – contributing factors were the lack of contraception and the dire living conditions plus the increased availability of cheap gin that came with industrialisation – and the rhetoric adopted was crucial to Coram's fund-raising. He did badly at first, because he emphasised the 'Fallen' women's 'shame', engendering fear in 'respectable' ladies that his proposed home might actually encourage women to be wanton.

When Coram won the support of six dukes, eleven earls and the painter William Hogarth, he was awarded a royal charter to found the hospital in November 1739, but he was clearly not a tactful man. He was booted off his own project when he became 'meddlesome' and, amongst other indiscretions, loudly and falsely accused the new institution's chief nurse of immodesty, dishonesty and drunkenness. Hogarth, however, remained closely associated with the Foundation and helped it to prosper, giving two paintings (the 1740 portrait of *Thomas Coram* and the 1750 *March of the Guards to Finchley*, both on display today) and encouraging his wife Jane to join the Hospital's fostering scheme. George Frederick Handel raised the then stupendous sum of £7,000 by leading a 1753 charity concert of *The Messiah* (you can see displayed Handel's 'a fair copy' of *The Messiah*).

Day-to-day life in the Hospital was described by its Treasurer, Sir Thomas Bernard: 'They rise at six in the summer and daylight in winter, part of them being employed before breakfast in dressing the younger children, in cleaning about the house, and the boys in working a forcing pump which supplies all the wards and every part of the hospital abundantly with water.' The girls were taught needlework and did housework:

> The little boys knit the stockings that are wanted for the children in the house: the elder boys, in their turn, work in the garden. ... They are all taught and make a proficiency in reading, writing and accounts. Different occupations and manufactures have been, at times, introduced into the Hospital. The last that has been tried, with much effect and continuance, has been the spinning of worsted yarn.

Punishments for wrong-doers ranged from 'severe' and 'slight' floggings to forced service aboard naval vessels and even deportation to Australia.

At first the Hospital took only twenty foundlings at a time, totalling a hundred in a year, all by ballot (red and black balls were pulled out of a hat). Some children were brought by well-to-do women, but most came from servants and daughters of tradesmen and farmers. In 1756 Parliament offered a grant of £10,000 on condition that the Hospital appoint places 'for the reception of all exposed and deserted young children', and an 'all-comers' basket' was hung up at the gate in which 117 babies were left on the first day to be taken inside by the porter. Some fatally ill children were left by families who were desperate to sidestep funeral costs.

As admissions went up the Hospital went down in the public's estimation, the all-comers' system was ended due to seriously depleted funds in 1769, and although in 1853 Charles Dickens gave the Home a favourable mention in *Household Words*, by this century the future of Thomas Coram's Foundation looked shaky. In 1926 the Foundation was saved, but the building was nearly lost when the originally dirt-cheap Bloomsbury site's value soared as a result of the nearby railway. The Foundation sold out to developers and moved to country premises in Berkhamsted; a public campaign led by Fleet Street magnate Lord Rothermere raised the money to buy back the Hospital site for Coram's Fields Children's Playground in 1936 (see Children). Gradually the Foundation's policy changed to favour fostering, and by 1954 the last of the fifty 'foundlings' had been sent to foster homes. The 40 Brunswick Square headquarters continue to operate a research institute and serve as a base for several other voluntary childcare organisations. As you explore the two floors of the museum, you might occasionally glimpse one of their members scribbling furiously at a desk by a casement full of eighteenth-century foundlings' tokens.

CHARING CROSS SEE MAP ON P.46

When Edward I's wife Eleanor of Castile died in 1290, Edward ordered that crosses be erected at all the twelve resting places of the funeral cortege between Nottinghamshire and Westminster, the last of which was here, in the village of Charing. A statue of Charles I now stands just south of Trafalgar Square in place of Eleanor's Caen stone cross, which was pulled down when it had deteriorated in 1647 to be made into paving stones and knife handles.

The **National Gallery** and the **National Portrait Gallery** are wonderful reasons for visiting what has become a rather traffic-choked Central London junction, and in the centre of it all, pigeon-splatted **Trafalgar Square** continues to have a wide appeal that lies somewhere between that of an Italian piazza and an English village fête. A haven for eating, taking tea and resting is the buffet-café in the crypt of **St Martin-in-the-Fields** on the north-east corner of the square.

Trafalgar Square

Children love to sit on the lions that guard Nelson's base; to splash in the fountains, where a surprised mermaid clutches two spouting dolphins; to watch occasional expert rollerskaters in the south-west corner; and above all, they love to feed the pigeons. Bring your own birdseed, or buy it from the Trafalgar Square vendor (someone sells birdseed almost every day of the year in the south-east corner). Built between 1820 and 1840 on the site of the royal mews where falconers and hawks lived, Trafalgar Square was planned by John Nash as part of a road improvement scheme linking Westminster to North London. Favoured for political rallies because it can accommodate crowds of around 50,000, the square fills with representatives of the Norwegian Embassy in traditional costume when Norway's annual gift of a massive pine tree to Britain since the Second World War is erected every Christmas. On New Year's Eve the square and its fountains fill with revellers and amused police waiting for the chimes of Big Ben to liberate cheers, bottle corks and streamers;

some find the celebrations claustrophobic and object to those strangers who use the occasion to excuse bullying attempts to kiss everyone long before and after the stroke of midnight. On a sunny weekday it can be pleasant to sit on the edge of the fountain writing postcards. And it is curious to see in the granite, so to speak, the oft-reproduced fluted Corinthian column topped by the three-times-bigger-than-life-size Horatio Nelson that appears from the ground to be a pigmy version of the celebrated admiral. The extravagant lifestyle of his mistress, **Lady Emma Hamilton**, soon accounted for the wealth she had inherited after Nelson's death at the 1805 Battle of Trafalgar, and twenty-seven years before this column was erected in 1842 to commemorate Nelson's last battle, she died a bankrupt prison escapee. Lady Emma Hamilton is represented at the National Portrait Gallery by one of the twenty portraits George Romney painted of the famous aristocrats' mistress who was born a rural blacksmith's daughter.

St Martin-in-the-Fields

Trafalgar Square, WC2.

This church, built by James Gibbs between 1721 and 1726, is an odd mix. Steps as busy as those of an Italian church lead up to a pillared portico that could have been shipped in from Ancient Greece, and the whole is surmounted by a wedding-cake spire that was at least partly influenced by the work of Sir Christopher Wren. Despite being set a little way up from Trafalgar Square, it is one of the most eye-catching buildings in the area. Inside, you can see an impressive plasterwork ceiling by the Italian craftsmen Artari and Bagutti, and every Sunday except Christmas week you can come to choral evensong at 5 p.m. In the eighteenth-century crypt you can choose from a selection of eighteenth-century brass lords and ladies and rub a bit of history at the **Brass Rubbing Centre** (*Mon–Sat, 10 a.m.–6 p.m., Sun. noon–6 p.m.*). The crypt also contains the café in the crypt (see Eating and Drinking).

The National Gallery

North side of Trafalgar Square, WC2, tel. 071 839 3321. Open Mon–Sat 10 a.m.–6 p.m., Sun 2–6 p.m., closed 1 Jan, Good Friday, first Monday in May, 24, 25, 26 December. Free. Disabled access via the Sainsbury Wing and Orange Street entrance. Gift shops.

Boasting 'one of the world's finest collections of Western European painting from about 1260 to 1920', Wilkins's 1838 long classical pillared and porticoed National Gallery building, despite taking up the whole north side of Trafalgar Square, is unimpressive. You could, instead, consider the statue of a seated woman on the east façade by Flaxman. Flaxman decided that the statue, originally destined for Marble Arch, should represent Britannia, a figure who was invented by the Romans to personify a conquered Britain and became for the Victorians a symbol of Britain as conqueror; when Flaxman discovered that his statue was going to the National Gallery instead, he decided that Britannia should become Minerva, so the face that had once been modelled on Frances Stewart, a mistress of Charles II, came to stand for Minerva, the Roman goddess of Wisdom, who, in Victorian Britain, embodied Prudence.

Once you're inside, it's hard to know where to start, because the National Gallery has good examples of works by most of the major artists who painted from the thirteenth century onwards. There are three rare works by Piero della Francesca (?1420–92), including the formal yet intensely human fifteenth-century *Baptism of Christ*. Leonardo da Vinci's (1452–1519) large-scale 'cartoon', the bewitching *Virgin and Child with Saints Anne and John the Baptist*, is fascinating for its insight into the genius of da Vinci. Hans Holbein the Younger's (1497–1543) double portrait *The Ambassadors* is mysterious for the strange, free-floating, elongated skull at the bottom. The attention to detail of Jan van Eyck's (d. 1441) *The Marriage of Giovanni Arnolfini* could absorb you for hours. The National's Rembrandts include an intimate study of *A Woman Bathing in a Stream* and one of his very last self-portraits, *Self-Portrait Aged Sixty-three*.

The National Gallery began in 1824, when Parliament voted to buy John Julius Angerstein's collection of paintings. Today the Gallery displays Angerstein's contribution and works collected since in rooms that revel in the Victorian taste for maroon and forest-green silk wallpapers. That's until you reach the Sainsbury Wing (opened 1991), which was specifically designed by Robert Venturi to house the Early Renaissance Collection of Italian and Northern Works as well as the techno-impressive Micro Gallery (look up any of the Gallery's paintings on the computer), a swish cappuccino bar/restaurant and a smart lecture hall. Pick up a floor plan from the Information Desk to see how the works are divided chronologically between wings. Almost all the Gallery's 2,300 paintings are on display at any one time.

Rokeby Venus Perhaps the most famous painting in the National Gallery is the one that was nearly destroyed during an axe attack on 10 March 1914 by a small woman in a neat grey suit, suffragette **Mary Richardson**. She declared, during her trial for damaging Velázquez's *The Toilet of Venus* (known as 'The Rokeby Venus'): 'I have tried to destroy the picture of the most beautiful woman in mythological history as a protest against the Government destroying Mrs Pankhurst, who is the most beautiful character in modern history.' The nation was outraged – not just at the damage but because, as a result of Mary Richardson's protest, the National, then the Wallace Collection, the Tate and other galleries in the country were closed to the public while trustees reconsidered the guard and alarm situation.

The Times described the 'Rokeby Venus' as 'perhaps the finest painting of the nude in the world'; 'She is ... the Goddess of Youth and Health, the embodiment of elastic strength and vitality – of the perfection of Womanhood at the moment when it passes from the bud to the flower.' Mary Richardson was condemned to six months, the most the judge could give for her crime, but since she was only on temporary release from Holloway under the 'Cat and Mouse Act' (i.e. until she recovered health after hunger-striking), when she returned to gaol it wasn't clear which sentence she was serving. Linda Nead notes that it wasn't until 1952 that Richardson gave an additional reason for choosing the Velázquez: 'I didn't like the way men visitors to the gallery gaped at it all day.'

Leyster, Ruysch, Vigée-Lebrun: three women who made it

The paintings of **Judith Leyster** (1609–60) are represented in the National Gallery by *A Boy and a Girl* (late 1630s), which may have been an illustration of the Dutch proverb on children's carefree nature, 'to hold an eel by its tail'. Leyster, daughter of a Haarlem brewer, gained such renown in her day that she was able to take on three male pupils and even sue her former tutor, Frans Hals, for stealing one from her. By the 1890s, however, she was forgotten, and Frans Hals was in great demand. Cunning dealers deleted Leyster's star monogram and substituted the initials FH, and major international galleries bought Leysters as Hals. This 'offers a sober warning to art historians committed to a view of women's productions as obviously inferior to those of men,' says Whitney Chadwick in *Women, Art and Society*. '"Some women artists tend to emulate Frans Hals," noted James Laver in 1964, "but the vigorous brush strokes of the master were beyond their capability. One has only to look at the work of a painter like Judith Leyster to detect the weakness of the feminine hand." Yet many have looked and not seen.'

Although Leyster is known for her genre paintings, to boost her income she also did watercolour tulip illustrations for sales catalogues known as 'Tulip Books'. It may have been the sixteenth-century boom in botanical publishing that brought flower paintings in oils to prominence in Holland in the early seventeenth century. **Rachel Ruysch** (1664–1750) gained international status in the field. The National Gallery holds a classic example of her work, *Flowers in a Vase*, which Whitney Chadwick describes as balancing 'a swirl of twisting blossoms along a diagonal axis'. Ruysch – who, says art historian Maurice Grant, was 'as great in her line as Rembrandt in his' – was born in Amsterdam to an anatomy and botany professor who dabbled in oils, encouraged Rachel's interest in his collection of minerals and animal skeletons, and apprenticed her to a top flower painter, William van Aelst, at the age of fifteen. In 1701 she married the painter Juriaem Pool, joined The Hague painters' guild, had ten children and still managed to continue working. From 1708 to 1713 she was court painter in Düsseldorf. She commanded high sums for her works, which numbered at least a hundred and probably over two hundred by the time of her death.

Parisian Royalist **Elisabeth Louise Vigée-Lebrun** (1755–1842) rivalled Angelica Kauffmann for acclaim as the eighteenth century's best-known, most flamboyant woman painter. Vigée-Lebrun's prolific output (around 1,000 works) is represented at the National Gallery by *Self-Portrait in a Straw Hat*, which is almost certainly a reference to Rubens's famous *The Straw Hat*, also at the National Gallery.

Born to a hairdresser and a pastel portraitist whose friends gave her art lessons, Elisabeth completed her self-training by copying old and modern masters, and started to do portraits in oils after her father's death in 1770 to pay for her brother's schooling. Some portraits were of aristocrats, and her marriage to the well-connected but money-careless J.B.P. Lebrun ensured her entry into the privileged *salon* world, where artists could mix socially with upper-class patrons. In 1779 she painted her first portrait of Marie Antoinette, who became a personal friend and assisted her election as one of only four women members to the French Academy in 1783 at the age of twenty-eight. Instead of elaborate court costumes, Vigée-Lebrun took the convention-breaking step of showing her sitters in simple white Grecian gowns. Her work was acclaimed, but trouble was brewing.

While J.B.P. Lebrun was fast frittering away Elisabeth's substantial earnings, the backlash against her work came in the form of attacks on her reputation – she was accused, amongst other things, of having 'intimate' knowledge of her sitters. By 1789 a tarnished reputation was the least of her worries: the French Revolution was under way. In October, after the march of the market women on Versailles, Vigée-Lebrun upped sticks and left France with her daughter. What became a twelve-year exile resulted in renown abroad. In Rome she painted portraits of the royal court and Emma Hamilton, and met Angelica Kauffmann. In England at the turn of the century she painted portraits of the Prince of Wales and Lord Byron.

You can go back to paintings in the National Gallery again and again and still want more, in which case you might want to buy the book of the pictures, *The National Gallery Collection* (National Gallery Publications), which has 250 reproductions chosen by Michael Levy with accompanying text.

ART, GREATNESS AND THE FEMALE NUDE

Women's absence as artists and presence as nudes is a time-worn art debate. Feminist art historians began questioning the litany in the early 1970s, when some set out to find forgotten or underrated women artists (such as Rachel Ruysch and Anne Damer); others, including Linda Nochlin, ask: 'Why have there been no great women artists?' In *Women, Art and Power and Other Essays* (Thames & Hudson), Nochlin knocks the notion that 'great' men are simply 'born genius', saying that 'greatness' is largely down to training in accepted institutions, from which women have historically been barred. She goes on to wonder: 'What of the small band of heroic women, who, throughout the ages, despite obstacles, have achieved preeminence?' Are there any qualities that characterise them as a group? 'Almost without exception, [they] were either the daughters of artist fathers, or, generally later, in the nineteenth and twentieth centuries, had a close personal connection with a stronger or more dominant male artistic personality.' Mme Vigée-Lebrun, Angelica Kauffmann, Gwen John and Rachel Ruysch all fit the first category.

In *The Female Nude* (Routledge), Linda Nead notes: 'More than any other subject, the female nude connotes "Art". The framed image of a female body, hung on the wall of an art gallery, is shorthand for art more generally; it is an icon of Western culture, a symbol of civilization and accomplishment.' She asserts that the female nude has almost always presupposed a male painter and a male viewer, and that the female nude 'proposes particular definitions of the female body. ... The obscene body is the body without borders or containment.' Nead considers the dilemma feminist artists face, quoting Lucy Lippard's 1976 *Art in America* article: 'A woman using her own face and body has a right to do what she will with them, but it is a subtle abyss that separates men's use of women for sexual titillation from women's use of women to expose that insult.'

National Portrait Gallery

St Martin's Place, WC2, tel. 071 306 0055. Open Mon–Fri 10 a.m.–5 p.m., Sat 10 a.m.–6 p.m., Sun 2–6 p.m., closed New Year's Day, Good Friday, first Monday in May, Christmas Eve, Christmas Day and Boxing Day. Admission free except for special exhibitions.

Tucked round the corner from the National Gallery you'll see one of the world's most comprehensive historical surveys of one nation's men and women in paintings, photographs and sculpture. There are images of many women mentioned in this book, from Elizabeth I to Elizabeth Fry, Mary Wollstonecraft to Margaret Thatcher, and many more in between. Amongst the works is a 1942 self-portrait by Hannah Gluckstein – or, as she preferred to be known (refusing to use 'Miss' as a prefix), **Gluck** (1895–1978). The daugher of tea-shops founder J. Lyons, Gluck 'ran away with 2s. 6d. in my pocket and no food card, a necessity during the [First World] war', to don a man's suit, crop her hair and become a painter, first doing 'instant portraits' in the Oxford Street department store, Selfridges. 'I never "pose" a sitter,' she wrote, once she had set up her own studio. 'I spend much time watching them at work and at ease, then seize that split second when the whole personality is involved.' Gluck became known for staging exhibitions with panache after she decorated the Fine Arts Society gallery in 1932 as a 'Gluck room', with stepped three-tier 'Gluck' frames on white-panelled walls set off by Constance Spry flower-and-vegetable arrangements.

Regarding the new mid-nineteenth-century craze for photography, the novelist Elizabeth Gaskell said: 'Other women may not object to having their portraits taken for the public, and sold indiscriminately, but I feel a strong insurmountable objection to it.' Every household simple *had* to have a photograph album, featuring the royal family, celebrities and, finally, themselves. 'Pictorially, the professional photographers still had little to contribute,' says David Piper in *The English Face* (National Portrait Gallery Publications). 'The most remarkable work was being done by amateurs like Lewis Carroll, and most notably, by Julia Margaret Cameron.'

Having retired to England with her Anglo-Indian jurist husband and six children, **Julia Margaret Cameron** (1815–79) – ' a woman of noble plainness', as a friend described her – was forty-eight when her daughter gave her a newfangled present, a camera. Undaunted by the cumbersome equipment, she turned a glazed-chicken house into a studio, a coal-hole into a darkroom, and pressed everyone from her maid to members of her distinguished circle of friends (including Tennyson, Browning and Darwin) to sit for her, sometimes for up to twenty minutes at a time.

Her work fell into two categories. Her 'mythological' tableaux – or 'fancy' pictures, as she called them – proved instantly popular. Invited to illustrate Tennyson's *Idylls of the King* in 1874, she found that a quayside porter in Yarmouth, Isle of Wight, near her home in Freshwater Bay, made an excellent King Arthur.

But today it is for her portraits of friends including Virginia Woolf's mother, Julia Stephen, that she is revered. When the trend was for conventional full-length poses with Grecian urn- and pillar-painted backdrops, Julia Margaret Cameron 'concentrated on the seat of intellect, the head, often wrapping the shoulders in a loose dark drapery,' says David Piper. She wrote of her subjects: 'My whole soul has endeavoured to do its duty towards them in recording faithfully the greatness of the inner as well as the features of the outer man.' Her approach was unconventional in every way: she used extra-large plates and an unusually long exposure (three to seven minutes) which, of course, meant that sitters moved at least slightly during the process. 'When focusing and coming to something which to my eye was very beautiful,' she wrote, 'I stopped there, instead of screwing on the lens to the more definite focus which all other photographers insist on.'

David Piper judges that 'The success of her portraits rested on the excellence of her eye, her insistence on a beautiful effect, and the deliberate "imperfection" of her technique.' Her photographs could even suggest, says Piper, 'a failure of the sitter to wash beforehand'. Of Julia Margaret Cameron's portrait of historian Thomas Carlyle (in the National Portrait Gallery), Roger Fry wrote: 'Neither Whistler nor Watts come near to this in the breadth of the conception, in the logic of the plastic evocations, and neither approach the poignancy of this revelation of character.' Perhaps this is why Carlyle felt equivocal: 'It is as if suddenly the picture began to speak, terrifically ugly and woebegone, but has something of a likeness – my candid opinion.'

The National Portrait Gallery also holds a marble bust of Elizabeth Farren, Countess of Derby, as Thalia, Muse of Comedy (*c.*1789) by **Anne Seymour Damer** (1749–1828), the only pre-twentieth-century British woman sculptor of note. The only daughter of Field Marshal Henry Seymour Conway, Anne had, as a child, seen an Italian pavement artist modelling a wax head, and decided she could do better. Her father's cousin, the writer Horace Walpole, took her under his wing and helped her through an apprenticeship that included time with the sculptor John Bacon. She did marry at eighteen, but after accruing heavy debt, John Damer shot himself in 1776. The yearly allowance of £2,500 that remained allowed her to devote herself to her art and become a professional sculptor, dividing her time between England, Italy and Portugal.

Damer, an enthusiastic society hostess, had to suffer snide comments from friends and the press. One satiric 1789 engraving condemning her for daring to carve academic nude figures shows her chiselling the nude backside of Apollo wearing modesty-protecting gloves. Casting aspersions on the nature of Damer's relations with women, a pamphlet called *The Whig Club* wrote of Elizabeth Farren: 'She is supposed to feel more exquisite delight from the touch of the cheek of Mrs. D–r than the fancy of any novelties which the wedding night can promise with such a partner as His Lordship.' Despite all this, Damer gained renown and large-scale commissions including 'Isis', sculpted in 1785 for the Thames bridge at Henley. 'She models like Bernini,' wrote Horace Walpole, '[and] has excelled moderns in the similitudes of her busts.'

WESTMINSTER SEE MAP ON P.89

There are some magnificent major sights in Westminster, including the Tate Gallery and Westminster Abbey, and a few lesser ones, such as the Jewel Tower. It can be tricky, though, finding a relaxing place to eat or just rest for half an hour.

Undulating, beautiful leafy **St James's Park** gets jam-packed on sunny days. Sunbathers stretch out in green-striped deck chairs, gruff local pensioners bulldoze parties of school children out of

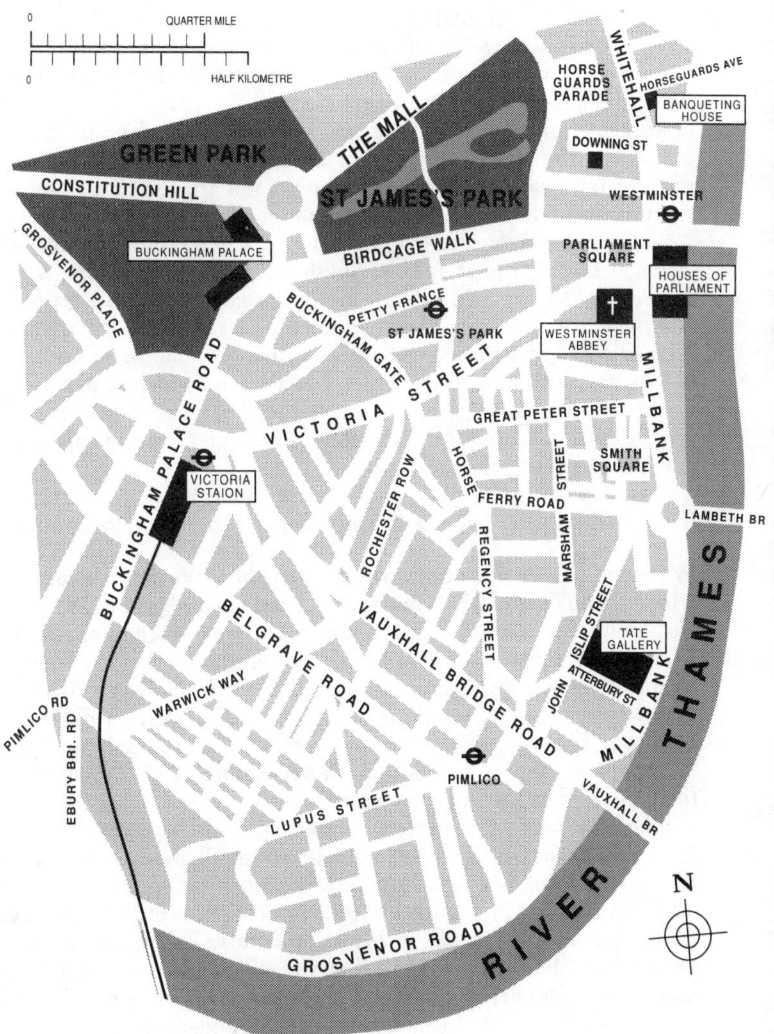
0
QUARTER MILE
0
HALF KILOMETRE
GREEN PARK
CONSTITUTION HILL
THE MALL
ST JAMES'S PARK
HORSE GUARDS PARADE
WHITEHALL
HORSEGUARDS AVE
BANQUETING HOUSE
DOWNING ST
WESTMINSTER
BUCKINGHAM PALACE
BIRDCAGE WALK
PARLIAMENT SQUARE
HOUSES OF PARLIAMENT
GROSVENOR PLACE
BUCKINGHAM GATE
PETTY FRANCE
ST JAMES'S PARK
WESTMINSTER ABBEY
BUCKINGHAM PALACE ROAD
VICTORIA STREET
GREAT PETER STREET
MILLBANK
SMITH SQUARE
VICTORIA STAION
HORSE FERRY ROAD
ROCHESTER ROW
MARSHAM STREET
LAMBETH BR
REGENCY STREET
BELGRAVE ROAD
VAUXHALL BRIDGE ROAD
ISLIP STREET
TATE GALLERY
JOHN
ATTERBURY ST
MILLBANK
WARWICK WAY
PIMLICO RD
EBURY BRI. RD
PIMLICO
VAUXHALL BR
LUPUS STREET
RIVER THAMES
GROSVENOR ROAD
N

their way and tourists cluster round the lake path photographing each other with sparrows eating out of their hands. Along Whitehall, visitors don't know which imposing grey-white Portland stone building to focus on first, while the mounted guard, splendid in crimson jacket and sprouting gilt helmet, remains stoically oblivious to the taunts of passers-by and mischievous children for an hour, until another guard replaces him. The formal **Changing of the Guard** takes place *between 11 a.m. and noon at Whitehall and Buckingham Palace*. Time of year and weather affect the exact time, so ring 0839 123411 for details. Around Victoria there are office blocks and a scattering of chemists, newsagents and sandwich takeaway shops with shades pulled down unless it's the lunchtime rush of businessmen and women, hectic nurses from nearby St Thomas' Hospital and grey-uniformed teenage escapees from the St Paul's School dining-hall.

The place to go for good food and high-class lunchtime BBC classical concerts is **St John's,** Smith Square (*off Millbank, up Dn Stanley St, tel. 071 222 1061 for programming details*; go to the basement for the licensed Footstool buffet restaurant). A riverside rectangle of grass that is usually less crowded than St James's Park is **Victoria Tower Gardens,** which has a small children's playground at the Lambeth Bridge end, and at the Abingdon Street entrance you'll find a statue of Emmeline Pankhurst and a plaque to Christabel Pankhurst.

The Pankhursts, like women after them, made their presence felt in Westminster because it was the seat of national government.

Women in Parliament: most notably Nancy Astor and Margaret Thatcher Constance **Markiewicz** (1868–1927), an Irish deb who married a Polish count and was nicknamed 'the Red Countess' for her Sinn Féin activism, became in the 1918 general election, after a campaign conducted from Holloway prison, the first woman to be elected an MP (for the St Patrick's division of Dublin). But as a Nationalist protest she refused to go to Westminster, and so it was that **Nancy Astor** (1879–1964) became the first woman MP in Parliament.

Gender was an issue from the start. Some suggested that the American society hostess was pulled into the Plymouth seat only on the coat-tails of her rich husband, Waldorf Astor, after he stood down as MP for Plymouth in 1919 in order to accept his peerage. Certainly, she was elected in his place with less than half the votes her husband had won in 1910, but she still had a majority of more than 5,000, and her campaigning style was very much her own. She was known for great effrontery, charm and unusual tactics such as – towards the end of a public address – to approach 'some old woman scowling in a neighbouring doorway, who simply hated her,' recalled one admirer, 'take both her hands and kiss her on the cheek or something of that sort'. She found heckling positively helpful: 'It takes opponents to get me gingered up,' biographer John Grigg (*Nancy Astor*, Sidgwick & Jackson) records her saying during the by-election. And she did not compromise to win votes. After asking the driver of a petrol lorry how he intended to vote, she noticed that he was smoking and said, 'If you don't put out that cigarette you won't vote for anybody'.

It's hard to imagine the effect the very presence of Nancy Astor must have had when, on 1 December 1919, she was introduced to the long-time all-male House of Commons. Much attention was paid to her attire – black coat and skirt – and to her demeanour (would she use feminine wiles or attempt to become an honorary man?). '[F]rom the first moment of her appearance in that exclusive club a terrifying responsibility rested upon her. She carried the repute of future women MPs in her elegant gloved hands,' wrote Mary Stocks later. 'Everybody waited to see what she would say or do; and those who resented female incursion into that sacred male preserve devoutly prayed that she might do or say the wrong thing. She did not say or do the wrong thing, but she often said and did the unexpected thing.' Lord Campion wrote: 'She would keep up a running and very audible commentary on a speech with which she disagreed, or continue to interrupt when the Member speaking refused to give way.' One final resort was to pull Sir Frederick down physically by his jacket.

Nancy had personal admiration for the Pankhursts; she would not have called herself a feminist but did decide that as the only woman in the House she should prioritise women's issues. She began in her maiden speech with a request for state control of drink, saying that she spoke 'for hundreds of women and children throughout the country who cannot speak for themselves. I want to tell you that I do know the working man, and I know that, if you tell him the truth about drink, he would be as willing as anybody else to put up with these vexatious restrictions.' She became active in campaigns for women police, slum clearance and nursery facilities. From the mid-1920s onwards she fought for more recreational space for children, and helped to found the National Playing Fields Association. 'To me there is no more tragic figure than the small boy or girl taken up for playing in the streets. He may be fined, but it is we grown-ups who should be convicted and condemned,' she announced at the Albert Hall launch of the Association, and added:

> There is an old notion that girls ought to be always at home darning stockings and cooking meals. . . . Of course, there is a right thought at the back of this old idea. I am all for women and girls knowing about housework – they are the first to suffer if they don't. But good housekeeping nowadays demands an iron constitution, and an iron constitution demands fresh air and exercise.

PR AND BODY LOTION: TWO 1980s WOMEN

Champagne and Buddhism, 'green' ethics and a multi-million-pound turnover – **Lynne Franks** (b. 1948), London's PR Queen, and **Anita Roddick** (b. 1942), founder of the Body Shop, exemplify key aspects of the 1980s.

'Throughout the eighties, there wasn't much going on that we weren't involved in,' says Franks of her PR firm. 'Live Aid, Swatch watches, Brylcreem.' Initially suspicious of pushy PR people, she was persuaded to set up in business by Katharine Hamnett, who became her first client in the 1970s. Lynne Franks soon represented almost every major fashion designer and celebrity figures such as pop star Annie Lennox, and she really hit the headlines when the Labour Party became a client in the mid-1980s.

While enthusiastically enacting the 'I shop, therefore I am' 1980s buzz phrase, Franks embraced the creed of the Nichirin Shoshu Buddhists, who were rumoured to chant for material gain. She once confessed to chanting for taxis. She installed a Buddhist shrine in her North London home, and had gold cushions made to match. She became a totem for the Filofax-, designer-crazed eighties when she was cited as part-inspiration for Edini, the central character of comedienne Jennifer Saunders's 1990s TV spoof of eighties greed, *Absolutely Fabulous*. But the 1980s are over. The Lynne Franks PR Agency is being renamed more anonymously LFPR, leaving Lynne Franks free to spend more time in her house in Majorca, where she can, she says, 'become a real human being'.

Anita Roddick has no intention of bowing out in the 1990s. Indeed, she decries the eighties, which she recalls opening with 'the emergence of "gimme" capitalism and the supposition that the first duty of business was to look after Number One'. She concludes her autobiography-come-business handbook *Body and Soul* (Vermillion) with the words, 'Make no mistake about it – I'm doing this for me.' She is seen by many as a perfect example of a Thatcherite entrepreneur. Tory politician Edwina Currie described her as 'a beautiful and original woman who deserves her success'. Yet Roddick sells her Body Shop products on ideals. 'I hate the beauty industry,' she says. 'It is a monster industry selling unattainable dreams ... Our concept of beauty is Mother Teresa, not some bimbo.'

Roddick's business started as one small shop in Brighton in 1976, when she decided to 'address a whole group of women like myself, who are not stupid and don't want to pay a fortune for a moisture cream that is nothing more than an oil and water emulsion'. She rejected expensive packaging, condemned animal testing, and searched out ancient herbal remedies. 'Bedouin tribes cover their corpses with basil to stop putrefaction. I thought it would be good for deodorants.' Runners in the London Marathon complained of sore feet, so the Body Shop handed out free samples of peppermint foot lotion to the runners, and the product became a bestseller. Soon Body Shops were opening all over the country. But 'we did not get much attention in the press until our first London shops opened, in Portobello Road and Covent Garden.' Suddenly Anita was in demand on all the women's magazine programmes on afternoon TV, talking about 'things like how to make a face mask with a boiled lettuce and blended avocado ... demonstrating how to make all this stuff in the kitchen like a latter-day green Fanny Craddock'. In 1985 she was made Veuve Clicquot Businesswoman of the Year, and in 1988 she was awarded an OBE. The company, which was started on £4,000 on a back street, has a current market value of £365 million.

Many veteran suffragettes found it distressing that British women's first official political representative was such a firm believer in women's traditional roles. Yet the woman who rushed up to Nancy on her inaugural day while she was changing trains at Paddington and said, 'It is the beginning of our era. I am glad I have suffered for this', had not misplaced her faith. Many of the women who entered the House during Nancy Astor's twenty-five years in Parliament were, regardless of party affiliations, taken under her wing, starting in October 1921 with Liberal Mrs Wintringham and including Margaret Bondfield (see East End), who became the first woman Cabinet Minister in 1929.

After only a year in Parliament, Nancy Astor called a conference on 1 March 1921 at her 4 St James's Square home of more than forty representatives from the confusion of women's groups to advise them from her insider's experience of the best way to become more politically effective, mainly by setting up a 'headquarters organisation'. 'By the middle of the year,' records John Grigg, 'a Consultative Committee of Women's Organizations had come into being. Its object was to improve the political, economic and social status of women.'

In 1943, when Nancy Astor was in her sixties and still an MP after twenty-four years, 'a whole Parliamentary debate assumed', writes Wendy Webster in *Not a Man to Match Her* (Women's Press), 'that the menopause disqualified women between the ages of forty-five and fifty from war work'. Wendy Webster takes it as evidence of changed perceptions that when Margaret Thatcher 'stood for the leadership of the Conservative party some thirty years later, at the age of 49, the menopause was scarcely mentioned', yet it may simply have been that double standards still operated – and were indeed perpetuated by Thatcher herself.

In May 1979 **Margaret Thatcher** (b. 1925) became the first woman Prime Minister of any major industrial nation and almost immediately, *Newsweek* journalist Alan Meyer noted, the number of women in the House of Commons fell by nearly a third: to 19 out of 635, the smallest number since 1951. 'The battle for women's rights has largely been won,' she said. 'I hate those strident tones we hear from some Women's Libbers.' She prided herself on a reputation as 'the best man in the country', yet played on her femininity. A 'housewife' image was devised by her media adviser, Gordon Reece, during the leadership contest. 'Some say I preach merely the homilies of housekeeping or the parables of the parlour,' she told the Lord Mayor's Banquet in 1982, 'but I do not repent. Those parables would have saved many a financier from failure and many a country from crisis.'

Even before she was Prime Minister, Labour Cabinet Minister Barbara Castle noted in her published diaries that Mrs Thatcher's wardrobe practically took over the lady MPs' room in the Commons: 'There would be half-a-dozen garments hanging up there and underneath them a tidy row of at least eight pairs of shoes.' Margaret Thatcher discussed her complexion; for example, in the 1971 radio interview Wendy Webster records: 'The first impression you create is a terribly important one. I don't wear a lot of cosmetics, I'm not heavily made up, but I like fairly good ones, and ones that suit my skin.' In 1986 she went further and invited the BBC to film her wardrobe. 'This black one came through the Falklands war all right,' she said, fondly fingering a suit, and in the same programme she made the famous declaration that all her underwear came from Marks and Spencer's. By the time Mrs Thatcher had won three consecutive terms in office, however, her housewife image had largely been displaced. Media stories came to concentrate on her 'glamour'. The sum of her new teeth, voice, hairstyle, clothes and accessories caused Russell Davies to say in 1989: 'She has changed more than any authentic human being should', except for 'the low, scuttling run, with bent knees and that stiff clockwork arm batting metronomically to and fro'.

From the day she became Prime Minister, Margaret Thatcher sparked contrasting violent reactions. 'We are quite depressed by her election,' the feminist magazine *Spare Rib* wrote. 'We think it will work against Feminism.' 'I think she's shown that anything's possible for women,' said Joanna Foster in 1989 when she was chairperson designate of the Equal Opportunities Commission, 'and she's got there on her own merits and hard work and skills, which is wonderful.'

In *One of Us* (Pan), Hugo Young paints a picture of her as a Grantham grocer's daughter with plodding determination who barely scraped into Cambridge University's Chemistry Department and escaped jobs, including cake-filling-tester at J. Lyons in Hammersmith, only when, through Conservative Party campaigning, she met independently wealthy Denis Thatcher, whom she described later as acting as 'a shock absorber'. Having believed that the Treasury was as high as a woman could go (after her marriage she had concentrated on studying law, specifically taxation), Margaret Thatcher won first the leadership of the Party and then, in 1979, the general election. Her rhetoric was anti-socialist. She said that anyone who went through the Welfare State turned into a caged bird: 'It has social security. It has food and it has warmth, and so on. But what is the good of all that if it has not the freedom to fly out and live its own life?' She opposed consensus politics and declared her aim to be 'not the extension but the limitation of government' through tax incentives, reducing the money supply to attack inflation, cuts in public spending and high interest rates, with the final goal of relaunching Britain as a player on the international board.

Wendy Webster interprets Thatcherism as a 'toughocracy' rather than a 'meritocracy': 'It is to depend on no one'. Unemployment soared to three million. The official Soviet news agency TASS's nickname for her, 'The Iron Lady', gained common currency after her hardline reaction towards the USSR over the invasion of Afghanistan, and she set her image as a woman who could be relied on to stand firm with the famous phrase 'the Lady's not for turning'. This intransigence and repeated autocratic Cabinet reshuffles led to her downfall after three successive terms in office. On the run-up to the next general election, Labour's popularity in the polls had increased to a substantial lead, and by autumn 1989 Margaret Thatcher had been deposed in favour of John Major.

THE SUFFRAGETTE PANKHURSTS: EMMELINE, INSTIGATOR/FACILITATOR; CHRISTABEL, LAWYER/ORATOR; SYLVIA, ARTIST/IDEALIST

The three Pankhursts who came to lead the fight for women's suffrage in England were, it seems, detested and adored in equal measure. 'Really the pair are not seeking democratic freedom, but self importance,' wrote Independent Labour Party (ILP) Chairman Bruce Glasier after a meeting with Christabel and Mrs Pankhurst shortly after the two women had left the ILP to found the Women's Social and Political Union (WSPU) in Manchester; he continued: 'Christabel paints her eyebrows grossly and looks selfish, lazy and wilful. They want to be ladies, not workers, and lack the real humility of heroism.' Despite his misogynistic 'scorn of their miserable individual sexism', his remark highlights a number of pertinent issues, including motive. There were already several suffrage societies in and around Manchester in 1903 – why found another? In *The Strange Death of Liberal England* (MacGibbon and Kee) George Dangerfield wrote that Mrs Emmeline Goulden Pankhurst (1858–1928) who, as her liberal textile factory father's favourite, had been educated in Paris in place of the eldest son, would not remain behind the lines if she could stand in front. Martin Pugh added that Mrs Pankhurst and her eldest daughter Christabel (1880–1958), who trained in law and reportedly disliked grass-roots involvement, could not deal with the working-class women textile workers and consequently soon 'went in pursuit of the drawing rooms of London'.

The Manchester–London move was partly facilitated by Emmeline's daughter Sylvia (1882–1960), who won an art scholarship and moved to London to study at the Royal Academy and soon found her Park Walk flat used as a base by Mrs Pankhurst on her vote-lobbying trips to Parliament. Sylvia's relationship with the fight for suffrage was equivocal at this stage, largely because she felt deeply jealous of Christabel as her mother's favourite.

In 1905 Christabel was charged with the 'crime' of addressing her previously ignored question: 'Will the Liberal Party give Votes for Women?', direct to Sir Edward Grey at a political rally in the Free Trade Hall, Manchester. On hearing that her sister had been arrested, Sylvia noted that 'Mrs. Pankhurst, to whom her first born had ever been the dearest of her children, proudly and openly proclaimed her eldest daughter to be her leader.' Patricia W. Romero writes in *E. Sylvia Pankhurst* (Yale): 'Seeing herself on the sidelines, Sylvia responded by founding the first London branch of the

WSPU' and devoted her art to producing banners (later the 'Suffragette Tea Service' and 'The Holloway Brooch'). Mrs Pankhurst and Christabel moved the WSPU base to London after Christabel had graduated in law with first-class honours in 1906, by which time Sylvia had already resigned the honorary secretaryship (against her mother's instructions). Christabel almost instantly ruled out the use of support crowds of East End working-class women and established the use of militant tactics. The wealthy recruit Emmeline Pethick-Lawrence chose green, white and purple (representing hope, purity and dignity) as the WSPU colours.

Christabel was clearly a charismatic figure. David Mitchell records in *Queen Christabel* (Macdonald & James) how men as well as women flocked to hear her speak, shouting 'We want Chrissie!' Her face was on badges, photos and postcards distributed by the WSPU, and celebrity status was indicated when Madame Tussaud's made a wax model of her. Emmeline Pethick-Lawrence hailed Christabel as the 'Maiden Warrior' who would 'go forth with the flat of the future, strong in the gladness and youth of your dauntless spirit, to smile with your sword of destiny the forces of stupid and unreasoning prejudice and blind domination'. Henry Nevinson admired her impudent dismissal of MPs as a 'rudimentary organ like the buttons in the middle of a tail-coat's back'. Nevinson believed that her law-breaking activities, such as arson and window-smashing, far from alienating wealthy subscribers, 'gave a more satisfying sensation of blood, of vicarious danger ... The more violent and dangerous the proposals for others the more vehemently they applauded, just as Spanish spectators applaud most when a horse is disembowelled and a man or bull drips blood.'

By 1909 journalists were referring to Christabel's 'witchery', an image Christabel recognised as powerful, writing on 19 September in the *Suffragette*: men 'are afraid of women's blows ... they have a superstitious terror of women in revolt'. Christabel had her detractors. George Bernard Shaw spoke of 'the henpecking and want of effective political capacity behind the huge resources of the WSPU. What are you to say to grown-up women who think that their dear jolly blithering Christabel is the greatest political genius since Richelieu?'

Sylvia has been perceived as the saint who stuck to her socialist principles when Emmeline and Christabel embraced autocratic rule and toured England during the war lecturing for the patriotic cause. Her biographer, Patricia W. Romero, suggests that Sylvia may have retained her belief in socialism specifically to annoy her sister and mother. She was certainly no angel. 'Sylvia,' George Bernard Shaw wrote to her on 12 September 1929, 'You are the queerest idiot genius of his age – the most ungovernable, self-interested, blindly and deadly wilful little rapscallion-condottiera that ever imposed itself on the infra-red end of the revolutionary spectrum as a leader.' It is unclear, then, if Sylvia founded a rival East End WSPU (see East End) in support of the 'feminine proletariat' Christabel dismissed as politically useless, or out of spite, or both.

Despite many reservations about their character and methods, few could deny the Pankhursts' achievements. The non-militant suffrage leader Millicent Fawcett admitted that the Pankhursts were responsible for bringing the issue of suffrage out of the shadows and 'sent it sweeping like a flame throughout the country'.

By the time women over the age of thirty were given the right to vote in 1918 (the age limit was reduced to twenty-one ten years later, and to eighteen in 1969), Sylvia had thrown herself into socialism, amongst other things running a co-operative toy factory throughout the war and travelling secretly to the USSR in 1920 to meet Lenin. Emmeline and Christabel had thrown themselves into patriotism, Mrs Pankhurst impressing Nancy Astor as the best speaker she had ever heard with a recruiting speech, and in 1926 standing for Whitechapel as a Conservative. The December 1918 general election took Christabel back to thoughts of Parliament, this time not petitioning for suffrage but standing as one of seventeen women candidates. She stood, with a manifesto that advocated collectivism and automation as the way to industrial salvation, for the Women's Party at Smethwick where, despite the lack of funds available to those without official party backing and the supposed disadvantage of a militant background, she lost by only 775 votes.

Banqueting House

Whitehall at Horseguards Avenue, SW1, tel. 071 930 4179. Adult £2.95, child £1.60, concessions £2.30; or can be seen on inclusive ticket for 'all five palaces' including the Tower of London and Hampton Court. Open Mon–Sat 10 a.m.–5 p.m., closed Bank Holidays and sometimes at short notice for government functions. Flight of stairs.

If you take this at face value it is a grand, not very clean building much like all the others on Whitehall, with a hall inside that can be perambulated in seconds. But if you watch the video in the crypt and use the Acoustiguide included with the admission price, you'll get a vivid picture of Inigo Jones's ground-breaking 1622 architectural memorial to the Stuart monarchs' divine right to rule.

Today, florists and government officials may be spraying wreaths gold and shifting stacks of chairs for a forthcoming function in this relatively simple first-floor box rectangle. In the heyday of the Stuart monarchs from James I to William and Mary of Orange (see Kensington Palace) the hall rang with the sounds of royal banquets and theatrical masques performed by members of the court in elaborate costumes under the lush Rubens ceiling paintings (commissioned by Charles I) which you can see more easily with the aid of thoughtfully placed mirrors on wheels.

Houses of Parliament

Entrance at St Stephen's Porch on St Margaret Street. Residents of the UK can write to their MP with as little as two days' notice to ask for a tour. Anyone can queue for admittance to the strangers' galleries during committee debates in the House of Commons and the House of Lords. Tues and Thur it's usually difficult to get into the Commons; the Lords is easier all round. For information on sittings tel. 071 219 4792.

As the powers to make policies for England passed from the hands of the monarchs to an elected government body, so Edward the Confessor's medieval Palace of Westminster became, after several fires and rebuildings, the Houses of Parliament. It is well worth the trouble of writing a letter or queueing to see inside the place where the laws of this land are debated and made, partly for the surprise of finding a mix of archaic traditions, lavish neo-Gothic décor and occasional evidence of run-of-the-mill office activities such as a working post-office counter in the mosaic-lavished, glittering **Central Lobby.**

Westminster Hall, which you'll see on your left as you are put through a rigorous X-ray security check, is the only part of the original medieval palace to have survived intact both the devastating 1834 fire and World War II bombing. Once the site of joustings and royal Christmas festivals, it is now empty, slightly dank-feeling and impressive, especially for its timber roof: the supporting hammerbeam alone reportedly weighs 660 tons. The hall's authentic Gothic style was the starting point for the 1835–60 construction of the Houses of Parliament by Charles Barry and Augustus Welby Pugin in eye-catching neo-Gothic. The profile as seen from Westminster Bridge, with spiky pinnacled 336-foot Victoria Tower at one end and the slightly smaller 320-foot Big Ben clock tower at the other, is immediately recognisable from a thousand postcards.

Inside, the layout is simple. The predominantly green-decorated House of Commons is to the north of the Central Lobby, and the lush red House of Lords is to the south. If you go to see a debate, you will glimpse Westminster Hall, pass through the amazing Central Lobby and sit in the cramped, discreetly raised **Strangers' Gallery** of your chosen House. If you're on a tour, the official 'Line of Route' takes you first to the high-Victoriana **Robing Room**, in which you are surrounded by legends of King Arthur's Round Table in big pictures and carvings; then you pass the collection of paintings in the **Royal Gallery** and through the sumptuous **Prince's Chamber** before you reach the **House of Lords**, where you'll find the crimson Woolsack that serves as the Lord Chancellor's seat. The statue of Churchill at the door of the Chamber in the Members' Lobby has one very shiny foot, because it is rubbed by MPs on their way into the **House of Commons** for good luck. Once inside you'll find out why, during televised debates, MPs can be seen craning uncomfortably into their seats: a grille motif repeated along the backs of benches disguises a series of amplifiers. The two red lines on the carpets in front of the government and opposition benches have no such practical use – they are the distance of two swords apart, honouring the centuries when opposing Members were required to stand behind their respective lines to stop fights breaking out.

As you leave the Houses of Parliament, if you look up at the corner of Bridge Street you'll see a yellow box saying 'Taxi', which lights up whenever a Member needs a cab.

The Jewel Tower

Opposite south end of the Houses of Parliament (Victoria Tower), tel. 071 222 2219. Open daily April–Sept 10 a.m.–6 p.m.; Oct–Mar Mon–Sat 10 a.m.–4 p.m. Adults £1.80, concessions £1.40, children 90p. Many awkward steps.

Built to house Edward II's jewels, the moated fourteenth-century Jewel Tower is one of the least altered of London's medieval buildings; on three (small) floors it houses an exhibition that traces the history of English Parliaments from the Magna Carta to Margaret Thatcher, with text, pictures and, on the top floor, a video. Displays include the Speaker's Robes and a suffragette cartoon showing a battered policeman, an angry woman brandishing an umbrella, and the Houses of Parliament, with a rhyme:

This is the house that man built,
And this is the policeman all tattered and torn
Who wished women voters had never been born,
Who nevertheless
Tho it gave him distress
Ran them all in,
In spite of their dress:
The poor suffragette
Who wanted to get
Into the House that man built.

Westminster Abbey

Entrance off Broad Sanctuary. Tel. 071 222 7110 for guided tour information and 071 222 5152 for information on services. Open Mon–Fri 9 a.m.–4.45 p.m.; Sat 9 a.m.–2.45 p.m./3.45 p.m.–5.45 p.m., admission to the Royal Chapels costs £3 adults, £1.50 concessions, £1 under-16s (the nave and cloisters can be accessed free of charge). On Wed 6–7.45 p.m. the whole Abbey is open free of charge. The Westminster Abbey Chapter House charges separate admission – £2 adults, £1.50 concessions, £1 children – and opens 10 a.m.–4 p.m. daily. Awkward ramps and turnings; staff available to assist.

William Morris and Pugin complained of the Abbey's tomb-and-effigy clutter, and architect-critic Nikolaus Pevsner describes the Abbey's skyline as 'disappointing', yet both the tawdriness of the blackened Reigate stone twin-towered medieval Gothic exterior and the surprising sense, once inside, that you have invaded a grand, echoing secret of magical chaos are appealing. You should bear two things in mind when you visit: (1) the cost – if you want to 'do' the Royal Chapels with audioguide and full colour brochure plus the Chapter House and Brass Rubbings, you could come out over £10 poorer; (2) there's a vast amount to see via a system of walkways that is maze-like and often crowded. Go with the flow to prevent exasperation then afterwards, if you have missed particular effigies, ask a guide to direct you.

In *London, Volume One* (Penguin), Pevsner treats the early history of Westminster Abbey as something of a detective story. He speculates on Roman fragments, Edward the Confessor's major eleventh-century involvement and the nationality of the architect, Henry of Reynes (English or French), who was commissioned by Henry III in 1245 to rebuild the Abbey as we see it today in French High Gothic style. Pevsner goes on to point out that 'We are so used to this cathedral-like building in the middle of London that we may forget to ask why it is that all other great English abbeys lie in ruins', and suggests that 'The answer is the unique connexion of the abbey with the king and the state. The church was the Reims and the Saint Denis of England put together, coronation as well as burial church of kings and queens.'

Elizabeth II was crowned in the Coronation Chair in June 1953, Princess Anne was married at the High Altar in 1973, and around the thirteenth-century shrine of Edward the Confessor 'a garland of royal tombs appeared' (Pevsner) from the fourteenth century onwards. Today, in the **Royal Chapels**, memorials to medieval queens lie next to statues of Victorian philanthropists. You can see the black marble tomb of Edward II's queen, Philippa of Hainault (1314–1369), the grandiloquent white marble tomb of Elizabeth I (see Greenwich) and the iron-fenced tomb of Lady Margaret Beaufort (1443–1509), who encouraged her son, Henry VII, to rebuild the Abbey and called to inspect the 'new work' in 1501.

A floor plaque in **Poets' Corner** commemorates George Eliot, wall plaques celebrate Jane Austen and the Brontë sisters near the entrance to St Faith's Chapel, and above the organ loft door there's a memorial to Henrietta Barnett. Aphra Behn is buried under the first-floor slab in the refreshingly airy east **cloister**, and back in the **nave** on the left as you enter you'll find a black diamond shape on the floor for Angela Burdett Coutts and, near the north wall, a floor slab to Sidney and Beatrice Webb.

Apart from the effigies of queens, the Abbey's memorials to women can be small and hard to find. The statue of Saint Wilgefortis, also known as Saint Uncumber, is no exception. This bearded saint is at the far right of an overfilled niche above the tomb of Ludovic Stuart.

Buckingham Palace

SW1, tel. 071 930 4832. St James's Park or Victoria Underground.

A small country house was transformed into Buckingham Palace only after national embarrassment at having no permanent residence for royalty caused George IV to commission architect John Nash to create, between 1825 and 1830, a gold-tinted bath stone building. Despite a classical frieze in the middle and pedimented pavilions on either side, 'Buck House' still looks more like an expanded country house than a palace. Dame Jennifer Jenkins of the Royal Parks Review Group considers the Palace's setting 'quite simply a national disgrace. Pedestrians risk limb, even life,' she says, dodging cars to get from the Mall to the Queen Victoria memorial to the Palace, where visitors mistakenly think they'll get a better view.

The August 1993 test run of opening the Palace to the public for eight weeks may or may not be repeated. Visitors have confirmed that George V's description of the interior – as rather like a huge hotel – still holds good, only it's a rather dilapidated hotel now. Sure, there's gilding on the ballroom ceiling, and the music- and drawing-rooms are tranquil, but the carpets are a rather too lurid red; electric fires have been stuck in marble grates. There's undoubtedly a thrill to seeing how the royal half lives, but most architects agree that the **Royal Mews** are more stimulating (*open Tues, Wed, Thur 12–4 p.m. from around Apr–Sept, and Wed 12–4 p.m. only through winter; admission charge*). The lion-and-unicorn archway indicates that you are about to enter very grand stables indeed. The **Queen's Gallery** (*Buckingham Palace Road, open Mon–Sat 10.30 a.m.–5 p.m., Sun 2–5 p.m. admission charge*) is an uninspiring space to see temporary exhibitions selected from the extensive royal collection of paintings (a Van Dyck and a Rembrandt will usually be on display) and works of art including Sèvres porcelain and French furniture by Riesener.

From Queen Victoria to the Squidgy Tapes During a reign that lasted longer than that of any other British monarch, strong-willed **Queen Victoria** (1819–1901) saw her country rise to industrial greatness while the monarchy lost power to become little more than ceremony.

After a relatively frugal childhood dominated by her mother at Kensington Palace, Victoria asserted her independence as soon as she became queen in 1837 and moved to Buckingham Palace. It seems that she derived a naive pleasure from her political duties. A few days after her accession she wrote in her journal: 'I have so *many* communications from the Ministers, and from me to them, and I get so many papers to sign every day, that I have always a *very great* deal to do. I *delight* in this work.' A Mr Creevey observed: 'A more homely little being you never beheld, *when she is at her ease*, and she is evidently dying to be always more so. She laughs in real earnest, opening her mouth as wide as it can go, showing not very pretty gums. ... She eats quite as heartily as she laughs, I think I may say she gobbles.' But she was rash. Actions that threatened her popularity early on included refusing to dismiss Whig ladies of the bedchamber in recognition of Sir Robert Peel becoming Prime Minister in 1839. Her 1840 marriage to her cousin, Prince Albert, went down better, partly because he proved an enthusiastic patron of the arts, sponsoring the Royal Exhibition in 1851. Albert's death in 1861 caused two years of severe depression, after which Jubilee celebrations of her fiftieth and sixtieth years on the throne caused a final upsurge in her popularity. Always a staunch upholder of family values, by the time she died, aged eighty-two, she had thirty-seven grandchildren.

Soon after the accession five decades later of **Elizabeth II** (b. 1926), the reigning monarch again came to represent good old-fashioned family values – which was ironic, since she became a likely heir to the throne only after Edward VIII abdicated in order to marry an American divorcee, Mrs Wallis Simpson.

Elizabeth was popular from the start, pressing her father to allow her to volunteer as a trainee driver when World War II broke out. A 1945 newspaper photograph showed her as 'one of the girls, No. 230873 subaltern of the Auxiliary Transport Services, examining a piece of machinery'. After she became queen in 1953, her many foreign tours became famous for including 'walkabouts', during which she would chat to members of gathered crowds. Brian Hoey's *Monarchy: Behind the Scenes with the Royal Family* (BBC Books) furthered the image of Elizabeth as a down-to-earth woman with all the usual kinds of chores. She's called at 7.30 a.m. daily with a cup of tea, Hoey informs readers, and for breakfast she prefers something simple like a boiled egg. She's also loved for her devotion to her many corgi dogs, and for her refusal to update the style of her wardrobe. She cuts a distinctive figure at state occasions wearing a triangular headscarf tied under her chin.

But the marriage of Elizabeth's son Charles to Diana Spencer in 1981 turned out to be just the beginning of a series of royal marital bust-ups, culminating in what the Queen described in 1992 as her *annus horribilis. Daily Mail* journalist Nigel Dempster claimed that Diana had been doubtful about the marriage even during the engagement, but that her sisters had said: Tough, you're on the commemorative tea-towels. Newspaper magnates rejected almost entirely the kind of 'responsible' editorial approach that had kept Mrs Simpson secret for two years; sensational scoops were the order of the day. Tapes of Diana talking over the telephone to an alleged lover whom she fondly called 'Squidgy', and of Prince Charles telling Camilla Parker Bowles that he'd like to be her Tampax, became hot news and perhaps helped to precipitate the breakdown of their marriage. The question mark that hovers over the future of the British royal family ensures continued spectacular in-depth press coverage of every royal going-on from state visits to private holidays.

The Tate Gallery

Millbank at Atterbury Street, tel. 071 821 1313 or 071 821 7128 for information. Open Mon–Sat 10 a.m.–5.50 p.m., Sun 2–5.50 p.m. Free (except for rooms 28–30 when they house a special exhibition). Access for disabled visitors in John Islip Street, through the car park at the back of the Gallery. Wheelchairs available on request. Phone for information on Sculpture Tours for visually handicapped visitors. Feature films screened in the Clore Gallery auditorium. If you want to view works in store, pick up an application form at the information desk or write to Study Collections Manager, Tate Gallery, Millbank, London SW1P 4RG.

The Tate was built as a gift to the nation from sugar broker Sir Henry Tate on the site of a 1,100-cell penitentiary in what is generally considered a dull late-Victorian example of the grand Classical manner style of architecture. The building opened in 1897 as the 'Gallery of Modern British Art', when 'modern' was defined as post-1790. Today the collection is split in three: the pre-twentieth-century **British Collection**; the international post-1860 **Modern Collection**; and the **Turner Bequest**, which is marvellously displayed in the celebrated 1987 extension, the Clore Gallery (Stirling and Wilford), which can be 'read as a garden pavilion attached to a large house' complete with lily pond (Jones and Woodward, *A Guide to the Architecture of London*, Weidenfeld & Nicolson).

Inside, the décor's sometimes odd – grand marble fittings next to woodchip wallpaper – but the space is airy and laid out simply. Start on your left at the far end of the ground floor, and you can do a roughly chronological circuit. Only about an eighth of the Tate's collection is on display at any one time, and although rooms 1–10 remain pretty much the same, paintings are rehung annually, so some of the works mentioned below may not be on view when you visit. Before, during or after, it's worth investing in Simon Wilson's *Tate Gallery, An Illustrated Companion* (Tate Gallery).

In the **Tudor and Stuart** galleries you may see work by the Lely-influenced Covent Garden-based portraitist **Mary Beale** (1633–99), whose popularity allowed the high charges of £5 for painting a head, £10 if she included the body. You will almost certainly see *The Cholmondley Sisters* (*c.*1600–10, artist unknown), an eerily immediate two-dimensional depiction of 'Two ladies of the Cholmondley Family/Who were born on the same day/Married the same day/And brought to bed the same day', a story that is unlikely in fact but is pursued in the depiction of the 'sisters' as practically indistinguishable except for the colour of their eyes.

In 1768 the Royal Academy was founded, with Joshua Reynolds as its first president, and even before the end of the century Reynolds's taste for 'historical attitudes' in a 'Grand Style' version of Italian Renaissance masters was accepted nationally as a benchmark of quality. Luke Gardiner's commission of a painting of his fiancée with her two sisters inspired Reynolds to portray them as Greek goddesses worshipping the god of marriage, Hymen, in *Three Ladies Adorning a Term of Hymen (The Montgomery Sisters)* (1773).

William Blake (1757–1827) was RA-trained but almost immediately dismissed by contemporaries as an eccentric for expressing his highly personalised view of man's relationship with God through poetry and works such as the darkly powerful *Elohim Creating Adam* (1795, one of the Large Colour Print series) and the delicately coloured whirl *Beatrice Addressing Dante from the Car* (1824–7, part of the set of illustrations for Dante's epic, the *Divine Comedy*). Today, his dense, often disturbing visions make him one of the most interesting and important artists of his generation.

The Pre-Raphaelite Brotherhood, consisting of John Everett Millais, William Holman Hunt and Dante Gabriel Rossetti, also rejected the conceits of the RA. They looked back (before Raphael) and advocated idealised medieval values, rejecting industrialisation in favour of craftsmen. Elizabeth Siddal, a cutler's daughter and bonnet-shop assistant, became the lover, then wife, of Rossetti. She has been celebrated for forging a career not only as a model but as an artist in her own right. In the pomegranate-red Room 9 is Rossetti's moving tribute to Elizabeth Siddal, *Beata Beatrix* (*c.*1864–70), which was painted after Siddal's death from a laudanum (opium) overdose in 1862. Nearby you may see an example of Siddal's work, *Lady Affixing a Pennant to a Knight's Spear*.

Beyond the Pre-Raphaelites, you'll find works representing **Gwen John** (1876–1939), who started in childhood imitating Welsh beach painters, but was overshadowed in her lifetime in Britain by her brother, Augustus John, and in Paris by her lover, Augustus Rodin. Today Gwen John's acclaim exceeds her brother's. Of the Tate's fourteen Gwen John works, Simon Wilson praises *Nude Girl* (1909–10) for 'an intimacy, objectivity and grasp of the physical reality of the body, unprecedented in English painting', and goes on to suggest that the realism of this picture may have come largely from her dislike of the model. He quotes a September 1909 letter to Ursula Tyrwhitt: 'It is a great strain doing Fenella. It is a pretty little face, but she is *dreadful*.' **Vanessa Bell** (1879–1961) is represented at the Tate by eleven works including a 'Fauve' pale pink and acid yellow portrait of a friend, *Mrs St John Hutchinson* (1915), whom Vanessa and Duncan Grant painted during the same sitting.

Vanessa wrote to Roger Fry: 'On Friday we painted Mary. Duncan got very desperate and began his again, which I think I ought to have done but I didn't. It is a frightfully difficult arrangement for I am bang in front of her and everything is very straight and simple and very delicate colour.'

Compared for the realism of their nude portraits, both Stanley Spencer (1891–1959) and Lucien Freud (b. 1922) are striking not for the cool objectivity with which the veins and sags of the human body are rendered but for the compellingly self-revelatory choice of subjects and composition. Freud's *Girl With a White Dog* (1950–51) shows his first wife, Kitty Garman, on a sofa in a green dressing-gown cradling the pet's head in the bend of her knee; her bared right breast rests in the crook of her right arm. Spencer's *Double Nude Portrait: The Artist and his Second Wife* (1936) shows Hilda Carline stretched beside a joint of meat beneath him, he looking down, perhaps in worship. Very different from this 'varied anthology of flesh textures showing skill, tenderness and objectivity' (as the Gallery's Trustees described *Double Nude Portrait* on its acquisition) is Spencer's series of biblical events imagined taking place in his native village, Cookham-on-Thames. Even the Bloomsbury critic Roger Fry, who generally disapproved of narrative painting, wrote of villagers emerging from coffins and tombs in *The Resurrection, Cookham* (1923–7): 'It is highly arresting and intriguing ... a very personal conception carried through with unfailing nerve and conviction.'

Set apart in the excellent Clore Gallery you'll find a collection of works by the man considered by many to be Britain's greatest artist, J.M.W. Turner (1775–1851), whose watercolour landscapes – some violently stormy, others ethereally tranquil – broke free from conventions of realistic depiction over a century before abstraction. Back in the main gallery, unless there has been a major curatorial rearrangement, you'll pass through 'Art in Wartime Britain' and a room displaying works by **Barbara Hepworth** (1903–75), daughter of a Yorkshire County Surveyor, who, on leaving the RA, committed herself to promoting abstract art through the radical Seven and Five Society and later – in 1939 – helped to challenge London's supremacy in the British art world by setting up studio in St Ives, Cornwall, where young artists went on learning pilgrimages.

The final rooms are often given over to changing exhibitions, for which you may have to pay an admission fee. See p.86 for Art, Greatness and the Female Nude.

The cloakroom is free, the gift shop is chock-a-block with reproduction posters and cards of the paintings on display, and the imaginatively designed self-service basement restaurant is known for its good – if not cheap – buffet food.

MAYFAIR SEE MAP ON P.46

The rich moved in when Mayfair's namesake, the cattle and general May fair, was kicked out in 1708 for its associated 'drunkenness, fornication, gaming and lewdness'; today, in quintessentially monied English Mayfair, Christie's and Phillips's moustachioed auctioneers use nasal 'gnoing once, gnoing twice' pomp and ceremony to sell antiques; high-class prostitutes serve top-star-rated hotels on roaring Park Lane, and Coutts bank serves the Queen; some of the dark-brick, pale-blue and primrose-yellow flower-box-bedecked streets of Georgian houses and grand five- and seven-storey mansion blocks are so unchanged that TV aerials look out of place; the six-acre eighteenth-century Grosvenor Square, now dominated by the vast gold eagle of the American Embassy, attracts snuff, rifle and porcelain shop staff with Marks & Spencer's sandwiches on sunny lunchtimes; the local cinema (the Curzon Mayfair) is almost as well known for its blue velvet seats as for its film programming, and the shops – which are the main reason for coming to Mayfair, unless you're booked into a hotel – are all about luxury: spot the newest Vivienne Westwood shop by its towering gilt mirrors; buy some of London's most expensive nylon tights at Fogal on Bond Street, one-time home to Nelson and his mistress Lady Hamilton; ogle fabulously expensive frocks on pedestrian South Molton Street; and when you've not even a little finger left to hang another shopping bag on, go for lunch or high tea at one of the cafés or Edwardian pubs in quaint cobbled Shepherd Market (established 1735).

Prestige and Philanthropy Everywhere in Mayfair you'll see blue plaques to eminent Marquesses and RAs, for Mayfair has long been a destination for those wanting a high-class ring to their postal code. **Margery Hurst** (OBE), winner of the Pimms Cup for Anglo-American business friendship in 1962, chose Brook Street to set up the agency that helped to make the formerly male domain of secretarial employment a decent, upright occupation for respectable girls after the Second World War (the Brook Street Bureau is still one of London's best secretarial agencies). **Constance Spry** (OBE), daughter of a railway clerk, founded her famous school of floristry on South Audley Street and went on in 1953 to win the ultimate accolade of the commission to do the floral décor for Elizabeth II's coronation.

Angela Burdett Coutts, by contrast, was handed 1 Stratton Street by her family when she didn't need a prestigious Mayfair address at all. In 1837, at the age of twenty-three, she had inherited the vast fortune of her grandfather, Thomas Coutts, banker to George III, after Coutts cut the rest of his family out of his will for disapproving of his remarriage, at the age of eighty, to a young actress who became a favourite butt of the gutter press, Harriot Mellon. Miss Angela Burdett Coutts (1814–1906) immediately received innumerable offers of marriage – 'You, like me, are supposed to be made of Gold,' wrote the old Duke of Wellington – but she refused them all, and in 1838 or 1839 she met Charles Dickens, who immediately saw in the quiet heiress an overwhelming desire to help others. She didn't know how; for twenty years Dickens supervised her activities, which – even though they were, at her insistence, done largely anonymously – brought her the admiration of her peers, the devotion of the destitute, the nickname Queen of the Poor, and a posthumous reputation as the greatest Victorian philanthropist. If travellers on the omnibus saw outside her house the white cockatoo indicating that Miss Coutts was 'in', then they would cheer.

Like other women of her time, but on a phenomenally larger scale, Angela Burdett Coutts made philanthropy her career and, in the course of it, gave away an estimated three or four million pounds. At first these gifts took the form of one-off payments that showed up on bank statements as 'Donation' – for example, to a regularly complaining clergyman's wife in a damp vicarage in Kendal. Under Dickens's influence she invested in projects. Her response to Florence Nightingale's description of the sodden misery of soldiers in the Crimea in 1855 was to send a specially designed drying machine. The *Illustrated London News* reported: '1,000 articles of linen can be thoroughly dried in 25 minutes with the aid of Mr. Jeakes "centrifugal machine".'

In 1847 Dickens wrote to one Dr Brown of the success with thirty of the fifty-six girls who had passed through a Home founded by Miss Coutts in Shepherds Bush for 'starving needlewomen, poor needlewomen who had robbed ... violent girls ... poor girls from Ragged Schools, destitute girls who have applied at Police offices for relief ... domestic servants who have been seduced, and two young women held to bail for attempting suicide'. The Home was run in a conventionally disciplinarian Victorian fashion, but Angela was unconventional in disagreeing with Dickens on the point of marriage: Miss Coutts said that girls could be single and still saved. Many girls were sent, with smart clothes and learned manners, to start a new life in the colonies.

The Home was too expensive to continue for long, but it proved the blueprint for Miss Coutt's model villages. One of these was Holly Village, Hampstead, which was originally built for retired servants and bank clerks but is now – ironically – a desirable and pricey middle-class enclave. In Bethnal Green – where outsiders went only if they were escorted by the police – Miss Coutts commissioned a Mr Darbishire to build flats in Columbia Square to house 'the poor' (owing to a mixture of outdated design and neglect, the flats were condemned in the 1950s as unfit for human habitation, with allegations that one child in three contracted pneumonia). Other examples of her practical philanthropy included aid to the East End weavers and Bermondsey tanners and a 'sewing school' in Spitalfields, but all this and more was apparently forgotten during 'the scandal' of 1880–81.

For her support of the RSPCA, Angela had won the heartfelt gratitude of Queen Victoria, who wrote to her: 'It is a great satisfaction to me to know what a friend you are to dumb animals – who are in many cases man's best and kindest friends.' But when Miss Coutts appeared at a Buckingham Palace drawing-room reception as 'Mrs', Queen Victoria wrote in her journal: 'That poor foolish old woman Lady Burdett Coutts was presented on her marriage with Mr. Bartlett, 40 years younger than herself. She looked like his grandmother, & was all decked out with jewels – not edifying.' Rumours spread that the American Ashmead-Bartlett, her former private secretary, brought his mistresses to her house, and that he was 'cut' at the clubs for remarks like, 'By Jove, I must go and look after my grandmother.'

Angela's biographer, Diana Orton, points out that although Ashmead's marriage undoubtedly opened doors to a political career, it did not make him especially rich: Angela had already given away much of her wealth, and a condition of her inheritance had been that she never 'intermarry with any person being by birth an alien', in which case she would forfeit all benefit, 'as if she were dead'. Contrary to malicious society gossip, Archdeacon Wilberforce was one who believed that the marriage made Angela happy.

By the time she died, obituarists had forgiven her indiscretion. *The Daily Telegraph* declared her life 'one of the proudest and most satisfactory that the history of the nineteenth century can exhibit, for it is a record full of generous acts, of unstinted benevolence, and noble aspirations'. *The Times* said: 'Nothing can deprive the Baroness Burdett Coutts of her claim to lasting public gratitude.'

The Church of the Immaculate Conception and Mount Street Gardens

Entrances on Farm Street and Mount Street at Carlos Place.

A modest façade belies the echoey Gothic grandeur inside this 1844–9 church of the Jesuit community. Another surprise haven targeted by footsore shoppers in the know and locals after a bit of fresh air and relaxation is the garden behind, where benches bear memorials to past residents who loved the leafy greenness and occasional flowerbeds that are unusually pigeon-free thanks to stern 'Do not feed' signs.

BAKER STREET, ST MARYLEBONE SEE MAP ON P.46

The pipe-and-deerstalker-hat motif of the fictional Baker Street resident Sherlock Holmes repeats along the neat tiled walls of the Underground station, suggesting that you might emerge to find a smog-clad, gas-lamp-lit scene of hansom carriages and skulking villains when in fact there's little to see of Holmes's and Watson's world but a few touristy pub and café namesakes around 221B Baker Street, an address that was non-existent when Conan Doyle was writing the doctor–detective's adventures. The dirty brick nine-storey-high mansion blocks seem to be rearing back from the choky, thundering nine lanes of traffic that converge outside Baker Street Station, but walk fast off the main thoroughfares and you can escape into the most atmospheric travel bookshop in London (**Daunt,** *83 Marylebone High St, W1*), then relax with a sandwich in hidden-away Paddington Gardens (Paddington St at Luxborough St); shop at designers' bijoux showcase stores and take tea or champagne cocktails in pedestrian-only St Christopher's Place, and in the evening enjoy a chamber music concert or recital at the Wigmore Hall; appreciate the almost rurally leafy Manchester Gardens, with the magnificent and surprisingly under-visited Wallace Museum of Art; and, back near Baker Street Station, after long queues and many thin steep stairs, you finally reach the famous and creepily fascinating Madame Tussaud's.

If you're booked into a St Marylebone hotel, don't be unnerved when the streets empty at night, for the area is generally considered safe and there are a handful of decent restaurants for a range of budgets and needs, including a quick meal alone, and a friendly place to take children (see Eating and Drinking).

Browning to Bowen: Implementing Change From the 1830s, for over a century, Marylebone housed more than its fair share of dynamic women. Why?

In 1756 the Marylebone Road had been built as a City-to-West-London bypass, and in the burst of growth that came with industrialisation – including the opening in 1838 of the first passenger train station, Euston – the area was targeted by developers. The quickly constructed exclusive homes were far from slum areas (such as the East End), and therefore ideal for wealthy middle-class men seeking respectable surroundings for their daughters, who struggled to reconcile Victorian ideals and desires for personal fulfilment. With time on their hands and, in many cases, annuities from their fathers, these women were able to instigate change. Writing could be done secretly and anonymously.

The poet **Elizabeth Barrett Browning** (1806–61), a precocious child who read Greek at the age of eight, was at once hopeful and depressed by the family's move in 1835 to Gloucester Street, then 50 Wimpole Street, in London after the sale of their grand country house, Hope End, due to her father's financially straitened circumstances. London was England's literary nerve-centre, where she might meet writers she admired and could more effectively submit work to magazines and newspapers; but all she saw was soot and bricks and more bricks, and the rattling carriages gave her headaches. She used what biographer Margaret Forster calls 'invalid props' such as addictive nightly doses of opium to keep 'stuck close to the fender', where she could continue writing and quietly contemplate the potential for independence presented by payments for her writing. At thirty-two she became tired of anonymity; simultaneously, her tyrannical father had a change of heart on reading 'The Seraphim', of which he was so proud that he at last allowed Elizabeth to put her name to her work. Having work published under her own name brought money, status and passionate declarations of love from Robert Browning: in 1846, aged forty, Elizabeth finally gained freedom from her father, who opposed the courtship – her first – but this time Elizabeth did not submit to his wishes. She and Robert Browning eloped to Italy where, although she was haunted by unrealistic hopes of making peace with her father, Elizabeth's health improved and her reputation swelled to such proportions that she was considered for Poet Laureate.

Three years after Elizabeth Barrett Browning had escaped to Italy, twenty-two-year-old **Barbara Leigh Smith Bodichon** (1827–91) was complaining about 'the unjust laws of society and country which crush women, ... but now I hope that there are some who will brave ridicule for the sake of common justice to half the people in the world'. Barbara Leigh Smith was well placed to fight for justice – partly because she had braved ridicule by her very birth: her father, a Liberal MP, and her mother, a milliner's apprentice thirty years his junior, never married; the illegitimate Smiths were known by their cousins, who included Florence Nightingale, as 'the tabooed family'. Mr Smith was atypical in two other things that instilled productive determination in Barbara. First, he made sure she was educated not in lady's manners by a governess but in subjects like art, Classics and arithmetic alongside boys at the then radical Westminster School (which her father had helped to found). Second, not only did he give her an annuity, which was unusual, but he made the annual £300 automatic on her coming of age and unconditional, which was unheard of (Florence Nightingale's father grudgingly allowed her an annuity only once he had approved of her project).

Barbara Leigh Smith quickly concluded that she must fight for women's economic rights, which meant challenging the received opinion (that it was degrading for women to accept *paid* work; that a woman's career should be helpmate in marriage), and she set about identifying changes necessary for women to earn independent incomes: they must be entitled to education, to rights over their property in marriage, and to employment opportunities.

In 1854 at the age of twenty-one, she inherited from her father and ran Westminster School which, she insisted, should train girls for employment, not in 'vanity, false ideals of what is lady-like'. In the same year she published *A Brief Summary, in Plain Language, of the Most Important Laws of England concerning Women* – mainly the laws that made a wife's property her husband's. When Millicent Garrett Fawcett had 'a purse containing £1.18s.6d.' stolen at Waterloo Station, it was recorded in the police report as 'the property of Henry Fawcett'; the income earned by Mrs Gaskell's writing went straight to her husband, who gave her an allowance.

In 1855 Barbara Bodichon's Married Women's Property Bill committee gathered 26,000 signatures, including those of Elizabeth Barrett Browning, Harriet Martineau and Elizabeth Gaskell, and on her marriage to Eugene Bodichon in 1857, Barbara Leigh Smith insisted on retaining financial autonomy. In 1858 she founded and financed *The English Woman's Journal*, which remained Britain's principal feminist voice for the rest of the century. In the first issue, Bessie Rayner Parkes wrote of the need for new opportunities for women. Barbara Leigh Smith Bodichon exposed the plight of 'distressed needlewomen ... the decayed gentlewomen and broken-down governesses', and proposed a practical solution: 'Apprentice 10,000 to watchmakers; train 10,000 for teachers for the young; make 10,000 good accountants; ... educate 1,000 lecturers for mechanic's institutions; 1,000 readers to read the best books for working people; train up 10,000 to manage washing-machines, sewing-machines etc.'

The journal attracted women with radical tendencies including Jessie Boucherett, who was so impressed by her first skim-read of *The English Woman's Journal* at a railway-station bookstall that she rushed to meet the editors, and in 1859 the journal's 19 Langham Place offices became the base for Boucherett's Association (later Society) for Promoting the Employment of Women, whose members included founder of the Victoria Press Emily Davies (see The City), and whose successes included encouraging women to learn to swim (the Committee persuaded the manager of St Marylebone Baths to admit women on Wednesday afternoons).

But the 'Ladies of Langham Place', as the radical group under the guidance of Barbara Leigh Smith Bodichon became known, split over the question of suffrage. Just as Barbara had insisted on a woman's right not just to employment but to *paid* employment, so she demanded women's equal place in politics. Florence Nightingale refused an invitation to join her cousin's suffrage committee, saying, 'It makes me mad, the Women's Rights talk,' and even the other Langham Place women were at best tentative. Bessie Rayner Parkes suggested in 1863 that women could form political opinions 'intelligently and gracefully, in a manner suitable for a woman', and that they could then express them 'in a gentle, unobtrusive way'. Frances Power Cobbe feared that women might use political freedom 'as a facility for licentiousness'. Emily Davies resigned.

Barbara's close friend, the novelist **George Eliot** (1819–80), was also ambivalent. Certainly, she thought, women should have the vote, but change should be moderate and gradual. She believed that men and women were inherently different. '[Y]ou can never imagine what it is to have a man's force of genius in you, and yet to suffer the slavery of being a girl,' she wrote in *Daniel Deronda*. Eliot thought the goal should be partnership, not personal fulfilment. Leigh Smith Bodichon, supposedly the inspiration for the tenacious redhead *Romola*, was always welcome at the Priory in North Bank near Regent's Park, Eliot's home from 1863, but Eliot refused to join the activities of the Langham Place women – partly because of their difference in outlook but partly, Eliot's biographer Jennifer Uglow suggests, because she suspected that her personal reputation would damage rather than help the cause. That she was living with a married man, George Lewes, and was changed from country girl to urban intellectual of 'The Order of the Quill' so incensed her favourite brother Isaac that he forbade her family to have any contact with her.

The married life of Sir Arthur Conan Doyle (1859–1930), creator of Marylebone's most famous resident, Sherlock Holmes, illustrates how, despite all 'the Women's Rights talk', much remained the same. His marriage in 1885, when he was a doctor, to the sister of a patient, Louisa (or Louise) 'Touie' Hawkins, was almost astoundingly conventional. 'Louise was not gifted or well-read,' says Conan Doyle's biographer, Charles Higham, 'she made the ideal Victorian housewife, with sewing, mending, and cleaning her chief interests. Her femininity and total lack of complication, her motherliness and warmth, her sheer common sense, appealed to Conan Doyle and his mother. ... When he was racked by some complex question of metaphysics, Louise could fix a cup of tea.' Through Conan Doyle's transition from struggling Southsea doctor to successful Montague Street- then Baker Street-based crime writer, 'the relationship worked perfectly'. In 1897 Conan Doyle fell in love with a beautiful young woman in her twenties, Jean Leckie, whom he married in 1906 after Louisa died of TB. Although Jean Leckie, unlike Louisa, had 'a fine intellect, read extensively, and was a skilled conversationalist', she was nevertheless 'emphatically feminine', a 'quintessential Victorian' who believed that 'men should be worshipped'.

But while Jean Leckie was content with adoring her husband, **Elizabeth Bowen** (1899–1973) was trying art school and journalism, and by the time Conan Doyle died she was an acclaimed writer with a stable, supportive husband. By now all sorts of business avenues were open to women; in direct opposition to George Eliot's notions of inherent male genius, Bowen could describe himself in *Why Do I Write?* as a 'free-lance maker', saying that if she had not written, 'I should probably have struck out in designing and making belts, jewellery, hand bags, lampshades or something of that sort'. Several of Bowen's novels and stories provide powerful evocations of this area of London in the 1930s and 1940s (see Recommended Books).

The Anglo-Irish debutante's literary career had begun after World War I, when she moved to London to live with her Great-Aunt Edith. She started writing and going to readings at the Poetry Bookshop: 'upstairs, after dark, in a barn-like room, I listened to Ezra Pound reading aloud what was hypnotically unintelligible to me by the light of a candle'; and when she was twenty-four her first collection of short stories, *Encounters*, was published. In the same year – 1923 – she married Alan Cameron, whose work took them to Oxford, then back to London in 1935, by which time Elizabeth was moving in high-powered literary circles. She first met Virginia Woolf at tea in Lady Ottoline Morrell's Gower Street garden, where Elizabeth and Virginia talked about ice cream.

By the time Elizabeth and Virginia were described by Hugh Walpole in 1938 as sitting together 'like two goddesses from a frightfully intellectual Olympus', the two women had already been on letter-writing terms for some years. In 1935 Elizabeth wrote to Virginia Woolf how she had fallen in love 'at first sight' with 2 Clarence Terrace:

> It is about 3½ minutes from Baker St Station and overlooks the park lake with those coloured-sail boats and a great many trees. It is a corner house, which I think is nice, don't you, as the windows look different ways. ... The reason for taking it is that it is, in a bare plain way, very lovely with green reflections inside from the trees such as I have only seen otherwise in a country house.

Through the last years before the Second World War Elizabeth Bowen was an enthusiastic hostess; Elizabeth Jenkins called her 'the last *salonnière*'; her husband called her guests 'the black hats' because when he came back from work at the BBC, the hall of 2 Clarence Terrace was always lined with writers' and critics' black hats. After World War II, Elizabeth and Alan returned to Ireland.

Marylebone was hit hard by the World War II bombing – although stately white-stuccoed Clarence Terrace survives – and today most of the grand houses are office space.

SWIMMING DISPLACES CROQUET: WOMEN AND EDUCATION

The official opening in 1848 of Queen's College for Women in Harley Street marked the beginnings of better education for girls and women, but in 1871 Maria Grey still felt impelled to complain, in a paper read to the Society of Arts:

> What [women] are educated for is to come up to a certain conventional standard accepted in the class to which they belong, to adorn (if they can) the best parlour or the drawing-room, as it may be, to gratify a mother's vanity, to amuse a father's leisure hours, above all, to get married.

Until nearly the end of the nineteenth century, there were more institutional education opportunities at elementary level for working-class than for middle-class girls. However, the 'dame schools' were dismissed by many as run by widows profiteering from working mothers by offering not schooling but childminding; the Victorian reformer Charles Booth declared that working-class parents sent their children to Sunday School only so that they could have sexual intercourse in the afternoon; and the curriculum at the weekday schools consisted mainly of prayers, ciphering, religious exercises, knitting and sewing.

The basic mass state elementary system, which existed mainly in the form of the weekday schools, was run by philanthropists and religious reformers who were keen to convert the working classes to the ways of God and 'civilised' Victorian society. No mother 'of good position', wrote education reformer Dorothea Beale, 'would have thought of sending her daughter to a day school – those were only for the lower classes'. A few lucky girls were sent to ladies' seminaries where, 'at considerable expense' – writes Josephine Kamm in her biography of Miss Beale and Miss Buss (*How Different From Us*, Bodley Head) – 'she might acquire enough superficial information to enable her not to appear an ignoramus'. Miscellaneous facts were learned parrot-fashion using the question-and-answer method: 'Q. What is Whalebone used for? A. To stiffen stays, umberellas and whips.' Frances Power Cobbe said of the typical fashionable finishing school she was sent to at a cost of £2,000 for two years: 'If the object had been to produce the minimum of result at the maximum of cost, nothing could have been better designed for the purpose.' She went on: 'Everything was taught in the inverse ratio of its true importance ... at the top music and dancing.'

Most middle-class girls could hope at best for an *enthusiastic* governess, for the proposal for Queen's College came only when idealistic Christian Socialists, including the Reverend F.D. Maurice, realised the absurdity of teachers who had not been taught. Queen's College was founded, with the support of one of Queen Victoria's maids of honour, Miss Murray, primarily to provide secondary education for governesses, but it was also open to all 'ladies' over the age of twelve. Among the first students were **Frances Mary Buss** (1827–94) and **Dorothea Beale** (1831–1906), who did not meet at the time, for Miss Buss had been teaching with her mother at a school in Kentish Town, North London since the age of fourteen, so she could take only the evening classes; while Miss Beale, thanks to her Liberal surgeon father, was a day student.

Miss Beale went on to teach at Queen's College from 1849 to 1856, while Miss Buss pioneered secondary-school education for girls by running the North London Collegiate School for girls in Camden from 1850 as a democratic day school with low fees and high academic standards. In 1871, when Miss Buss's Camden school became public, it had already been used as a model for several other secondary schools around the country. In 1828, aged twenty-seven, Miss Beale became Principal of Cheltenham Ladies' College (which had opened in 1854) and transformed it into a famous and financially secure school which was used as model for girls' boarding-schools that opened at the end of the century, including Roedean, Benenden and Wycombe Abbey.

It is ironic that these expensive, primarily upper-class boarding-schools are ridiculed by some today for placing an undue emphasis on sports; in the 1860s, when walking and croquet provided most of the exercise a respectable girl wished for, Miss Buss introduced robust swimming lessons and Miss Beale provided skipping ropes and swings. That neither of the pioneering headmistresses married gave rise to the well-known rhyme:

Miss Buss and Miss Beale
Cupid's darts do not feel,
They leave that to us,
Poor Beale and poor Buss.

Although in company Miss Beale objected to any reference to the rhyme, her friend Annie Ridley said that Dorothea and Frances Mary chuckled about it in private, and Annie likened them to two queens who, in each other's company, could 'for a brief respite … escape from the loneliness of royalty'.

Miss Buss and Miss Beale were fifty-one and forty-nine respectively by the time Bedford College was finally awarded university status. Set up in 1849, only a year after Queen's College, by Mrs Reid, who recognised that Queen's was basically a school, Bedford was to offer women higher education. In 1892 Dorothea Beale established St Hilda's Hall, Oxford, to give trainee teachers a year at the University; and at the turn of the century June Purvis's depressing declaration in *A History of Women's Education in England* (Open University Press) that from 1800 to 1914 the literacy rate of women was persistently below that of men was on its way to being falsified. Today Queen's College (where feminist writer Katherine Mansfield studied) still operates from the Tuscan-porticoed Nos 43–49 Harley Street, now offering secretarial courses and domestic science.

Madame Tussaud's

Marylebone Road, NW1, tel. 071 935 6861. Open May–Sept 9 a.m.–5.30 p.m. daily; Oct–June 10 a.m.–5.30 p.m. daily. Admission £5.95 adults, £3.95 under-16s, £4.55 OAPs; combined ticket with Planetarium £7.40 adults, £4.85 under-16s, £5.85 OAPs (go to the Planetarium first and you miss the usually long Tussaud's queue).

Madame Tussaud fine-tuned her modelling skills making death-masks during the French Revolution; she left her husband and child behind in Paris to set up a waxworks in London in 1802, and nearly two centuries later, Madame Tussaud's – still one of London's top tourist attractions – continues to move with the times, whether it's the subtle moves of Princess Diana three inches away from Prince Charles twenty-four hours after the public announcement of their February 1993 estrangement, or major moves, such as installing a new multi-million-pound **Spirits of London** exhibition in which visitors are moved physically in replica black cabs through 400 years of London's history up to the psychedelic swinging sixties and Twiggy, and including Queen Victoria taking a 'hands-on' role in the Industrial Revolution (she drinks a cup of tea). The black cab ride is short but generally thought wonderful.

The recent regrouping of old with additions of new wax models, including Australian soap-star-turned-pop-queen Kylie Minogue and rebel footballer 'Gazza', all under snazzy exhibition titles, has succeeded in attracting troupes of snap-happy teenagers. Giggle and pose with waxy media stars under a night sky to the tinkling sound of light jazz in **The Garden Party** exhibition, where adventuring TV presenter Anneka Rice is halfway up a tree on a rope ladder and a koala bear is halfway up satirical Aussie 'housewife' Dame Edna Everage's evening dress. In **Hollywood Legends**, Marilyn Monroe beats down her billowing white skirts.

The **London Planetarium** offers ecologically sound messages, newly installed interactive video and live weather coverage; the **Pier Café**, too, is new, with simulated sounds of the seaside (cawing seagulls) and Edwardian slot machines.

All this is great fun, but it is in more traditional sections like the **Great Hall** and the **Chamber of Horrors** that the wax figures become more than just disappointing – or, as comedian Lenny Henry put it 'gobsmacking' – for the success or failure of their likeness to the original. The sight, near George Bush and King Hussein, of – on a red velvet sofa – a slumped-asleep woman visitor who, on second glance, turns out to be wax is at once comic and rather eerie. By the time you've passed Hitler on the stairs and the bell is tolling for the executions by garrotte, guillotine and electric chair, and in a grim Victorian cobbled street you stumble across the mutilated corpse of Jack the Ripper victim Catherine Eddowes, the wax models can become positively sinister. The **200 Years of Madame Tussaud's** exhibition is curtly dismissed at first by most teenagers as boring old history. But then they get to the video of the making of Texan blonde model Jerry Hall, and then they see a gory waxwork of Madame Tussaud herself moulding a mask from the severed head of Marie Antoinette after her execution in 1793, and gradually the bizarre and macabre story of Madame Tussaud begins to fascinate.

Marie Tussaud Soldier Joseph Grosholtz died before his daughter Marie was born in 1761 in Strasbourg, so the widowed mother took work immediately in Berne, Switzerland, as housekeeper to Philippe Curtius, a German-born doctor who also made wax models and took the fascinated six-year-old Marie with him when his models were shown at the fashionable Palais Royal in Paris. The future Madame Tussaud's apprenticeship had begun, and in 1778, at the age of seventeen, she was so skilled that Curtius asked her to model Voltaire (whose model is still on display). When Marie was twenty, Louis XVI's sister Elisabeth appointed her Art Tutor Royal at Versailles, where she lived for nine years that proved the most settled she was to have been until her seventies. In 1789 Revolution broke and Curtius called her back to Paris, where she was mainly safe because of Curtius's friendships with all the key revolutionaries, and because of her skills. She was ordered by the regime to make public-warning death-masks, including those of family she had lived with (Louis XVI's and Marie Antoinette's masks are on display today in the Chamber of Horrors).

In 1784 Curtius died, leaving Marie sole heir to his exhibition (you can see Curtius's 'Sleeping Beauty' model of Louis XV's mistress, Madame du Barry, in the '200 Years' exhibition), but attendance dropped, the man she married in 1785 and had two sons by, civil engineer François Tussaud, developed a gambler's streak, so Madame Tussaud set out in 1802 for London and success with her eldest son, Joseph (her younger son was sent on later).

Wax modelling was not new in England. The 1272 funeral effigy of Henry III was probably the first full-sized wax figure, and by the eighteenth century having your likeness in wax was the height of fashion: modeller Mrs Patience Wright amused her high-society clients by putting a wax housemaid on the stairs, and Catherine Andras, who showed at the Royal Academy, was appointed 'Modeller in Wax' to Queen Charlotte in 1801. But Madame Tussaud had skills they lacked: she saw how to make her art popular entertainment. When one Colonel Despard, who had conspired to assassinate King George III, was hanged, then beheaded, in 1803, Madame Tussaud applied for permission to take a plaster mould of his severed head. Gate admission at her temporary show at the Lyceum went up immediately, and heads made from the death-masks of executed criminals became popular viewing for family parties.

For over three decades, Madame Tussaud toured England with death-masks and royal personages including George III and the Duchess of York, and at the age of seventy-four she finally decided to settle down with her show, first in Gray's Inn, then in the high-class neighbourhood of St Marylebone. The site was perfect – respectable enough for visiting royalty and convenient for customers whom she called the 'labouring classes', who travelled the trolley buses on nearby Oxford Street. Success was fast and sure. The 1850 model of herself made by herself in 1850, dressed in a favourite bonnet and cloak, was so convincing that acquaintances started to say hello, and today Madame Tussaud still greets visitors from school children to the rich and famous. Margaret Thatcher has been modelled four times and come to see each likeness; when actor Larry Hagman was asked if he was pleased to see himself as J.R. Ewing in stetson and white tuxedo standing on a piece of turf from Southfork Ranch in Texas, he said, 'Are you kidding? That's having arrived, you know, to be at Madame Tussaud's.'

Wallace Collection

Hertford House, Manchester Square, W1M 6BN, tel. 071 935 0687; open Mon–Sat 10 a.m.–5 p.m., Sun 2–5 p.m., closed 24–26 December, New Year's Day, Good Friday and first Monday in May; free; wheelchair available at the front desk.

A steamy family saga of wealth and illegitimacy spanning nearly two centuries produced one of London's finest collections of art and *objets d'art*, including Catherine II of Russia's eighteenth-century Sèvres porcelain ice-cream cooler. Victorian Lady Wallace's bequest instructions that her late husband's collection be preserved intact without addition in grand Hertford House ensured an appealing hidden-away timeless quality that attracts savvy local office workers, St Christopher's Place shoppers and, in Iris Murdoch's novel *Under the Net* (see Recommended Books), the rakish narrator Jake, who 'made for the nearest quiet place I knew of, which happened to be the Wallace Collection', where he considers his conundrum 'sitting facing the cynical grin of Frans Hals's Cavalier'.

It all began with a descendant of Queen Jane Seymour, the 1st Marquess of Hertford (1719–94), whose kernel collection of six Canalettos was expanded by his son, the second Marquess of Hertford (1743–1822). The second Marquess's prestigious position as Lord Chamberlain had been facilitated by his wife's 'protracted liaison' with the Prince of Wales and, in turn, facilitated the leasing of Hertford House in 1797 for its proximity to good duck-shooting. His extensive acquisitions of notable English portraits included Sir Joshua Reynolds's of the mistress of the 3rd Viscount Bolingbroke, **Miss Nelly O'Brien**, and Thomas Gainsborough's of the actress mistress of the Prince of Wales (later George IV), **'Perdita' Robinson**. The son of the 2nd Marquess, the 3rd Marquess of Hertford (1777–1842), married an illegitimate beauty, Maria Fagnani, then embarked on a life of dedicated dissipation that inspired Thackeray's sinister Lord Steyne in *Vanity Fair*. The third Marquess was accidentally responsible for purchase of one of Titian's most important works, **Perseus and Andromeda**, which the 3rd Marquess thought was by Domenichino and so had it hung in Hertford House bathroom. His son, the 4th Marquess of Hertford (1800–70), presented himself as the perfect Edwardian gentleman, shunning marriage and devoting himself to collecting art on a grand scale. He peppered his taste for the decorative (some say sentimental) work of eighteenth-century French painters (Fragonard, Boucher and Watteau) with high-priced purchases of now world-famous paintings including Frans Hals's intriguing **Laughing Cavalier** and the seventeenth-century Spanish court painter Velázquez's **The Lady with a Fan**. The 4th Marquess left his title to a second cousin and his great collection to the man he had made his secretary and agent, and who was his unacknowledged illegitimate son, Richard Wallace (1818–90). Wallace quickly married a Paris perfume shop assistant, Julie-Amélie-Charlotte Castelnau, and carried on collecting works his father would have approved of while adding the core of the finest collection of European armoury outside the Tower of London. The English society which had, owing to the circumstances of his birth, declined to know him for twenty years awarded him a baronetcy for his philanthropy and gladly accepted from his widow, on behalf of the nation, his family's collection. In places it is awkwardly hung, but it is constantly curious and compelling.

BLOOMSBURY SEE MAP ON P.55

The main appeal of Bloomsbury is the grand, echoey British Museum, which in winter is swathed in the aroma of chestnuts roasting on braziers at the gates. The area also boasts a small toy museum (see Children), a celebrated alternative dance venue (The Place; see Entertainment), two of London's major points of entry (King's Cross and Euston train stations), some beautifully English squares and two jarringly modern landmarks, the thirty-five storey flat rectangle that is **Centrepoint** at the Tottenham Court Road end of shoppers' Oxford Street, and the 620 foot top-heavy metallic tubular Post Office Tower, now called **British Telecom Tower**, which was built tall in 1965 so that the capital's telecommunications system would not be jangled by jutting rooftops.

Development of the area began in 1661, when the 4th Earl of Southampton conceived a novel idea: he designed Bloomsbury Square so that three sides would house his well-to-do friends and one side, plus some streets behind, would house their servants. His only daughter, Rachel, united his with another great estate by marrying the 1st Duke of Bedford, and in 1775 the widow of the 4th Duke, Gertrude, followed the Earl's example by building Bedford Square. Today many of the one-time lords' and ladies' living-rooms are littered with the institutional purple-and-orange furniture and polystyrene cups of faculties, institutes and students' common rooms that are attached to the ever-expanding London University, which moved to Bloomsbury after the Second World War.

North of the well-stocked, user-friendly university bookshop, Dillons, Gower Street, WC1, the area around King's Cross continues to be an infamous favourite haunt of prostitutes and drug addicts, melodramatically and not entirely fairly labelled 'the Bronx of Britain' by the tabloids. Still, King's Cross is worth avoiding at night: if your train arrives late, walk purposefully to the official cab stand, which is marked by a queue of suitcase-laden passengers snaking slowly but surely into a line of black London taxis. South again, around Charlotte Street (W1), chi-chi hair salons and jolly restaurants are kept in business by staff from TV's Channel 4 headquarters. Tottenham Court Road's (W1) innumerable indistinguishable electronics goods stores fill at lunchtime with hi-fi buyers and staff from local publishers buying computers and compatible game programmes for their children. Bloomsbury can feel bleak at night, but actually, King's Cross apart, it is only quiet, and the most hassle you're likely to get is polite requests for loose change from occasionall homeless men and women in sleeping bags in shop doorways.

Women alone are well served for lunch by many cappuccino cafés, **Pizza Express** and the bring-your-own-bottle, highly acclaimed **Museum Café**. You can pick up free lesbian and gay weeklies plus herb tea or a healthy pasta bake at the lively café and bar, **First Out** (see Eating and Drinking). In Russell Square on sunny summer days half-dressed students lie chatting while women with children gratefully cluster round the outdoor café (north-east side). As you wander, you can consider some of the women who trod the pavements of Bloomsbury before you. In Queen's Square, novelist and campaigner for women's education Mrs Humphry Ward became the first president of the Anti-Suffrage League in 1908 (she is commemorated today by the Mary Ward education centre at number 43 Queen's Square, WC1). Perhaps most of all, the area is associated with the Bloomsbury Group.

DR ELIZABETH GARRETT ANDERSON (1836–1917) BREAKS INTO 'THE FORTRESS'

'I am thoroughly ordinary,' protested the teenage Elizabeth Garrett. Yet by the age of thirty she had founded a dispensary for women and children (the yellow and red brick building on Euston Road at Churchway that is now called the Elizabeth Garrett Anderson Hospital). At thirty-two she gained the right to practise in England as a physician and surgeon. From 1873 to 1892 she was the only woman member of the British Medical Association, and at the age of seventy-two she was elected Mayor of Aldeburgh, so becoming the first woman mayor in England.

Elizabeth Garrett was first inspired by an article in *The English Woman's Journal* on the pioneering American physician Dr Elizabeth Blackwell. Her social circle took her at eighteen to tea at the house of artist Barbara Bodichon, who immediately pressed on Elizabeth a letter of introduction to her heroine, Dr Blackwell, who in turn addressed the nervous young woman as a future colleague. 'She assumed that I had made up my mind to follow her,' Elizabeth Garrett recalled. The final push came from her childhood clergyman's daughter friend Emily Davies, who had done parish visiting in urban tenements and become convinced of the need for women doctors to attend women and children, but found the idea of doing it herself distasteful. Emily explained to the still slightly reluctant Elizabeth the qualities that made her the perfect pioneer: good health, energy, and a father who was prepared to support her morally and financially.

Elizabeth left Suffolk and her nine brothers and sisters for Middlesex Hospital, London, where she started as a nurse in order to gain access to dissections and operations. By 1863 she had studied in both London and Scottish hospitals, but urgently needed to work in practical anatomy. Replies to her letters were discouraging. 'I must decline to give you instruction in Anatomy,' wrote an Aberdeen surgeon.

> I have so strong a conviction that the entrance of ladies into dissecting rooms and anatomical theatres is undesirable in every respect and highly unbecoming that I could not do anything to promote your end ... it is not necessary that ladies should be brought into contact with such foul scenes.

Undeterred, Elizabeth dissected cadavers in her bedroom until L.S. Little, demonstrator at the London Hospital Medical School, agreed to take her for the full course. She sailed through the questions on medicine, midwifery and medical pathology at her examinations so smoothly that two examiners, conferring afterwards, agreed it was a good job they did not have to put the three students awarded final certificates in order of merit, for they would have had to put Elizabeth Garrett first. The medical journal *The Lancet*, which had celebrated her expulsion from the Middlesex four years earlier (when male students threatened to leave if she stayed), condescended to congratulate her, under the heading 'Frocks and Gowns'. In a draft for a speech to the Royal Free Hospital School of Medicine, Elizabeth wrote: '*I was in the fortress* as it were, but alone and likely to be for a good long time.'

Soon after opening the Euston Road hospital, Elizabeth was pressed by husbands and fathers of her dispensary patients to stand for the London School Board. At the age of thirty-four she fell completely in love with a fellow member of the Board, James Skelton Anderson. Having always put her work first, she agreed to be married, but her worst fears appeared in print in the *British Medical Journal*: 'It is announced that Miss Elizabeth Garrett M.D. is about to marry. The problem of the compatibility of marriage with female medical practice ... will thus be tested.' However, she managed to enjoy marriage and motherhood, without slowing her pioneering lead in the medical profession. Even though she was in her seventies when the suffragettes enlisted her support, she gave her all. In *Elizabeth Garrett Anderson* (Methuen), Jo Manton records a Tuesday evening in 1908 when

> she prepared to join a raid on Parliament and the inevitable scuffle with the police. [Suffragette] Millicent Fawcett, who knew the risks her sister would run, was appalled. On the morning of the raid, Lady Frances Balfour found her walking up and down her room at Gower Street in real agitation. 'Elizabeth is over seventy and not fit to be arrested,' she said.

Secretly, Lady Balfour went to the Home Secretary to secure a written promise that Mrs Garrett Anderson would not be arrested, and sure enough, through the turmoil of the raid, when women were torn from railings, Mrs Garrett Anderson remained untouched. Her son 'walked back beside his mother along the last stretch of Whitehall', notes Jo Manton. 'He observed that she was mystified and indeed rather put out at not having been molested in some way by the police. If she had known the reason she would have been furious.'

The Bloomsbury Group, including Virginia Woolf (1882–1941) and Vanessa Bell (1879–1961) Today the words 'Bloomsbury Group' evoke respectable images of eminent men and women of letters and established artists – Lytton Strachey, Maynard Keynes, Virginia Woolf; Vanessa Bell and Roger Fry – but in 1904 the move by the two beautiful young Stephen sisters Virginia and Vanessa from their Kensington childhood home to 46 Gordon Square in Bloomsbury, even though their two brothers moved with them, was considered not just daring or foolish but socially disastrous.

Bloomsbury was then a 'bad' area; Virginia and Vanessa's parents were relatively liberal, but in their upper-to-middle-class social milieu Music, Drawing and Deportment were considered the only suitable education for girls, and servile marriage their only decent aspiration. Virginia and Vanessa, already close, were drawn closer together by Virginia's two nervous breakdowns (in 1895 and 1904) and by three bereavements (their mother died in 1895, their half-sister in 1907 and their father in 1904). So although Quentin Bell suggests in his introduction to *The Diary of Virginia Woolf* (Penguin) that Vanessa was more keen to defy convention than Virginia, Vanessa's move to Bloomsbury at the end of 1904 without Virginia would have been unthinkable. Once there, they 'did not dress or behave in a decorous manner', explains Quentin Bell:

> their days were given to the desk and the easel, they largely neglected the duty of accepting or leaving cards, of paying calls or even of dressing for dinner ... not only were there no chaperones and no small talk but there were grave positive evils in the form of quite ineligible young men and conversation on quite unsuitable topics.

The ineligible men were their brother Thoby's Cambridge graduate friends; their unsuitable conversation was more often than not intellectual. Vanessa had a tendency to fall asleep on the sofa, but Virginia used the debates to complement avid reading and piece together an education she had been deprived of.

The sisters' daring attracted attention, whether it was to fascinate or alienate: well-bred contemporaries demonstrated acute hostility by giving them 'the cut direct', and a number of Thoby's friends fell instantly in love with both at once. Lytton Strachey, who called them 'the two most beautiful and wittiest women in England!', imagined being married to each on separate occasions (although he retracted his 1909 proposal of marriage to Virginia). Leonard Woolf's autobiography describes his first sighting of Vanessa and Virginia aged twenty-one and nineteen respectively:

> It was almost impossible for a man not to fall in love with them, and I think I did at once. ... In white dresses and large hats, with parasols in their hands, their beauty literally took one's breath

away, for suddenly seeing them one stopped astonished [as] when in a picture gallery you suddenly come face to face with a great Rembrandt or Velásquez.

The casual fireside evenings debating and laughing at Gordon Square could be said to have more formally become the 'Bloomsbury Group' in 1905, when Thoby started his intellectual 'Thursday Evenings' and Vanessa started the 'Friday Club' for painters who were keen to break with tradition to discuss art, and to exhibit. The following year, after a trip to Greece, Thoby died of typhoid fever, Vanessa agreed to marry Clive Bell, and the focus of the Bloomsbury Group began to disperse. Vanessa set up her beloved Charleston home in Sussex. Virginia moved first with her brother Adrian to 29 Fitzroy Square, then with Adrian, Duncan Grant, Maynard Keynes and Leonard Woolf to 38 Brunswick Square; finally, after marrying Leonard Woolf in 1912, she moved with him to Richmond, where on doctors' orders Leonard insisted that Virginia should rest to rebuild strength after another nervous breakdown and a suicide attempt.

Vanessa gained some renown as an artist before the First World War broke out, exhibiting in the first Post-Impressionist exhibition at the Grafton Galleries in 1910 and co-founding the Omega Workshops with Roger Fry in 1913, but Virginia had only reviews published until 1915, when she and Leonard bought a printing press. They founded the Hogarth Press in 1917, and published Virginia's third novel, *Jacob's Room*, in 1922 (the first two novels were published by Duckworth). From then on, Vanessa and Virginia continued to collaborate, Vanessa designing covers for books produced by the Hogarth Press and Virginia writing two catalogue introductions for Vanessa's increasingly respected exhibitions.

Vanessa kept a London home and studio in Bloomsbury, and Virginia and Leonard Woolf's Hogarth Press remained Bloomsbury-based. But after the war new people motivated the Bloomsbury Group. Virginia had already gained wide respect as a prolific novelist of calibre and Vanessa had become a mother of three, content in a country routine of walks by the pond, when Virginia described the Bloomsbury Group in a letter to her nephew Quentin Bell in 1930 as 'merely wild, odd, innocent, artless, eccentric and industrious beyond words'. Virginia Woolf is commemorated with a blue plaque at 29 Fitzroy Square.

Women's Institutes, Land Girls and the 'Kitchen Front' Four months before she drowned herself in the River Ouse, Virginia Woolf acknowledged the significance Women's Institutes had acquired locally and nationally throughout the Second World War by agreeing, in November 1940, to become the Treasurer of the

Rodmell branch of the Women's Institute (she was then living at Rodmell in Sussex). In *All Work and No Play?* (OUP), Rosemary Deem suggests that the membership rate of Women's Institutes continues to be high because husbands don't consider WI meetings a threat, quoting a conversation with a new town WI member: 'He thinks I won't get up to any mischief while I'm here – mind, I have to leave everything just so ... meal ready to eat when he comes in ... house tidy ... kids doing their homework upstairs ... or it's murder when I get back.' The official WI handbook describes a higher purpose, 'which is to improve and develop conditions of country life' by bringing subjects voted by two-thirds of WI members to be of national concern before relevant government departments.

The contribution of women during the Second World War was undoubtedly essential, but afterwards they were strong-armed by government propaganda, and sometimes by union legislation, to leave 'men's' jobs – in factories, for example. Even during the war, women easily retained power only in comparatively insignificant and generally traditionally 'feminine' areas such as food, through organisations like the Women's Institutes and the Women's Farm and Garden Association, which had its headquarters in Bloomsbury's Byng Place under the direction of Miss K.M. Courtauld throughout the 1930s. Founded in 1899 to help women to get careers in agriculture, the Women's Farm and Garden Association was effectively tamed when it was made responsible for organising the Women's Land Army. Food was, of course, crucial during the war (Britain needed healthy soldiers). Women were entrusted with ensuring quality and quantity by working physically tilling fields and operating thresher machines as members of the Land Army, and by fighting on the 'Kitchen Front', a term devised by the government's Ministry of Food as part of its high-budget advertising campaign.

Women were told by the Ministry how to produce maximum nutrition and the illusion of variety, so that families would eat heartily, from supplies that were limited by rationing. Kitchen Front ads had titles like 'Medals for Housewives', which promised '*A medal for this* ... Saving all bread crusts', 'Never accepting more than the rations' and 'Making delicious dishes from home-grown vegetables, with just a *flavouring* of meat or fish'. The 'Dig for Victory' campaign declared: 'Women! Farmers can't grow all your vegetables', so London back gardens were sown with wheat, barley and potatoes, and sections were wired off for poultry. One East London woman remembers: 'A neighbour of ours in West Ham kept rabbits and chickens, she used to go out to feed them with a tin bath on her head, right through the bombing. It sounds ridiculous now, but they were so important then.'

ELIZA LYNN LINTON: EMANCIPATED ANTI-SUFFRAGIST

'She fought for Women: yet with women fought,' wrote Walter Besant in poetic tribute to Victorian journalist and novelist Eliza Lynn Linton after her death in 1898. He congratulated her for beating back the 'sexless tribe, the shrieking sisterhood' 'with gibe and scorn and jest' while 'the world glorified in their show of shame' ... 'brave woman!' he hailed her, 'Farewell!'

In *Woman Against Women in Victorian England* (Indiana University Press), Nancy Fix Anderson explores the contradictions of a woman who sought and gained her own freedom, then bitterly fought others who tried to do the same. Anderson looks back to Eliza Lynn Linton's Lake District childhood, when she alienated her vicar father by embracing religious excesses including self-tortures (such as digging out a tooth with a knife) and felt that she could never win the approval of the heavenly Father because she was 'hopelessly in the clutch of the devil!' She preferred nights on the floor, for sleeping on beds she denounced as 'unrighteous effeminacy'; her penances resulted in hallucinations and brought her to the point of nervous breakdown, after which she suddenly rejected religion and in 1845, when she was twenty-three, set out alone for London to become a writer. This was an extraordinary venture for a young provincial clergyman's daughter in mid-Victorian England, when the most daring thing a middle-class girl unhappy with her lot could respectably do was live with another family as a governess.

Despite her father's vehement opposition, and with the help of his London solicitor, William Loaden, Eliza secured meagre rooms in a Russell Square boarding-house near the British Museum reading rooms, where she researched her first novel, *Azeth, the Egyptian*, which she published in 1847 with £50 borrowed from Loaden. She said later that her move to London made her 'one of the vanguard of the independent women'; her boarding-house life she called 'my first field of personal freedom'; and her risk-taking was vindicated by *Azeth*'s reception: 'The flatteries and congratulations I hear everywhere, the being made a full-grown lion of, the reviews, and my own hopes are almost turning my head.'

But there was trouble on the horizon. Her marriage in 1858 to a poor engraver, W.J. Linton, was not happy. Linton was shorter than she was, and in reference to what she considered his consequently diminished manhood she derisively nicknamed him 'Manny'. Eliza was also richer than he, and when they married she insisted on having a settlement drawn up that gave her control of her own inheritance in order to circumvent the laws that incorporated a woman's legal personality and property into that of her husband. She maintained her 'cherished individualism' and at the same time passionately defended the strong manly husband who was 'always in a sense [woman's] master. ... Anyone who has ever been under such guidance as this knows the gladness of worthy living.' The marriage soon collapsed; Eliza tried to set herself up as hostess of a literary *salon*, but nobody came, and bitterness set in.

By the 1860s Florence Nightingale had made nursing respectable, and Elizabeth Garrett was 'the first English woman doctor'; education denied to Eliza had been available at Queen's College and Bedford College since the 1840s, and now middle-class Victorian girls were graduating. Eliza's own work was falling from critical favour, and George Eliot – just when invitations to her Sunday afternoon receptions were becoming socially prized – cut Eliza from her circle. Furious, Eliza mocked Eliot for letting George Lewes coddle her, and described her as 'artificial, *posée*, pretentious, unreal.

... In her endeavour to harmonize two irreconcilables – to be at once conventional and insurgent – the upholder of the sanctity of marriage while living as the wife of a married man ... she lost every trace of that finer freedom and whole-heartedness.'

In 1866 Barbara Bodichon spearheaded the formation of the first Women's Suffrage Committee, and in that same year Eliza Lynn Linton began writing for the *Saturday Review*, which had made its position clear in 1855, its founding year, when it stated: 'Anything that draws women away from their own firesides [will] in the end be more productive of harm than good.' In her famous March 1868 *Saturday Review* article 'The Girl of the Period', Eliza attacked the 'modern phases of womanhood – hard, unloving, mercenary, ambitious, without domestic faculty and devoid of healthy natural instincts' as 'a pitiable mistake and a grand national disaster'.

Biographer Nancy Fix Anderson concludes that 'Eliza's success lay not in stemming the tide of women's emancipation. It was rather in her own personal victory in emancipating herself from the dictates of Victorian patriarchy.' Whether Eliza liked it or not, other women saw her lead and followed.

The British Museum

Great Russell Street, W1, tel. 071 636 1555 or 071 637 7384 for recorded information for visitors with disabilities. Open Mon–Sat 10 a.m.–5 p.m., Sun 2.30–6 p.m. Closed during Christmas period, New Year's Day, Good Friday and the first Monday in May. Essential work occasionally necessitates closing areas without notice. Admission free. The First Aid room off Room 25 may be used as a baby-changing area; the public toilets are generally crowded. Blind and partially sighted visitors can do the touch tour of Roman Sculpture. Tours of the collection cost £6 adults, £3 children and last one and a half hours. Decent stripped-pine-and-pastel-look café/restaurant. Special children's shop sells 'Fun with hieroglyphics stationery' and Roman pop-up books.

The British Museum has inspired many, including toddler **Dorothy Eady** (1904–81) who, after a fall at the age of three, dreamed of a temple and realised, during a visit to the British Museum the next year, that the temple of Abydos was her true home. At the first opportunity she moved to Egypt, married an Egyptian, and by the time she died she had long been Keeper of the Temple of Isis, happy in the knowledge that she was a reincarnated minor priestess; as well as being revered locally she was an internationally recognised expert on hieroglyphics.

The beginnings of the museum's collection of architectural trophies from Greece, Rome and Asia Minor were crammed into a grand house for the first five decades until 1823, when Robert Smirke began his twenty-year commission to design and construct a suitably pompous public building which, he decided, should have a massive sweep of Ionic colonnade for a façade. He did not bank on the bathos of the elegant stone benches being sat on by local cleaners and shop workers munching sandwiches from Tupperware boxes surrounded by scavenging pigeons; but still, the British Museum is impressive. Its well-labelled collection is fascinating – and huge. Make good use of the many leather-topped wood benches that are scattered liberally through the halls and often placed in front of important or famous exhibits, amongst them the Sculptures from the Parthenon or, more commonly, the **Elgin Marbles**, so-called because they were brought back to London from the 1801–6 travels of Lord Elgin.

The remnants of the Parthenon, which was built on the Acropolis at Athens between 447 and 438 BC and dedicated to Athena, patron goddess of the city, are in the ground-floor **Duveen Gallery**. Time-eaten stone-carved pediments featuring headless, armless gods and goddesses and bits of horses tell Athena's story. The East Pediment records how she was born fully grown and fully armed from a wound Hephaistus caused with an axe to the head of her father, the mighty Zeus. The West Pediment tells of the contest between Athena and Poseidon for the right to protect the land of Attica: Poseidon struck the rock of the Acropolis and brought forth salt water to show his strength, while Athena gave Greece the olive tree, which sprung suddenly out of dry earth. King Cecrops decided this time that Athena's gift was best, but when he was asked again to arbitrate between Athena and Poseidon, the Oracle advised him to ask *every* Athenian to vote, and so Cecrops stirred up the wrath of the other gods because women outnumbered men and Athena won. The gods avenged themselves by depriving women of the vote from that day forth, and decreed that women should be known through their husbands or fathers as 'daughter of so-and-so' or 'wife of so-and-so', and no longer as 'woman of Athens'.

Negotiate stairs lined with mounted and hung Roman mosaics or pierced by a Canadian totem pole, and you'll come to the light-filled **Egyptian Galleries**, where the eerie and beautiful **Mummies** fascinate children and have tourists reaching for their cameras – 'snap me with Henutmehit!' The **Domestic Objects** section displays hand-shaped bone 'clappers', which were clapped together as percussion instruments, and nearby there's a fine array of Egyptian cosmetics. Eye make-up was much used for adornment and, explains a curator's blurb, for general physical comfort. Mineral preparations that were used in Ancient Egypt as eye paints – malachite for lurid green and galena for sultry black kohl – also helped to soothe the eyes after exposure to Egypt's bright sun and swirling dust. Red ochre was used as rouge, and henna for dying fingernails, the soles of the feet, the palms and the hair. Exhibit 65242 is a kohl pot with a wooden kohl stick, held by a figure of the god Bes, who looks like an influence for one of children's writer Maurice Sendak's beast of the night illustrations.

Last but by no means least, since you still have the extensive **Assyrian, Prehistoric and Medieval galleries** to see, back on the ground floor is the dark wood-panelling and gilt **British Library Museum**, where sturdily elegant glass cases show pages of Charlotte Brontë, Jane Austen and George Eliot manuscripts. Students on the book-binding course at the London College of Printing come to examine the elaborate goatskin and copper wire works of their predecessors under the 'Bookbinding Competition' banner.

MARY WOLLSTONECRAFT'S VINDICATION

'Would men but generously snap our chains, and be content with rational fellowship instead of slavish obedience, they would find us more observant daughters, more affectionate sisters, more faithful wives, more reasonable mothers – in a word, better citizens,' wrote Mary Wollstonecraft (1759–97) in the chapter titled 'OF THE PERNICIOUS EFFECTS WHICH ARISE FROM UNNATURAL DISTINCTIONS ESTABLISHED IN SOCIETY' in *A Vindication of the Rights of Woman* (published 1792). She wrote the book from a house in Store Street, Bloomsbury, at a time when the area around Tottenham Court Road was considered suspect but was cheap and convenient and so leapt into by writers, artists and theatrical people who did not care about propriety.

Mary was hailed as Britain's first feminist. It seems that her early bid for independence was spurred by an unhappy, turbulent family life in Essex, Yorkshire and poverty-stricken Spitalfields, each move dictated by the dwindling fortunes of her failed gentleman-farmer father, whose drinking and physical abuse of his wife created an atmosphere Mary found intolerable. She grasped at each of the few options open to females of the petty-bourgeois class – first chaperoning a wealthy Bath family's children, then teaching. After her mother's death in 1782 she opened a school in the London suburb of Newington Green with her beloved Fanny Blood. Although the school failed and Mary was nearly destroyed when Fanny died in childbirth in 1875, Mary's time in Newington Green brought her into contact with the ideas of a radical group, the North London Rational Dissenters.

Mary was hailed as an 'Amazon!'. By 1787 she had published *Thoughts on the Education of Daughters*, and was working for the radical St Paul's Churchyard publisher Joseph Johnson, reading, writing articles and translating. Her social circle soon included pro-revolutionary Dissenters Thomas Paine, William Blake, Henry Fuseli and William Godwin. She wrote *A Vindication of the Rights of Woman*, enthused by the outbreak of revolution in France, and in December 1792 she left London alone for Paris at the height of revolutionary tumult. There she began a love affair with the dashing American author and entrepreneur Gilbert Imlay, with whom she had a child, Fanny. But back in England, having ecstatically defied convention by refusing to accept formal marriage ties, Mary found it impossible, in her unhappiness, to shake off the humiliation of Imlay's infidelities – he began openly preparing to set up house with an actress – and she attempted suicide twice in 1795: once with laudanum and, in October, by throwing herself off Putney Bridge.

It was in her effort to forget Imlay that Mary undertook what biographer Claire Tomalin calls a characteristically impulsive action: on 14 April 1796 she called alone and uninvited on her old philosophical anarchist friend William Godwin, who was at the height of his fame ('he blazed as a sun in the firmament of reputation', wrote Hazlitt) and in a good position to help her professionally on her way back into a leading role in the London intellectual scene. Godwin claimed that he had fallen in love with her when he read *A Vindication*, yet he still proposed unsuccessfully to Amelia Anderson in 1796 before beginning an affair with Mary. When she became pregnant, this time Mary agreed to marry – at St Pancras church in March 1797 – but ten days after the birth of her daughter, Mary Shelley (later the author of *Frankenstein*), Mary Wollstonecraft died of puerperal fever and was buried in the same St Pancras churchyard. Grief-stricken, Godwin wrote memoirs to vindicate his dear wife's memory. But his frank discussion of her insistence on the need for divorce reform and the excusability of adultery, as well as the facts of her love affairs and suicide attempts, fascinated but also alienated even those who had initially felt some sympathy with the doctrines laid out in *A Vindication*. Later, radical thinkers, including Virginia Woolf, returned to her life and work; today Mary Wollstonecraft's *A Vindication of the Rights of Woman* is considered seminal in the tradition of liberal feminism (for further reading, see Claire Tomalin's biography, *The Life and Death of Mary Wollstonecraft* [Penguin]).

THE CITY SEE MAP ON P.130

London's Square Mile is packed with history and financial corporations. Come to the Tower for medieval armour and eerie Tudor tales, then see the sci-fi Lloyds building from the top of Sir Christopher Wren's triumph, the landmark St Paul's Cathedral (see on). Meander past photocopy and chocolate shops and fast-talking paper boys with mobile phones at newsstands by alehouses where the seventeenth-century diarist Samuel Pepys liked to 'take a knipp'. Negotiate maze-like back alleys to find Dr Johnson's House, or take Stonecutter Street, Love Lane and a concrete walkway over a bit of Roman wall to the Museum of London, where you can learn about the remnants of history that didn't survive the Great Fire and World War II air raids. Lastly, at 5 p.m. sharp, either get mown down by brolly-bearing city traders and brokers in Burberry-style macs or follow the brogues and occasional court shoes down uneven stone steps to crowded wine bars where deals are diagnosed and oysters enjoyed before commuter trips home from Liverpool Street Station.

The **Lloyds Building** (best seen from Tower Bridge at dusk; *Leadenhall Street EC3*) at night is lit blue; during the day it justifies several walks round for its mesh of external pipes and gliding transparent elevators. Few of the City's other law and finance institutions offer much to the casual visitor, but some significant ones are worth knowing about in passing. The **Bank of England** (*Threadneedle Street EC2*), nicknamed 'The Old Lady of Threadneedle Street' by Richard Brinsley Sheridan in 1797, is today housed in a plain-walled grey 1920s monolith by Sir Herbert Baker that is generally

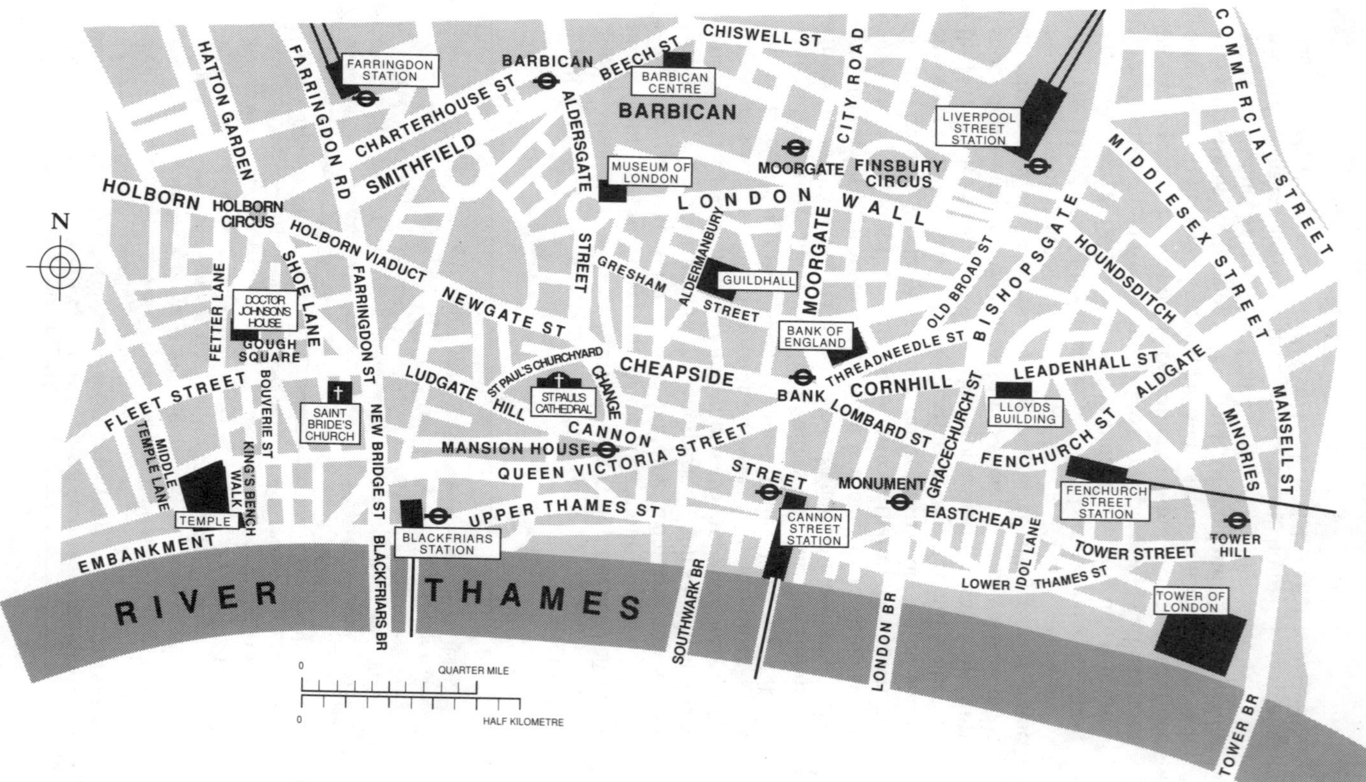
N
HATTON GARDEN
FARRINGDON STATION
FARRINGDON RD
CHARTERHOUSE ST
BARBICAN
BEECH ST
BARBICAN CENTRE
CHISWELL ST
CITY ROAD
COMMERCIAL STREET
BARBICAN
SMITHFIELD
LIVERPOOL STREET STATION
MUSEUM OF LONDON
MOORGATE
FINSBURY CIRCUS
HOLBORN
HOLBORN CIRCUS
ALDERSGATE STREET
LONDON WALL
MIDDLESEX STREET
HOLBORN VIADUCT
GRESHAM
ALDERMANBURY
GUILDHALL
MOORGATE
STREET
HOUNDSDITCH
FETTER LANE
SHOE LANE
FARRINGDON ST
NEWGATE ST
OLD BROAD ST
BISHOPSGATE
DOCTOR JOHNSONS HOUSE
GOUGH SQUARE
BANK OF ENGLAND
THREADNEEDLE ST
ST PAUL'S CHURCHYARD
CHEAPSIDE
LEADENHALL ST
ALDGATE
FLEET STREET
BOUVERIE ST
LUDGATE HILL
ST PAULS CATHEDRAL
CHANGE
BANK
CORNHILL
GRACECHURCH ST
LLOYDS BUILDING
MINORIES
MANSELL ST
SAINT BRIDE'S CHURCH
NEW BRIDGE ST
CANNON
LOMBARD ST
MIDDLE TEMPLE LANE
KING'S BENCH WALK
MANSION HOUSE
QUEEN VICTORIA STREET
STREET
FENCHURCH ST
MONUMENT
TEMPLE
UPPER THAMES ST
EASTCHEAP
FENCHURCH STREET STATION
CANNON STREET STATION
IDOL LANE
TOWER HILL
EMBANKMENT
BLACKFRIARS STATION
TOWER STREET
LOWER THAMES ST
RIVER THAMES
BLACKFRIARS BR
SOUTHWARK BR
LONDON BR
TOWER OF LONDON
0
QUARTER MILE
0
HALF KILOMETRE
TOWER BR

panned by architecture critics (although there is a small museum). The nearby 1840s Sir William Tite **Royal Exchange** building (*Threadneedle Street and Cornhill, EC2*) has a much more engaging façade – Corinthian pillars topped with lounging deities and a dainty spire – but unfortunately you can't go in. The sprawling **Temple** complex (*King's Bench Walk, EC4*), which has spawned law students since the Middle Ages, has a Norman-Gothic church where knight effigies are sometimes joined by nervy twentieth-century law students cramming for lessons, but an idle walk around is a mainly sedate and uninspiring experience.

The City also boasts innumerable churches, of which two contrasting examples are profiled here. If you want to see more, you could contact the St Paul's Information Centre, or follow the various brown signs to churches of note in an *ad hoc* exploratory fashion that will reward you with trips down curious alleyways. If you're on the way to or from the Tower of London and need a rest, **St Dunstan's-in-the-East** (*off Idol Lane, EC3*) is worth searching out, for in the ruins there is a magnificent garden with benches and walls of climbing plants to block out the surrounding noise of Embankment traffic and City building projects. Another good place for a characterful break is the elaborately gilt-decorated late-nineteenth-century **Leadenhall Market** (*Leadenhall Street, EC3*), where at lunchtime teenagers in crimson-braided caps offer Victorian shoeshines outside purveyors of fish, poultry and game, and you can join pinstriped fund managers and insurers in a sawdust-scattered bar, a tapas bar, or the Croissant Express, depending on your needs and your finances.

The City is at its best midweek, for at weekends almost all the shops close and the area, although not unsafe, is uninviting and lifeless. For information leaflets and general inquiries go to **St Paul's Information Centre** on *St Paul's Churchyard, EC4*, which is *open Mon–Fri 9.30 a.m.–5.30 p.m. all year; May–Oct it is open Sat and Sun 9.30 a.m.–5 p.m.; Nov–Apr Sat 9.30 a.m.–12.30 p.m.*

Roman London and Boudicca Despite muddy streets that spoiled expensively imported thong sandals and flowing togas, life was comfortable for the wives and daughters of early Roman occupiers of a wattle-and-daub settlement turned busy riverside trading centre called Londinium – but not for long. In AD 62 the angered widow queen of the nearby Celtic Iceni tribe took a revenge that razed the infant capital of the province of Britain.

The Queen of the Iceni, whose name meant 'Victory', continued long after her death to inspire awe, ridicule and chauvinism. Tennyson described her in his poem 'Boadicea' as

… standing loftily charioted,
Mad and maddening all that heard her in her fierce volubility

Bill Belcher wrote that she was 'rather a dear', who

> ... drove about with great abandon
> And left her critics without a leg to stand on
> (*Other People's Clerihews*, ed. Gavin Ewart);

and the archaeologist Sir Mortimer Wheeler reportedly complained, when the name 'Boadicea' fell out of favour, that one simply would not dine with a lady called 'Boudicca'.

What little is known of Boudicca is unreliable, because it was recorded by Romans. Since the Celts trained both men and women in war, it seems likely that she was a fierce warrior as well as an able leader. The historian Ammianus Marcellinus wrote that 'A whole troop ... would not be able to withstand a single Gaul if he called his wife to his assistance. Swelling her neck, gnashing her teeth and brandishing her sallow arms of enormous size, she begins to strike blows mingled with kicks as if they were so many missiles sent from the string of a caterpault.' The historian Dio Cassius described Boudicca as 'very tall, in appearance most terrifying', with 'a great mass of the tawniest hair' and, around her neck, 'a large golden necklace'. She had two teenage daughters and a husband, King Prasutagus, who settled for peaceful coexistence with Rome, and so made his daughters and the Emperor co-heirs. When Prasutagus died, Rome decided to take the whole kingdom, but in flogging Boudicca and raping her daughters, the Romans miscalculated. Boudicca led her Iceni tribe and the neighbouring Trinobantes in a rebellion that took them first to Camulodonum (Colchester) and Verulanium (St Albans), then to Londinium, by which time her 20,000-strong troops were, according to Dio Cassius, battle-crazed:

> Those who were taken captive by the Britons were subjected to every form of outrage. The worst and most bestial atrocity committed by their captors was the following. They hung up naked the noblest and most distinguished women and then cut off their breasts and sewed them to their mouths, in order to make the victims appear to be eating them; afterwards they impaled the women on sharp skewers run lengthwise through the entire body. All this they did to the accompaniment of sacrifices, banquets and wanton behaviour.

The historian Tacitus claimed that 80,000 Britons were slaughtered. The city was burnt to the ground.

Boudicca – 'mounted in a chariot with her daughters before her' according to Tacitus – was finally defeated in Leicestershire after a rousing speech that caused the Roman leader Suetonius to break his customary silence and command his men to 'ignore the noise and threats of these savages', who were, he assured them, more women than men. Dio Cassius wrote that Boudicca fell sick and died; Tacitus asserted that she took poison to avoid captivity and humiliation. You'll find an 1850s Thomas Thornycroft statue of Boudicca and her two daughters in a chariot pulled by wild unreined horses on Victoria Embankment, SW1, at Westminster Bridge.

A charred layer is all that remains of London before Boudicca. Soon afterwards a city wall was built, and a Roman life that was civilised and luxurious for some and wretched for others was re-established. Evidence has been found of sophisticated villa central-heating systems, and items unearthed from wealthy Romans' dressing-tables include boxwood combs, lip rouge pots and manicure sets; grimmer remnants include a plaited bronze wire scourge used to flog disobedient servants, and a Roman wax tablet reading 'TAKE GOOD CARE THAT YOU TURN YOUR SERVANT GIRL INTO CASH'. By the time the Roman Empire collapsed in the fourth century, Londinium had become a thriving administrative, financial and commercial capital.

Women and Life in Medieval London, Featuring 'Brewsters'

Several centuries of sackings and burnings by Franks, Picts, Scots, Saxons and Danes followed the fall of Rome, yet London emerged from the Dark Ages a centre of commerce that was fierce enough in its independence for Edward the Confessor to move the seat of national government beyond the surrounding walls to Westminster. His Norman successor, William the Conqueror (crowned in 1066), granted London – the richest town in his new kingdom – rights of self-determination, and he built several strongholds, including the White Tower (now the centre of the Tower of London, see p.151), as precautions against the 'fickleness of the vast and fierce populace'. In 1215, King John was pushed further and gave the citizens the right to elect their own mayor. The Corporation of London still celebrates each new mayor's accession annually with the Lord Mayor's Show, on the second Saturday of every November.

The worst smells and ribaldry that characterised life in medieval London could largely be avoided by ladies of noble birth, who might ride at countryside hawking parties or sit elegantly at spinning wheels while young squires and noblemen rampaged through the city streets provoking fights with workmen and each other long past the early-evening curfew. 'Beautiful virgin girls' had the honour of being required to stand 'motionless like statues, decorated with very elegant ornaments' for important processions, when the inches of mud and refuse would be almost completely cleared by the official street-rakers. More often than not, however, the gutters were clogged with offal, fishheads and excrement, pigsties were built outside front doors, and only the wealthier traders could afford to build their homes high above the streets and counter noxious fumes by filling every room with strong perfumes, bunches of herbs and smoking incense.

Whores – also known as Winchester geese because their houses were owned by the Bishop of Winchester – could perhaps count themselves lucky to be cast out, along with Jews and lepers, and based over the wooden London Bridge in Southwark. It was the unlucky wives and daughters of humble tradesmen who had to live closest to the city's unsavoury street level, often cramped in one room that served both as home and as workspace.

Thoroughfares earned names like Ironmonger Lane and Bread Street because workers of the same trade tended to huddle together in order to control the quality of their goods, to prevent undercutting, to share tools and to help those of their number who were no longer able to work. These links were formalised as Guilds, early trade unions which were all-powerful in the city and granted widows partial membership. The ale trade was almost exclusively headed by women, who were known as 'ale-wives' or 'brewsters'.

Ale had been brewed in the home by women since Saxon times. Water, as Roger Protz explains in his *Great British Beer Book* (Impact Books), was not safe to drink. Consequently, ale was drunk not only at celebrations and funerals but during all meals, including breakfast. It was normal for medieval lords, ladies and their children to drink one quart of ale with breakfast; the ladies' gentlewomen took a more modest two pints. Since demand often outstripped supply, some houses began to specialise in brewing. When a new brew was ready, the ale-wife would erect a pole bedecked with a branch or bush above her door.

As ale-houses became established, permanent wooden signs replaced occasional poles, and Henry III took steps to ensure honest trading and a high quality of basic foodstuffs. The official post of ale conner, or ale taster, was created (the conners, usually men, could be recognised by their shiny red noses); the 1267 Assize of Bread and Ale required that ingredients be strictly monitored and only pots with official seals be sold as measures; and the Tumbril and Pillory Statute detailed punishments for lawbreakers. Many ale-wives, including the sixteenth-century Elynoure Rummynge, who was said to have a hideous visage but a superb 'noppy ale', were held in high regard, but those who cheated on the measurements were fined the first time; if they were found guilty again, the law stated that 'he or she shall suffer corporal punishment, to wit the baker to the Pillory, the brewster to the Tumbril or the Flogging'. Roger Protz notes that in a fourteenth-century Chester Miracle Play Christ redeems all the characters from the fires of Hell except the brewster with the short measure, who is flung back to the demons after admitting:

Some time I was a taverner
A gentle gossip and a tapster
Of wine and ale a trusty brewer
Which woe hath me bewrought.
Of cans I kept no true measure,
My cups I sold at my pleasure,
Deceiving many a creature,
Tho' my ale were nought.

Women and Publishing in the mid-nineteenth Century, Notably Mrs Beeton and Sensationalist Victorian Mary Braddon Mary Wollstonecraft's *Vindication of the Rights of Woman* was published by Joseph Johnson from St Paul's Churchyard in 1792; Anne and Charlotte Brontë stayed at the Chapter Coffee House when they were visiting their publisher on Paternoster Row during the 1840s and 1850s. Publishing was still based in the City when the mid-nineteenth-century spread of literacy beyond the privileged classes facilitated a massive boom in the industry that saw women's domestic magazines and sensational fiction emerging as the biggest sellers. Two of the most famous examples were first serialised in magazines, then appeared as books within a year of one another: *Mrs Beeton's Book of Household Management* by **Isabella Beeton** (1837–65) in 1861, and *Lady Audley's Secret* by **Mary Braddon** (1837–1915) in 1862.

Cheapside-born Isabella Mayson became the eldest of twenty-one children when her widowed mother married a printer-turned-Epsom-racecourse-clerk whose home grew so crowded that some of the children had to be raised in the Grandstand by their grandmother. At twenty-one Isabella married an ambitious young Bouverie Street-based publisher, Sam Beeton, who was overwhelmed by demand from the burgeoning railway station W.H. Smith stalls for his threepenny *English Woman's Domestic Magazine*, which mixed recipes, house management, fiction and a problem page, and proved the forerunner of today's popular women's magazines. Once Sam had managed to persuade his shy and conscientious wife to contribute articles, Isabella's heartfelt advice, written to others as one thrown suddenly into wife- and motherhood, became immensely popular.

Isabella embarked on a book version, collating recipes and suggestions sent in by the magazine's readers as well as providing her own. She shared a remedy for toothache that involved a piece of zinc and a shilling; she told the housemaid how to whiten scorched linen using 'dried fowl's dung'; she gave the lady's maid a 'very superior' recipe for boot polish using red French table wine and brandy; and in making sure to embrace all points of view she turned to letters such as this one, which was published in the *New Monthly Belle Assemblée:*

> My mistress is what in perlite society is called wimsical; she makes more errands in one Hour than can be counted in two; and then if the meat is not Dun to a Turn, and the vagetables Biled to a T, the consequence is sich Disagreement as need not be *subscribed*, and aught not in a genteel family to eggsist ...
>
> I am well awear that Servants are frequently trubblesome people; but surely, maddam, the same may be said (with all dew Difference) of employers.

Within one year of publication *Mrs Beeton's Book of Household Management* had sold 60,000 copies, but Isabella's husband soon found a taste for reckless speculation. Bereaved of two children, Isabella worked all hours as joint editor of Sam's publishing business to keep the family's finances going, and so added poor health to the stress her sisters had noticed. Mrs Beeton's accomplished life was cut short at the age of twenty-eight by an attack of puerperal fever shortly after the birth of her fourth child.

Mary Braddon, born in Soho in the same year as Mrs Isabella Beeton, also turned to writing and editing to conquer financial instability, but generally her life was very different, and often frustrating, for in many ways it exemplified the contradictions inherent in Victorian moral standards.

Lack of funds made divorce impossible for Mary Braddon's mother, Fanny, who suffered the disgrace of an adulterous husband. 'Papa had whiskers,' recalled Mary Braddon in memoirs written shortly before her death, 'and was always what is called nowadays well-groomed. I think he wore a blue, or perhaps a bottle-green coat, with a suspicion of brass buttons ... Papa was nobody's enemy but his own.' This Mary knew because she was 'told much that is not generally told to a girl before her kenwiggs pigtails are exchanged for a coil of plaits in a tortoise-shell comb'.

When her abandoned mother was forced to move with her two daughters to Camberwell, Mary turned her thoughts to a now desperate need: making money. In 1857 she tried acting which, even though she was accompanied everywhere by her mother, was 'a thing to be spoken of with bated breath, the lapse of a lost soul, the fall from Porchester Terrace to the bottomless pit'. She left the stage for writing in 1860 and met the publisher of *Temple Bar* and *St James's Magazine*, John Maxwell – 'a big burly florid-faced loud-spoken Irishman', as Robert Buchanan described him – who had a wife in a Dublin lunatic asylum. They fell in love and lived in sin, Mary looking after John's five children and bearing six of her own, until 1874, more than a decade later, when Maxwell's wife died and they could legally marry.

It is not surprising, perhaps, that Braddon's first bestseller, *Lady Audley's Secret*, featured bigamy, madness, sexual passion and a strong-willed heroine who was quite different from 'proper' women of Victorian fiction who stood for propriety, domesticity, chastity and the maternal. *Lady Audley's Secret* inaugurated the vogue for the melodramatic sensation novel, and launched a writing career that was to produce nearly eighty books in only fifty years, during which time the printer's boy was often waiting outside Mary's door. 'I have never written a line that has not been written against time,' she told her friend Bulwer Lytton in December 1862, adding that serial-writing was a curse which accounted for the 'errors, absurdities, contradictions and inconsistencies', for which she apologised.

Described by Robert Buchanan as a 'plump, fair-haired, unassuming girl', Mary Braddon was by 1901, wrote Arnold Bennett, 'a part of England ... she has woven herself into it; without her it would be different'. He continued: 'There are thousands of tolerably educated English people who have never heard of Meredith, Hardy, Ibsen ... but you would have to travel far before you reached the zone where the name of Braddon failed of recognition.' Admired by Dickens, Gladstone and Ford Madox Ford, Mary Braddon was quickly forgotten after her death until she was reappraised by feminists in the 1970s.

Museum of London

London Wall, EC2Y 5HN, tel. 071 600 3699. Open Tues–Sat 10 a.m.–6 p.m. (last admission 5.30 p.m.), Sun 12–6 p.m., closed every Monday except Bank Holidays (10 a.m.–6 p.m.). Admission, £3 adults, £1.50 students/unemployed/children aged 5–17, or £7.50 family entrance (tickets valid for 3 months). Located at the top of a pedestrian walkway, The Museum – distinguished by a Dick Whittington logo – is well signposted from nearby Underground stations (Barbican, St Paul's, Moorgate, Bank). Baby-changing facilities. Good disabled access.

Well laid out to entertain and inform for hours, the Museum of London is an excellent first stop if you want an overview of the city's history, and it is exceptionally child-friendly. Ramps and lifts make every section of the museum accessible to buggies, which are available from reception free with the deposit of a credit card or driver's licence. Older children will be surrounded by school groups of contemporaries drawing, taking notes and giggling, and the museum operates a good events schedule that might include children's lectures, film presentations or holiday activities. Last but not least, if you want to save money, use the family picnic area outside the main entrance.

The Museum of London combines objects and a lively text to chart London's history, starting near the upper-floor main entrance with skulls that may have been the heads of victims of the AD 60 massacre led by Boudicca. Walk through Roman interiors, medieval and Tudor London to the Great Fire Experience before going down to the lower floor, which begins in Late Stuart London and takes you through the Imperial Capital to Second World War London, featuring Selfridges Lifts and the Lord Mayor's Coach. Each floor has a decent-sized temporary exhibition gallery showing archive material gathered into regularly-changing themes. In the centre of the museum is a peaceful and beautiful Nursery Garden; the Coffee Shop serves good shortbread and the airy Terrace Café and Restaurant serves hot and cold food at fair prices.

Barbican

Bounded by London Wall, Beech Street, Moorgate, Aldersgate Street, Chamerlin Powell and Bon. No charge for entrance to estate; individual charges for events in Arts Centre (see Entertainment).

Within this residential and arts centre complex are a good art gallery and a pleasant atrium. The arts centre is renowned amongst families for its great children's programmes; residents would not live anywhere else. But the Corporation of London received few accolades for the design of the post-Second World War concrete Barbican, built as a city-within-a-city on the site of the bombed-out Cripplegate. Begun in 1963 and comprising a mixture of forty-storey blocks, bleak walkways and terraces, all on a roughly triangular plan, the estate comprises over 2,000 executive-priced flats, the lauded Guildhall School of Music and Drama and the City of London School for Girls as well as the Royal Shakespeare Company, the London Symphony Orchestra, a movie theatre and exhibition space to tempt you into the maze of paths that might be comprehensible but for the signposts, which often lead you back where you started.

St Bartholomew the Great

Entrance on Little Britain.

Parts of the inside of this dour flint-faced, square-towered nineteenth-century shell are the remains of London's only surviving medieval monastic church.

History St Bartholomew the Great was founded in 1123 by Rahere, an ambitious court jester of humble origins who – probably influenced by Matilda, the wife of King Henry I – decided to transform his life of triviality with a pilgrimage to Rome and, on his return, a 'Smedfeld'-based building project: the linked St Bartholomew's Priory and hospital, of which he became Prior and master respectively. Because ill-health was considered punishment for sin, medieval citizens turned to holy men and women to cure them, and by the thirteenth century it was the duty of all churches to help the sick as well as provide 'hospitality' for pilgrims and travellers. Under Church auspices, apothecaries used herbs and roots to make medicines, and by the fourteenth century St Bartholomew's, which was run by eight Augustinian brothers and four sisters, had widened its remit to look after women who were pregnant and any children born there up to the age of seven.

The medieval tradition of executing criminals within sight of the Priory was extended in Tudor times to include heretics, amongst them Anne Askew, a young woman of noble Lincolnshire family who split with her husband over religious differences and came to London, possibly to obtain a divorce; she joined the court of Henry VIII's sixth wife, Catherine Parr, and distributed Protestant tracts. Tortures on the rack made her so weak that she had to be carried in a chair to her death by burning at the stake in July 1546, aged twenty-five.

During the three hundred years before restoration began in 1863, various uses of St Bartholomew's included the Lady Chapel as a squat and later a printers' workshop; the North Transept as a forge (note the blackened walls); and the cloisters as a stable.

Today The thirteenth-century gateway is inconspicuous below a black-timber and white classic Tudor gatehouse. Walk past a small graveyard which serves as occasional lunch-spot for city chaps and into the impressive, sombre Nave. You'll find much of the earliest architecture in the Choir, including the plain, sturdy tiers of surrounding Norman arches. Saint Bartholomew the Great's sparse decorations and monuments include, on top of Rahere's tomb, a full-colour and newly touched up fifteenth-century conjectural model of the man.

Central Criminal Courts (The Old Bailey)

At Newgate Street and Old Bailey. Group tours Mon–Fri at 11 a.m. and 3 p.m. when the courts are not sitting; Sat. 11 a.m. Visitors admitted to the public galleries via the Newgate Street entrance at 10.45 a.m. and 1.15 p.m. weekdays when the courts are sitting, except in August.

The gold-clad, sword-wielding figure atop the shiny green dome of the Baroque 1907 Portland stone Central Criminal Courts has featured in many films for her potency as a symbol of justice, and in some cases injustice. Various murder trials – including that of Ruth Ellis, the last woman to be hanged in Britain – have made the Old Bailey famous, as has its previous site: the notorious Newgate Prison. For grisly memorabilia and reconstructions of Newgate, go to Madame Tussaud's and the Museum of London.

Newgate Prison and Elizabeth Fry Right from its 1180 beginnings, the gaol at the medieval city wall's New Gate was an overcrowded breeding-ground of vice and disease that few entered willingly. One notable exception was the seventeenth-century Catholic midwife Elizabeth Cellier who, after tending interned pregnant women, wrote such a horrifying exposé of prison conditions that she was fined £1,000 for libel; but one of the most famous was **Elizabeth Fry.**

Many thought Elizabeth Fry a saint for daring to enter Newgate, and many considered her dangerous: 'We long to burn her alive,' wrote the Reverend Sydney Smith in 1821. 'Examples of living virtue disturb our repose and give birth to distressing comparisons.' Elizabeth Fry exposed and then improved prison conditions while showing that, contrary to popular belief, criminal women were not only human but reformable.

Born to a wealthy Norfolk Quaker family in 1780, highly strung young Betsy Gurney was, like many of her contemporaries, accustomed from her mid-teens to taking large quanities of strong drink and the opiate laudanum to counter recurring toothaches, stomachaches and attacks of 'nerves'. But she was also wilful, and – despite great fear of thieves and footpads – in 1798 she made a trip to London where, with her hair dressed up, she 'felt like a monkey', 'vain and proud and silly'. Fired by the Evangelical American preacher Savery, whose voice gave her 'quite a palpitation at my heart', she decided to abandon all fripperies and become a Plain Friend. She needed a pliant husband. She was unsure of her feelings towards her brother's friend Joseph Fry, but he agreed to support her unquestioningly all his life, and they married in 1800. It wasn't until 1809, when she was already a mother of ten, that her father died and Elizabeth Fry felt free at last to preach, commenting that she felt like 'a bottle that has been corked up and pressed down and now there is an opening inside, there is much to run out'. She set herself a task: to 'live to a better purpose'; and within a year she had stormed London.

In her biography *Elizabeth Fry* (Papermac), June Rose describes the scene that must have greeted Elizabeth when her interest in reforming country prisons took her on to Newgate:

> half-naked, drunken women clawed through the iron railings with wooden spoons tied to sticks to beg the public for pennies for porter or for 'garnish money', to be paid to their fellow pris-

> oners to buy them a sight of the fire. Shrieking curses, brawling, spitting and tearing each other's hair ...

Women in prisons ate and slept in the same cramped straw-covered rooms that often served as 'a mere brothel for the turnkey'. Elizabeth Fry was at first concerned for the pale, ragged children: 'I understand that the first language they began to lisp was generally oaths or very bad expressions' (*Mrs Fry's Evidence to the House of Commons Committee on Prisons*, 1818). She appealed as a mother direct to the coiners, forgers, thieves and prostitutes who were prisoners, and won their support for her plan to found a school for their children. The authorities patiently explained that the vicious women prisoners would turn her school into a roughhouse, but when Mrs Fry persuaded the prisoners to give up one of their smaller cells for a schoolhouse, the authorities reluctantly allowed her to try her 'benevolent but almost hopeless experiment'.

The school, taught on the first day by the educated Mary O'Conner, who had been imprisoned for stealing a watch, was fully and enthusiastically attended, but outside, women continued to chew and spit tobacco and cavort in men's clothes. So Mrs Fry and her Bible-bearing helpers conceived a plan for penal reform that would give employment and instruction to women prisoners. Even her brothers-in-law, both long concerned with prison reform for delinquents, thought her plan ridiculous, so Elizabeth forged ahead without them. She set up a committee of Quaker women; she and her devoted husband entertained the prison authorities at home; then Mrs Fry called together seventy women prisoners whom even sheriffs and turnkeys had been unable to call to order, and asked the now demure gathering if they would obey any rules that had to be made as part of a new system which would introduce occupation, instruction, religion and cleanliness. The women gave their earnest assurance, and the authorities had to agree.

By 1820 the flogging of women had been abolished, conditions for women in prisons had improved considerably, and Elizabeth Fry's plans for a Ladies' Association had gone national. Over a thousand people flocked to her funeral in 1845 at the Friends' burial ground at Barking. An 1874 bronze medallion of Elizabeth Fry (artist unknown), which you might be interested to know about but probably won't want to see, is over the entrance of Wormwood Scrubs Prison, W12.

Dr Johnson's House

17 Gough Square, accessible from Fetter Lane, Fleet Street and Shoe Lane (follow the signposts). Tel. 071 353 3745. Open Mon–Sat 11 a.m.–5.30 p.m. (Oct–Apr 11 a.m.–5 p.m.), closed Bank Holidays. Admission £2 adults, £1.50 unemployed, students and children under 18. Whole house open to the public. Brochure warns 'Many Unavoidable Steps'. Dull for most children.

Dr Johnson – famous for, amongst other things, compiling the first comprehensive English Dictionary (published 1755) and saying 'The man who is tired of London is tired of life' – is shown in a cartoon by Max Beerbohm, which is on sale as a postcard in the gift section, having a joke with Boswell that the house without him is as useless as an eggshell without the yolk. Today it has his spirit. Although it is spartan and now surrounded by offices with only a few pieces of period furniture (including his friend Mrs Carter's mahogany bureau-bookcase and whatnot), this typical sturdy four-storey seventeenth-century house – which Johnson chose to rent for its large attic workspace and proximity to the printers – is suffused with atmosphere. You can see a number of portraits of his friends and family, read handboards with photocopied information sheets stuck on; and if she has time, the curator-receptionist-coat-checker might tell you how Dr Johnson was physically imposing at almost seven foot when the average man was nearer five, how he lifted a pipsqueak who insulted him into a tree and left him there, and how he respected women.

Dr Johnson and his Women: Wife, Adoptive Sister, Actresses and Bluestockings One of the first portraits you'll come across is of the tiny, spirited and generally well-liked **Mrs Hester Thrale** (1741–1821), intellectual and author of the popular *Anecdotes of the Late Samuel Johnson* (1786). Johnson was great friends with her until, after the death of her rich brewer-businessman husband Henry Thrale in 1781, Hester fell in love with and married Italian music teacher Gabriel Piozzi, an act that maddened Johnson enough, he told Fanny Burney, to make him burn all her letters.

Acclaimed novelist and sometime keeper of the Robes of Queen Charlotte **Fanny Burney** (1752–1840) was not so spurned. In the **Dining Room** you'll find a portrait of Johnson's favourite protégée. Dismissed in 1815 by the critic William Hazlitt as 'a mere common observer of manners', Fanny wrote novels, including *Evelina*, which was praised by, amongst others, her father, who said it was 'the best novel I know, excepting Fielding's, and in some respects better than his.'

On the question of politics in novels, Fanny wrote: 'Once I had had an idea of bringing in such as suited me, but that, upon second thought, I returned to my more native opinion that they were not a feminine subject for discussion.' Of women's education she wrote: 'It has no recommendation of sufficient value to compensate its evil excitement of envy and satire'; yet in many respects she broke with convention – for example, by writing in the first place, and by remaining single until the age of forty. When she finally married, she wrote to a friend:

> I remember … when I was thirteen, being asked when I intended to marry! and surprising my playmates by solemnly replying, 'when I think I shall be happier than I am being single.' … I have only this peculiar, – that what many contently assert or adopt in theory, I have had the courage to be guided by in practice.

Over by the window on the first **Landing** of Dr Johnson's House is a small portrait of **Kitty Fisher**, whose sullied reputation as mistress of several eminent men and ballad-singer between acts at Drury Lane did not make Johnson ashamed to be seen in her company, since he judged her 'kind and charitable'. The **Withdrawing Room** features a large portrait of the fierce **Mrs Elizabeth Montagu** (1720–1800), who said in 1750: 'Wit in women is apt to have bad consequences; like a sword without a scabbard, it wounds the wearer and provokes assailants. I am sorry to say the generality of women who have excelled in wit have failed in chastity.' Known as the Queen of the Blues for allowing 'blue stockings' instead of the formal black silk at her literary parties, she quarrelled with Johnson over his *Life of Lyttelton* and struck him off her visitors' list, at which Johnson commented: 'Mrs Montagu has dropped me. Now, Sir, there are many people one should like very well to drop, but would not wish to be dropped by.'

He had fondness and respect in equal measure, however, for **Elizabeth Carter**, whose portrait by Catherine Read in the **Library** was commissioned by Mrs Montagu. Daughter of a liberal Kent clergyman, Elizabeth had the privilege then usually denied women of a scholarly education, which equipped her to contribute in 1734 to *The Gentleman's Magazine*, through which she met fellow contributor Johnson, who remained a firm friend while she established her career by editing Mary Talbot's letters and translating Epictetus. Johnson signed his letters to her 'Yours with a respect which I neither owe nor pay to any other'.

In **Miss Williams' Room** you will find a portrait of 'My Tetty', the beloved **Mrs Johnson**, from whose death in 1752 (only three years before the publication of the Dictionary) Johnson never quite recovered, still saying 'I wish Tetty had seen this' many years later. Many were baffled that a wealthy widow with three children should marry the penniless Johnson; Johnson's friend David Garrick couldn't stand her. Her friend Anna Williams admitted that Mrs Johnson 'inclined to be satirical', but Johnson remembered her brown eyes and mass of soft golden hair, stating that she read comedy aloud better than anyone he had heard.

By the time Mrs Johnson met **Anna Williams**, cataracts had put paid to the living Anna was earning through writing, and because the operation proved unsuccessful, when Mrs Johnson died she begged her husband to 'take care of Anna', who had some independent income, including an annuity from Mrs Montagu, but continued to rely on Johnson for lodgings. Her sight problems caused her to develop odd habits, which guests calling for tea commented on. Boswell concluded that Miss Williams was measuring her guests' tea by placing her finger inside the cup; Miss Reynolds agreed about her motive but swore that the finger was outside, measuring by feeling the rising heat. Miss Williams's post as President of the Ladies' Charity School for poor children did not stave off boredom, and she became crotchety with age. Johnson, who had to bribe her maid to stay, said: 'Had she had a good humour and prompt elocution, her universal curiosity and comprehensive knowledge would have made her the delight of all that knew her.'

The last stop in Dr Johnson's house is his quiet, roomy **Garret**, which Boswell speculated would have been 'fitted up like a countinghouse' while the Dictionary was being compiled – that is, with a high desk running the length of the room at which Johnson's six paid clerks wrote standing up.

St Bride

Bride Street, off Fleet Street. Free entry to the Crypt Museum. A few awkward steps down to the Museum.

St Bride, often called St Bride's, has several claims to fame, amongst them one culinary, one architectural and one bibliographical. An eighteenth-century Ludgate Hill-based apprentice pastry-cook called William Rich gained fame in his trade for modelling his wedding cake on the St Bride spire, which he could see from the windows of his lodgings; the Baroque white spire in question, made up of four tapering octagonal arcades pulled out 'like a telescope' (Pevsner) is, at 226 feet, the tallest Wren built after the Great Fire of 1666; in 1500, Wynken de Worde brought Caxton's first moveable-type printing press to a workshop next to the churchyard, sealing St Bride's reputation as the 'Printers' Cathedral' and the 'Journalists' Church'.

Visiting St Bride In 1940 a bomb proved near-disastrous but also fortuitous, since although it destroyed most of the church, the cherished landmark spire survived, and the damage revealed Roman wall foundations, which you can see today in the **Crypt Museum**. Alongside a section of Roman pavement, various artefacts include Delft pots uncovered by archaeologists on the site, printed ephemera telling the Wynken de Worde story and, displayed in a cabinet donated by the Worshipful Company of Cooks, the golden silk party dress of Susannah Rich, wife of the pastrycook who used only the best French brandy in his white-tiered cakes, 'even when it cost one guinea a bottle'.

Upstairs the church, which is colourful and squeaky-clean since the post-war rebuilding, still functions as the Journalists' Church, with newspaper proprietors and colleagues commemorated by plaques along the rows of pews.

MOLL CUTPURSE, HIGHWAYWOMAN

In an unmarked St Bride churchyard grave lies the daughter of a respectable Barbican shoemaker, Mary Frith (1584–1659), who had, long before her teens, if her 'autobiography' is to be believed – tired of the restrictions that went with being female, preferring 'very *Tomrigg* or *Rumpscuttle*' games with boys, such as 'Sword and Dagger for a bout at Cudgels', to 'that sedentary life of sewing or stitching'. And so she abandoned petticoats for one of the few professions of her time that could earn women fame: she became Moll Cutpurse, 'pickpurse, fortune teller, receiver and forger'; she was portrayed in Middleton and Dekker's popular play *The Roaring Girl* in 1611; and she went on to live prosperously until the then grand old age of seventy-five.

Three years after her death, her 'autobiography' was published to great success that was perhaps partly due to the book's promise to 'all ye *Pick-pockets, Lifters, Heavers, Rumpads, Bawds* &c. ... the discovery of all those Arts and Artifices' for which Moll Cutpurse, 'the Oracle of Felony', was famous. The introduction to *The Life and Death of Mrs M.F., commonly called Mal Cutpurse* (1622) sketches Moll as an honest, upright thief, lamenting the 'sad decayes' of the trade after 'the losse of this Monopolizing Improver' who had thieved with such 'Discretion and Judgement'. But the 'autobiographical' part of the book is almost certainly within the 'rogue literature', or 'jest-biography' tradition – that is, suggests *A Biographical Dictionary of English Women Writers 1580–1720* (Harvester Wheatsheaf), not written by Moll at all. Indeed, it was probably written by a man. Questions of authenticity do not, however, make the book any less enlightening or entertaining: Moll was real, and some of the incidents are likely to be based in fact; even if the author did not know Moll's real character or motivations, it is interesting to read how a seventeenth-century man interpreted them.

At twenty, explains the introduction, Moll decided she was truly estranged from the 'Manners and Customes of the Age', and 'resolved to set up in a neutral or Hermaphrodite way', but fell at first into bad company: 'having entered and initiated her self into a private crue of some loose Women, who had undertaken to manage the promptness and dexterity of her wit to some notable advantage. Their trade being to receive Goods which were lifted: that is to say, stollen by Thieves.' Moll quickly learned from others' mistakes. The above-mentioned bad 'crue' were soon 'either Hanged or Runne away', and Moll observed that showy villainy attracted unwanted attention. She used as an example

> that memorable Story of the five *Women-Shavers* in *Drury-lane*, which I was very glad to hear; for it was a most impudent debaucht piece of malice and lessened the envy of my Actions; these five Furies had got a poor Woman, (whom they suspected the princi pal'st Shavers Husband had to doe with) and having stript her, whipt her with rods most terribly, and shaved off all the Hair about her, and they souced her in suds till they had almost killed the poor Wretch, whose tears, cries and protestations prevailed not a rush. They were afterward prosecuted for the riot, and con-

demned to the Pillory, for which one or two of them suffered, and the rest fled to *Barbadoes*; but all of them ruined their poor husbands.

Although she reportedly rose to become head of a gang of thieves, she managed to avoid court appearances. Knowing the common defence against pickpockets – to sew a fish-hook in the lining of your pockets – she was not about to get caught so easily. By the time she was convicted for robbing and wounding General Fairfax while he was crossing Hounslow Heath, she was rich enough to buy herself out of Newgate for £2,000, and later apparently had the gall to set up a pawnshop on Fleet Street where victims could buy back their stolen goods.

Known to the end, her 'autobiography' says, as a 'good *Fellow*' who 'loved good *Liquor*', Moll lived her life in the belief that 'the Universe consists and is made up of Cheaters and Cheatees ... and there is no great difference below between them; To be excellent and happy in Villany, hath been alwayes reputed equal with a good Fame ... as I have in my LIFE been preposterous, so I may be in my Death'.

St Paul's Cathedral

Ludgate Hill. Open daily 9 a.m.–6 p.m. Galleries closed Sun; crypt sometimes closed Sat; access limited during services. Admission £2.50 adults, £1.50 children/concessions, half-price after 4 p.m.; same charges again to climb to the galleries. Crypt free. No charge if entering for a service or private prayer.

'It is a commonplace, but we cannot help repeating it, that St. Paul's dominates London,' wrote Virginia Woolf in *The London Scene*. 'It swells like a great bubble from a distance; it looms over us, huge and menacing as we approach. But suddenly St. Paul's vanishes. And behind St. Paul's, beneath St. Paul's, round St. Paul's when we cannot see St. Paul's, how London has shrunk!'

Since Virginia Woolf wrote *The London Scene*, the sombre grey dome of St Paul's, topped with a gold ball and cross, has been dwarfed in height by surrounding tower blocks, but not in stature. Enter the nave, and Wren's cathedral inspires still deeper awe – the space is huge. You are drawn towards the dome by glittering mosaics. To your right is the entrance to the galleries, well worth the additional expense, but only if you are in good health and free of luggage/pushchairs, for you must tread over 500 dizzying steps to reach the top. The **Whispering Gallery** offers a bird's-eye view of the choir, arches and clerestory as well as the surprise of being able to hear, as if they were next to you, strangers chatting in low voices behind the stone balustrade on the opposite side of the dome's interior. The **Stone Gallery** and the more dramatic higher, smaller **Golden Gallery** both run round the outside of the dome and offer spectacular views of London. Even on a sunny day it will be crisp, so wrap up warm if you want to relax on one of the stone benches. Before you leave, go down to the labrynthine, white-arched **Crypt** –

the largest in Europe – which features, in one darkened section, an entertaining fifteen-minute slide-show with voice-over, and throughout commemorates many significant figures through British history, including Florence Nightingale, who is shown in her nurse's cap on a brown marble frieze.

Building St Paul's The wooden medieval structure was burned down in 1087, the Norman and Gothic cathedral was destroyed by the 1666 Great Fire, and in 1669, thirty-seven-year-old Christopher Wren (1632–1723) was appointed Surveyor General by the king and asked to draw up plans to rebuild not just St Paul's but also much of the city. The fast rise of mathematician and rationalist philosopher Wren can be charted by his marriages. The relatively low-key 1669 wedding to Faith, daughter of an old family friend, Sir Thomas Coghill, took place in the modest Temple Church; in 1677, after Faith's death in 1675 from the then prevalent disease of smallpox, Wren's marriage to Jane, daughter of Lord Fitzwilliam, was solemnised in – no less – the chapel royal of St James's Palace.

The building of St Paul's dominated Wren's career until its completion in 1710, when he was seventy-nine, but little is known of his private life. His friend John Flamsteed, the first Astronomer Royal, described him as 'the only honest person I have to deal with', although another friend, the scientist Robert Hooke, recorded that sometimes Wren was 'surly', 'not kind', and 'even jealous of me'. Hooke also says that Wren cured worms with 'burnt oyle', and 'cured his Lady of the thrush by hanging a bag of live bog-lice about her neck' – perhaps under the instructions of his sister, Susanna Holder, who attained a small amount of fame for developing medicinal remedies that helped to prevent miscarriages.

Wren was commissioned by King Charles II, but soon after Queen Anne's succession to the throne in 1700, he had won her lasting support for a number of reasons. Wren backed her attempt to quash licentiousness by informing his workmen that anyone caught swearing on the cathedral site would be liable to instant dismissal. Anne was fiercely anti-Catholic, pro-Church of England, and not much interested in the arts – Wren's aptitude for building houses of worship at once satisfied her religious fervour and staved off cultural critics. The steps of St Paul's later served as the platform for a violent falling out between Anne and Sarah, Duchess of Marlborough, who was succeeded as the queen's favourite by Abigail Masham (see West London).

St Paul's was reduced for a time to functioning as a short cut through the City. Its period of disrepair ended only when Queen Victoria complained that it was 'dreary, dingy and undevotional'. The renovation included the glittering mosaics, which Wren would, by all accounts, have judged garish. The fifteen-year-old Katherine

Mansfield, on her first trip to London in 1903, was, however, mainly impressed: 'The building of St Paul's is very fine but I don't like all the pigeons that are constantly flying about.'

FLEET STREET: WOMEN AND JOURNALISM

Before newspaper magnates Tiny Rowland and Rupert Murdoch relocated and modernised their printing operations, leaving Fleet Street to the property developers, the 'Street of Ink' was, as national disseminator of information, a key target for anyone with a message, and women forged two main routes in. A handful, including Harriet Martineau and Rebecca West, penetrated the ranks of mainstream journalists. Others, including Emily Faithful and the suffragettes, founded independent presses.

Harriet Martineau (1802–76), educated daughter of a Norwich textile manufacturer, overcame illnesses, including deafness, at the age of twenty-eight to become a children's writer, novelist and London journalist on the *Daily News* for fourteen years (1852–66). In her lifetime she was widely known for her dogmatic newspaper articles on topics ranging from the Married Women's Property Bill, which she supported, to the new subject of political economy, which she popularised, to licensed prostitution, which she deplored; but she was quickly forgotten after her death for reasons partly of her own making. Martineau was clearly wilful – if a conversation took a turn she didn't like, she simply put her ear trumpet down – yet she managed to counter the distaste men and society had for intelligent single working women by maintaining an aura of receptive femininity. In 1837 the well-connected Unitarian barrister Henry Crabb Robinson was greatly impressed to find her 'agreeable in person and manners ... not old maidish and not offensively blue in the colour of her conversation'. She kept up a front of modesty. When she was seriously ill in 1855, for example, she wrote an obituary of herself for the *Daily News* that ventured: 'Her original power was nothing more than due to earnestness and intellectual clearness within a certain range ... In short, she could popularise while she could neither discover nor invent' (this obituary turned out to be twenty-one years premature).

Emily Faithful (1835–95), freed by the relatively liberal education granted by her Epsom rector father and inspired when she learned that women had been active in the fifteenth-century printing industry, decided to improve career opportunities for women in 1860 by founding the Victoria Press in London, which trained women in the printing trade and operated commercially. 'We ventured to call it the Victoria Press,' said Emily in October 1860, 'after the sovereign to whose influence English women owe so large a debt of gratitude, and in the hope also that the name would prove a happy augury of victory.' Emily Faithful ascertained through personal experiments that 'if women were properly trained, their physical powers would be singularly adapted to fit them for becoming compositors, though there were other parts of the printing trade – such as lifting of the iron chases – [which entailed] an amount of continuous bodily exertion far beyond average female strength'. For these tasks a small number of men were employed. Emily received requests from girls and women all over the country, and from the outset in 1860 the Press kept both a mainstream and an alternative profile. In 1862 Emily became Printer and Publisher in Ordinary to the Queen; the feminist publications *English Woman's Journal* and *Victoria Magazine* peeled regularly off her steam presses between 1863 and 1880. When a Women's Printing Society was founded in 1876 Emily's battled seemed – at least to some extent – won, and from then on she slowed her activities, which had included some poetry and prose writing and dramatic reading tours.

A decade after Emily's death, **Christabel Pankhurst** (1880–1958) adopted the 4 Clement's Inn home of social worker and charismatic suffragist fund-raiser **Emmeline Pethick-Lawrence** (1867–1954) as the headquarters for six years of the Women's Social and Political Union, for its location. 'Adjacent to Fleet Street,' said Christabel, Clement's Inn 'was highly convenient for the newspapers, which were ever interested in the militant movement. ... Even exaggerated and distorted reports, which made us seem more terrible than we really were, told the world this much – that we wanted the vote and were resolved to get it.' In 1920 Viscountess Margaret Rhondda founded the feminist-socialist weekly *Time and Tide*, which was published from 88 Fleet Street and attracted writers including Virginia Woolf and Rebecca West.

Feminist journals gave women a chance to prove their journalistic skills, which Cicily Isabel Fairfield, or **Rebecca West** (1892–1983), did before she was twenty. Cissie, daughter of an Irish soldier and war correspondent, went to London's Academy of Dramatic Arts intending to become an actress; instead she became a writer 'without choosing to do so' after the *Evening Standard*'s regular theatre critic was unable to go to Gorky's *Lower Depths*, and gave Cissie the free tickets. Cissie's review went down well, so because she needed money, and 'at home we all wrote and thought nothing of it', Cissie called on the London bureau chief of the Melbourne *Argus* – who had previously given her father work – only to be told that she should 'find something more suitable to do than writing'.

She immediately contacted the new feminist weekly, *The Freewoman*, and wrote a book review for the second issue which featured in the first line the word 'bloody' two years before 'Not bloody likely' in Shaw's *Pygmalion* caused horrified giggles in a liberal London audience. Cissie took a pseudonym the next spring, mainly to pacify her mother, choosing the name of the heroine she had recently played in Ibsen's *Rosmersholm*, Rebecca West.

The Freewoman went bust after W.H. Smith, the major newsagent chain, declined to stock it; and although Rebecca was appointed assistant editor of *The New Freewoman* in 1913, she was beginning to be annoyed by the paper's lack of literary content. 'I don't see why a movement towards freedom of expression in literature should not be associated with your gospel,' she said to the original paper's founder, Dora Marsden. She invited the poet Ezra Pound to become literary editor, but even so, Rebecca resigned after only four months. Her biographer Victoria Glendinning records that 'She had been horrified by the proofs of the first issue: "My lord, the printing! The carelessness, the dirt, the shakiness! ... And can't we stop attacking the WSPU? The poor dears are weak at metaphysics but they are doing their best to revolt."' (*Rebecca West*, Papermac). Rebecca began to write for the socialist newspaper the *Clarion*, chastising Labour and Liberal politicians 'for their pusillanimity over votes for women' (Glendinning), and she began writing book reviews regularly for the *Daily News*.

Indeed, by the time she was contributing regularly to the feminist *Time and Tide* in the late 1920s, she had already concluded the two affairs for which – unfairly – she is most famous in the minds of many. For personal pride and public discretion she tried to keep secret both her ten-year affair with H.G. Wells, with whom she had a son, and her distressing liaison with the Fleet Street newspaper magnate Lord Beaverbrook, for whose papers she often worked as a journalist. By now she had already written two novels, and was an acclaimed journalist.

When Beaverbrook invited her to contribute regularly to his paper the *Evening*

Standard, when she was in her fifties, he billed her as 'The Greatest Journalist of Our Time' – not out of sentimentality for their affair but because that was how she was perceived. She wrote regularly for papers including *The Sunday Tmes, The Daily Telegraph* and *The New Yorker*, but she particularly enjoyed working for the *Standard*: 'a peculiar, amiable, self-satisfied bedlam that never sought to correct its faults. And it was a great paper.' In 1949 she was created CBE and in 1959 she became a dame. In September 1982, a few months before she died, she wrote an ironic, punchy piece for *Vogue* on what it felt like to be ninety.

Guildhall

At Gresham Street and Aldermanbury, tel. 071 606 3030 ext. 1460 for information and to book tours with the beadle. Open 7 days a week 10 a.m.–5 p.m. May–Sept including Bank Holidays; Oct–Apr Mon–Sat 10 a.m.–5 p.m. Free. Important to phone ahead – the Guildhall is closed to the public for special occasions, including the Booker Prize, addresses by heads of states, the Lord Mayor's Banquet and bomb-searches before the Lord Mayor's Show. Some steps.

If you have time to spare, it is worth fixing up a tour of the Guildhall to see what remains of the seat of Medieval City government.

In the **Great Hall**, the walls are the original 1411 constructs, but the 9 foot 6 inch tall models, Gog and Magog, are reduced post-war replicas of the 14 foot 3 inch mischievous warrior giants that were paraded in midsummer pageants in the fifteenth and sixteenth centuries. The ground-floor **Library** is now a corporate space given over to functions. Downstairs the **East Crypt** is an impressive low spread of pale stone fan vaulting that was at street level when it was built in 1411. The **Guildhall Clock Museum** (*entrance at Aldermanbury; open Mon–Fri 9.30 a.m.–4.45 p.m.*) is low-key and mesmerising, lined with quietly ticking grandfather clocks and elaborately decorated eighteenth-century verge watches displayed in glass cases.

Tower Bridge

Near Tower Hill Underground, tel. 071 403 3761. Open Apr–Oct 10 a.m.–6.30 p.m., Nov–Mar 10 a.m.–5.15 p.m., closed New Year's Day, Good Friday, Christmas Eve, Christmas Day and Boxing Day. Admission £3.50 adults, £2.50 children aged 5–15 and OAPs, £10 family ticket. Stairs make it unsuitable for disabled people and those with awkward, heavy baggage including children's buggies.

After all the revamping, including 'a unique themed gift shop' and the introduction of a 'resident animatronic worker-guide', the best thing about visiting Tower Bridge is still the view up and down the Thames from the two high-level enclosed walkways.

When Tower Bridge was built between 1886 and 1894, the two spiky Gothic-Victorian steel-framed towers served to support the split-level bridge and housed both the stairs to the pedestrian walkways and the steam pump engines that hydraulically lifted the road-traffic lower level to let boats through. In the first month of the 1894 opening river traffic was a priority, and the bascules were raised 655 times. Today they open electronically on average ten times a week. You can see exhibitions about the construction and history of the bridge in the north and south towers, and the original Victorian steam pump engines have been kept in working order.

Tower Hill Pageant

Tower Hill Terrace, near Tower Hill Underground, tel. 071 709 0081. Open daily Apr–Oct 9.30 a.m.–5.30 p.m., Nov–Mar 9.30 a.m.–4.30 p.m. Admission £4.50 adults, £2 children under 16 and OAPs, £12 family ticket. Tour takes approximately one hour. Staff will assist disabled people.

This new and rather gimmicky but nevertheless amusing and informative 'dark ride museum' carries you physically in a 'time car' that resembles a black-hooded Wurlitzer through 2,000 years of the sights, smells and sounds of London's history. See a medieval knight puppet stick his head out of an ale-house, hear the crackling Great Fire, smell cloves shipped from the spice islands and block your nose for the putrid Plague. Experience the Tower Hill Pageant if you still have time and money left after the Museum of London.

The Tower of London

North bank of the Thames to the west of Tower Bridge. Tel. 071 488 5694. Open Mar–Oct, Mon–Sat 9.30 a.m.–5.30 p.m., Sun 10 a.m.–5 p.m.; Nov–Feb Mon–Sat 9.30 a.m.–4 p.m.; closed 24–26 Dec, 1 Jan, Good Friday. Admission £6.40 adults, £3.90 children aged 5–15, £4.80 student and unemployed, £17.50 family ticket; or buy the £14.50 all-in ticket which admits you to four other palaces (Hampton Court, Kensington Palace, the Banqueting House and Kew Palace). Free Yeoman Warder guided tours at regular intervals throughout the day; last tour leaves 3.30 p.m. summer, 2.30 p.m. winter, weather depending. Access to some parts of the Tower is difficult and tiring if you have an infant and a buggy. Poor disabled access.

If you take a tour, even before you've passed over the grassed moat and through the portcullised main gate, the Tower of London site is entertaining. Only warrant officers with twenty-two years' service in the armed forces behind them qualify to wear the red tabard and wreathed blue hat that is the Tudor-style royal livery of a Yeoman Warder, or 'Beefeater', so the bloodthirsty and comic tales are delivered in deafening barks, as if assembled tourists are unruly troops. Yeomen's tour scripts obviously vary, but you are likely to hear descriptions of how beheadings on Tower Hill served as popular entertainment, of how the moat once filled with the Tower community's detritus, and that even today anyone wishing to enter the Tower after hours must know the password, which is changed daily.

Inside, William the Conqueror's eleventh-century toy-like grey Caen stone White Tower, with fourteenth-century cupolas adorning the four corner turrets, is just the centrepiece of an eighteen-acre site that grew over the centuries as successive kings varied their priorities. Twelfth-century Richard the Lionheart ordered more fortifications; Henry III opted for amusement in the form of a royal menagerie; and Henry VIII made the complex the chief state prison. He offered Tower Green as a more private site for the execution of noble traitors and wives who had failed to bear him sons (see Greenwich for more on Henry VIII's wives). Women executed on the Green in the sixteenth century included the beautiful 'Nine Days' Queen', Lady Jane Grey, whose stay at the Tower awaiting coronation became imprisonment when her rival Mary I won overwhelming national support. It is said that Anne Boleyn's ghost haunts the Tower, accompanied by a vast retinue of knights and ladies. Women prisoners included goldsmith's wife and mistress of Edward VI, Jane Shore, who was accused of sorcery by Richard III. The eighteen-year-old Elizabeth I, after two months of interrogation on plots against her half-sister, Mary I, refused to set foot in the Tower again, except briefly for her own coronation.

What You'll See Because all the Yeomen live in the Tower grounds with their families you might, as you wander, glimpse a teddy bear in a window or an off-duty warder taking a guard dog for a walk, but the village atmosphere does not last beyond the homey green, parish church and doctor's house. From cold stone steps the legendary black ravens eye visitors beadily, and – with the exception of the glittering **Crown Jewels** in the **Jewel House** of the Waterloo Barracks – the sections that are open to the public boast either murder-and-imprisonment- or war-and-torture-related exhibitions. In the **Bloody Tower**, for example, the two little princes Edward and Richard were allegedly killed to assure Richard III's accession, and you can see the desk where Sir Walter Raleigh wrote a history of the world while captive for thirteen years. In the **Martin Tower** you can see **instruments of torture** and in the central **White Tower**, which is considered one of Britain's most important examples of Norman military architecture, you can visit the **Royal Armouries** and the **National Museum of Arms and Armour**. This vast, morbidly compelling collection includes ivory and wood medieval crossbows, lances blunted with use, and – upstairs – Henry VIII's Armour Garniture, which has a metal codpiece protruding so far from between the metal skirts that a Warder overheard one young boy cry out: 'Cor! Look at the size of that man's willy!'

When you've finished at the Tower of London you can stroll the river promenade or picnic on a pleasant moat-path bench.

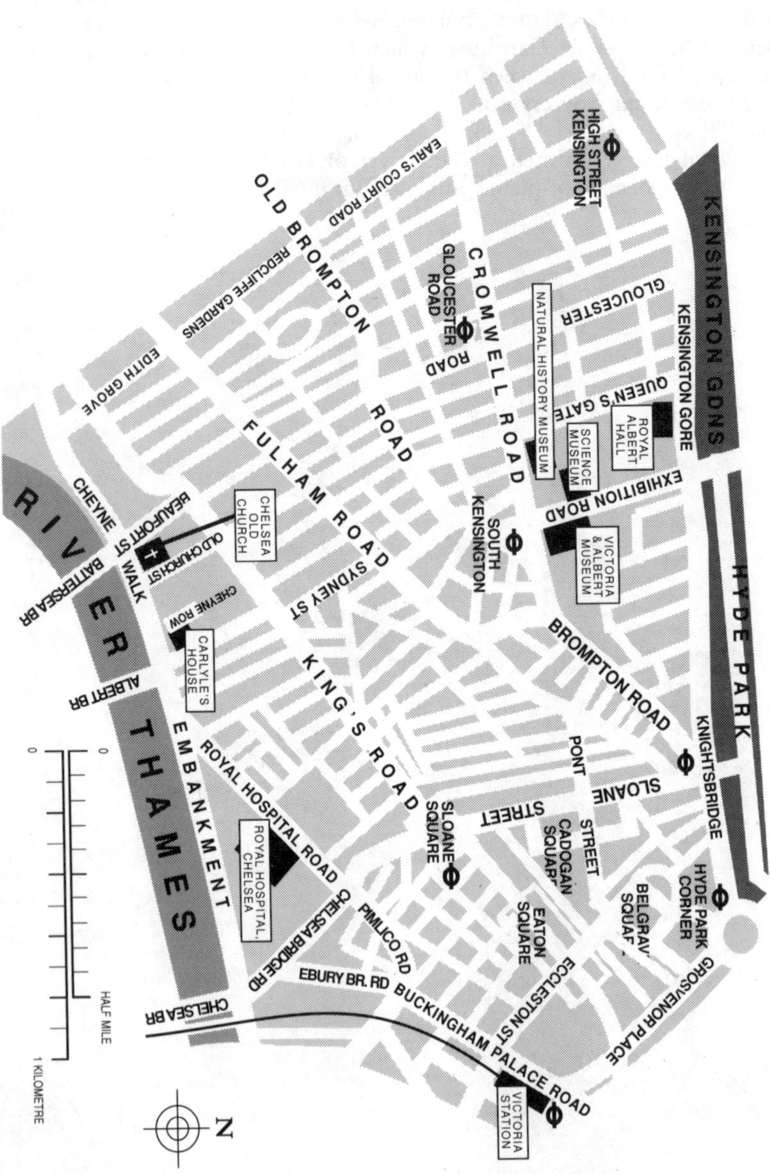
KENSINGTON GDNS
HYDE PARK
HIGH STREET KENSINGTON
KENSINGTON GORE
GLOUCESTER
ROYAL ALBERT HALL
QUEEN'S GATE
NATURAL HISTORY MUSEUM
SCIENCE MUSEUM
EXHIBITION ROAD
VICTORIA & ALBERT MUSEUM
CROMWELL ROAD
GLOUCESTER ROAD
SOUTH KENSINGTON
EARL'S COURT ROAD
OLD BROMPTON ROAD
REDCLIFFE GARDENS
EDITH GROVE
FULHAM ROAD
BROMPTON ROAD
KNIGHTSBRIDGE
HYDE PARK CORNER
SLOANE STREET
PONT STREET
CADOGAN SQUARE
SLOANE SQUARE
KING'S ROAD
SYDNEY ST
CHELSEA OLD CHURCH
OLD CHURCH ST
BEAUFORT ST
CHEYNE WALK
CHEYNE ROW
CARLYLE'S HOUSE
RIVER THAMES
BATTERSEA BR
ALBERT BR
EMBANKMENT
ROYAL HOSPITAL ROAD
ROYAL HOSPITAL, CHELSEA
CHELSEA BRIDGE RD
PIMLICO RD
EATON SQUARE
ECCLESTON ST
GROSVENOR PLACE
EBURY BR. RD
BUCKINGHAM PALACE ROAD
CHELSEA BR
VICTORIA STATION
HALF MILE
1 KILOMETRE
0
0
N

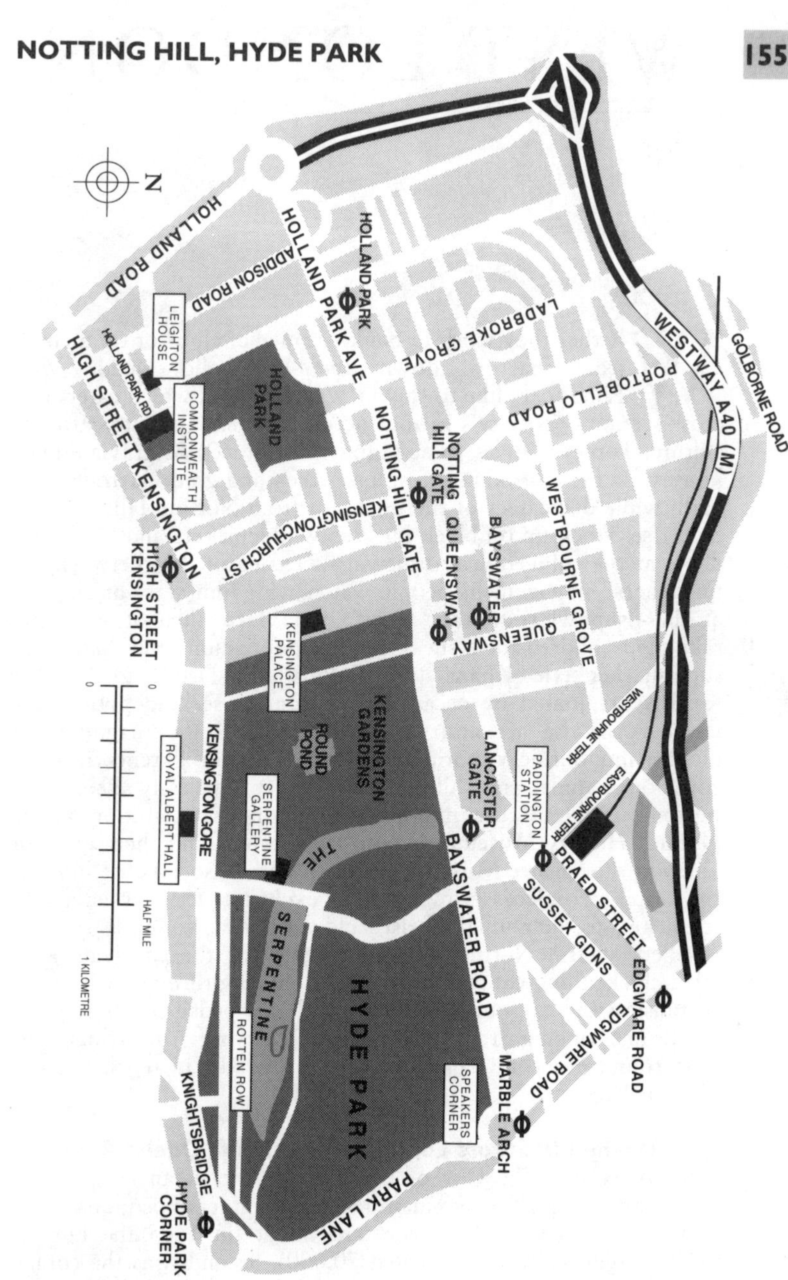
N
HOLLAND ROAD
ADDISON ROAD
HOLLAND PARK AVE
HOLLAND PARK
LADBROKE GROVE
PORTOBELLO ROAD
WESTWAY A40 (M)
GOLBORNE ROAD
LEIGHTON HOUSE
HOLLAND PARK RD
HIGH STREET KENSINGTON
COMMONWEALTH INSTITUTE
HOLLAND PARK
NOTTING HILL GATE
NOTTING HILL GATE
KENSINGTON CHURCH ST
HIGH STREET KENSINGTON
QUEENSWAY
BAYSWATER
WESTBOURNE GROVE
QUEENSWAY
KENSINGTON PALACE
KENSINGTON GARDENS
ROUND POND
WESTBOURNE TERR
EASTBOURNE TERR
PADDINGTON STATION
LANCASTER GATE
ROYAL ALBERT HALL
KENSINGTON GORE
SERPENTINE GALLERY
THE SERPENTINE
BAYSWATER ROAD
PRAED STREET
SUSSEX GDNS
EDGWARE ROAD
HYDE PARK
ROTTEN ROW
EDGWARE ROAD
SPEAKERS CORNER
MARBLE ARCH
KNIGHTSBRIDGE
PARK LANE
HYDE PARK CORNER
0
0
HALF MILE
1 KILOMETRE

WEST LONDON

Whether they work in banking, media, clubs or on a cheap jeans barrow down the Portobello Road, West Londoners like to stay in West London, which caters to a cross-section of society's various needs, from shopping to eating to culture. Top executives value grand white stucco Belgravia Square houses for their proximity to plush green-and-gold Harrods Food Hall, while dedicatees of the punk era from Notting Hill concrete high-rises stock up on black-buckled winklepickers and Goth pendants at the subterranean timewarp Kensington Market. Penguin publishers' management people-watch with film stars and agents at the fishbowl restaurant **Kensington Place**, then at weekends take their children for a cheap treat of poppadums and dhal at the supermarket-style **Khans** (see Eating and Drinking). Milling tourists are joined by occasional inspiration-seeking potters and jewellers in the art and design galleries of the magnificently gloomy monolithic **Victoria and Albert Museum**. Parents, fashion-conscious nannies and children alike all get hopelessly absorbed in button-pushing at the interactive arthropods exhibition at the **Natural History Museum** or with corn chutes and themselves on video at the **Science Museum's** Launch Pad. A social elite in tasteful pastel two-pieces crowned with exclusive designer hats fight for tickets to the annual Chelsea Flower Show. Young Rastas and revellers swarm Notting Hill in August for the carnival, when fried chicken and canned beer sustain dancing through a weekend of music systems pounding from residents' bedsitting rooms and oil drums ringing from beauty-queen-carrying truck floats. All year round everyone can enjoy leisurely walks in regal, relaxing Hyde Park.

Two Women in Stuart London, 1603–1714: Queen Anne and Queen Mary The City of London was life-endangering during the Stuart dynasty for two main reasons. First, cramped, unsanitary conditions made plague a constant threat (in 1665 the bubonic Great Plague killed an estimated 70,000). Secondly, as the conflict between pro-Parliament Puritan merchants and the court intensified into the Civil War, which was concluded in 1649 with the execution of Charles I, the City became the Whig stronghold, where Puritan Roundheads doused invading Royalist Cavaliers with cauldrons of boiling water while unemployed oysterwomen shouted 'Privilege of Parliament!'. So the wealthy moved west, most decisively William of Orange and his wife Mary in 1689 to the then remote palace of Kensington.

Since it was generally held that women's predominantly cool and moist humours made them physically and emotionally weaker, and therefore unfit for heavy work or public life, despite Mary II's rights of succession she insisted on sharing reign equally with William. Both she, and particularly her sister Queen Anne after her, were dogged by the desire and failure to produce a male heir as well as by political intrigues and parliamentary crises inherited from the liberal Whigs v. Royalist Tories Civil War period.

Although she was a daughter of the Catholic James II, Princess Mary (1662–94) was raised a Protestant by command of her uncle, Charles II. In 1677 she married her cousin, the Dutch Protestant leader William of Orange, and in 1688 she supported her husband's deposition of her father. Events surrounding her refusal to be made queen with William as prince consort had far-reaching implications. The mere fact that varying proposals were made, by Mary and by Parliament, at once undermined the issue of the Divine Right of succession and heralded the Parliament's independence of the crown (this independence was clearly signposted in 1696 by the Demise of the Crown Act, which allowed Parliament to exist for six months after the king's death). Furthermore, it was no longer only preferable to be Protestant – from now on, any future monarchs had to make formal anti-Catholic declarations.

The joint crowning of William and Mary was a compromise that dissatisfied both the left and the right, and even though it assured Anne's rights of succession, the sisters were already regularly having bitter quarrels. Mary ruled only reluctantly during William's war absences, preferring to consider science, geography and theology while walking for exercise with her maids in the Kensington Palace Queen's Gallery and sipping chocolate, a drink she popularised in England. Indeed, her great popularity, her hereditary title and her undeviating Anglicanism were such a buoy to William's rule that many thought that her death in 1694 would cause his downfall, but – presumably to Anne's disappointment – he survived without apparently difficulty until 1702.

Many criticisms have been levelled at Anne (1665–1714). For a long time she was dismissed as a squabbling ministers' puppet with a dubious reigning passion for members of the same sex. But in *Stuart England* (Penguin) Stuart Kenyon argues that she had 'a mind of her own, and her most successful ministers, Godolphin and

Harley, were those who took her most seriously'. Inded, it is much to her credit that she remained so in control when pressures included her exclusion from her sister's favour until Mary's death, the death of her husband Prince George in 1708, seventeen miscarriages and stillbirths in as many years, with her only son dying at the age of eleven, and the impossibility of making or breaking a personal friendship without having to consider constitutional implications.

One of her first acts as queen was to dismiss every Whig in sight and replace them with firm Tories, and by 1707 her relationship with Sarah Duchess of Marlborough – close companion and confidante since the age of eight, but a supporter of pro-Spanish War Whig ministers – was over, with lasting acrimony. Sarah was immediately replaced as favourite by Abigail Masham, who was related to Harley, a Tory whom Anne recalled to parliamentary power after the Whig defeat of 1710. By the time Anne died, she had apparently turned to food for consolation and, weighing 20 stone, had to be buried in a square coffin. The independence of Parliament was signalled, but the dominance of the constant Lords over the dismissable Commons left England, Kenyon argues, not yet a parliamentary monarchy but an aristocratic monarchy. Any hopes of the Stuart line continuing were dashed by the succession of George I.

In front of St Paul's Cathedral you can see the 1886 Richard Belt copy of the 1712 Francis Bird original of the statue of Queen Anne. The statue's position and the Queen's reputation as a brandy-lover gave rise to the rhyme:

Brandy Nan, Brandy Nan, you're left in the lurch,
Your face to the gin shop, your back to the church.

Other Women in Stuart London: Spinsters and Handmaids

With rare exceptions like Moll Cutpurse (see The City), Nell Gwyn (see Piccadilly) and Aphra Behn (see Covent Garden), life in Stuart London was grim for unmarried women, who were soon lumped together under the term originally used to describe women employed in spinning, 'spinsters'. Aphra Behn's biographer, Angeline Goreau, reports that the government agency for Poor Relief, not known for its generosity, named five shillings a week as the minimum one adult could live on. A spinster could, if she worked a seven-day week, earn two shillings and fourpence; in 1638 a bushel of grain cost six shillings. Teachers could earn more than spinsters, but hardly a decent living wage. In 1672 Mary Sutton earned five shillings, probably for a week, for teaching workhouse children lacemaking; another schoolmistress said: 'It's little they pay, and it's little we learn 'em.'

Women agricultural labourers earned about the same as spinsters, and many came to the city hoping for more lucrative work, but although there were more options – 'as to cry matches, small-coal, blacking, pen & ink, thread-laced, and a hundred more such kind of trifling merchandises,' observed one American visitor – the wages were often worse. In *The Gentlewoman's Companion* (1675), Hannah Woolley cautioned young women to become waiting-maids, lest they end up thieving or in 'bawdyhouses'. But although a washmaid, cook, dairymaid or lady's maid at least had bed and board guaranteed, she could never hope to leave that profession. Washmaids were paid about £2 a year in 1685 and accomplished lady's maids no more than £7. Samuel Pepys spent more buying a servant girl a suit of clothes – so that she looked merely passable – than he gave her in a whole year's wages. Sexual harassment was an accepted part of the servantgirl's job. If a girl got pregnant she was dismissed immediately. The situation for women still hoping to avoid prostitution was often so desperate that, as the brother of Jane Martindale from Yorkshire wrote, 'her money grew so near running to an end that she had thoughts to sell her hair, which was very lovely for both length and colour'.

The 1960s and 1970s: Quant, Biba, Westwood, Siouxsie 'It was tough, in the fifties. Girls wore white gloves,' wrote novelist Angela Carter in *Very Heaven: Looking Back at the 1960s* (Virago). *Very Heaven* editor Sara Maitland found many of her contributors embarrassed to recall themselves in the 1960s, when they were full of unpoliticised, pre-feminism arrogance and 'belief that if we smoked enough dope and screwed enough people the world would be transformed'. Actress Julie Christie found something

> very oppressive about that time: the peer pressure – the whole business of being as freaky as possible and if you weren't you were labelled 'straight' or 'square'. There was definitely status within that apparently no-status 'classless' society … and it hung on how much drugs you took or how you dressed or just how freaky you were.

Angela Carter, however, remembered: 'Truly, it felt like Year One, when all that was holy was in the process of being profaned.' She and her friends could enjoy being poor – squatting, on the dole, and still able to afford London Transport: '… the relaxation of manners, the sense of intellectual excitement, even the way, oh, God, you didn't have to shave your *armpits* … hemlines, politics, music, movies, everything … there was a yeastiness in the air that was due to a great deal of unrestrained and irreverent frivolity'.

With the sixties came many things that were taken for granted even by the seventies: the Pill; the freedom to read thirty-two-years-censored *Lady Chatterley's Lover*; the everyday road-fact of the

Breathalyser, introduced by Harold Macmillan's daring new Minister of Transport appointment, Barbara Castle; and, above all, with the sixties came Youth Culture.

'Teenagers were defining themselves against their families within the support of a tight peer group identity,' writes Sara Maitland. The booming postwar high-employment society gave this distinct group more money and leisure than previous generations, manufacturers sought to capture this new market, and suddenly every hip, with-it teenage girl *had* to at least aspire to look like the model Twiggy, have a favourite Beatle and save pocket money for the group's latest LP. Since fashion in music and clothes was central to teenagers' existence throughout the sixties and seventies, sights were set alternatively on Kensington and Chelsea as Mecca shifted between Kensington High Street and the King's Road.

By the early 1960s the sprawling department store was deemed old-fashioned, and in 1965 Mary Quant, a Goldsmiths' art graduate with a radically geometric haircut and a penchant for short skirts opened on Chelsea'a King's Road the mould-breaking and subsequently much-copied first 'boutique', Bazaar. The boutique was intimate, with an informal café downstairs, and stocked only Mary Quant's op-art gymslip designs. 'It was the *make-up* we liked most,' recalls one ex-punter dreamily. Elizabeth Wilson writes in *Adorned in Dreams* (Virago) that the significance of well-heeled Mary Quant and her upper-class backer husband, Alexander Plunket Green, 'was that they were able to transform themselves from "zany" students whose boutique was a kind of permanent party for their friends, into business tycoons who married their own flair for style to the most modern American methods of sizing and mass marketing'.

Quant, famous for shaving her pubic hair, capitalised on being a member of the 'Chelsea Set', 'whose parties', commented George Melly, 'and general way of carrying on had won the total attention of the gossip writers of the period'. Yet Quant described her phenomenon with the rhetoric of democracy. 'Once only the Rich, the Establishment set the fashion,' she said. 'Now it is the inexpensive little dress seen on the girls in the High Street. ... They may be dukes' daughters, doctors' daughters, dockers' daughters. They are not interested in status symbols. They don't worry about accents or class. ... They represent the whole new spirit that is present-day Britain – a classless spirit that has grown up out of the Second World War. ... They are the mods.'

But by the end of the sixties the supposedly independent-minded mods were replacing white lipstick with dark, and donning vast floppy hats and elegant floaty prune, aubergine and sage hippie dresses from Bazaar's rival, Biba, founded in Kensington by Barbara Hulanicki. 'And then, Kensington began to lose its stuffiness,' wrote one-time Chelsea's Bazaar devotee Alexandra Pringle in *Very Heaven*.

> A small shop had opened on the Abingdon Road which was to end its days in that bastion of old-ladyhood – Derry and Tom's. Perhaps it was the greatest frivolity of the sixties, but to me it also seemed awesome. It was black and gold, it had brothel-like interiors of palms, ostrich feathers and glittering sequins. It was Biba's.

Hulanicki was canny in producing a Biba catalogue, which was passed round eagerly amongst fashion-conscious undergraduates, but expanding from Abingdon Road boutique to department store proved Biba's downfall ... 'how many people really wanted an aubergine-coloured fridge, or baked beans with a Biba label?' asks Elizabeth Wilson. In 1975 the store closed. The King's Road was once more the place to be seen to be buying.

The Beatles and being 'zany' went out. Spitting and swearing and the Sex Pistols came in with Malcolm MacLaren and Vivienne Westwood's anti-design King's Road boutique, Sex, as style-leader. The *Sex Pistols, The Inside Story* (Omnibus Press) by Fred and Judy Vermorel paints an unappealing picture of MacLaren and his young male acolytes as surrounded by put-upon women – at first.

MacLaren, a mod and Harrow Art School student, was soon booted out by his mother, and met **Vivienne Westwood** when he was sleeping rough in her brother's car. Vivienne apparently fell in love with him over a bowl of Shredded Wheat, and later called him 'the most extraordinary person I've ever met'. But he spurned her, moved into a brothel, then a shoemaker's flat in Berwick Street, and finally lodged with film students in Chiswick where Vivienne, having left her husband, tracked him down, and – Malcolm complained – repeatedly appeared naked in his bedroom. Ten months later, Vivienne gave birth to their son Joe.

Fred and Judy Vermorel say that MacLaren owes his success to 'Vivienne Westwood's Northern determination to MAKE GOOD'. He had 'crazy ideas' – she ran them up as costumes. First she made a bright-yellow 'boiler suit', then jewellery, which she sold on Portobello Road to supplement her small primary-school-teaching income, and so support the family. Malcolm inherited money from his grandmother, Vivienne borrowed money from her retired shopkeeper parents, and they leased the back part of 430 King's Road. Initially it was Paradise Garage, then 'Let it Rock' for teddy boys and finally 'Sex' after Malcolm chanced upon a Walthamstow lingerie catalogue advertising 'scandalous lingerie and glamourwear'.

Malcolm sprayed the shop with fluorescent pink death-to-men slogans from Valerie Solanis's SCUM manifesto and Vivienne ran up versions of Soho pornshop fetish clothes – and the Punk Rock look was born. Malcolm began to nurture an ambition to form the most notorious rock band ever. Leaving the practicalities of managing the shop to Vivienne, he went to New York, where he heard of a street gang called the the Sex Pistols ... he'd got the name; now he needed the members of the band, who could be – indeed, *should* be – talentless. The look was crucial: spiked hair, safety pins and (of course) clothes from Sex.

'The Sex Pistols have burst into the Top Ten with a record which calls the Queen a "moron",' wrote the *Sunday Mirror* in its June 1977 'disturbing report on the amazing new cult', Punk Rock. Vivienne Westwood discussed her views on the queen that month in *No Future*: 'You can talk about her having killed many people too by smiling on hypocrisy. Like entertaining the Brazilian ambassador on a business level, while his country is daily torturing people to death.' But, she went on: 'I feel sorry for her ... she is a symbol of the total wastage of potential. She's prevented from being some kind of wild, crazy, intelligent, creative human being and has to be some kind of zombie instead.'

A year later, in October 1978, the Sex Pistols' singer, Sid Vicious, was arrested, accused of stabbing to death his blonde American go-go dancer girlfriend – dubbed 'Nauseous Nancy' Spungen by the *Daily Mail* – in a New York hotel room. During the trial, 'Sex Pistols' manager Malcolm MacLaren [was] accused of cashing in on the stabbing death,' wrote the *Evening Standard* when a new line of T-shirts went on sale in MacLaren's shop. 'The T-shirts, at £6.50 each, show Vicious surrounded by a bunch of dead roses. Across the front are the words: "I'M ALIVE. SHE'S DEAD. I'M YOURS."' When MacLaren arrived in New York with the $30 million bail, he also began negotiations for the Sid Vicious story. Four months later Sid Vicious was dead of a heroin overdose in the arms of his sleeping new girlfriend, discovered by his mother, Mrs Ann Beverley, when she brought them a morning cup of tea. Having campaigned to prove him innocent of murder, she now delcared to the *Daily Express* that he couldn't have died of a heroin overdose: 'I know he didn't have any more that night, because I had the packet in my pocket ... There is no way Sid could have slipped the smack from my pocket. He wasn't like that. He would have waited until the next day and said, "Can I have some more?"'

By now, MacLaren had long split with Vivienne Westwood, who went on to win international acclaim as one of Britain's foremost designers (see and buy her clothes today at the King's Road 'World's End' shop), Punks were photographed as sights by tourists on the King's Road, and a group of Sex Pistols fans were gaining infamy in their own right.

Nearly two decades before the scandal of Madonna's conical bra, Janet Ballion – a.k.a. Suzie Sioux, then **Siouxsie of the Banshees** – was noticed by the press for attending a 1976 Paris Punk Rock festival wearing 'a bra top with cut-out cups', for which, reported the *Sun* newspaper, she 'got punched in the face'. Nineteen-year-old Siouxsie, who explained that her attire was 'to show that erogenous zones are overrated and tits are no big deal', established herself as leader of the most dedicated group of early Pistols fans, known as the Bromley Contingent. Later admitting that the first record she ever bought was 'ABC' by the Jackson 5, Siouxsie proceeded to break the Punk mould by becoming a *female* swearing, spitting, outrageously underdressed star, dubbed the 'suburban saboteur' by *Sounds* magazine.

Siouxsie's début with three members of the Bromley Contingent, renamed the Banshees, was in 1976 at the first British Punk Rock festival at the 100 Club in Oxford Street, the idea being that they would play so badly they'd get bottled off. To Siouxsie's surprise, another band, the Clash, objected to her swastika armband. She said: 'As a symbol of shock the swastika was the best thing around. I meant it to be nothing more.' At the time of the gig, *Melody Maker* magazine commented that Siouxsie's inventive clothes were street theatre that was bound to end up on the stage: 'She'll wear black non-existent bras, one mesh and one rubber stocking, and suspender belts (various), all covered by a polka-dotted, transparent plastic mac.'

A year after the band's success at the 100 Club, Siouxsie still refused to sign up a record deal: 'We'll do it on our own terms. We're not gonna water down things to make it acceptable to the people who sit behind desks.' Describing the music, she said: 'Nobody in the band's into melody, thank God,' and she explained that the songs' subject matter came from stories she read in the *Sun*. 'It'll be great when people realise that a woman musician isn't a miracle, isn't anything to laugh at either,' she told one interviewer. 'I don't see myself as a Joan of Arc or anything, but it would be great if other women follow in my footsteps.'

In 1978 the Banshees signed with Polydor, and by the early 1980s Siouxsie could boast big sales and did things like New York magazine photoshoots in furs that were so expensive they came with an armed guard. A newspaper reported: 'Siouxsie's dad is dead now, but her mum is pleased with her success in the music business. "She still asks me when I'm going to learn to be a secretary," Siouxsie added. "She doesn't think music is a very safe way of life."'

KENSINGTON SEE MAP ON P.154

For museums come to South Kensington, where wide avenues are lined with grand biscuit-coloured six- and seven-storey terraces and sleek-coiffured ladies in hacking jackets pass with the golden Labrador on their way into Hyde Park for a brisk walk past the indefinitely scaffolding-covered 175 foot spiky neo-Gothic mid-Victorian **Albert Memorial** (opposite the Albert Hall). High Street

Kensington was described in 1846 by Thackeray's eldest daughter as 'a noble highway, skirted by beautiful old houses with scrolled iron gates', and by Thackeray himself as rumbling with 'omnibuses every two minutes'. Today it is an assault course of impatient high-style businesswomen shouting into their mobile phones while muddy schoolboys scoot through hooting traffic after rugby practice and keen shoppers weave in and out of glass-fronted high-street fashion stores, Afghan/used Levi 501-strung Kensington Market and disco-pumping Corinthian-pillar-fronted independent British designers emporium Hyper Hyper (see Shopping).

The attractions of cosy **Holland Park** (W8) include a peaceful Japanese garden, freely roaming peacocks, locals practising t'ai chi on Sunday mornings and the children's One O'Clock Club play-group every weekday lunchtime (see Children). Further north still and you're in Notting Hill, where academics and TV producers daily pass groups of homeless and alcoholics huddled under grubby blankets and nylon sleeping bags near Ladbroke Grove Underground station (you might find the straggled groups depressing, but they're rarely threatening). In Notting Hill you can enjoy a thriving café and bar scene and the famous market on winding Portobello Road (W11), which was once a cart track through the fields from Notting Hill turnpike.

Follow Portobello Road down from the pretty pink and primrose yellow terraces around Chepstow Road, and you first pass stalls and shop fronts laden with antiques. As you reach the repertory Electric Cinema the stalls are all knock-off priced hosiery and vegetables, then past seedy pubs and trendy bars up towards the Westway and you can buy dated and high-trend knick-knacks from patchouli oil to hand-made hats. On to the Golborne Road (W10) and you can rummage through stalls boasting purple flared jeans, mohair jumpers, holey curtains, empty picture frames; mostly second-hand, much of it overpriced, some of it useless and all of it part of the absorbing Portobello Road experience. You can end your visit with Cellnet-bearing market traders, aspiring actors and students hiding hangovers behind Ray Bans at the **Lisboa Café**, or in summer climb to the rooftop **Café Grove** (see Eating and Drinking).

Hyde Park

It is possible, although perhaps a little ambitious, to walk from the West End to Notting Hill or South Kensington through 600 acres of London's largest park. On the way you can see a contemporary art exhibition at the **Serpentine Gallery**, historic costumes at **Kensington Palace**, and sometimes forget that you're in the middle of a metropolis, which was the original intention when the gardens of Kensington House and Henry VIII's royal hunting grounds were combined for public use in 1637. Since then, different parts of Hyde Park have served varying functions.

Now dominated by Speakers' Corner, the gathering point for political rallies from National Front to CND, the area near Marble Arch was a place of popular entertainment from the fourteenth to the eighteenth century. Public holidays were declared for hangings at the Tyburn Tree, when popular victims were toasted by crowds with gin and ale, and flowers were strewn in front of them by girls in white dresses. The lake that was formed as a picturesquely irregular water feature in 1731 out of the Westbourne Brook at the suggestion of George II's wife, Queen Caroline, was used as an ice rink through nineteenth-century winters, and today you can go boating across it or – if you don't mind a thin coating of algae – swim in the lido. Women still trot horses down sanded **Rotten Row**, but this century they tap withers past teenagers playing frisbee.

A hundred years ago, when Rotten Row was *the* place to be seen, ladies had to contend with 'Skittles' Walters. A courtesan who became known as 'Skittles' for telling some insulting drunken guardsmen that 'if they didn't hold their blood row, she'd knock them down like a row of bloody skittles', Catherine Walters was amongst the first to take up roller-skating in the 1880s. Her appearance on Rotten Row was celebrated by Poet Laureate Alfred Austen: 'though scowling matrons stamping steeds restrain, she flaunts propriety with flapping mane'.

In the eighteenth century anyone passing through was likely to spy a duel and was at the mercy of thieves and footpads; in the 1940s you could still see sheep grazing. The poet and novelist Stevie Smith, of whom Seamus Heaney says: 'She reminds you of two Lears, the suffering king and the nonsense poet', enjoyed walking in Kensington Gardens. In Stevie Smith's novel *The Holiday* (1949) the narrator walks one day from the Round Pond to the Statue of Physical Energy by G.F. Watts, and comments on the fearsome upper-class children:

> Once I met a crocodile of them, out walking from some high-class baby school in the neighbourhood. ... They walked listlessly, in a lackadaisical manner, they wore a great mixture of garments; a little girl, for instance, was wearing a hand-woven light fawn overcoat above a longer tartan kilt, she had a Fair Isle knitted tam on her head. ... Some of the little boys had wind-breaker jackets and short knickers made of this expensive hand-woven material. So the children strung along, staring vacantly about them, and hanging on to the arm – those who could get near her – of a nanny-governess brisk person.

Today you can feed the geese on the **Round Pond** and be interrupted only by a jogger determined to tell you her love life, or you can lounge in a striped deck chair for hours. Take children to the (free) **Playground** in the north-west corner, or to the famous kitsch **Peter Pan** statue. If you want to be alone with a book, discover the Edwardian **Sunken Garden**, where benches are backed by pleached limes and overlook kaleidoscope flowerbeds that have a small canal as their centrepiece.

Kensington Palace

On the West edge of Hyde Park; entrance at the north-east corner of the building, near the Orangery. Open daily 9 a.m. (1 p.m. Sun) to 5 p.m.; closed New Year's Day, Good Friday and 24, 25, 26 December. Admission £3.90 adults, £2.60 children, £2.95 seniors/students, £11.30 family. Some unavoidable stairs if you want to see the State Apartments. You can take a tour, but the labelling throughout the Palace is more than sufficient in terms of information and entertainment.

Although it is now called a palace, the plain red-brick Kensington building was intended as a low-key royal abode away from the smoke and oppressive air of London, which was aggravating King William's asthma. By his accession in 1689, this had become chronic. William and Mary instructed Christopher Wren *not* to embellish when he began work in 1689 converting the £14,000 Jacobean mansion into Kensington House, as their new home. Mary felt 'long condemned' in Whitehall, where she could 'see nothing but water or wall', so she went 'often to Kinsington [*sic*] to hasten the workmen, and I was to [*sic*] impatient to be at that place, imagining to find more ease there'. By August 1690 Mary told her husband, 'Kensington is ready' and 'looks very well', but in 1694 she had contracted smallpox, and she died in December at the early age of thirty-two.

Except for some interior redecorations and occasional hidden extensions – for example, more rooms added behind the King's Gallery for Queen Anne in 1706 – Kensington House remained a long, two-storey house with only four urns on the roof and a finely carved foliated white hood over the Garden Door for decoration. Queen Anne, who succeeded to the throne in 1702, loved gardening, so she rooted up 'the Box', the smell of which she apparently disliked, and had formal English gardens constructed in place of Mary's Dutch layout. The formidable Queen Caroline also busied herself with the gardens, and her rearrangement of furniture led to the celebrated discovery, in a bureau drawer, of the Holbein drawings now at Windsor. After Queen Caroline's death in 1737 half the Palace was closed up, and it was saved from demolition in 1898 only by Queen Victoria's fond childhood memories of the 'three large, lofty, fine cheerful' second-floor rooms in which she was born and brought up, and of 'pleasant balls and *delicious* concerts'. Parliament was persuaded to vote £36,000 for its restoration, and in January Victoria announced that the State Apartments, 'which have been closed and unoccupied since 1760 ... shall after careful restoration be opened to the public'.

What You'll See Today In accord with its status as a house, not a palace, the rooms comprising the State Apartments are mainly small, and – apart from those later occupied by Princess Victoria, which are stashed with Victoriana clutter – the chambers and galleries are largely elegantly panelled in plain wood. There are many royal portraits and a vast louche Rubens in the **King's Gallery** depicting 'Satyrs and Sleeping Nymphs' or 'Jupiter and Antiope' (art historians cannot agree). Queen Mary's midnight-blue **Bedchamber** features George IV's semi-precious-stone-and-marquetry-decorated writing cabinet, and the **King's Staircase** has a dizzying illusionist gallery of chatting courtiers and courtesans painted on the walls by William Kent (?1685–1748).

Downstairs on the ground floor you'll find several darkened glassed-off corridors displaying the **Court Dress Collection**, starting with a heavily embroidered 1760 square box mantua and petticoat. By the next century dress was less restrictive (silk trains, puffed sleeves and bodices), and King Edward VIII had altered the time ladies were presented at court from mid-afternoon to the more relaxed evening. Twenties flapper style with trains added characterised the period after the First World War, when courts were revived for twenty years. In 1936 King Edward VIII held two Afternoon Receptions at which young ladies were presented, and the last Evening Court was in 1939. Princess Diana's 1981 wedding dress is the last dress you see before passing through the lavishly stocked gift shop and, if you're in need of refreshment, head down to the very English 'Winter Café' to eat scones and fruit cake.

Commonwealth Institute

Kensington High Street. Open Mon–Sat 10 a.m.–5 p.m.; Sun 2–5 p.m. Closed New Year's Day and 24, 25, 26 December. Admission free. Wheelchair access from car park entrance; ask staff for assistance. Book in advance for the Activities Room. Phone for details of special events for children, Christmas, summer and Easter.

Described by one Kensington-based mother as 'the poor man's Science Museum', the Commonwealth Institute is a great place to entertain children for free – perhaps to cheer them up after a Kensington High Street shopping trip – and adults may find it engagingly dated. The building, a tent of green-copper roof on a vibrant blue rectangle, was opened in 1962 by the Queen 'to increase, throughout Britain, knowledge and understanding of the Commonwealth'. Inside, the stepped layers of galleries represent each Commonwealth country with exhibitions: stacks of giant building blocks have doors to open that might reveal a country's natural habitat; sometimes there's a Perspex barrel to 'spin and see' a country's innovations ... in Canada you can look in on a now rather shabby stuffed porcupine; you can spin and see a faded box of Magic Pantry Chicken, a hockey visor and a paint roller.

Pick up idiosyncratic presents like Nigerian thornwood figurines and Dragon's Breath Mustard from the gift shop as you leave.

Leighton House

12 Holland Park Road, tel. 071 601 3316. Open Mon–Fri 11 a.m.–5 p.m.; closed Sun and Bank Holidays. Phone for a full programme of classical concerts and art lectures.

Another freebie, but this time for adults, the otherwordly oddity Leighton House is worth a special trip if you're not in the area.

Built as a shrine to art and a studio-house for Victorian artist Frederic Leighton, the house embodies Leighton's belief that beauty is an end in itself, life-enhancing. His designer friend and fellow Royal Academician George Aitchison was instructed to cram it with beautiful objects and details, and to create a showcase for tiles Leighton collected during travels to Tangier. The result includes a dense rich blue-and-gold centrepiece, the amazing Turkish Delight- and belly-dancer-evoking **Arab Hall** (to your left as you enter).

Raised in Europe because of his ill mother's need for warmer climes, young Frederic gained his first reputation in Rome as a dashing addition to the *salon* of the opera singer Adelaide Sartoris. His English acclaim came in the 1850s, when Queen Victoria bought *Cimabue's Madonna* after it was shown at the Royal Academy, and suddenly Leighton was moving in royal circles, visiting the Prince and Princess of Wales regularly at Marlborough House; but he was also much criticised.

The writer Vernon Lee thought him a stuffed shirt when she met him in 1844, describing him as a cross between Olympian Jove and a head waiter. Many thought him a mediocre artist taking himself laughably seriously, surrounded in his **Dining Room** and **Drawing Room** with excesses of William Morris wallpaper and Pre-Raphaelite Burne-Joneses hanging next to Leighton's own work. But he was not someone contemporaries ignored. Some of the greatest musicians of the age, including Clara Schumann and opera singer Pauline Viardot, performed at his famous musical evenings, which were usually held on the eve of the Sending-in Day for the Royal Academy Summer Exhibition. Bernard Shaw certainly knew and disliked Leighton, and may have used as a source for his play

Pygmalion Leighton's Platonic but adoring relationship with his favourite actress model, Dorothy Dene, who Leighton painted as Desdemona and Bianca. Broken by crippling attacks of angina by the 1890s, Leighton created a trust fund for Dorothy Dene and left the house to his sisters, who were persuaded by Emilie Barrington, Leighton's future biographer, to preserve the house as a museum with only a small section closed to the public.

The Royal Albert Hall

Kensington Gore, opposite the Albert Memorial, SW7. Tel. 071 589 8212.

The round red-brick Royal Albert Hall (built 1867–71) was one of the first parts completed of a grand educational centre, including three museums, proposed by Prince Albert to make use of the nearly £200,000 profit left over from the Hyde Park Great Exhibition of 1851. It rings through each year with the sounds of pop and jazz concerts and political meetings, but most famously for eight weeks every summer with the Promenade Concerts, when thousands of excited students and composers queue for tickets, then spend intervals picnicking in the Park. At the turn of the century the Hall was a key suffragette venue.

Dame Ethel Smyth, Composer and Suffragette Despite – or perhaps because of – opposition from her traditional army family, the young Ethel Smyth (1858–1944) studied music in Germany. She was recognised as the first significant English woman composer after the 1893 performance of her Mass in D at the Albert Hall. The difficulties of getting her work widely accepted, combined with the personal charisma she found in Emmeline Pankhurst on their first meeting in 1919, turned her to suffragism: 'At that moment I was deep in certain musical undertakings. These liquidated, I decided that two years should be given to the WSPU after which, reversing engines, I would go back to my job.' At first the woman with 'the soft bright eyes that on occasion could emit lambent flame' scorned Smyth for her apolitical absorption in the arts, but soon Mrs Pankhurst embraced Ethel, and by 1911 Smyth had composed the WSPU's theme tune, the *March of the Women*. Her memoirs recall a great meeting at the Albert Hall:

> one of those astounding money-making efforts so often put through by the WSPU, and on this occasion Mrs Pankhurst and Annie Kenney – most irresistible of blue-eyed beggars – were the chief protagonists. Sometimes as much as £6000 to £7000 – on one occasion, late in the fight, £10,000 – would be raised in a couple of hours, but as 'money talks', these painful facts found no mention in the Press!

She goes on to record a telling incident:

> Militancy was a costly business and much depended on these Albert Hall meetings; hence it is not surprising that as the day approached the faces of the leaders grew grave. On the way to the hall Mrs Pankhurt's silence seemed to me to betoken a touch of nervousness, and as the Union car, flaunting its purple, white and green colours, passed slowly down Piccadilly, booing and jeering men and women lined the pavement, only held back from more active demonstrations by the presence of the police.
>
> Suddenly the car pulled up with a jerk; a woman was down, caught by our mudguard; there was hatred and menace in the air and loud execrations. In a twinkling Mrs Pankhurst was on the pavement, her arm round the blowzy victim of Suffragette brutality, while with the innate authority that never failed her she ordered a policeman to fetch an ambulance. And so manifest was her distress, so obviously sincere her bitter regret that because of the meeting she could not herself take the injured one to the hospital, that in less time than it takes to tell the story it was the crowd that was comforting Mrs Pankhurst, assuring her (which was the case) that no harm had been done, that the lady was quite all right. And all this time Mrs Pankhurst's face, soft with pity, radiant with love, was the face of an angel, and her arm still encircled the lady, who was now quite recovered and inclined to be voluble. Finally the crowd of late enemies urged her to get back into the car, 'else you'll be late for the meeting!' Half-crowns passed, and we drove off, cheers speeding us on our way. But as she settled down somewhat violently in her seat, Mrs Pankhurst might have been heard ejaculating in a furious undertone, 'Drunken old beast, I wish we'd run her over!'

Smyth herself frequently caused exasperation, as Vita Sackville-West observed: 'Blinkered egotism could scarcely have driven at greater gallop along so determined a road. But although a nuisance, Ethel was never a bore.' Sylvia Pankhurst recorded in *The Suffragette Movement*:

> I stood with her on the quay at Southampton, bidding goodbye to Mrs Pankhurst, on board for America. At the moment of parting the siren blew hugely. The adored Mrs Pankhurst, smiling and waving to us from the deck, was forgotten by the musician, who snatched a notebook from her pocket and scribbled eagerly, exclaiming in her ecstasy, 'A gorgeous noise!'

Ethel was known for violent passions – for Lady Ponsonby, then for Virginia Woolf – and for her ear trumpet. Cursed by deafness before the age of fifty, 'She was vastly entertaining,' wrote Elisabeth Lutyens in her memoirs of Ethel,

> with enormous, vociferous vitality for which one needed to be in exceedingly rude health. In later years her shouting through the wrong end of the ear trumpet, necessitated by her deafness, doubled the volume of her voice and shut off all incoming sound. As hers was, anyhow, the only voice to be heard in her presence, this seemed unnecessary.

Ethel could not hear the concerts given in 1934 to celebrate her seventy-fifth birthday, and was in any case annoyed that this Festival was intended 'to get at long last [her] output into the mainstream. ... Ah! it's a queer business,' she wrote in her memoirs.

> Because I have conducted my own operas and love sheepdogs; because I generally dress in tweeds, and sometimes, at winter afternoon concerts have even conducted in them; because I was a militant Suffragette and seized a chance of beating time to *The March of Women* from the window of my cell in Holloway prison with a toothbrush; because I have written books, spoken speeches, broadcast, and don't always make sure that my hat is on straight; for these and other equally pertinent reasons in a certain sense I am well known. If I buy a pair of boots in London, and not having money enough produce an envelope with my name, the parcel is pressed into my hand: 'We want no reference in *your* case, madam!' This is celebrity indeed! – or shall we say notoriety? – but it does not alter the fact that after having been on the job, so to speak, for over 40 years, I have never yet succeeded in becoming even a tiny wheel in the English music machine.

Science Museum

Exhibition Road, SW7 (tel. 071 938 8000/8080; recorded information on 071 938 8123). Open Mon–Sat 10 a.m.–6 p.m., Sun. 11 a.m.–6 p.m. Admission £3.50 adults, £1.75 under-16s, students, UB40s, free under–5s, registered disabled and after 4.30 p.m. Baby-changing area. Wheelchair access.

Seven acres of revamped exhibition space chart the history of invention with well-labelled exhibits from power on the Ground Floor through food and telecommunications on the First Floor, printing and chemistry on the Second, oceanography and aeronautics on the Third and medicine on the Fourth and Fifth Floors. Children from nine months to ninety-nine years old love the sleek glass elevators and then run wild in the hands-on **Launch Pad** exhibition, which has human 'explainers' to answer any questions. The less swish basement **Children's Gallery** has a mini operative 1920s lift and a periscope. Nearby you can chortle at historic domestic objects, including the pre-1596 water closet invented by Sir John Harington, a godson of Queen Elizabeth.

Natural History Museum

Cromwell Road, SW7, tel. 071 938 9123. Open Mon–Sat 10 a.m.–6 p.m., Sun 11 a.m.–6 p.m. Admission £4 adults, £2 5–17-year-olds, OAPs, students, UB40s; free under-5s and after 4.30 p.m. Baby-changing area. Wheelchair access and wheelchair, available at main and side entrances.

This is fascinating for everyone, but a special treasure trove for anyone with children to entertain. The sprawling pale yellow and grey nineteenth-century building, modelled on twelfth-century Rhineland Romanesque cathedral architecture, is a visual feast even before you get to its contents, which include some 40 million specimens and, in the vast, echoey, Gothic-arched main hallway, the skeleton of the dinosaur Diplodocus, one of the largest land mammals that ever lived. After the Diplodocus-dominated Central Hall, the archaic feel of the museum is largely gone, although travelling between flashing techno exhibitions you do occasionally stumble across Victorian wood and glass cases displaying, for example, hummingbirds, and bearing now apologetic labels for the occupants' demise.

Take seven-to-elevens to the hands-on natural world **Discovery Centre** in the basement. At the 'Please Touch' table you can feel python skin and penguin wing; then test your wits with your fingertips in the surprise-filled 'Feely Box'. During the Easter and summer holidays special events include model-making and short talks by Museum scientists. Children aged six and upwards also love the **Creepy Crawlies** exhibition, which boasts interactive videos and apparently utilitarian chrome tube lacing set incongruously beneath an ornate original stonework roof. Those aged eight or more enjoy the **Stories of the Earth**, where they can ride an earthquake machine, and every newcomer should meet the **Dinosaurs in the Ronson Gallery**. The bone walk, a raised 'skeletal' walkway, takes you past vast dinosaur skeletons looming in the gloam, and on to robotic dinosaurs – watch a Deinonychus tear at the flesh of a freshly killed Tenontosaurus before retiring, possibly quite shaken, to the elegant Central Hall café or the more functional basement eatery.

BEATRIX POTTER'S INSPIRATION

Born in 1866 and raised in a quiet Kensington square by well-to-do parents whom she rarely saw, Helen Beatrix Potter entertained herself from early on by sketching the menagerie of pets she kept secreted in her nursery. When she'd drawn the lizards, mice, rabbits and insects once too often, she began visiting the Natural History Museum and the South Kensington Museum (now the V&A). She began to write stories at the age of twenty-seven, and noted in her journal on 7 January 1896: 'To Museum, studying labels and insects, being in want of advice – and not in good temper. It is the quietest place I know – and the most awkward. The staff here have reached such a pitch of propriety that one cannot ask the simplest question.' It was at the South Kensington Museum that Beatrix spotted the mouse-tailor's waistcoat that featured in her second published book, *The Tailor of Gloucester*: 'I have been delighted to find I may draw some most beautiful 18th century clothes at the South Ken Museum.' Having lived at her autocratic lawyer father's home till the age of thirty-nine, she married – against his and her mother's wishes – Norman Warne, the son of her publisher, and although he died a few months later she had by then made enough money from her books to move independently to a farm in the Lake District, where she became a successful hill farmer.

Victoria and Albert Museum

Cromwell Road, SW7, tel. 071 938 8500. Open Mon 12–5.50 p.m., Tues–Sun 10 a.m.–5.50 p.m. Suggested admission £4.95 adults, £3.50 concessions and children under 17; £12 family ticket; but any amount offered must be accepted. Wheelchairs available at main entrance. Tours introducing British collection at 11.30 a.m. (Tudor/Stuart period) and 1.30 p.m. (Victorian) during the week; tours of the whole museum at 11 a.m., noon, 2 p.m. and 3 p.m. weekdays and weekends. Special tours for children at Easter, summer and Christmas. Galleries often closed at short notice owing to reorganisation or shortage of staff.

' ... it has an almost naughty looseness', says architect critic Nikolaus Pevsner of the V&A building. His comment applies equally well to this magnificent institution's history and to its fascinating contents.

The museum was founded in 1851 by Prince Albert to improve the technical and art education of designers and art manufacturers at a time when Britain seemed to be falling from its lauded position of supreme industrial nation. Its first director, Henry Cole, energetically assembled collections of *objets d'art* such as ceramics, furniture and tapestries from around the world, but was given to house them only temporary iron and glass buildings left over from the Great Exhibition that were so hotchpotch ugly that they were known as the 'Brompton Boilers'. Not for another four decades (1891) was Aston Webb commissioned to build the present terracotta, red-brick and mosaic gâteau 'mixture of Franco-Flemish motifs jostling with Wrenaissance and even Gothic ones ... crowned by a cupola consisting of a classical octagon with columns and a lantern' (Pevsner). Gifts and bequests multiplied, until today the V&A's vast brief, as Britain's National Museum of Art and Design, is to display 'the fine and applied arts of all countries, all styles, all periods'. The types of gallery are divided into two. **Art and Design** galleries display varieties of arts assembled to evoke a period or civilisation. **Materials and Techniques** galleries show particular types of objects, for example silver or porcelain.

Don't expect to 'do' the V&A in one visit. The seven miles of corridors are maze-like – your plan or a porter may well tell you first left after the stairs is British pottery, but then, unaccountably, you stumble into cases and cases of smirking centuries-old Northern European wax effigies. Take a tour for orientation, or give yourself over to the pleasure of random discoveries.

The airy open-brickwork and a pale-wood basement restaurant, which has papers hung up for you to read if you're on your own, is a good starting and finishing point. Nearby you'll find the museum's original refreshment rooms, the **Morris, Poynter and Gamble rooms**, which are oppressively ornate with forest-green William Morris wallpaper, tile panels featuring pained Pre-Raphaelite redheads, stained glass by Gamble and sparse heavy furniture by Burne-Jones (Level A). Next door to the delicate tapestries and carved leopards of the **Nehru Gallery of Indian Art 1550–1900** is the exhibition of **European Dress 1600 to the Present**. Here, Rifat Ozbek stretchy feathered leggings are near floaty Georgian gowns, and further on there's a glass case full of underwear, from mid-eighteenth-century sidehoops made of linen stiffened with cane to less formal mid-nineteenth-century drawers of the wife of a Dorset shipbuilder, to a late-nineteenth-century Meccano-style metal bustle designed to compress without damage when the wearer sat down (Level A). On Level 6, in the Henry Cole Wing, is the largest collection in the world of **Paintings by John Constable**, bequeathed by the artist's daughter. Throughout the museum examples in such varied fields as metalwork, textiles, sculpture and musical instruments come from – as well as Europe – the Far East, South Asia and the Islamic World.

WOMEN IN DESIGN: FROM POMEGRANATES TO POLKA DOTS

For centuries a woman's touch has traditionally transformed a house into a home. In *A Woman's Touch* (Virago), Isabelle Anscombe dates women's entry into commercial British design back to the 1860s, when William Morris advocated socialism and the glorification of the tradesman through the new Arts and Crafts movement, and Pre-Raphaelite painters' medieval visions, including the chatelaine at work on her embroidery, introduced a new ideal of feminine beauty. At first women worked in the their mid-forties were striking out independently, and by the Second World War women in design could claim equal status with men.

Dante Gabriel Rossetti spotted the teenage beauty Jane (Janey) Burden at the theatre in Oxford in 1857, painted her, and introduced her to his circle of idealistic young friends, including William Morris. Within a few months she was engaged to Morris, and at the age of forty she was a much-painted mythologised beauty. 'Those dear and much abused "prae [*sic*]-Raphaelite" painters', wrote Mrs Hawes in *The Art of Beauty* (Chatto & Windus),

> are the plain girls' best friends … Morris, Burne-Jones, and others have made certain types of face and figure once literally hated, actually the fashion. Red hair – once, to say a woman had red hair was social assassination – is the rage. A pallid face with a protruding upper lip is highly esteemed. Green eyes, a squint, square eyebrows, white-brown complexions are not left out in the cold. In fact, the pink-cheeked dolls are nowhere; they are said to have 'no character' …

Morris idealised his 'glorious lady fair'. Henry James described her as 'very quaint and remote from our actual life … this dark silent medieval woman with her medieval toothache'. In the 1870s the stage designer W. Graham Robertson said: 'I fancy that her mystic beauty must sometimes have weighed rather heavily upon her … I feel sure she would have preferred to be a "bright, chatty little woman" in request for small theatre parties and afternoons up the river.'

Jane's daughter **May Morris** had more practical involvement in Morris & Co., the interior decorating company Morris founded in 1861 to spread his ideas of a socialist utopia in homes. May was appointed manager of the embroidery section in 1885, but Isabelle Anscombe argues that any creativity was subsumed in adoration of her father. May devoted years of her life after his death to editing his complete works, and to organising the building of a Memorial Hall for Morris at Kelmscott.

Attitudes were beginning to shift, but even though Mrs M.J. Loftie, a contributor to *Saturday Review*, applauded young girls who showed 'some ambitions besides those of being fashionably dressed', it was difficult for women of May Morris's generation to persuade employers that they were not physically so weak that training would be wasted on them. **Agnes and Rhoda Garrett**, sister and cousin of the pioneering medic Elizabeth Garrett Anderson, wanted to become architects, but opposition to the idea of women in trailing skirts inspecting muddy building sites was great, and they finally founded a decorating firm, concerning themselves with providing decent interiors for clients unable to afford the prices of companies like William Morris's. Rhoda told a meeting of the National Society for Women's Suffrage that she knew women who had tried to learn a useful trade, 'and whose difficulties lay, not in their want of power to acquire the requisite knowledge, but in the almost over-whelming prejudice of those already in possession of the vantage ground which stops them at every turn'. Gertrude Jekyll's solution was to create her own career.

Having attended the South Kensington School of Art in 1861, at the age of eighteen, **Gertrude Jekyll** developed an interest in natural beauty and found initial direction through William Morris, whom she met in 1869 and who introduced her to embroidery. She received prestigious commissions for her pomegranate, dandelion, periwinkle and mistletoe designs from Lord Leighton, the Duke of Westminster and Burne-Jones, but it was artist Barbara Bodichon, whom she met in 1873, who commissioned her first garden. While planning and digging Bodichon's small cottage garden in Sussex, Jekyll conceived revolutionary ideas – that gardens should not be formal; that exotic plant species could be used, but only to complement natural habitat; that garden design was a fine and delicate art, but that non-experts should be able not only to appreciate but also to tend the end results. Gardening projects multiplied, and by 1890 Gertrude Jekyll's eyesight was too poor for embroidery. She devoted herself entirely to gardening and went on to gain international renown for the fourteen books on garden design she wrote after the age of fiifty-seven.

While Janey Morris's health and confidence were near final collapse and May Morris continued to be firmly under her father's thumb, in 1879 an entirely different kind of woman was born: **Syrie Maugham**. The daughter of the altruist Dr Barnardo, Syrie exchanged her sober Plymouth Brethren background for a complex love life and a reputation as one of London's first women to gain fame in what quickly became the woman-dominated world of interior design. By 1913 she had tired of her pharmaceutical company founder husband, Henry Wellcome, and become fascinated by the work of the interior decorator hired by her wealthy department store founder lover, Gordon Selfridge. She served an unpaid apprenticeship and began to win her own commissions while having an illegitimate child by Somerset Maugham in 1915. She persuaded Maugham to marry her to mask his homosexuality, converted 213 King's Road so that Maugham had a separate entry and living quarters in order to ensure his proximity while she established herself as a society hostess, using Maugham's literary success by association to promote her business.

In April 1927 she threw a midnight party to show off her 'all-white' room. Fellow decorator Ronald Fleming said: 'The effect was sensational, and, as a setting, filled with pretty women in coloured dresses, it was most effective. … As propaganda the idea was certainly brilliantly conceived, and the firm of "Syrie" was launched in a big way.' By 1930 she controlled workshops in Chelsea and employed 20 people. Noël Coward, Gertrude Lawrence, Tallulah Bankhead, Mrs Wallis Simpson and the Prince of Wales were among her clients. But she had a Chelsea-based rival.

Interior decoration became a firmly respectable profession when a member of the upper classes fallen on hard times, society hostess **Sybil Colefax** took it up. When Colefax, whose eminent friends included Neville Chamberlain, Winston Churchill and Maynard Keynes, lost most of her money in the Wall Street Crash: 'She said,' wrote Virginia Woolf, 'I will not be beaten; and promptly turned house-decorator; ran up a sign in Ebury Street, sold her Rolls-Royce and is now, literally, at work, in sinks, behind desks, running her fingers along wainscots and whipping out yard measures from 9.30 to 7.' Friends drawn from a circle including Edward VIII and Mrs Simpson, Noël Coward and H.G. Wells came to her for restrained chintzy good taste and the social value of her good name. Isabelle Anscombe says that Colefax contributed little that was original in style, but proved that women with no preparation for a working life could go into business and succeed – indeed, 'far from being socially ostracised because of her need to earn a living, she gained the admiration of her friends for her unabashed commercialism'.

Meanwhile, **Clarice Cliff** and **Susie Cooper** were interwar contemporaries who identified an untapped market: tableware for professional people who had taste but not necessarily money. Clarice Cliff has the greater renown today for her bold, quirky designs, but – even though she married her firm's director, and the prestige of her name was recognised when it was attached to a series designed by artists including Vanessa Bell – Cliff always remained an employee, and her output slowed to a trickle after her marriage in 1940. Susie Cooper attributes her own success to her independence. As early as 1929, at the age of twenty-seven, she felt confident enough to leave her post as resident designer at a small pottery, Gray's, to set up her own firm and, helped by the boost in designer tableware given by Cliff, cornered the popular market. First the John Lewis Group of department stores bought her 'Polka Dot' line of tableware, Selfridges followed suit, and Cooper cleverly supplied each store with different colours – all muted – so that each had an exclusive range. Although the business arrangements were conducted mainly through her brother-in-law, who was her London agent, Cooper kept ultimate control, and production at the Susie Cooper works continued expanding until 1961, when she merged with a larger firm and five years later was bought out by Wedgwood, for whom she continues to design.

A large Morris & Co. embroidery on which May Morris probably worked is displayed in the Textiles Galleries of the V&A, as are textiles collected by Gertrude Jekyll, including one piece of Russian lace and pieces of French and Italian embroidery. The V&A also holds representative examples of Vanessa Bell and Clarice Cliff pottery, and a comprehensive collection of works by Susie Cooper, mostly in Gallery 137.

CHELSEA SEE MAP ON P.154

Residents of Chelsea enjoy a mainly privileged existence. Wizened red-coated war pensioners shuffle contentedly through the grand Royal Hospital grounds; countrified Barbour-outfitted old-monied establishment figures stroll from bijoux converted stables or cottage-style terraced houses to the King's Road Waitrose supermarket for basic foodstuffs, or to one of the innumerable interior décor shops to replace an apéritif-soiled scatter cushion. Visitors come for the Royal Court Theatre at night, for a handful of sights on fresh summer days, and all year round for shopping. At the base of the elegantly decayed gabled red-brick houses and occasional grey concrete 1940s blocks that run all down the King's Road are shop fronts boasting 'Pizza Hut', 'Jean Machine', 'quality shoes', 'designer clothes', 'antique market'. Catch a bus down to the World's End for acclaimed alternative designer Vivienne Westwood clothes and then go for cappuccino at the spruced-up Dôme brasserie, or visit the good-value, high-quality 'never knowingly undersold' Sloane Square department store Peter Jones, which boasts – on a floor above fabrics, perfumery and sensible sweaters – a café with a panoramic view of South London, where a woman alone can muster her energy before the Underground trip back home.

Young teenagers can join school classes brushing up on their English Civil War history at the stuffy, gung-ho **National Army Museum** (*Royal Hospital Road, tel. 071 730 0717, open daily 10 a.m.–5.30 p.m., free*). Toddlers can cavort in the **Adventure Playground** at the south-west corner of the Royal Hospital grounds. But otherwise Chelsea offers mainly adult excursions, many of them based on eating and drinking (see Eating and Drinking).

Royal Hospital

Entrance on Hospital Road at West Road and Franklin's Row, and on the Chelsea Embankment. Chapel, Great Hall, Museum and Ranelagh Gardens open daily 10 a.m.–noon, 2–4 p.m. Children barred from playing in the Ranelagh Gardens, where wheelchairs are admitted only with permission from the Secretary's Office.

Topped and toed by wired-off tennis courts, the Figure Court, which is framed on three sides by long, regular pedimented brick ranges designed by Christopher Wren, is at the centre of the Royal Hospital grounds and bears the explanatory Latin inscription: 'For the support and relief of maimed and superannuated soldiers, founded by Charles II, expanded by James II and completed by King William and Queen Mary – 1692'.

It is widely thought that Nell Gwyn's (see Piccadilly) compassion prompted Charles II to offer a hostel, in the absence of pensions, to regular army veterans who were too old or maimed during service to serve any longer. Since then, women's involvement has been rare. In the museum there is a model of a 1692 matron bearing food on a tray, and one wall displays photos of celebrated occasions when royal women, most frequently the Queen, shook hands with some or all of the four hundred in-Pensioners.

The doddery, relaxing **Museum** consists of one room that hums with classical music and features glass cases displaying in-Pensioners' costumes through the ages, many tarnished medals and two large German bombs secured to the wall near a radiator. The undulating bloom that is **Ranelagh Gardens** occasionally offers concerts in the Rotunda, and if your visit to the **Chapel** and the **Great Hall** is anywhere near lunchtime – when everything closes – you will experience an overpowering smell of canteen school dinners.

Carlyle's House

24 Cheyne Row, tel. 071 352 7087. Open Apr–Oct 11 a.m.–5 p.m., closed Mon except Bank Holidays, Tues and Good Friday. Admission £2.50 adults, £1.25 under-16s. Unavoidable steps.

Years of damp and mustiness add to the authenticity of this red-brick Queen Anne house, memorial to the forty-seven years Victorian man of letters Thomas Carlyle and his wife Jane lived here. The writer's hat is still on the peg, and the screen Jane decorated is still in the Library, where she entertained friends, including John Stuart Mill and John Ruskin while dour Thomas was sent down to the kitchen so that his smoking with Alfred Lord Tennyson didn't irritate her lungs.

Jane Welsh Carlyle: Wit and Disappointment Born to a strict disciplinarian East Lothian doctor, Jane (1801–66) was enjoying a rigorous boys' classical education from the age of five and writing gory tragedies at thirteen. When she was eighteen her father died, leaving her a considerable income, and when she was twenty she met Thomas Carlyle. After a long-drawn-out courtship, through which she wrote reams of witty, intelligent letters, she married him in 1826 despite her mother's strong objections. For all Jane's protestations of her beloved's genius, all Mrs Welsh could see was that he was poor.

Life on a remote Dumfriesshire farm became frustrating for socialite Jane, and in 1834 the Carlyles left Scotland for Cheyne Row. 'Some new neighbours,' wrote Jane to Mrs Carlyle in May 1839, 'that came a month or two ago, brought with them an accumulation of all the things to be guarded against in a London neighbourhood, viz., a pianoforte, a lap-dog, and a parrot.' Jane and Thomas quickly became known for Jane's skills as a forthright and entertaining hostess, and also for their raging arguments. In 1826 Jane had written adoringly to an aunt of Carlyle: 'He possesses all the qualities I deem essential in *my* husband, – a warm true heart to love me, a towering intellect to command me, and a spirit of fire to be the guiding starlight of my life ... a scholar, a poet, a philosopher, a wise and noble man, one who holds his patent of nobility from Almighty God.' But Jane had to suffer years of poverty and demeaning household tasks normally reserved for servants before Carlyle finally gained recognition amongst the literati in 1834.

Although both Carlyles loved the Cheyne Row house, Jane frequently felt excluded – when Carlyle was not working in the attic, he was taking refuge walking in the garden with his pipe, wearing a dressing-gown and a straw hat, beneath two vines and a walnut tree that yielded sixpence worth of nuts a year. Jane loved festivities – such as Christmas dinner with the Sterlings, for which she made a red and black tartan dress with sleeves as large as 'bushel-sacks' – but Thomas said, 'All dinners make me feel unwell for days after'. Besides, at home, 'with a dull book even, one has more sovereignty, a royaller time'.

Illness plagued them. In her biography *Jane Welsh Carlyle* (Michael Russell Publishers), Jane Surtee marvels at the scrupulous detail with which the couple chronicled their health in letters when they were apart: 'biliousness and sick headaches follow with impressive regularity upon nervous prostration, influenza, high fever and dyspepsia'. Constipation also featured regularly – 'not surprisingly,' says Surtee, 'in a household whose diet of potatoes, porridge and mutton chop found rare variety in vegetables and fruit. An unprecedented assault on five grapes leaves Jane poisoned and suffering from "stomach cramp" for twenty-four hours.'

Friends and biographers have speculated that throughout the forty-year marriage Carlyle was impotent, and perhaps the last straw was his obsession from 1842 to 1857 with the aristocratic

Lady Harriet Ashburton. By 1843 Jane had rewritten the history of her courtship with Carlyle in a letter to her niece:

> Just because in virtue of his being *the* least unlikeable man in the place, I let him dance attendance on my young person, till I came to *need* him – all the same, as my slippers to go to a ball in, or my bonnet to go out to walk. When I finally agreed to marry him, I cried excessively and felt excessively shocked – but had I then said *no* he would have left me – and how could I dispense with what was equivalent to my slippers or my bonnet?

By the early 1860s Jane's health had collapsed, and despite a period of convalescence in Scotland in 1864, and an apparent improvement on her return to Cheyne Row, she died suddenly in April 1866.

Chelsea Old Church
At Old Church Street and Chelsea Embankment, SW3.

This church evokes history precisely because it was so badly bombed during the Second World War. Monuments dating back to the thirteenth century were extricated from the rubble and lovingly restored, and a peacetime project was begun to embroider kneelers celebrating Chelsea residents through the ages. **Magdalen Herbert** was remembered with love by the poor of London for altruism during the Plague year 1625, and by today's churchwarden with amusement for a reprimand ('For God's sake,' she was overheard saying to hasten her children on the way to church, 'let us be there at the confession'); and she was remembered on her death with tears by her friend John Donne, who wrote of her:

> No spring nor summer's beauty hath such grace
> As I have seen in one autumnal face.

This century, **Yvonne Green** was a Canadian living in Chelsea during the Second World War who volunteered to take fire-watching duty in place of an ill colleague, and was killed on the night of the 1941 bombing; on her kneeler the words of Laurence Binyon are embroidered beside Canadian maple leaves: 'They shall grow not old, as we that are left grow old'.

Looking up from the kneelers behind the pews, you'll see to the left of the church, in the **Lawrence Chapel**, an elaborate sixteenth-century memorial arch within a solid postwar arch, and nearby an imperiously reclining figure in grey stone by the Italian Giovanni Lorenzo Bernini. This is the much-loved benefactor of Chelsea village, Lady Jane Cheyne, daughter of a Royalist who barricaded her house with her sisters for several days against Cromwellian forces, and later sold her jewels to help her father in exile. In the centre is the **Altar**, which dates back to the seventeenth century, and the surrounding rails comply with regulations laid down by the Bishop of Norwich in 1636: 'Neer one yarde in height, so thick with pillars that dogges may not get in'. To the right is the **More Chapel**, where a small, delicately enamelled bronze frieze on rough stone dating back to 1555 commemorates Lady Jane Guildford, mother of thirteen children, one of whom was Queen Elizabeth's favourite, Leicester; another was executed for being the Catholic husband of Lady Jane Grey.

On your way out, pass the (literally) **chained books**, including a 1717 Vinegar Bible, a 1723 Prayer Book and 1683 Homilies, which are of note for being the only chained books in any London church, but unfortunately went behind glass under orders of the insurers after visitors took to ripping out pages as mementoes.

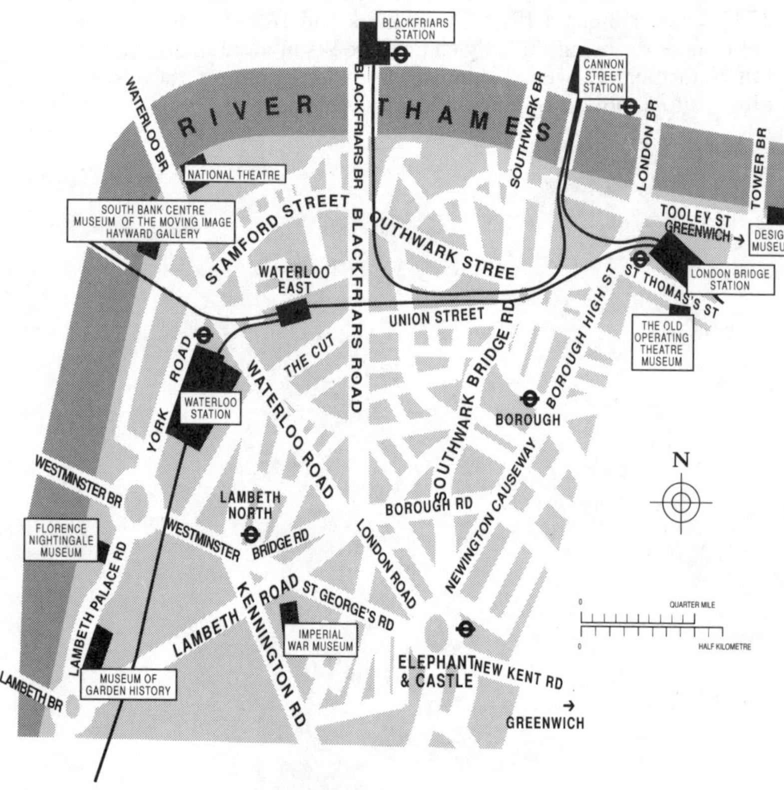
BLACKFRIARS STATION
CANNON STREET STATION
RIVER THAMES
WATERLOO BR
BLACKFRIARS BR
SOUTHWARK BR
LONDON BR
TOWER BR
NATIONAL THEATRE
SOUTH BANK CENTRE
MUSEUM OF THE MOVING IMAGE
HAYWARD GALLERY
STAMFORD STREET
BLACKFRIARS ROAD
SOUTHWARK STREET
TOOLEY ST
GREENWICH →
DESIGN MUSEUM
LONDON BRIDGE STATION
ST THOMAS'S ST
WATERLOO EAST
UNION STREET
SOUTHWARK BRIDGE RD
BOROUGH HIGH ST
THE OLD OPERATING THEATRE MUSEUM
THE CUT
YORK ROAD
WATERLOO ROAD
WATERLOO STATION
BOROUGH
N
WESTMINSTER BR
LAMBETH NORTH
BOROUGH RD
NEWINGTON CAUSEWAY
FLORENCE NIGHTINGALE MUSEUM
WESTMINSTER BRIDGE RD
LONDON ROAD
LAMBETH PALACE RD
LAMBETH ROAD
KENNINGTON RD
ST GEORGE'S RD
IMPERIAL WAR MUSEUM
0
QUARTER MILE
HALF KILOMETRE
ELEPHANT & CASTLE
NEW KENT RD
LAMBETH BR
MUSEUM OF GARDEN HISTORY
→ GREENWICH

SOUTH LONDON AND THE RIVER

A riveting nineteenth-century operating theatre, the Royal Observatory perched high on idyllic parkland, Bakelite radios in a chic museum above a river-view café, a seventeenth-century walled garden. ... If anyone tries to tell you to avoid South London, defy them.

'First impressions of South London are likely to be disappointing,' writes Bridget Cherry in *London 2: South* (Penguin), speaking of the lack of both countryside and metropolitan buzz and suggesting that, 'slowed down by the press of traffic, the traveller has more time to contemplate the apparently interminable sequence of dingy Victorian and Edwardian shopping parades before being whipped around the occasional bleak concrete roundabout'. True, but as Cherry notes, 'the persistent explorer' will be rewarded. Some of London's best and most quirky museums are tucked down unlikely alleys in the sprawl of South London, hemmed in by magnificent royal parks and residences that are all accessible by boat down perhaps the most fascinating route through London, the **Thames**. The bus travel alternative is slow and exhausting; Underground train is the cheapest and fastest way to tackle this area.

Women with children and women with an interest in gardens are especially well catered for. The **Imperial War Museum**, the **Maritime Museum** and the **Museum of the Moving Image** all throng with squealing, squabbling, delighted parties of schoolchildren. An afternoon at the Museum of Garden History could precede the two or three visits it takes thoroughly to enjoy and investigate Kew Gardens. Battersea Park contains a garden for the handicapped and a Buddhist Peace Pagoda (1985) with gilded wind bells that is lovely to walk by for a view of the City over the Thames. Or, if gardens and museums just aren't your thing, you might like to soak up the cultural vibrancy of Brixton, through its cafés and bars (see Eating and Drinking), through its plantain, sarong and seasonal vegetable market on Electric Avenue (see Shops and Markets), or through festivals held in Brockwell Park. These include Gay Pride and a bizarre inner-city version of a country show (tiny tent for the one pig bearing a sign saying 'Good for bacon', and a massive marquee for the gas cooker showroom).

A major not-to-be-missed gallery which has changing exhibitions of modern and historical art is the **Hayward Gallery** (*Belvedere Rd, South Bank Centre, SE1, tel. 071 928 3144; open Tues, Wed 10 a.m.–8 p.m., Thur–Mon 10 a.m.–6 p.m.; admission £5 adults, £3.50 concessions*). **Southwark Cathedral** (*Montague Close, SE1*), the oldest Gothic Church in London, is a haven in the middle of Southwark road and rail madness for its services and the attached Pizza Express (*Montague Close, SE1, tel. 071 407 2939 for the cathedral, 071 378 6446 for the restaurant, or see Eating and Drinking*). **Dulwich Picture Gallery** (*College Road, SE21, tel. 081 693 5254; open Tues–Sat 11 a.m.–5 p.m., Sun 2–5 p.m.; admission £2 adults, £1 concessions, children free, West Dulwich BR*) is hopelessly stuffy if you have children and rather awkward to get to, but it has a celebrated permanent collection of works by Rembrandt, Rubens, Poussin, Gainsborough and Canaletto.

South London has been a mix of rich and poor since medieval times, when it was a rural hinterland of marshes with the occasional monarch's palace retreat. The prospect of pleasure attracted a cross-section of city-dwellers over the river by boat when the New Spring Gardens (later the Vauxhall Gardens) opened in 1660. The nights were lit by hundreds of lamps strung along tree-lined walkways. The air filled with the sounds of fiddles and harps, the cries of meat and pasty sellers, and the whispered seductions of young rakes to titled ladies and lords to blushing servant girls, for this was one of the only places where men and women could mix socially across class boundaries. 'Women squeak and men drunk fall', went a contemporary ballad, 'Sweet Enjoyment of Vauxhall'. In 1816, with a fanfare of fireworks, Madame Saqui made her début walking a tightrope tied to a sixty-foot mast. In the same year Vauxhall Bridge opened; this helped to ensure the closure of the gardens two decades later by offering easy access to more exciting West End entertainments and, for the same reason, encouraged City businessmen's suburban building projects in place of exhausted brick-fields and market gardens. Later, the roaring and smoke-belching that came with the steam railways sent the wealthy out to leafy suburbs such as Richmond, and filing clerks and theatre people took lodgings in their vacated once-grand houses. Today, South London remains an unsettling mix of heavy industry, yuppie havens and poverty-trap high-rise blocks.

Women in Tudor and Elizabethan London While Greenwich was favoured for its river access and leafy outlook as birthplace and later residence of both King Henry VIII and Elizabeth I, Southwark was flocked to by would-be revellers escaping restrictive City night-time regulations to enjoy bear-baiting and, as the Elizabethan era dawned, the new theatres around Clink prison and Paris Garden. The Rose, built in 1587, first staged the plays of Marlowe. The Swan was built in 1596 and three years later the Globe, in which Shakespeare owned a one-tenth share. Women were present in large numbers as whores, and women of all ranks were allowed to enjoy bears being baited by mastiffs in gardens near the Globe. Queen Elizabeth had her own bear pit, the more easily to watch the 'byting, clawying and roring' described by Robert Laneham, Clerk of the Council Chamber Door. She was also entertained by the spectacle of a monkey being set to fight a horse.

But it was not thought seemly for women either to attend cock-fighting, or to appear on stage. Unwed girls went bareheaded to set them apart from married women, who wore hats or a hood and veil indoors and out. Husbands were held responsible for their wives' behaviour, so any woman who stepped out of line was likely to be dealt with harshly. Wife-beatings were accepted. In 1610 MPs attacked the Ecclesiastical Commission for granting alimony to separated wives, 'to the great encouragement of wives to be disobedient and contemptuous against their husbands'. Women did not count politically as individuals: society was made up of patriarchal household units. The commonwealth was confined to free men, for bondmen 'be taken but as instruments and of the goods and possessions of others,' wrote Sir Thomas Smith in *De Republica Anglorum*. 'And in this consideration also we do reject women, as those whom nature hath made to keepe home and to nourish their familie and children, and not to medle with matters abroade, nor to beare office in a citie or commonwealth no more than children and infants.'

Nevertheless, 'common law' was frequently displaced by common practice. Many women in the gentry and trades, for example, made marriage settlements to protect their property. Widows could take over and run their late husbands' businesses, even though they would not appear on official records. And perhaps because painting was considered a craft and held in low regard, Levina Teerlinc was able to become gentlewoman painter to both Queen Mary and Queen Elizabeth, and she probably trained one of the finest Elizabethan painters, Nicholas Hilliard.

Henry VIII's desperation for an heir and his six wives' failure to produce a robust male child meant that there were a lot of queens of England through the fifteenth and sixteenth centuries, most famously Elizabeth I, renowned then and now as the Virgin Queen. Both her childhood and that of her half-sister and queen before her, Mary Tudor, were riven by political intrigues of international consequence that surrounded their father Henry's state of wedlock. It all started well enough. Kings were expected to ally themselves to foreign powers by marriage after protracted negotiations with the father of a woman whom they might not meet until the wedding day. Indeed, Holbein's introductory portrait of Henry's fourth wife, Anne of Cleves, was so overly flattering that Henry bemoaned 'the fate of princes to take as is brought them by others, while poor men be commonly at their own choice'. Catherine of Aragon, however, seemed ideal in almost every respect.

Life expectancy for women was not much beyond thirty years of age, so Catherine was rather old at twenty-four, in 1509, when she became Henry's first wife, but she was of Spanish royalty and 'She thrilled the hearts of everyone,' declared Thomas More in 1501. 'There is nothing wanting in her that the most beautiful girl should have.' Except the ability to give birth to a healthy son. By the time Catherine had miscarried three times and been delivered of one stillborn and one sickly boy, with only a daughter, Mary, surviving, Henry was growing anxious, and when one of his mistresses, Elizabeth Blount, produced a bouncing boy in 1519, the marriage began to break down completely. Over the next few years he might have toyed with two options: marrying Mary off young in the hope that she would produce a male heir in Henry's lifetime; and legitimising his bastard son, Henry Fitzroy. By 1527 he was moving instead towards a third option: remarriage. But this required the sanction of the Church.

The question of succession was of such international consequence that the Pope might have agreed if approached tactfully, but Henry chose to declare his marriage to Catherine an offence against divine law on the grounds that she had originally come to England as the bride of his brother, Arthur, who had died within a year in 1502. The Pope was hardly likely to accept a lecture on canonical law, and matters were made worse by Catherine's conviction not only that the marriage was valid but that divine intervention had brought it about. So Henry simply decided to displace the Pope's jurisdiction in favour of the secular rule of princes and magistrates over the Church in England, and in 1533 he secretly married the already pregnant Anne Boleyn.

Anne, one of Catherine's maids of honour, was the second commoner to become Queen of England, and for her perceived wiles she won unprecedented unpopularity. In November 1531 she narrowly escaped by barge a mob of seven or eight thousand women (or men dressed as women) who set out to lynch her when news spread that she was dining with friends at a house near the Thames. She was openly called a whore and a heretic, and in March 1532 the Abbot of Whitby was the first to receive punishment for declaring her a 'common stewed whore'. But Alison Weir suggests in *The Six Wives of Henry VIII* (Pimlico) that Anne Boleyn's greatest crime may simply have been that she did not know her place.

She was not suitably demure. Even the clothes prescribed by convention required a bearing that resembled submissive dignity. Agonising corsets of stiff leather or wood were worn with cumbersome oversleeves and heavy damask trains. Henry had to remind Anne, when she became angry at his unfaithfulness, that adultery in men was perfectly acceptable.

After Anne had produced only a surviving daughter, Elizabeth, Henry made adultery a treasonable offence by accusing her of having taken five lovers, including her brother. She was beheaded on 19 May 1536 on Tower Green, and minutes after the Tower guns were fired, signifying that her head had fallen to the grass, the king was rowed at full speed down the Thames to Jane Seymour, whom he married less than two weeks later. Within a year Jane Seymour had died in childbed, having produced a son, Edward (infection, then puerperal fever, was so common that women, as a matter of course, made arrangements during pregnancy for someone else to look after their child should they die giving birth). It is an indication of Henry's love for Jane Seymour that he did not marry Anne of Cleves until 1540. Happy at the prospect of independence, Anne agreed to a divorce the same year, and by August Henry's new bride, Catherine Howard, was infuriating court elders with her overt greed, flaunting new gowns and jewels daily. This time it was not only Catherine's failure to produce a son but her Catholic backing that hastened her downfall. The king was entirely unaware of her infidelities, but when Archbishop Cranmer learned of them from a Protestant called John Lascelles, he saw a chance to have the queen removed. In February 1542, after a calm request to practise resting her head on the block the night before, she was beheaded for treason.

Catherine Parr felt terror when she was first proposed to by Henry VIII, but in 1543 she became his sixth and final wife. She had an equable personality; she managed to modify some of his policies, such as the persecution of Roman Catholics under the Act of the Six Articles, and she was unconventionally learned. Fluent in Latin and competent in Greek as well as other European languages, she championed the new Humanist approach of men such as Juan Luis Vives and Sir Thomas More, who maintained that women could be erudite and still dignified. She and Catherine of Aragon between them ensured that Mary and Elizabeth had the best education available for women at the time. Catherine Parr still condoned women's inferior status, however. In *The Lamentations of a Sinner* (published 1548), she said that wives should wear 'such apparel as becometh holiness and comely usage with soberness', and young women must be 'sober minded, love their husbands and children, and be discreet, housewifely and good'.

Henry VIII had left instructions that in the event of his sickly six-year-old son Edward's death, the crown was to pass to Mary and then, in default of heirs, to Elizabeth. Henry's death in 1547 was followed by Edward's in 1553, and a succession crisis during which the Duke of Suffolk tried to realise his ambitions through his daughter, Lady Jane Grey, a niece of Henry VIII's, by naming her as successor. National support was for Mary, however, and within days Lady Jane Grey had been executed on Tower Green for treason.

Mary I Mary (1516–58) had also been a political pawn as a child. Within the space of five years she found herself betrothed first to the Dauphin of France and then to the Emperor Charles V of Rome, depending on her father's changing allegiances. Her education by Vives, although liberal for the time, did not diminish her keenness for hunting and card games, but she was not trained for political responsibility. She was made Princess of Wales in 1525, then declared illegitimate when Henry broke with her mother, Catherine of Aragon, in 1534; and was even required at one point to act as lady-in-waiting to her infant half-sister Elizabeth I.

Mary remained loyal to her mother, whom she never saw again after 1534, and to Catholicism, with a high-principled abrasiveness that was to make her perhaps England's most unpopular monarch. As soon as she became the first woman to rule England in her own right, at the age of thirty-seven, she did two rash things: she married the widely disliked twenty-six-year-old Philip of Spain, and she restored the papal supremacy. A year later, in 1555, she introduced anti-heresy laws that caused countless hangings and burnings at the stake, and earned her the name Bloody Mary. She also allowed Philip to draw England into the war between France and Spain, even though he had left her that year in frustration that Parliament would not crown him king. In 1558, still desperate for a child, lonely and ill, famines having further incensed her people, Mary died on 17 November. Philip – who could have been, but did not bother to be, present – wrote to his half-sister: 'I felt a reasonable regret for her death'.

Elizabeth I Through all this, **Elizabeth** (1533–1603) had kept a low profile, narrowly escaping execution for suspected involvement in the Protestant Sir Thomas Wyatt's uprising in 1554 (she was imprisoned in the Tower, but released after two months when no evidence was forthcoming). Once she was queen, Elizabeth gave vent to stubborn fits of temper. She refused to have a tooth pulled until the Bishop of London had one extracted in front of her to demonstrate how painless the procedure was. 'When her Highness is angry or not well disposed, trouble her not with any matter which you desire to have done,' warned Clerk of the Council Robert Beale, in a memorandum on how to discuss matters with the queen. But through the succession crisis Elizabeth was careful to bow four or five times every time she greeted her half-brother Edward, who called her 'sweet sister Temperance'; and when Mary was crowned, Elizabeth made a formal trip to congratulate her, expertly suppressing the hatred she felt, which was returned by Mary in equal measure.

Elizabeth's first task when she became queen in 1558 was to appease the Catholics of her nation, which she did with a tolerant religious settlement, the Acts of Unity and of Supremacy, in 1559. Then she tackled the appalling economic situation with currency reforms, employment laws and poor relief. Beale and most of her councillors thought her a 'princess of great wisdom, learning and experience'. 'She was so expert in the knowledge of her realm and state,' said Cecil, 'as no counsellor she had could tell her what she knew not before.' Indeed, concluded John Oglander, she lacked nothing 'that could be desired in a prince, but that she was a woman'.

The question of marriage was tricky, bound up as it was with international politics. Elizabeth managed to end Mary's war with France and refuse Philip II of Spain's offer of marriage, and to keep an uneasy peace with both countries. Despite her deep affection for Robert Dudley, Earl of Leicester, it seems unlikely that she would have married him even without the 'grievous and dangerous suspicion and muttering' that a local clergyman described surrounding the death of Dudley's wife in 1560. In 1569 Parliament begged her to marry anyone she chose, just so long as she married, but Elizabeth repeatedly declared her intent of dying the Virgin Queen. 'I know the truth of that, madam,' the Scottish diplomat Sir James Melville claimed to have replied to her on one occasion. 'Ye need not tell me. I know your stately stomach. Ye think, gin ye were married, ye would be but Queen of England, and now ye are King and Queen baith. I know your spirit. Ye cannot suffer a commander.'

Mary, Queen of Scots, having been deposed in Scotland in favour of James, found 'refuge' in England, but her claim for succession to the English throne caused Elizabeth to keep her in virtual imprisonment for nineteen years, declining to recognise her as heir, knowing 'the inconstancy of the people of England, how they ever mislike the present government and have their eyes fixed upon that person who is next to succeed'. Finally in 1587, after the treasonous Babington Plot and Mary's part in it had been discovered, Elizabeth – still reluctantly – signed the warrant for Mary's execution, after which she suffered a severe breakdown in her health. The execution convinced Philip of Spain that he must rule England, and the Spanish Armada was launched in 1588 to invade the country. Elizabeth personally addressed her troops at Tilbury, offering 'to lay down for my God, and for my Kingdom, and for my people, my honour and my blood, even in the dust. I know I have the body of a weak and feeble woman, but I have the heart and stomach of a king, and a king of England too.' Although the Armada was defeated, the war lingered on until her death at the then astoundingly old age of seventy. She had brought her country out of poverty into world greatness, creating an ebullient nationalism which was evident in the enlightened culture that flourished in the court of her time. You can see a 1586 stone statue by William Kerwin of Elizabeth I at St Dunstan in the West, Fleet St, EC4.

FROM WHITE LEAD TO VASELINE: WOMEN AND MAKE-UP

Elizabeth I was lucky: she was born with the pale skin and strawberry-blonde hair that was all the Renaissance rage. While she merely dabbed a little marjoram for scent, other Elizabethan women took drastic measures.

Though it was time-consuming, it was at least not too unpleasant sitting for hours in the sun gripping a face mask between the teeth so that the hair would be bleached without the face being browned. And not all the whitening skin applications were toxic. Powder made out of ground alabaster was all right; so were potions made of ingredients such as beeswax and ground hogs' jawbone. But for the *really* white look, women used white lead mixed with vinegar, or with borax and sulphur. To achieve contrast, lips were reddened with madder, or crystalline mercuric sulphide. Turpentine and sublimate of mercury dealt with spots and freckles, rather too effectively – the skin was left pitted and in need of even more cover-up potions, which were then glazed with egg white for a shiny, professional finish.

The use of lead went out only when the natural look came in with the nineteenth century. Obvious facial adornment was unacceptable for upright Victorian women. But since a pale face was still desireable, vinegar was imbibed in the belief that it whitened, as was arsenic. By World War II make-up was becoming not just acceptable but downright desirable. There was one big drawback: wartime shortages. Vaseline was dabbed on the eyelids for added glitter when going to a dance; the seams of silk stockings were simulated with a deft stroke of an eye pencil down the backs of the legs.

WATERLOO AND THE SOUTH BANK SEE MAP ON P.182

You could do some or even all the sights listed below on the same day, but you would emerge worn and bad-tempered. The area is dominated by large roads and heavy traffic; eye-relief in the form of pleasant architecture is generally well hidden. Instead, try targeting one major museum and one curiosity, breaking up the day with a leisurely light meal (see Eating and Drinking) or a walk along the river between Waterloo Bridge and Southwark Bridge.

Imperial War Museum

Lambeth Road, SE1, tel. 071 735 8922. Lambeth North, Elephant and Castle or Waterloo Underground. Open daily 10 a.m.–6 p.m. Admission £3.30 adults, £1.65 concessions, £8 family ticket.

Removed from the roaring traffic under an imposing green dome guarded by rose-surrounded cannons is an award-winning museum that covers British and Commonwealth warfare since 1914 with the intention of honouring those who served without glorifying war.

As you approach the 1815 building, which was designed to be a lunatic asylum (some cells are now administrative offices), you'll see a piece of Berlin Wall featuring bubble-writing graffiti that declares 'Change your life'. Pass through grand Corinthian pillars, and you enter the impressive **Large Exhibits Gallery**. Large exhibits hanging from the ceiling include the rickety propeller plane Sopwith Camel 2F1. Nearby, ready to trundle across the sleek floor, is the earliest of the museum's five Second World War tanks, 'Matilda'. Among hands-on exhibits is a German mast periscope that attracts queues of day-glo knapsack-bearing schoolchildren who walk away grumbling disappointment that the eyepiece offers only an obscured view of St Paul's Cathedral. The ground floor also features art galleries, a thematic temporary exhibition and a modern chrome/brickwork café that serves reasonably priced coffee and sandwiches. Upstairs are viewing galleries with different perspectives on the large exhibits, and on the Lower Ground Floor you'll find **Historical Displays** of artefacts including World War II recruiting posters: a mother and daughter are shown nobly holding back the tears as uniformed men march away from the window below the caption 'WOMEN OF BRITAIN SAY – GO!'

Bedlam Although the present building dates back only to 1812–15, the Royal Bethlehem Hospital for the Care of the Insane (or Bedlam) itself dates back to before Henry VIII's reign. For a long period through the seventeenth and eighteenth centuries the hospital was also one of London's most popular sights: admission was charged, and patients were chained in cages as if in a zoo. Whipping was common until public outrage caused by accounts of the abuse of 'delicate' women led to legislative reform. Even then, various instruments used to restrain patients during the eighteenth century included, for noisy women, the brank or 'scold's bridle'.

By the mid-nineteenth century, a plant-decorated gallery that was the women's ward in the present building was described by a journalist: 'Every conceivable kind of needlework is dividing their attention with the young lady who reads aloud "David Copperfield" or "Dred"; while beside the fire, perhaps an old lady with silver locks gives a touch of domesticity to the scene.' Women were put in solitary confinement in the basement 'on account of being violent, mischievous, dirty or using bad language'. A

Victorian atmosphere persisted into the twentieth century. 'Wax flowers under cases, and engravings of Queen Victoria and Balmoral,' wrote Antonia White in her autobiographical novel *Beyond the Glass* (Virago), recalling the ten months she spent in Bedlam in 1922, during which time she was forcibly fed, drugged, tied down to her bed, straitjacketed and put in a padded cell. 'It is ironically appropriate', writes Elaine Showalter in *The Female Malady; Women, Madness and English Culture 1830–1980* (Virago),

> that in 1930, when Bethlem Hospital moved to new facilities, its former buildings became the Imperial War Museum. Despite the lingering male mental casualties of the postwar period, as soldiers returned to take over their former places as social leaders, women returned to *their* former places as the primary psychiatric patients.

Women and World War II Whether World War II helped or hindered the advancement of women's equality has been debated since the 1960s. Betty Friedan and Juliet Mitchell argue that sure, women got jobs owing to men's absence during the war, but immediately peace was declared, government and employers pushed women back into domesticity. Arthur Marwick disagrees, arguing that permanent changes included state provision for childcare, access to men's jobs, and equal pay. One thing is certain: no woman in London could remain unaffected, for the Second World War, unlike previous wars, caused as much destruction amongst civilians as soldiers in action. More men, women and children were killed at home within the first three years (by 1942) than troops in action.

An early trauma for mothers was the evacuation of children, who were dropped at collection points with no idea where they were going or for how long, carrying only a change of underclothes, sandwiches and gas masks, a favourite toy, and a name and address label attached to the overcoat. After the Germans began bombing the East End docks and surrounding houses at about 5 p.m. on 7 September 1940, women of the East End quickly grew used to preparing food and bedding, and travelling every afternoon to the West End, where bombing was less severe and shelters were deeper. Many bought tickets for the Underground and camped out on station platforms because they were warm, dry and well-lit, with plenty of people around for moral support.

In January 1940 food rationing was introduced, ration books being issued in different colours for adults, children, pregnant women, travellers and seamen. The way women fed their families became a subject of national importance, and Ministry of Food propaganda posters declared: 'Food is a munition of war, don't waste it'. Wasting food was a fineable offence, as this 20 January 1943 *Bristol Evening Post* reports: 'Miss Mary Bridget O'Sullivan ... was fined a total of ten pounds, with two guineas costs, at Baret today for permitting bread to be wasted. ... It was stated that the servant was twice seen throwing bread to the birds in the garden.'

Women were invited by posters to fill jobs in industry and agriculture vacated by soldiers. Oliver Lyle, the owner of the Tate & Lyle sugar factory in Plaistow, recalled in 1960:

> We had no lack of volunteers and the girls did a splendid job and quickly learned to be good process hands and promising mechanics ... The mud presses were 'manned' by girls. ... In the can-making Grace Ranger became a neat fitter and could clear a jammed Angelus double seamer ... Gladys and Ivy Lewil could adjust Southall and Smith weighing machines.

Mrs Groves, who went to a munitions factory, remembered:

> We were allocated to different sections, the girls that were really A1 were put into the part that made the most dangerous shells and bullets. I was sent to make bullets, small bombs and shells, we used TNT, gelignite and neonite. The work was dangerous, sometimes people got fingers blown off, or it could be more serious, you just got used to it. If you worked with TNT, you'd get a nice rash and also your face and hair would go yellow. The work was always boring.

Florence Nightingale Museum

In the grounds of St Thomas' Hospital, 2 Lambeth Palace Road, SE1, tel. 071 620 0374. Nearest Underground stations Westminster and Waterloo. Open 10 a.m.–4 p.m. Tues–Sun and Bank Holidays. Closed Christmas Day, Boxing Day, New Year's Day, Good Friday, Easter Sunday. Admission £2.50 adults, £1.50 children, OAPs, students.

This compact, immaculate, pleasant space can be hard to find. Don't go into St Thomas' Hospital itself – come to the museum from Lambeth Palace Road at Westminster Bridge Road, where you'll find a sign pointing down a ramp. The museum's on your right, at the bottom. 'There is nothing like the tyranny of a good English family,' reads a blown-up extract from Florence Nightingale's note-journal on the first wall. Sketchbooks and household artefacts chart her childhood up to her momentous decision to enter nursing, when you see a plaster-cast grouping of Crimean soldiers, with – through a sheet of gauze – a man having his leg amputated by saw. 'May the methods by which every human being will have the best chance of health ... be learned and practised!' wrote Florence in 1893. As well as charting Florence's life, the museum puts hers in context with other women of her time. There is also an entertaining slide-show.

Florence Nightingale, A Woman of Destiny At No. 1 Harley Street, W1, in 1853, Florence Nightingale finally got the chance, at the age of thirty-three, to act on the direct call of God which she had received at the age of seventeen: on 7 February 1837 she recorded: 'God spoke and called me to His service'. She shunned suitors and rejected social rounds in favour of visiting the poor and sick with her mother. She discussed her infant ideas with her father's visiting high-powered friends, daring in 1844 to ask the American philanthropist Dr Samuel Gridley Howe if he thought it would be 'a dreadful thing' if she were to devote herself to nursing, to which he replied – not at all: 'go forward ... act up to your inspiration and you will find there is never anything unbecoming or unladylike in doing your duty for the good of others'. Her friends and family heartily disagreed; in any case, no formal training was available. She proposed that she should invite herself to Salisbury Infirmary 'to learn the "prax"'. The idea didn't go down well. Florence's mother was terrified, her daughter wrote, not only by 'the physically revolting parts of a hospital, but things about surgeons and nurses which you may guess'; her father flatly refused.

Florence Nightingale's biographer, Elspeth Huxley, describes the hospital situation 'before Pasteur's discoveries of how germs spread infection': 'The patients were filthy and verminous; bedding stank and was seldom changed; infections of every kind were prevalent; gangrene was rife.' Florence later wrote: 'It was *preferred* that the nurses should be women who had lost their characters, i.e. should have had one child,' for doctors considered sex with nurses on demand a perk of the job, and if the nurse did not sleep in the less afflicted male patients' beds, then she spent the night in a wooden cage on the landing, which was so noisy that she could generally sleep only if she was blind drunk.

Once she had decided the direction of her destiny, it was almost a decade before Florence could act on it. In February 1853 she was invited to nurse her ninety-five-year-old grandmother through her last days, and in April her name was put forward by her friend Liz Herbert to be head of a planned Institution for the Care of Sick Gentlewomen in London. Although Florence disapproved of the charitable ladies in charge, whom she called 'fashionable asses', she leapt at the job, and the titled committee ladies soon found her hard to handle. Florence Nightingale's revolutionary and practical proposals included a 'windlass installator', or lift, to bring the patients' meals up from the kitchen, and bells fitted with 'a valve which flies open when the bell rings, and *remains* open in order that the nurse may see who has rung'.

The Committee thought that only members of the Church of England should be admitted. Florence argued that any woman who was sick and poor, regardless of her faith, should be admitted – and she won.

Because she inevitably had difficulty finding trained nurses, Florence acted as both house surgeon and dispenser. Most patients considered her a saint, but her sister wrote in a letter to Mary Mohl: 'When she nursed me, everything which intellect and kind human intention could do was done but she was a shocking nurse,' and declared: 'I wish she could be brought to see that it is the intellectual part which interests her, not the manual.' Certainly, once 1 Harley Street was up and running, it seems that Florence got bored.

In August 1854 an outbreak of cholera in the slums of Soho took her to Middlesex Hospital to nurse prostitutes and drunken bawds, 'putting on turpentine stupes' and holding the women in her arms as they died. 'The prostitutes came in personally,' she told Mrs Gaskell in October 1854, 'poor creatures staggering off their beat! It took worse hold of them than of any. One poor girl, loathsomely filthy, came in, and was dead in four hours.' Perhaps to relieve tension, Florence sometimes injected comedy into her stories, such as this one recorded by Elizabeth Gaskell of a woman who got better:

> I never heard such capital mimicry as she gave of a poor woman, who was brought in one night, when FN and a porter were the only people up – every other nurse worn out for the time. Three medical students came up, smoking cigars, and went away. FN undressed the woman, who was half tipsy but kept saying, 'You would not think it ma'am, but a week ago I was in silk and satins; in silk and satins dancing at Woolwich. Yes!'

In October 1854 Florence heard that in the war England and France had declared on Russia in March that year, casualties were numerous and cholera had broken out. She set off immediately for the Bosporus with a quickly gathered assortment of thirty-eight women, from Roman Catholic nuns to the old-style drunken nurses of lost character.

Known as the Lady with the Lamp for the Turkish lamps she carried while attending soldiers at night in the Crimea, she returned home a hero in 1856 and was immediately called to the audience of Queen Victoria and Prince Albert, an occasion Florence used to practical purpose: '[Miss Nightingale] put before us all the defects of our present military hospital system, and the reforms that are needed. We are much pleased with her; she is extremely modest.' Florence then turned her mind to the £45,000 Nightingale Fund that had been raised by the grateful British public and decided to use it to start the Nightingale School of Nursing at St Thomas' Hospital in 1859.

At the end of 1859 she published *Notes on Nursing: What it is, and what it is not*, which emphasised the importance of hygiene and the psychological aspect of care, saying that the least thing could alarm a patient, even a nurse's cumbrous dress: a 'nurse who rustles is the horror of a patient'. *Notes on Nursing* was, even at the then high price of 5 shillings, a bestseller, and the St Thomas' school's success was immediate. Of the fifteen probationers, thirteen qualified and were employed by infirmaries and hospitals. Even though increasing ill-health made her an invalid, Florence Nightingale was influential until the end of her life, and frequently consulted on matters of nursing and hospital administration.

Museum of Garden History

Lambeth Palace Road opposite Lambeth Bridge, SE1, tel. 071 261 1891. Waterloo Underground then 15-minute walk or 507 bus to Lambeth Palace stop. Free. Open Mon–Fri 11 a.m.–3 p.m., Sun 10.30 a.m.–5 p.m. Wheelchair access.

This is one of those homespun museums that survives almost entirely because of the enthusiasm of its staff. A seventeenth-century walled garden and exhibitions in church premises chart the development of gardens from monastery enclosures to present-day suburban gardens. The museum celebrates the work of two John Tradescants, a father-and-son team who gardened for – amongst others – Queen Henrietta Maria at the then famous gardens of Lambeth Palace, of which nothing now remains. Museum exhibits include 1920 insecticide puffers. The garden has plants for sale and there's a cheery café.

Museum of the Moving Image (MOMI)

Near Belvedere Road and Waterloo Road junction in the South Bank Centre, tel. 071 401 2636 (24 hours). Follow signs for 'South Bank' from Waterloo or Embankment Underground. Allow time to find the entrance, near the National Film Theatre, because the South Bank Centre can be confusing. Open daily (except 24–26 Dec) 10 a.m.–6 p.m. Admission £4.95 adults, £3.50 under-16s/disabled/OAPs/UB40s, £4.20 students, under-5s go free. Wheelchair access by prior arrangement.

Make your own zoetrope, watch an actress-guide do her best to remain enthusiastic in the face of sullen schoolchildren refusing to join her line of chorus girls, read your own news bulletin and stand on a blue ramp so that you can see yourself flying over London.

With an astounding array of exhibits including a large number that are hands-on, the museum charts the history of the moving image from oriental shadow puppets through cinema during World War I to TVs that look like fish tanks and alternative video, including work by America's video art pioneer, Maya Deren. Apparently maze-like but with good signposting, this museum is great for children and anyone with an interest in TV or film.

Shakespeare Globe Museum

Bear Gardens, Liberty of the Clink, Bankside, SE1, tel. 071 928 6342 or 071 620 0202 for information on the project. Mansion House or London Bridge Underground. The museum is tucked away on the riverside – follow a map. Open Mon–Sat 10 a.m.–5 p.m., Sun 2 p.m.–5.30 p.m. Admission £2 adults, £1 under-16s, OAPs, students UB40s, Southwark residents. Unavoidable stairs.

In terms of price, this rates well compared to London's bigger museums, but until the project's ultimate aim is realised – the completion of a full-size replica of the Elizabethan Globe Theatre – the displays will continue to be rather shabby.

On the site of Tudor pleasure grounds and bear-baiting gardens (hence the address, Bear Gardens), the museum rather grandly advertises itself as 'the only exhibition in the world wholly dedicated to Shakespeare's Elizabethan stage and London's historic Bankside area of Southwark, the cradle of Western civlization's theatre'. There are some lovely models and costumes plus interesting text, and until Globe Theatre II is finished (scheduled for April 1995), during the summer you should be able to go and see the work in progress. A must for lovers of theatre history.

The Old Operating Theatre, Museum and Herb Garret

9a St Thomas's Street, SE1, tel. 071 955 4791/081 806 4325. Open Tues–Sun 10 a.m.–4 p.m. Admission £2 adults, £1 concessions. Two minutes' walk from London Bridge BR and Underground station – follow the signs. Special lecture 2.30 p.m. first Sun of every month. Not wheelchair-accessible; awkward with buggy/heavy shopping.

At the top of a square brick tower, up thirty-two thin spiral stairs with a rope for a banister, you'll find one of London's most jam-packed fascinating sights, which can be broken down into three main components. Nestled in a wooden horseshoe of rising viewing platforms is the oldest **operating theatre** in the country, which was built exclusively for the St Thomas' women's ward and features an original nineteenth-century wooden operating table with, underneath, the sawdust-filled box that the surgeon kicked around to wherever there was most blood dripping.

The source of sweet smells is the **herb garret**, which was used by the hospital's apothecary, and in front of the corner filled with bunches of dried herbs and jars and colourful powders is the **museum.**

It seems at first that you will whizz round the sectioned-off roof eaves that comprise the museum, but the history of St Thomas' Hospital from the medieval generosity of Alice de Bregerake to the nineteenth-century Florence Nightingale is told on information boards in a compelling combination of words and pictures, and the collection of objects deepens a morbid fascination with the horrors of medicine before the age of science. The instruments for cupping and bleeding and a midwife's nineteenth-century brass tube fumigator are innocuous beside the perforator and decapitating hooks in the eighteenth-century 'obstetrics' case of Dr Smellie, and the amputation saw accompanied by an illustration showing how the involved parties should arrange themselves – amputee on a chair; assistants to keep him or her there; while the surgeon saws in without the benefit of anaesthetic.

London Dungeon

28–34 Tooley Street, SE1, tel. 071 403 0606. Near London Bridge Underground. Open from 10 a.m. seven days a week all year except Christmas Day, last admission 4.30 p.m. (close 5.30 p.m.) Oct–Mar; 5.30 p.m. (close 6.30 p.m.) Apr–Sept. Admission £5, £3 under-15s, free disabled.

A tacky, exploitative museum which tires even the children it's aimed at. Exhibits that are billed as 'spine-chilling' – including pressing, boiling and the gibbet cage – are made scary not by the rickety models but through setting the imagination working by taped screams, and the fact that it's so dark that you can't see where you're walking. The new 'Jack the Ripper Experience' has been condemned by many women as sensationalist, and children visiting it are anything from bemused to traumatised by the flashed images of decapitated East London prostitutes.

Design Museum

Butlers Wharf, Shad Thames, SE1, tel. 071 403 6933. London Bridge Underground then 47 or P11 bus, or Tower Hill Underground then walk over the bridge. Admission £3.50 adults, £2.50 concessions (students, under-18s, UB40s and disabled). Open 10.30 a.m.–5.30 p.m. every day except 25, 26 and 27 Dec and 1 Jan. Good wheelchair access, and concessionary rate for disabled visitor's companion.

It is appropriate that the building that contains the Design Museum should itself be of striking design: the assembly of white square 1930s liner-cruiser architecture shapes looks set to rumble through the elegant patio down to the Thames and out to sea. Inside, everything from the Blueprint Café to the attendants to the white echoey gallery space to, of course, the exhibits themselves is designer. The second-floor **Collection Gallery** illustrates the development of design in mass-production through selections of everyday objects such as pottery, Tupperware, radios and cars. Changing exhibitions in the first-floor **Review Gallery** illustrate innovative and current design. There are also interactive video databases that you can tap into. Older children will enjoy this, but it's really an adult experience. Despite – and because of – the emphasis on chic it's worth a visit, and on a sunny day combine it with a riverside walk.

THE RIVER THAMES SEE MAP ON P.182

The Thames, which was called the river Tamesis by Julius Caesar, changes character completely between the functional East End docklands, where you can do high-speed watersports (see p.330), and towards Richmond, where you can lounge beneath romantic willow trees as swans sail majestically by. If you're up at dawn, when the tide's out, you might spot enthusiasts digging about for bits of Roman pottery amongst rusted debris in the silt. On sunny days, video directors in shades sometimes choose Thames moorings for fashion shoots. You should not miss the chance to appreciate views of the city from at least one of the bridges in Central London (you could try Tower Bridge and/or Westminster Bridge). Another way of appreciating the Thames is to go on a **Thameside Pub Walk** (*tel. 071 624 3978; £4 adults, £3 children/concessions; meet at Blackfriars Underground*).

Sights along the Thames include **Cleopatra's Needle** (*Victoria Embankment, SW1*). This 186-ton obelisk was carved in honour of Egyptian gods in about 1475 BC, and shipped as a gift from Egypt to England in 1878. Incarcerated underneath, the obelisk included some of the day's newspapers, and photographs of twelve women considered the most beautiful of their time. Today the monument is greyed and rather obscured by trees. It is easier to spot the tourist trade that has grown up around it, such as the gift-selling Cleopatra Kiosk. The nearby **Victoria Embankment Gardens** (*SW1*), with its lawnmower-striped lawns and red-and-white-awninged café, is a beautiful place to relax on a summer's day. To find out about a programme of free concerts from Gilbert and Sullivan to the London Dixieland Allstars, tel. 071 375 0441 or go to the bandstand and look at the noticeboard.

Travelling the Thames by Boat The boats you'll ride in are generally small and chugging, most with a sardonic commentary crackling through loudspeakers from the captain, who'll tell you a mixture of historical facts and river gossip, such as the calculation that by the year 2000 tides will have changed so much that the Thames Barrier will be redundant. Westminster is not Central London's only landing pier, but it is the biggest and the one to target for upriver destinations. For general information on Thames boat services, including boats from Tower Pier, Charing Cross and

Greenwich, tel: **Riverboat Information** on *0839 123 432* or **Thames Passenger Services Federation** on *071 231 7122*. For **Recorded River Trip Information** tel. *071 730 4812*. To get through direct to **Westminster Passenger Services**, tel. *071 930 2062/071 930 4721/081 940 3891*.

Westminster Pier is located at Victoria Embankment down steps at Westminster Bridge; nearest Underground station Westminster.

Boats to Kew take approximately one and a half hours, cost £5 single/£7 return adults, £4 single/£5 return children aged 4–14 and leave Apr–Oct 10.15 a.m., 10.30 a.m., 11 a.m., 11.30 a.m., noon, 12.30 p.m., 2 p.m., 2.30 p.m., 3 p.m., 3.30 p.m. Always phone to check times and prices.

Boats to Richmond take two and a half to three hours, cost £6 single/£8 return adults, £4.50 single/£6 return 4–14s, and leave Apr–Oct 11.15 a.m., noon and 12.30 p.m. Always phone to check times and prices.

Boats to Hampton Court take three to four and a half hours, cost £7 single/£9 return adult, £5 single/£6 return 4–14s, and leave Apr–Oct 10.30 a.m., 11.15 a.m., noon, 12.30 p.m. Always phone to check times and prices.

GREENWICH SEE MAP ON P.182

Treat Greenwich as a day trip, for it has a market, the fascinating Royal Observatory, several sights that are great for children (including the *Cutty Sark* and the Maritime Museum), and it's a fine excuse to travel along the Thames (see above). To get a view from the Isle of Dogs that inspired Canaletto, go under the Thames through the Victorian-tiled echoey foot tunnel which children find strangely memorable; it's marked at each side of the river by red-brick-supported glass domes sprouting weeds (open daily; to reach the north bank entrance of the Greenwich Foot Tunnel take the Docklands Light Railway to Island Gardens stop; on the south bank, you'll find the entrance near the *Cutty Sark)*. Greenwich British Rail station is a relatively fast and cheap but unromantic way to get to Greenwich. If it snows in winter, Londoners skive off school and work to rush to the steep slopes of Greenwich Park with sledges; and in summer, Greenwich Park is a great place to picnic. The park also has a children's boating lake, an extensive flower garden, one of the best views of London from the site of the General Wolfe statue, and a café. There are a lot of mediocre sandwich bars and touristy maritime theme pubs – see Eating and Drinking for a couple of reasonable places to eat.

Cutty Sark

King William Walk, SE10, tel. 081 853 3589. Greenwich or Maze

Hill BR. Passport ticket to Cutty Sark, *Maritime Museum, Queen's House and Old Royal Observatory costs £7.45 adults, £5.45 children and OAPs. Entrance to* Cutty Sark *only £3 adults, £2 under-15s/OAPs. Open Apr–Sept Mon–Sat 10 a.m.–6 p.m., Sun noon–6 p.m.; Oct–Mar Mon–Sat 10 a.m.–5 p.m., Sun noon–5 p.m.*

This impressive 1869 sailing vessel, the only surviving tea and wool clipper, was named the *Cutty Sark* after the short (which is 'cutty' in Scottish) shift ('sark') worn by the witch in Robert Burns's poem 'Tam o' Shanter' – a drunken Tam, fleeing from a witch, Nannie, manages to escape, but without his horse's tail. The tail remains in Nannie's hand as part of the ship's figurehead today. You can roam all over the *Cutty Sark*, past information boards detailing the history of the China tea trade and the ship's maiden voyage; you can see an eerie selection of figureheads with names including Cleopatra, Florence Nightingale, Elizabeth Fry and Amphitrite (goddess of the sea); and on deck you can see into the crew's bunks.

Royal Naval College

King William Walk, SE10, tel. 081 858 2154. Greenwich or Maze Hill BR. Open Fri–Wed 2.30 – 5.30 p.m. Admission free. Wheelchair access by prior arrangement.

Now a naval university, this grandiose complex of classical buildings was constructed on the site of Greenwich Palace in 1694. The ceiling of the **hall** that was started by Wren and finished by Hawksmoor and Vanburgh is the main thing to see: painted between 1707 and 1726, it's the most lavish secular interior of its period in England – William and Mary are swimmingly surrounded by representations of virtues. The Wren **chapel** is also open to the public.

National Maritime Museum

Romney Road, SE10, tel. 081 858 4422. Greenwich or Maze Hill BR. Passport ticket to Cutty Sark, *Maritime Museum, Queen's House and Old Royal Observatory costs £7.45 adults, £5.45 children and OAPs. Entrance to museum only, £3.75 adults, £2.75 children/OAPs. Open Mar–Oct Mon–Sat 10 a.m.–6 p.m., Sun 2–6 p.m.; Nov–Feb Mon–Sat 10 a.m.–5 p.m., Sun 2–5 p.m. Stairs and lifts.*

Despite nods towards women – such as featuring a portrait of Lady Hamilton in amongst Lord Nelson regalia, including his stockings – this is primarily about naval heroes and their vessels. Boys and girls love it, and the museum's commitment to tying exhibitions in with the national school curriculum makes sure English children come in droves. The museum charts maritime history from the golden royal barge of 1732 to the present day with a rather endearing mix of decrepit-looking exhibits, such as the penguin Captain Scott brought back from the Antarctic in 1904 and super-swish high-tech sections such as the 'video wall' in the Twentieth-century Seapower gallery. The temporary exhibitions are especially well done.

Queen's House

Romney Road, SE10, tel. 081 858 4422. Greenwich or Maze Hill BR. Passport ticket to Cutty Sark, *Maritime Museum, Queen's House and Old Royal Observatory costs £7.45 adults, £5.45 children and OAPs. Entrance to Queen's House only, £3.75 adults, £2.75 children/OAPs. Open May–Sept Mon–Sat 10 a.m.–6 p.m., Sun noon–6 p.m. Awkward stairs.*

'The Queen ... is building somewhat at Greenwich wch must be finished this sommer, yt is saide to be some curious devise of Inigo Jones, and will cost about 4000li,' noted a courtier in 1617 a year after Inigo Jones had begun England's first Palladian villa for Anne of Denmark. When Anne died in 1619 he completed it as Henrietta Maria's 'House of Delights', and it is now Jones's earliest surviving work, having narrowly missed demolition during the Civil War only because Cromwell thought he might like to live there himself at some point.

Acoustiguide wands talk visitors round the history of the newly opened Queen's House. The wand system invokes slapstick scenes of adults bending and stretching to find the point in the room where they can get close to what they want to see and still pick up the radio signals that make their wand work. Child-friendly signs warn parents where balconies and balustrades have dangerously large gaps.

The Old Royal Observatory

Greenwich Park, 5 minutes' walk from the Maritime Museum, tel. 081 858 4422. Greenwich or Maze Hill BR. Passport ticket to Cutty Sark, *Maritime Museum, Queen's House and Old Royal Observatory costs £7.45 adults, £5.45 children and OAPs. Entrance for Royal Observatory only, £3.75 adults, £2.75 children/OAPs. Open Mar–Oct Mon–Sat 10 a.m.–6 p.m., Sun 2–6 p.m.; Nov–Feb Mon–Sat 10 a.m.–5 p.m., Sun 2–5 p.m. Unavoidable stairs if you want to get to the top.*

This distinctive red-brick and white toy castle on a hill with an observatory ballooning behind it is the best of all the Greenwich sights for adults and children alike, at once momentous and hilarious.

Designed by Sir Christopher Wren 'for the observator's habitation ... and a little for pompe', the oldest part of the Observatory, Flamsteed House, was built after Charles II appointed John Flamsteed as his first Astronomer Royal in March 1675 'so as to find out the so much-desired longitude of places for the perfecting the art of navigation'. As you approach the **Meridian Courtyard** you'll see a line of people photographing each other astride the greeney-blue meridian line; as you go in towards the cash desk you can check your watch against the Greenwich Mean Time 'pips'. Exhibitions in words, prints, videos and interactive science stations consider 'The Theme of Time-keeping' and 'Exploring the Universe', and chart the history of how the zero meridian line, which each navigator at one time picked arbitrarily, came to be fixed; in the Flamsteed House **Octagon Room** an example of the long wood box telescopes of the age is propped on a ladder (currently the view through it turns reverence into giggles, for you see a picture of the cartoon dog Pluto). In the **Meridian Building** you can see a collection of telescopes including, at the top of steep stairs, the 28-inch refracting telescope of 1893.

Ranger's House

Chesterfield Walk, Blackheath, SE10, tel. 081 853 0035. Greenwich or Maze Hill BR. Admission £2 adults, £1 children/OAPs/UB40s. Open daily 10 a.m.–5 p.m. (4 p.m. Nov–Jan); closed Good Friday, 24, 25 Dec.

If you need a reason to walk through the park, come to the Ranger's House, a grand brick eighteenth-century house that was built for Admiral Francis Hosier but became the park ranger's residence in the nineteenth century and today holds the **Suffolk Collection** of 53 paintings, including full-length Jacobean portraits by William Larkin. The house leaves you conveniently close to one of the few decent eateries, Escaped Coffee House (see Eating and Drinking).

Fan Museum

12 Crooms Hill, SE10, tel. 081 858 7879. Greenwich or Maze Hill BR. Open Tues–Sat 11 a.m.–4.30 p.m., Sun 12–4.30 p.m., closed Mon, 24, 25, 26 December and 1 January. Admission £2.50 adults, £1.50 children 7–16 and OAPs.

Over a period of forty years, Hélène Alexander sought out fans until she had the most comprehensive collection in the world. The Fan Museum was created in 1991 to house her treasures and to serve as a centre for fan-making and fan research. Do you mean *air-conditioning* fans? you might ask, and some did, so the curators included some plastic electric fans almost as a joke in a case at the end of the 'orientation' room which shows how fans – the kind you wave elegantly by hand – are made. The collection consists of over 2,000 fans from all over the world, made of feathers and tortoise-shell, ivory and silk, a great many of them from the eighteenth century. One, on permanent display behind special glass in the admission hall, is sixteenth-century French. Since fans can be on display for only up to a couple of months before deteriorating, the exhibitions rotate bimonthly; they are curated thematically (for example, 'Flowers', 'Children'). If you look carefully at each exhibit, you'll get round the three rooms of the Georgian house that make up the museum in about fifteen minutes.

Kew, Richmond, Hampton Court

See map on p.viii

Really, these constitute three separate day trips, possibly more, for countless return trips to see Kew would be rewarding. A slow but enjoyable way to reach all three destinations is by river boat (see The River Thames), but the time factor will probably limit you to returning by train or Underground.

Kew Gardens

Kew Road, Richmond, Surrey, tel. 081 940 1171. Kew Gardens Underground, or Kew Gardens BR. Open Nov–Jan 9.30 a.m.–4 p.m. daily; Feb 9.30 a.m.–5 p.m. daily; Mar 9.30 a.m.–6 p.m. daily; Apr–mid-Sept 9.30 a.m.–6.30 p.m. Mon–Sat, 9.30 a.m.–8 p.m. Sun, Bank Holidays; mid-Sept–Oct 9.30 a.m.–6.30 p.m. daily. Admission £3 adults, £1 under-16s, £1.50 OAPs/students, free under-5s, £12 season tickets.

Whether you're interested in plants or not, Kew is a rare treat. If you've been before it's probably larger than you remember, and if you're new to Kew and the word 'gardens' conjures up either domestic-sized or even grand landscaped gardens, you'll also find that Kew's bigger than you think. The map/leaflet you get with your ticket advises you to explore *either* the East or North section, not all at one go. Kew – or the Royal Botanic Gardens – which Princess Augusta commissioned and George III continued after her death in 1772, covers 300 acres.

One of the great pleasures is simply to roam and see what you find – giant redwoods in the Woodland Glade, Capability Brown's Rhododendron Dell near the Bamboo Garden – but there are a few highlights to pick out – not with the idea that you see them all, but so that you can begin to choose between them. The distinctive Victorian glass and wrought-iron architecture complete with winding stairs that take you close to giant palm trunks and leaves keeps the **Palm House** popular. The modern jutting **Princess of Wales Tropical Conservatory** contains what seems to be a series of sci-fi film sets. Triffid-like plants quiver over your head as you enter, and water sprays out automatically at intervals as you pass over a mangrove swamp towards the sounds of softly whirring fans in the Mohave desert diorama, which has a sad tribute at the exit to the large number of school parties that stampede through. Under an already heavily scored cactus there's a sign asking visitors to refrain from signing their names in the exhibits.

The compact **Marianne North Gallery** is wallpapered with the works of Victorian Marianne North who, self-trained as an artist, devoted her life after her father's death to often hazardous worldwide travels so that she could paint flowers in their natural habitat. The reopened small royal Jacobean country retreat **Kew Palace**, which features, in the bedroom, the small black chair where Queen Charlotte died surrounded by her family, has a separate door charge (£1 adults, 50p under-16s, 70p students/OAPs). But more fascinating, and without any extra charge, is the seventeenth-century **Queen's Garden** behind the palace, where labels display herbs' names alongside appropriate seventeenth-century instructions for use. For example, 'Double Feverfew' was 'held to bee a speciall remedy to helpe those that have taken opium too liberally', and 'Small Bastard Rubarbe' was said to 'somewhat moove the belly'.

Kew is one of the few places some mothers will bring toddlers to, confident that the grass is clean enough to crawl around in. Unless you want a high-priced formal sit-down lunch in the **Orangery**, bring a picnic, as the so-called **Bakery** sells only stodgy overpriced donuts and greasy pasties. Or splurge on cream tea at the **Maids of Honour** (see Eating and Drinking).

Richmond

Richmond was originally a place to retire to from the pressures of London. Queen Elizabeth I died in the peace of Richmond Palace. As late as the 1920s, after instructions to rest, Virginia and Leonard Woolf ran the Hogarth Press from blue-plaque-marked Hogarth House, Paradise Road. Today the main attraction of Richmond is still its quiet holiday atmosphere, best appreciated in the rambling park and on the oddly twee yet still appealing riverfront walk, which can be followed by a wander through the cobbled, geranium-basket-strung streets. If you go to the Tourist Centre at the **Richmond Riverside Centre** (the classical façade at Richmond Bridge on the riverfront, tel 081 940 9125) you can get a series of leaflets detailing 'Richmond Heritage Walks'. These cover: **Richmond Green**, where joustings and tournaments took place in the fifteenth century when Henry VII held court at the Richmond Palace (now destroyed except for two castellated gatehouses); and

Maids of Honour Row, a handsome row of Georgian houses (not open to the public) built around 1725 by George II for maids attending the Princess of Wales.

The stretch of buildings called **Richmond Riverside** (down the stairs at Richmond Bridge) was condemned by many when it was formally opened in 1988 by Queen Elizabeth II as a soulless classical pastiche, but Prince Charles declared it 'an expression of harmony and proportion'. The two-mile walkway that goes by it, however, appeals to a wide variety of people. On a sunny day the willow-tree-lined promenade, which sometimes attracts a stray waddling goose, is a mix of 'Wet'n Wild' T-shirted beer lads out with their mates, families eating ice creams and playing frisbee, and amateur watercolourists at easels reproducing the grand lines of Richmond Bridge but omitting the 'No Swimming' warning signs and advertising boards for trips in Edwardian rowing skiffs. Resist the temptation to go into one of the riverside pubs or cafés, which are mainly tourist traps – see Eating and Drinking for more pleasant alternatives.

If you go to Richmond Park by winding up through the flower-bedecked terraces and gardens of **Richmond Hill**, you'll be rewarded at the top with a view of river and countryside that has inspired many painters, including Turner. Once in **Richmond Park**, you'll see different kinds of people depending on the time of year – guffawing picnickers with Pimms and cucumber sandwiches in summer, earnest wiry twenty-year-olds with spiked black hair and plastic carrier bags meticulously seeking out magic mushrooms as autumn draws in, and then through winter scatterings of hardy women in Barbours striding out to walk their Labradors. The park has been prized for its wildlife since Charles I enclosed 2,470 acres as a royal chase in 1637. Today there are badgers (rarely seen) and red and fallow deer (avoid when rutting). On a fine day the view from the top of the King Henry VIII mound extends to St Paul's Cathedral.

Hampton Court Palace

East Molesey, Surrey, tel. 081 781 9500. Hampton Court BR. Open Apr–Oct 10.15 a.m.–6 p.m. Mon, 9.30 a.m.–6 p.m. Tues–Sun; Oct–Mar 10.15 a.m.–4.30 p.m. Mon, 9.30 a.m.–4.30 p.m. Tues–Sun. Last admission half an hour before closing. Park open dawn to dusk daily. Admission, inclusive ticket to Palace, courtyard, cloister and maze £4.60 adults, £2.90 under-16s, £3.50 OAPs, under-5s free. Admission to maze only Mar–Oct £1.25 adults, 80p under-16s, 75p OAPs. Wheelchair access.

Here you can chat with actors in period costume while surveying England's Tudor masterpiece, see Surrey locals trying to get to grips with fifteenth-century tennis on original Tudor courts, or become thoroughly lost in the famous maze and enjoy wandering the grounds as far as a section known as 'the Wilderness', where you might like to pause for a picnic.

Although Hampton Court Palace was one of the favourite royal Tudor residences – first of Henry VIII and later of Elizabeth I – it was actually built in 1514 by Cardinal Wolsey, whose wealth was said for a time to exceed Henry's, until he gave much of it to Henry in the form of Hampton Court. His 1529 gift did not have the desired appeasing effect at all. Henry began work on the Palace immediately, and still had Wolsey executed in the Tower for treason.

Henry's court was so huge (over 1,000 people) that his enlargements included quadrupling the size of the kitchens. The next substantial changes came during the reign of William and Mary, when William decided to make Hampton Court his Versailles, and Mary commissioned Sir Christopher Wren to rebuild entirely – a plan that was halted by her death in 1694 at a point when Wren had got only as far as the Fountain Court, the Clock Court and the Orangery. Little work was done by succeeding monarchs (Queen Anne simply occupied the King's Apartments), until finally Queen Victoria opened the Palace to the public, and today it is divided into historical routes: the Tudor Royal Lodgings; the Queen's Apartments; the Georgian Rooms; the King's Apartments; the Wolsey Rooms; and the Tudor Kitchens. Through these, the massive kitchens that are laid out as if a feast is being prepared, complete with mock food, are a highlight; as is the spectacular Tudor roof of the Royal Chapel.

There are many splendid – if sometimes bordering on monotonous – rooms to walk through, including the Communication Gallery, which features 'The Windsor Beauties', a collection of Sir Peter Lely's representations of the ladies of Charles II's court which caused the Victorian historian Ernest Law to remark: 'No more congenial task could have been selected for the pencil of Lely than that of portraying on glowing canvas the sensuous contours and lovely features of the frail and seductive nymphs in the amorous court of the Merry monarch.' In the Wolsey Rooms, Renaissance paintings from the Queen's collection are on display. Outside there is, of course, the famous maze, which is rather small, with iron railings to support the thinning hedges. The grounds merit a long walk, and if you haven't brought a picnic, don't despair, for the restaurant and café are run by restaurateur Prue Leith – the usual kind of major-sight-café cake and sandwich fare is served at the typically slightly inflated prices, but it is much better quality.

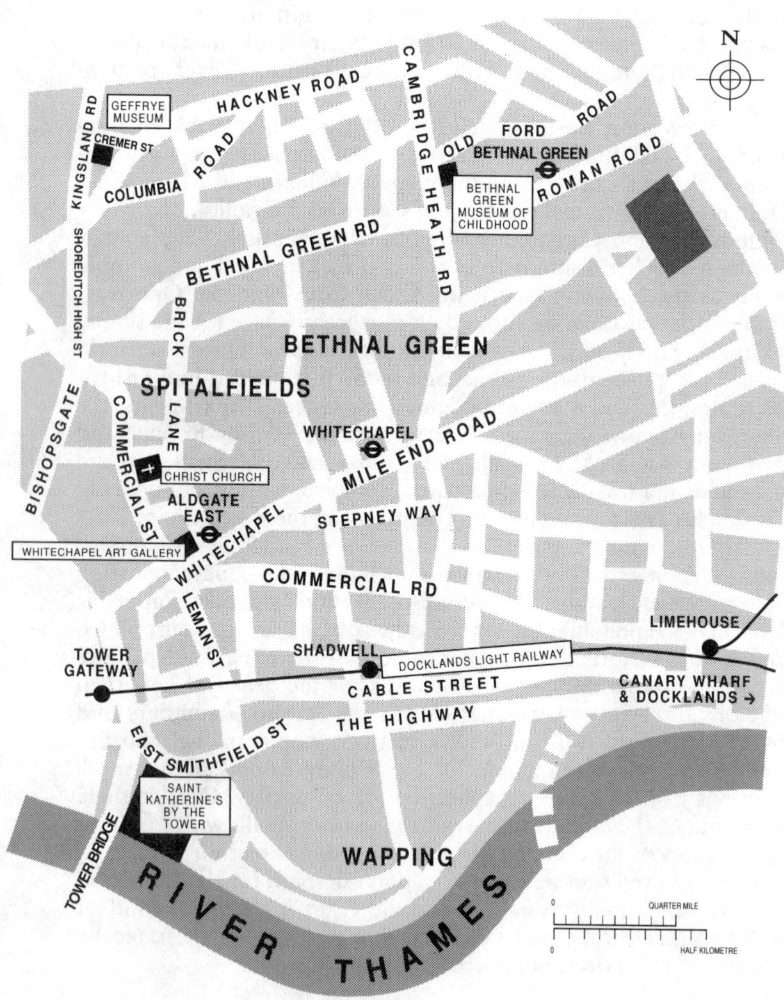
N
GEFFRYE MUSEUM
HACKNEY ROAD
CAMBRIDGE HEATH RD
OLD FORD ROAD
KINGSLAND RD
CREMER ST
ROAD
BETHNAL GREEN
ROMAN ROAD
COLUMBIA
BETHNAL GREEN MUSEUM OF CHILDHOOD
BETHNAL GREEN RD
SHOREDITCH HIGH ST
BRICK LANE
BETHNAL GREEN
SPITALFIELDS
BISHOPSGATE
COMMERCIAL ST
WHITECHAPEL
MILE END ROAD
CHRIST CHURCH
ALDGATE EAST
STEPNEY WAY
WHITECHAPEL ART GALLERY
WHITECHAPEL
COMMERCIAL RD
LEMAN ST
LIMEHOUSE
TOWER GATEWAY
SHADWELL
DOCKLANDS LIGHT RAILWAY
CABLE STREET
CANARY WHARF & DOCKLANDS →
THE HIGHWAY
EAST SMITHFIELD ST
SAINT KATHERINE'S BY THE TOWER
TOWER BRIDGE
WAPPING
RIVER THAMES
0
QUARTER MILE
0
HALF KILOMETRE

THE EAST END

The reputation of the East End as a melting pot of different cultures, classes and industry was established in the sixteenth century when the 'fayre hedges and long rows of elms' (John Stow) east of the City were razed as London became a leading centre of European trade. The port, and later the docklands, attracted a mixture of prosperous merchant shippers, foreigners escaping religious persecution and paupers in search of cheap or free accommodation until World War II, when the docklands were bombed and new waves of immigrants settled in other areas, including Brixton and Hackney. Luxury flat and shop complexes created for City high-fliers in the 1970s and 1980s by dockland redevelopers became white elephants with the 1990s recession.

Today, the East End sprawls beyond the River Lea into Essex, but just two or three short exploratory trips can reveal its diverse history alongside some of London's most rewarding sights, vibrant streetlife and authentic Indian restaurants. A weekday walk through the area called Spitalfields (near Aldgate East Underground) takes you past 'import'/'wholesale' warehouses and stalls selling knock-off priced handbags and pastel shell suits around Fashion Street, E1. On Brick Lane, E1 walking south, street and shop signs are in Bengali; women wearing sarees under nylon puffa jackets and serenaded by car stereo sounds of Hindi pop stars.

After a couple of defiant Stan's cafés, you come to the traffic-roaring Whitechapel Road, E1. Look left and you see the Georgian building that houses an Elizabethan bell foundry (at No. 34), the shuttered headquarters of the Salvation Army, and the moons and minarets of the modern brick East London Mosque. Turn right and you can go to the Whitechapel Art Gallery, then to the famous Jewish restaurant Bloom's for a salt beef sandwich (see Eating and Drinking). If you prefer bustle and you want purchases, go to Brick Lane on a Sunday for the market (see Shopping), perhaps combined with a brief visit to Christ Church and a browse around Old Spitalfields Market. All week the Old Spitalfields Market echoes with the chimes of Rowland Emmett's giant clockwork 'Quiet Afternoon in Cloud Cuckoo Valley'. On Sundays it fills with stalls selling organic food and crafts, and in the north-east corner there's a straw-littered showcase for the Three Farms Association, where children can meet the animals before rushing off to buy a piece of sugar-free flapjack.

Of all the dockland redevelopments, the best to target is **St Katharine By The Tower** (*entrance on East Smithfield, E1*), known as Katharine Docks, which, despite a laboured mariners' theme that dictates the stock of the quayside shops, has been impressively restored featuring a stately yacht haven. It is convenient for a walk along the **Ornamental Canal** (*entrance on Thomas More Street*) to the boutiques of Tobacco Dock or on to the Shadwell Basin, where under twenty-ones can join in water activities including canoeing (see Children).

The **Docklands Light Railway** (*LDR, board at Bank Underground; no service weekends; tel. 071 918 4000*) is fun. Either ride it for its own sake or head for 'Mudchute' city farm. Don't get off at Canary Wharf. If LDR publicity claiming that the glinting glass 800-foot obelisk Canary Wharf Tower is 'the tallest building in Britain and the very symbol of London's Docklands', is correct it's depressing: an on-site LDR member of staff, when pressed for what's there to do or see, said, 'Not a lot. It's like a ghost town.' With or without children, the **Bethnal Green Museum** of Childhood is almost a day trip in itself, as is the **Fawcett Library** for any feminist or researcher of women's history (see Women and Feminism, p.25). The alluring tucked-away **Geffrye Museum** can be combined on a sunny day with a promenade along Grand Union Canal to the Angel Islington's antique shops and café/bar/restaurant scene. For a brief history of London's immigrants, see Women and Culture, p.29.

Victorian London The combination of factories and slum conditions that characterised the worst of Victorian times (1837–1901) concentrated in the East End because of its docks, which serviced the export/import trade of an empire that spanned one-fifth of the globe, and because it was out of the way, so need not offend the sensibilities of London's affluent. Far from operating quietly as a cog in the 'Great Engine' of the Industrial Revolution, the East End became a battleground of Victorian values. On the one hand, says David Thomson in *England in the Nineteenth Century* (Pelican), Victorian Liberalism's 'quest for a new morality' promoted the Radical goal of 'the greatest happiness of the greatest number' over and above the welfare of individuals, and prized as virtues 'Industriousness, tolerance, self-reliance and self-help, earnest endeavour, liberality of mind'. On the other, from mid-Victorian England's 'evangelicalism, its fear of an after-life and its Protestant Christianity' came a belief in the importance of 'Piety, fidelity to the pledged word, good faith in human relationships, charity'. Liberalism required industrious Victorians to leave the destitute to their self-inflicted fate, while evangelicalism compelled charitable Victorians to enter the worst slums as angels of mercy. Evangelicalism kept 'good' women at home as pious wives and mothers, sweat workshop conditions and threat of starvation forced women on to the street as prostitutes in desperate bids to help themselves, whilst 'liberality of mind' (or middle-class hypocrisy) led men to seek sexual pleasure outside the marital bed.

Victorian East End life was portrayed in fiction by Dickens (see Recommended Books) and recorded by journalist and social historian Henry Mayhew in *London Labour and the London Poor* (written and published between 1849 and 1861; selection now available from Penguin). Mayhew provides vivid descriptions. You can practically smell the Brick Lane gasworks, dockland lodging-houses (where sleeping on the kitchen floor got a penny reduction in the fee) and street traders' chestnut stoves and ginger-beer fountains. You can hear the chatter in 'tally-shops', where women bought shawls and dresses on credit, and the guffaws at 'penny gaffs', where entertainment consisted of obscene songs and suggestive dances, and refreshments included pigs' trotters and oranges.

Mayhew's book is also an early example of the value of oral histories. The eight-year-old watercress girl who shuffled about in carpet slippers crying 'Four bunches a penny, water-creases' and thought nowhere could be handsomer than Farringdon-market told Mayhew:

> 'I used to go to school, but I wasn't there long … mother took me away because the master whacked me. … We never goes home to breakfast till we've sold out; but if it's very late, then I buys a penn'worth of pudden, which is very nice with gravy … I always give my mother my money, she's so very good to me. She don't often beat me. She's very poor and goes out cleaning rooms sometimes. I ain't got no father, he's a father-in-law. … He grinds scissors, and he's very good to me. No; I don't mean by that that he says kind things to me. He hardly speaks. When I get home, after selling creases, I puts the rooms to rights. I clean the chairs, though there's only two to clean, and scrubs the floor. … Sometimes we has a game of "honeypots" with the girls in the court, but not often … 'cos going out with creases tires me.'

Successful watercress girls could become coster girls – street sellers of oranges, apples or violets, depending on the season – who, if they earned scant money, preferred spending the night under a dry arch or behind a market stall to braving recriminations at home. Courtships, promising a degree of independence, were described by Mayhew as usually short:

> The coster-lads see the girls at market, and if one of them be pretty, and a boy take a fancy to her, he will make her bargains

> for her, and carry her basket home. ... A girl seldom takes up with a lad before she is sixteen, though some of them, when barely fifteen or even fourteen, will pair off. They court for a time, going to raffles and 'gaffs' together, and then the affair is arranged. The girl tells her parents 'she's going to keep company with so-and-so', packs up what things she has and goes at once. ... A furnished room, at about 4*s*. a week, is taken, and the young couple begin life. The lad goes out as usual with his barrow, and the girl goes out with her basket.

Mayhew was bemused by the cultural behaviour of the few who did marry:

> The costermongers strongly resemble the North American Indians in their conduct to their wives. They can understand that it is the duty of the woman to contribute to the happiness of the man, but cannot feel that there is a reciprocal duty from the man to the woman. The wife is considered as an inexpensive servant, and the disobedience of a wish is punished with blows. She must work early and late, and to the husband must be given the proceeds of her labour. Often when the man is in one of his drunken fits – which sometimes last two or three days continuously – she must by her sole exertions find food for herself and him too. To live in peace with him, there must be no murmurings ... for if there be, she is either beaten into submission or cast adrift to begin life again – as another's leavings.

Mayhew meticulously categorised his interviewees:

> The women engaged in street-sale are of all ages and of nearly all classes. They are, however, chiefly of two countries, England and Ireland. There are (comparatively) a few Jewesses, a very few Scotchwomen and Welchwomen who are street-traders ... of foreigners there are German broom-women, and a few Italians with musical instruments.

His category 'Those that will not work' included prostitutes, many of whom were young girls, as this extract from the May 1835 opening address of the London Society for the Protection of Young Females, and Prevention of Juvenile Prostitution, makes clear:

> It has been proved that 400 individuals procure a livelihood by trepanning females from eleven to fifteen years of age for the purposes of prostitution ... no sooner is the unsuspecting helpless one within their grasp than ... she is stripped of the apparel with which parental care or friendly solicitude had clothed her, and then, decked with the gaudy trappings of her shame, she is compelled to walk the streets ... producing to her master or mistress the wages of her prostitution. ... After this it is useless to attempt to return to the path of virtue or honour, for she is then watched with the greatest vigilance. ... It rarely occurs that one so young

> escapes contamination; and it is a fact that numbers of these youthful victims imbibe disease within a week or two of their seduction ... and it is not uncommon circumstance that within the short space of a few weeks the bloom of health, of beauty, and of innocence gives place to the sallow hue of disease, of despair, and of death.

In the 1860s – not including the uncounted thousands of amateurs called 'dolly mops' who worked the streets of London – an estimated 80,000 professional prostitutes occupied nearly 3,000 brothels, the worst of which were down by the docks (convenient for sailors), in Whitechapel, Shadwell and Spitalfields.

Drunken brawls, violent thieving and even murder in these areas was not uncommon or cause for much concern, but at a time when table legs were kept modestly covered, and the very word prostitute caused morbid shudders in polite society, all London was shocked by the savagery of the murders between August and November 1888 of at least five prostitutes, whose bodies were found with uterus and viscera removed. Their killer was never caught but was nicknamed when an anonymous letter was received by the Central News Agency on 28 September 1888: 'I am down on whores, and I shan't quit ripping them until I get buckled.' At the time, Jews were blamed – in 1965 Robin Odell narrowed the suspect's occupation down to *shochet* – that is, a ritual slaughter man who prepares kosher meat – and in 1888 the *Jewish Chronicle* reported that it was not safe for Jews to go outside their homes at night: 'Without a doubt the foreign Jews in the East End have been in some peril during the past week owing to the sensationalism of which the district has been a centre.'

Conflicting theories on the Ripper's identity developed immediately. In 1929 Leonard Matters argued that the Ripper was a Harley Street surgeon avenging the death of his son by syphilis contracted from a prostitute; in 1939 William Stewart concluded from evidence, including the medical precision of the mutilations, that the killer was a midwife; by 1960 Dr Stowell's theory was favoured – that the Ripper was the Duke of Clarence, grandson of Queen Victoria, a homosexual equipped with a rudimentary medical knowledge picked up while dissecting venison on the hunting fields; and by the 1970s Michael Harrison had a theory that it was in fact the Duke of Clarence's tutor and later boyfriend, J.K. Stehpen, Virginia Woolf's cousin. Judith R. Walkowitz argues in *Feminist Studies 8* (Fall 1982) that the killer's identity quickly became irrelevant, and the murders became 'a modern myth of male violence against women, a story whose details have become vague and generalized, but whose "moral" message is clear: the city is a dangerous place for women, when they transgress the narrow boundaries of home and hearth and dare to enter public space'.

Certainly, few Victorian women dared venture outside their allotted realms unless protected by the halo of evangelical philanthropy; sometimes an additional direct call from God was necessary – for example, in the case of radical Methodist **Catherine Booth** (1829–90), who took the precaution of marrying a man who shared her belief in women's intelligence. But she stood to address the congregation herself only when one day, in the middle of her husband's sermon, she realised it was God's command. By the 1860s Catherine was beginning to recognise the limits of both street-corner preaching in the East End and the 'Hallelujah Band' (formed from converted criminals), and in 1877 the evolution of a military structure was recognised with uniforms, designed by Catherine, and a new name, the Salvation Army. 'Christianity is necessarily aggressive,' explained Catherine, who believed the urban poor had to be marched to 'Holiness'. Christianity could not, she said, 'shine for itself; it must go out, and out, and out to the uttermost part of the earth'. A 1929 bronze statue of Catherine Booth by G.E. Wade is at the William Booth Training College, Champion Park, SE5.

Angela Burdett Coutts (see Mayfair) was directed less by evangelicalism in her philanthropy than by Dickens, who informed her that workers brought in to build roads and railways and relegated to East End slums needed decent lodgings. In 1851 Miss Coutts planned a model development and chose its location: Bethnal Green, the place where Nancy died in *Oliver Twist*, described by Engels as 'a towering crag of refuse and an enormous ditch or stagnant lake of putrefying matter; in this Pandora's box dead cats and dogs were profusely scattered, exhibiting every stage of disgusting decomposition'.

Dickens was largely responsible for the vogue of blocks of flats which, in most cases, proved worse than the terraces they replaced; but his rhetoric convinced: if 'large buildings had been erected for the working people, instead of the absurd and expensive separate walnut shells in which they live,' he argued, 'London would have been about a third of its present size, and every family would have had a country walk, miles nearer to their work and would not have had to dine at public houses'; furthermore, in flats 'they would have had gas, water, drainage and a variety of other humanizing things which you *can't* give them so well in little houses'. In 1862, in *All the Year Round*, Dickens hailed the opening of Miss Coutts's Columbia Square, describing the exact dimensions of the flats. The living-room contained a range, a boiler and an oven, and was twelve foot by ten. The bedroom, in which the entire family slept, was twelve feet by eight.

By the time **Octavia Hill** (1838–1912) came to East End housing reform, she had learnt only that smaller blocks were preferable, and believed that existing dwellings should be redeveloped. A block at St Jude's seemed perfect, but she wrote in July 1874 to her friend and colleague, the Reverend Samuel Barnett: 'I find the difficulties of management in Whitechapel greater than ever I anticipated, property and people being equally impossible to deal with.' Landlords were unwilling to give up even derelict and deserted buildings until they had received the government compensation due once the dwelling had been declared uninhabitable.

Samuel Barnett's wife, Henrietta, sold some of her jewels and, for around £500, the block of St Jude's was secured. 'So we bought the rickety dwellings,' wrote Henrietta, 'gave its degraded inhabitants the chance of reform before turning them out, tidied up the property, and used its rents to the day of its final destruction.' By 1881 Samuel Barnett had been installed in the district as vicar, which was exactly what he and Henrietta wanted but proved distressing, since as their home was surrounded by brothels, they were constantly confronted with not just the issue but the practice of sex. If a girl from Henrietta's class fell victim to the white slave traders, Henrietta fell ill for a week. She sold more jewels to buy three nearby properties which had been used as brothels, and used the rent to rehabilitate prostitutes. Believing in the rich dwelling among the poor, she and Samuel held monthly entertainments and endured 'greasy heads leaning against Morris wallpapers and dirty garments ruining furniture covers'.

Octavia shared few of Henrietta's dilemmas. Although Henrietta was devoted to her, she still found Octavia's views too simplistically harsh, commenting: 'She expected the degraded people to live in disreputable conditions, until they proved themselves worthy of better ones.' Cardinal Manning was so unhappy with her methods in the Charity Organisation Society, which involved rigorous inquiries before allocating relief, that he resigned in protest, saying: 'The good Samaritan did not delay to pour oil into the wounds of the man half-dead until he had ascertained whether he was responsible for his own distress.' Octavia herself wrote in *Macmillan's Magazine* in 1869: 'Where a man persistently refuses to exert himself, external help is worse than useless.' Clearly, Octavia Hill embraced the ideals of her time, categorically opposing state intervention, yet perhaps the root of her harshness is revealed by this comment in an 1876 letter to Henrietta: 'The many poor ... are dear to me because they are poor and needy, but ... are not individual men and women to me.'

WOMEN IN TRADE UNIONS

The Industrial Revolution took women into factories as sweat labour. They were – as women's trade-union leader Mary MacArthur said of her own times more than a century later – low-paid because they were unorganised and unorganised becaus the were low-paid; men often excluded them from trade unions (societies born from medieval guilds) because they were seen as rivals. In London women were at first mainly employed in bookbinding and the rag trade. In 1834 the fight of 200 women folders and sewers against a reduction in wages by the British and Foreign Bible Society was successful largely because they had the support of the male London Union of Journeymen Bookbinders.

The plight of young girls employed in 'the dressmaking establishments' in the 1840s was described by Englels:

> During the fashionable season, which lasts some 4 months, working hours, even in the best establishments, are fifteen, and, in very pressing cases, eighteen a day. … The only limit to their work is the absolute physical inability to hold the needle another minute. … Enervation, exhaustion, debility, loss of appetite, pains in the shoulders, back and hips, but especially headaches, begin very soon; then follow curvatures of the spine, high, deformed shoulders … coughs, narrow chests. … In many cases the eyes suffer so severely that incurable blindness follows … consumption usually soon ends the sad life of these milliners and dressmakers.

Many of the girls were naive, fresh from the country, and slaves to their employers partly because the only alternatives were the dreaded domestic service and prostitution. It took outside intervention by philanthropic middle- and (more frequently) upper-class women to help women in the sweat trades to help themselves.

Emma Paterson (1848–86), the educated daughter of a poor schoolteacher, identified the problem, travelled the United States seeking models for women's industrial organisations, and founded in July 1874, on her return to London, the Women's Protective and Provident League to help women in trades including bookbinding, dressmaking, millinery and upholstery to form unions. Although she was recognised by Beatrice and Sidney Webb in their *History of Trade Unionism* as 'the real pioneer of modern women's trade unions', she lacked funds, and on her death the WPPL leadership passed to **Lady Emily Dilke** (1840–1904), whose wealth ensured the WPPL's survival (she gave £100 annually); and while Lady Dilke was able to impress workers by climbing over bales of rags in a warehouse to learn about rag sorting, her aristocratic background carried weight during negotiations with employers. **Annie Besant** (1847–1933) also came in from outside, most famously as chief organiser of the Bryant and May Match Girls' Strike in 1888.

At a Fabian Society meeting on 15 June, Clementina Black, secretary of the WPPL, proposed a Consumers' Union whose members would buy only goods whose manufacturers treated employees, particularly women, fairly; and Annie Besant, attending the meeting as a socialist journalist, agreed to investigate the allegations of East End vicar the Reverend Adamson against the Bryant and May factories in Bromley-by-Bow. The match girls had staged an unsuccessful strike three years previously, and would talk to the flamboyant one-time religious flagellator and accomplished society lady only if she gave assurances that she would be personally responsible for paying the wages of anyone dismissed as a result. In the 23 June issue of the *Link*, Annie Besant's article appeared under the title 'White Slavery in London':

> A typical case is that of a girl of 16, a piece worker; she earns 4s a week and lives with a sister employed by the same firm who earns 'good money, as much as 8 or 9s a week'. Out of the earnings 2s a week is paid for the rent of one room. The child lives on only bread and butter and tea alike for breakfast and dinner, but related with dancing eyes that once a month she went to a meal where she got, 'coffee and bread and butter and jam and marmalade and lots of it'. … The splendid

salary of 4s is subject to deductions in the shape of fines: if the feet are dirty, or the ground under the bench is left untidy a fine of 3d is inflicted; for putting 'burnts' – matches that have caught fire during the work – on the bench 1s has been forfeited. … If a girl is late she is shut out for half a day … and 5d is deducted out of her day's 8d.

Besant went on to describe the factory conditions:

> These female hands eat their food in the rooms in which they work so that the fumes of the phosphorus mix with their poor meal and they eat disease as seasoning to their bread. Disease I say; for the 'phossy jaw' that they talk about means caries of the jaw, and the phosphorus poison works on them as they chew their food and rots away the bone.

Besant's article stirred up public sympathy, so knocking the bottom out of the market for Bryant and May shares, and it got three girls dismissed. On 8 July over 1,400 match girls met with organisers, including Besant and Clementina Black, and voted to come out on strike, and 'that a union be formed, to be called the Matchmakers' Union', of which Annie Besant became secretary. A deputation was sent to the House of Commons. Onlookers stared, laughed and applauded as the match girls passed in draggled skirts, broken boots and vast black velvet hats worn 'clapped on the head like a clam shell'. Donations kept the strikers from starving, and in less than two weeks the Bryant and May directors had agreed to all demands.

In Charrington Hall on 17 July the girls shouted out 'Yes' to every proposal, including: the abolition of all fines, and of deductions from wages for any purpose; an increase in the rate for piecework; all strikers to be taken back without exception; barrows for transporting boxes formerly carried on the head. Annie set about raising money for a members' club in Bow with a piano, games and light literature, 'so that it may offer a bright homelike refuge to these girls who now have no real homes, no playground save the street'. Relations with management improved quickly, and in 1893 Annie wrote: 'We have found the manager ready to consider any just grievance and to endeavour to remove it, while the company have been liberal supporters of the Women's Club at Bow.'

Although Annie Besant helped women in other industries, including tin box makers, boot finishers and the fur pullers of Bermondsey, direct action by women in low-paid, unspecialised jobs without the support of male trade unions was always perilous. More usual was the government intervention policy pioneered by Lady Dilke, who fought for legislative enactments – for example, on working conditions and equal pay. Once women's trade unions had been formed – and, after World War I, amalgamated with men's unions – the involvement of philanthropists faded, and women workers were pushed by personal experience to fight for prominence within national trade unions and the TUC. Once in influential positions, they then had to somehow champion women workers' issues without alienating either employers or male trade unionists.

Margaret Grace Bondfield (1873–1953), for example, the tenth of a Somerset lace-maker's eleven children, learnt the hard way about living-in as a West End shop assistant working a seventy-five-hour week for £25 a year. She read on her fish and chips newspaper a piece on the National Union of Shop Assistants, Warehouse Men and Clerks, and applied for the post of assistant secretary. **Florence Hancock** (1893–1974) sweated from the age of twelve in a café and condensed milk factory, joined the Workers' Union at twenty and had risen by 1928 to the rank of chief woman officer in its new merged form as the Transport and General Workers' Union

(TGWU), when she campaigned for equal pay, childcare and aid for married women workers.

Margaret Bondfield became the first woman delegate of a Trade Union Congress as early as 1899, but it wasn't until 1942 that the TUC elected their first woman President, **Dame Anne Loughlin** (1894–1979), and the Equal Pay Act was not finally passed until 1969. Even then, Beechey and Whitelegg write in *Women in Britain Today* (OUP), 'in the 1970s unions in many workplaces actually went along with management attempts to evade the requirements of the Equal Pay Act by regrading or redefining jobs'. Feminists have argued for additional positive measures to improve the situation of women at work. Beechey and Whitelegg report: 'Positive action programmes have been introduced in a number of companies (e.g. Thames Television and Sainsbury's)', but 'they are entirely voluntary, and they are unlikely to be successful unless negotiated and agreed between management and unions'.

Geffrye Museum

Kingsland Road (near Cremer Street, south of Grand Union Canal), E2, tel. 071 739 9893. Old Street Underground. Open Tues-Sat 10 a.m.–5 p.m., Sun 2–5 p.m., closed 1 Jan, Good Friday, 25, 26 Dec. Free. Wheelchair access to most rooms and herb garden. Children under 8 must be accompanied.

Set back from the urban nightmare of thundering heavy goods vehicles, cheap shoe manufacturers, welfare offices and shady stripper pubs that characterise the Kingsland Road are plane-tree-shaded eighteenth century ex-Ironmongers' almshouses built on three sides of an immaculately kept lawn. In these modest buildings you can enjoy a series of period rooms, all with accompanying handboards or wall-signs featuring information such as how the lighting worked and the name and address of the Covent Garden artisan whose 1702 inventory was used for the faithful reconstruction of the William and Mary room.

First you'll see an Open Hearth Kitchen, fully kitted out with implements that changed little from 'early times' to the nineteenth century, including: griller with provision for catching dripping; beer warmers shaped conically with handle to facilitate being thrust into embers; and clockwork spitjack for roasting. Your walk along the length of the building takes you chronologically through time up to a mid-1950s council flat plus discussion of the desperate postwar housing shortage and finally to a late-1950s suburban lounge, which is almost eerie for being relatively recent yet utterly dated. The dark oak-panelled Georgian room is adjacent to an airy curving country-garden-muralled coffee bar that serves a well-priced mixture of healthy and indulgent cakes and biscuits. Beyond the Bakelite and home-appliance-filled 1930s room is a display of Clarice Cliff pottery (see p.176). On your way out, take handfuls of printed literature from the well-stocked central reading area, and peruse them in the beautiful secret herb garden (open Apr–Oct). Adults are served by talks on each period room and occasional concerts, and the museum runs an impressive series of 'workshops for young people' which is divided into groups aged ten and over, aged five to ten and under five during Easter, Christmas and summer holidays.

Bethnal Green Museum of Childhood

Cambridge Heath Road (between Roman Road and Old Ford Road), E2, tel. 081 980 3204 or 081 980 2415 for recorded information. Bethnal Green Underground. The building looks more like a train station than a museum; look for the primary-coloured sign. Open Mon–Thur and Sat 10 a.m.–6 p.m. (including Bank Holidays), Sun 2.30–6 p.m., closed first Monday in May, 1 Jan, 24, 25, 26 December. Free. Prior arrangement requested for wheelchair access.

This branch of the Victoria and Albert Museum delights adults perhaps even more than children. Housed behind a three-bay red-brick nineteenth-century façade in aircraft-hangar-like cast-iron galleries that tempt children to scream and test the echo, you'll find a prized collection of doll's houses which dates back to 1673, includes the Billiard Table Makers' doll's house that was personally decorated by doll's house devotee HM Queen Mary (1867–1953), and encourages infant voyeurism (toddlers point and peek to see the rat in Dingley Hall's kitchen).

Indeed, children can become frustrated by the museum's old-fashioned approach. It's all see, no touch, with a curatorial aversion to those newfangled 'hands-on' exhibits. The mezzanine-level doll collection features fashionable 1920s adults' 'Boudoir Dolls' opposite teenage Sindy and her lesser-known rival, Dashing Daisy. Upstairs, the porcelain 'pap boats' that were used for weaning in the seventeenth and eighteenth centuries are part of the 'Growing Up' exhibition, and over the other side 'Trash or Treasure' invites you to 'dip into 400 years of children's books', including a 1950s pamphlet on sex by the Reverend Wm P. O'Keefe entitled 'The Young Lady says "No"!'. Walk on and find model trains, hobbyhorses and much, much more. Phone for details of Saturday workshops and special summer activities. There's a gift shop; a café is scheduled for autumn 1994.

Whitechapel Art Gallery

80 Whitechapel High Street (at Angel Alley), E1, tel. 071 377 0107. Open Tues–Sun 11 a.m.–5 p.m., Wed 1–8 p.m., closed Good Friday and Easter Sunday. Free. Wheelchair accessible.

The distinctive turn-of-the-century asymmetrically twin-towered windowless façade, with two small doors framed by a grand arch, is easy to miss because it soars up sheer from the pavement. Inside, the 1984 renovation has made the purpose-built art gallery – commissioned by philanthropists, including Henrietta Barnett, to bring culture to the impoverished East End – a white, airy, streamlined two-level space that shows generally two-month-long exhibitions of contemporary work by non-established artists who included, in the past, Barbara Hepworth. Once every eighteenth months, winning competition submissions provide a showcase of work by chosen East End artists. If you don't fancy Bloom's next door, try the Whitechapel Café at the back of the gallery, and on your way out you can browse the specialist Zwemmer Art Bookshop.

Christ Church

Commercial Street (at Fournier Street), E1, tel. 071 377 0287. Aldgate East or Liverpool Street Underground.

Nicholas Hawksmoor's landmark early-eighteenth-century English Baroque white spire was made stark by a nineteenth-century rebuild, but is currently being restored to its original splendour. The interior – one of Hawksmoor's most sumptuous and complex, with its clerestory aisles roofed by elliptical barrel vaults – is currently dominated by large hand-made fluorescent banners declaring, in bubble-writing, messages including 'What a joy to know the grace of God'. Christ Church works for the community – a rehabilitation centre for homeless alcoholics is housed in the crypt; 'crisis' news reports and contacts are pinned to the board in the narthex – and it is the venue for concerts in the annual June Spitalfields festival (phone for details or pick up a leaflet).

SYLVIA'S PEOPLE'S ARMY

Opting for a working-class mass movement rather than Christabel's favoured 'feminine Bourgeoisie' (see Westminster), Sylvia Pankhurst took her suffrage campaigning to the East End, where, says Patricia W. Romero in *E. Sylvia Pankhurst* (Yale):

> The enthusiasm of Sylvia's following was as much an outpouring of frustration against the conditions of life in East London as it was a desire for the vote. ... Even before [Sylvia] moved to Bow, she visited the area from her rooms nearby, walking through streets full of garbage and human waste. ... It was to cure these ills that Sylvia launched her utopian campaign for the vote in East London.

It was also because while Christabel was in exile in Paris (to escape imprisonment) she chose Annie Kenney, not Sylvia, as deputy leader in her absence.

In Christabel's paper, *The Suffragette*, Sylvia wrote primarily of her East End campaigning; even in Australia, their sister Adela Pankhurst recognised that Sylvia had 'started a party', so Christabel must have known in Paris; and Sylvia may have been responsible for leaking to the *Daily Mail*, in summer 1913, information suggesting that the WSPU was suffering financially from loss of membership and disorganisation. Emmeline and Christabel's decision to expel Sylvia from the WSPU was not immediate but inevitable; it was implemented in the autumn after the *Daily Mail* leak. Sylvia refused to renounce the WSPU name, however, and by May 1914 she claimed eight branches in the East End, with some sixty active members.

When Sylvia first moved to Bow, neighbours were suspicious, but even if there was a 'kind of inverted snobbism' on her part (Lord Brockway) she soon convinced them that she wanted to improve conditions and win the vote and, co-worker Annie Barnes said, 'everyone she knew came to love her'. She led demonstrations to Downing Street and Parliament, held regular meetings in Victoria Park and off Old Ford Road, and sent organisers from Bow to Stepney, Hackney, Bethnal Green and Poplar. But the East End working women had little spare time or money. Amongst Sylvia's more unrealistic pleas was for her East End supporters to practise 'self-denial' weeks – i.e. to deny themselves already paltry rations – to support the paper and the Federation, a WSPU method that worked amongst the middle classes but was hardly likely to be successful in the working-class East End.

Sylvia's fight for suffrage did not long survive the outbreak of World War I. Anyone of German extraction was abused and attacked, the Zeppelin raids caused extensive damage, and rioting frequently broke out. 'Alas, poor Patriotism,' concluded Sylvia, 'what foolish cruelties are committed in thy name.'

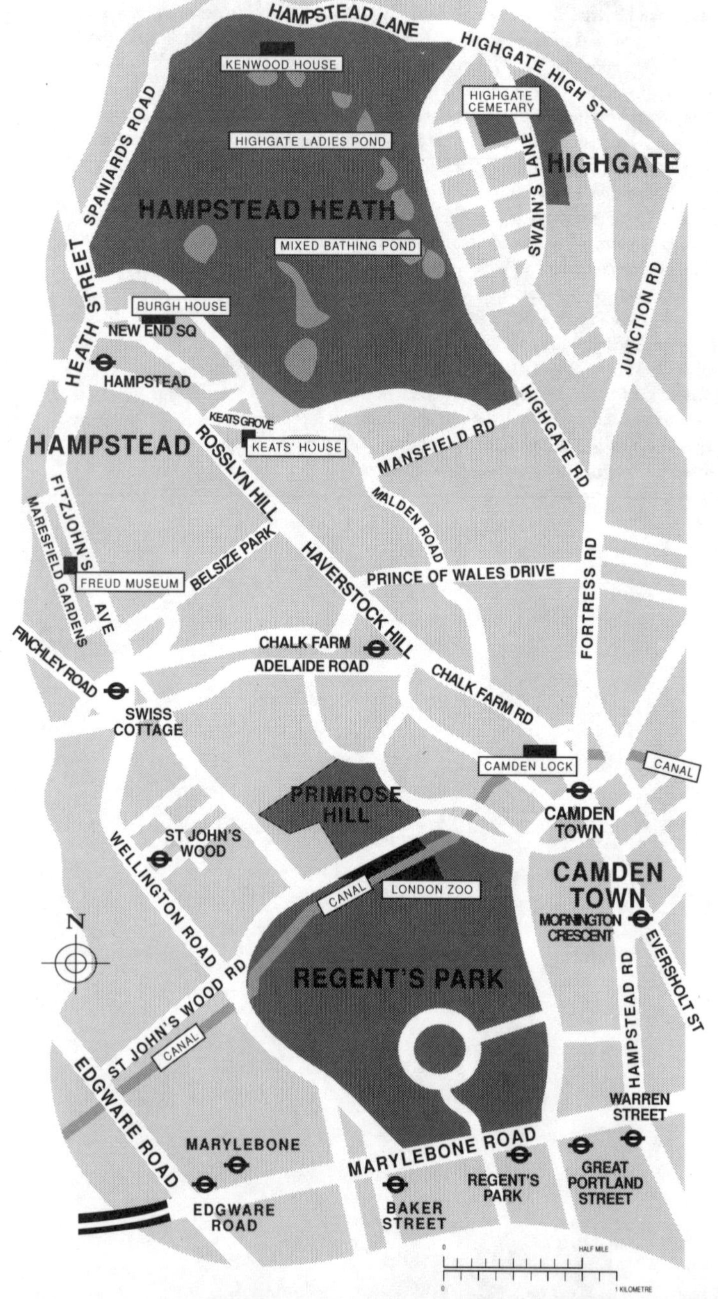
HAMPSTEAD LANE
KENWOOD HOUSE
HIGHGATE HIGH ST
HIGHGATE CEMETARY
SPANIARDS ROAD
HIGHGATE LADIES POND
HIGHGATE
SWAIN'S LANE
HAMPSTEAD HEATH
MIXED BATHING POND
HEATH STREET
JUNCTION RD
BURGH HOUSE
NEW END SQ
HAMPSTEAD
HIGHGATE RD
KEATS GROVE
KEATS' HOUSE
MANSFIELD RD
HAMPSTEAD
ROSSLYN HILL
FITZJOHN'S AVE
MARESFIELD GARDENS
MALDEN ROAD
BELSIZE PARK
HAVERSTOCK HILL
FREUD MUSEUM
PRINCE OF WALES DRIVE
FORTRESS RD
FINCHLEY ROAD
CHALK FARM
ADELAIDE ROAD
CHALK FARM RD
SWISS COTTAGE
CAMDEN LOCK
CANAL
PRIMROSE HILL
CAMDEN TOWN
WELLINGTON ROAD
ST JOHN'S WOOD
CAMDEN TOWN
CANAL
LONDON ZOO
MORNINGTON CRESCENT
N
EVERSHOLT ST
REGENT'S PARK
ST JOHN'S WOOD RD
CANAL
HAMPSTEAD RD
EDGWARE ROAD
WARREN STREET
MARYLEBONE
MARYLEBONE ROAD
REGENT'S PARK
GREAT PORTLAND STREET
EDGWARE ROAD
BAKER STREET
HALF MILE
1 KILOMETRE

NORTH LONDON

North London has urban village appeal – knots of thriving restaurants, bars and cultural life resulting from the area's historical development (a spread of wealthy spas and merchants' manors) and North Londoners' insularity. For residents of leafy Primrose Hill, antique-shop-lined Islington and 'the village' (Hampstead), anyone who lives almost anywhere else, but especially 'South of the river', is to be pitied (those in South London, of course, defend their patch with equal fervour). This feisty loyalty makes for great atmosphere. As well as the Zoo to visit and places of literary/psychoanalytic pilgrimage (Keats's and Freud's houses, there are lots of places to eat, drink or just 'hang out'.

Watch baseball games in **Regent's Park** and savour the central Queen Mary's rose garden before meandering up towards **Primrose Hill** (NW3), where there's sunbathing in summer, kite-flying in spring and autumn, and tobogganing if it snows in winter (watch out for improvised sledges, including erratic tin trays and dangerously bouncy industrial tyres). Or you could take the **Regent's/Grand Union Canal** route, which can – despite fast-pedalling cyclists on the walkway and flotsam and rusted debris in the water – be romantic at sunset. It can also be an enjoyable way of avoiding the Camden Town Underground crush if you're headed for **Camden Market** (NW1), and great for children – phone the **Laburnum Boat Club** on 071 729 2915 to find out about canoeing and narrow boating, or the **Pirate Club** on 071 267 6605 to find out about canoeing, dinghies and theatre events. Leave the canal at Angel Underground station, and at the south end of Upper Street you can join a young arty crowd in a proliferation of bars, cafés and brasseries, then take in a film (**Screen on the Green**, see Entertainment) or a theatre/dance production (the **Almeida** or **Sadler's Wells**, see Entertainment) or a puppet show (**Angel Marionette Theatre**, see Children).

North London Literary Women, particularly Sara Coleridge and Joanna Baillie Novelist George Eliot is buried in Highgate cemetery, poet Stevie Smith lived with her 'Lion of Hull' aunt in Palmers Green, short-story writer Katherine Mansfield worked from East Heath Road and contemporary novelist Margaret Drabble fought to save Hampstead's local library in 1993.

Sara Coleridge (1802–52) devoted herself in her Hampstead home to organising, editing and annotating the works of her father, Samuel Taylor Coleridge. She was determined to counter De Quincey's charges of plagiarism and wanton self-indulgence, despite personal difficulties (including recurrent bouts of severe depression) and the fact that she had hardly known her father (she said herself that she was more intimate with his friend, Wordsworth). She was clearly intelligent – having received no formal education, by the age of twenty-two she had mastered six languages – yet she insisted on describing her work as a series of 'humble tasks', and began her twenty-six-page autobiography only in 1851, when she was close to death, suffering from breast cancer. In September 1940, Virginia Woolf mourned a woman of unrealised potential – an 'unfinished masterpiece' – yet celebrated her editorial work as 'not self-sacrifice, but self-realization', saying that she 'found her father, in those blurred pages, as she had not found him in the flesh; and she found that he was herself'. Biographer Bradford Keyes Mudge (Yale) notes that 'Toiling in the service of Coleridge's reputation, Sara pieced together his fragments at the price of her own'; so that, even though by 1850 'she was an established figure among the London literati, as comfortable discussing politics with Carlyle or Macaulay as she was sharing literary gossip with Henry Crabbe-Robinson', she received 'little recognition for her labors'.

Sara Coleridge's intimates came to number another of her father's friends, **Joanna Baillie** (1772–1851), who is acknowledged with a blue plaque at Bolton House, Windmill Hill, NW3, and whose greatest asset was thought by some to have been her role as hostess of London's first literary *salon* and by others her breeding. In the *Blue Plaque Guide to London Homes* (Queen Anne Press), Martin Hall dismisses Joanna Baillie's poetry as 'little more than derivative, if not imitative of other great talents who were members of her circle'; Wordsworth said: 'If I had to present to any foreigner any one as a model of an English gentlewoman, it would be Joanna Baillie', and Crabbe-Robinson wrote in 1812: 'She is small in figure and her gait is mean and shuffling; but her manners are those of a well-bred lady. She has none of the unpleasant airs too common of literary ladies, even her conversation is pleasant!' Certainly, she is largely forgotten now, and she was perhaps best known during her lifetime for the famous men she brought together. Nevertheless, she did gain fame for her ten blank-verse *Plays on the Passion* (published in 1798 and 1812). One of these, *De Montfort*, was made into a popular play starring Sarah Siddons, and whether or not

Walter Scott was exercising 'patronising flattery', as the *Blue Plaque Guide* asserts, when he described Baillie as 'now the highest genius in our country', the comment is indicative of the wide renown she had gained under her own name.

HOLLOWAY PRISON FOR WOMEN

Holloway was described in 1862 as a 'noble building of the castellated Gothic style'. This 1849–51 prison building was demolished in the 1970s with only two decorative griffins saved, plus the foundation stone and its inscription: 'May God preserve the City of London and make this place a terror to evil doers'. Edward Jones and Christopher Woodward concede in *A Guide to the Architecture of London* (Weidenfeld & Nicolson) that for its function the 'castle' was outdated, 'but at least the building looked like a prison. The trouble with the new Holloway [on Parkhurst Road, N7] is that it resembles a local authority housing scheme with bars over the windows.' Chris Tchaicovsky of the organisation Women in Prison maintains that Holloway is, as prisons go, one of the best in the country. Built of red brick, it has been laid out on the village green principle, with grass and trees and accommodation in units of 16 and 32, each centred around common dining and TV areas.

Holloway became exclusively a women's prison in 1902, and by 1906 its first group of famous residents were passing in and out of the castle gates regularly: the suffragettes, who – many for the first time – now came in contact with women from different social backgrounds. Sylvia Pankhurst (see Westminster and The East End) described 'the shrunken forms of frail old grannies' and 'the tense, white looks and burning eyes of younger women'. Dr Mary L. Gordon, appointed inspector in 1908, contrasted most inmates' reactions to prison life with the suffragettes' complaints. Tasks in the kitchens and laundries – shovelling coal into the furnaces and polishing furniture for example – were considered light labour except by the middle-class women, who were used to servants and declared it demeaning. 'O! the ravages of prison fare on delicate digestions could hardly be exaggerated!' wrote suffragist composer Ethel Smyth (see p.169) of the food, which was, for many, nourishing. Studies showed that a large number of women gained weight during their sentence. 'In so far as the coarse food and clothing is a punishment to the well-brought-up prisoner,' wrote Gordon, 'it perhaps equalized things a little.'

Sylvia Pankhurst described the ordeal of prison reception. First breasts were bared for a perfunctory examination by a male doctor, then prisoners were required to bathe in a 'miserable place with piles of dirty clothing heaped on the floor. ... The baths were indescribably dirty', and the water was 'clouded with scum of previous occupants'. The prison outfit was 'dark, chocolate-coloured serge', and in the cell, mattress and pillow were filled with 'some kind of shrub'. For meals, matron banged the door demanding to be passed her 'pint' (mug), which was then filled with oatmeal gruel and water. Ethel Smyth found in March 1912 that she 'never got accustomed to an unpleasant sensation when the iron door was slammed and the key turned'.

The authorities' reaction to suffragettes' hunger strikes was force feeding. To highlight the horrors of this, Emily Davison attempted suicide in 1911 by throwing herself downstairs. After public outrage at force feeding, the Cat and Mouse Act was introduced instead, whereby women who had become dangerously ill from hunger-striking were released, only to be rearrested immediately they were well and showed signs of becoming active again. 'We were also charged not to submit meekly to "silly" rules,' wrote Ethel Smyth,

> commanded to rage against the dubious complexion of bath water, and generally render the lives of the Governor and his visiting magistrates intolerable. ... How we got the materials – calico, purple, white and green tissue paper and so on, not to speak of hammer and nails – I cannot remember, but designs and mottoes breathing insult and defiance would embellish the courtyard walls for hours before they were discovered and torn down.

It seems that warders often turned a blind eye. Mrs Pankhurst and Ethel Smyth 'saw more of each other than the protocol permitted. For instance she [the merciful matron] would often leave us together in Mrs Pankhurst's cell at tea-time "just for a moment", lock us in and forget to come back.'

REGENT'S PARK SEE MAP ON P.222

The land that was appropriated by Henry VIII from the Abbess of Barking for hunting grounds during the Dissolution of the Monasteries became Regent's Park between 1817 and 1825, when John Nash presented the Prince Regent with plans for a park that would bring profit for the crown by featuring grand stucco-terraced houses round the perimeter. Despite World War II bombing, most of the elaborately corniced and Corinthian-pillared terraces – named after the titles of some of George III's fifteen children (i.e. Clarence and Suffolk) – survive today. So too do Nash's plans for a curiously shaped lake (where there is boating), an arm of Regent's Canal framing up the west side, and a circular botanical garden, Queen Mary's Gardens, where in summer there's a riot of sweet smells and colours in the beautiful **Rose Garden**. A welcome addition that takes up a sizeable chunk of the north of the park is the **Zoo**. The park is bordered by Primrose Hill, a smaller, less formal park. In nearby Camden Town there is the famous wharves- and lofts-housed **Camden Lock Market** (see Shopping). Just south of the park is Madame Tussaud's (see Baker Street, and St Marylebone), and to the west is the area of exclusive canal-side houses known as Little Venice (for canal boat trips from Little Venice to the Zoo to Camden Lock or back again, contact the **London Waterbus Company** on *071 482 2550; boats leave from moorings at the corner of Warwick Crescent and Westbourne Terrace, W9, Warwick Avenue Underground or Camden Lock, Camden Underground; prices if you want to include Zoo admission are around £8 adults, £5 children; or without Zoo admission, £4 adults and around £2.50 children; the service is more frequent during the summer months – phone for details*).

London Zoo

Regent's Park, NW1, tel. 071 722 3333. Open Apr–Oct daily 9 a.m.–6 p.m.; Nov–Mar daily 10 a.m.–dusk. Admission £5.30 adults, £4.40 students/OAPs, £3.30 under-16s under-4s free.

Wheelchair access. Phone ahead to check opening hours of the children's Discovery Centre, and the various rides and feeding times.

The Zoo has various appeals, many of them unexpected.

If you come towards it from the Park, you'll see the landmark listed Mappin Terraces, which have long been deserted by their intended inhabitants, bears, and are described by architecture critic Gillian Darley as 'a ghostly range of sandpaper mountains'. First off, pick up a programme of events with a map of the Zoo from the information booth and decide if you want to meet Ming Ming and Bao Bao the Giant Pandas, or watch the elephant weighing, or get a special introduction to the Asiatic Lions. All eyes focus on the soft-bottomed bucket-beaks of the Pelicans as fish lash about inside during feeding time. The gorillas' similarity to humans, and their terrifying strength, keep a constant audience outside the circular Gorilla House. An architect asked, off the record, to name a favourite London building declared unequivocally: 'The Penguin Pool', a clean-lined white structure that suggests a 1950s Mediterranean lido. The Discovery Centre offers mask-making and the chance to look through a giant giraffe neck periscope for a giraffe's-eye view. All in all, judged nine- and fourteen-year-old sisters, 'better than Madame Tussaud's', but that's not counting the restaurant and snack kiosks, which are limited and pricey. You'd be better off picnicking in the park.

HAMPSTEAD AND HIGHGATE SEE MAP ON P.222

Centred round country manors that were desirable for being rural yet still within relatively easy reach of London, the neighbouring villages of Hampstead and Highgate developed in tandem through the sixteenth and seventeenth centuries until Hampstead got the edge in the eighteenth century, when supposedly health-giving waters were found and it became a fashionable spa. Today, with its smart High Street restaurants/bistros, chi-chi shops and glitterati residents, Hampstead is considered by some the St Tropez of London. The locals have long been committed to honouring Hampstead's past (see on for Burgh House). The area's attraction remains much as it was when Virginia Woolf discussed 'Great Men's Houses' in *The London Scene* (Hogarth Press), in which she contemplates the literary legacy: 'To look over London from this hill [Parliament Hill] Keats came and Coleridge and Shakespeare perhaps.' She notes that life goes on: 'the butcher delivering his meat from a small red motor van. ... And here at this very moment the usual young man sits on an iron bench clasping to his arms the usual young woman'; and evokes the sense of being outside London yet above it, not away from it:

we shall find ourselves on top of the hill and beneath shall see the whole of London lying below us. It is a view of perpetual fascination at all hours and in all seasons. One sees London as a whole – London crowded and ribbed and compact, with its dominant domes, its guardian cathedrals; its chimneys and spires; its cranes and gasometers; and the perpetual smoke which no spring or autumn ever blows away. London has lain there time out of mind scarring that stretch of earth deeper and deeper, making it more uneasy, lumped and tumultuous, branding it for ever with an indelible scar. There it lies in layers, in strata, bristling and billowing with rolls of smoke always caught on its pinnacles.

Hampstead

Burgh House

New End Square, NW3, tel. 071 431 0144. Hampstead Underground or Hampstead Heath BR. Near Hampstead High Street. Free. Open Wed–Sun noon to 5 p.m. except Christmas and Good Friday; Bank Holidays 2–5 p.m. Limited disabled access.

This cheerful local museum celebrates Hampstead and the history of the house, a square three-floor 1703 Queen Anne house that was, throughout the 1720s, the house of Dr William Gibbons. Gibbons was the canny physician who declared Hampstead's water medicinal and so enticed up to Hampstead Wells a cross-section of society, from court ladies to seamstresses, to take the waters, promenade in Well Walk and enjoy concerts in the Great Room after dusk. Later Burgh House residents included Rudyard Kipling's daughter Elsie, who wrote that 'the delightful old house and garden which we rented in Hampstead was a source of happiness to my father to the end of his life'. It was also a source of concern. 'Dear Babe', Kipling wrote to Elsie in January 1934, 'Now *re. William and Mary* [the house]: – Actuarially, one's rent ought not to exceed 10% of one's income – even with low rates. So, you see, you are rather committing yourselves at Hampstead. (By the way, no tenant that I've ever heard of does *outside* repairs on a three year lease ...).'

The ground floor features a room for art exhibitions (often of local work) and up the barley-sugar-balustered staircase (probably the original) on the first floor you'll find the local historical exhibitions. Hand-drawn maps and family trees trace D.H. Lawrence and his circle, Daphne Du Maurier's childhood haunts, and Mr and Mrs Constable's Hampstead life in the early nineteenth century. Hampstead artefacts, including nineteenth-century oil jars, are lovingly displayed; and the curators say they would welcome any additions. In the basement is a licensed buttery, or a short walk away there are the Hampstead Tea Rooms (see Eating and Drinking).

Keats's House

Keats Grove, NW3, tel. 071 435 2062. Hampstead Underground or Hampstead BR. Near Hampstead High Street. Open Apr–Oct Mon–Fri 2–6 p.m., Sat 10 a.m.–5 p.m., Sun 2–5 p.m.; Nov–Mar Sun 1–5 p.m. Admission free. Stairs. An appointment is always necessary to use the Memorial Library.

Although this square 1815–16 white stucco Regency house illustrates well how houses of its period were equipped and used, it is not exceptional in architectural terms. But it is sadly compelling for its literary legacy, for it was here that the poet John Keats lived from 1818 to 1820, when he was close to death from consumption and racked with love for his young neighbour, Fanny Brawne, to whom he became engaged but did not survive to marry.

'I will be as patient in illness and as believing in Love as I am able –' he wrote to Fanny in 1820, when she was nineteen. But he was beset with worries – first that she might want to break their engagement (which, he conceded, would have been 'very reasonable!') and, once she had refused to do so, he became concerned about alleged flirtation after he learnt that she had attended an intimate party of Maria Dilke's unchaperoned in May 1820. 'I *will* resent my heart for having been made a football,' he wrote. 'You must be mine to die upon the rack if I want you.' Fanny replied with some spirit that it was not her behaviour that was at fault but those 'friends' who chose to gossip about their love; he did not recant, but did plead that he had spoken 'not in the spirit of a Threat to you – no – but in the spirit of Wretchedness in myself'.

Well-wishers travelled out from London to see Keats, ladies of the local Hampstead gentry lavished him with jam and blackcurrant jelly, and Fanny kept him supplied with oranges. But friends worried that they spent too much time together – that her presence might cause the agitation doctors had told him to avoid, and that she might be exposed to infection. Nevertheless, they continued to grow closer, Fanny sending notes every evening, even if it was only to say 'Good night' – words he would then keep under his pillow. In September 1820, Keats set off on a supposedly health-restoring voyage to Rome, where he was to die. He could not help wondering: 'Is there another Life? Shall I awake and find all this a dream? There must be,' he wrote to his friend Brown. 'We cannot be created for this sort of suffering.' And tortured by thoughts of Fanny, he wrote: 'I should have had her when I was in health, and I should have remained well. I can bear to die. I cannot bear to leave her.'

In the right-hand parlour of the house, which was once the Brawnes' (what is now one house was two), you'll see tragic trinkets including locks of hair and engagement gifts; the left-hand parlour, which was Keats's, displays penned memorials. Upstairs you'll find the bedroom that overlooks the garden where Keats wrote 'Ode to a Nightingale'. The basement features a sparse kitchen and the gift shop.

Hampstead Heath

In the twelfth century it was prowled by wolf packs; during Henry VII's reign it was strewn with nobles' clothes being dried by washerwomen. Since then, the rambling Heath has been fiercely protected from development by Hampstead residents. Today it is big enough to accommodate a lido, three bathing ponds, a sports ground, an open-air stage, a museum, regular fairs, and winding paths into woods you can still get lost in. Sometimes on weekend afternoons you can hear the sounds of opera singers or violinists practising for an approaching Kenwood classical concert (see Entertainment).

If you're not native to London, a stroll on the Heath is a great way of becoming familiar with the peculiarities of Londoners' leisure habits. Couples who could clearly afford sleek mountain bikes prefer to creak across the Heath on second-hand 'boneshakers', a picnic balanced in the handlebar basket, suit tails and floral skirts fluttering in the wind. Some of the kites flown on the Heath's Parliament Hill, by contrast, are of the very latest design. The most up-to-date thing about the women-only **Highgate Ladies' Pond** is the concrete diving platform – the rest is, as the name implies, literally just a pond, with a boat floating in the reeds at the edge and birds' feathers floating on the surface of the roped-off swimming area. Most women who like swimming outdoors prefer it to the men's and women's **Mixed Pond**, for there is a spacious grass area by the Ladies' Pond that's screened off by trees. Even on not especially warm days, hardy Londoners sunbathe topless here (note: young children are not allowed in the Ladies' Pond).

Kenwood House

Hampstead Lane, NW3, tel. 081 348 1286. Highgate, Archway or Golders Green Underground. On Hampstead Heath. Expect to walk across the Heath to get there. Open Apr-Sept 10 a.m.–6 p.m. daily; Nov-Jan 10 a.m.–4 p.m. daily; Feb, Mar, Oct 10 a.m.–5 p.m. daily. Free. Wheelchair access.

Set high on Hampstead Heath, the house that was probably owned by the king's printer in the seventeenth century was revamped in the eighteenth century as a 'gentleman's country house' by Robert Adam for the Earl of Mansfield, and is best known today for the serene Kenwood Lakeside Concerts (phone for details) and as home to the Iveagh Bequest.

The house itself, grand white stucco apparently stretched wide across the brow of the hill, is a mixture inside of run-down and lavish. The library is spectacular, for holding books was only its secondary function – it was intended as 'a room for receiving company' – so Adam gave it fluted Corinthian columns and visions of majestic animals beneath a curved ceiling which he described as 'extremely beautiful'. The Iveagh Bequest is displayed with minimum labelling, as if in a home rather than a museum: key attractions are the Rembrandt *Self-Portrait in Old Age*, Vermeer's ringleted girl *Guitar Player*, and a whole host of posing and demure Gainsborough and Reynolds society ladies. The museum is a wonderful way to spend a sunny Sunday, perhaps combining it with a stroll on the Heath, a swim in the bathing ponds and/or cake and tea at the café's walled garden tables.

Freud Museum

20 Maresfield Gardens, NW3, tel. 071 435 2002. Finchley Road Underground. South of Hampstead High Street. Open Wed–Sun noon–5 p.m. Admission £2.50, £1.50 concessions, children under 12 free. Stairs.

First stop for most people visiting Freud's house is the couch – a cushion-and-tapestry-covered sofa – where the 'talking cure' took place; turn round and you'll see his study chair, which, American sex therapist Dr Ruth noted, is shaped like a woman embracing the sitter. The antiquities Freud liked to surround himself with make the **Consulting Room** rather like a museum. With the exception of the **Conservatory**, which has been converted into a Freud-artefacts shop, the other ground-floor room – the **Dining Room** – has also been kept as it was when Freud lived here. Upstairs has been changed to accommodate the museum's exhibitions and his daughter Anna's furniture, most notably her large weaving machine (she was a keen knitter and weaver – rugs are still made on her loom and sold to raise money for the museum; you may see bits of thread, clues to work in progress). The numerous photographs and texts (with English translations) in the **Anna Freud Room** are fascinating; the changing exhibitions in the **Exhibition Room** are thoroughly researched and illuminating; and in the **Video Room** you can see old footage modestly and engagingly narrated by Anna Freud, much of it shot by Marie Bonaparte, of Freud, often with his nose in a book or with all attention focused on his beloved dog, Jofi. You can ask for a leaflet, *Anna Freud; Her Life and Work*, which talks through her life with reference to various items in the museum.

Freud and Women 'Initially, Freud's critics ... refused to believe that women could suffer frustrations of sexual desire, since they were not supposed to have any,' writes Elisabeth Young-Bruehl in

Freud on Women (Hogarth Press). Three-quarters of a century after Freud had fathered psychoanalysis in Vienna, sexual desire in women was taken for granted and feminists were up in arms with charges against him including, write Lisa Appignanesi and John Forrester in *Freud's Women* (Virago), that 'Freud was merely a conservative Victorian patriarch who saw woman's primary place as being that of reproductive servant of the species or, at idealised best, as a civilising and nurturing angel, "an adored sweetheart in youth, and a beloved wife in maturity". To be part of one's epoch may not be a first-degree offence, but to universalise time-trapped prejudices may.' Some feminists, however, are wary of dismissing Freud completely, most notably Juliet Mitchell: 'a rejection of psychoanalysis and of Freud's works is fatal for feminism. ... If we are interested in understanding and challenging the oppression of women, we cannot afford to neglect it.' The British Kleinian analyst Hanna Segal is at once more dismissive and positive about Freud's input:

> I think Freud's theory that little girls think they have got a penis and then discover they don't is bunko. On the other hand, Freud was the first to treat women as human beings in the sense that he gave a proper place to female sexuality. ... And even more important, I think, psychoanalysis is the first organized profession in which from the beginning women were treated exactly the same as men.

Appignanesi and Forrester concur, saying that Freud was revolutionary because 'he listened acutely to his female patients and heard – beyond tics, paralyses, phobias, losses of voice – what they said, however disruptive this content may have been to current opinion'. He identified marriage and the *coitus interruptus* that almost inevitably went with it as a danger point for a large number of his women patients, positing that many neurasthenias and hysterias were results of 'dammed-up libido' and an unchallenged intellect during married life. For academics and visitors to the museum, an irrepressible question has often been: what of Freud's own married life and his personal relations with women?

After a stream of courtship letters to his future wife Martha Bernays, celebrating their 'courage to get fond of each other without asking anyone's permission', there is scant mention of her through fifty-three years of marriage that began in 1886. To his friend, patient and colleague Marie Bonaparte he wrote in 1936: 'It was really not a bad solution of the marriage problem, and she is still today tender, healthy and active.' Freud described in his dream book a woman whom he would 'not have liked to have as a patient, since I had noticed that she was bashful in my presence and I could not think she would make an amenable patient. ... The person in question was, of course, my own wife.' Freud's biographer, Ernest Jones, says: 'His letters and his love choice make it plain that he had only one type of sexual object in his mind, a gentle feminine one', but 'Freud was also interested in another type of women, of a more intellectual and perhaps masculine case' – including, he says, Marie Bonaparte.

Great-grand-niece to Emperor Napoleon I, and described by Freud as the 'energy devil', Marie Bonaparte was a woman who felt equally comfortable dining at Buckingham Palace or lecturing on female sexuality. Despite losing faith in Freud's conviction that therapy could solve her problem of sexual frigidity ('that nature made me, by sex, a female misfit – but otherwise, in the brain, almost a man'), Marie remained his devoted friend to the end, using her many diplomatic connections to facilitate the Freuds' flight from the Nazis to England in July 1938. By the time Freud arrived at Maresfield Gardens, it seems clear that the most important woman in his life had for some time been his daughter, Anna.

Anna Freud (1895–1982) remembered a childhood scarred by a dislike of school and an intense jealousy of her pretty elder sister, Sophie, yet for her '*Unartigkeit*' – saucy disobedience – she gained her father's favour; in 1899 he wrote to his friend Wilhelm Fliess: 'Anna has become downright beautiful through her naughtiness.' Once she reached the age of fourteen he let her listen in on the Wednesday evening meetings of the Vienna Psycho-Analytical Society. By 1922, Anna's first paper, 'Beating Fantasies and Daydreams', had come out of her analysis with her father, as had the confidence to deliver the paper to the Vienna Society and so gain membership. In 1923, after Freud's first cancer surgery, she became his chief nurse, secretary, spokesperson and colleague, and by 1925 she had become close friends with an American analysand of Freud's, Dorothy Burlingham, who had four children. It was in the analysis of children, mainly during her years in Maresfield Gardens, that Anna made her mark on the world of psychoanalysis.

But it was not easy, for London was the stronghold of Anna's rival in the field, Melanie Klein. 'For Klein,' write Appignanesi and Forrester, 'the child in analysis is no different from an adult'; whereas for Anna, 'the child is not a minuscule adult. He or she is *sent* to analysis, does not come of her own accord and therefore must be won over.' Alongside conducting fiery public 'scientific' debates with Melanie Klein and her supporters which became known as the Controversial Discussions, Anna and Dorothy Burlingham developed their Viennese experimental nursery project in a London ravaged by the wartime Blitz. The two Children's Rest Centres they founded in Hampstead in 1941 had obvious immediate war work functions, and offered insights which 'significantly shaped fostering and welfare policy, social work and paediatrics after the war in Britain and America', suggest Appignanesi and Forrester. Anna and Dorothy Burlingham concluded that for small children, air raids were 'simply a new symbol for old fears': 'We shall know that peace has returned when nothing is left for the children to be afraid of except their own former ghosts and bogeymen.' Until the 1970s, Anna Freud and Dorothy Burlingham continued to write key books that still provoke debate, and when Dorothy died in 1979, 'Anna mourned, wrapped herself in Dorothy's hand-knitted sweaters and carried on, battling against her severe anaemia, against a new host of her father's detractors ... and organising the second and third of the Hampstead Symposia' (Appignanesi and Forrester) until she too died in October 1982.

Highgate

Highgate Cemetery

Swain's Lane, N6. Archway Underground. East of Hampstead Heath. Western cemetery open daily 10 a.m.–4 p.m. with guided tours on the hour; Eastern cemetery open Mon–Sat 9 a.m.–3 p.m., Sun 2–4 p.m. Admission charge.

Come here to see the graves of famous people including George Eliot, Christina Rossetti and, perhaps most famously, Karl Marx; and for an eerily pleasant stroll in an overgrown nineteenth-century cemetery which was landscaped with winding paths and an Egyptian theme. 'In such a place the aspect of death is softened,' praised the *Lady's Newspaper* in 1850, when the cemetery had already been, for a decade since its 1839 opening, a fashionable place not only to be buried but to visit for the architecture and the views of London.

ACCOMMODATION

HOTELS

London's hotel trade has spent the past two or three years in a notable doldrum, and overall, it is definitely still a buyer's market. If you aren't too fussy about precisely where you stay, you should be in a strong position to bargain for a discount on that curiously apt term, the rack rate (i.e. the first faint-inducing room price quoted). That said, certain hotels will always be popular and heavily booked, including many of the recommendations below, so reserve a room well in advance if you have a specific location in mind. Peak bookings are caused in certain areas by major events such as the Chelsea Flower Show, or the Ideal Home Exhibition, as well as national holidays. The most prestigious hotels can still command very high tariffs, often exclusive of breakfast or VAT, or added service charges (check when you book). You can find accommodation in London from about £20 per night (for bed-and-breakfast, hostel or hall-of-residence rooms – less if you are prepared to share) up to around £2,500 for the poshest suite at the newly opened luxury Lanesborough Hotel. For a mid-range single-occupancy room with private facilities in a respectable central area, expect to pay between £40 and £100 per night, including VAT and breakfast.

Single travellers are always penalised in London hotels. Of the few single rooms available, most are unpleasant and poky or poorly equipped, while single occupancy of a double room costs something like 80 per cent of the double rate. If you are travelling alone you're bound to be clobbered, but at least make sure you get a decent room. If you have children, however, you can probably find a good deal (many hotels, particularly the chains, offer free stays for children under twelve or fourteen – sometimes even older children – sharing rooms with parents. Check that you get the right discount if you're a single parent, obviously; some deals specify children staying with *two* adults). Cheap deals are nearly always available through the large chains for weekends and short breaks (usually two or three nights' accommodation, with special deals for children). These can be excellent value, and are well worth looking out for. Pick up their brochures from any travel agent or tourist office.

In British hotels the time-honoured practice of tipping comes nowhere near the blatant extortion racket operated in some countries (for example, the USA). The successful campaign in recent years by such prestigious publications as *The Good Hotel Guide* and *The Good Food Guide* deploring the practice of obligatory service charges has shamed many hotels into a reassessment of their policy. Few hotel staff will refuse tips, of course, and you may well find the wheels oiled more smoothly if you produce a little financial sweetener for services rendered, especially if you stay for more than a night or two. But there is no reason to feel blackmailed into greasing every palm on the payroll for the normal service you would expect in a hotel. If staff go out of their way to be particularly helpful, such as booking theatre tickets or restaurants, some acknowledgement seems only reasonable, but it is entirely at your discretion.

London hotel rooms tend to be small, but all except the cheapest provide a telephone and television (often cable or satellite). Many hotels are undergoing constant modernisation and refurbishment, and have all mod cons, some with individual room safes, video recorders and fax machines. Increasingly, the needs of women travellers are being met with hair dryers and irons automatically provided in every room, heightened security measures, useful toiletries in the bathroom (one hotel group specifically trains its concierges not to blanch if asked for a Tampon!) and less depressingly institutional décor. If you are on a strict budget, go for a room without bath or shower in an older, mid-priced hotel (often 20 per cent or so less than an en-suite room). There are usually comparatively few of these, so you're most unlikely to have to queue for the loo, even if you have to walk a pace or two to reach it. Beware of pricey extras, such as telephone calls made from your room, minibar drinks, garage parking, and laundry services.

There is no universal system of hotel classification in Britain: the well-known motoring organisations such as the AA or RAC award stars according to the facilities offered, and the London Tourist Board awards crowns (for hotels) and keys (for apartments), plus a complex series of 'quality' gradings designed to indicate how pleasant an establishment is (obviously a somewhat subjective rating). Every classified hotel in London has to have a Fire Certificate and public liability insurance (regulations in Britain are stricter than in many other countries). The definition of a B&B is very flexible in London. Price tag gives no indication – high-class places in Kensington advertise as B&Bs yet will provide room service snacks; other places call themselves hotels yet have no restaurant facilities.

Payments are usually accepted by credit card (Access/Eurocard and Visa are the most widely usable; many larger hotels also accept charge cards such as American Express or Diners). If you arrive without making an advance reservation and without much luggage, you may be asked to pay in advance or sign a credit card slip. Ask to see the room first. Smaller places and guesthouses naturally prefer cash. You can book accommodation by writing six weeks or more in advance to London Tourist Board, 26 Grosvenor Gardens, SW1W 0DU, stating your budget limit (no charge is made). If you make a reservation through the Tourist Board less than six weeks ahead a booking fee is levied, and a deposit taken (subsequently deducted from your bill).

Hotels suitable for women travelling with children

British hotels have taken quite a pasting in recent years for their unwelcoming attitude to children, and comparatively few now dare admit to age restrictions. In practice, many town hotels are simply not suitable for children, and have no facilities for them. If you want to bring children to London, the best bet is to choose somewhere fairly functional, with hard-wearing, practical fittings and space to run around.

The large hotel groups make special efforts to attract families, particularly at weekends when business trade dips. Some very good deals are available. If you are travelling from another part of the UK, look out for packages including free transport on British Rail for children under twelve. At Ibis hotels, all bedrooms contain a softly upholstered bench seat which can double as a mattress to accommodate a smallish child (up to ten or so) for no extra charge (a protective wooden bar is added). There are three Ibis hotels in London (Heathrow, Greenwich and Euston). At Holiday Inns, children and teenagers stay free up to the age of nineteen if they share with parents on Weekender rates. (Holiday Inns in London are at Heathrow and Gatwick, Kensington, King's Cross, Mayfair and Brent Cross). Forte's Leisure Breaks offer no single room supplements and free accommodation for children under sixteen (separate rooms at Crest hotels – Bloomsbury, Regent's Park, St James's and Heathrow – or sharing with adults at the other Forte brands, such as Posthouse or Grand). Children under five get free meals. Lots of facilities are available for children (cots, highchairs, playrooms, leisure clubs with supervised activities, fun packs of crayons and puzzles, complimentary soft drinks as well as tea and coffee, 'Hungry Bear' menus for the beans-and-fish-fingers brigade, babysitting services, etc.).

Many of the hotels recommended in the following pages offer some children's facilities, including virtually all the top-grade (i.e. expensive) ones. Less pricey choices include the Bonnington (spacious public rooms, special family rates, unstuffy atmosphere), the Mornington (relaxed Swedish staff, light, modern rooms, filling buffet breakfasts), Knightsbridge Green (extra sitting/playing space), the Rembrandt (spacious public areas, swimming pool, undaunting restaurants), Edward Lear (low-key, relaxed atmosphere, some large family rooms), Swiss Cottage (leafy and gardened, spacious rooms, welcoming family atmosphere, children under eight stay free, some self-catering cottages). Avoid the chic hotels of Chelsea and South Kensington where lack of space, hushed tones and house rules prevail. Anywhere with priceless antiques is likely to look gloomily at prospective junior guests (though many a hotelier will ruefully admit that light-fingered adults are more of a risk than butter-fingered children).

Self-catering may be the easiest solution. Here you can come and go as you please, don't have to worry about getting anyone marshalled for breakfast at a particular time, and if you need to heat up some baked beans hurriedly at 4 p.m, there's no problem. The London Tourist Board produces a useful free leaflet listing approved self-catering agencies, and by far the majority of these accept children of any age. Ask for 'Self-catering apartments and accommodation agencies in London'. As an example, Aston's studios, for two, three or four people provide secure, peaceful accommodation near late-opening supermarkets and public transport at basic or more luxurious standards. (Astons, 39 Rosary Gardens, SW7 4NQ, tel. 071 370 0737; fax 071 835 1419 – very near Gloucester Road Underground).

Choices for Businesswomen

Many British chain hotels pay some attention to the real or perceived needs of the female business traveller, though in practice this may be little more than lip service. Women are now a significant potential market, and the hotel trade teeters uneasily from patronising gestures with bunches of flowers to an awesome barrage of security devices. Holiday Inns make more effort than most to satisfy lone women guests; company policy includes great care over details like not divulging room numbers without permission, and seating women sensitively in restaurants. Forte's Lady Crest rooms have good security systems, better lighting and a large proportion of non-smoking rooms (it's not that women don't smoke; but the ones who don't object to the smell more than men, so it's said). Most 'lady executive' bedrooms verge towards the pastels and florals in decorative style, with more than averagely ruched curtains and matching tiebacks. They contain hair dryers rather than trouser presses, and possibly even an iron. Freebies in the bathroom will probably be more lavish and feminine, and doors sport peepholes and safety chains. Good choices at the top end of the scale include Belgravia's Hyatt Carlton and its small sister the Lowndes; the orthodox, well-established Athenaeum, and the superbly equipped Inn on the Park. And if money is no object at all, there's always the newly opened Lanesborough, with its formidable emphasis on security and privacy. If you need somewhere to work or hold business meetings, the luxury suites of 22 Jermyn Street or Le Gavroche at 47 Park Street are extraordinarily comfortable and well fitted with faxes and phones – at a price. Somewhat less expensive are the sleek modern Scandic Crown hotels, with their fitness centres; The Edwardian group's successful evocation of those comfortable last days of the Raj; or mid-priced smaller hotels such as the Linbar group (Alexander, Executive, etc).

Apartments

For a good range of serviced flats in London (mostly at the top end of the scale), contact The Apartment Service (tel. 081 748 4207). As a general rule of thumb, one-bedroom apartments work out about 25 per cent less expensive than the equivalent standard of hotel accommodation. Most generally operate on weekly rates; others allow shorter stays.

Dolphin Square

SW1 3LX, tel. 071 834 3800

This large brick complex of serviced suites, handily placed for Westminster and Victoria, is definitely on the upmarket side, but tariffs are based on suite size, not the number of guests, so by sharing you can make considerable savings. Its attractively furnished apartments contain irons and hair dryers, decent cooking facilities and sufficient equipment to entertain. Other appealing features (all on-site) are the health club, with a large heated pool, a range of useful shops (bakery, dry cleaner, hairdresser, grocer, newsagent, wine merchant, etc.), an attractive restaurant, coffee shop and cocktail bar, squash, tennis, travel agency and booking service, etc. Prices range from £92 per night for a single studio to £228 for a three-bedroom apartment (three bathrooms); weekly rates are lower.

Royal Court Apartments

51 Gloucester Terrace, W2 3DH, tel. 071 402 5077

Eight large Victorian town houses close to Lancaster Gate and Hyde Park make a useful base of 80 apartments, all with private bath or shower. Facilities are not especially luxurious, but recently refurbished and clean. Some have hard-wearing floor-coverings suitable for children. Business facilities, a fitness room with sauna and jacuzzi, and 24-hour reception are provided, and rooms are serviced daily. Useful shops and restaurants lie just a stone's throw away, and the nearest Underground is a safe three-minute walk. Single studios go from £60 per day; three-bedroom apartments cost £200. Again weekly rates are lower. Superior double studios (£90) sleep three.

Hostels and budget accommodation

It is possible to stay in London very cheaply, if you're prepared to accept basic facilities or share rooms with groups. It's important, though, to look for somewhere with adequate security measures. If the front door is constantly left open, with no one watching who is wandering about, avoid it. Hostels, cheap hotels, halls of residence and other places housing young women in multi-occupancy blocks are regular targets for men with suspect intentions. The Tourist Information Centre at Victoria Station can make bookings in YHA or other approved London hostels for a modest fee, and you can obtain lists of these from the LTB at 26 Grosvenor Gardens, SW1W 0DU, tel 071 824 8844 for reservations. It's inadvisable to accept offers of accommodation from touts at stations or other arrival points.

Hostels

There are seven official youth hostels (i.e. run by the Youth Hostel Association) in the London area – at Earls Court, St Paul's, Holland Park, Oxford Street, Hampstead, Highgate and Rotherhithe (the last is the newest, with good modern facilities). To stay in them you must be a member of the YHA, and produce a valid card when you book. You can purchase a four-day membership for £3 at any hostel; otherwise YHA membership is valid for twelve months. Any hostel will book a bed in another hostel for you, and you can make advance payments by credit card to confirm your reservation. There's no upper age limit now on YHA membership. All YHA hostels have limited kitchens for simple meal preparation, and several London ones provide cafeterias too. Bed linen is usually charged extra – take a sheet sleeping bag if you have one. Rates are around £13 per night for an adult in shared dormitories, but concessions are available (UB40, etc.). Don't confuse YHA hostels with independently run ones – there are several in the Earls Court area, for example, not all of which are recommendable. An exception is Curzon House Hotel, at 58 Courtfield Gardens SW5 (tel. 071 373 6745) with cheap single, double and dormitory accommodation in reasonably acceptable surroundings. Guests get their own front-door key, and closed-circuit TV monitors comings and goings.

Alternative hostel-type accommodation is provided by the YWCA's Central Club, a listed building at 16/22 Great Russell Street, WC1B 3LR, tel. 071 636 7512; fax 071 636 5278. Rooms are fairly spartan and institutional but have TV, radio, drinks and telephone. Communal facilities include a coffee shop (vegetarian and health foods available), TV lounge, hair salon, gym and swimming pool (single rooms about £30, much less if you share). Both men and women can stay in YWCA or YMCA accommodation. Other addresses worth contacting are the Independent Youth Hostel Group (IYH), Glendale Hotel, 8 Devonshire Terrace, W2, tel. 071 262 1770 (smart student hostels in West London), International Students House, 229 Great Portland Street, W1N 5HD, tel 071 631 3223 (student accommodation with good facilities), or the London Hostels Association, 54 Eccleston Square, SW1V 1PG, tel. 071 828 3263 (over 1,000 beds in acceptable areas).

City of London Youth Hostel

36 Carter Lane, EC4V 5AD, tel. 071 236 4965

The latest jewel in YHA's crown opened in 1992. It is allegedly very popular with overseas visitors and young women travellers, though of course all YHA hostels are mixed and generally contain more men than women. It lies just a stone's throw from St Paul's Cathedral, and is thus ideally suited for exploring the fascinating City area, where there is in any case little choice of accommodation at any price. The City of London Tourist Information Centre is just a minute or two away. Inside the hostel is clean and bright, though the building is historic (formerly the Choir School of St Paul's). Rates are a little higher than in some of the older hostels (£19.30 including breakfast). Some single rooms are available, though none has private facilities.

London Hostels Association

071 828 3263

This non-profit-making organisation, designed to provide inexpensive accommodation for students and working people in London, runs ten centrally situated hostels. Many occupants are long-term, but there is no minimum stay period and rooms are available for single-night stays. Most are in pleasant Holland Park/Bayswater/Earls Court areas, close to Underground stations, and all are well kept, usually in large Victorian terraced houses which blend in discreetly with their smart residential neighbours. Facilities are fairly simple with washbasins only in bedrooms, but furnishings are clean and modern, with sitting- and dining-rooms, laundry facilities, TV rooms, etc. Security is generally good; doors are kept locked, and someone is always on duty to see who is coming in and out. Rates are usually quoted half-board, with good-value set three-course meals, but B&B rates are also available.

Railton House

10 Craven Hill, W2 3DT, tel. 071 723 5643

is one of the nicest and best-managed of the LHA hostels, with a garden and small patio (continental breakfast only). Rates go from £14 per night for a single room with breakfast.

Educational establishments everywhere are keen to maximise revenue in today's economic climate, and out of term time many student rooms become vacant. Systems for letting these are now much more organised than they used to be. A few examples: Goldsmiths College (071 692 7171); Passfield Hall (071 387 3584); Queen Mary College (081 504 9282); Polytechnic of Central London (071 580 2020), or contact Senate House in Gower Street (071 636 2818) for any of the London University accommodation. Short lets are not always possible, but it's always worth a try. Book well ahead if you can.

The Vacation Bureau (tel. 071 351 6011) books single and twin rooms during vacation periods at King's College's seven halls of residence. Some of these are modern functional boxes, but an exception is **Wellington Hall** on Vincent Square, a little way from the Underground stations but an altogether pleasant and thoroughly interesting location. The Horticultural Halls and salubrious residences of local MPs lie nearby, and the area is under constant discreet police surveillance, so it is relatively safe at night, though very quiet. The building itself is a splendid Edwardian pile in Tudor style. Rooms are large and light (the best overlook the leafy square) with washbasins only (women are usually allocated rooms close by the single-sex showers and bathrooms). Many original features have been retained (Edwardian fireplaces, mullioned windows, stained-glass windows and plasterwork ceilings in the dining-room). Public areas are sociable, and facilities for laundry, preparing your own meals, ironing, etc., are provided. Security is much better than in some student blocks in London, with video cameras and strategically placed reception staff, and the bar is open only to residents. Another of King's College's halls, **Elizabeth House** on Warwick Way, is allocated to women only.

En Famille

Another way to beat the fearful cost of London accommodation is to stay with a family. Various agencies will find you a room (LTB lists some of those it approves of in a leaflet called 'Accommodation with Families in London', but there are many others, some perfectly respectable). Sometimes you stay *en famille*, but this can't always be guaranteed (or avoided!), so make it clear what kind of experience you are expecting when you book. Some agencies have minimum stay requirements of two nights or more. You can book these rooms through the LTB's Tourist Office at Victoria, but you will be charged a fee and have to pay a deposit. Most cater for children. Check any supplements payable for private bathrooms, single rooms, etc., and whether breakfast is included. Location is all-important when choosing accommodation. Always find out how far you'll have to walk for public transport, and what kind of area it is. Wolsey Lodges, a consortium of private homes offering interesting hospitality and often a good dinner in high-quality accommodation (often of historic or architectural merit), has four properties in London. Contact The Secretary, Wolsey Lodges, 17 Chapel Street, Bildeston, Suffolk IP7 7EP, tel. 0449 741297 for a brochure.

Bed and breakfast

Many of the nicest B&B houses in London do not advertise themselves with 'Vacancy' notices on the street, and the only way you can find out about them is to contact an agency. One of the most impressive of these is **At Home in London**, run by Maggie Dobson (tel. 081 748 1943), who inspects all the 60 properties she recommends. Most of the owners are professional or retired people, including single women who specify that they prefer to take women-only guests for security reasons. Usually these private homes are elegant period-style residences in attractive, safe areas near public transport, mostly in West London between Kew and Knightsbridge. Vetted B&B in a pleasant home is an ideal and congenial solution for women travelling alone, whether on business or for pleasure, particularly if you don't have a limitless budget. Some houses welcome children, but make this requirement clear when you book. Non-smokers, pet phobics, vegetarians, etc., can all be catered for. Prices range from about £20 in the outer London areas to £40 more centrally. Another agency with properties in the West London area is **London Home to Home**, based in Ealing (tel. 081 567 2998).

Hotels

South Kensington/Chelsea

This classy bit of London has a good many smart, small hotels which feel personal, and are often beautifully decorated and furnished. Some are so discreet that they are all but indistinguishable from neighbouring residential houses. Sumner Place and other side streets off the Old Brompton Road are good hunting grounds. The area is pleasant and safe to walk about in at night, well served by public transport and black cabs, and excellent if you enjoy posh window-shopping and intimate restaurants. The price range is wide: if you are prepared to walk or take a bus a few blocks, you can find some surprising bargains. Further north-west is Earls Court, bursting with hotels and hostels, cheap, though rarely noteworthy.

Expensive

Blakes

33 Roland Gardens, SW7 3PF, tel. 071 370 6701; fax 071 373 0442. Seven to ten minutes from either Gloucester Road or South Kensington Underground, south of Old Brompton Road.

Fashion designer Anouska Hempel's exotic hotel is justly famous. Each room is a gorgeous, individual fantasy of silks, antiques and *objets d'art*, decked out in powerful colours (black is a favourite) and luxurious furnishings using classical and oriental themes. Inside, the real world evaporates. Public rooms are limited – a chic basement restaurant where celebrities waft through the soft lighting to nibble expensive, exquisite delicacies, and off it the small, opulently cushioned Chinese Room lounge and streamlined cocktail bar. Retreat to the bedrooms for total privacy and relaxation. For sheer style and hedonism. Blakes is hard to beat. It is discreetly well-equipped for business travellers too (full secretarial facilities, fax, courier service). For romantic interludes, some of the walls could be better soundproofed.

Beaufort

33 Beaufort Gardens, SW3 1PP, tel. 071 584 5252; fax 071 589 2834. Five minutes from Knightsbridge Underground, off Brompton Road, in a cul-de-sac next to Beauchamp Place.

Tariffs may make you reel at this small, privately owned hotel, but a glance at the tasteful lavishness of any of its 28 individually designed rooms gives some clue to its popularity with well-heeled Knightsbridge types. Fresh flowers and cool airy colours give the whole place a restful, feminine feel, and the elegant house cat Harry sets the tone, luxuriating on a sofa in the sitting-room. Personal pampering is the watchword here: a panoply of thoughtful extras deck the rooms, including fruit, chocolates and brandy decanters, video recorders and the sort of umbrella you'd be happy to carry down Sloane Street. Light meals can be served in bedrooms from 7 to 9 p.m., and continental breakfast is included in the rack rate; but there's a wide choice of eating places nearby. Owner Diane Wallis provides a handwritten appraisal of some personal favourites. Guests are given a front-door key.

Cranley

10–12 Bina Gardens, South Kensington, SW5 0LA, tel. 071 373 0123; fax 071 373 9497. Five minutes from Gloucester Road Underground, off north side of Old Brompton Road.

This small, American-owned hotel in three converted town houses is smart enough to feature in luxury Concorde tour packages for the American market, alongside Grosvenor House and the Ritz. It aims (more or less successfully) to give guests the feel of staying in a private home – 'as if your aristocratic friends have given you full use of their well-run London town house', boasts the brochure. Inside it's an extravagant experience of expensive fabrics and antiques. All the rooms are fairly spacious, and some have kitchenettes equipped with microwave ovens and fridges. Each floor of bedrooms is decorated differently in bold luxurious flourishes, and the bathrooms are particularly opulent. Meanwhile, classical music plays in the drawing-room by the entrance door, and breakfast is served in a civilised room downstairs. There is no restaurant, but snacks are served until 11 p.m. One floor is reserved for non-smokers.

REMBRANDT
Thurloe Place, SW7 2RS, tel. 071 589 8100; fax 071 225 3363. Two minutes from South Kensington Underground, close to the V&A opposite the Brompton Oratory.

There's nothing remarkable about the corporate style of this large well-placed hotel in the heart of South Kensington. On the other hand, its quasi-classical public rooms have a comfortable and relaxing air, full of plants, winged armchairs and sink-into sofas. A pianist strums from time to time, and there are plenty of spaces to read, work or sit alone without feeling awkward. Bedrooms are smart and well-equipped, and facilities include a health club with one of London's most attractive hotel swimming pools.

Moderate

NUMBER SIXTEEN
16 Sumner Place, SW7 3FG, tel. 071 589 5232; fax 071 584 8615. A hundred metres from South Kensington Underground, off Old Brompton Road.

Four adjacent town houses on this early-Victorian street have been skilfully converted into a most peaceful hotel with a casually urbane atmosphere. Security is reassuring (entryphone system) but unobtrusive. A recent programme of extensive refurbishment has smartened up many of the older bedrooms; all differ with a colour-co-ordinated mix of stylish fabrics, period furnishings and useful mod cons such as hair dryers. A number of singles are available. Rear rooms and the attractive conservatory overlook a quiet walled courtyard garden of classical statuary. There are two elegant sitting-rooms with open fires, comfortable sofas, masses of glossy magazines and an honour bar for drinks. Children under ten generally discouraged. Residents enjoy membership of a local health club at reasonable rates.

SYDNEY HOUSE
9–11 Sydney Street, Chelsea SW3 6PU, tel. 071 376 7711; fax 071 376 4233. Seven minutes from South Kensington Underground, near the Fulham Road end of Sydney Street.

Recently opened, this hotel is steadily finding its mark among the smarter sort of interior décor magazines. The moment you enter the reception foyer of this discreet town house, you realise you are in a world of self-conscious, deliberate Style. The walls have undergone expensive *palazzo* treatments to impart an instant patina of age and distinction. Bugatti furniture and Baccarat chandeliers adorn public areas, while bedrooms luxuriate in mini-fantasy worlds of Biedermeier, canopied toile or leopard skin. The dining-room glows in Chinese yellow and navy-blue wicker. Some may find it oppressively overdone, but aesthetes and eager frequenters of those classy designer shops along the Fulham Road will love a look at this place. It successfully escapes the tedious conventions of hotel décor. The ambience, though highly fashionable, is welcoming rather than supercilious, and the tariff is reasonable for this area.

ALEXANDER

9 Sumner Place, SW7 3EE, tel. 071 581 1591; fax 071 581 0824. Two minutes from South Kensington Underground, off Brompton Road.

This is one of the smartest of the Linbar hotels, set in several of the white porticoed town houses in this elegant Victorian street. Many of its neighbours are also hotels, so discreet that you'd never guess from outside, for there are no signs to tell you so. Behind the gracious façade lies a handsome reception lounge, curtains all swagged and draped, parlour palms in corners. Breakfast (a buffet-style affair – no enforced fry-ups) is served downstairs in a room of pale Chinese Chippendale chairs. Next to it is a small cosy bar-lounge with newspapers where residents only can have a peaceful drink without fear of being pestered or propositioned. The bedrooms are not exceptionally stylish, but restfully decorated in soft colours. All are provided with hair dryers and irons. There is also a cot available if you turn up with a child. Outside a pretty paved patio with dribbling fountains suggests tea or drinks on sunny days. The front door is kept locked to ensure privacy and security.

ASTER HOUSE

3 Sumner Place, SW7 3EE, tel. 071 581 5888; fax 071 584 4925. Location as above.

A winner of various Tourism awards for outstanding bed and breakfast, this family-run guesthouse offers civilised, comfortable accommodation at a reasonable price for this expensive location. It's a no-smoking house where many regular women guests appreciate the respectable atmosphere and good security, though if you detest a few mild 'house rules' it may not be for you. The front door is kept locked and guests are given a key to come and go as they please. Health-conscious buffet breakfasts are served in a greenhouse-like room (L'Orangerie) on the first floor, filled with plants and white garden furniture. Each bedroom has its own bathroom, a fridge and fresh flowers.

FIVE SUMNER PLACE

South Kensington, SW7 3EE, tel. 071 584 7586; fax 071 823 9962. Location as above.

Highly commended for B&B by the tourist authorities, this converted town house in a street full of similar establishments scores for its attractive single rooms and a pretty rear conservatory and adjacent patio garden where breakfast is served, and where you can sit at any time during the day. As is usual in these smart guesthouses, the front door is kept locked and you get your own key. Lighting and surface space are generous, hair dryers and steam irons are provided on request. All 11 rooms have TV and radio; some also have a fridge.

Inexpensive

HOTEL 167

167 Old Brompton Road, SW5 0AN, tel. 071 373 3221; fax 071 373 3360. Ten minutes from Gloucester Road Underground, near The Boltons.

This smart little place has aroused much interest in recent years, being that rare commodity, the affordable and acceptable B&B. It's slightly further from the shops and museums of South Kensington than many much more expensive hotels, but the massive saving on rooms outweighs the price of a brief walk or bus ride. Inside it has a positive, slightly outré style, with curious modern abstracts in hall and foyer. Public areas are limited to a simple breakfast room in the reception area, and one large squashy sofa. Bedrooms are attractive and practical, containing small fridges, Venetian blinds, and well-lit bathrooms with good storage and surface space. Furnishings are a mix of imaginative modern or more traditional Art Deco styles. Double-glazing screens most of the passing traffic. Children are accepted, but it is not really suitable for small infants. The ambience is relaxed, but an entryphone system ensures that Irish owner Frank Cheevers knows exactly who's going in and out.

SWISS HOUSE
171 Old Brompton Road, SW5 0AN, tel. 071 373 2769. Ten minutes from Gloucester Road, next to Hotel 167.

Lightning doesn't often strike twice in such close proximity, but here is yet another civilised B&B that won't break the bank, albeit with a very different atmosphere from its next-door neighbour. Plants and windowboxes grace the exterior portico and balconies of this Victorian terraced guesthouse; inside the family atmosphere is quickly apparent (in a slightly Spanish-sounding mode – the owner is Columbian-born). Public rooms consist simply of a country pine breakfast room with dressers full of china and dried flower arrangements. The bedrooms are neat, fresh and light, in fairly conventional decorative styles, but some are unusually spacious. There are no restrictions on children. Hair dryers and irons can be provided on request. Credit card payments are surcharged.

Knightsbridge/Chelsea

A cluster of hotels cater for the smart shoppers converging on Harrods and Sloane Street – many of those, predictably, are women. But you don't necessarily have to be rich to stay in this area; some places offer quite reasonable tariffs for this part of town. Several secluded places around Pont Street or Cadogan Gardens have good business facilities and quiet, well-equipped rooms.

Expensive

THE BERKELEY,
Wilton Place, Knightsbridge, SW1X 7RL, tel. 071 235 6000, fax 071 235 4330. Short walk from Knightsbridge Underground, past chic boutiques; unostentatious sandstone building just off busy road.

Elegance, authenticity and discretion are bywords of the Berkeley, newly reopened complete with the original writing room and Edwin Lutyens wood panelling. Counties women in town shopping with their daughters treat it as their town house – indeed, if you grow especially fond of your room's antiques and individual plush yet restrained décor, then the guest directory will ensure, if possible, that you stay in it again on your next visit. Entertain in the fine, formal restaurant, or dine alone in the

Mediterranean-style Perroquet – and later work up another appetite in the Roman-bath-like rooftop pool.

HYATT CARLTON
Cadogan Place, SW1X 9PY, tel. 071 235 5411; fax 071 235 9129

Large modern international chain hotels usually imply impersonality, but somehow the Hyatt Carlton avoids it. The plate-glass foyer leads effortlessly into the charming Chinoiserie lounge in sunshine yellow where tempting arrays of cakes are served, sometimes to the accompaniment of a harp. It's an excellent place to relax after battling round Knightsbridge shops, and if you can afford to stay, the facilities offered are exemplary. Bedrooms are spacious and restful with lavish furnishings. For the health-conscious or those smitten with guilt after the cakes, the Peak Health Club offers a panoply of keep-fit equipment (no pool).

LOWNDES
Lowndes Street, SW1X 9ES, tel. 071 235 6020; fax 071 235 1154. Four minutes from Knightsbridge Underground, east of Sloane Street.

This small luxury hotel is now part of the Hyatt group, and has had an extensive refit. Guests resident here can take advantage of the opulent facilities at the top-class Hyatt Carlton just round the corner. But the Lowndes is a much smaller and more intimate place, where country-house themes have been imported into the welcoming lounge by the reception entrance – a relaxing place to have coffee with the papers by the Adam-look fireplace. Snacks are available all day in the undaunting Brasserie, and the light, cheering bedrooms have many facilities amid good-quality repro or contemporary furnishings. Many of the hotel's guests are women, and it makes special efforts to make them feel welcome.

L'HOTEL
28 Basil Street, SW3 1AT, tel. 071 589 6286; fax 071 225 0011. One minute from Harrods and Knightsbridge Underground, in a quiet street between Brompton Road and Sloane Street.

A younger sister of the Capital a few doors away, L'Hotel has fewer facilities and less on-tap service, but feels more personal and secluded. It's also a lot cheaper (all things are relative!). Bedrooms are just as stylish, with Ralph Lauren fabrics in a French *fin-de-siècle* setting. Kettles and fridges stocked with wine and soft drinks are also provided. Downstairs the Metro wine bar is a convivial, chic place to meet friends, or dine happily alone on good French café fare, much less daunting than the august and celebrated Capital restaurant with its oppressively ruched Austrian blinds. Rooms directly above the Metro can be noisy. Women travelling with children will not be shunned.

Moderate

KNIGHTSBRIDGE GREEN
159 Knightsbridge, SW1X 7PD, tel. 071 584 6274; fax 071 225 1635. Two minutes from Knightsbridge Underground, opposite Hyde Park.

Though it's only a block or two from Harrods overlooking the hurly-burly of Knightsbridge traffic, the secluded air of this private, residential-looking block screens out stress. Its location and atmosphere make it particularly popular with women, and the feel within is predominantly feminine.

Décor is stylish, but restrained and unfussy. Tea and coffee are available all day in the Club Room, where a collection of smart magazines reclines on a large central coffee table. Many of the bedrooms are spacious and have sitting-rooms where breakfast (English or continental) is served. Lighting, storage, and soundproofing have been thought out carefully. The welcome is genuinely warm and personal.

Basil Street

Basil Street, SW3 1AH, tel. 071 581 3311; fax 071 581 3693. Two minutes from Harrods and Knightsbridge Underground, between Sloane Street and Brompton Road.

This tranquil, unusual hotel is much loved by regular visitors, many of whom are women. Staying there gives guests automatic membership of the women-only Parrot Club downstairs – a relaxed meeting-place of invitingly arranged sofas and chairs. On upper floors are an intimate restaurant, and a most comfortable, welcoming bar-lounge where one of the best-value hotel teas in London is served (a good place for a chat after Sloanish shopping bouts, or even a discreet assignation). Next door (same management) are a cheery basement wine bar and a cheap carvery and salad bar, both excellent and inexpensive places for lunch. Bedrooms are comfortable, but gently old-fashioned and unpretentious, some soothingly plain. For those on a budget, the ones without bathrooms are very cheap for this fashionable part of London. Regular 'Basilities' get discounts.

Fenja

69 Cadogan Gardens, SW3 2RB, tel. 071 589 7333; fax 071 581 4958. Just off Sloane Square, two minutes from Underground.

A distinctive, quiet hotel in a maze of dignified red-brick mansion blocks. It offers classy B&B, and its 13 rooms are all named after artists and writers with Chelsea associations – Turner lived here once. Paintings and sculpture fill the house, and many original features remain. Soft colours in bedrooms contrast with richer hues in the hall and fine stairway. Breakfast is served in the bedrooms; light meals are available at other times. The small lounge is less appealing than the rest of the house.

Mayfair/Piccadilly

The ritziest bit of the West End, and sure enough, The Ritz itself is here for those wealthy enough to enjoy it. And there are other choices, including such old retainers as Browns (perfect for tea and post-shopping fatigue), or the swanky five-stars on the corner of Hyde Park (Dorchester, Hilton, Inn on the Park, Intercontinental). Few, if any, match budget requirements, and women travelling alone may well be scrutinised carefully in certain hotels (well-known assignation points for the more upmarket sort of call-girl). Shepherd Market is where the streetgirls work.

Expensive

ATHENAEUM
116 Piccadilly, W1V 0BJ, tel. 071 499 3464; fax 071 493 1860. Midway between Green Park and Hyde Park Corner Underground stations.

One of Mayfair's most prestigious locations overlooking Green Park sets the scene for this long-established, civilised hotel. The Lady Athenau Club ensures a special welcome for lone females. As you approach the doormen are friendly, and staff give the impression of having steady hands on this Rank flagship's tiller. The clubby cocktail bar and its awesome collection of malt whiskies may suggest a predominantly masculine atmosphere, but the comfortable Windsor lounge is equally popular with men and women alike for morning coffees and afternoon teas with the papers. It's a place to sink into wing armchairs in pink brocade or Regency striped sofas, softly lit by Chinese lamps. The French-style restaurant's intimate alcoves and soft colours make it an inviting place to eat, even if you are alone. Bedrooms are exceptionally comfortable, spacious and well-equipped, some a little bland and over-co-ordinated, but all of very high quality. Those at the back lack leafy views but are slightly quieter. Bathrooms luxuriate in Italian marble and mountains of towels. The apartments, approached from a quiet neighbouring side street, are very luxurious and more adventurously decorated. Business facilities are readily supplied. If you're particularly energetic you can even take a jogging suit for a trot round Green Park.

THE FOUR SEASONS (FORMERLY, INN ON THE PARK)
Hamilton Place, Park Lane, W1A 1AZ, tel. 071 499 0888; fax 071 493 6629. In a small side street off the north side of Hyde Park Corner, overlooking Hyde Park.

Reckoned by some to be the most attentive of London's top hotels, this place prides itself on service. So if you fancy some smoked salmon sandwiches at 4 a.m. or a spot removed from your skirt late on Sunday evening, don't hold back. You'll be paying for it! Bedrooms and suites are superbly well-equipped; they even have US-style sockets, so transatlantic visitors don't need an adaptor. They are marvellous places to work, and most are large enough to hold a meeting of three or four comfortably. The conservatory rooms are unashamedly pretty, with glazed sitting sections full of plants. Among its opulent and extensive public areas, the foyer and lounge downstairs where teas are served beneath glittering Venetian crystal, or the prettily decorated all-day Lanes buffet, are two of the most relaxing. Bar areas, if fairly mannish in décor, are none the less salubrious and inviting to any lone traveller, and you can always go the whole hog in the formal Four Seasons restaurant, where Bruno Loubet's culinary muse presides.

Soho/Covent Garden

What a mix, from downright sleaze to the toffiest-nosed evening wear. There aren't many hotels here, but several can be classed among the most fascinating in London, matching that creative-and-media clientele. Most charming of these is Hazlitt's on Frith Street. For value, head towards the Fielding, just behind Bow Street Magistrates' Court. Most comfortable, if you can afford it, are Forte's flagship, the Waldorf Astoria, or two of the finest of the Edwardian group (Hampshire and Mountbatten). Parts of the area can be seedy at night, but it is well populated and rarely threatening.

Expensive

HAMPSHIRE

Leicester Square, WC2H 7LH, tel. 071 839 9399; fax 071 930 8122. On Leicester Square, two minutes from Underground.

This luxury hotel was recently created within the distinguished red-brick shell of the old Dental Hospital, and is the central London flagship of the Edwardian group. Facilities are sharp enough to please the most exacting business executive, yet the ambience is a clever pastiche of gentler and more courteous times, namely the Edwardian era. Décor and furnishings evoke gracious country-house living and relics of empire. Ceiling fans stir the air above fat-cushioned sofas, classical fireplaces, long-case clocks and oriental jars. The bedrooms are beautifully decorated in warm traditional styles – immaculate and inviting, though no discreet mod cons are omitted. The Hampshire's less expensive smaller sister hotels share similar style and facilities, though all are subtly different. For more affordable single rooms, try the intimate Cheshire on Great Russell Street, Bloomsbury, or the Savoy Court on Granville Place behind Oxford Street.

HAZLITT'S

6 Frith Street, Soho Square, W1V 5TZ, tel. 071 434 1771; fax 071 439 1524. In heart of Soho, off Old Compton Street. Nearest Underground Tottenham Court Road.

Hazlitt once lived in one of the three eighteenth-century houses that now comprise this enchantingly different hotel. It is one of the most idiosyncratic anywhere in London, and one of very few at all in this part of the city. Its proximity to theatreland, the opera houses, and a host of advertising agencies and publishers means that its clientele tends to the arty, creative, media sort, who breeze in clutching film scripts or music scores and retreat to bedrooms they regard by habit as 'theirs'. The hotel is by no means opulent or luxurious, but it is resoundingly stylish and interesting. The atmosphere is peaceful, private and notably lacking in hotelish trappings. Pictures festoon the walls, bedrooms are restrained in shades mostly of green and cream, with mahogany, pine and oak furnishings. Antiques and quaint objects abound, classical busts peering over the rims of vast Victorian baths, jardinières of ferns poised on every suitable ledge. Classy continental breakfasts with croissants and fresh orange juice are served in your room. A small sitting-room with an open fire behind reception is the only public room – a quiet space for reading.

Inexpensive

FIELDING

4 Broad Court, Bow Street, WC2B 5QZ, tel. 071 836 8305; fax 071 497 0064. Tucked down a pedestrianised enclave by the Magistrates' Court, opposite the Royal Opera. Nearest Underground Covent Garden.

This unusual find is much frequented by opera buffs and theatregoers. It isn't luxurious, but it isn't expensive either. The exterior looks much like a private house, an eighteenth-century listed building with diamond-paned windows. Smoky the parrot guards the reception area in a small pink bar, and may greet you with some squawked insult on arrival; other staff are more than civil. Rambling floors of small, simply furnished bedrooms lead off the narrow stairway, some split-level and oddly shaped, with bathroom fittings ingeniously shoehorned into minuscule spaces. Several have useful desks for guests who need to do some work, and hair dryers are provided. Hard to beat for an inexpensive, personally run B&B in this fascinating part of London, and there's a good proportion of singles. Children are welcomed too. If you can't manage the stairs, several rooms are on the ground floor.

Kensington/Holland Park/Notting Hill

Smartly residential, within easy reach of the Albert Hall and the shops of Kensington High Street. High-profile modern palaces like the Royal Garden look after you handsomely, but tucked away in the quieter streets lie smaller places of real charm, from Georgian style in Pembridge Court to that idiosyncratic collector's item, the Gore. The best of these hotels are affable to all comers, undaunting to stay in alone, and decoratively easy on the eye.

Expensive

GORE

189 Queen's Gate, SW7 5EX, tel. 071 584 6601; fax 071 589 8127. Top end of the street near the Albert Hall, just off Kensington Gore. Nearest Underground Gloucester Road, but closer access by bus.

Under the same imaginative ownership as Hazlitt's (see above), the Gore shares similar qualities of quirky, indefinable charm and flair. Frogs and hares sit at the feet of a shapely nymph by the entrance, though some guests have a habit of wandering off with these quaint bits of statuary from time to time. The welcome is personal, friendly, unobsequious, assured. The walls throughout this spacious building are plastered with a multitude of prints and paintings, an obsession of one of its art-dealer directors. Bedrooms vary greatly from tiny singles with stripped pine washstands to extraordinary fantasies of Tudor panelling, tiled frescoes and minstrel's galleries. All are distinctive and tasteful. The bar and restaurants attract a knowing crowd of outsiders who flock to sample Antony Worrall-Thompson's inventive cuisine, either in the august and sybaritic dining club called One Ninety Queen's Gate, or in the much cheaper but equally stylish Bistro 190, where you could certainly dine alone and be happily entertained by food, surroundings and unstarchy service.

Abbey Court

20 Pembridge Gardens, W2 4DU, tel. 071 221 7518; fax 071 792 0858. Off Notting Hill Gate, two minutes from Underground.

This exquisitely kept small hotel has recently changed hands, and is still settling down under a new regime. The owners aim to follow substantially the same formula of classy, discreet town house accommodation in this sought-after and convenient location. Inside, the elegant, well-proportioned rooms are beautifully furnished with antiques and lavish personal touches. Bedrooms vary in size and style – and in price, but singles are available. Children under twelve, however, are not accepted. 24-hour room service provides light meals. The reception lounge is the only sitting-room, and though gracious indeed, it is something of a thoroughfare. Breakfast can be served in bedrooms (continental only) or the conservatory (full English). The cheaper Holland Park Hotel (see below) is under the same management.

Pembridge Court

34 Pembridge Gardens, W2 4DX, tel. 071 229 9977; fax 071 727 4982. Just north of Notting Hill Gate, near the Underground.

An elegant, family-owned town house where the welcome is cheerful, personal and enthusiastic, and prices for this attractive part of London not unreasonable. The mood is upbeat, the touch sure, for this thriving business has grown steadily over the past twenty years. An unusual feature of the hotel is its collection of costume accessories (gloves, purses, fans) displayed in many of the rooms. Celebrities stay here from time to time, and it's popular with musicians and antique dealers. All the bedrooms are comfortable, stylish without being too insistent, and well-lit, with hair dryers and a fair number of singles. A newer extension houses a sitting-room and a jolly wine-bar restaurant (evenings only) called Caps (the owner's school nickname), where some Thai specialities are served.

Inexpensive

Abbey House

11 Vicarage Gate, Kensington W8 4AG, tel. 071 727 2594. Just off Kensington Church Street. High Street Kensington or Notting Hill Gate Underground.

This well-kept porticoed Victorian house suggests exclusivity, and probably a steep tariff, but the owners' deliberate and unusual decision *not* to go in for en-suite bathrooms and the latest designer fetish keeps prices remarkably reasonable in this fashionable part of the city. The original features of the house, particularly the graceful plant-filled stairwell and some splendid plasterwork, are much in evidence, but expect no luxury in the bedrooms. These are definitely without frills, though some are very spacious – useful if you're travelling with children. Breakfast is served in a light, attractive basement room. The owners live in the central section of the house (its grandest rooms), and keep a watchful eye on comings and goings, so a sense of security prevails.

HOLLAND PARK

6 Ladbroke Terrace, W11 3PG, tel. 071 792 0216; fax 071 727 8166. Between Holland Park and Notting Hill Gate Underground stations, just north of Holland Park Avenue.

A newly renovated upmarket B&B, inexpensive for this area. Bedrooms are given a theatrical theme, but furnishings are decent and tasteful rather than desperately *à la mode.* A small garden adds a dimension at the rear. There are plenty of attractive eating places nearby, and the neighbourhood towards the south of Ladbroke Grove is architecturally interesting and highly desirable, with easy access to public transport along well-lit streets.

Bayswater/West End

Plenty of choice here, but be picky – not all of it is recommendable or good value. For more peace, stay off the busier road systems or request rear rooms. Sussex Gardens and Queensborough Terrace are lined with hotels and guesthouses. Some bits around Paddington aren't very respectable, and some surprisingly prestigious hotels in the West End take backhanders from working prostitutes, so don't be surprised if you're eyed up in the bar.

Moderate

MORNINGTON

12 Lancaster Gate, W2 3LG, tel. 071 262 7361; fax 071 706 1028. Just north of the Bayswater Road, screened from busy traffic. Closest Underground Lancaster Gate.

This hotel has a distinctive feel the moment you walk into it. Perhaps it's the intimate book-lined library bar-lounge to one side of the panelled reception foyer, or the courteous and efficient welcome. The Mornington is Swedish-owned, which shows most obviously in the clean-lined, voguish décor of its light, immaculate bedrooms, its unobtrusive mod cons (including sauna and satellite TV), and the wholesome buffet-style Scandinavian breakfasts served downstairs. Staff are noticeably helpful and agreeable, standards of housekeeping are quietly high, the atmosphere is dignified but unstuffy.

CONCORDE

50 Great Cumberland Place, W1H 7FD, tel. 071 402 6169; fax 071 724 1184. Just north of Marble Arch, three minutes from the Underground.

A modest, somewhat old-fashioned hotel, pleasantly small-scale, family-run, and friendly for such a central and bustling location. The Concorde is a little sister of a larger hotel a few doors away with rather more facilities, the Bryanston Court. Both share the same cosy ambience of battered leather armchairs and oil paintings of unidentifiable worthies. Both are recommendable, but if you're on a budget the Concorde will save you a few pounds. It is well kept, but don't expect decorative perfection. Rear rooms are quieter; many are quite small and simple. Most have showers. All have hair dryers. A good base for West End shopping, and a more salubrious and personal choice for lone women than some larger and more prestigious hotels in this area, where prostitutes cruise the bars.

DELMERE
130 Sussex Gardens, Hyde Park, W2 1UB, tel. 071 706 3344. Between Paddington Station and Hyde Park. Paddington, Lancaster Gate, or Edgware Road Underground.

This street is packed with guesthouses of many kinds, some exceedingly dim. The Delmere is one of its brightest stars, well-kept inside and out, though its tariff is a lot keener than those of many of its neighbours. Some bedrooms are inconveniently small, and furnishings could be accused of prissiness in places, but all are in sparkling condition and very clean. The atmosphere is civilised, the management sure-footed. An attractive, comfortable sitting-room downstairs, with a gas coal fire and the daily papers, is a signficiant plus point. Weekend breaks are good value.

BYRON
36–38 Queensborough Terrace, W2 3SH, tel. 071 243 0987. Off the Bayswater Road, near Queensway Underground.

A more agreeable and friendly place than many around Bayswater, though there is no shortage of accommodation to choose from here, much of it ludicrously expensive. The Byron's effortful decorative ambitions fall short in some quarters: the *faux* marbling below dado rails fails to convince; the vending machine in an otherwise cosy country-house-look lounge is a mistake. Some bedrooms verge on bleak; others are much more appealing, perhaps prettily stencilled with prints of grand houses. Colour schemes are tasteful and modern with plenty of practical appliances, including controllable heating and air-conditioning, hair dryers and free in-house videos. Upstairs buffet breakfasts are dispensed in a chic café-style room with dashing modern chairs and stained-glass windows. The tariff is reasonable for the facilities provided, and there are quite a few single rooms, some reserved for non-smokers. Children are welcome.

Inexpensive

PARKWOOD
4 Stanhope Place, W2 2HB, tel. 071 402 2241; fax 071 402 1574. Two minutes west of Marble Arch, off Bayswater Road.

Few would expect such a friendly, family-run B&B house so close to the West End. The street's imposing architecture of classical porticoes and black wrought-iron railings hints at gracious living, and the reception lounge is certainly elegant. Upstairs, the bedrooms are simply furnished and show some signs of wear, though recent refurbishing has produced more co-ordinated effects in many rooms. Breakfast is served in the basement, in a cheerful room of bentwood chairs and framed posters.

EDWARD LEAR
28–30 Seymour Street, W1H 5WD, tel. 071 402 5401; fax 071 706 3766. A couple of short blocks north of Oxford Street, near Marble Arch Underground.

Blue awnings and a proudly displayed blue plaque declaring 'Edward Lear lived here' distinguish this small B&B hotel from the rest of its seemly brick terrace. Room sizes cater well for single travellers and families as well as the orthodox twosomes most hotels prefer. Guests are courteously received and then left largely uninterrupted. Public rooms consist of two pleasantly decorated sitting-rooms and a breakfast room lit by enormous French windows. Edward Lear nonsense is much in evidence on walls and bookshelves. Bedrooms have inoffensive floral themes, and some have their own bath or shower. Choose a back room if traffic noise disturbs you. The tariff is quite reasonable for a base this close to Oxford Street.

Marylebone/Regent's Park

Not exactly bristling with hotels, though there is a wide range, from the clean-shaven, well-equipped White House to lusciously interior designed Dorset House. For motherly guesthouses offering reassuring, good-value B&B, try La Place or the Blandford, both a deerstalker's throw from Baker Street.

Expensive

WHITE HOUSE

Albany Street, Regent's Park, NW1 3UP, tel. 071 387 1200; fax 071 388 0091. Just north of Euston Road, a stone's throw from Great Portland Street Underground (also near Regent's Park and Warren Street).

This interestingly designed block of flats was first built during the 1930s, originally very much with the 'man-about-town' wanting a discreet *pied-à-terre* in mind. Now in respectable ownership with Abela Hotels, it can afford a bit of mild titillation about its misspent youth and raffish associations with the Profumo scandal. A well-thought-out array of business and leisure facilities will appeal to men and women alike. Security is good, service is efficient, and its varied public rooms are perfectly pleasant for single women: among them a rusticised basement wine bar of beams and copper knick-knacks, a smart classic restaurant with a comfortably chintzy lounge area attached, and a spacious, airy Garden Café, which serves healthy but not obsessive coffee-shop food most of the day. Amenities include sauna and keep-fit equipment. US-style electric sockets. Weekend breaks can be good value if the weekday rack rate is too startling. A highly recommendable base in the King's Cross area, where a careful choice of accommodation is especially important for women.

DORSET SQUARE

39/40 Dorset Square, NW1 6QN, tel. 071 723 7874; fax 071 724 3328. North of Marylebone Road, near Regent's Park. Marylebone or Baker Street Underground.

A gorgeous Regency house on a corner site in a dignified square, which formerly served as the site of Lord's cricket ground. Cricketing themes echo throughout the hotel in commemoration of this association, but the exuberant panache of its décor and furnishings shows an entirely feminine hand, that of owner Kit Kemp. (Two sister establishments, South Kensington's Pelham and the Durley apartments on Sloane Street, show similar flair, but Dorset Square is better value for lone travellers.) Antiques, expensive fabrics, glorious flower arrangements and interesting paintings merge in harmonious but inventive schemes – each bedroom is a separate, dramatic statement, and a delight to behold. All have sofas and many generous extras. The restaurant and bar downstairs are plainer and a little easier to digest than some of the overegged sitting-rooms.

BLANDFORD

80 Chiltern Street, W1M 1PS, tel. 071 486 3103. In a quiet side street parallel to the north end of Baker Street, three minutes from the Underground.

This establishment is run by a hospitable but businesslike Asian couple, who offer simple, inexpensive accommodation and a lavish breakfast, for which they have won numerous awards. Public rooms by the entrance offer little more than a perch to wait for taxis, but the bedrooms themselves are well-equipped and unpretentious with modern, calm colour schemes. The welcome is friendly and caring, the housekeeping exemplary (the kitchen would put many a London restaurant to shame), and the atmosphere homely but unclaustrophobic.

LA PLACE

17 Nottingham Place, W1M 3FB, tel. 071 486 2323. Quiet street leading south off Marylebone Road, four minutes from Baker Street Underground.

The most appealing of several small hotels in a decent street of no great charm, but relatively peaceful and very convenient for Marylebone or the West End. An enterprising mother-and-son team run it, and have steadily upgraded it over recent years, so the interior may surprise in its ambitious, high-quality furnishings and stylish décor. Tall windows are opulently swagged and draped, bedrooms sport an array of mod cons, and downstairs are a comfortable reception lounge and a plant-filled bar of blond bentwood and rattan chairs. A simple menu is available in the evenings as well as at breakfast, though there is no shortage of choices nearby. Owner Mrs Jaffer is particularly aware of the problems faced by women travelling alone, and places a high emphasis on security.

Bloomsbury/Euston

Literary types converge here. It's also the haunt of many student and package hotels. Some near Woburn Place are very impersonal – no more than bed-boxes – but there are some nuggets of real character around the University area, such as the remarkably civilised Academy. Take care as you approach the King's Cross area. Tariffs may be low, but when you get there, you'll see why – it's London's prime red-light area. Cartwright Gardens is a good bet for inexpensive respectable guesthouses.

Moderate

EUSTON PLAZA
17/18 Upper Woburn Place, WC1H 0HT, tel. 071 383 4105; fax 071 383 4106. South of Euston Road, near Euston Station.

This Scandinavian-style hotel in Euston combines convenience of location with other attractions most successfully. It is modern and practical in style, so don't come here for any fuddy-duddy traditionalism. What you will get is startling efficiency and a friendly welcome, stylish surroundings, and superb facilities including free use of the on-site health club with jacuzzis and Finnish saunas galore. Perhaps with reference to the great Victorian railways nearby, an eye-catchingly designed garden-look conservatory restaurant called the Terrace sports curvaceous white wrought-iron pillars and spandrels. Light meals are available all day. Restful colour schemes and blond wood prevails in bedrooms. For business travellers facilities are excellent. The atmosphere in all is youngish, relaxed and non-sexist.

BONNINGTON
92 Southampton Row, WC1B 4BH, tel. 071 242 4848; fax 071 831 9170. Between Holborn and Russell Square Underground stations, near the British Museum.

At first glance there seems little to single this hotel out from various other functional bed factories in this area, but a short acquaintance with the place soon reveals a much more personal charm. Owned by the same family for many years, this hotel has changed much in recent times, but keeps its air of sure-footed management and friendliness. Décor and furnishings are fairly bland and predictable, but new facilities have been added throughout, and now it boasts a comfortable new bar-lounge area and a modern restaurant to one side. Bedrooms have also been upgraded, and many are reserved for non-smokers. Choose rear ones to avoid traffic noise. Families with children are welcome, and good-value weekend breaks are available.

ACADEMY
17–21 Gower Street, WC1E 6HG, tel. 071 631 4115; fax 071 636 3442. Near the University Senate House and the British Museum. Nearest Underground stations Goodge Street and Euston Square.

A tastefully sophisticated environment at an affordable price. Three Grade II listed Georgian houses have been skilfully converted (retaining original features) into a charming private hotel. A small cosy library overlooks a pretty garden where drinks and tea can be served in summer. Downstairs is an unusual and stylish restaurant and dining club called GHQ, offering interesting menus (including vegetarian dishes) in intimate surroundings, sometimes enlivened by jazz recitals. Bedrooms are attractive and individual, but some are smallish and insulation from road and internal noise is a little weak. Ask for a rear room.

Inexpensive

MABLEDON COURT
10–11 Mabledon Place, Bloomsbury WC1H 9BA, tel. 071 388 3866. South of Euston Road, between Euston and Kings Cross/St Pancras Stations.

The building is plain, and the surrounding area none too exciting, but the tariff of this newly renovated guesthouse is strikingly reasonable, and if you need a simple base near these northern stations, this is a good bet in an area where some care is advisable. Inside it's as neat as a doll's house (with similar dimensions), and all the rooms are fresh and clean. Downstairs a stylishly furnished breakfast room and tiny lounge with a modern sofa are the only public areas.

Victoria/Pimlico

Like most of London's main train station areas, Victoria is well-served with inexpensive hotels and hostels. Many of them are pretty dim, so choose carefully. Ebury Street is a convenient starting place to look if you have nowhere specific in mind. Several agencies at the station will find you a room anywhere in London, but all charge a booking fee (around £5). For more luxury there's the Grosvenor, of course, with an entrance inside the station, or the highly traditional Goring.

Expensive

GORING

Beeston Place, Grosvenor Gardens, SW1W 0JW, tel. 071 834 8211; fax 071 834 4393. In a quietish side street just off Grosvenor Gardens, two minutes from Victoria Station.

Three generations of Gorings have built up the formidable reputation of this old-fashioned Edwardian hotel, with meticulous attention to every last detail of housekeeping. It gives the impression of being thoroughly safe, respectable, and old-fashioned, even a bit staid. Décor is smartly contemporary in a traditional idiom. Service belongs to a bygone era, and staff are welcoming to any unannounced arrival. The bar-lounge is a charming room for tea or coffee, alone or accompanied. A life-size model sheep snuggles by an open fire, and there are plenty of papers and magazines to read. The glazed bar area overlooks a peaceful, private formal garden (no access, unfortunately, to hotel guests). The restaurant (no jeans allowed) is flamboyantly decorated and eye-catching in royal blue and yellow – though food is not the hotel's strongest point. Bedrooms vary, but are mostly quite restrained in warm deep colours, with Edwardian brass beds. All are exceptionally comfortable and well-equipped.

Moderate

EBURY COURT

24/32 Ebury Street, SW1W 0LU, tel. 071 730 8147; fax 071 823 5966. Three minutes from Victoria Station.

This rambling warren of a hotel occupies several adjacent Victorian terraced houses in a street of many small guesthouses. It has been in the same family for many years, and feels very much like a private home. Recently, after a change of ownership (from mother to daughter and son-in-law), it has been extended and renovated, with a corresponding increase in tariffs. But to the relief of many regular visitors, the essential simplicity and personal feel of the place remain. It is by far the best bet for accommodation on this street, with plenty of inexpensive single rooms (some tastefully plain and without bathrooms) and a family room. Other rooms are more elaborately furnished with four-posters and canopy drapes. Antiques and traditional furniture are sprinkled throughout the hotel. Public rooms are small but numerous, including a pretty basement breakfast room with cushioned alcoves, a black leather bar, a smarter restaurant upstairs serving a short lunch and dinner menu, and a dignified little sitting-room. Breakfasts are notably good, with eggs six ways and haddock or kippers if you're lucky. Bathrobes are provided in rooms without private facilities. Discounts and weekend breaks make it more affordable in the winter months.

Inexpensive

ELIZABETH

37 Eccleston Square, SW1V 1PB, tel. 071 828 6812. A short walk south-east of Victoria Station.

This tall Victorian house overlooks a pleasant London square, and is one of the better-kept buildings among faded terraces of erstwhile grand buildings. Neither public rooms nor bedrooms give much lift to the heartstrings, being furnished in a mix of genteel dowdiness and functional modern fittings, but the place is well run and clean, welcoming and salubrious, and above all, inexpensive. Recently the Elizabeth won an award for service, and was commended for good breakfasts. You could do a great deal worse round here for these prices.

WINDERMERE

142–144 Warwick Way, SW1V 4JE, tel. 071 834 5163. Seven minutes south of Victoria Station.

The road is busy, the surroundings are somewhat bleak, but the well-kept exterior of this Victorian house stands out from the neighbours – its period architectural features carefully preserved, welcoming carriage lamps by the door. Inside, the favourable impressions are sustained. It is modern, perhaps a little grandiosely soft-furnished in parts, but certainly effortful, with a pleasant breakfast-room-cum-coffee-shop downstairs, where snacks and drinks are available all day. Bedrooms are light and clean, with curtains of heavy glazed chintz and sensible modern fittings.

COLLIN HOUSE

104 Ebury Street, SW1W 9QD, tel. 071 730 8031. West of Victoria Station, a block from Buckingham Palace Road.

Little but an almost illegible nameplate distinguishes this small private guesthouse from many others in the street at first, but a tap at the door quickly identifies this as one of the stars. It's not at all fancy, but it is friendly and reliable, with neat little bedrooms, practically fitted. Breakfast is served in a minute basement room cheered up with landscape photographs and honey pine furnishings.

WOODVILLE HOUSE

107 Ebury Street, SW1W 9QU, tel. 071 730 1048. Location as above.

Another welcome addition to that rare breed, the agreeable, affordable B&B.

Though it's a little more expensive than Collin House, in the same street, this well-kept shuttered Georgian guesthouse offers slightly more in terms of facilities, having a more spacious breakfast room – imaginatively, if rather busily, decorated in a series of intimate spaces – and a garden for summer use. None of the bedrooms, however, has an en-suite bathroom. Maximum use is made of the house's limited internal dimensions, and bedrooms are cleverly squeezed into apparently impossible spaces, with doll's house armchairs and plumbing arrangements. All the rooms have hair dryers, and both single and family rooms are available. If you don't mind sharing a bathroom and keeping your elbows in, Woodville House makes a thoroughly civilised and convenient base. It's worth booking ahead; competition from discerning budget-conscious visitors can be fierce.

Outer suburbs

It seems a mystery, but some of London's apparently most attractive areas are virtual deserts as far as hotels are concerned. Kew, Chiswick, Hampstead, Highgate, are very poorly served with anything other than commercial hotels. Yet there are great advantages in staying outside the Great Wen. Besides the fact that it's a lot quieter, you can bring a car, ditch it locally and travel up to town by public transport. The best bet for value and general pleasantness is to choose a bed-and-breakfast home from a reputable agency (see page 243). The few hotels listed here are far-flung geographically, but among the scarce places of real character. Richmond has several acceptable hotels (best is the Petersham, with a splendid view of the Thames), but beware aircraft noise.

Moderate

SWISS COTTAGE

4 Adamson Road, NW3 3HP, tel. 071 722 2281; fax 071 483 4588. Two minutes north-east of Swiss Cottage Underground station.

The neighbourhood is desirable, transport connections are good – and you even stand the chance of a parking place outside this place, where you're promised a highly respectable and pleasantly old-fashioned stay. Solid antiques mingle casually with contract repro and a slightly bizarre collection of paintings. The bedrooms are mostly spacious and comfortably furnished, and there are many homely touches such as bowls of fruit and plenty of flowers. Sandwiches and snacks are served in the bar, and an appetising range of à la carte dishes in the dining-room. Breakfasts are recommended. Garden cottages and various annexes offer additional accommodation, some self-catering. A healthy proportion of single rooms suggests a welcome for lone travellers. Children under eight stay free if they share a room with parents.

Inexpensive

NO. 7 GUEST HOUSE

7 Josephine Avenue, SW2 2JU, tel. 081 674 1880, fax 081 671 6032. On an elegant curving avenue set back from the road; about a ten minute walk from Brixton Underground; some women are wary of Brixton – arrive by taxi and use cabs until you feel comfortable with the area.

This is primarily for gay men, but lesbian women are more than welcome and bi-sexual women 'will be accepted', says the manager. The four en-suite rooms are done out pine and patchwork country style with TVs secreted near the ceiling. Warm and friendly large breakfast room and conservatory seating area. You can track down some of Brixton's size-able lesbian population at the gay-friendly Fridge nightclub and – along with a large number of trendy south Londoners – at the Brixtonian (see Entertainment and Eating and Drinking).

Kingston/Teddington

Moderate

KINGSTON LODGE

Kingston Hill, Kingston upon Thames, Surrey KT2 7NP, tel. 081 541 4481. Five minutes' walk from Norbiton BR Station.

There are many good reasons for staying out of town, and this suburban outpost of the Forte empire isn't a bad option, especially if you want to bring a car with you. It's on a fairly busy road, but there are plenty of rear rooms, and the location is attractive, with several BR stations an easy short drive away, where you can park and get up to town on reasonably efficient and regular train services. Public areas ramble from the reception desk, split-level and open-plan but given homely touches with relaxing blue and cream colour schemes and Adam-style fireplaces where gas coal fires burn. A conservatory extension overlooking a pretty courtyard garden houses the dining area down a few steps, shielded from bright sunlight by soft, billowy white blinds. Rooms are pleasant and unsurprising, and the hotel has a small-scale, personal feel, albeit with a few signs of wear.

Inexpensive

CHASE LODGE

10 Park Road, Hampton Wick, Kingston, Surrey KT1 4AS, tel. 081 943 1862. Three minutes' walk from Hampton Wick Station.

If you have a car, you can park outside; if you don't have one, it's a very short safe walk to the nearest station with regular services up to town. Hampton Wick is one of the pleasantest of London's outlying village suburbs, with the wide green spaces of Hampton Court and Bushy Park to roam in, the river, and plenty of upmarket shops and restaurants within walking distance or in nearby Richmond or Kew. You're just off the flight path here, so plane noise isn't a serious problem as it is further north. Nigel and Denise Dove have run this enterprising B&B in a modest Victorian house for the past few years, and steadily upgraded it. Now dinners are served in an airy conservatory room and smart little bar-lounge. Bedrooms are generally small, but pretty and personal in cotttagey styles with pine or Victorian furnishings. Bathrooms are squeezed in wherever possible. Several rooms are in a garden annexe. One, for more romantic interludes, has an exotic tented ceiling of green and red fabric.

EATING AND DRINKING

EATING

You'll find a wider range of international cuisines in London than in any other city in Europe. Until cookery writer Elizabeth David introduced Britons to Mediterranean cooking in the 1960s, the British were on the whole uninterested in experimenting with other nations' cuisines, which meant that when Thai, Swedish, Lebanese, Indian restaurants and more opened, they remained untampered with, and most continue to be deliciously authentic. You can also try an impressive variety of traditional British foods, from cheap snack jellied eels and whelks bought on street corners to big bacon-and-egg breakfasts in cafés known as 'greasy spoons' to hearty dinners of steak and kidney pudding in the oldest restaurant in London, Rules. Eating healthily is getting easier and more enjoyable as a fast-increasing number of restaurants reduce the cream factor and include vegetarian and steamed fish dishes on their menus. 'In' food has been new-wave Italian for a while, and it is becoming increasingly popular to serve traditional 'grandmothers' cooking-style English food – oxtail soup, bread and butter pudding, etc.

The recession has helped diners. Poor-value restaurants have closed; top-quality restaurants have started offering low-priced set lunches and pre-theatre menus. Eating with a female friend in a Michelin star restaurant is not likely to be an awkward experience, because the staff and other diners are there primarily for the food. Dining alone, however, is another matter. The British are not very good at making solo women feel comfortable. The formal yet still amiable service of French waiters and the frank, chatty approach of American staff can make French and American restaurants sound choices. Always reserve in advance to let the restaurant know you'll be a woman alone, and take a book or notepad so that you can feel busy if people-watching makes you uncomfortable. If there's any attempt to put you by the toilets in a dingy corner, simply politely demand a better seat.

If you want a high-quality evening meal, smart restaurants such as the Dorchester, Claridges, the Intercontinental and the Four Seasons have staff who are old-fashionedly polite and tables that are widely spaced. Since women alone are often more welcomed at lunchtime by restaurants, you'll get a greater choice of places where you feel comfortable if you swap your main meal to lunchtime and have a light beer-and-sandwich supper in relaxed brasseries and grills in the evenings. (Women with children see Children in Practicalities.) Over the Christmas period many restaurants close – hotel restaurants are the best bet, but for Christmas Day itself you should book well ahead. Some restaurants close in August for a holiday break.

AFTERNOON TEA

Afternoon tea – that is, tea and cakes and small crustless sandwiches at about 3–4 p.m. – is a British institution, and here are some of the places where it's traditionally taken (expect to pay around £10–£15 for the full works):

The Dorchester (*55 Park Lane, W1, tel. 071 629 8888*). Fresh flowers, dainty china, black-tails service and often Gershwin played on the piano while you luxuriate in the newly done out grand chandelier and gilt Dorchester hotel for hours. There's no pressure to hurry your Viennese pastries and scones with thick Devon cream.

Palm Court, the Ritz (*Piccadilly, W1. tel. 071 493 8181*). This is such a tourist attraction that it's wise to book well ahead, and you can't expect to hang around for long. Amazing chintzy setting with lots of marble, mirrors, pink damask and tinkling live harpsichordist.

Fortnum and Mason (*Fountain Restaurant and St James Restaurant, 181 Piccadilly, W1, tel. 071 734 8040*). Tea in the St James Restaurant is more old-fashionedly formal, with military pictures and heavy wallpaper; the Fountain Restaurant is the airy ground-floor one with delicately coloured murals of Mr Fortnum and his associate Mr Mason on trips round the world in search of the very best tea (if you don't want the cream tea, the Fountain's ice creams and sorbets are considered by those in the know to be excellent). Lots of silver; great dated atmosphere.

Browns (*Dover St, W1, tel. 071 493 6022*). 1950s-style nursery tea in an English country-house setting with lots of sofas and a roaring fire in winter. No pressure to eat up and leave.

Many women won't go alone to pubs and some make a rule of avoiding them even when they're with friends, preferring wine bars. Most Central London pubs are fine midweek, though, and unless you get harangued by someone who is very drunkenly persistent, most chat-ups are quite easy to put off. Not replying is one of the best options. Often it is the pubs that serve real ale that are least threatening, because punters are there for the quality of the beer (the Campaign for Real Ale, or CAMRA, publishes guides – see Recommended Books). Friday and Saturday nights in pubs, however, can be rowdy and boys-out-on-the-towny, which is OK if you're with friends but best avoided if you're alone. Hotel bars are not necessarily good places to drink alone, as there's an outside chance that you might be taken for a prostitute looking for work. Sit near the bar staff, say you won't be joined by anyone and ask if they'd see to it that you remain undisturbed.

The listings below give you an idea of what to expect, and pick out some of the best restaurants and bars for women. A good up-to-date annual restaurant listings that is pretty comprehensive but, some say, not so good on top-range restaurants is the *Time Out Guide to Eating and Drinking in London* (£6.99, available from good newsagents and most bookshops). Of the newspaper restaurant critics, the *Evening Standard*'s Fay Maschler is one of the most accurate. If a restaurant is bad she'll say so, regardless of the establishment's prestige; and she'll pick out tiny back-street restaurants that are wonderful value. *Time Out* magazine's weekly restaurant highlight section is also good, picking out new and newly refurbished restaurants.

Regarding categorisations of the listings, **budget** means you can eat for around £5 and certainly not much more than a tenner per person. **Moderate** means you can spend anything between £10 and £50, depending how you order. **Expensive** means you can't get away with spending much less than £50 a head, and you might receive a bill of substantially more.

Please note that all the opening hours listed are correct at the time of going to press, but restaurants do change their hours.

LESBIAN PUBS, BARS AND CAFÉS

London's lesbians are celebrating the power of the pink pound, noting that many of the new bars that are opening are lesbian and gay, and declaring that the trend will continue.

Angel Café and Bar (*65 Graham Street, N1*). This chic airy chrome bar/café hidden behind Venetian blinds can be hard to find but is worth the effort. Friendly, with a mixed clientele, it has gay and lesbian newspapers spread about for you to read; it's popular with women. Good food selection.

Brixtonian Backayard (*4 Neal's Yard, WC2, tel. 071 240 2769; Covent Garden Underground*). At the moment Saturdays are women-only nights (phone to check). All week though, this colourful designery mauve-and-orange washing-strung rum bar in the heart of Covent Garden is lesbian-friendly. As it's a bit hard to find, tucked into a new brick complex, there's an outside chance that it may not last – it's well worth checking to find out.

Duke of Clarence (*140 Rotherfield Street, N1, tel. 071 226 6526; Highbury and Islington Underground*). A friendly pub with an open fire and a women-only room.

Duke of Wellington (*119 Ball's Pond Road, N1, tel. 071 249 3729; Highbury and Islington Underground then 30 or 277 bus*). There's a women-only back room (with pool table), which some find a bit tuah-edged, preferring to stick to the mellow, lesbian-friendly main bar of this traditional English pub. When lesbian/women bands play, the entire pub becomes women-dominated. A fair way out of the centre of London but in the heart of Hackney, the area that's said to have the largest lesbian population in Europe.

Drill Hall (*16 Chenies Street, WC1E 7ET, tel. 071 631 1253; Goodge Street Underground*). Women-only bar Monday nights; vegetarian Greenhouse Café downstairs.

The Edge (*11 Soho Square, W1, tel. 071 439 1223; Tottenham Court Road Underground*). Swish new mixed bar where even the ashtrays are so designer-appealing that customers consider appropriating them. Bang in the centre of town; jam-packed on Friday and Saturday nights till 2 a.m. (and later if the owners can get a licence).

First Out (*52 St Giles High Street, WC2, tel. 071 240 8042; open 11 a.m.–11 p.m. Mon–Sat, 1–10.30 p.m. Sun; Tottenham Court Road Underground*). London's first gay and lesbian café serves salads, baked potatoes and healthy cakes. It's now making a name for itself as an in-town pre-club bar. Women's night is Saturday in the ochre, turquoise and brick basement. Come here to pick up all the free gay and lesbian newspapers.

Mildred's (*58 Greek Street, tel. 071 494 1634; Tottenham Court Road Underground*). An enthusiastic lesbian following for this cosy friendly café/restaurant that serves some dire food but generally good soups and falafels.

Rosanna's (*17 Strutton Ground, off Victoria Street, SW1, tel. 071 233 1701; Victoria Underground*). On Thursday nights this café/bar attracts a designer dyke, cruisey, richer crowd.

Stephs (*39 Dean Street, W1, tel. 071 734 5976; Leicester Square, Piccadilly Circus, or Tottenham Court Road Underground; open for lunch and dinner Mon–Sat*). Gregarious Lancashire-raised Steph serves average-to-poor food (stick to the simplest dishes) in a flamingo-decorated restaurant in the heart of Soho to a mainly male gay clientele who absolutely adore her. According to one female client, Steph's not so keen on gay women, but the staff are friendly and the restaurant's great for anyone who enjoys a high-camp atmosphere. Steph regularly hosts gay carnivals and charity events.

Soho

Don't miss a night in Soho – the buzzing bar and restaurant scene attracts an invigorating mix of Londoners from fashion models to 5 a.m. breakfast clubbers, student strippers, resident video editing house runners and expense-account eighties-style coke-snorting power diners. The many sex shops are not a threat – along with the concentration of clubs, the sex shops help to make Soho one of the safest early-hours districts in London: the place is always humming with workers and happy good-timers. A great way into London if you're alone or with friends, Soho's not the best place to bring children.

BAR ITALIA

22 Frith Street, W1, tel. 071 437 4520. Open 24 hours except Sun, when it closes between 5 a.m. and 7 a.m. Leicester Square or Tottenham Court Road Underground.

Look for a first-floor-level neon clock that tells the wrong time and, spring-autumn, Ray Ban-clad trendsters crammed round pavement tables. If you like, you can bring a paper to read while you enjoy a powerful espresso and slice of panettone perched on a bar stool any time of the day or night in this long, thin, neon-lit, Formica café/bar, or you can watch MTV on the massive video screen at the end, or you can people-watch an entertaining mix of Italian expat and Soho cool media crowd regulars – and you can listen: the usual British reserve doesn't seem to apply here, so you're likely to overhear loud gossipy confessionals. Be warned, though, that if there's a football match being screened, you won't get through the door.

BUTLERS TEA AND COFFEE COMPANY

26 Rupert Street, W1, tel. 071 734 5821. Open 8.45 a.m.–8 p.m. weekdays, 10 a.m.–9 p.m. Sat, noon–8 p.m. Sun. Leicester Square Underground.

A tiny shop front decorated with wooden coffee barrels and assorted tea caddies. Conveniently close to the Metro cinema, this elegantly casual forest-green coffee and tea parlour is for more serious caffeine drinkers in ones and twos who want a choice of 65 teas or 23 coffees (try Trafalgar, Jamaican Blue Mountain or 'coffee of the week'). Regular customers include staffs' family on the way home from shopping trips, occasional leather-clad media dynamos and pre-theatre single businessmen and women with papers and notebooks. Butlers' brioches are shipped down from the Hampstead Tea Rooms, and as well as decaffeinated tea and coffee, there's a fine sparkling elderflower drink on offer.

CAFÉ BOHÈME

13 Old Compton Street, W1, tel. 071 734 0632. Open 8 a.m.–3 a.m. Mon–Sat, 9 a.m.–11 p.m. Sun. Tottenham Court Road or Leicester Square Underground.

After the exclusive, minimalist designerism of the 1980s, Café Bohème is very 1990s – unostentatious chic that's welcoming to all at all times of the day until late into the night, when it bursts into rip-roaring club atmosphere. Tables for breakfast with the papers, a bar to stand at while you take a swift espresso, and for evening all the requisite trendy bottled beers but also cider and champagne by the glass.

HARRY'S BAR

19 Kingly Street, W1, tel. 071 434 0309. Closed Sun and 6–11 a.m. through the rest of the week. Oxford Circus Underground.

An unobtrusive café down a dark, scaffolding-lined back street that looks alarming after dark but is actually quiet and made safe by the frequent passage of clubbers on their way to Harry's. Harry's is pleasant any time of day. Local office staff enjoy the choice of 'Harry's Continental' (croissants) or traditional 'greasy spoon' breakfast-lunches in the squeaky-clean jolly green and muralled tiny room. And the café/bar really comes into its own at night, when the pull-down screen over the bar crackles with MTV, clubbers sober up over coffee and sausage-egg-chips around 2 a.m., and at 4 a.m. the club staff debrief each other over scrambled eggs and orange juice. Rowdiness is rarely a problem (Harry's licence to sell alcohol ends at midnight), and you'd have no worries coming here on your own – women staff work unhassled all hours.

Maison Bertaux

28 Greek Street, W1, tel. 071 437 6007. Open 9 a.m.–7.30 p.m. Mon–Sat, 9 a.m.–1 p.m. and 3–7.30 p.m. Sun. Leicester Square Underground.

Set up by a French pastrycook in 1871, Bertaux's hasn't changed much, and today's owners – partners dry, Austrian Johann Steinecker and ever-friendly English Michelle Wade – keep a loyal clientele who swear that the almond croissants are the best in town and heartily approve of Bertaux's resistance to the cappuccino trend – this is a French patisserie, so you get *café au lait*. The cakes are delectable, the layout of cosily rickety furniture upstairs and the two booths downstairs are equally conducive to a solitary book-reading/postcard-reading/people-listening session and an intimate chat with a close friend.

The Nuthouse

26 Kingly Street, W1, tel. 071 437 9471. Open 8 a.m.–7 p.m. weekdays, 10.30 a.m.–7 p.m. Sat. Oxford Circus Underground.

Near Liberty's on a thin unlikely-looking street between Hamleys on Regent Street and Carnaby Street. This hidden-away gem serves good, cheap sit-down or takeaway 'unique vegetarian food variety of many ethnic traditions' in cosy dark terracotta and duck-egg blue back-room surrounds. Try the peanut butter and carrot savoury crêpe, or perhaps a chilli tofu burger, or help yourself from the (sometimes mediocre) salad bar – or just enjoy a steamed almond milk (there's no minimum charge). For its lovely service and good value, the Nuthouse is a favourite with nearby clotheshop workers and publisher employees. Great alone; perfect for friends on a budget.

Patisserie Valerie

44 Old Compton Street, W1, tel. 071 437 3466. Open 8 a.m.–8 p.m. Mon–Fri, 8 a.m.–7 p.m. Sat, 10 a.m.–6 p.m. Sun. Tottenham Court Road or Leicester Square Underground.

Anyone fresh over from Paris will be disappointed by the croissants and should choose from the Sicilian pastry chef's impressively indulgent cakes, but all walks of London life, from skint Soho artisans to City wheeler-dealers and many tourists, love the croissants, especially when they come in baskets first thing in the morning. Plain café tables below Toulouse-Lautrec-style café society murals in a long, low-lit room are nearly always jam-packed with lovers, shoppers, workers, business meetings and lots of women alone contentedly taking their time over the papers. The staff don't, however, take kindly to note-scribbling – they say it's a place of rest, not work.

Star Café

22B Great Chapel Street, W1, tel. 071 437 8778. Open 7 a.m.–6 p.m. Mon–Fri. Tottenham Court Road Underground.

The building on the corner of Hollen Street looks like a pub, until you see 'Star Café' blazoned across the window. Classic British roast lamb and apple crumble café lunch for under-a-fiver prices that belie the central, just-off-Oxford-Street location. Old ads including a rust-edged Lyons Tea plaque prop up the walls, industrial lampshades light your way to red-checked tablecloths, and a swift, friendly service provides hearty early-morning fry-ups that ease hungover articled clerks and hipsters into fresh working days. Decent vegetarian selection; fine alone.

Budget

BAHN THAI: THAI
21A Frith Street, W1, tel. 071 437 8504. Ground floor open daily noon–11.15 p.m. Leicester Square or Tottenham Court Road Underground.

Recently revamped at the expense of atmosphere, Bahn Thai is known for presenting a winning combination of good, cheap Thai food, attentively served. The seafood dishes are especially commended. Idiosyncrasies include stewed pigs' trotters. Special efforts have been made to produce vegetarian dishes to match the meat-based ones. Bahn Thai is one of the few places in Soho where children are welcome (highchairs available).

GOVINDA'S: INDIAN
9 Soho Street, W1, tel. 071 437 3662. Open Mon–Sat noon–8.30 p.m. Tottenham Court Road Underground.

Cheap, good Indian vegetarian food at stripped-pine tables in a community café run by followers of Radha Krishna. Almost everyone who works in the area comes here as a cheap healthy fallback at some point, whether they're in banking, TV or high-street fashion.

JIMMY'S: GREEK
23 Frith Street, W1, tel. 071 437 9521. Open 12.30–3 p.m. Mon–Sat, 5.30 –11 p.m. Mon–Wed, 5.30–11.30 p.m. Thur–Sat Leicester Square or Tottenham Court Road Underground.

Seedy-looking entry leads into seedy-looking hall and steps into seedy-looking basement, which is Jimmy's. This low-ceilinged café has long been first stop for already cheerily tipsy parties in search of non-vegetarian raucous party-time meals. The best (some say, the only edible) starter is the calamari; the stifados and moussakas – inevitably with chips – usually go down well, partly because even including carafes of the (often sticky) house wine, the bill stays low.

KETTNERS: ENGLISH-AMERICAN
29 Romilly Street, W1, tel. 071 437 6437. Open daily 11 a.m.–midnight. Leicester Square or Tottenham Court Road Underground.

Fast food in nearly elegant white tablecloth/wine-bucket surroundings of a century-old building. Kettners hasn't been in vogue for ages but it's always packed because it appeals to everyone from City whizz-kids who like the champagne bar to jazz supremos who appreciate the informality and find the prices and deteriorating glam décor (peeling gold wall sconces and seventies-era pot plants) perfect for a big birthday bash. Expect to queue most nights.

MEN'S BAR HAMINE: JAPANESE
84 Brewer Street, W1, tel. 071 439 0785. Open noon–3 a.m. Mon–Fri,

noon–2 a.m. Sat, noon–midnight Sun. Piccadilly Circus Underground.

The name's a joke. 'Men' is short for 'Ramen', which is Japanese for noodle, the dish that this small, amenable restaurant made its name for serving. Lots of Japanese come to watch the Japanese telly broadcasts while slurping noodles and eating very good meat dumplings.

MILDREDS: VEGETARIAN
58 Greek Street, W1, tel. 071 494 1634. Open noon–11 p.m. Mon–Sat. Tottenham Court Road Underground.

Despite some disappointing or even disgusting dishes, Mildred's has a varied faithful following from, to and including literary agents/lesbians/late-night groovers, partly because the relaxed classy cafeteria atmosphere and close but not claustrophobic green functional tables are congenial for a woman alone. The soup of the day is nearly always good in terms of value and taste. Vegan dishes are marked with a 'V'. Mildreds will take bookings for parties of six or more; otherwise, if it's busy, you have to queue or wait in the pub across the road.

POLLO: ENGLISH-ITALIAN
20 Old Compton Street, W1, tel. 071 734 5917. Open noon–11.30 p.m. Mon–Sat. Leicester Square or Tottenham Court Road Underground.

On your own or with friends, you can't help people-listening in this crammed basic Formica/booth eatery that serves English-Italian food such as omelette and chips, rigatoni spinaci and chicken in mushroom sauce to soul jazz record store-owners discussing publishing deals, theatre box-office staff bemoaning the success of a current production and media kids shouting 'Yo'-this and 'Man'-that at each other over a beloved car stereo. If you just want to read a book, your best chance is between 2.30 and 5 p.m.; if there's a queue, the efficient (sometimes bullying) staff make sure it moves fast. **Presto** at *4 Old Compton Street (tel. 071 437 4006)* serves similar food at slightly higher prices but it gets less full and the staff remember you after only a couple of visits – the restaurant's a special favourite with the male gay population because rumour has it that Derek Jarman picked at least two film extras from tables at Presto.

Moderate

ANDREW EDMUNDS: MODERN BRITISH
46 Lexington Street, W1, tel. 071 437 5708. Open 12.30 – 2.30 p.m. for lunch, 6 – 10.30 p.m. for dinner weekdays; Sat lunch 12.30–2.30 p.m., Sun 1–2.30 p.m. and 6–10.30 p.m. for dinner Sat and Sun. Oxford Circus Underground.

This looks deceptively like someone's home, which is part of the appeal – you may spot chairs outside bearing seasonal flowers in a pot. Everything about this front-room-sized, good-value bistro is mellow, from the staff and the crowd of regulars right down to the tail-thumping resident mongrel dog, Heathcliff. At lunch, film and advertising bosses forge dynamic deals over the daily changing menu that includes dishes like baked onion soup and duck breast with lentils; and in the evening it's the bosses' unostentatiously fashion-aware staff who murmur and chortle in the wooden pews lit by candles stuck in bottles cased in dripped wax with a backdrop of forest-green walls. There's always a vegetarian dish; although the quality of the food can be up and down, the prices are always pleasing. Great alone or with friends.

BISTROT BRUNO: FRENCH
63 Frith Street, W1, tel. 071 734 4545: Open for lunch 12.15 Mon–Fri and dinner 6.15 (last orders 11.30 p.m.) Tottenham Court Road Underground.

A Michelin star chef, Pierre Condou, produces gutsy French bistro food with a twist in a cosily chic sand/concrete Soho restaurant at bistro prices. This is a welcome new addition to Soho – high-quality food at affordable prices in an atmosphere that's comfortable for women alone or in pairs. Join a media/publishing crowd at lunchtimes; popular for pre-theatre meals in the evening. Friendly, helpful staff; good selection of half bottles of wine.

THE GAY HUSSAR: HUNGARIAN
2 Greek Street, W1, tel. 071 437 0973. Open Mon–Sat 12.30–2.30 p.m. for lunch, 5.30–10.45 p.m. for dinner. Tottenham Court Road Underground. Red front with horse head, bugle and crossed-keys motif over the door.

This is not an on-your-way-somewhere-else restaurant: the menu exhorts you to 'JÓL ENNI', 'JÓL INNI' and 'JÓL ÉLNI' – Eat Well, Drink Well and Live Well – and the staff encourage you especially to 'drink deep' before, during and after Hungarian dishes that include the popular chilled wild cherry soup, pressed boar's head, Transylvanian stuffed cabbage and chicken paprikash with thimble egg dumplings. By the end you'll be slumped in your red-velvet banquette, gazing at the wood-panelled walls, able to do nothing more than stagger happily into a taxi. The small library displayed over the bar area represents the Gay Hussar's legendary left-wing following – you'll spot books by *Mirror* journalists, Neil Kinnock and Michael Foot. The vegetarian dishes are carefully prepared, but few and far between. Although you might feel comfortable here on your own after a few drinks, entering and sitting down would require some bravery.

THE LINDSAY HOUSE: BRITISH
21 Romilly Street, W1, tel. 071 439 0450. Open for lunch 12.30–2.30 p.m., dinner 6 p.m.–midnight Mon–Sat; Sun lunch 12.30–2 p.m., dinner 7–10 p.m. Leicester Square or Tottenham Court Road Underground.

Discreet house front; necessary to ring the doorbell. The food is not exclusively British (woodpigeon terrine, roast breast of duckling and saddle of hare appear alongside sun-dried tomatoes with grilled goat's cheese) but the sumptuous décor of this tall, narrow eighteenth-century house is rich in original features, from the welcoming fireplace in the ground-floor drawing-room up the historic wood-panelled staircase to the period antique-strewn first-floor dining-room. The combination of the staff's brief (to be courteous and attentive to everyone, whether they're wearing Dior or denim) and the vague feeling that you're being entertained in someone's sumptuous fabric-draped home makes the Lindsay House ideal for a solo pre-theatre meal, and even the birdcage-designed ladies' toilets will get you in the mood, for here are displayed framed costume designs from Covent Garden opera productions. Lindsay House lovers reportedly include Elaine Paige and Kiri te Kanawa.

Pubs and Bars

Coach and Horses

29 Greek Street, W1, tel. 071 437 5920. On the corner of Romilly Street. Tottenham Court Road or Leicester Square Underground.

Notorious for its newspaper hack serious boozer regulars and for always being jam-packed, the Coach and Horses is a fun central meeting-place with an attraction for budget travellers: the beer's cheaper than elsewhere in Soho.

The Dive Bar

King's Head, Gerrard Street, W1, tel. 071 437 5858. Leicester Square or Piccadilly Circus Underground.

In the basement of the King's Head pub, this bar featuring two seat-filled brick tunnels has long been a favourite trendy students' pre-club meeting-place. Loud old Beach Boys numbers, camp staff who'll ward off unwanted attentions if you're sitting alone at the bar.

French House

49 Dean Street, W1, tel. 071 437 2799. Leicester Square Underground.

A makeshift meeting-place for the French Resistance during World War II and run for years by the charismatic Gaston, the French House still has signed photos of famous French people on its walls, but Gaston has gone, and with him much of the atmosphere. The beer is expensive and comes only in half-pints, the staff often spend more time chatting to their friends than serving, and it's a rare visit when you don't get approached by one of a handful of local homeless male alcoholics in his sixties or seventies ("Ave you 'eard of parallel orgasm?' was one opening gambit). However, The French House remains a favourite meeting-place – for art students at the start of art gallery opening crawls, birthday drinks, aspiring actors after class – and local shop workers collapse in briefly before staggering home. Those in the know skip the beer and select from the good wine list.

Shampers Wine Bar

4 Kingly Street, W1, tel. 071 437 1692. Oxford Circus Underground.

A dark and friendly green-fronted wine bar to escape into after shopping at nearby Liberty's for a lunchtime glass of good wine and a salmon pâté snack, or in the evening just for the wine – a wide selection comes by the glass. Although there are a lot of suits, it doesn't feel oppressive.

Soho Brasserie

23–25 Old Compton Street, W1, tel. 071 439 9301. Leicester Square or Tottenham Court Road Underground.

The Soho Brasserie deserves a prize for thoughtfully and repeatedly making women alone feel at home drinking just coffee or a bottle of champagne either in the airy cane-chair/tiled-floor front section or in the sultry low-lit back dining area. The day's papers are laid out on the bar, or you can people-watch out of the window. It's been rather untrendy for some time, so it can be the ideal place to meet friends – it might be the one place in Soho where you can get a seat.

Some people find Covent Garden all brash trash, no class; others love it for the chance to make a pick-up in some bars/restaurants, or to do some high-price people-watching in others. Star-studded audiences surge in and out of the Royal Opera House and thespians in and out of the stage doors; shoppers and shop workers let their hair down after a hard day's work. It's rarely quiet in Covent Garden – fun for those of you who love crowds; a nightmare for anyone who wants seclusion.

Snacks and Cafés

CAFÉ CASBAR
52 Earlham Street, WC2, tel. 071 379 7768. Open daily 10 a.m.–9 p.m. Covent Garden Underground.

A great place for a woman to come alone for decent coffee and/or food that won't break the bank. Also a favourite for women meeting in town for shopping or cinema-going, for dancers after a dance class at Pineapple studios and trendsters just generally hanging out. Inventive sandwiches (ham and Brie with glazed cranberries) that have a generous helping of side salad. Almost always loud music.

CAFÉ IN THE CRYPT
St Martin-in-the-Fields, Duncannon Street, WC2, tel. 071 839 4342. Open 10 a.m.–8.30 p.m. Mon–Sat, 10 a.m.–6 p.m. Sun. Charing Cross Underground.

A community church café that does healthy hot and cold food (good soups; interesting salads) in smart surroundings. Canny tourists, shoppers and worshippers choose between the self-service counter and the separate cakes and espresso bar. Near the National Gallery.

CAFÉ PELICAN
45 St Martin's Lane, WC2, tel. 071 379 0309. Open 11 a.m.–midnight Mon–Sat, 11 a.m.–11 p.m. Sun. Charing Cross Underground.

Café Pelican is perfect as a mid-shopping coffee stop-off or for a pre- or post-theatre snack. Lots of snacks and salad brasserie fare in *faux*-grand surroundings. Children and babies will be accommodated. Good for women alone. Near the National Gallery and the Opera House.

Budget

AFRICA CENTRE: AFRICAN
38 King Street, WC2, tel. 071 836 1976. Open 12.30–3 p.m. Mon–Fri, 6–10.30 p.m. Mon–Sat for dinner. Covent Garden Underground.

Failed attempt to make an institutional space homely with African print strips of cloth for décor; dishes such as hot chicken stews and fried fish in a restaurant that's cheap and rarely packed, and practically next to the chi-chi Covent Garden piazza.

ECOLOGY CENTRE: VEGETARIAN
45 Shelton Street, WC2, tel. 071 379 4324. Open 10 a.m.–6 p.m. Mon–Sat.

Covent Garden or Tottenham Court Road Underground.

Cheap vegetarian food (salad, quiche, sandwiches, etc.) in a café that lacks atmosphere but is quiet even on a hellishly busy weekday lunchtime.

FATBOY'S DINER: AMERICAN
21–22 Maiden Lane, WC2, tel. 071 240 1902. Open 11 a.m.–midnight Mon–Sat, 11 a.m.–10.30 p.m. Sun. Covent Garden Underground.

This is popular with families for Sunday brunch – kids love the diner food (burgers, cream soda, cherry pie) and the chrome/Formica décor of this original caravan-style 1940s New Jersey diner.

FOOD FOR THOUGHT: VEGETARIAN
31 Neal Street, WC2, tel. 071 836 0239. Open noon–8.30 p.m. Mon–Sat, noon–4.30 p.m. Sun. Covent Garden Underground.

Might look rather like a tired old 1970s veggie restaurant, but it's not. Certainly there's lots of stripped pine, but the clichéd quiche is almost entirely avoided – the daily changing menu draws from international cuisine and includes wicked extras such as sumptuously healthy trifles for pudding. Not much room in the downstairs café/restaurant, so a constant queue puts pressure on punters to eat up and leave quickly.

NEAL'S YARD BAKERY AND TEA ROOM: VEGETARIAN
6 Neal's Yard, WC2, tel. 071 836 5199. Open 10.30 a.m.–4.30 p.m. Mon–Sat. Covent Garden Underground.

Tranquil upstairs café and tea room that feels almost rural, and serves good vegetarian food and a variety of herbal teas.

Moderate

BERTORELLI'S: MODERN ITALIAN
44A Floral Street, WC2, tel. 071 836 3969. Open noon–3 p.m., 5.45–11.30 p.m. Mon–Sat. Covent Garden Underground.

This quietly bustling Naples-yellow-and-blue-decorated restaurant, newly refurbished and serving fine modern Italian food, is good for semi-formal business meetings and pre-theatre meals with a friend.

CHRISTOPHER'S: AMERICAN
18 Wellington Street, WC2, tel. 071 240 4222. Open 12.30–2.30 p.m. lunch, and 6–11.30 p.m. dinner Mon–Fri, dinner 6–11.30 p.m. Sat. Covent Garden Underground.

For the main courses there are lots of simple meat grills plus an eclectic selection of dishes (from carpetbag steaks to pigs' trotters) and – perhaps most popular – there's Maine lobster. Even with the spectacle of whole lobsters arriving at tables, though, it's still the décor and the clientele that are really remarkable. Frescoed stairwell ceiling, hand-printed fleur-de-lis on the walls of a Rococo dining-room that attracts courting diners and business parties. Celebrities are regularly spotted here having a relaxed chat with agents and colleagues. Book well ahead.

THE IVY: MODERN BRITISH
1 West Street, WC2, tel. 071 836 4751. Open noon–3 p.m., 5.30–midnight daily. Leicester Square Underground.

When asked where they'd go for a good meal on their own, many women reply 'The Ivy', because the new owners have retained the old 1930s restrained, clubby feel (green banquettes, wood-panelled walls, stained-glass windows) and added new touches such as commissioned pieces of art (for example by Howard Hodgkin). The menu also mixes old and new – eggs Benedict and mixed grill, or galettes and Parma ham salad. Popular destination for a special-occasion treat.

JOE ALLEN'S: AMERICAN

13 Exeter Street, WC2, tel. 071 836 0651. Open noon–1 a.m. Mon–Sat, noon–midnight Sun. Aldwych or Covent Garden Underground.

This has long been a fun place to people-watch the theatre folk who come here for Caesar salads and pecan pie, so book ahead. Theatre posters and red-checked tablecloths adorn this old pineapple warehouse basement space that's friendly and busy.

MON PLAISIR: FRENCH

21 Monmouth Street, WC2, tel. 071 836 7243. Open noon–2.15 p.m. Mon–Fri, 6–11.15 p.m. Mon–Sat. Covent Garden or Tottenham Court Road Underground.

All sorts of cosy nooks where you can eat piles of frites with delectably cooked pieces of meat. Interesting dishes for vegetarians too. Sullen but wry-humoured staff.

ORSO: ITALIAN

27 Wellington Street, WC2, tel. 071 240 5269. Open daily noon–midnight. Covent Garden Underground.

Busy, noisy, sometimes rushed, but long extremely popular with a whole range of people who want to splash out on a treat occasion or conduct a fun, impressive business meeting. Ingredients like arugula, sun-dried tomatoes and ricotta recur.

RULES: BRITISH

35 Maiden Lane, WC2, tel. 071 836 5314. Open noon–midnight Mon–Sat, noon–10.30 p.m. Sun. Covent Garden or Charing Cross Underground.

If you're dining alone, phone ahead to book table 42, which has the day's papers hanging above it, or if that's taken, go for table 22. The warren-like old room cluttered with Edwardian memorabilia and a cosy mix of tables and banquettes makes Rules unusually intimate. It's undoubtedly a tourist spot (take souvenir envelopes on your way out), but it's also a place hardened Londoners love to come for a treat. Not entirely but primarily British cooking, including 'Furred Game' (wild Highland/fallow deer), treacle sponge, Stilton and port. The menu suggests: 'Eat game for health, free range, low in fat'; good-value pre-theatre and weekend specials available.

SOLANGE'S: FRENCH

11 St Martin's Court, WC2, tel. 071 240 9936. Open noon–3 p.m., 5.30–11 p.m. Mon–Fri, 5.30–11 p.m. Sat. Leicester Square Underground.

A good place to eat alone. Matter-of-fact, mainly French staff will give you one of the best tables and remain courteous however much or little you order. Theatre posters on the wall, red banquettes, odd music selection (i.e. the Bee Gees). Solange's strengths are Brittany crêpes (lavishly sweet or savoury) and omelettes.

Expensive

SAVOY RIVER ROOM RESTAURANT: INTERNATIONAL
The Savoy, The Strand, WC2, tel. 071 836 4343. Open 7–10.30 a.m. Mon–Sat, 7.30–10 a.m. Sun; daily 12.30–2.30 p.m.; 6–11.30 p.m. Mon–Sat, 7–10.30 p.m. Sun. Charing Cross Underground.

As the name implies, this restaurant gives you a view of the river (although only from a few tables). Eating at the Savoy is about the experience rather than the food. The whole place glitters gold and mirrors while you eat well-prepared food that's served by glove-and-tails-formal waiters. Afterwards, incongruous bands serenade diners for a romantic dance in front of a pagoda. If you're a woman alone, the Savoy Grill – despite lots of suits at lunchtime – might be more suitable. River Restaurant breakfasts (full English or continental) don't come cheap, but the Savoy breakfasting experience makes you feel like a millionaire.

Pubs and Bars

CAFÉ PACIFICO
5 Langley Street, WC2, tel. 071 379 7728. Covent Garden Underground.

Up a few stairs in an old banana warehouse, this noisy, echoey Tex-Mex bar and restaurant fills with young good-timers – that's not to say that you'll definitely get chatted up, but it's pretty likely. Tequila and margaritas relax inhibitions.

FREUDS
198 Shaftesbury Avenue, WC2, tel. 071 240 9933. Covent Garden or Tottenham Court Road Underground.

Down some rattly iron railing stairs, this concrete-and-metal-decorated basement has long been a cool place to hang out and tap time to loud music against designer bottled beers. Also good during the day for coffee and imaginative sandwiches.

MARQUIS OF GRANBY
51 Chandos Place, WC2, tel. 071 836 7657. Leicester Square Underground.

Triangular bar, Hooper's Brighton Seltzer ad over the fireplace, bohemian poet types scribbling on pads. One of the more downbeat, casually friendly pubs in the area.

SHERLOCK HOLMES
10 Northumberland Street, WC2, tel. 071 930 2644. Charing Cross or Embankment Underground.

This is praised in CAMRA's 'Best Pubs in London Guide' as one of the earliest theme pubs. Memorabilia of the detective Sherlock Holmes (TV stills, a violin case, a magnifying glass) surround you while you taste ales including Brakspear Bitter and Whitbread Flowers Original.

TGI FRIDAYS
6 Bedford Street, WC2, tel. 071 379 0585. Charing Cross Underground.
This is not intended as a pick-up joint, say the managers, but effusive staff do match up members of the opposite sex at a corner of the bar, and get conversations going by helpful questions and frequent refills of a wide variety of cocktails. Oddities like rowing boats festoon the candystripe theme décor. On the more civilised side of Café Pacifico.

Whether you're in Piccadilly shopping for gym shoes and Ferragamo, or to see an art exhibition at the Royal Academy then a theatre extravaganza on Shaftesbury Avenue, or because you're staying at one of the high-class hotels on Piccadilly itself, there's a place to eat to suit every budget. After hours, Piccadilly Circus can feel a bit seedy, although the usually milling crowds make it pretty safe.

Snacks and Cafés

CAFÉ DE COLOMBIA
Museum of Mankind, 6 Burlington Gardens, W1, tel. 071 287 8148. Open 9 a.m.–4.30 p.m. Mon–Sat, 12.30–6.30 p.m. Sun. Green Park or Piccadilly Circus Underground.

This is ideal if you've just been to the Museum of Mankind, but oddly enough, considering the museum's popularity with children, it's not ideal if you're with young children, unless they're very well-behaved. Once chicly trendy, the café has seen better days, but when everywhere else is full up, this is very useful to know about during a tiring shopping expedition.

THE WREN
At St James's, 35 Jermyn Street, SW1, tel. 071 437 9419. Open 8 a.m.–7 p.m. Mon–Sat, 10 a.m.–5 p.m. Sun. Piccadilly Circus or Green Park Underground.

Attached to the side of the Wren-designed St James's church, with white plastic tables spilling outside into the leafy churchyard in summer, this is a superb-value snackery considering its location, slap in the middle of Piccadilly. No smoking allowed, no alcohol licence – just good healthy cakes such as walnut and banana, or if you're hungrier have a vegetarian casserole. Women alone will feel perfectly comfortable. The outside seating is good for women with young children in summer.

Budget

NEW PICCADILLY: ENGLISH-ITALIAN
8 Denman Street, W1, tel. 071 437 8530. Open daily 11 a.m.–9.30 p.m. Piccadilly Circus Underground.

Not at all new, and that's part of the charm of this 1950s-feel banquette-and-Formica café, along with the fact that you can bring your own drink and there's no charge for corkage. Basic food dishes include a good canelloni, lots of chip-and-omelette kinds of dishes and stodgy puddings with custard. Vegans stand little chance of being able to order much more than water, vegetarians get only a couple of dishes, but meat eaters with a taste for slumming it with itinerant trendies will love it.

Moderate

CAFÉ FISH, RESTAURANT AND WINE BAR: FISH
30 Panton Street, off Haymarket, SW1, tel. 071 930 3999. Wine bar open 11.30 a.m.–11.30 p.m. Mon–Sat. Leicester Square or Piccadilly Circus Underground.

Fishy prints and artefects are strewn around the aquamarine-blue and sandy-coloured restaurant which bright young things enjoy for a fun night out of – surprise, surprise – dishes of fish – mussels, calamari, shallow-fried plaice, and for the extra health-conscious, a trout steamed in a paper bag. The downstairs wine bar has a pruned-down version of the menu. Don't expect efficient service – the place is always packed.

Chez Gerard: French

31 Dover Street, W1, tel. 071 499 8171. Other branches. Open noon–3 p.m., 6 p.m.–11.30 p.m. Mon–Sat. Green Park Underground.

Jam-packed with suits at lunchtime, and quiet at night when it's just right for a very good pre- or post-theatre French meal. Wood panelling, French gallery prints on the wall, intimate banquettes, staff who are delightful if it's someone's birthday.

The Criterion: International

Piccadilly Circus, tel. 071 925 0909. Open Mon–Sat noon–11.30 p.m. Piccadilly Circus Underground.

A Byzantine extravaganza of tulip lights, palms, marble walls and a gold mosaic ceiling stretching across a glittering hall that manages to feel hugely grand and opulent yet still intimate for a midday snack by yourself or with a friend. The eclectic menu is filled with surprises – caramelised pizza, fried spaghetti – and traditional favourites such as steak frites and roast cornfed chicken. Afternoon tea is served from 3 p.m. to 5 p.m.; minimum charge operates, so no hanging around for hours with only a coffee.

Green's Champagne and Oyster Bar: Fish

36 Duke Street, St James's, SW1, tel. 071 930 4566. Bar open 11.30 a.m.–3 p.m., 5.30–11 p.m. Mon–Sat; noon–3.30 p.m. Sun. Piccadilly Circus Underground.

A lot of dandies in pinstriped suits surrounded by mahogany panelling at the marble-topped oyster bar or in green banquettes. This feels very much like a gentlemen's club, which for some women is precisely its appeal. Don't go alone; go with a friend and revel in the dated luxury. Fare is, of course, champagne and oysters, and also lobster, crab, wild salmon.

Mulligans: Irish

13–14 Cork Street, W1, tel. 071 409 1370. Open 12.30–2.15 p.m. Mon–Fri, 6.15–11.15 p.m. Mon–Sat. Oxford Circus or Piccadilly Circus Underground.

Irish stew, oysters, smoked salmon, herring and beetroot salad ... In a relatively new restaurant that's a cross between a gentlemen's club and a homey Irish bar, you'll get robust food served by quietly friendly staff.

Quaglinos: International

16 Bury Street, SW1, tel. 071 930 6767. Open lunch and dinner, last orders midnight Fri–Sat, 11 p.m. Sun.

Terence Conran's 1993 revamp of the old Quaglinos (where Barbara Cartland claims to have found a pearl in her dish of oysters) elicits a mixed reaction. It seems that most of the staff don't know a good bottle of wine from a bad one, and you might have to resort to swigging from a hip flask before your choice finally arrives. There's almost inevitably an annoying wait for the food, too – first in a queue on the stairs above the huge dining-room, then at a table that's prime-placed if you're an easily recognisable celebrity and on the sidelines if you're not. Mixed reports on the food – overcooked Canadian lobster, superb chips, dry fruit dessert tarts – but the thirties-style glamour gets constant applause. Pillars painted by a mixture of known and upcoming artists, including Estelle Thompson; flouncy staff uniforms designed by Conran's son, designer Jasper Conran.

Expensive

THE OAK ROOM: FRENCH
Le Meridien Hotel, 21 Piccadilly, W1, tel. 071 734 8000. Open Mon–Fri noon–2.30 p.m., 7–10 p.m., 7–10 p.m. Sat, closed Sun. Green Park or Piccadilly Circus Underground.

The newly restored Edwardian grandeur (pale oak panelling, festoons, chandeliers) of this restaurant attracted royal clients when it opened in 1908, and helped to make dining out quite the rage. In 1911 the *Gentlewoman's Court Journal* wrote: 'it is now quite the correct thing to dine at a restaurant', especially at 'this haunt of sybarites' where 'crowds of epicures' gather to celebrate the saying that it is 'a delight to live and eat'. The Michelin star Oak Room restaurant divides its menu into *cuisine traditionelle* and *cuisine créative* – for example, dishes such as Gazpacho with Warm Langoustines and Quenelles of Courgette as well as Roasted Squab Pigeon on a Nest of 'Couscous' and Aubergine. The room and the food are a treat.

Pubs and Bars

CAFÉ ROYAL
68 Regent Street, W1, tel. 071 437 9090. Piccadilly Circus Underground.

Refurbishment hasn't stopped this classy bar feeling sophisticatedly old-fashioned. Frescoes and gilded mirrors surround while you swizzle sticks in cocktails at tables where New Zealand writer Katherine Mansfield liked to come, and Charlie Chaplin was once spotted.

Westminster

It can be a bit of a nightmare finding a decent place to eat after going to visit the Houses of Parliament or the Tate Gallery – indeed, if you're not already at the Tate, it might be worth targeting its downstairs restaurant. Or you could catch a bus back up into Soho/Covent Garden, or try one of the suggestions below.

Budget

THE WELL: BRITISH
2 Eccleston Place, SW1, tel. 071 730 7303. Open 9 a.m.–6 p.m. Mon–Fri, 9 a.m.–5 p.m. Sat. Victoria Underground.

This is inevitably packed with backpackers from Victoria Station who are pleased to have found a reasonably priced, airy and friendly basic café to buy filling baked potatoes, good soups of the day with granary bread, a range of sandwiches, or just a strong cup of tea. Vegetarian dishes available every day.

Moderate

THE FOOTSTOOL WINE BAR AND RESTAURANT: INTERNATIONAL
St John's Smith Square, SW1, tel. 071 222 2779. Open 12.15–2 p.m. Mon–Fri; open in the evening only if there is a concert in the church. Westminster Underground.

In the crypt of St John's Smith Square's Baroque church is a haven where you can have cheap snacks (pies and pâtés) in the wine bar section or a three-course meal – selection of dishes such as galantine of duck, tagliatelle, millefeuille and sticky toffee pudding. Both have no-smoking sections.

POMEGRANATES: INTERNATIONAL
94 Grosvenor Road, SW1, tel. 071 828 6560. Open 12.30–2 p.m., 7–11.15 p.m. Mon–Fri, 7–11.15 p.m. Sat. Pimlico Underground. Take a cab at night, as it's on a rather bleak-looking stretch of riverside road down some steps in a basement.

Along with a select few other restaurants in the area, Pomegranates has a division bell, the bell that rings to tell parliamentary whips who are dining here that they must rush posthaste to Parliament to organise a vote. When it opened in the 1970s it was, says owner Patrick Gwynne-Jones, the only truly cosmopolitan restaurant in London, frequented for years for its hidden-away qualities by showbiz folk from Laurence Olivier to Diana Ross. The 'cosmopolitan peasant' menu reflects Gwynne-Jones's world travels ... Australian oyster-filled carpetbag steak, Welsh salt duck, Jamaican curried goat. Gwynne-Jones's entertaining explanation of how dishes came to be on the menu makes even unspectacular choices thoroughly enjoyable, especially if you're on your own. Mellow plinky jazz plays in a cosy clublike atmosphere to international custom from the booze industry to single American businesswomen to families from the nearby council flats celebrating special occasions.

Mayfair

Many women refuse to eat here after dark at all unless it's in a smart hotel restaurant, saying it's a notorious red-light district – which may be true but does *not* mean the area is threatening. And there are a couple of jewels that you should not dismiss. Finding a cheap place is more tricky, but possible – read on.

Cafes and Snacks

VILLAGE COFFEE SHOP AND GALLERY
27 Shepherd Market, W1, tel. 071 499 4592. Open 7 a.m.–9 p.m. Mon–Fri, 9 a.m.–7 p.m. Sat and Sun. Green Park Underground.

Dating back to the eighteenth century, this quaintly rickety-looking building has served as a sweetshop, an ironmonger's and, for the past four decades, as a coffee shop. Red-checked tablecloths, black beams, jazzy music, laidback yet still efficient staff; clients range from other nearby restaurants' staff to Goldie Hawn and Dustin Hoffman popping in on their way back to high-class Mayfair hotels. Owners boast club sandwiches you could hold the door open with. Lots of herbal teas, full English breakfast and baked potatoes as well as coffee. Don't expect to get a table to yourself if you're here alone during a busy period, but don't expect any hassle either.

Moderate

HARD ROCK CAFÉ: AMERICAN
150 Old Park Lane, W1, tel. 071 629 0382. Hyde Park Corner Underground. Open 11.30 a.m.–12.30 a.m. Mon–Thurs, Sun, 11.30 a.m.–1 a.m. Fri, Sat.

You can spot this one by the long queues outside. The food's lots of burgers and meat grills, and the appeal for many is the possibility of buying Hard Rock Café T-shirts; or for £250 there's the Hard Rock Café leather bomber jacket.

Expensive

LE GAVROCHE: FRENCH
43 Upper Brook Street, W1, tel. 071 408 0881. Open noon–2 p.m., 7–11 p.m. Mon–Fri. Marble Arch Underground.

Michel and Albert Roux produce classic, elegant French food which keeps this London's only three-star Michelin restaurant. Some complain that the cooking's overrated, but men and women – including *Vogue* food reviewer Arabella Boxer – have long enjoyed the consistently high-quality food in convivial surroundings.

LE SOUFFLÉ: FRENCH
Hotel Inter-Continental, 1 Hamilton Place, W1, tel. 071 409 3131. Open 12.30–3 p.m., 7–11 p.m. Mon–Fri, noon–4 p.m. Sun. Formal dress. Hyde Park Underground.

Unfailingly courteous, expert French staff in this hotel restaurant that narrowly lost its Michelin star but still serves excellent food. Soufflé (potato or hazelnut, for example) is the chef's highlight. There's a special section on the menu for healthy eaters called 'Cuisine de Vie'. Relaxing yellow surroundings, pianist quietly tinkling. Good for a romantic dinner, or alone, or for an impressive business dinner.

ZEN CENTRAL: CHINESE
20–22 Queen Street, W1, tel. 071 629 8103. Open noon–2.15 p.m., 6.30–11.15 p.m. Mon–Sat, noon–2.15 p.m., 6.30–11 p.m. Sun. Green Park Underground.

Possibly the most expensive Chinese food in London, and arguably the best. You can eat for around £20 in the evening, but the cross-section of loyal Londoners who are prepared to travel some distance to come here would advise splashing out to make the most of the sumptuous dishes that are detailed in a flower-decorated menu the size of a book. Give 24 hours' notice for the Kwantung suckling pig, or if there are two of you try the double-boiled fluffy supreme shark's fin. The menu promises to 'admit only first-class produce' so that 'you will understand something of the heights to which Chinese cooking can soar'. Despite frosted glass and metal minimalist décor, the airy room where ivy sprouts round the skylight feels happily busy and buzzing.

A big area with a lot of pubs, bars and sandwich cafés that serve local office workers and Madame Tussaud's visitors. There are a couple of places that are handy to know about after shopping on nearby Oxford Street. Nico Central's for a special but not extortionate night out.

Budget

RANOUSH JUICE BAR: MIDDLE EASTERN
43 Edgware Road, W2, tel. 071 723 5929. Open 9 a.m.–2 p.m. daily, Marble Arch Underground.

It can be a scrum to get served, but local office workers love it for lunchtime and clubbers love it late night for freshly squeezed juices including melon, and for sandwiches including falafel and sharwarma. Pay before you eat.

Moderate

NICO CENTRAL: FRENCH
35 Great Portland Street, W1, tel. 071 436 8846. Open noon–2 p.m., 7–11 p.m. Mon–Fri. Oxford Circus or Great Portland Street Underground. Other branch 90 Park Lane, W1, tel. 071 409 1290.

This is the site where Nico Ladenis earned the Michelin stars that allowed him to open another restaurant, Nico at Ninety, at a prestigious Mayfair address. Here the idea is that you get the same quality food but it's all less formal. Smiley staff, good selection for vegetarians, and generally simple dishes such as succulent lamb with puréed potatoes for meat eaters. Good everything-on-one-plate pudding choice that gives you the chance to try all the sweet options. Blue canopy outside; Juan Gris prints adorn marbled cream walls. Clients remain loyal and say *Au revoir* to the staff as they would to old friends.

TOPKAPI: TURKISH
25 Marylebone High Street, W1, tel. 071 486 1872. Open daily noon–11.30 p.m. Baker Street or Bond Street Underground.

Good family choice if you're staying in a hotel in the area or need a hearty meal after Madame Tussaud's in a place where children are welcome. Lots of brass plates and hanging lamps combine for a fun décor feel. Impressive mixed meze including bayildi and cacik to start with. Generous portions of main-course kebabs including breast of chicken. Vegetarians should stick to the starters.

ZOE'S: INTERNATIONAL
St Christopher's Place, W1, tel. 071 224 1122. Open 11.30 a.m.–11.30 p.m. Mon–Sat. Bond Street Underground.

A relative newcomer to the scene, Zoe's has already become popular with showbiz folk including – rumour has it – pop star Lulu, and local snazzy-clothes-shop workers. In an airy upstairs café you can get light snacks such as mushrooms on toast or mozzarella salad, or full meals such as grilled Barnsley chump chop. The downstairs restaurant is done out in a daring mixture of purple, orange and aquamarine colours that succeed in being cheerful and chic. Here you can order from a Country or City menu – hearty stews, pigs' trotters, asparagus tarts; chargrilled pizza, cornmeal 'blinis', smoked duck broth. Many dishes can be had as starter or main course, so it's great for anyone trying to keep a low calorie count (have the starter as the main course). Vegetarians are served well too. If the service remains as amiable and the food quality as high, then this is a good place to meet a friend after Oxford Street shopping, or for an entertaining evening.

Bloomsbury

Local staff of literary publishing houses, TV production companies, the British Museum and Great Ormond Street Hospital are served by a clutch of French, Greek and Italian restaurants on Charlotte Street and Indian bhelpoori houses on Drummond Street, and by innumerable pubs that tend to fill to capacity at around 5.30–7 p.m. then empty as workers wend their way home.

Cafés and Snacks

COFFEE HOUSE GALLERY

23 Museum Street, WC1, tel. 071 436 0455. Open 8 a.m.–5.30 p.m. Mon–Fri, 10 a.m.–5.30 p.m. Sat, 12.30–6 p.m. Sun. Tottenham Court Road, Holborn or Russell Square Underground.

There are plenty of bad coffee shops in Bloomsbury – this is possibly the best. Large pottery cups of cappuccino with a hint of cinnamon while you read the café's papers and wonder if you can resist the daily changing menu of imaginative salads and sandwiches made from only the best fresh and Italian ingredients. Cakes and croissants for breakfast. Airy front room and sunny yellow back room, both displaying Sicilian, Amalfi and Bassano del Grappa pottery that is for sale. Amenable for solo coffee drinkers except at lunchtime, when it gets very full.

THE HERMITAGE

19 Leigh Street, WC1, tel. 071 387 8034. Open 10 a.m.–3 p.m., 5–11 p.m. Mon–Fri, 10 a.m.–2 p.m. Sat and Sun. Russell Square or King's Cross Underground.

Although the pebbledashing and velveteen décor is beginning to look decidedly shabby, the Hermitage is a good stop-off coffee place to know about for two reasons: it's well situated if you're on your way on foot either to a dance performance at The Place or to catch a train from King's Cross Station; it's fine if you're alone. Opening hours are flexible – if you walk through the door between 3 and 5 p.m. you'll almost certainly be served.

Budget

DIWANA: BHELPOORI HOUSE, VEGETARIAN

121–123 Drummond Street, NW1, tel. 071 387 5556. Open daily noon–11.30 p.m. Euston Underground.

The first and, many still think, the best of the Drummond Street bhelpoori houses that have earned the area the label 'Little Bombay'. The functional stripped-pine décor and no-fuss practical plastic menus are matched by the no-nonsense service but belie the standard and presentation of the food. The Thali gives you a chance to try a selection of the food on offer; the paper dosas are a visual feast that beg the tricky question of how to eat these spectacular curled fan pancakes with fillings. Not licensed, but the yoghurt drink lassi is good, and there's an off licence just down the road. The rest of 'Little Bombay' consists of **Ravi Shankar** (*131–136 Drummond Street, tel. 071 388 6458*), which is similar to Diwana but licensed and therefore often with a bigger bill at the end; and **Chutneys** (*124 Drummond Street, tel. 071 388 0604*), which is also licensed but of an immaculate white modern décor.

MANDEER: INDIAN
21 Hanway Place, W1, tel. 071 323 0660. Canteen open noon–3 p.m. lunch Mon–Sat. Tottenham Court Road Underground.

As you go deeper into this apparently seedy-looking back alley, you think this can't *possibly* lead to a healthy, cheap fun vegetarian Indian lunchtime curry canteen/buffet service, but it does. The attached restaurant is more plushly decorated and consequently more expensive.

OCTOBER GALLERY CAFÉ: INTERNATIONAL
24 Old Gloucester Street, WC1, tel. 071 242 7367. Open 12.30–2.30 p.m. Tues–Sat. Holborn Underground.

Plenty of vegetarian food available in this tucked-away café that's half indoors next to the October Gallery and half outdoors in a foliage-swathed courtyard. Food generally high-quality and inventive. Get there early – they tend to run out of food by about 2 p.m.

WAGAMAMA: JAPANESE
4 Streatham Street, off Coptic Street, WC1, tel. 071 323 9223. Open 12–2.30, 6–11 p.m. Mon–Fri, 1–3.30, and 6–11.30 p.m. Sat, closed Sun. No bookings.

New healthy fast-food Japanese noodle bar in a designer concrete and pine basement where students, solo female accountants, Japanese businessmen and trendsters line up at the bench-tables to slurp noodles during the day and at night, at around 8 p.m. the queue that twists upstairs and out on to the street is served drinks. If you're alone, this is one of the few places where you might get chatting to someone. If you're vegetarian, health-conscious and/or a no-smoker you'll probably find yourself coming back again and again. If you're not familiar with the dishes, Wagamama is cheap enough to experiment, and the booklet-sized menu contains comprehensive information on each dish and a glossary at the back. Staff are helpful too.

Moderate

AUNTIES: BRITISH
126 Cleveland Street, W1, tel. 071 387 1548. Open 12–3 p.m. Mon–Fri, 5.30–10.30 p.m. Mon–Sat. Goodge Street Underground.

Good filling winter food – cosy surroundings for cosy English stodge such as steak and kidney pudding and sticky toffee pudding.

Costa Dorada: Spanish
47–55 Hanway Street, W1, tel. 071 636 7139. Open 5.30 p.m.–3 a.m. Mon–Sat, 5.30 p.m.–midnight Sun. Tottenham Court Road Underground.

The appeal of this restaurant and tapas bar, hidden down an unlikely-looking back alley, is decent tapas (snacks of fried calamari, Spanish omelette, etc.) and the atmosphere, which is kept lively by blaring Spanish TV and wild flamenco dances performed by professionals and Spanish customers and waiters who just can't stop themselves joining in. Children welcome before 10 p.m. No jeans or trainers.

Museum Street Café: Modern British
47 Museum Street, WC1, tel. 071 405 3211. Open 12.30–2.30 p.m., 7.15–11.15 p.m. Mon–Fri. Essential to book, and to turn up on time. Tottenham Court Road, Holborn or Russell Square Underground.

This is extremely popular, small and good value, so you have to book ahead for this fêted lunch and dinner spot. Minimalist décor and minimalist choice scribbled on a blackboard of delectably prepared dishes that might be Mediterranean-influenced salad or grilled fish but will certainly be made from top-class ingredients. The vegetarian dishes tend to be good but less imaginative. Prix-fixe menus; unlicensed, so bring your own bottle of wine. The squashedness of it means you should prepare to enjoy the conversation at the next table.

Pizza Express: Italian
30 Coptic Street, WC1, tel. 071 636 3232. Other branches. Open daily 11.30 a.m.–midnight. Tottenham Court Road, Holborn or Russell Square Underground.

Pizza Express is the best and most reliable of the pizza chains, and the one that many credit with introducing pizza to London in the late 1960s, an era that's reflected in the Biba-style swirling décor and sprouting pot plants. If you order the Veneziana – onions, capers, olives, pine kernels, sultanas, mozzarella, tomato – 30p goes to the Venice in Peril fund. Salade niçoise and a plate of doughballs are a popular pizza alternative. At quieter times you could happily eat here alone; highchairs are available and children are welcomed – in theory.

White Tower: Greek
1 Percy Street, W1, tel. 071 636 8141. Open 12.30–2.15 p.m. Mon–Fri, 6.30–10 p.m. Mon–Sat. Tottenham Court Road or Goodge Street Underground.

For five decades this famous Greek restaurant has been a favourite hideaway place for writers, artists, politicians and TV celebrities who love it for the timeless shop/taverna décor – a portrait of Byron jostles with an assortment of old plates, a rifle and dated net curtains – and for the high-quality Greek food. The taramasalata is mixed on the premises to an old family recipe, the 'mezedes à la grecque' features turbot, artichoke hearts and stuffed aubergine. Certainly not one of the cheapest Greek restaurants, but many still consider it the best.

Pubs and Bars

Bradleys Spanish Bar
48 Hanway Street, W1, tel. 071 636 0359. Tottenham Court Road Underground.

This is bizarre – Thai staff, German

beer, tatty Formica and ripped velveteen décor, Spanish serenades and soul hits on the jukebox, precariously small toilets and regulars (including businessmen, students and flaky media trendsters) who love it with a fiery loyalty and would like to keep it to themselves. Why? It's not entirely clear ... try it for yourself.

LAMB
94 Lamb's Conduit Street, WC1, tel. 071 405 0713. Russell Square Underground.

This old-fashioned pub with lots of original Victorian etched glass, privacy screens and photos of old showbiz stars serves a cross-section of the area's workers – academics, students, hospital staff – and Londoners who travel in for the real ale.

TRUCKLES OF PIED BULL YARD
off Bury Place, WC1, tel. 071 404 5334/8. Open 11.30 a.m.–3 p.m. Mon–Sat, 5.30–9 p.m. Mon–Fri. Holborn Underground.

Early evenings and lunchtimes in summer the table- and chair-filled secluded yard fills with the smells of char-grilling meat and grateful garden-less Bloomsbury residents.

The City

Weekday lunchtimes and early evenings the wine bars and smart restaurants in the heart of 'the square mile' throng with networking men and women in suits, which can be threatening but is also fascinating and makes for an unmatchable anthropological experience. Leadenhall Market is an atmospheric place to snack. The Tower Hotel (in St Katharine's Dock) is thought horrifically ugly by some but invaluable for its river-view greenhouse conservatory, where you can take a refreshing cup of tea. If you're sightseeing, note that at weekends everything closes down and you might have trouble finding somewhere to eat. Cafés and restaurants at the edges of the City have a more mixed clientele.

Budget

DIANA'S DINING ROOM: BRITISH
30 St Cross Street, EC1, tel. 071 240 0272. Open 7 a.m.–8 p.m. Mon–Sat, 8 a.m.–6 p.m. Sun. Farringdon Underground.

Grab a takeaway sandwich or sit for a full English breakfast, or try falafel in pitta in a licensed café/restaurant run by Diana and her daughter on the edges of the City. Certainly it's café fare, but generally healthier and lots of it.

EAST/WEST: MACROBIOTIC
188 Old Street, EC1, tel. 071 608 0300. Open 11.30 a.m.–7.30 p.m. Mon–Fri, 11.30 a.m.–3 p.m. Sat and Sun. Old Street Underground.

You're talking about a bit of a walk to get here from the City, but if you want macrobiotic food, that's a small price to pay. And if you're not familiar with macrobiotic cooking, don't expect unappetising food – after snacks like hummus or the set meal of the day, there are luscious dairy-less puddings including things like tofu cheesecake. Also a range of beers for sale in this clean, friendly white room.

Moderate

THE ALBA: MODERN ITALIAN
107 Whitecross Street, EC1, tel. 071 588 1798. Open noon–3 p.m., 6–11 p.m. Mon–Fri. Barbican or Moorgate Underground.

This is perfectly sited for a snack in the wine bar (ciabatta sandwiches) or a full meal (raw veal starter and grilled swordfish main) in the warm pink and marble restaurant before or after attending an arts event at the Barbican Centre.

LE POULBOT: FRENCH
45 Cheapside, EC2, tel. 071 236 4379. Open Mon–Fri 7.30 a.m.–3 p.m. Bank or St Paul's Underground.

This is a City stronghold, particularly the downstairs restaurant, which is wall-to-wall suits, but the ground-floor red, white and blue decorated Brasserie is good if you're alone. The day's papers are hung near the door. You can have just coffee and a patisserie in the morning, and at lunch there are classic dishes like omelettes and steak frites. Popular with chic City women.

QUALITY CHOP HOUSE: MODERN BRITISH
94 Farringdon Road, EC1, tel. 071 837 5093. Open noon–3 p.m. Mon–Fri, noon–4 p.m. Sun for lunch; 6.30–11.30 p.m. Mon–Sat, 7–11.30 p.m. Sun. Farringdon Underground.

This is cited again and again by Londoners as a favourite. Contradictory mix of regressively nostalgic dishes such as lamb chops and corned beef hash plus fashionable European and American dishes such as Caesar salad plus souped-up golden oldies, for example salmon fishcakes. The setting is complementarily contradictory: original greasy café that's barely been done up since it was taken over by the celebrity Le Caprice chef Charles Fontaine. You'll probably be sharing a packed bench table with staff from the nearby *Guardian* newspaper offices. Simple things like moules marinière are done well. Sunday brunch is fun.

Knightsbridge

Hotels and shops are the main reasons for being here unless Knightsbridge is your home. Lots of high-class restaurants – especially around the chic shopping area Brompton Cross – and also some hidden-away budget gems.

Cafés and Snacks

CAFÉ MINEMA
35 Knightsbridge, SW1, tel. 071 823 1269. Open 11 a.m.–midnight Mon–Sat, 1–9 p.m. Sun. Hyde Park Corner or Knightsbridge Underground.

Standing outside you can see, through two floors of glass, trendy staff and clients in a chic pale-green, black and chrome café that serves food supplied by the Savoy kitchens. Weary shoppers welcome it, as do audiences of the Minema Cinema next door. Good cappuccinos and cakes; or go for a light salad, perhaps Caesar or goat's cheese.

Budget

STOCKPOT: INTERNATIONAL
6 Basil Street, SW3, tel. 071 589 8627. Open 8 a.m.–11 p.m. Mon–Sat, noon–10.30 p.m. Sun. Knightsbridge Underground.

Two or three pounds will buy you things like spaghetti bolognese, breadcrumbed chicken, or a range of vegetarian dishes. Grateful students laugh, chat and eat squashed into segregated benches.

Moderate

BIBENDUM OYSTER BAR: FISH
Michelin House, 81 Fulham Road, SW3, tel. 071 581 5817. Open noon–10.30 p.m. Mon–Sat, noon–3 p.m. Sun. South Kensington Underground.

Joan Collins has been spotted in the restaurant upstairs, but the ground-floor oyster bar's more fun, and it's a first choice for women alone who want a civilised and enjoyable light meal. Few mind having to queue, for the oyster bar's in an amazing tiled building that flourishes the jolly tyre Michelin man motif; a Renault van out front sells fresh oysters to passers-by. Once at one of the few tables, surrounded by gleaming white tiles, you can have, of course, oysters, and also selections from a honed-down version of the upstairs restaurant menu – for example, chilled cucumber soup or a plate of Parma ham and figs.

CHICAGO RIB SHACK: AMERICAN
1 Raphael Street, SW7, tel. 071 581 5595. Open 11.45 a.m.–11.45 p.m. Mon–Sat, noon–11 p.m. Sun. Knightsbridge Underground.

Children thoroughly enjoy the Chicago Rib Shack, because American owner Bob Payton has dedicated it to fun, with staff instructed to keep children happy. Special children's menus and food like ribs, burgers and fries.

DAPHNE'S: MODERN ITALIAN
112 Draycott Avenue, SW3, tel. 071 589 4257. Open daily lunch and dinner, including Sun brunch 11 a.m.–4 p.m. South Kensington Underground.

Famous for being favoured by showbiz and royalty when it was founded in the 1960s by casting director Daphne Rye. Now newly opened in 1993, Daphne's fills with super-rich sex kittens and sleekly groomed executive men and women in ice-green and fuchsia suits who are famous or like to be in the place where famous people are said to dine. The service is friendly, though not always fast, and the décor is convivial – a biscuit-coloured front room with a gold square motif and a conservatory back room, both with real fires for winter. As for the food, mixed feedback so far. Stick to the simple dishes – mushroom and cheese soufflé starter good but a little watery, whereas calf's liver with spinach is excellent. Go with a friend for a fun night out in a bustling restaurant.

FIFTH FLOOR: MODERN BRITISH
at Harvey Nichols on Knightsbridge, separate lift on Sloane Street, SW1, tel. 071 235 5250. Open noon–3 p.m.

lunch, 6–11.30 p.m. dinner Mon–Sat. Knightsbridge Underground.

In celebrated designer surroundings on top of the department store you may well have just been shopping in, you can join well-heeled Knightsbridge-ites dining from a Modern British menu that might include black pudding and lobster. Dainty salads also feature. Prix-fixe and à la carte menus.

LE METRO: BRASSERIE
28 Basil Street, SW3, tel. 071 589 6286. Open 8 a.m.–11 p.m. Mon–Sat. Knightsbridge Underground.

This regularly fills with women diners, who've come after a shopping trip at Harrods or because they're staying in the attached hotel, the Capital. Consequently, the staff are thoroughly used to treating sole women diners – lunchtime or evening – with due courtesy. Despite its proximity to the main shopping drag, it feels secluded because it's indicated by a discreet sign, then you have to go down some unlikely-looking stairs. Unspectacular white and cane décor includes Toulouse-Lautrec lithos; a light meal with a glass of wine need not come to much more than £10. Dishes like sweet red pepper soup, squid risotto and lots of desserts including banana bread with butterscotch sauce. Good place for vegetarians.

GRILL ST QUENTIN: FRENCH

2 Yeoman's Row, SW3, tel. 071 581 8377. Open 12–3 p.m., 6.30–11.30 p.m. Mon–Sat; 12–3.30, 6.30–10.30 p.m. Sun. Knightsbridge Underground.

You can sit here with a girlfriend with just a glass of good wine and a dish of oysters, or you can have a delicious light meal. High-powered executive women from the City target it after a total makeover at the Harvey Nichols or Harrods beauty salons.

South Kensington

A day in Hyde Park or the South Kensington museums (the Victoria and Albert, the Science and the Natural History Museum) will leave you in need of refreshments. Here are some suggestions.

Cafés and Snacks

DAQUISE
20 Thurloe Street, SW7, tel. 071 589 6177. Open daily 10 a.m.–11.30 p.m. South Kensington Underground.

If the threatened closure hasn't happened (phone to check), be thankful, for this is a rare place: you can sit alone with nothing but a coffee during the busiest period, and no one will mind one bit. Indeed, there will probably be several other women doing the same – perhaps one in a Windsmoor coat just back from shopping at Foyles, and a student desperately swatting from a book beside a table full of Poles tucking into pierogi, dumplings and fried buckwheat sausage. Fustily delightful brown hessian and plastic décor. Good for tea-time poppyseed cake and apple strudel.

Moderate

BOMBAY BRASSERIE: INDIAN
Courtfield Close, Courtfield Road, SW7, tel. 071 370 4040. Open daily 12.30–2.45, 7.30–11.45 p.m. Gloucester Road Underground.

An international reputation guarantees lots of tourists and businesspeople at this old-fashioned restaurant that is reminiscent of the Raj. The prices are high in the evenings, but the lunchtime buffet is a bargain, and a good informal choice for a woman alone. Cooled by whirring fans and surrounded by potted palms, you can choose from several different curries that will be of a higher quality than your local takeaway, although you shouldn't expect anything extraordinary.

OGNISKO POLSKIE: POLISH
55 Prince's Gate, Exhibition Road, SW7, tel. 071 589 4635. Open daily 12.30–3 p.m., 6.30–11 p.m. South Kensington Underground.

Some come here for the decent food – which includes borscht, stuffed fish in aspic, and flaki (strips of tripe in broth) – but more come for the atmosphere, which becomes increasingly merry as you try more of the flavoured vodkas from a wide selection that ranges from cherry to pepper. Although it's part of the Polish Club, the restaurant welcomes non-members through its poster-spatted hallway into a high-ceilinged room with pillars, a fireplace, and the bar where you begin your vodka experimentation.

TUI: THAI
19 Exhibition Road, SW7, tel. 071 584 8359. Open noon–2.30, 6.30–11 p.m. Mon–Sat, 7–10.30 p.m. Sun. South Kensington Underground.

The high number of Thai diners at this inoffensively decorated modern chrome and black restaurant suggests that the food's authentic, and it's opposite the V&A.

Pubs and Bars

BAR ESCOBA
102 Old Brompton Road, SW7, tel. 071 373 2403. Gloucester Road or South Kensington Underground.

Popular with the striped-shirt-and-pearls Chelsea set, and also with well-heeled foreign students. Loud atmosphere.

Chelsea

The shoppers' King's Road is in Chelsea; there are some sights and a huge number of restaurants, many of them celebrated and very pricey. Come here to see how the monied Chelsea set live.

Budget

CHELSEA KITCHEN: INTERNATIONAL
98 King's Road, SW3, tel. 071 589 1330. Open 8 a.m.–11.45 p.m. Mon–Sat, noon–11.30 p.m. Sun. Sloane Square Underground.

School-dinner-type food in a budget eatery that clamours with the sounds of squashed art students and relieved backpackers diving into an eclectic menu which can put chicken Madras next to spaghetti Bolognese, then follow with apple pie and custard.

Moderate

CHUTNEY MARY: ANGLO-INDIAN
Plaza 535, 535 King's Road, SW10, tel. 071 351 3113. Open 12.30–2.30 p.m., 7–11.30 p.m. Mon–Sat, Sunday Buffet 12.30–3 p.m., 7–10.30 p.m. Fulham Broadway Underground; at night take a cab.

This looks like nothing from the outside, but downstairs the restaurant spreads out into a plant-filled conservatory scattered with cane chairs and well-separated tables, many of which have a view on to a modern courtyard with a fountain sprinkling in the middle. A rich, fast set likes coming here for innovative dishes that have days of the Raj stories attached, for example: a servant's mispronounced 'cutlets' became 'memsahib cutless', which are served alongside the country captain (chicken and rice). The food is well worth the trip. The range of cocktails is popular.

THE ENGLISH HOUSE: BRITISH
3 Milner Street, SW3, tel. 071 584 3002. Open 12.30–2.30 p.m., 7.30–11.30 p.m. Mon–Sat, 12.30–2 p.m., 7.30–10.30 p.m. Sun. Sloane Square or South Kensington Underground.

This couldn't feel more British, with blackcurrant and autumn leaves wallpaper, a Victorian terrace and Victoriana clutter, all in an authentically rickety-feeling old town house. Not as high-powered as sister restaurant **Waltons** (*121 Walton Street, 071 584 0204*), where politicians and earls dine. The English House is consequently more convivial for a woman alone or with a woman friend. Americans and Germans come here in the certainty that royalty dine at the English House. Traditional English recipes have been modified for the modern palate – for example, no overfloured sauces. Starters like rabbit terrine with apricot chutney, or watercress mousse followed by roast beef and Yorkshire pudding or roast rack of spring lamb (season depending). Vegetarians are served better by the larger evening menu.

Expensive

LA TANTE CLAIRE: FRENCH
68 Royal Hospital Road, SW3, tel. 071 352 6045. Open 12.30–2 p.m., 7–11 p.m. Mon–Fri. Sloane Square Underground.

'A supremely grand experience without snootiness'; 'My first choice for a special-occasion dinner' ... professional and amateur women foodies again and again pick out London's only three Michelin star restaurant for special praise. Most diners think chef-owner Pierre Koffman gets everything right, from the elegant blond-wood surroundings to Matisse reproductions on the menus to details of presentation that make dishes such as his famous recipe for pigs' trotters, or coquilles St-Jacques, a visual feast before the sublime experience of eating them. Of the Michelin star restaurants, this is favoured as the place that would be most welcoming to a woman dining alone.

Pubs and Bars

HENRY J. BEAN'S BAR AND GRILL
195–197 King's Road, SW3, tel. 071 352 9255. Sloane Square Underground.

Residents of Chelsea don't much like going to pubs, so most of the pubs are tourist traps or suits galore, neither especially suitable for women. Henry J. Bean's is popular with a healthy mix of young Sloaney locals, tourists and student trendsters, and because it serves food as well (burgers, etc.), you could slip behind a table and keep a low profile. Some come here, though, to get picked up. Early-evening happy hours, bouncer on weekend nights.

Kensington

The area around Notting Hill is all about hanging out with a cool media and artsy set – at Portobello market and at innumerable bars and restaurants, or with top-scale business executives at top-range restaurants. You'll be spoilt for choice – here are some of the best, and a few starting points.

PRUE LEITH, EATER EXTRAORDINAIRE

The catering company she started in a bedsit in 1962 is now Britain's third largest. In 1989 she was awarded an OBE for promoting higher standards in British cuisine. Yet Prue Leith freely admits that she's 'certainly not the best cook in my business'. However, 'I am a very good *eater,*' she says. 'You have to enjoy eating to enjoy cooking, and I do so love food.'

She first developed a passion for eating when her parents sent her, aged nineteen, from her home in Cape Town, South Africa, to the Sorbonne in Paris to study history, which left her cold. Having been refused apprenticeship by top French kitchens, she set out for London. She began catering for a firm of solicitors from a rented room in Barons Court that was basic but fine – until her landlady found a lobster on the dressing-table and a lettuce in the bath, and chucked her out. Undeterred, she continued to build up her freelance catering business and develop the Leith philosophy: no trends, no cans, just good, wholesome food.

It was work as a food stylist for TV commercials that decided her on the subject of honesty. After spraying cream cheese with water to make it glisten for the camera, she was required to tackle 'a ludicrous, small inedible fruit pie. A voice-over said, "They don't just ooze!" But they did.' At a time when high-class restaurants might serve up monkfish as lobster, Prue Leith pioneered the 'don't cheat' principle at her flagship restaurant, Leith's (see below), and at her cooking school. 'Fifteen years ago,' she recalls, 'I'd got girls into the Dorchester, Claridges, the Roux brothers,' but the Savoy held out. So she paid a personal visit to find out why. She expected all the usual excuses – women can't stand the heat of the kitchen, can't lift the stockpot, will take men's minds off the job – but instead, she says, Trompetto declared: 'At a certain time of the month they'll curdle the mayonnaise.'

Although there is still prejudice, Leith's year-long food and wine course injects a stream of women chefs into the top kitchens of London. Leith herself continues to embark on new ventures. In 1992 she accepted 'the hardest challenge in catering', doing the food for Intercity train travellers. Indeed, if it's not a challenge, then ten to one Prue Leith won't take it on. Skills learnt during a stint studying acting in her teens have resurfaced in a developing taste for political lobbying. One current concern is raising the profile of the trade in schools. But she always returns with relish to tastings at Leith's, when new dishes created by her chef are laid out on a table. 'It's such an *interesting* hour,' she says. The perfect job for a woman who says, with an engaging laugh, 'Both my parents were greedy and I am greedy, too.'

Cafés and Snacks

CAFÉ GROVE

253 Portobello Road, W11, tel. 071 243 1094. Open 9 a.m.–11 p.m. Mon–Fri, 9 a.m.–6 p.m. Sat, 10.30 a.m.–5 p.m. Sun. Ladbroke Grove Underground.

Above a bookshop, and in the summer out on a balcony that has a bird's-eye view of the market, this perennially trendy café serves *caffè latte*, cappuccino, herb teas, scrambled eggs on toast and cakes – everything you need for a lazy, hanging-out breakfast or Sunday brunch. In the evenings it turns into a Mexican restaurant.

LISBOA PATISSERIE

57 Golborne Road, W10, tel. 081 968 5242. Open daily 8 a.m.–8 p.m. Ladbroke Grove Underground.

Despite the popularity that keeps this plain counter-service café buzzing with Portuguese families and sunglasses-and-Levi-501-adorned Notting Hill cool dudes, the prices for Portuguese coffees and superb cakes have stayed low, on market days attracting long queues of both shoppers and market traders bearing mobile phones and lots of gold jewellery. Rather than asking for a coffee, ask for a *galão*, a rich, milky coffee in a glass. Keep children happy with custard tarts.

Budget

GEALE'S: FISH

2 Farmer Street, W8, tel. 071 727 7969. Open noon–3 p.m., 6–11 p.m. Tues–Sat. Notting Hill Underground.

This could slip into the £10 range, but only if you came out really quite drunk and stuffed to the gills. To make sure you stay within budget, go for the set lunch. Batter inevitably features high in the food content, but it's an especially high-quality batter (made with beef dripping) and not all cod fillings: the unconventional salmon in batter gets a thumbs-up, as do the deep-fried clams. The small wine list is good value – try a glass of the white Mâcon. Congenial atmosphere; a cross between hip café (young staff) and downbeat tea shop (yellow tablecloths and dark wood).

KHANS: INDIAN

13–15 Westbourne Grove, W2, tel. 071 727 5420. Open daily noon–3 p.m., 6–11.45 p.m. Bayswater, Royal Oak or Queensway Underground.

This aircraft hangar of a place is, say some locals, going downhill and now inferior to the nearby Standard (see below), but it still regularly fills to its 300 capacity. Good fun. Drink lots of the potent beer and you'll forget about the erratic service and only reasonable-quality curries.

STANDARD: INDIAN
21–23 Westbourne Grove, W2, tel. 071 727 4818. Open daily noon–3 p.m., 6–midnight. Bayswater, Royal Oak or Queensway Underground.

This is the oldest Indian restaurant on Westbourne Grove, serving a chana masaladar (chickpeas in spicy masala sauce) that many Londoners will go out of their way for.

Moderate

L'ACCENTO: ITALIAN
16 Garway Road, W2, tel. 071 243 2201. Open 12.30–2 p.m. Mon–Fri, 6.30–11 p.m. Mon–Sat. Bayswater Underground.

This new restaurant seems to have been surprised by its own popularity, which looks set to continue as the emphasis is entirely on the food. In a small room done out simply to look like rough-hewn stone you can choose from an imaginative daily changing menu that might include black squid ink risotto or wild mushroom polenta or pumpkin-purée-filled ravioli. Book ahead so you're sure to get a table amongst the jostle of Notting Hill trendies, friends after work on their way home, and cosy couples.

CHEZ MOI: FRENCH
1 Addison Avenue, Holland Park, W11, tel. 071 603 8267. Open 12.30–2 p.m. Mon–Fri, 6.30–11 p.m. Mon–Sat. Holland Park Underground.

This restaurant has been serving high-quality food from an` always-up-to-date menu for nearly three decades to Londoners who become such loyal regulars that it's a first choice for special occasions such as marriage proposals. The décor's odd: bottle windows send a wobbly daylight on to elaborate furnishings that include pink-striped wallpaper, lots of gilt mirrors, wooden busts and society portraits. The menu's mainly French – restaurant critic Fay Maschler recommends the *carré d'agneau* and saddle of hare – and there's a *'quelque chose de différent'* section, from which Maschler recommends the scallops with fuot-maki roll and sa-teh of chicken. Better than average selection for vegetarians.

CLARKE'S: MODERN BRITISH
124 Kensington Church Street, W8, tel. 071 221 9225. Open 12.30–2 p.m., 7–10 p.m. Mon–Fri. Notting Hill Gate or High Street Kensington Underground.

Sally Clarke's Mediterranean-influenced cooking is bound in by a restriction she found and liked in California: her lunch and dinner menus are set. There is no choice, which most customers love because – after they have been greeted personally by Sally at the door – it feels as if they are at an extremely smart dinner party, at which the starters, entrées and desserts have all been designed to complement each other perfectly. Clarke is so determined that ingredients are fresh that she flies her pigeons and fish in from Calais and gets her mushrooms from her mother. One autumn day's menu read: Buckwheat blini served with salmon eggs, warm dill butter and watercress salad; poached guinea fowl with horseradish *salsa verde* and spiced lentils; cheeses with oatmeal biscuits and celery; warm moca custard with biscotti and marzipan panforte. If you're vegetarian, phone ahead and a special dish will be prepared for you. A first choice for many Londoners for a special occasion such as a birthday; it's so romantic that if you went there on your own you might feel rather lonely.

KENSINGTON PLACE: MODERN BRITISH
201–205 Kensington Church Street, W8, tel. 071 727 3184. Open 12–3 p.m. Mon–Fri, 12–4 p.m. Sat and Sun; 6.30–11.45 p.m. Mon–Sat, 6.30–10.15 p.m. Sun. Notting Hill Gate Underground.

This designer warehouse with chrome trimmings and a massive windowed front is just made for 'rubber-necking' – inside and outside literary and film agents, editors and producers check who's doing deals with whom. And the food's good, with careful attention to detail (e.g. nice bread). If you're most interested in the food, come in the evening when diners are concentrating on dishes like chicken and goat's cheese mousse and braised rabbit with thyme instead of rubber-necking, although a bit of entertaining eavesdropping is unavoidable because the tables are packed so close.

Expensive

LEITH'S: BRITISH
92 Kensington Park Road, W11, tel. 071 229 4481. Open daily 7.30–11.30 p.m. Notting Hill Gate Underground.

Leith's stands out for a number of reasons, including these: it is run by and named for the doyenne of British restaurateurs, Prue Leith; it offers a separate menu for vegetarians plus the assurance that all the fresh produce is grown on Leith's own farm; and it operates the rare trolley system, a WYSIWYG (what you see is what you get) approach to the starters, which appear on a trolley for you to choose from. The introduction of swivel chairs is a surprisingly good idea, although it does add to the executive feel that's engendered by the mainly male business clientele. Nevertheless, the restaurant is broken up with walls and mirrors so that tables are intimate, and the atmosphere is comforting. Even if they're slightly disappointed by a dish (e.g veal scallops in lime gravy), diners are won over by the honest feel that pervades; more often, the dishes are excellent (e.g. langoustine ravioli), and the wine list is well-respected. The staff are affable and quietly attentive.

Bars and Pubs

BEACH BLANKET BABYLON
45 Ledbury Road, W11, tel. 071 229 2907. Notting Hill Gate Underground.

It looked for a while as if this might be a passing phase, but trendy bars around the country have modelled themselves on Beach Blanket Babylon – not literally copying the fireplaces set in the roaring mouths of wild beasts, but trying to match the regressive pub-fixtures-and-fittings-meet-lunatic-interior-decorator feel. Some find it too trendy by half; others love the bustle of dudes in obscure name label designers. It's wine-bar-y enough for women friends who don't like pubs to feel comfortable in.

JULIE'S BAR
137 Portland Road, W11, tel. 071 727 7985. Open 11 a.m.–midnight Mon–Sat, noon–10.30 p.m. Sun. Holland Park Underground.

Interior designer Julie Hodgess created the rambling Victorian Gothic look in this wine bar. Julie's has long appealed to conservative Kensington-ites looking for a touch of bohemianism, and slightly tired ravers who appreciate the sturdily romantic atmosphere. Food on the evening menu is good (big sirloin steaks or light leek and watercress soups) and Sunday-afternoon tea is popular. The manager's baby's highchair is always available.

Hammersmith

Moderate

RIVER CAFÉ: ITALIAN
Thames Wharf, Rainville Road, W6, tel. 071 381 8824. Open 12.30–2.30 p.m. Mon–Fri, 1–2.45 p.m. Sat, Sun; 7.30–9.30 p.m. Mon–Fri. Hammersmith Underground.

Although some complain that this restaurant is 1980s-dated décor, few have anything but praise for the food, which is simple Italian with only the best ingredients – for example, saffron soup, bresaola (northern Lombardy dried salt beef), calf's liver with polenta. You must book, and unless you're in the area already – for example, to see a show at the Riverside Arts Centre – prepare for a long journey.

Waterloo and the South Bank

Most of the eateries listed here are convenient for the sights including the Imperial War Museum, the St Thomas' Old Operating Theatre, Museum and Herb Garret and the Design Museum.

Budget

BENKEI: JAPANESE
19 Lower Marsh Street, SE1, tel. 071 401 2343. Open noon–3 p.m., 6–10.30 p.m. Mon–Fri, 6–10.30 p.m. Sat. Waterloo Underground.

Japanese red lanterns and black-lacquered counter where you buy for takeaway or perch on a stool to eat dishes like tempura and beef teriyaki for around a fiver. Handy stop-off place before going to the Old Vic for a performance, although the bustling market that makes the street feel safe during the day is not there after 5 p.m.

MARIE'S: THAI
90 Lower Marsh Street, SE1, tel. 071 928 1050. Open 7 a.m.–5.45 p.m. Mon–Fri, 7 a.m.–3 p.m. Sat. Waterloo Underground.

You'll probably go past this the first time, as it looks like the seediest 'greasy spoon' on the street. It does do egg and chips, but you'll also see, under Thai tourist posters, market traders and local office workers tucking into dishes like Neau Phad Nummon Hoi, which are written up on day-glo boards in the window. Weekdays, you can stock up on fruit from the market afterwards.

PERDONI: ENGLISH-ITALIAN
18–20 Kennington Road, SE1, tel. 071 928 6846. Open 7 a.m.–6.30 p.m. Mon–Fri, 7 a.m.–noon Sat. Lambeth North Underground.

Practically opposite Lambeth North Underground station in the middle of a row of shops on a main road, this smart, clean, fudge, orange and copper-coloured Italian café/restaurant is a good place to start, end or punctuate your visit to the sights around Waterloo. Many women eat alone here, although it's not brilliant for vegetarians (omelette-and-chips fare) or children. Meat eaters are in for a cheap treat: say a dish of the day is *fegato alla rosmarino*, the calf's liver will be fine, the rosemary in healthy sprigs and the sauce genuinely wine-tasting. Creamed potato piped round the edges of most dishes as if they're cakes. Sandwiches also available.

Moderate

BLUEPRINT CAFÉ: MODERN ITALIAN
Design Museum, Butlers Wharf, SE1, tel. 071 378 7031. Open noon–2 p.m., 7–11 p.m. Mon–Sat (last booking 9.30 p.m.), Sun noon–3 p.m. Tower Hill or London Bridge Underground.

Designer location for designer food that attracts sussed City folk over the river for a chi-chi lunch. Italian influence to much of the menu (frequently pasta plus dishes such as *vitello tonnato*). Excellent river views. If you fancy something more formal but along the same lines, go to the nearby **Le Pont de la Tour** (*The Butlers Wharf Building, 36D Shad Thames, Butlers Wharf, tel. 071 403 8403*). Both venues are owned by design king Terence Conran.

THE CHAPTER HOUSE: ITALIAN
Pizza Express at Southwark Cathedral, Montague Street, SE1, tel. 071 378 6446. Open 10 a.m.–4 p.m. Mon–Fri. Closed weekends. London Bridge Underground.

You know you're getting decent-quality pizzas at decent prices at any branch of Pizza Express, and here, in a grey extension next to Southwark Cathedral, you can join local office workers and worshippers in clean modern pine surroundings for a hearty lunch in between the Waterloo–South Bank sights.

GABRIEL'S WHARF: INTERNATIONAL
Embankment or Waterloo Underground.

This is not one restaurant or bar but a complex where there are several serving corporate executives from nearby businesses, including London Weekend Television and an arty crowd who work at or are visiting the neighbouring South Bank centre. An oasis for locals, it's perfect if you've just been to something at the Hayward Gallery, the NFT or one of the theatres or concert halls. Pizza, Japanese food and sandwich fare are available amongst craft gift shops.

MESON DON FELIPE: SPANISH
53 The Cut, SE1, tel. 071 928 3237. Open noon–11 p.m. Mon–Sat. Waterloo Underground.

Although this is considered one of the decent Spanish tapas restaurants in London, a visit is still more about the socialising atmosphere than the food. Tortilla, gambas alioli, olives and other tasty Spanish snacks are served along the square bar or at more intimate side tables. Terracotta walls are splashed with bright colours in the form of plates and flamenco posters. Near the Old Vic theatre and relatively near the South Bank arts complex, this is one of the more fun pre- or post-theatre options, partly because it's not the bar's prime function – all kinds of Londoners, mainly from South of the river, come here for a good night out.

RSJ: French

13A Coin Street, SE1, tel. 071 928 4554. Open noon–2 p.m. Mon–Fri, 6–11 p.m. Sat. Waterloo or Embankment Underground.

Perfectly sited for pre- or post-theatre/event meals if you're going to something at the South Bank centre. Because it's off the beaten track on an empty but safe road (look for an unobtrusive white building with blue woodwork), it doesn't get too full. The expensive sunny yellow upstairs restaurant attracts rather a lot of men in suits, especially during the day – the less pricey, cheerful basement brasserie with a Mediterranean feel to the décor might be more enjoyable. An imaginative English-customised French menu will give you basic pasta or complex dishes such as duck legs cooked slowly in vegetables, herbs and spices served crisp with crisps, red wine sauce and roast apples and peaches. Melon-motif-decorated tablecloths and tasteful prints surround you.

Pizzeria Castello: Italian

20 Walworth Road, SE1, tel. 071 703 2556. Open noon–11 p.m. Mon–Fri, 5–11 p.m. Sat. Elephant and Castle Underground (insalubrious subways – take cabs if you're unfamiliar with the area).

The four-cheeses pizza is favoured, as is the garlic bread, but the dough balls leave something to be desired at this pizzeria that's popular partly because there's little competition in the immediate vicinity. A homey local feel to the place.

The Tall House: Modern British

134 Southwark Street, SE1, tel. 071 401 2929. Open 9 a.m.–4 p.m. Mon–Fri. Blackfriars or Waterloo Underground.

A tall, thin stack of relaxed café, spacious brasserie and restaurant, this is a haven for local office workers and handy if you're stranded between sights, desperate for a coffee and a snack. The brasserie café area is all 1970s-look plants and Biba-style easy-wipe tablecloths. It's airy, with lots of stripped pine. You can have a selection of cheeses or a Waldorf salad for under a fiver.

Brixton

A relatively little-known, lovely park; the Ritzy, a new multiscreen cinema; the Fridge nightclub and the gig venue the Academy are in Brixton, which has a reputation of being rough but is loved by students and trendy thirty-something residents who wouldn't live anywhere else and ensure a lively café and bar scene. If you're not familiar with the area, take cabs at night.

Budget

PIZZERIA FRANCO: ITALIAN
4 Market Row, Brixton Market, Electric Lane, SW9, tel. 071 738 3021. Open 9.30 a.m. – 5 p.m. Mon, Tues, Thurs–Sat. Brixton Underground.

Before 11.30 a.m. you can have just coffee and croissants to the strains of opera highlights and Abba in the tiny panettone-strewn pizzeria with outside tables, but the sight of the pizza dough being worked behind the counter and the smells as Napoletanas and calzones go into the oven may well tempt you to stay. Good pizza bread sandwiches too. No special provisions for children, but long-time customers bring them and share in an atmosphere of happy chaos.

Pubs and Bars

THE BRIXTONIAN
11 Dorrell Place, off Nursery Road, SW9, tel. 071 978 8870. Open 5.30 p.m.–midnight Mon, 11 a.m.–midnight Tues–Thurs, 11 a.m.–1 a.m. Fri and Sat, 5.30-11 p.m. Sun. Brixton Underground.

There's a Caribbean restaurant above, but the main appeal of the Brixtonian to a cultural cross-section of Brixtonites is the 100 different kinds of rum sold in its ground-floor rum bar. The décor is camped-up Caribbean with cane furniture and splashes of purple, orange and pink over the walls. Outside in winter heating lamps extend the bar's capacity, and indoors there's sometimes blues and jazz bands.

Clapham and Wandsworth

As residential areas, Wandsworth and Clapham have a sturdily respectable appeal for well-heeled folk in business/the arts who want bigger houses than they could afford in Chelsea or don't mind smaller houses than they had in Brixton because of the increased feeling of safety that goes with the area. The Battersea Arts Centre attracts custom from other areas of London, but the knots of bars and restaurants are kept thriving mainly by people who live locally, so they maintain a relaxed, homey atmosphere.

Moderate

GRAFTON: FRENCH
45 Old Town, SW4, tel. 071 627 1048. Open 12.30–3.30 p.m., 7 p.m–midnight Mon–Sat. Clapham Common Underground.

As other restaurants go in and out of fashion, here in a quiet, seventeenth-century building you'll get good French food with formal service in a dining area that feels rather like an archetypal grandmother's living-room.

OSTERIA ANTIC BOLOGNA: ITALIAN
23 Northcote Road, SW11, tel. 071 978 4771. Open noon–11 p.m. Mon–Sat, 12.30–10.30 p.m. Sun. Clapham Junction BR/35, 37 bus.

Lively menu and a lively atmosphere at this local restaurant which serves above-average-quality dishes such as young goat and stew of cuttlefish and prawns.

Expensive

HARVEY'S: FRENCH
2 Bellevue Road, SW17, tel. 081 672 0114. Open 12.30–2 p.m. Tues–Sun, 7.30–11 p.m. Tues–Sat. Wandsworth Common BR.

Roux-brothers-trained Marco Pierre White, the youngest chef to be awarded two Michelin stars, has gained due fame for his food – which elicits subdued cries of velvety, sensuous, sophisticated, sublime – and as a bit of a ladykiller. Some women positively exult at the idea of dining alone at Harvey's, in case Marco saunters over for a flirtatious chat. But few actually venture out there *toute seule*, thinking first of the thirty-minute cab ride from Central London and then of the size of the white room, which is pleasantly decorated but small. Harvey's is perhaps better as a place to dine *à deux*. Share the delights of dishes such as Bresse pigeon with *cèpes* ravioli and wild mushrooms bathed in a truffled sauce followed by a *harlequin de chocolat* with cinnamon sauce.

Pubs and Bars

TEAROOM DES ARTISTES
697 Wandsworth Road, SW8, tel. 071 720 4028. Open 6 p.m.–midnight Mon–Fri, noon–midnight Sat and Sun. Wandsworth Road BR, or a 15-minute walk from Clapham Common Underground.

The Tearoom serves decent vegetarian food but is most popular as a coolly bohemian-feeling bar where all the furniture is meant to be mismatched in the crooked interweaving of ground-floor, first-floor and outdoor yard sections. Sometimes there are bands. A good place to while away a Sunday from late brunch through Aqua Libras to in-vogue bottled beers.

Greenwich

If it's a sunny day and you're visiting maritime sights, including the *Cutty Sark* and the Royal Observatory, your best bet is to take a picnic and enjoy it in spacious Greenwich Park. If it's raining, here are some alternatives.

Budget

ESCAPED COFFEE HOUSE: VEGETARIAN
141–143 Greenwich South Street, SE10, tel. 081 692 5826. Open 10 a.m.–10.30 p.m. Mon–Sat, 11 a.m.–8 p.m. Sun. Greenwich BR.

If you're coming from the station, the market or the *Cutty Sark*, it's a fair walk up the hill; it's quicker to approach the café from the top end of the park after you've done the Royal Observatory and the Ranger's House. Hanging plants, art posters, mismatching wood tables and chairs, and so much stripped pine you could be in a Swedish sauna. Evidence that children are truly welcome is the highchair already at one of the tables and the chalked blackboard note: 'Half-price portions available'. Daytime fare is salads, sandwiches and healthy cakes. In the evening the candles-in-bottles come out and it's the same kind of food plus soups and specials of the day, but a pound or two more expensive. Light meal for around £5.

Moderate

SAIGON: VIETNAMESE
16 Nelson Road, SE10, tel. 081 853 0414. Open daily noon–11 p.m. Greenwich BR.

Convenient for the market and Greenwich's maritime sights, this restaurant serves decent food to a mixture of tourists and locals in a friendly atmosphere, at prices that won't break the bank. Dishes like squid balls for starter then grilled fish with chopped lemon grass, chilli and spring onions.

Pubs and Bars

TRAFALGAR TAVERN
Park Row, SE10, tel. 081 858 2437. Greenwich BR.

A great riverfront location for this pub, which has just changed hands, so the rather dull interior décor may be spruced up. Because food's currently served at lunchtime, children are allowed in during the lunch period. It's near a rowing club, so picturesque views in fine weather.

Richmond and Kew

Most visitors from Central London come for the Royal Botanical Gardens at Kew and the lazy-atmosphere riverside walk at Richmond.

Snacks and Cafés

MAIDS OF HONOUR
288 Kew Road, Kew Gardens, Surrey TW9 3DU, tel. 081 940 2752. Open 9.30 a.m.–1 p.m. Mon, 10 a.m.–6 p.m. Tues–Fri, 9 a.m.–6 p.m. Sat. Kew Underground and BR.

This legendary tearoom is ideally placed for refreshments after a day at Kew Gardens. The Maids of Honour is classic English, complete with chintzy curtains, plastic candle hanging lights, paper doilies and a heavy tacky feel that's somehow warm and cosy. All the meat in pies and sandwiches, etc., is 'organic farm produce', but the main things to come here for are the cream teas and the original Maids of Honour cakes, which are small curd tarts. Children are welcome but are expected to be well-behaved, which shouldn't be a problem once they're involved with the ritual of scones and jam or equivalent.

Moderate

CAFÉ FLO: FRENCH
149 Kew Road, Richmond, Surrey, tel. 081 940 8298. Open daily 12.30–11 p.m. Other branches. Kew Underground/BR, North Sheen BR, Richmond Underground/BR.

Café Flo serves brasserie food at acceptable prices. Children are welcome, and this branch of the French-style brasserie is equally well-placed for the sights of Richmond and Kew. The prix-fixe meal is always a bargain, or you could just stick to soup and coffee.

PIERRE'S: INTERNATIONAL
11 Petersham Road, Richmond, Surrey, tel. 081 332 2778. Open daily 8.30 a.m.–11 p.m. Richmond Underground/BR.

Richmond has *lots* of places to eat and drink, but not all of them are good value and many of them get uncomfortably full. An airy marble-table and geranium-window-plant atmosphere plus patisseries, home-made tabouleh and rolled pitta falafel sandwiches make Pierre's well worth the short walk from the tourist trap riverfront venues. Good snack lunch for under a fiver.

Pubs and Bars

RICHMOND ARMS
Waterloo Place, Richmond, Surrey, Richmond Underground/BR.

In Richmond's centre, this gay-friendly pub is frequented by many air stewards because of Richmond's proximity to Heathrow.

THE WHITE SWAN
Old Palace Lane, Richmond, Surrey, tel. 081 940 0959.

This off-the-beaten-track pub serves average food but is one of the nicer places to have a relaxed beer during or after a riverside walk.

The East End

Although there aren't a huge number of wonderful restaurants in the East End, there are a few that are well worth the journey and a couple that are handy to know about if you're going sightseeing to, for example, the Whitechapel Art Gallery, or Brick Lane market, or London's Docklands. Going for an Indian meal down Brick Lane is a regular pilgrimage for many Londoners. Indeed, there are so many cheap neighbouring rivals that it's almost impossible to pick one out for recommendation. Below are a couple that give an idea of the range.

Snacks and Cafés

BRICK LANE BAGEL BAKERY
159 Brick Lane, E1, tel. 071 729 0616. Open 24 hours daily. Shoreditch (peak hours only) or Whitechapel Underground.

A churn-'em-out Formica shop front serves cabbies and clubbers through the small hours and market traders and shoppers on weekends with bagels, plain and with fillings including the traditional smoked salmon and cream cheese.

Budget

CHERRY ORCHARD: VEGETARIAN
241–245 Globe Road, E2, tel. 081 980 6678. Open 11 a.m.–3 p.m. Mon, Thur, Fri; 11 a.m.–7 p.m. Tues, Wed. Bethnal Green Underground.

This is handy after the Bethnal Green Museum of Childhood and especially lovely in summer, when the garden opens (fountain and flowers and outside seating). The Cherry Orchard is run by five Buddhist women who serve imaginative vegetarian and vegan dishes including things like cauliflower and cashew filo pie. There's also food for anyone on sugar-free and wheat-free diets. Bright orange and blue rag-rolled décor. No smoking in restaurant; can smoke in garden.

SHAMPAN: BANGLADESHI
79 Brick Lane, E1, tel. 071 375 0475. Open daily noon–3 p.m., 6 p.m.–midnight. Aldgate East Underground.

This is one of the best of the new kind of Brick Lane restaurants. Smarter décor and specifically Bangladeshi cuisine attract even well-heeled City types who might worry about hygiene in nearby equivalents. The excellent range of dishes includes marinated arr, a Bangladeshi fish, and chicken spiced with shatkora, a Bangladeshi fruit.

SWEET AND SPICY: INDIAN
42 Brick Lane, E1, tel. 071 247 1081. Open 8 a.m.–10 p.m. Mon–Sat, 8 a.m.–6 p.m. Sun. Aldgate East Underground.

This is a basic Brick Lane curry-caff of the old school. Scruffy floor, metal beakers for water with dhal, roghan josh and mixed vegetable dishes making up the bulk of the menu that's enjoyed hugely by arty sets after shows at the Whitechapel, and Asian regulars.

Moderate

BLOOM'S: JEWISH
90 Whitechapel High Street, E1, tel. 071 247 6001. Open 11 a.m.–9.30 p.m. Sun–Thur, 11 a.m.–3 p.m. Fri, Sat closed all day. Aldgate East Underground.

In the 1920s, Morris Bloom began experimenting with kosher foods and found a new way of pickling salt beef. His sandwiches became so popular that his café turned into a restaurant, and today you can buy salt beef sandwiches done his way at the sandwich bar, or go back to the corrugated-wood, skating-rink-shaped restaurant for heimishe barley soup, turkey schnitzel or Bloomburger and onions. Old-fashioned waiters make children welcome in a quiet way with highchairs and reduced-price portions.

Pubs and Bars

CAPTAIN KIDD
108 Wapping High Street, E1, tel. 071 480 5759. Wapping Underground.

This modernised pub has a recurring theme through the décor – Captain Kidd – and a great view of the river from a lovely beer garden and a family room with Dumbo, Scooby Doo and Tweety Pie murals. A warning on the door says 'No admittance without a child'. Many families find this pub the perfect place to spend a sunny Sunday afternoon.

Hang out in Hampstead after spending a day on the Heath.

Cafés and Snacks

HAMPSTEAD TEA ROOMS
9 South End Road, NW3 tel. 071 435 9563. Open daily 9 a.m.–7 p.m. Belsize Park or Hampstead Underground.

Big, cream-lavished cakes and patisseries are the things to come here for. It gets packed at around 4–5 p.m. on weekends when families and friends from all over London spill from the Heath into this cosy haven.

Moderate

CAFÉ DES ARTS: INTERNATIONAL
82 Hampstead High Street, NW3, tel. 071 435 3608. Open daily 12–4 p.m., 6–11.30 p.m. Hampstead Underground.

This relatively new addition to Hampstead's not hugely inspiring restaurant scene is generally welcomed. Dishes such as chargrilled radiccio with marinated vegetables come in starter or main-course sizes. The menu is characterised by unexpected mixes. Roast lamb with dhal, stir-fried beef with brandy-soaked apricots. Because it's Hampstead, single well-behaved children are often in evidence, brought out by parents not prepared to have their lifestyle hampered by family life. No pipes or cigars are allowed in this oak-panelled seventeenth-century dining-room. As well as wine, you can order Kulta, a strong beer brewed by women in Lapland 'for the liberality of mankind'.

Pubs and Bars

EVERYMAN CAFÉ
Holly Bush Vale, NW3, tel. 071 431 2123. Open 11 a.m.–11 p.m. Mon–Fri, 10.30 a.m.–11 p.m. Sat, 10.30 a.m.–10.30 p.m. Sun. Hampstead Underground.

Before or after you've been to a screening at the Everyman Cinema (of which the café is part), this downstairs arty café-cum-brasserie is the perfect place to have a relaxed beer or bottle of wine. Brunch and full meals are also served.

SPANIARDS INN
Spaniards Road, NW3, tel. 071 455 3276. Golders Green Underground or, during the day, Hampstead Underground then a pleasant walk over Hampstead Heath.

Low-ceilinged pub on a car-scrapingly narrow bit of road. Pleasant and atmospheric, with a range of dishes that have got it into the *Good Pub Food* guide (see Recommended Books). Popular with families.

Islington

One of Islington's main attractions is the thriving bar and restaurant scene. Make a day of it and combine café-ing with a walk along the canal. Or make a night of it and go to the Sadler's Wells or the Screen on the Green cinema as well.

Cafés and Snacks

PATISSERIE BLISS
428 St John Street, EC1, tel. 071 837 3720. Open 8 a.m.–7 p.m. Mon–Fri, 9 a.m.–6 p.m. Sat, Sun. Angel Underground.

Some say you get the best croissants in London here (all patisseries are baked on the premises); others complain that the staff are too concerned with nightclub chat to get round to serving in a tiny room that fills to capacity with a cross-section of loyal Islington-ites, from trendies to monied City types plus baby.

Budget

ALFREDO'S: BRITISH
4–6 Essex Road, N1, tel. 071 226 3496. Open 7 a.m.–2.30 p.m. Mon–Fri, 7 a.m.–noon Sat. Angel Underground.

This has something of a cult status for its unchanged Deco Formica caff décor, its well-prepared caff food, and its courteous service.

RAVI SHANKAR: VEGETARIAN INDIAN
422 St John Street, EC1, tel. 071 833 5849. Open noon–2.15 p.m. daily; 6–10.30 p.m. Mon–Thur and Sun, 6–11 p.m. Fri and Sat. Angel Underground.

Very convenient for a pre-Sadler's Wells meal. A clean, sparsely decorated restaurant (just a few atmospheric photos of India). At lunchtime, Ravi Shankar fills with local office workers grateful for the cheap set lunch. The bhelpoori food, including spectacular paper dosas, is made in the kitchens of Chutneys (see Bloomsbury).

Moderate

ANNA'S PLACE: SWEDISH
90 Mildmay Park, N1, tel. 071 249 9379. Open 12.15–2.15 p.m., 7.15–10.30 p.m. Tues–Sat. Angel Underground then 73 bus.

French and English food is also served in this blue, plant-scattered room that has a relaxed conservatory feel about it, but as garrulous Anna talks you through her menu, everything Swedish sounds too irresistible to miss, from dishes such as lax pudding (salted salmon baked with onions, potatoes and cream) and fresh terrines made of pike and eel. Saturdays are popular with families, when children tuck into the home-made ice cream with glee. It's certainly a bit off the beaten track, but the fact that it's worth a visit is indicated by its popularity – make sure to book in advance, especially for dinner.

CASALE FRANCO: ITALIAN
Round the back of 134–137 Upper Street, N1, tel. 071 226 8994. Open 12.30–2.30 p.m. Fri–Sun, 6.30–11.30 p.m. Tues–Sat, 6.30–11 p.m. Sun. Angel or Highbury and Islington Underground. No pizzas at lunchtime.

Secreted in an alley behind a lighted red-and-white Citroën Garage sign, the lighting-laced ceiling and red-brick walls give Franco's a ruddy, friendly atmosphere that is as conducive to a woman alone as to a birthday party. Franco, who started small running a tiny pizza café in Brixton, is the pizza expertise behind possibly the best pizza restaurant in London. He can be seen by the ovens, tossing pizza dough or putting finishing touches to one of his superb calzones. Most of the non-pizza entrées are excellent, and both sweets and starters come in generous portions (note that pizzas aren't on offer at lunchtime). Ever since celebrities such as Julie Christie were spotted dining here, there've been complaints that service can be surly.

IZNIK: TURKISH
19 Highbury Park, London N5, tel. 071 354 5697. Open daily 10 a.m.–3.30 p.m., 6.30–11 p.m. Highbury and Islington Underground.

Behind an unostentatious glass front is a visual feast of kilims and arty blue-glass candelabras, and that's before you've even begun to look at the menu, which goes on and on and is surprisingly good for vegetarians. Hot starters include cigar-shaped parcels of fetta cheese in filo pastry and chickpea rissoles; for main course you can have oven-baked lamb in a paper bag, *menemen* ('scrambled eggs Turkish-style') or a traditional shish kebab (marinated lamb grilled on skewers). This can be budget, but the dishes are so good that it's best to decide to blow out.

WILLOUGHBY'S: MODERN BRITISH
26 Penton Street, N1, tel. 071 833 1380. Open noon–3 p.m. Mon–Fri, 6.30 –11 p.m. Mon–Sat. Angel Underground.

This restaurant's a real treat. Don't be fooled by the unassuming café front. In a quiet, pleasant back area that is simply decorated in green, you can enjoy dishes from a seasonally changing menu that is good for vegetarians and will more than satisfy meat eaters. The Glamorgan sausages and salmon fishcakes are signature dishes that get the thumbs-up; Willoughby's won the Hotel and Restaurant Wine Magazine award for serving the best house red.

Pubs and Bars

OLD QUEEN'S HEAD
44 Essex Road, N1, tel. 071 354 9273. Angel Underground.

Medieval-looking wood-and-stone-carved fireplace in a large square room with industrial lampshades over the bar and flowers such as thistles in jars on the tables. Not so many of the boisterously bright young things of Islington's main drag (Upper Street) – a funky, mellower crowd.

Camden

Camden Market's the big crowd-puller here. Less boisterous delights around Camden include Primrose Hill and Regent's Park, as well as the canal. The centre of Camden has a couple of cinemas.

Snacks and Cafés

CAFÉ DELANCEY
3 Delancey Street, NW1, tel. 071 387 1985. Open daily 8 a.m.–11.30 p.m. Camden Town Underground.

The day's newspapers hang at the door for you to read at bijoux round tables or in cane chairs by the window. Cappuccino, chocolate and numerous high-calorie-count cakes. A nice place for two women friends to snack at almost any point through the day (it can get crowded at lunchtime).

MARINE ICES
8 Haverstock Hill, NW3, tel. 071 485 3132. Open 10.30 a.m.–10.45 p.m. Mon–Sat, 11 a.m.–8 p.m. Sun in summer. Chalk Farm Underground.

Here you can have peanut butter ice cream, ice-cream sundaes in tall glasses with cherries on top, an ice-cream cake cassata, a lemon or strawberry and melon water ice, for Marine Ices is an ice-cream parlour where children will bliss out for so long that you'll get the chance to read the paper from cover to cover ... that's if you haven't succumbed yourself. There are also basic pasta dishes.

Budget

EL PARADOR: SPANISH
245 Eversholt Street, NW1, tel. 071 387 2789. Open noon–3 p.m. Mon–Fri, 6–11 p.m. Mon–Thur,. 6–11.30 p.m. Fri and Sat,. 7–10.30 p.m. Sun. Mornington Crescent Underground (if open), or ten minutes walk from Camden Town Underground.

This is so underdecorated, unlike most tapas bars, that the front part feels almost like a 'greasy spoon'. The real treat here is being able to eat some of the best Spanish snacks in London at reasonable prices outside on the patio in summer. Good, reasonably priced Spanish wine and beer list.

MANNA: VEGETARIAN
4 Erskine Road, NW3, tel. 071 722 8028. Open daily 6.30–11 p.m. Chalk Farm Underground.

Detractors say it's dated (1970s brown décor), but it's heaven-sent for vegetarians, for there's little else for non-meat eaters in the area. Good variety of starters – seaweed salad, Mexican chilli pâté – and the salads go down well.

Moderate

BELGO: BELGIAN
72 Chalk Farm Road, NW1, tel. 071 267 0718. Open noon–3 p.m., 6–11 p.m. Mon–Fri, noon–1 a.m. Sat, noon–11.30 p.m. Sun. Chalk Farm Underground.

Yes, the improbable concrete façade does lead through a tunnel-like passage to a long, light dining-room where you can get good-value set meals (boar sausage and beer will probably feature). Media trendy set enjoy the matey service and a good range of beers, including cherry and raspberry.

CAMDEN BRASSERIE: FRENCH
216 Camden High Street, NW1, tel. 071 482 2114. Open noon–3 p.m. Mon–Sat, 12.30–3.30 p.m. Sun; 6–11.30 p.m. Mon–Sat, 6–10.30 p.m. Sun. Camden Town Underground.

Staff at Camden publishing houses remain fiercely loyal to either Café Delancey or Camden Brasserie when it comes to lunch. Brasserie fans say this one really does feel like a French brasserie, and the salads – with things like grilled swordfish or chicken livers – are lovely. Wood floors, changing art exhibitions on the walls, friendly atmosphere.

Pubs and Bars

THE BUCK'S HEAD
202 Camden High Street, NW1, tel. 071 284 1513. Camden Town Underground.

Women who don't like pubs feel comfortable here at lunchtime – it's very light, with wood floors and tables and friendly staff. Good cheapish, above-average-quality food on the lunch menu (e.g. smoked chicken and Stilton salad). In the evenings it gets busy and buzzing with a younger crowd.

CROWN AND GOOSE

100 Arlington Road, NW1, tel. 071 485 2342. Camden Town Underground.

Cosy trendy décor including blue walls, gilt cherubs and flowers attract a laidback North London set. One of the better pubs for women.

ENTERTAINMENT

London has something for everyone, and then some... Soho's 'More than Vegas' stripper bar has been judged A-OK for 'politically correct' women by the *Guardian*; Princess Diana has been seen stepping out of members-only Knightsbridge bop-venue Annabel's; soap stars appear as thigh-slapping boy heroes and busty male Ugly Sisters in role-reversal Christmas pantomimes; the West End stage version of Agatha Christie's whodunnit *The Mousetrap* is into its fifth decade; an ex-ballroom off cinema-lined Leicester Square is once-monthly home to one of Europe's hottest lesbian clubs; bingo devotees descend on Essex Road for its lavish Art Deco Egyptian-style Bingo Hall; expense-accounters can test Radio 4's 'Week Ending' (unfair) skit on the Royal Opera House's pricing policy, 'La Travestyata', which featured the aria 'I want to buy a ticket, not a bungalow' ...

NIGHTLIFE AND GIGS

Women have blunderbussed the male domains of London's club and gig scenes. Take DJ-ing: 'There's quite a male, boffin quality to being a DJ, with all the knobs – it's like being able to fix your own car,' says Kleavage Sisters DJ Katrina Boorman; she adds: 'If anyone comes near my knobs, I tell them to sod off.' Soul and R&B DJ Wendy May is one of a growing number of women who've fought past what DJ Dominique calls 'the train-spotting attitude' into a position of crowd-pulling power that commands fees of up to £100 an hour. Other women decided: forget controlling the music – we want our own clubs. Look out for safe-sex-promoting raunchy club one-nighters organised by girl gangs with names like Pussy Posse.

Sisters are out there doing it for themselves, and the more they do, the easier it gets for you to join them and have a rip-roaring good time. If you're solo, here are a few handy hints: at sit-down gigs in smaller venues, if you're steered towards a dingy corner simply demand a better seat, and prepare a couple of barbed comments if you don't want to be chatted up (at larger venues you'll be allotted a seat, and fans will be intent on the gig, not on chatting you up); at rock gigs, know your fellow fans and judge for yourself if you'll be happy alone amongst them; 'ladies free' nights and clubs advertised by slick guys distributing flyers on Oxford Street on Friday and Saturday nights are known as 'cattle markets'.

Time Out magazine offers the most comprehensive listings across the board. Although it often skimps on lesbian information, info on straight clubs is, on the whole, reliable and easy to negotiate (the listings are divided by music type). Look in magazines including *ID, The Face, Mix Mag* and *Straight No Chaser* for selective coverage of happening clubs and gigs; for reviews of major jazz and rock gigs, see the 'Arts' sections of the national press and the *Evening Standard*. The underground 'house' parties with names like Bob's Full House and Kinky Disco are, as ever, by their nature hard to find out about – shops are your best bet: pick up flyers and tickets in advance (you can't always pay at the door) from Black Market Records (25 D'Arblay Street, W1, tel. 071 437 0478), Quaff (4 Berwick Street, W1, tel. 071 287 0705), and Catch A Groove (94 Dean Street, W1, tel. 071 494 0208) for dance and hip-hop; Soul Jazz (12 Ingestre Place, W1, tel. 071 494 2004) for soul jazz, and for reggae try Daddy Kool (9 Berwick Street, W1, tel. 071 437 3535). Trendy clubs do operate door policies – a club 'uniform' that pretty well always guarantees entry is 501 Levi jeans and a plain T-shirt.

The lesbian club scene is getting easier to break into – visit one of the cafés/bars listed in Eating and Drinking, where you'll find tables groaning with current flyers and, if they're not too busy, counter staff will fill you in on the latest.

Clubs

Weekend prices are around £10 until 3 a.m. when they drop – partly because of the licensing laws (only non-alcoholic 'psychoactive' drinks after 3 a.m.) and also to encourage club-crawling. To get round licensing laws that forbid alcohol sale outside members-only clubs after 11 p.m., most clubs will include a token membership fee in the admission price. Smarter, executive-league clubs are the best places for women alone who don't want to get hassled, but these clubs are likely to operate a members-only rule for real, and bar anyone wearing jeans and sneakers. Some allow visitors temporary membership (try **Annabel's,** *44 Berkeley Square, 071 629 3558* if you want to mix with royalty; and **Tramp,** *40 Jermyn Street, 071 734 3174* for pop star/TV celebrities and the sight of late-teen and early-twenties getting blind drunk with an assurance that comes from substantial/vast inherited wealth); two that are possibly most amenable for businesswomen alone are **Harry's Bar** *(26 South Audley Street, 071 408 0844)* and **Mortons** (*28 Berkeley Square, 071 499 0363*). Hotel clubs can be good to target if you're alone – for example, the club at the **Dorchester Hotel**, which is exclusive and provides entertainment as well. If in doubt about membership, phone ahead to avoid disappointment. If you're alone, *don't* take an unlicensed minicab home – if possible, arrange for a black taxi cab beforehand (see Getting Around and advice in Police and Crime); night buses are a slow and not always pleasant but relatively reliable alternative.

CRAZY LARRY'S

533 Kings Road, SW10, tel. 071 376 5555; Fulham Broadway or Sloane Square Underground; open till 3 a.m.; admission highest Thur–Sat.

A bit more civilised than average, this disco-&-restaurant attracts completely different crowds on different nights – could be rockabilly, or lots of Sloane Ranger Tom Cruise lookalikes, or the teen clubbers' Deb set. Phone ahead or check listings to get an idea of what you can expect.

FRIDGE

Town Hall Parade, Brixton Hill, SW2, tel. 071 326 5100; Brixton Underground; admission around £5; open till 3 a.m.

Recognisable by the fridges strung out front, this massive warehouse of a club is known for serving the hip lesbian and gay community, and is one of the clubs where you're perhaps less likely to get unwanted attention – go for solid grooving.

HIPPODROME

Cranbourn Street, WC2, tel. 071 437 4311; Leicester Square Underground; open till 3 a.m.; admission £6–£12.

'This is an absolutely foul tourist trap,' warns one woman who strayed into the Hippodrome by chance. So, warning: ignore the flyers that are handed out on busy corners on Friday and Saturday nights unless you want to be sized up by leery men hoping to pick up young tourists.

LIMELIGHT

136 Shaftesbury Avenue, WC2, tel. 071 734 4111; Leicester Square Underground; open till 4.30 a.m. Fri and Sat; admission £7–£10.

Most hipsters feign boredom at the mention of the Limelight, but the warren of rooms in a converted church continues to attract glitzy launches, and at the weekends the well-rated sound system pumps out a not-too-safe/not-too-daring mix of musics. Pop celebrities can be seen on occasions weaving in and out of the pillars, in-vogue beer grasped tight in hand.

MADAME JOJOS

8–10 Brewer Street, W1, tel. 071 734 2473; Leicester Square or Tottenham Court Road Underground; open till 3 a.m.; admission £6–£10.

At London's original transvestite club you can stay seated to watch the drag acts while astounding transvestites serve you drinks. Favourite haunt of media-industry gangs on outrageous nights out.

SUBTERRANIA

12 Acklam Road, W10, tel. 081 960

4590; Ladbroke Grove Underground, though you'd be best to take a cab after dark if you're unsure where it is; open till 2 a.m.; admission £3–£6.

This is where you'll find the grooving wealthy and wasted trendy youth of Notting Hill – wild children of film- and music-biz bigwigs. A sleek, hard-to-find eighties club that has a balcony for people-watching and maintains a consistent reputation for a decent night out.

WAG
35 Wardour Street, W1, tel. 071 437 5534; Leicester Square or Piccadilly Circus Underground: open till 3.30 a.m.; admission £5–£8.

Inevitably no longer the hyper-trendy place it was, but this unexceptionally done-out venue keeps up with trends, so it's not a bad centre-of-town starting place.

XENON
196 Piccadilly, W1, tel. 071 743 9344; Piccadilly Circus or Green Park Underground; open till 3 a.m.; admission £5–£10.

This is variously described as brash trash, a favourite haunt of German students and an Essex Girl's hangout – it's a safe-ish bet club: it's not just a cattle market, as many Central London clubs are; and the disco-funk may be dated, but most find it enjoyably danceable.

Lesbian Clubs

A growing number of out lesbians reject the sober attire of women they call 'diesel dykes' and 'woolly jumpers'; instead they dress glam and go out wild-clubbing as the 'baby doll dyke' set. Club and bar managers are beginning to take seriously the lesbian and gay community's current buzz phrase, 'the power of the pink pound', so lesbian clubs are getting better slots for more regular one-nighters and moving to more glamorous central venues. Look in *Time Out* and the gay press available free at bars and cafés listed in Eating and Drinking to confirm details of the best current clubs.

ACE OF CLUBS
52 Piccadilly, W1, tel. 071 408 0226; Green Park Underground; 9.30 p.m.–3.30 a.m. Sat; admission £3.50.

A long-standing friendly favourite that gets everyone from baby doll dykes to sex-politics campaigners to seventies bikers grooving on a packed disco floor to golden oldies like Gloria Gaynor's 'Survive' and 'Freak!' by Chic.

CLIT CLUB
at The Elephant and Castle, 2 South Lambeth Place, SW8, tel. 071 582 8764; Vauxhall Underground; 10 p.m.–2 a.m. last Sat of every month; admission £4.50, £2.50 concessions with proof.

This women-only leather/fetish club with changing themes is, say most London lesbians, for the brave.

GIRL BAR
at Heaven, Under the Arches, Villiers

Street, WC2, tel. 071 839 3852; Charing Cross Underground; open till 3.30 a.m.; admission £6 or £4 with a flyer.

'Boot girls, cute girls, fruit girls, suit girls, queer girls, beer girls, glam girls, wham girls' (and more) now welcome at this famous camp gay venue – cruisy, voyeuristic, stylish Girl Bar with DJs Princess Julia and Sister Bliss, and access to Heaven mixed dance floor.

PALM BEACH

at Palm Beach Suite, 386 Streatham High Road, SW16, tel. 081 769 7771; Brixton Underground and a bus up Brixton Hill, or Streatham BR – it seems a long way out, but you shouldn't have personal safety worries in Streatham; 9.30 p.m.–2 a.m. Fri; admission £3.

'Tacky, wacky and wild' say Central Londoners travelling down to suburban South London's longest-running mixed gay and lesbian venue for dancing under plastic palm trees with Jason Donovan and Kylie Minogue lookalikes to more Village People numbers than you've heard since the 1970s.

THE PASSION PIT

at Hash Eleven, 11 Wardour Street, W1, tel. 071 437 7301; Oxford Street Underground; Sat 10 p.m.–4 a.m.; admission £4 before 11 p.m. then £6 till 3 a.m.

Varied music from fêted DJs Slamma, Queen Maxine, Rachael Auburn and Mazz for a young, relaxed Designer Dyke crowd.

PUSS PUSS

at the Fridge, Town Hall Parade, Brixton, SW2, tel. 071 326 5100; turn left out of Brixton Underground, cross at lights then left past Town Hall to low, battered-looking building strung with fridges; 1st Wed of every month; open till 3 a.m.; admission £5.

Unfortunately, this currently clashes with the more in-vogue Café de Paris Venus Rising – go to both if you're in for a club-crawling night; pick Puss Puss if you like a 'Brixton, slightly rougher edge', says one discerning clubber, noting the Fridge's renown for introducing lesbian go-go girls in cages. Combine Puss Puss with a visit to the lesbian-friendly Brixtonian (see Eating and Drinking).

ROSANNA'S

at 17 Strutton Ground, off Victoria Street, SW1, tel. 071 233 1701; Victoria Underground; 7–11 p.m. Thur; free.

This already popular café serving hot and cold vegetarian food gets crammed with a Designer Dyke, cruisy, richer crowd on women-only nights.

TATTOO

at First Out Café, 52 St Giles High Street, behind Centrepoint, WC2, tel. 071 240 8042; Tottenham Court Road Underground; 8–11 p.m.; free.

This 'dare to bare it' women-only weekly one-nighter is really a pre-club bar, but there is music, so you can start practising your disco steps.

VENUS RISING

at Café de Paris, 3 Coventry Street, W1, tel. 071 287 3602; Leicester Square Underground; open till 6 a.m. first Wed of every month; admission £5.

The largest lesbian club in Europe has moved from the Fridge to the decayed glamour of a Central London ex-ballroom where Marlene Dietrich once sang. Women – lipsticked, checked-shirted, bisexual and straight – save through the month so they can blitz the night on drink, manic dancing and anything else they can lay their hands on. Canny customers empty bladders before they go – queues for everything are long.

WOW BAR

at Brixtonian Backayard, Neal's Yard, WC2, tel. 071 240 2769; Covent Garden Underground – it's off Shelton Street (and although the walk through the chi-chi yard looks unlikely it is not unsafe); Sat till late, peaks around 11 p.m.; admission £1 before 10 p.m., £1.50 after.

Veteran respected lesbian events organiser Sue Wade's WOW Bar is about relaxed drinking/chatting rather than dancing. Rumours that it's pretentious are unfounded – the crowd's mixed.

Pick-Up Scenes

Most Covent Garden bars are patronised on Friday nights by at least a handful of young bank clerks and City trader types who are after a good time, probably already drunk, and primed with traditional/corny/schoolboy chat-up lines ('I'm a gynaecologist – share your problems with me'). Supermarkets are being billed as *the* hot pick-up spots on the basis of little evidence – the Sainsbury's at 17 Camden Road NW1, with its late-night opening hours and wealthy-trendy mix of customers, wide aisles and browsable magazine racks, seems a good bet. So too does the Bedford Street Tesco's (Covent Garden), which has a Customer Advertising Board where you might strike up conversations over notices on everything from flats advertised to parrot cages for sale. Openings at commercial galleries are also being targeted, the idea being that here you'll get a cleaner, richer, more sophisticated kind of pick-up – wander up Cork Street midweek early evening in the hope that you'll stumble across one. Leicester Square on Friday and Saturday nights is full of people, many of them looking to meet new friends or have a one-night stand.

If you don't want to leave it to chance, send a 'Lonely Hearts' in advance to *Loot* (Free-Ads, 24 Kilburn High Road, NW6 5UA), *Time Out* (Tower House, Southampton Street, WC2E 7HD; £30 for up to 20 words including PO Box number) or the *The Pink Paper* (Classifieds, The Pink Paper, 77 City Garden Row, N1 8EZ; first 20 words free, £4 for box number).

Gigs

World music, US pop celebrities, small-town Indie bands …

London offers a great variety of live gigs with a corresponding spread of prices, from free at local pubs to £20 at major venues (or more for black-market tickets). If you're going alone, pubs and smaller venues can offer welcome intimacy but may involve undesired jostling, while the anonymity of larger venues can be depressing or liberating. Assess your mood and consider the character of bands' fans before making your choice. Below is a selection of key venues, but you should always check listings in *Time Out* and *New Musical Express* to find out what's going on during your visit, as some of the best gigs can be held in offbeat venues like churches, warehouses and on London's parkland, as well as in pubs and clubs.

Rock and Pop

Two London-based women who've made their mark on the pop scene as more than backing bimbos are Neneh Cherry, who insisted on continuing a programme of energetic disco performances in tight lycra outfits while pregnant, and Siobhan of Shakespeare's Sister, who renounced the glam-girlie image of Bananarama, the band she started with in the 1980s, in favour of dour dark clothes/make-up and lyrics that sometimes tackle sexual politics.

Academy, Brixton

211 Stockwell Road, SW9, tel. 071 326 1022. Brixton Underground.

Some women are nervous of Brixton – if you're at all worried, take a cab there and book one beforehand for the way back – but you'll find that if you arrive by tube on gig nights a river of fellow fans will carry you safely and swiftly to the Academy and back to the station afterwards. Gigs are big and sweaty, with sometimes needlessly aggressive bouncers. The main floor slopes, so it's easy to see and the bars aren't impossible to get to. Most love the atmosphere and freedom to dance at gigs that are often reggae or rap and include comebacks, for example of Iggy Pop.

Borderline

Orange Yard, Manette Street, WC2, tel. 071 437 8595. Leicester Square or Tottenham Court Road Underground.

Bizarre mixture of country and Western, new Indie band promotions by record companies, office parties and individuals after a pick-up in basement sawdust surroundings.

Hackney Empire

291 Mare Street, E8, tel. 081 985 2424. Overground BR train to Hackney Central or Hackney Downs; buses include 38, 106, N11, N96.

It can be a trek to get here, even from within Hackney (bus is easiest), but the programming range is good – from alternative comedy benefits to free jazz – and the renovated music-hall venue is a spectacle in itself. Tables in the auditorium make it one of the more pleasant places for a woman alone to watch a gig.

The Grand

Clapham Junction, St John's Hill, SW11, tel. 071 738 9000. Clapham Junction BR.

This converted theatre is one of the nicest gig spaces. Big blues gigs and successful rock bands trying to get away from soulless stadiums play here just for the joy of it.

HAMMERSMITH APOLLO
Queen Caroline Street, W6, tel. 081 748 4081. Hammersmith Underground.

Hammersmith isn't particularly appealing at night, but neither is it known as dangerous. At one of London's biggest, longest-established rock venues you'll find international big star acts (pay accordingly), but you have to watch them from your seat.

MARQUEE
105 Charing Cross Road, WC2, tel. 071 437 6603. Leicester Square or Tottenham Court Road Underground.

A venue that's so intimate you can touch the bands. Popular current Goth, heavy rock and metal bands attract, the bouncers find, an alarming number of fifteen-year-olds pretending to be eighteen. Big names do warm-up gigs here. You'll come away very sweaty.

MEAN FIDDLER
24–28A Harlesden High Street, NW10, tel. 081 965 2487. Willesden Junction Underground.

The folk music the Fiddler's famous for staging has been relegated to the Acoustic Room – the main trade is now Indie rock bands. As it's a pub with informal seating available, the Fiddler can feel more comfortable than the big venues for a woman alone, although the rooms are nothing special, and it can sometimes be difficult to see the band.

POWERHAUS
1 Liverpool Road, N1, tel. 071 837 3218. Angel Underground.

This one-time pub does Indie rock.

WEMBLEY ARENA
Empire Way, Wembley, Middlesex, tel. 081 900 1234. Wembley Park Underground.

If the band you want to see is playing somewhere else as well, forgo the massive Arena, as it lacks atmosphere.

WEMBLEY STADIUM
Empire Way, Wembley, Middlesex, tel. 081 900 1234. Wembley Park Underground.

Another of the BIG venues, and one where there's a lot of waiting around for temperamental stars finally to make their appearance, so it's not a good place to come without a crowd of happy people. If you sit in the stands you don't get soaked with rain and alcohol; on the pitch you get a marginally better view – not of the band/singer but of the gargantuan video screens showing the performance simultaneously. May as well stay home and watch it on the telly.

Jazz

BASS CLEF
35 Coronet Street, London N1 6NU, tel. 071 729 2476/2440. Old Street Underground.

Often cheap/free admission if you arrive before 9.30 p.m. for the Latin and World music gigs that encourage dancing during and also before and after, with DJs in a small space that some say is claustrophobic and others say is wonderfully sweaty-atmospheric. Prepare for a sense of achievement when you find the venue, which is tucked down a back alley. See also Tenor Clef.

JAZZ CAFÉ

5 Parkway, NW1, tel. 071 916 6000. Camden Town Underground.

Trendy venue, trendy programming, trendy twenty-something clientele. You could happily come here alone (sit at a minimalist steel table or a stool at the cool bar). Seems more formal than even the legendary Ronnie Scott's because of the reverential bluey space around the stage. Vogue-ish young names that may be big in a few years come here. Concrete washrooms with disconcerting doors.

100 CLUB

100 Oxford Street, W1, tel. 071 636 0933. Tottenham Court Road Underground.

Many find this London's best venue for smoky, basement, laidback jazz atmosphere, although others complain about the absence of air-conditioning and preference for eclectic programming, which can feature an internationally acclaimed modern jazz twenty-piece band one night and an obscure three-man rockabilly set the next. Arrive early to get a good seat, or you'll be stuck behind a pillar with punters crushing you on their way to the food and drink bars.

RONNIE SCOTT'S

47 Frith Street, W1, tel. 071 439 0747. Tottenham Court Road Underground.

If a big name's coming to London, they'll probably play here. If you want a good seat you should book a table, where you'll be pressed to order food and find it's easier to avoid unwanted attentions. Low ceilings, maroon décor and a committed audience of regulars make for a good atmosphere.

PIZZA EXPRESS

10 Dean Street, W1, tel. 071 437 9595. Tottenham Court Road Underground.

This can end up being a pricey evening, as on top of admission you have to pay for food too, but the food is good. The Pizza Express Allstars and the P.E. Modern Jazz Quartet alternate.

TENOR CLEF

1 Hoxton Square, N1, tel. 071 729 2440. Old Street Underground.

Bigger names attract more serious music listeners to this smaller, more chi-chi venue upstairs from the Bass Clef.

VORTEX

Stoke Newington Church Street, N16, tel. 071 254 6516. Stoke Newington BR or 73, 106 bus.

Above a rickety-looking bookshop, this jazz venue is the only one in London that seems to practise a positive discrimination policy of scheduling women and local jazz musicians into their programming. If you're not based in Hackney, it's well worth the trip.

THE ARTS

For fairly comprehensive listings of what's on, turn to *Time Out* magazine; and for reviews turn to the daily and weekend broadsheets. The *Evening Standard* is best for early reviews; *The Independent* prides itself on wide arts coverage.

Classical Music and Opera

Classical opera always did have plenty of parts for women, but they were 'Dead women, dead so often', lamented Catherine Clément in *Opera, or The Undoing of Women* (Virago). Anne Manson was told repeatedly that a career in opera conducting was 'hopeless', so she started her own company and 'made opportunities for myself'. 'Changes happen when women move into influential positions,' says composer Nicola LeFanu, citing the appointment of Sian Edwards to the directorship of the English National Opera.

On any one night, London offers perhaps the best classical music and opera choice of any cultural capital for a range of prices, from free church recitals to international superstar line-ups at the Royal Opera House. Festivals to look out for include the excellent-value **South Place Sunday Concerts** from beginning Oct to end Apr (*Conway Hall, Red Lion Square, tel. 071 242 8032*). Also, the summer **Spitalfields Festival** (*Christ Church, Commercial Street, E1, tel. 071 377 0287*). Free tickets are available for **BBC Wednesday Lunchtime Concerts** (*Broadcasting House, Portland Place, W1, tel. 071 580 4468 or look in Radio Times*).

Almeida

Almeida Street, N1, tel. 071 359 4404; about a 15-minute walk from Angel Underground.

Primarily a theatre, this serves also on occasional weekends as one of London's more avant-garde music venues.

Barbican Centre

Silk Street, EC2, tel. 071 638 8891. Barbican Underground or, on Sundays, Moorgate Underground.

This astoundingly ugly arts centre is home to the London Symphony Orchestra and the English Chamber Orchestra, and boasts a warm pine-feel 2,026-seat auditorium that provides surprisingly good views from all seats, and has good acoustics. Programming includes celebrity recitals and visiting orchestras. It's worse for orientation and for women's loos than the South Bank Centre.

Blackheath Concert Halls

23 Lee Road, Blackheath, SE3, tel. 081 318 9758 box office or for information 081 463 0100; Blackheath BR.

Unless you live nearby you have to be fairly committed to hearing a concert here, for it is a fair trek from London, and ticket prices are often high. However, the programming is impressive, as is the lavish hall, which regularly fills to capacity.

Fenton House

Hampstead Grove, NW3, tel. 071 435 3471; Hampstead Underground.

Top musicians perform recitals in a venue that is also a museum for a prized collection of early musical instruments.

ICA

The Mall, SW1, tel. 071 930 3647; Piccadilly Circus or Charing Cross Underground; day membership must be bought for a couple of pounds.

Another venue for avant-garde performances.

Kenwood Lakeside Concerts

Kenwood House, Hampstead Lane, NW3, tel. 081 348 1286; Archway, Highgate or Hampstead Underground.

You must allow time to get here, because the chance to roam the surrounding Hampstead Heath is part of Kenwood's appeal. You can bank on popular classics by good orchestras and wafty acoustics, for the concerts are held literally by the side of the lake. Take a picnic, grab a deck chair, and relax.

The London Coliseum

St Martin's Lane, WC2, tel. 071 836 3161 box office or 071 240 5258 credit card bookings; Leicester Square or Charing Cross Underground.

This is celebrated for innovative ENO (English National Opera) productions which often give young men and women chances in powerful creative positions, and appeal to a wider cross-section of society than Covent Garden. The ENO is the only full-time opera repertory company in the country. The productions are all given in English.

Royal Albert Hall

Kensington Gore, SW7, tel. 071 589 3203 or for credit card booking, 071 589 9465; High Street Kensington Underground.

Crowds of Londoners, classical music students and their tutors queue with sandwiches for the BBC Henry Wood Promenade Concerts, more widely known as 'The Proms', from mid-July to mid-September to see internationally renowned musicians and choirs in a venue of breathtaking architecture.

Royal Opera House

Covent Garden, WC2, tel. 071 240 1066; Covent Garden Underground.

Patented by Charles II in the seventeenth century, the then-called 'Theatre Royal' was rebuilt after an 1808 fire with the help of Sarah Siddons (see Covent Garden); requisitioned during the First World War by the Ministry of Works for use as a furniture repository; became a Mecca Dance Hall during the Second World War. In 1946, Ninette de Valois's Sadler's Wells Ballet was offered residency; in 1947 the infant Royal Opera Company gave its first performance of *Carmen*. Today the Royal Opera, the Royal Ballet and the Birmingham Royal Ballet give some 450 performances a year at prices ranging from under £10 (take binoculars) to well over £100, and absurd amounts for star billings or charity events. Fairy busts prop up the balconies; if an opera's in Italian the English version is projected over the stage; in the stalls bar, champagne and salmon are consumed in large quantities during intervals. Sometimes giant screens erected in Covent Garden Piazza crackle the performance live to excited crowds who can't see or hear much, but enjoy the atmosphere.

St James's Church Piccadilly

Piccadilly, W1, tel. 071 734 4511; Piccadilly Circus Underground.

This is a favourite haunt for lovers of Baroque music from the resident St James's Baroque Players or at the summer Lufthansa Festival. Pick up a brochure for details of lunchtime and evening recitals.

St John's Smith Square

Smith Square, SW1, tel. 071 222

1061; Westminster Underground.

Loved for its bargain BBC Monday lunchtime concerts, St John's frequently hosts chamber orchestras and soloists. Good café in the crypt.

St Martin-in-the-Fields

Trafalgar Square, WC2, tel. 071 930 0089. Charing Cross Underground.

A range of lunchtime recitals in a magnificent Wren church.

South Bank Centre

South Bank Centre, Belvedere Road, SE1, box office 071 928 8800, information 071 928 3002; from Waterloo Underground follow the signs.

People who positively favour the cold concrete design of this massive arts centre are the skateboarders who find that shielded swoops and pillars make a perfect skate-park. You'll hear the echoes of their skattling wheels as you try to find your way about – allow a good ten minutes extra to locate your destination if you've not been here before (although it's not nearly as bad as the Barbican).

Within the complex, which has all been purpose-built with much money and attention paid to acoustics: the seductive, spaceship-like **Royal Festival Hall** is the largest classical venue, hosting orchestras with international reputations and impresarios from soloist pianists to pop stars like Dionne Warwick; much about the **Queen Elizabeth Hall** is scaled down, from its size to the drama of the décor to – sometimes, but not always – the status of the programmed stars; the **Purcell Room** hosts heralded quartets and musicians making their début – for its intimate acoustics it is the musicians' musician venue, and audiences are infectiously enthusiastic. The South Bank is home to the acclaimed Opera Factory. Pick up leaflets and pore through them for some time to get to grips with the month-long theme-based festivals that are frequently staged. Good bookshop and plenty of unexceptional cafés and restaurants. Instead, take a picnic to eat on the banks of the Thames.

Wigmore Hall

36 Wigmore Street, W1, tel. 071 935 2141; Bond Street Underground.

The Wigmore is loved for its beauty, its fine acoustics, its intimacy and the quality of its programming, which often includes heralded quartets. Favourite musicians' location for recitals and chamber music. There is now a much-improved bar and a good restaurant. Sunday-morning concerts are popular.

Theatre

London is not short of eminent women who have come out of its theatreworld – Peggy Ashcroft and Vanessa Redgrave, to name but two. Women in key positions of managerial power, however, have been fewer. Even when she was Associate Director of the Royal Court, Jules Wright remained frustrated by the lack of directing opportunities. So she founded the Women's Playhouse Trust (WPT) in 1983 – you could look out for their productions, which promote women's involvement from writing to directing to the technical crew.

Many of London's theatres are sights in themselves: four Edwardian-Victorian theatres on Shaftesbury Avenue alone. You'd be wiser, though, to base your theatre choice not on the décor but on the production being staged. The three stages that comprise the **National Theatre** – the Olivier, Lyttelton and Cottesloe – are housed in the modern South Bank Centre yet attract some of the country's most exciting theatre productions featuring top actors, directors and technicians. The Cottesloe also stages an impressive programme of talks with acclaimed writers. The Barbican, also a concrete nightmare, is London home to the renowned **Royal Shakespeare Company (RSC)**. The **Royal Court**, known as the Writers' Theatre, remains scruffy despite a revamped coffee/drinks bar. The **West End** means the theatres around Shaftesbury Avenue, where you might see one of the big musicals such as *Phantom of the Opera* or *Cats*, or a long-running play such as *The Mousetrap*. Beyond the West End is the **Fringe**, which is a blanket term for the hotbed of small, alternative theatres that can be in a pub back room or one of the bigger venues, including the Bush and the Almeida (more listed below). If you coincide with the biennial summertime **London International Festival of Theatre** (LIFT) you'll be spoilt for choice of city-wide fringe productions.

To get cheap tickets: phone ahead to see if you can queue on the day for cut-price expensive tickets; get seats in 'the gods' (at the top at the back – take binoculars and prepare to become hot and sweaty); go to a matinée; or go to the **Society of West End Theatre (SWET)** ticket booth, which won't deal with fringe tickets and charges commission, but after a long queue will save you a lot of money on big productions (*Leicester Square, WC2; open noon till 30 minutes before start of last matinée and 2.30–6.30 p.m. for evening performances Mon–Sat*). To decide what you want to see, turn to *Time Out* for comprehensive listings and for reviews to the *Evening Standard*, because it will concentrate on London productions.

ALMEIDA
Almeida Street, N1, tel. 071 359 4404; a safe ten-minute walk from Angel Underground.

Almost West End. The Almeida manages to be both chic and cosy, and to attract important troupes and actors who are between feature films.

BATTERSEA ARTS CENTRE
176 Lavender Hill, SW11, tel. 071 223 2223; Clapham Junction BR.
Fringe. 'BAC' is a pain to get to and some of the productions are dire, but the programming is adventurous – wait for the reviews before risking the journey.

BUSH THEATRE
Shepherds Bush Green, W12, tel. 081 743 3388; Goldhawk Road or Shepherd's Bush Underground.

Fringe. This small theatre, above a pub, has made a name for nurturing new writers.

Drill Hall

16 Chenies Street, WC1, tel. 071 637 8270; Goodge Street Underground.

Fringe. The Drill Hall is rare and ahead of its time for providing crèche facilities some evenings (phone for details). The productions don't always get good reviews, but the Drill Hall is celebrated for its continued commitment to feminist, gay and lesbian, and political community works. Good vegetarian restaurant in the basement; women-only bar on Mondays.

Gate Notting Hill

The Prince Albert, 11 Pembridge Road, W11, tel. 071 229 0706; Notting Hill Gate Underground.

Fringe. Another pub theatre, this one's known for high-standard stagings of obscure European plays.

Hen and Chickens

Hen and Chickens Pub, Highbury Corner, N1, tel. 071 704 2001; Highbury and Islington Underground.

Fringe. The upstairs pub room often stages political feminist productions.

ICA Theatre

The Mall, SW1, tel. 071 930 3647; Piccadilly Circus or Charing Cross Underground; day membership must be bought for a couple of pounds.

Fringe. The Institute of Contemporary Arts prides itself on producing the most experimental works in the city. Chic bar and café with good salads and vegetarian food.

King's Head

115 Upper Street, N1, tel. 071 226 1916; ten-minute walk from Angel Underground or the same from Highbury and Islington Underground.

Fringe. The ambitious productions at the King's Head, the oldest and possibly the best pub theatre, often transfer to the West End.

National Theatre

South Bank Centre, South Bank, SE1, tel. 071 928 2252; Waterloo Underground.

Major. Within the National, the **Olivier** is the biggest theatre; the proximity of audience and players at the **Lyttelton** can make for intense theatre experiences; and the flexible **Cottesloe** can accommodate formal talks or audience-participation events. There are almost always free musical events in the foyer which showcase young and new talents before performances begin. Well-stocked theatre bookshop and pleasant but pricey eatery.

Old Vic

Waterloo Road, SE1, tel. 071 928 7616; Waterloo Underground.

Major. In the past this has been the theatrical home to Lilian Baylis and Laurence Oliver's National Theatre, and although today it is less remarkable for the people and productions attached to it, it has recently been done up and is a pleasant place to go to see decent productions of classics.

Riverside Studios

Crisp Road, W6, tel. 081 748 3354; safe ten-minute walk from Hammersmith Underground.

Almost West End, this is the ICA of West London. Two large and flexible spaces are used for experimental pieces, sometimes multimedia. The canteen-style café is decent.

Royal Court

Sloane Square, SW1, tel.071 730 1745; Sloane Square Underground.

Major main theatre; fringe upstairs. Shaw directed his own plays here until it became a cinema in 1934 for a while; in the 1950s the late Peggy Ashcroft made her acting mark on the theatre scene under George Devine, and through the 1970s Caryl Churchill's plays put her on the map as one of the most interesting up-and-coming playwrights. The Royal Court programmes productions that aren't always entirely successful but are always challenging and interesting. The enthusiasm of the audiences is infectious.

RSC Barbican

Barbican Centre, Silk Street, EC2, tel. 071 638 8891; Barbican Underground; on Sundays go to Moorgate Underground and follow the signs.

Major. It can be a major headache locating first an entrance to the Barbican Centre and then the right bit of it – allow a good extra quarter of an hour to get there, and once you have, you'll appreciate the very good theatre space and excellent productions. After Stratford the Royal Shakespeare Company productions come here, where they are received rapturously by a loyal audience.

Theatre Royal Stratford East

Gerry Raffles Square, E15, tel. 081 534 0310; Stratford Underground.

Almost West End. This old Victorian theatre in a modern tower-block-filled bit of the East End has repeatedly served as training ground for great talents – for example, for producer Joan Littlewood – and also serves the local community.

Tricycle Theatre

269 Kilburn High Road, NW6, tel. 071 328 1000; Kilburn Underground.

Almost West End. The Tricycle is celebrated for its wide cultural remit and its work with children. It was a key venue through the 1970s for alternative theatre.

Dance

Having hit the glass ceiling at one of Britain's major dance institutions, the London Contemporary Dance Theatre, Siobhan Davies founded her own dance company in 1988 and went on to become the first British choreographer in the independent sector to receive an Olivier award for dance in 1993. Women of the next generation down decided to skip apprenticeship at the established companies and go straight for forming their own. Lea Anderson choreographs the all-women troupe called the Cholmondeleys and also the boys' equivalent, the Featherstonehaughs; Gaby Agis, who performs under her own name, earned infamy for dancing in heavyweight Doc Marten boots.

Dance is one of London's cheaper arts entertainments, and the range from mainstream to experimental is impressive. Phone to ask about standby tickets if you're trying to save money, and bear in mind that many theatres have a remit to keep back a certain number of cheap tickets for sale on the day. Check *Time Out* listings and look in your paper's review section. The now long-established annual autumn **Dance Umbrella** bills the most exciting of young British choreographers beside international touring troupes in a selection of the dance venues listed below.

ICA

The Mall, SW1, tel. 071 930 3647; Piccadilly Circus or Charing Cross Underground; day membership necessary.

This, along with The Place and the Riverside Studios, is one of London's key experimental/contemporary dance venues. At the Institute of Contemporary Arts it may take the form of mixed-media shows or performance art. Quality and entertainment value are generally high. The trendy bar is a chic place to hang out before and after.

The London Coliseum

St Martin's Lane, WC2, tel. 071 836 3161; Charing Cross Underground.

This *massive* venue is also home to the English National Opera. Ballet companies like the Bolshoi and the Dance Theatre of Harlem come here.

The Place

17 Duke's Road, WC1, tel. 071 387 0031; Euston Underground.

This is on a side street that is safe but can look grim if you've not been before, and once you get to the big, rather faded, hanging board saying 'The Place', you'll see from the milling students, noticeboard and lengths of mirror in the bar that this venue is primarily a dance school, home to London Contemporary Dance trainees. The annual **Spring Loaded** festival gives you a chance to see some of today's best young students, tomorrow's stars. The programming often features now internationally successful one-time students such as Lea Anderson (her two dance groups are the all-female **Cholmondeleys** and the all-male **Featherstonehaughs**) and Gaby Agis.

Riverside Studios

Crisp Road, W6, tel. 081 748 3354; Hammersmith Underground.

Bigger theatres and names that have gone one stage further down the well-known line than The Place, for example Siobhan Davies.

Royal Opera House

Covent Garden, WC2, tel. 071 240 1066; Covent Garden Underground.

This is home to the Royal Ballet. Celebrity-spotting happens in the upstairs bar.

Sadler's Wells Theatre

Rosebery Avenue, EC1, tel. 071 278 8916; Angel Underground.

The Sadler's Wells Royal Ballet is based here, and major companies stop by on their international tours (regularly, flamenco and the London Contemporary Dance Theatre). One of Britain's best children's companies, Whirlgig, does a run every autumn.

South Bank Centre

South Bank, SE1, tel. 071 928 8800; Waterloo Underground.

The huge Royal Festival Hall, small Purcell Room and middling Queen Elizabeth Hall each hosts appropriate-sized dance events.

Comedy

Jo Brand, Dawn French, Jenny Lecoat, Jennifer Saunders, Victoria Wood – and that's to name, in alphabetical order, just a few women comedians who got started in London's smaller comedy venues and went on to become TV mainstream; lesbian comedienne Donna McPhail is on her way. For a long time pub back rooms have been the traditional starting place for stand-up comics, and of course new venues pop up constantly. Look in the *Time Out* listings.

BANANA CABARET
The Bedford, Bedford Hill, SW12, tel.081 673 8904; Balham Underground.

A long way down the Northern Line, but many consider this one of London's most enjoyable and enterprising cabaret clubs.

COMEDY STORE
28A Leicester Square, WC2, tel. 071 839 6665; Leicester Square Underground.

Considered the place where alternative comedy was born, this Central London venue continues to programme some of the most interesting young comics just before they hit the big time, and the resident Comedy Store Players are, say regulars, consistently hilarious.

JONGLEURS AT THE CORNET
49 Lavender Gardens, SW11, tel. 081 780 1151; Clapham Common Underground then 45 bus, or Clapham Junction BR.

Also a bit off the beaten track, this attracts top players and a wildly enthusiastic audience. Book ahead.

RED ROSE CABARET
129 Seven Sisters Road, N7, tel. 071 263 7265; Finsbury Park Underground.

This is hosted by a top comedian – many rate Red Rose above the Comedy Store, saying that the programming is equally good and the tickets are half the price.

Cinema

Against all the odds, Sally Potter has been making films for years. Her first feature was the theoretical/formalist *Gold Diggers* (1981) about women and money, starring Julie Christie; it was described by one critic as a 'feminist torture session'. In 1993 she won international acclaim for her feature film of Virginia Woolf's novel *Orlando*, but that was after being turned down by every source of film finance in Britain and taking out a second mortgage on her home. 'I really do think Potter suffered for being a woman,' says young film-maker Isaac Julien.

With the closure of the run-down, massive muralled Scala in King's Cross and the dusting-down of the once famously flea-ridden, now newly enlarged Ritzy in Brixton, many Londoners fear for the survival of risk-taking repertory/alternative programming in their city. But the ICA keeps flying the banner for experimental film and video, and there are still independent cinemas to choose from.

Many women in London enjoy going to the cinema alone, and there are few, if any, where you'd have reason to feel uncomfortable, although late-night screenings do sometimes attract post-pub bored teenagers who may talk through the film and give minor aggro.

The ages that are allowed to see a film are indicated by cryptic letters and numbers that you'll find on the posters and incorporated in listings: 'U' means suitable for everyone; 'PG' means children under 13 must go with an adult; '12' means anyone over 12 can go alone; '15' is for anyone over 15; '18', 18 and over only. The classification relates to the amount of blood, guts and gore, sex and violence in the picture. Compared to America the classifications are careful; many in Britain think they're too liberal.

Obviously the cinema you go to will depend on what's playing; below is a selection of first-run and repertory venues, and a handful that are especially pleasant places to see a film. On Mondays and for matinées you can sometimes get cheap tickets. The Leicester Square cinemas are more expensive than others round London, but there is a buzz surrounding seeing a film on Leicester Square.

First-Run Cinemas

Cannon Tottenham Court Road

30 Tottenham Court Road, W1, tel. 071 636 6148; Goodge Street Underground.

Tucked away in a row of sport and audio-visual equipment shops, this is good for having smaller queues than most central cinemas. First-run programming of European and independent American and British films.

Chelsea Cinema

206 King's Road, SW3, tel. 071 351 3742; Sloane Square Underground.

Other cinemas show the same art-house films, but not with the panache and wine bar – come here if you want to mix your film-going with high Chelsea society's.

Curzon Mayfair

Curzon Street, W1, tel. 071 465 8865; Green Park Underground.

The best place in town to see European movies, say fans; middle-class and middle-of-the-road, say detractors. No one can fail to notice the astounding multicoloured bottle-end 1970s décor, or to be impressed by the sink-down luxury seats.

Empire

Leicester Square, WC2, tel. 071 437 1234; Leicester Square Underground.

This is perhaps the nearest to American movie-going that Central London has to offer. Lots of digital boards, buckets of popcorn, arcade and video bar, and laser shows before screenings. Major Hollywood blockbusters on vast screens with superb high-tech sound.

Gate Cinema
87 Notting Hill Gate, W11, tel. 071 727 4043; Notting Hill Gate Underground.

Come here to check out the trendy Notting Hill scene ... not many other places would have arty fruit baskets in the foyer. Mixture of independents and not-too-mainstream first runs.

ICA Cinema
Nash House, The Mall, SW1 tel. 071 930 0493; Piccadilly Circus or Charing Cross Underground.

Of the two screens here, this is the larger one and shows modern and archive films from all over the world (strong on Russia and China, for example), and at weekends there are the admired children's programmes.

Lumière
42 St Martin's Lane, WC2, tel. 071 836 0691; Leicester Square Underground.

Many think this beats the Curzon Mayfair for plushness; it programmes critically acclaimed films. Possibly the best Central London venue.

Metro
11 Rupert Street, W1, tel. 071 437 0757; Piccadilly Circus or Leicester Square Underground.

Trendy staff, trendy cakes, trendy art in the trendily concrete foyer, trendy foreign film programming; regularly hosts film festivals.

Odeon Marble Arch
10 Edgware Road, W2, tel. 071 723 2011; Marble Arch Underground.

Some films just have to be seen on a screen so wide it seems to curve round you, engulfing you in stereophonic sound, and this is the place to come. Blockbuster Hollywood first runs.

UCI Whiteleys
Whiteleys of Bayswater, Queensway, W2, tel. 071 792 3324; Bayswater or Queensway Underground.

This is an astounding complex. 'Youths' hang out by shop-surrounded marble-style fountains as if they're in an American shopping mall ... sail up the escalators and you're deeper in America with service and quick sales the name of the game, although the have-a-nice-day approach doesn't come easy to Londoners behind the counter. All the screens are big with good sound, and the largest screen has deafening THX (Lucasfilm) sound.

Repertory

If admission is limited to members, don't worry; membership is almost always instantly available at around £1.

Electric Cinema
191 Portobello Road, W11, tel. 071 792 2020; Ladbroke Grove Underground.

Revamped and beloved of Londoners, the beautiful Electric, the oldest purpose-built cinema in London, serves up a mixture of mainstream American, celluloid obscurities and, occasionally, live gigs.

EVERYMAN
Holly Bush Vale, NW3, tel. 071 435 1525; Hampstead Underground.

This, the oldest repertory cinema in London, does good triple- and double-bills and big revivals. It has a good café in the basement – the perfect way to round off a day on Hampstead Heath.

FRENCH INSTITUTE
17 Queensberry Place, SW7, tel. 071 589 6211; South Kensington Underground.

This has obscurity value – the relatively few people who know about it thrill at the thought of fixing a date to see a crackly French classic here. You have to book in person, and it's best not just to turn up because sell-outs are frequent.

ICA CINEMATHEQUE
Nash House, The Mall, SW1, tel. 071 930 0493; Piccadilly Circus or Charing Cross Underground.

Tiny place to see ambitious programmings of experimental/avant-garde films and video art that have to be *absolutely riveting* to stop the audience wriggling in the uncomfortable, creaky stack chairs.

NATIONAL FILM THEATRE
South Bank, SE1, tel. 071 928 3232; Waterloo Underground.

Themes and seasons dedicated to directors are favoured by programmers in this labyrinthine place. The London Film Festival is held here every November.

RITZY CINEMA CLUB
Brixton Road, SW2, tel. 071 737 2121; turn left out of Brixton Underground and it's on your left over Coldharbour Lane – some women say be careful in Brixton, but most think there's no need to be overcautious.

At the time of writing this is still undergoing major refurbishment that will transform a one-screen lovable fleapit into a multiscreen mega-cinema. If the home-made snacks are still served, they're worth saving a small appetite for.

RIVERSIDE STUDIOS
Crisp Road, W6, tel. 081 748 3354; Hammersmith Underground.

Here you'll see experimental video art during the BP Expo Student Film and Video Festival. British films often programmed.

HEALTH AND SPORT

See Fitness for gyms, steam baths, etc. Use the parks for jogging, playing frisbee and gentle ambling. Most parks have tennis courts, and many have bowling pitches. Look under Leisure Centres in the Yellow Pages for your nearest swimming/badminton/squash/aerobics venue.

Spectator Sports

You may have no interest in chaps in whites holding bits of willow batting a small red ball around, or no desire to see Gazza-style wide-boys kicking a bag of wind around a field, but you'll find that these games are quintessentially English, which can be interesting whether you're English or not. See Festivals in Practicalities for events such as Ascot which purport to be about horse-racing but turn out to be society occasions when the hats worn on Ladies' Day make front-page news.

ARSENAL, HIGHBURY STADIUM
Avenell Road, N5, tel. 071 226 0304; Arsenal Underground.

If you support one of the other London football clubs – Chelsea, Crystal Palace, Millwall, Queens Park Rangers, Tottenham Hotspur, West Ham United or Wimbledon – Arsenal obviously won't be your first choice, but if you're just doing a bit of cultural behaviour research, this one's easy to get to and in a quiet area. Football is not yet a family sport. The stadiums are notorious for urine-stinking passageways and beer-swilling 'hooligans'. The terraces are cheaper but offer worse views and more lager-loutism. If it's your first time, book a seat in advance. The football season runs from August to May.

LORD'S CRICKET GROUND
St John's Wood, NW8, tel. 071 289 1611; St John's Wood Underground.

This is more of a family game, with mum, dad and a couple of grumpy kids huddled round tea flask and Tupperware boxes filled with sandwiches. Up on the famous pavilion, the scene is a bit more classy – some say snooty. World cricket all summer; or you can book ahead to go and see the small museum.

Participation

BROADGATE ICE RINK
Eldon Street, EC2, tel. 071 588 6565; Liverpool Street Underground; open winter only.

Widely thought to be the best rink in London – it may be small, but it's immaculate and in the open air. Good-lookers with ambitions for success and wealth wear the latest gear.

PETER CHILVERS WINDSURFING CENTRE
Gate 5, Tidal Basin Road, west end of Royal Victoria Docks, E16, tel. 071 474 2500; Canning Town Underground.

Possibilities for networking with financial whizz-kids in unlikely surroundings of murky water and bleak modernist housing projects. Beginners and practised surfers accommodated.

REGENT'S PARK GOLF AND TENNIS SCHOOL
Outer Circle, Regent's Park, NW1, tel. 071 724 0643; Baker Street or St John's Wood Underground.

Pros are on hand (at a price) to comment on your forehand or putting techniques.

QUEENS ICE SKATING CLUB
17 Queensway, W2, tel. 071 229 0172; Queensway or Bayswater Underground.

A big rink and London's most famous – expect some seriously professional skating; phone beforehand if you want an appointment with an instructor, and bear in mind that Saturday night is disco night.

WIMBLEDON VILLAGE STABLES
24A High Street, SW19, tel. 081 946 8579; Wimbledon Underground.

Horse-riding within easy public transport access of Central London doesn't come cheap, but the Stables are good at matching mellow horses with nervous beginners, and the treks through Richmond Park and over Wimbledon Common are extremely popular.

Fitness

Look in the Yellow Pages under Leisure Centres to see if there's a swimming pool and/or gym nearby, and see Women and Feminism for the women-only Wesley Gym.

Forest Mere

Forest Mere Health Hydro, Liphook, Hampshire, GU30 7JQ. tel. 0428 722051, fax 0428 723501; less than one hour from London by train.

In a grand red-brick house beside a lake in woody grounds, and reportedly on a healing energy line, you can have your back tension erased by massage and heat treatment, then take yoga or step-aerobics before swimming in the pool, where squirrels play nearby; at lunchtime and in the evenings enjoy mountains of healthy food from the Savoy kitchens or simpler fare in the diet room with a mixture of high-powered executives, titled interior decorators, teachers who need three days compressed relaxation and women from Ireland, Australia and the States who find Forest Mere unmatched for value (3 days start at £300).

Jubilee Hall

The Piazza, WC2, tel. 071 836 4835.

Considering its central location, prices here are surprisingly low (around £3 or £4 per class). The gym is massive and the classes range from aerobics to pilates to jazzdance with occasional contemporary dance masterclasses.

Pineapple

7 Langley Street, WC2, tel. 071 836 4004.

There are 750 dance classes to choose from at this spacious dance studio complex, where beginners mix with Royal Ballet practising professionals.

The Porchester Spa

Queensway, W2, tel. 071 792 3980.

It costs around £15 for a day in the Porchester Turkish steam baths Russian rooms and swimming pool, where fried egg on toast is available in the echoey old-world ground-floor tiled lounging area, temporamental power showers grace the basement steam room area and a woman will give you a rough soap body scrub on a table slab for a small extra charge. Phone ahead to confirm details of which days are women's and which are mixed.

The Sanctuary

12 Floral Street, WC2, tel. 071 240 9635.

Housed in an old banana warehouse and now a cool mixture of pools, plants, Moorish white-pillared spaces and cushioned alcoves awash with the sound of running water, the women-only Sanctuary accurately advertises itself as offering 'pure self-indulgence' and 'a sense of timelessness' in a haven 'free from the pressures of everyday life'; it appeals to stressed executives and people treating themselves from teenager to septuagenarian (one woman celebrated her seventieth birthday here). Admission for a day (around £35) includes use of towels and a bathrobe and unlimited access to steam rooms, sauna, whirlpool and two swimming pools (one colder than the other). Extra treatments such as reflexology and aromatherapy cost about the same again, and the café serves a range of food from healthy salads to naughtily semi-healthy cakes with coffee. The Sanctuary gym next door is women-only.

SHOPPING

SHOPS AND MARKETS

London can be a shopper's paradise – or a nightmare: at every main bus and train station, all down Oxford Street, at most major sights you'll be confronted with legions of street vendors selling Made in Taiwan Kiss-Me-Quick hats, plastic policeman helmets and off-the-back-of-a-lorry royal souvenir mugs. If you've come for classic English goods, take note: you can buy a Burberry mac cheaper in Chicago. As for second-hand clothes, at famous markets such as Portobello, an old stained dress can cost more than a new one. London's markets are great fun, but if you want *cheap* cast-off clothes, prepare to queue and fight over rickety tables piled high indiscriminately with crumpled shirts and jumpers at **jumble sales** (look in *Time Out*'s 'Sales and Bargains' section or local newsagents' windows; target jumble sales in richer areas such as Hampstead or Kensington for the best bargains). It's always entertaining to browse in very English shops including Aquascutum and Simpson's of Piccadilly; go during the July and January sales for knock-down prices on raincoats and cashmere V-necks. For slightly faulty or dated top designers' goods at sometimes substantial discounts, look in the 'Sales and Bargains' section of *Time Out* for **designer warehouse sales**, go to designer sale shops including **The Designers Sale Studio** (*at 24 King's Road, SW3, tel. 071 351 4171*), or to wholesale outlets such as **Nicole Farhi** and **French Connection** (*at 75–83 Fairfield Road, E3, tel. 081 981 3931*; others detailed in *The Factory Shop Guide for East Anglia and South-East England*, available for £4.45 from Gillian Cutress, 34 Park Hill, London SW4 9PB, or leading bookshops). For shopping news turn to the 'Retail Therapy'/'Spending' section in the **Saturday Independent**.

If you ladder your tights on the way to a key meeting or find you failed to pack enough underwear, you'll be glad of the

Knickerbox and **Sock Shop** chains that revolutionised British high streets in the 1980s – you'll find their booth-sized outlets everywhere, along with **Body Shops** for animal-friendly, reasonably priced cosmetics and body hygiene products. The ubiquitous **Marks and Spencer**, known affectionately as 'Marks and Sparks', is good for fair-priced, no-nonsense basics from knickers and socks to crew necks and shirts, and the food departments sell an imaginative range of sandwiches for lunch plus quality pre-packed Meals for One.

Apart from the chains, shops of a kind tend to group together. You'll find, **by area:** books in Bloomsbury; electronic goods and sofabeds around Tottenham Court Road; top English stores such as Simpson's, Fortnum and Mason's and Aquascutum on Piccadilly and Regent Street; exclusive bespoke tailors and perfumeries that are reportedly frequented by royalty in Jermyn Street; *haute couture* and designer clothes around Knightsbridge and Bond Street (target St Christopher's Place, South Molton Street, Harvey Nichols and Beauchamp – pronounced Beecham – Place); new young fashion in Soho and Covent Garden (Neal Street is said to be the Carnaby Street of the 1990s).

If you've come from abroad, Britain's **Export Scheme** means you may be able to claim tax back on goods bought (VAT is currently 17.5 per cent). Two drawbacks: you sometimes have to spend £100 first; not all shops do it. Before you spend the money, ask the shop assistant for a form, which you fill in, they stamp, you hand in at Customs as you leave the country, and after a six-week wait you get your 17.5 per cent refund through the post.

For an exhaustive listing of shops and markets, see *Time Out*'s massive *Directory to London Shops and Services* (£6), or to encourage 'a complete women's economy' by giving shops run by women business, buy *The Everywoman Directory* (mail order £6.50 from Everywoman Sales, 34 Islington Green, London N1 8DU). Or see below for a selection of highlights and essentials.

OPENING HOURS

Most shops open Mon–Sat 9.30 a.m.–5.30/6 p.m. except Bank Holidays. Below are some notable variations:
Few shops in the City open at all on Saturdays;
a few fashion and accessories shops in Soho open on Sundays;
most shops around Oxford Street, Regent Street, Bond Street, St Christopher's Place and High Street Kensington stay open till 7 or 8 p.m. on Thursdays;
around Knightsbridge, Beauchamp Place and the King's Road, late-night opening (till 7 or 8 p.m.) is on Wednesdays;
during the fortnight before Christmas and the summer and winter sales, most department stores extend their late weekday hours and open on Sundays.

Don't go to London's markets just to *buy* – go for the *atmosphere.*

Berwick Street

Berwick Street, WC2; Oxford Circus or Tottenham Court Road Underground; open Mon–Sat 8 a.m.–5 p.m.

If you're working or sightseeing in the centre of town, come to Berwick Street to savour the vibrant colourful atmosphere and to buy picnic ingredients such as lumps of Gruyère and, depending on the season, lychees and oyster mushrooms.

Brick Lane Market

Brick Lane, E1; Aldgate East Underground; open Sun 5 a.m.–2 p.m.

This sprawling market sells just about everything from reject frozen food to saris. The sections that sell second-hand furniture, bikes and clothes have the best bargains at sunrise (traders put the prices up as tourists flood in), so if you're set on bargains but don't arrive till lunchtime, concentrate on the area nearby known as Columbia Road market, where flower vendors sell off potted plants at low prices and happy customers leave hidden by armfuls of bunches of cheap blooms. To keep you fuelled there are a number of bagel shops (see Eating and Drinking), and if you're after a curry go to one of the many cheap and extremely good Asian restaurants (see Eating and Drinking).

Brixton Market

Brixton Station Road and Electric Avenue, SW9; Brixton Underground; open Mon, Tues, Thur–Sat 8.30 a.m.–5 p.m., Wed 8.30 a.m.–1 p.m.

Visit the market with a friend on a sunny day to see Brixton at its best: survey yams and mangos on busy stalls that curve round with Electric Avenue to the covered section where you can choose from Afro-Caribbean fish, dreadlock wigs, Senegalese fabric and cheap cooking utensils before going to tiny **Franco's** for cappuccino and huge pizzas (see Eating and Drinking). Afterwards you could go for a walk in **Brockwell Park** (*entrance on Brixton Water Lane*) – where you should make sure not to miss the beautifully tended, other worldly walled garden – or take in an afternoon film at the **Ritzy** (see Entertainment).

Camden Market

Camden High Street to Chalk Farm Road, NW1; Camden Town Underground; open Sat, Sun 8 a.m.–6 p.m.

Originally a small collection of alternative stalls around Camden Lock (at the canal), Camden Market is now nearly mainstream and consists of several markets running from Camden Underground station halfway up Chalk Farm Road. It can get claustrophobically busy on a sunny weekend, but it's still a trendy fun place to buy Doc Marten boots – traditional black or silver-coloured – as well as lycra designs by aspiring Katharine Hamnetts, handmade earrings, African masks and healthy banana cakes and filled pitta. There are innumerable eateries, including – a little way out of the crush – **Marine Ices** (see Eating and Drinking), and a short walk away there's **Primrose Hill** for walking, sunbathing and kite-flying.

Chelsea Antique Market

245A and 253 King's Road, SW3; open Mon–Sat 10 a.m.–6 p.m., Sloane Square Underground.

Of the great many London antiques markets, this was the first, established in the 1960s by 'resting' actors and bohemians. There are beautiful leather-bound books, bird prints and maps, but stick to browsing, as prices are rarely reasonable.

Greenwich Open-Air Market

Greenwich High Road and Market Square, SE10; Greenwich BR or LDR to Island Gardens and walk through the tunnel; open Sat, Sun 7 a.m.–5.30 p.m.

This is best for antique bric-a-brac, crafts and jewellery, some of it surprisingly cheap. For a day out, combine a browse round the market with a visit to **Greenwich Palace**, the **Royal Observatory** or the ***Cutty Sark*** (see South London).

Petticoat Lane Market

Middlesex Street, E1; Aldgate or Aldgate East Underground; open Sun 9 a.m.–2 p.m.

Bear in mind the joke that you can lose your watch at one end and have it sold back to you at the other, and you'll have a fine time watching wide-boys demonstrating household gadgets like electronic vegetable peelers or kids' robot toys accompanied by neighbouring stallholders' bawled sales patter.

Portobello Market

Portobello Road, W11; Ladbroke Grove or Notting Hill Gate Underground; all of it open Sat 8 a.m.–5 p.m., everything except antiques also open 8 a.m.–3 p.m. Fri, vegetables section also open Mon–Wed 8 a.m.–5 p.m.

If you walk down Portobello Road from Notting Hill Gate towards the Golborne Road you'll pass – in order – antiques, fruit and veg and second-hand clothes on stalls patronised by locals including homeless people, who forage in discarded boxes, and media stars stocking up for dinner parties. Sounds include a bellowed 'Hurry, hurry, hurry; come and get your curry' and theatre students' arty busking near the Westway flyover; smells include fresh-baked organic bread from the health-food shop; and places to eat include the **Lisboa** and the **Grove Café** (see Eating and Drinking). Afterwards, go to a film at the **Electric Cinema** (see Entertainment), or for a walk in **Hyde Park** (see West London).

Department Stores

Department stores can be daunting and impersonal, but they often have everything you want in one place, and they're usually geared up for children, featuring baby-changing facilities plus special menus and highchairs in the restaurants.

Fenwick

63 New Bond Street, W1, tel. 071 629 9161.

Many women favour Fenwick's for its hosiery and blouse departments, which boast reasonable prices and a wide range of stock.

Fortnum and Mason's

181 Piccadilly, W1, tel. 071 734 8040.

Legendary for its food department – where a genteel atmosphere prevails despite crowds jostling for beautifully wrapped gifts of English jams, marmalades and teas – Fortnum's also has a good womenswear selection, a furniture and china department, a frieze of gentlemen in hunting pinks galloping round the old-fashioned first-floor restaurant/tearoom and a clock on the Piccadilly façade that bursts into charming mechanical action on the hour every hour.

Harrods

Knightsbridge, SW1; tel. 071 730 1234.

Covering 4.5 acres, some say green and gold Harrods lost its class when the Al Fayed brothers bought it, but the world-famous store continues to attract tourists for the window displays and rich locals for the gourmet delicacies including 130 types of bread in its warren of Victorian-tiled food halls. You can leave your dog in the Harrods kennels while you get lost wandering between Silverware, Perfumes, teenage fashion in 'Way In' and *haute couture* in 'International Designers' and the large childrens' department, which has a resident magician. If you can't tear yourself away from the magic tricks, get a Personal Shopper to search out gifts for your family, and buy theatre tickets through the Harrods agency.

Harvey Nichols

109 Knightsbridge, SW1; tel. 071 235 5000.

'Harvey Nicks' was considered Harrods' poor relation until in 1993 the fifth-floor restaurant and food hall designed by the in-vogue Julian Wickham opened. You don't have to fight to find it, since there's a special express lift to the glass-roofed restaurant which serves pricey modish snacks like buffalo mozzarella with truffle oil on big plates on small tables next door to a food hall that's more compact than Harrods' and easier to negotiate. The emphasis through the rest of Harvey Nichols is on designer clothes from saucy Helen Storey to quietly elegant Nicole Farhi; the tights section is extensive; and so too is the choice of shoes and accessories. And if you fly in and out of London a lot on business you can take advantage of Harvey Nichols' dressing service: go in for a fitting and thereafter you can phone to say you need an outfit for, say, an opera première or a charity ball and they'll send clothes in a selection of colours over to your hotel for you to choose from.

Peter Jones

Sloane Square, SW1; tel. 071 730 3434.

Peter Jones is many Englishwomen's favourite store for stocking an easily negotiable wide range of sensible goods at sensible prices from curtain fabrics to neat sweaters to household items such as wooden spoons.

Liberty

Regent Street, W1; tel. 071 734 1234.

This shop has a wonderful mock-Tudor exterior and a rich wood-panelled interior that stocks the famous Liberty print fabrics, classic men's silk handkerchiefs, designer tableware and a selection of designer clothes as well as antiques from pots to rugs, and there's a bargain basement for unusual gifts. A lovely shopping experience.

Marks and Spencer

458 Oxford Street, W1; 071 935 7954.

This is the biggest branch of 'Marks and Sparks', or 'M&S'. Like the others, it sells 'underwear' rather than 'lingerie', and this distinction is evident in the prices. Come for unglamorous, good-quality, fair-priced knickers, bras, shirts, T-shirts and jumpers. There are changing rooms now, but you can still exchange goods or get a refund as long as you keep your receipt.

Selfridges

400 Oxford Street, W1; 071 629 1234.

Legend has it that founder Gordon Selfridge wooed his mistresses by escorting them round his department store, letting them choose anything they wanted, gratis, and so went bankrupt. Today local office workers love it for the food department; the luggage section is good and the range of cosmetics and beauty products is unrivalled on Oxford Street.

Clothes, Alternative, Second-hand and Young

American Classics

404 King's Road, SW10, tel. 071 351 5229.

The rage for second-hand American fashion persists – come here for baseball caps and jackets and Levi 501s that cost nearly as much worn as new.

Cornucopia

12 Upper Tachbrook Street, SW1, tel. 071 828 5752.

Staff of *Vogue* magazine trawl the racks and rails of second-hand clothes and shoes. The dressing-room's big enough to test your bargain ballgown with a twirl.

Crazy Clothes Connection

134 Lancaster Road, W11, tel. 071 221 3989; open Sun, closed Thur.

Eight rooms of original 1920s–70s clothing for sale or for hire in an exuberant gossipy atmosphere maintained by the two women owners.

Duffer of St George

27 D'Arblay Street, W1, tel. 071 439 0996; one other branch.

Striped is about the most complicated pattern you'll find here. Duffer of St George has a faithful young-London following for the functional unisex jean trousers, flannel and T-shirt tops and pork-pie hat caps that manage to make an alternative fashion statement and still be restrained in design.

Flip

125 Long Acre, WC2, tel. 071 836 7044.

More Americana and second-hand 501s, some in worse nick and therefore cheaper than the pairs in American Classics. Flip's Bargain Basement is good for T-shirts and checked shirts, and there's usually something fun and affordable in the ground-floor selection of unisex hats.

HOBBS

Unit 17, The Market, Covent Garden, WC2, tel. 071 836 9168; other branches.

Cheaper than designer, classier than high-street fashion, the shoes and clothes – restrained yet still vogueish and sternly sexy – do equally well for work and pleasure.

HYPER HYPER

26–40 Kensington High Street, W8, tel. 071 937 6964.

Pass between pillars representing massive gold Classical Greek women and wander two floors of more than 70 individual stalls that have collectively been recently recognised internationally as a showcase for British fashion. Buy ethereal mauve floaty skirts from Ghost, a blue wig in the basement or a one-off fruit-design mohair jumper. Some say it's no longer on the cutting edge; others complain that the staff are too trendy for comfort; many wouldn't go anywhere else.

JIGSAW

Centre at the Circus, Regent Street, W1, tel. 071 734 7604; other branches.

Similar to Hobbs but only clothes, more of them, in more colours and considered slightly funkier.

MISS SELFRIDGE

40 Duke Street, W1, tel. 071 629 1234; other branches.

This is the biggest of several branches around the city, all selling high-street fashion that resembles catwalk designs at affordable prices.

PASSENGER

39 Beak Street, W1, tel. 071 287 3708; other branches.

Anyone who buys at Duffer of St George is likely to come to Passenger too – similar stock, but with a slightly more sporty emphasis. A trip to Passenger is often combined by clubbers and DJs with a trip to Soho's specialist record shops.

PINEAPPLE

6A Langley Street, WC2, tel. 071 836 4006.

Debbie Moore realised there was a market for cheap, streamlined leotards and leggings beyond the dance school next door, and has now shifted the emphasis to 'sporty', including cotton and lycra cycling shorts. Fair prices; clientele ranges from young and trendy to executives in need of a low-cut top to go under their suit jacket.

WAREHOUSE

116 Oxford Street, W1, tel. 071 436 4179; other branches.

Jeff Banks has been called ground-breaking for three things: he recently updated the design of the Girl Scouts' uniform; he is said to have revolutionised high-street fashion in the 1980s by making style affordable; and has been credited with introducing sales catalogues for the fashion-conscious. Warehouse clothes, which are generally slightly more stylish and less clubby than those in Miss Selfridge, attract young women with jobs who want to look fashionable and smart.

You can find good selections of designers' clothes in the major department stores, but the individual showcase shops can be much more fun and will stock the whole current collection. British women designers to look out for include: the internationally renowed populariser in the 1990s of stack heels, **Vivienne Westwood**; the woman who restyles military Wren outfits and got her picture in all the papers for wearing an anti-Pershing-missile T-shirt when meeting Margaret Thatcher, **Katharine Hamnett; Helen Storey** for her surprisingly wearable mad body-hugging mixes of materials such as PVC, denim and leather; and one-time Westwood assistant **Bella Freud**, who produces subtly saucy versions of staid English matron designs.

BROWNS
23–27 South Molton Street, W1, tel. 071 491 7833.

Even in the sales, this shop can be dauntingly quiet, and the staff are often haughty, but the walkthrough joined-up houses make an engaging setting for the impressive selection of designers' collections, including ranges from Donna Karan, Norma Kamali, Romeo Gigli and Alaia. Prices are high unless you go to the recent 'Labels for Less' section opposite, which sells out-of-season stock or seconds at discounts that are sometimes as high as 50 or even 90 per cent.

CAROLINE CHARLES
11 Beauchamp Place, SW3, tel. 071 589 2521.

The classy, costly eveningwear is favoured by the Princess of Wales, and actress Emma Thompson had Charles design a special outfit for the 1993 Oscar ceremonies.

EDINA RONAY
141 King's Road, SW3, tel. 071 352 1085.

Here you can buy pure silk sweaters for over £300 designed exclusively by the daughter of Egon Ronay, Edina, whose name has for many become synonymous with high-quality, creative knitwear.

ENGLISH ECCENTRICS
155 Fulham Road, SW3, tel. 071 589 7154.

Classic silk shirts have swirling gold-and-black unicorn and pocketwatch designs, traditional waistcoats imitate hedgehog skin – come here for elegantly eccentric English shawls, scarves, dresses, blouses.

JONES
15 Floral Street, WC2, tel. 071 379 4299.

Jones men's and nearby women's shop stock amazing and often difficult-to-wear clothes by young and outrageous designers – try on beaded bras by Helen Storey and lycra bodies by Junior Gaultier – as well as occasional almost classic designs.

JOSEPH
77 Fulham Road, SW3, tel. 071 823 9500.

Brompton Cross is considered by many to be one of London's most fashionable shopping areas, and it is dominated by branches of Joseph Ettedgui's fashion empire. You'll find restrained casual chic in them all and, specifically, machine-knitted jumpers and leggings in Joseph Tricot, T-shirts in Joseph Bis and classy suits in Joseph Pour La Ville.

KATHARINE HAMNETT
20 Sloane Street, SW1, tel. 071 823 1002.

Hamnett often uses utilitarian clothes and materials as her starting point, so you may find tough denim frocks, shirts made of parachute silk or perhaps suits that make their wearers resemble air-raid wardens. Prices can be high, but quality is good and the clothes generally weather several changes of fashion seasons.

MARGARET HOWELL
29 Beauchamp Place, SW3, tel. 071 584 2462.

In Margaret Howell's hands, the basic shapes and materials associated with traditional English gentlemen's suits, such as crisp white cotton and grey pinstripe, become exquisitely cut and finely finished trouser- and skirt-suits for women.

WHISTLES
12–14 St Christopher's Place, W1, tel. 071 487 4484; see phone book for other branches.

Come to Whistles for French and English designer suits, for example by Lolita Lempicka or Myrene de Premonville, for design-conscious and reasonably priced maternity wear such as generously elasticated leggings, and don't overlook Whistles' own label – a Whistles simple black top can become an indispensable part of your wardrobe.

WORLD'S END
430 King's Road, SW3, tel. 071 352 6551.

Westwood's clock-fronted small shop at the far end of the King's Road is worth a visit for its enjoyable barminess. Famous designs have included flesh-coloured leggings with a tactfully placed fig leaf, which Westwood herself wore for television interviews. Although the clothes often look too wacky to wear anywhere but on a catwalk, try them on – they're well made, and it sometimes takes only a bit of extra confidence to carry them off.

Clothes, Classic

AQUASCUTUM
100 Regent Street, W1, tel. 071 734 6090.

This large, elegant shop sells ladies raincoats for up to £1,000.

JAEGER
200–206 Regent Street, W1, tel. 071 734 8211.

Branches of Jaeger sell simply elegant suits in tweed, flannel, camel hair, cashmere for the high-powered businesswoman.

LAURA ASHLEY
7–9 Harriet Street, SW1, tel. 071 235 9796; see phone book for other branches.

Laura Ashley's trademarks are quintessentially English Victorian-style high-necked lacy blouses and flower-print bodiced dresses. Loyal customers love the nightdresses, which are in sturdy white cotton, affordable and tentatively romantic. The occasional T-shirt dresses are well made to last.

LONG TALL SALLY
21 Chiltern Street, W1, tel. 071 487 3370.

This shop stocks a wide range of clothes from classic to contemporary, casual daywear to eveningwear, all cut to fit women who are taller than average.

NICOLE FARHI
25–26 St Christopher's Place, W1, tel. 071 486 3416; see phone book for other branches.

Timeless clothes in soft moss greens, sand and mushroom made from linen for summer and wool gabardine for winter, sometimes in safari/nineteenth-century traveller themes. Trousers tend to be easy-to-wear 'slacks' even if they're part of a suit, and the most formal coats have smooth lines.

THE SCOTCH HOUSE
2 Brompton Road, SW1, tel. 071 581 2151.

Argyll socks and sporrans are of course on sale, alongside cosy cream Aran sweaters and other Scottish woollens.

SIMPSONS
203 Piccadilly, W1, tel. 071 734 2002.

Here you'll find the classic English-look Daks line in suits and casuals that some consider slightly dowdier than Jaeger, but still a good alternative.

TURNBULL AND ASSER
71 Jermyn Street, SW1, tel. 071 930 0502.

Perhaps you'd like a fine poplin man's shirt for yourself, or maybe you want to buy a man friend a dressing-gown or tie as a present from the shop whose famous clients incude the Prince of Wales.

Accessories and Lingerie

All major department stores stock lingerie, mid-priced conservative jewellery, leather goods including handbags and purses plus a range of shoes from sneakers to stilettos. Here are some alternatives to the big-store shopping experience.

BRADLEYS
85 Knightsbridge, SW1, tel. 071 235 2902.

Established as a specialist lingerie store over three decades ago, Bradleys sells everything from fluffy slippers to corsets to designer lingerie from all over the world to varied clients including royalty and nearby shop workers.

BUTLER AND WILSON
20 South Molton Street, W1, tel. 071 409 2955.

Butler and Wilson excels at high-class costume jewellery.

FOGAL
51 Brompton Road, SW3, tel. 071 225 0472.

Hundreds of stockings and tights here, some patterned, some nylon, some cashmere, many astoundingly expensive.

Janet Fitch

25 Old Compton Street, W1, tel. 071 287 3789.

Some of the jewellery pieces could set off a smart business suit nicely, and there's constant demand from clubbers for the jewelled metal whistles on sale in this very Soho store that has gained a name as an important showcase for new British jewellery designs. A shop assistant described this shop as 'spunky' and the 2 *Percy Street* branch as 'chi-chi'.

The Hat Shop

58 Neal Street, WC2, tel. 071 836 6718.

Berets to make you look like Ingrid Bergman in *Casablanca*, straw hats to protect you in the sun, mad orange matador's hats or eminently sensible hats for weddings – this shop will satisfy most hat needs and whims, but try and avoid Saturdays, when there's often queues outside.

James Smith and Sons

53 New Oxford Street, WC1, tel. 071 836 4731.

This is not the cheapest place to buy umbrellas, but it's one of the most atmospheric. 'Since 1830' declares the old green-and-gold sign grandly – you can buy brollies with animals' heads carved for handles, there are parasols, sword-concealing walking sticks, and you can have a cane made to order.

Janet Reger

2 Beauchamp Place, SW3, tel. 071 584 9360.

After World War II hardships Janet Reger hit big by designing a fantastical lingerie range featuring luxuriously unpractical camisoles, camiknickers, French knickers and suspender belts with a distinct whiff of Hollywood. She's still going strong.

VB Morrison Craft Shop

50 Neal Street, WC2, tel. 071 836 0928.

Come here for less refined, cheaper leather bags and purses, but be prepared to queue on Saturdays, as the shop's tiny and the chunky leather satchel is perennially popular.

Lock & Co.

6 St James's Street, SW1, tel. 071 930 5849.

Having supplied high-society Englishmen with traditional headwear such as bowlers, top hats and fishing hats since the seventeenth century, Lock & Co. recently began selling hats for women.

The Natural Shoe Store

21 Neal Street, W1, tel. 071 836 5254.

Clog-style Birkenstock 'made for walking' shoes go in and out of fashion in different countries, but are always ideal for traipsing round London's sights.

Russell and Bromley

24 New Bond Street, W1, tel. 071 629 6903.

This high-quality, well-respected shop is the perfect place to come and buy court shoes ('pumps') that will be just right for business meetings.

Shelly's Shoes

159 Oxford Street, W1, tel. 071 437 5842.

Come here for high fashion from customised Doc Marten boots to spangled 12-inch platforms, all at street prices – top names, including Katharine Hamnett, design some of the styles.

Health and Beauty

All major department stores sell good cosmetics ranges, and most will do you a facial and haircut as well – most notably Harrods, Harvey Nichols and Selfridges. For an expensive but heavenly three- or four-day health binge in beautiful country surroundings, see Health and Sport in Entertainment. For individual shops and services, see below.

Hair

ANDREW JOSE
Hyper Hyper, 26–40 Kensington High Street, W8, tel. 071 937 8810; 20 Charlotte Street, W1, tel. 071 323 4679.

Go to the disco-pumping Hyper Hyper branch for young hip cuts, or to the Charlotte Street branch for impeccable cuts that are perfect for high-powered business conventions from staff trained by Jose or from Andrew Jose himself, who is current holder of the Wella/*Vogue* 'best hairdresser of the year' award. Jose is the man many women trust when they want a radical change such as chopping long hair off into a style that suits their face and their day-to-day needs.

MCADAMS
14 Hay Hill, W1, tel. 071 499 8079.

Denise McAdams has made a name for herself as London's only top woman hairdresser, and when she set up independently she took clients such as Kathleen Turner, Prince Charles and the Princesses Beatrice and Eugenie with her to her new salon (cut by Denise costs around £50).

VIDAL SASSOON
130 Sloane Street, SW1, tel. 071 730 7288.

Vidal Sassoon himself has retired, but his skilled staff continue to execute the classic Five Point haircut, and those on a budget should try the **Vidal Sassoon Hairdressing School** (*56 Davies Mews, W1, tel. 071 629 4635*), where you can get cheap haircuts by nearly qualified trainees who remain under close supervision.

Scents and Cosmetics

CRABTREE AND EVELYN
6 Kensington Church Street, W8, tel. 071 937 9335; other branches.

Beautiful decorated wood, tin and paper instead of plastic packaging of natural avocado soap and peachy bath oil American products that are not tested on animals. A great place to buy gifts.

FLORIS
89 Jermyn Street, W1, tel. 071 930 2885.

Even if it's only an excuse to shop on Jermyn Street, come to Floris, 'purveyors of the finest English flower perfumes and toiletries to the court of St James's since the year 1730', for rose mouthwash and Lily of the Valley soap in elegant blue and gold packaging that bears the Royal Warrant.

NEAL'S YARD APOTHECARY
2 Neal's Yard, WC2, tel. 071 379 7222.

This is less quaint, more earthy – its 'natural' hair and body products are made of ingredients such as roots, leaves and beans (Slippery Elm, Prickly Ash and Squaw Vine, for example) and displayed in chunky luminescent blue glass jars.

PENHALIGONS
41 Wellington Street, WC2, tel. 071 836 2150.

Famous for prettily bottled toilet waters in fragrances including gardenia and orange blossom, Penhaligons is also known for the Lords line, which was created in 1911 for 'dashing young blades' and is still on sale today.

YVES ROCHER
7 Gees Court, W1, tel. 071 409 2975.

The range of cosmetics are all plant-based, and there's a beauty centre where you can get advice or treatment.

Books

Two areas that are great for book-browsing are Charing Cross Road, which is famous for being lined with second- and first-hand bookshops, and the streets below the British Museum, which are scattered with antiquarian book and print shops. For buying books on the hoof, you'll need to know about the city's best bookshop chains: **Dillons**, founded in the 1930s by pioneering businesswoman Una Dillon, sells fiction and general books but is especially good on academic books, for the helpful, knowledgeable staff, and for allowing you to browse without pressure to buy; the ever-expanding **Waterstone's** chain is good for highbrow fiction in plain but elegant shops – it offers a 25,000-title catalogue and will ship overseas; **W.H. Smith's** started small last century as magazine stalls in train stations – still great for its extensive magazine racks, Smith's also sells lots of hardbacks and paperbacks, mainly fiction, from Jackie Collins and Jilly Cooper blockbusters to Brontë bestsellers.

COMPENDIUM
234 Camden High Street, NW1, tel. 071 485 8944.

Two floors of books, almost always friendly staff and a wide selection of stock that includes North American imports. Camden residents often have to fight off the urge to come here several times weekly – the combination of convivial atmosphere and enticing titles can get too much for the bank balance. Good programme of readings.

Daunts

83 Marylebone High Street, W1, tel. 071 224 2295.

A bit off the beaten track, but well worth a visit if you're planning a trip or just interested in travel. This atmopsheric wood-balconied travel shop has shelves arranged cleverly so that next to sections displaying books on a particular country or city there will be shelves loaded with relevant novels.

Dillons

82 Gower Street, WC1, tel. 071 636 1577; other branches.

This huge, coolly blue decorated shop is wonderful. If you come in looking for something in the large children's section or the comprehensive poetry corner, you'll almost certainly be distracted and end up absorbed in the racks of books on tape, or perhaps the paperback fiction displays that pleasurably delay your arrival at the exit.

Foyles

113–119 Charing Cross Road, WC2, tel. 071 437 5660.

The staff are rude, and the appallingly organised shelves in the 29 departments make it nearly always impossible to find what you're looking for. London's largest and most famous bookshop is a nightmare – go to the nearby Waterstone's instead.

Hatchards

187 Piccadilly, W1, tel. 071 439 9921.

Year after year Hatchards gets the thumbs-up from punters who enjoy buying from its vast range of hardback and paperback general titles (religion-gardening-children) in elegant surroundings. London's oldest bookshop (founded in 1797) will also ship books anywhere in the world, and if you've been desperately trying to get hold of a remaindered book, try Hatchards search service.

Samuel French

52 Fitzroy Street, W1, tel. 071 387 9373.

Specialist theatre bookshop.

John Sandoe

10 Blacklands Terrace, SW3, tel. 071 589 9473.

The taste of the staff in this small, tucked-away bookshop is so trusted by customers that since the sixties Sandoe has operated a 'sight unseen' service whereby a lump sum can be paid monthly for a selection of current bests to be made on behalf of the customer, then forwarded by post.

Stanfords

12–14 Long Acre, WC2, tel. 071 836 1321; one other branch.

Internationally famous for its vast selection of maps; the two floors of Stanfords travel bookshop also boast a comprehensive collection of guides to countries and cities all over the world. Convenient for its central location, Stanfords has friendly staff, and the globe bedside lights near the main till make great gifts.

W.H. Smith

92 Notting Hill Gate, W11, tel. 071 727 9261; other branches.

Come here to combine magazine, stationery and book buying on your way to or from Portobello market (see Shopping).

Waterstone's

68 Hampstead High Street, NW3, tel.

071 794 1098; other branches.

Waterstone's staff love their work, which reflects in the friendly atmosphere you'll find at the impressive programme of author readings that take place at this branch. In keeping with the Waterstone's accessibility revolution which took bookshops on to the high street with a 'pile 'em high' approach, the doors are still open till 9 p.m. most nights, when the shop mills with Hampstead-ites distracted delightfully on their way home to supper.

Women's Bookshops

Centreprise
136 Kingsland High Street, E8, tel. 071 254 9632.

General and community bookshop that's strong on black fiction and non-fiction, lesbian and gay fiction, and children's books. Café next door that's at once echoey warehousey and cheerfully homespun. If you've come from the centre of town, you might want to combine your trip with a drink in the **Duke of Wellington** (see Eating and Drinking).

Gay's the Word
66 Marchmont Street, WC1, tel. 071 278 7654; open Sunday afternoons as well as through the week.

Lesbian, gay and feminist bookshop that also stocks cards, T-shirts, jewellery and badges, and has a noticeboard at the back featuring information on accommodation, work, readings and more. You can make use of the small seating area while you peruse notices from the board.

Silver Moon
68 Charing Cross Road, WC2, tel. 071 836 7906.

A great central location for the newly expanded Silver Moon, which has a wide, well-organised selection of fiction, political and general titles on and about women, including a fine section of fiction by and for lesbians (Silver Moon has begun publishing its own list of populist lesbian fiction), and there's a good children's section. Silver Moon has a noticeboard and regular author readings – phone for details or pop in.

CDs, Cassettes and Records

Soul Jazz
12 Ingestre Place, W1, tel. 071 494 2004.

The DJ's record shop. Come here to pick up flyers for happening clubs.

HMV Record Store
150 Oxford Street, W1, tel. 071 631 3423.

Knowledgeable but sometimes curt staff in the four-floor store that advertises itself as one of the biggest in Europe.

Music Discount Centre
10 Charlotte Place, W1, tel. 071 637 0129.

This intimate and seductive store sells discontinued classical records, tapes and CDs featuring acclaimed musicians, conductors and orchestras, all at knock-down prices. Helpful, friendly staff.

RAY'S JAZZ SHOP

180 Shaftesbury Avenue, WC2, tel. 071 240 3969.

This is the jazz person's used and new jazz records and cassettes shop – if you've questions about the old-sized 78 records or even want to buy something, you may have trouble distracting laid back assistants' attention from the famous jazz musician or journalist they're chatting with so amiably. Nice shambly atmosphere.

ROUGH TRADE

16 Neal's Yard, Covent Garden, WC2, tel. 071 240 0105.

Famous as the first independent record label and sales outlet for mainly Punk bands that wouldn't have been taken on by major labels in the 1970s, Rough Trade's first LP was 'Inflammable Material' by Stiff Little Fingers in 1979. Now that 'Indie' music's become almost mainstream-popular, you'll find numbers topping the charts in their record racks.

TOWER RECORDS

Swan and Edgar Building, 1 Piccadilly Circus, W1, tel. 071 437 1165.

Tower Records is known, as well as for its wide selection of youth market tapes, CDs and records, for its imaginative window displays that may promote a big-name pop star or a bravely alternative new film festival. Fine World Music section, and the store has a good selection of foreign newspapers.

VIRGIN MEGASTORE

14–30 Oxford Street, W1, tel. 071 631 1234.

This is a favourite with children: there is a large games section and a bookstore that features comic books and pop biographies. The extensive range of CDs, tapes and records runs the gamut from classical to thrash rock and grunge. There's a café upstairs if you need a rejuvenating coffee.

Gifts, Oddities and Specialist Stores

ATHENA

1 Leicester Square, WC2, tel. 071 437 6780; other branches.

In all the big museums and art galleries you'll find beautiful posters of exhibits past and present; at Athena you can buy Snoopy posters and the one of the woman tennis player idly scratching a naked buttock – it's said that this poster made the photographer a millionaire.

THE BACK SHOP

24 New Cavendish Street, London W1, tel. 071 935 9120.

'Personal care' is the buzzphrase in this Aladdin's cave of products designed to help all kinds of back problems at home, in the office, or while travelling for work or pleasure. Phone for a free full-colour catalogue or call in and have a free posture assessment, which will be given by David or Maura Macdonald, who are confident that they can help most back problems. If the answer costs £20 they won't try and sell you something more expensive, but if they recommend a product costing £400, it's because it's worth the investment. There's an in-shop bed to test pillows on, there are Cloud shoes, portable massagers, packable bed boards, easy-use car posture aids, sloping desk surfaces and, to encourage correct posture in children, the Swedish Tripp-Trapp chair. The range of office and leisure chairs will, if you've never tried an orthopaedic/ergonomic chair before, change your idea of what sitting should feel like, and even what chairs should look like. The range of Back Shop's own brand products is 25–40 per cent cheaper than equivalents currently on the market.

Button Queen

19 Marylebone Lane, W1, tel. 071 935 1505.

Thousands of antique and modern buttons with prices ranging from a few pence to astronomical.

Conran Shop

81 Fulham Road, SW3, tel. 071 589 7401.

From mauve velvet sofas to gold star design candle holders, this is the ultimate place to buy gifts and luxury household goods – and to people-watch.

Crafts Council Shop

Victoria and Albert Museum, Cromwell Road, SW7, tel. 071 589 5070.

Buy wooden toys, floral design notepads, designer jewellery and much more in a shop that's walled with real medieval shop fronts. Many gifts in the excellent range are made by British craftspeople.

Elizabeth David Cookshop

3 North Row, Covent Garden, London WC2, tel. 071 836 9167.

From the shop of the woman who introduced French peasant cooking to the British middle classes you can buy everything from a complete set of Le Creuset bakeware, including hob kettle, to a plain yet attractive tea strainer.

Gosh!

39 Great Russell Street, WC1, tel. 071 636 1011.

Of all London's comic shops, this is the least male-dominated. Buy the feminist 'Fanny' graphic short stories, and for children there's the whole range of Asterix, Tintin, etc.

Heal's

196 Tottenham Court Road, W1, tel. 071 636 1666.

This is the place hundreds of Londoners tell themselves they'll come to buy a sofa when they're rich ... meantime, Heal's ground floor is great for gifts, from designer kitchenware to candelabras to old-fashioned photograph albums.

Hope and Glory

131A Kensington Church Street, W8, tel. 071 727 8424.

Around half the pieces of commemorative pottery and glassware are pre-1940.

The Kite Store

48 Neal Street, WC2, tel. 071 836 1666.

Dragon and flower and numerous other designs of kites decorate the windows and hang all around you in this smart, enjoyable shop that can advise you on accessories including Parachuting Spider and Fluorescent Triblade. Fly your kite on Primrose Hill.

Anything Left Handed

57 Brewer Street, W1, tel. 071 437 3910.

The title says it all – scissors, pens, cups ... as long as it's for left-handed people, this shop stocks it.

Lots Road Chelsea Galleries

71 Lots Road, SW10, tel. 071 351 5784.

The *idea* of taking an antique back home can be more fun than the reality, unless you set your sights on something small and head for Lots Road, which is an entertaining jumble of Victorian washbowls, chenille curtains and pots and trinkets that you can view on Monday nights and may get for a bargain price at the auction.

Mysteries

9/11 Monmouth Street, WC2, tel. 071 240 3688.

At 'London's Psychic Shop and New Age Centre' you can buy crystals, books on t'ai chi, women's studies/psychology/spirituality. Head for the 'subliminal zone' (cassettes) or have a psychic reading.

Ray Man

64 Neal Street, WC2, tel. 071 240 1776.

A wonderful tiny shop resonating with the sounds of Eastern musical instruments from flutes to ankle bells to clay drums. Good for unusual gifts.

Sh!

22 Coronet Street, EC1, tel. 071 613 5458; open Wed–Thur noon–8 p.m. Fri and Sat till 10 p.m.; Old Street Underground.

A sex shop set up for women and their friends by accountant Kim de Testre when straight and lesbian friends persuaded her there was a big market of women who hated having to go to Soho's Ann Summers. Buy seamed black stockings, made-to-measure chaps, climax cream and more in a non-inhibiting environment.

Smythson

54 New Bond Street, W1, tel. 071 629 8559.

Fine-quality stationery is a useful and luxurious present; here you can buy with the knowledge that Smythson is a favourite of the Queen.

Studio 40

69 Berwick Street, W1, tel. 071 437 0811

Soho's longest-established gay shop stocks an extended and upgraded range of underwear, rubber clothing, and sex toys. For gay men and lesbians.

The Tea House

15 Neal Street, WC2, tel. 071 240 7539.

A tiny, absorbing shop that satisfies the English obsession for tea.

Wedgwood

266 & 270 Regent Street, W1, tel. 071 734 5656.

Whether it's a china napkin ring or an entire dinner set, you're bound to find something you like within your price range here.

The newest, slickest prestigious department store food and drink hall is the Fifth Floor of **Harvey Nichols**; the most atmospheric is **Harrods** for its linked tiled caverns filled with English and foreign delicacies; **Fortnum and Mason's** is perhaps best for gifts and most traditional, although it has been forward in its time, stocking Mr Heinz's new tinned products in 1886; **Selfridges** has a food hall that gets a long queue at the bread counter and smells deliciously of fresh-ground coffee; and **Marks and Spencer's** is good for lunchtime picnics and easy-cook evening meals for one. Of the supermarkets, **Kwik Save** is perhaps the best of the recessionary breed that forgoes fancy store interiors to keep named brands' prices low for the penny-counting customer; **Tesco's** is not especially adventurous but it is decently stocked, selling all the basics and organic vegetables in some branches; **Sainsbury's** is making a name for its user-friendly spaces and good-value own-brand products in everything from sardines to top-grade wine alongside a comprehensive selection of the usual supermarket goods. For fresh fruit and vegetables go to the markets in Berwick Street, Brick Lane, Brixton, Camden or Portobello Road. For drink, arguably the best off-licence chain is **Oddbins**, which stocks an impressively wide selection of cheap and vintage wines – the mainly young and admirably informed staff will give cheerful, reliable recommendations on best value wines.

André Simon

50 Elizabeth Street, SW1, tel. 071 730 8108.

Legendary glamorous publisher's publicist Caroline Michel shares the preference of London's glitterati for this Belgravia wine merchant.

Bendicks

20 Royal Exchange, EC3, tel. 071 283 5843.

Bendick's reputation is based on hand-made bitter-mint after-dinner chocolates, and although they are no longer hand-made they are still some of the best in London. This shop gives you a taste of the City as well.

Berry Bros & Rudd Ltd

3 St James's Street, SW1, tel. 071 839 9033.

Wooden panels, antique bottles and an ancient set of scales adorn the shop run by the Berry family since the 1700s. Staff are courteous; the claret and Burgundy stocks are particularly strong.

Carluccio's

30 Neal Street, WC2, tel. 071 240 1487.

This is for Italian specialist food in general, and mushroom lovers journey here for the selection of dried funghi.

The Drury Tea and Coffee Company

37 Drury Lane, WC2, tel. 071 836 2607.

The smell as you enter this shop is a caffeine fix in itself – the 22 blends from Brazil, Costa Rica, Mysore in

India and more can be mixed and ground to the customers' requirements.

I. Camisa & Son

61 Old Compton Street, W1, tel. 071 437 4686.

Come to this grocery store for everything Italian, from fresh-ground coffee to salami in all shapes and sizes, and hand-made pasta.

Justin de Blank

46A Walton Street, SW3, tel. 071 589 4743.

Treat yourself to bread baked in a 100-year-old brick oven, or at *42 Elizabeth Street, SW1, tel. 071 736 0605* try one of the French cheeses or a slice of roulade that's made to the specifications of the almost legendary caterer Justin de Blank.

Maison Bertaux

28 Greek Street, W1, tel. 071 935 6240.

This 'est. 1871' café and patisserie sells possibly the best almond croissants in London alongside little quiches and supremely indulgent cream gâteaux.

Neal's Yard Bakery Co-operative

6 Neal's Yard, WC2, tel. 071 386 5199.

Every loaf is made from 100 per cent whole wheat flour that is stoneground from organic wheat bought from the mill next door, and if you want to satisfy a sweet tooth healthily, try one of the sugar-free apricot and ginger cakes, or perhaps a carob brownie and an oat and raisin biscuit.

Neal's Yard Dairy

17 Shorts Gardens, WC2, tel. 071 379 7646.

Over 70 cheeses from Britain and Ireland are left to mature to peak condition in the Dairy's storerooms.

Rossyln Delicatessen

56 Rosslyn Hill, NW3, tel. 071 794 9210.

Dubbed by one well-heeled New York fan 'the Zabar's of London', the Rosslyn Deli's 4,000 lines from all over the world include 150 different cheeses, own-brand salad dressings and patisseries, and Iranian caviar. Buy for yourself, or they can make you up a gift basket.

Simply Sausages

341 Central Markets, EC1, tel. 071 329 3227.

You can get a huge variety of things in this shop, but they'll all be sausages – Lancashire and Cumberland sausages or spicy ones, and even vegetarian ones that taste too good to be true.

Twinings

216 The Strand, WC2, tel. 071 353 3511.

This shop is a shrine to the eighteenth-century tea merchant Thomas Twining: while you choose from the 100 varieties of tea in the long, narrow shop, you'll see pictures of the Twining family all around you, and in the back the museum celebrates Twinings as supplier to three generations of royalty.

GETAWAYS

In the time it takes you to cross Central London on a bus you could be whizzed from one of the capital's several train stations to a beach, hill-walking or a tea shop in a rural village.

The **British Travel Centre** (*12 Regent Street, SW1, Piccadilly Circus Underground, open 9 a.m.–6.30 p.m. Mon–Fri; May-Sept 9 a.m.–5 p.m. Sat, 10 a.m.–5 p.m. Sun; Oct-Apr 10 a.m.–4 p.m. Sat, Sun*) will give you heaps of brochures and advice, and once you've decided where you want to go, their **Room Centre** will, for a small charge, reserve appropriate accommodation anywhere in Britain.

Of the modes of **transport**, rail is often the fastest and most efficient, though rarely the cheapest. **Charing Cross** (*tel. 071 928 5100*) serves the South-East, Essex and East Anglia. **Euston** (*tel. 071 387 7070*) serves the Midlands, North Wales, the North-West and western Scotland. **King's Cross** (*tel. 071 278 2477*) serves the North-East and eastern Scotland. **Paddington** (*tel. 071 262 6767*) serves the West Country, South Wales and the West Midlands. **Victoria** (*tel. 071 922 6216*) serves the Sussex and Kent coasts and Europe. Special passes and deals to ask about that might save you money include Apex (which must be booked at least a week in advance), Network South-East Card, Family Railcard, Senior Citizen's and Young Person's Railcard.

Coaches are slower but cheaper, with minimal snack facilities. **National Express Coaches** cover most destinations (*tel. 071 730 0202, go to Victoria Coach Station, Buckingham Palace Road, SW1, ten minutes' walk from Victoria BR/Underground*). Travelling **by car** offers most flexibility. A big, reliable rental agency with lots of branches is **Hertz** on *081 679 1799*; also, **Godfrey Davies** on *071 723 9051*; for cheaper rental try **Holiday Autos** on *071 491 1111*. Finally, a romantic, if achey, option is **by bike** (contact the **Cyclists' Touring Club**, *Cotterell House, 69 Meadrow, Godalming, Surrey*

GU7 3HS, tel. 0483 417 217 for information including tour maps and bike rental). Most cyclists choose to take a train beyond London to pretty countryside before actually doing any cycling.

As for **accommodation,** B&Bs (Bed and Breakfasts) are often the best option unless you're going for luxury country-house hotels. **Stapleford Park** is one acclaimed example of a grand house hotel in lovely countryside, American-owned so equipped with all mod cons (*near Melton Mowbray, Leicestershire, LE14 2EF, tel. 057 284 522, fax 057 284 651*). The mid-priced hotels tend to be samey – ones with signs indicating that they have been awarded AA or RAC stars guarantee a certain standard of comfort and cleanliness (more stars equal more luxury). **B&Bs,** as the name implies, have breakfast thrown in with the price, and they are mostly cheap and friendly, almost always in homes and sometimes in working farmhouses. If you haven't fixed up accommodation before you go, find the nearest city or town's **Tourist Information Centre**, which will, for a small fee, fix you up with accommodation that suits your budget and needs.

Day Trips If your primary aim is to get away from the grime and smog of London for a day, bear in mind that Greenwich, Hampton Court, Kew and Richmond are all pleasant, escapist day trips (see South London and the River). If you have children you might want to go to **Brighton** (under an hour from London by train), where your children can run about on the pebbly **beach** (avoid swimming in the none-too-clean sea), play the amusement arcades on **Brighton Pier** or go to the **Sea Life Centre** in Madeira Drive (*tel. 0273 604234*); George IV's playtime mansion, the fairy-tale domed and minareted **Royal Pavilion,** is a must-see for anyone older than teenage, and the area known as **the Lanes** is pleasant to walk around.

You can see the sublime English gardens that writer Vita Sackville-West and her husband Harold Nicolson created for their home at Sissinghurst (Sissinghurst Gardens, Sissinghurst, Kent, *tel. 0580 712850*; about an hour from London by train to Staplehurst station, then about a 20 minute walk). June and July are the best times to visit, when the famous roses scent your walks around herb and cottage gardens and lakes. As well as a restaurant and a National Trust shop, there's plants for sale and a picnic site.

The cities of **Oxford** and **Cambridge** (about an hour away from London by train) appeal largely because of their grandly old-fashioned exclusive universities and the option of lazy punting on the river. **Stratford-upon-Avon** (about two hours from London by train), famous for having a theatre devoted to Shakespeare, is a key tourist destination for the Shakespeare industry of pubs and tea shops that has grown up around its history as Shakespeare's home town (go to the Tourist Information Centre for details of the five 'Shakespeare properties' that are open to visitors).

However, Oxford, Cambridge and Stratford-upon-Avon are all bustling, tiring day trips, and if you've decided you want to get away from London, you probably want a bit of peace and quiet. Indeed, if you're in London on business, countless meetings and brainstorms will leave you much in need of a **health farm** (see Health and Sport in Entertainment for Forest Mere).

Weekends For a weekend break, around three hours away from London is the area of lakes, fells and hard-to-climb pikes that inspired the poet Wordsworth and attracted children's story-writer/illustrator Beatrix Potter, the **Lake District** (contact the Tourist Information Centre at *Victoria Street, Windermere, Cumbria, tel. 05394 46499*). To the east there's **Yorkshire**, where the city of York is unique in England for still having its medieval walls intact (contact the Tourist Information Centre at *De Grey Rooms, Exhibition Square, York, tel 0904 624161*). But York, though lovely, is a big city. You could instead make a foray into Yorkshire's under-visited spectacular countryside, which features the dry-stone walls and bleakly attractive moors of **Brontë Land** (Haworth, near Bradford). In the village of Haworth itself, there's the **Brontë Parsonage Museum** (*tel. 0535 642323*), which illustrates the sad lives of the sisters who lived here, novelists Charlotte, Emily and Anne Brontë (in London, you can see a deep relief of the sisters in conversation at 32 Cornhill, EC3, in the bottom right-hand corner of the mahogany doors). The apothecary on Main Street promotes itself as the place where their brother Branwell bought the opium that contributed to his death. Shops and guesthouses all bear names like the Heathcliff Sweetshop, and Cathy B&B. Many of the country pubs have family rooms, and pub grub is generally a better option around Haworth than restaurants (take one of the CAMRA guides to pubs, pub food and/or real ale – see Recommended Books). Alternatively you could head off to Bradford, where there are some wonderful cheap, fun and authentic Asian restaurants. The nineteenth-century industrial mill town and city of Bradford also offers, at the *National Museum of Photography, Film and Television*, Britain's biggest cinema screen, IMAX, which makes the swooping plane or speeded-up growing flower so real that the audience gets motion sickness. Contact **Bradford Tourist Information Centre** at the **National Museum of Photography, Film and Television**, *Pictureville, Bradford BD1 1NQ, tel. 0274 753678*, or **Haworth Tourist Information Centre** at *2–4 West Lane, Haworth, BD22 8EF, tel. 0535 642329*.

CHILDREN

Chasing pigeons around Trafalgar Square; gobbling sweet gifts from occasional kindly newsagent owners; telling rib-ticklers to Buckingham Palace guards who are not allowed to laugh – and that's just some of the free-to-*cheap* thrills ...

Rain or shine, London is great for children, especially during the summer, Easter and Christmas holidays, when there's an abundance of special programmes. The British are not known, however, for liking children. Prepare for some primly disapproving looks.

You'll find while **getting around** on the Underground and buses that if you are pregnant people rarely stand – as a result of embarrassment rather than unkindness – but if you are struggling with infants and pushchairs you often can't fight off the helping hands. The old-style red double-decker buses are a good way of going places, seeing London and entertaining children all in one go (sit upstairs at the front), but they can be slow, especially during the rush hour, which is generally hellish, bus or Underground, and best avoided (Mon–Fri 8.30–9.30 a.m., 4.30–6.30 p.m.). Under-fives travel free on London Transport, and under-sixteens pay a child's fare until 10 p.m.; from then they must pay full. Children's travel cards are good value – around £1 for Central London's two zones for a day and around £6 for a week; fourteen- and fifteen-year-olds will need to provide a passport-sized photo.

Clean public **toilets** are hard to find, so use the bathrooms of department stores, museums, restaurants and cafés as you patronise them. Museums and department stores are likely to have decent baby-changing areas: use them to breastfeed if you are even a little cautious about breastfeeding in public. Women do occasionally breastfeed on buses or at tables in restaurants, but eyebrows go up, newspapers follow, and cutlery clatters in surprise and indignation. When **eating out** you'll find that a certain British prudery suffuses most cafés and restaurants, so even child-loving staff feel too inhibited to coochy-coo infants or chat with preteens. But if you avoid busy times – 1–2 p.m. for lunch and 7–9 p.m. for dinner – sometimes, cushions will be stacked up as highchairs, carrots puréed for toddlers, spices missed out for tender palates and the bill knocked down at the end.

When it comes to **entertainment** you'll find daytimes relatively unproblematic. In addition to specialist children's museums, innumerable easily accessible freebies include One O'Clock clubs in parks, spectacular adventure playgrounds, and public libraries children's sections.

Anyone with children and out working all day or searching for culture at night will be pleasantly surprised at the price of childcare in London. But if you want a family evening on the town, be warned: your discretion means nothing when taking your child to the movies if the film is rated 'X', '18' or (if your child is under twelve) '12', in which case your child is not, by law, allowed to see it; '**the pub**' is much more than a rather quaint British institution – it is *the* key social network, and children are generally barred. However, if you hear the common phrase 'Let's meet in a pub beforehand', don't despair. Know the rules: if your child is fourteen and older, she or he is, by law, allowed in a pub as long as he or she sticks to soft drinks; children of all ages are allowed in pubs that have 'family rooms' and into pub gardens. Two pubs where children are accepted are the **Prince Albert** (*11 Princess Road, NW1, tel. 071 722 1886*) near Regent's Park, and the **Spaniard's Inn** near Hampstead Heath (*Spaniard's Road, NW3, tel. 071 455 3276*). **The Surprise** (*16 Southville, SW8, tel. 071 622 4623*) in Larkhall Park, Stockwell, South London, is like a country pub in the middle of the city, and has a garden that's great for children in summer. To find out more, buy CAMRA's guide to *The Best Pubs for Families* (£4.95, Alma Books). Alternatively, suggest meeting in a café for coffee and a cake.

Resources

Information See the weekly ***Time Out*** magazine's 'Children' section for 'Activities and Fun' listings which are broken down into sports, exhibitions, eating out, workshops and classes. For similar information but spoken, not read, phone **Kidsline** (*071 222 8070, open term time Mon–Fri 4–6 p.m. and school holidays Mon–Fri 9 a.m.–4 p.m.*). Or phone **Circusline** (*0522 681591*) day or night for recorded information on circuses performing around Britain. And for information on children's playparks in your area – and all general child-related inquiries – telephone your local borough's **Town Hall**, which is required, under the Children Act, to provide information on activities for children.

Childcare One of London's largest and oldest babysitting services is **Childminders** (*9 Paddington Street, W1, tel. 071 935 2049 or 24 hours, 071 487 5040*). Childminders can provide 'absolutely dependable nurses, infant teachers, mothers and other suitably experienced staff' in most parts of London for a visitor's fee of £5 or £30 annual membership, then hourly rates between £2.50 and £4. The advertising section of *The Lady* magazine is generally thought reliable for babysitters. There is a crèche at the **Central YMCA** (*112 Great Russell Street, WC1, tel. 071 637 8131, admission £1*) on Tuesdays, Wednesdays and Thursdays for around £30 per annum, then £2.50 per session. For women who want to spend time in London without their children, **Pippa Poppins** (*430 Fulham Road, SW6, tel. 071 385 2458*) is a daytime and overnight nursery, or 'hotel for children', where you can leave your children for around £30 a night (charges higher at weekends).

Support If you are pregnant or have a young baby, you can contact the **National Childbirth Trust** (NCT) headquarters on *081 992 8637* and ask for your local branch, which can offer you practical information and advice and put you in touch with support groups and clinics.

Libraries Most libraries have at least a small children's section that you can use, although unless you can prove that you are resident in the area (for example, with a letter from a bank) you will not be able to take the books away. Ask about storytimes. One library with Wendy House, table and chairs with a teaset, and storytime on Tuesdays 10–11.30 a.m. is **Kensington and Chelsea Central Children's Library** (*Hornton Street, W8, tel. 071 937 2542*). Another well-stocked one is the jolly, cartoon-covered **Lewis Carroll Library** (*Copenhagen Street, N1, tel. 071 609 3051*).

Museums and Culture

Free sights and activities Entertaining children in London doesn't have to be expensive. Take them **kiteflying** on Primrose Hill (NW3) and then for stupendous sundaes at **Marine Ices**. Play round the **Statue of Peter Pan** in Hyde Park, then sail boats on Kensington Gardens' **Round Pond**. Watch the **changing of the guard** at Buckingham Palace, then take the bus to the **British Museum** (Bloomsbury, WC1), where children love the coins and **Egyptian mummies**. Stand for hours watching **jugglers and fire-eaters** on Covent Garden Piazza. There's no charge for the V&A Museum's famous collection of toys and toy theatres at the **Bethnal Green Museum of Childhood** (*Cambridge Heath Road, E2, Bethnal Green Underground, tel. 081 980 2415*), and the most you'll have to shell out if you want to give city-weary children a whiff of the country is a couple of sugar lumps for the ponies at the city farm **Spitalfields Farm Association,** where donkeys, sheep, bees and rabbits snuffle, buzz and bray round four acres of British Rail land and – if you book ahead – your child can ride on a horse (*Weaver Street, E1, Shoreditch or Bethnal Green Underground, tel. 071 247 8762, Tues-Sun 9 a.m.–5 p.m.*). Last and a long way away, but certainly not least, the **Horniman Museum** is celebrated for being child-friendly – the collection of ethnographic and natural history artefacts is supplemented by sound recordings and a children's club on Saturday morning in term time and every weekday morning as well during school holidays (*100 London Road, SE23, tel. 081 699 2339/1872, Forest Hill BR, open Mon–Sat 10.30 a.m.–5.50 p.m.; Sun 2–5.50 p.m.*).

Hands-on A perennial favourite, travelling by boat on the **Thames** or **Regent's Canal,** is free for under-fives (five-to-sixteens go half price) and a pleasurably traffic-free way of getting to Greenwich, Tower Pier or further to Kew, Richmond and Hampton Court (*contact the Riverboat Information Service on 071 730 4812 for trips down the Thames and London Waterbus Co. on 071 482 2550 if you want to explore the canal 'backwaters' of North London*). Indeed, the Regent's Canal Waterbus is the most exciting way to get to **London Zoo** (*Regent's Park, NW1, open Apr–Oct 9 a.m.–6 p.m. daily, Nov–Mar 10 a.m.–dusk; admission £5.30 adults, £4.40 students/OAPs, £3.30 under-16s, free under-4s*). The over-8,000-animal-strong Zoo boasts a penguin pool that architecture critics rave about, and activities to involve your children include, in summer, daily meet-the-animals sessions and camel rides, milking demonstrations if a cow is in milk in the Children's Zoo, weigh-in and bathtime for the elephants, and feeding time (check the Zoo's noticeboard for details). Picnic in the park afterwards to avoid exorbitant café prices.

Madame Tussaud's and the neighbouring **Planetarium** (see p.115) are favourites with older children, and those who didn't get nightmares from Tussaud's 'Chamber of Horrors' will enjoy the 'Medieval Horrors' at the **London Dungeon** (see p.198).

The **Imperial War Museum** (see p.190) and the floating naval museum that was once a World War II cruiser, **HMS Belfast** (*Morgan's Lane, Tooley Street, SE1, tel. 071 407 6434, admission £3.60 adults, £1.80 under-16s, free under-5s*) offer classic boys'-own entertainment.

'Launch Pad' at the **Science Museum** (see p.171), **MOMI** (Museum of the Moving Image, see p.196) and the **Natural History Museum** (see p.172) will have you fighting children to get a go on the hands-on exhibits; or for a quieter occupation go to the **Brass Rubbing Centre** in the crypt of St Martin-in-the-Fields (*Trafalgar*

Square, WC2, tel. 071 437 6023, open Mon–Sat 10 a.m.–6 p.m.; Sun noon–6 p.m., admission free then rubbings £1–£10 according to size).

Over fifty crazy and colourful coin-and-button-operated automata hand-made by contemporary craftworkers and inventors are crammed into **Cabaret Mechanical Theatre** (*33–34 The Market, Covent Garden, WC2, tel. 071 379 7961, admission £1.75, £1 under-16s/concessions, under-5s free*). Over in Bayswater, the **London Toy and Model Museum** houses an extensive collection of commercial European toys dating from 1850 (*21–23 Craven Hill, W2, tel. 071 262 9450, open Tues–Sat 10 a.m.–4.30 p.m.; Sun 11 a.m.–4.30 p.m., admission £3 adults, £1.50 under-16s, £2 concessions, under-4s free*); and back nearer the centre of town, behind Goodge Street you'll find a Victorian nursery, tin toys and old toys from all over the world in **Pollock's Toy Museum** (*1 Scala Street, W1, tel. 071 636 3452, open Mon–Sat 10 a.m.–5 p.m., admission £2 adults, 75 pence children*), which started in 1856 as a shop run by Benjamin Pollock, a cockney lad who'd had enough of the fur trade so took to selling theatrical prints (for example of Madam Vestris in breeches) and graduated to selling German toy theatres (which gave middle-class homes cachet) to customers including Charles Dickens and Ellen Terry. After Mr Pollock had died in 1937 and his shop was hit by a 'doodlebug' bomb during World War II, Marguerite Fawdry bought the ruins from Pollock's daughters and lovingly created the museum you can visit today.

Performances The **ICA** (see p.328) and the **Barbican** (see p.319) run special children's film clubs, and London has several lauded children's theatres, including: the only permanent puppet theatre in London, the 110-seater **Little Angel Marionette Theatre** (*14 Dagmar Passage, off Cross Street, N1, tel. 071 226 1787*); a purpose-built 300-seat theatre and adventure playground complex for under-twelves showing specially commissioned children's plays, the **Polka Children's Theatre** (*240 The Broadway, SW19, tel. 081 543 0363, wheelchair access, Wimbledon South Underground*); and, at over five decades old, London's oldest professional children's theatre, which stages, as well as commissioned plays, regular puppetry, magic and music, **Unicorn Theatre for Children** (*6 Great Newport Street, WC2, tel. 071 836 3334, Leicester Square Underground*). An adult theatre well known for its high-quality, highly enjoyable children's workshops is the **Tricycle Theatre** (*269 Kilburn High Road, NW6, tel. 071 328 1000 for info and 071 372 6611 for box office*).

Sports and Outdoors

Boating The lakes in Regent's Park and Hyde Park feature boats for hire. **Regent's Park Boating Lake** (*Maxwell's Boat House, NW1,* *tel. 071 486 4759, open Mar–Nov 9 a.m.–7 p.m. daily, charge £3.75 an hour rowing boat and £3.50 an hour pedal boat*); **the Serpentine** (*Maxwell's Boat House, Hyde Park, W2, tel. 071 262 3751, open summer 9 a.m.–7 p.m. daily; winter 9 a.m.–3.30 p.m. daily, charge £3.75 an hour rowing boat and £3.50 an hour pedal boat*). The **Shadwell Basin Youth Project** (*Shadwell Pierhead, Glamis Road, E1, tel. 071 481 4210*) offers canoeing, windsurfing and sailing to under-eighteens for around £1–£2 per session (parent's consent form, the ability to do a 50-metre swim and capsize a canoe are necessary).

Ice-Skating Skating the tiny outdoor Broadgate rink on a sunny winter day is amazing, but if you want classes or out-of-season ice-skating use the large, efficient Queensway rink: **Broadgate Ice Rink,** *Eldon Street, EC2, tel. 071 588 6565, Liverpool Street Underground, open 11 Nov–27 Mar, admission £3 adults, £1.50 under-twelves, phone for session times;* **Queens Ice Skating Club**, *17 Queensway, W2, tel. 071 229 0172, admission £3.50–£5 adults, £2.30–£5 under-fifteens, skate hire £1.20, phone for session times.*

Swimming There's no shortage of indoor swimming pools in London. Most have baby pools and baby changing areas, and if it's a 'leisure pool' you may be treated to wave machines and water chutes (look in the Yellow Pages under Leisure Centres), but on sunny days for health and recreation for you and your children, you can't beat outdoor swimming: if you go to Hampstead Heath you can take older children to the tree-surrounded, murky but refreshing **Mixed Bathing Pond** (*near Heath Road, free*), and if you're with younger children go to the slightly more sanitary red-brick evocative period tiled **Lido** (*entrance on Gordon House Road, NW5, free before 10 a.m.*). The **Highgate Ladies' Pond** on the Heath bars toddlers.

Running and Jumping Even small local parks usually have children's play areas, albeit just a rusty slide and a swing. Phone your borough's Town Hall to find out the location of your nearest rope-walk- and log-castle-filled **adventure playground**, or go to the ones in Holland Park and Battersea Park. Another worth targeting is **Coram Fields** (*93 Guilford Street, WC1, tel. 071 837 6138; no entry for adults unless accompanied by a child*). Coram Fields is an amazing find in the heart of London: seven acres of activities that are free or cheap to anyone under sixteen. A 'Pets' Corner', a sand-pit, separate play areas purpose-built for toddlers and older children are all enclosed from the busy streets of King's Cross and Holborn by plane trees and stretches of low, colonnaded Georgian buildings that once marked the grounds of Thomas Coram's Foundling

Hospital (see Holborn for the museum). The Under-5s Drop In Centre offers supervised indoor play at not more than £4 a day for non-Camden residents. Special early-evening activities include t'ai chi, arts and crafts, and photography. Children of all ages come from nearby housing association flats and council housing estates, and women working in Holborn drop their children here. Some mothers find the Fields a bit 'rough'; others welcome the boisterous inner-city atmosphere and good facilities.

Food for children

If your children want to try traditional English food, take them for decent sit-down **fish and chips** at Notting Hill's **Geales** (*2 Farmer Street, W8, tel. 071 727 7969*) or Bloomsbury's **North Sea Fish Restaurant** (*7–8 Leigh Street, W1, tel. 071 387 5892*), which are both rated for their battered fish but not for their rather pale, soggy chips (i.e. French fries) or their prices (£5–£6 for a piece of fish); both welcome babies and children and do reduced-price portions on request, and both are licensed. The traditional breakfast of bangers and beans, eggs and chips and bubble 'n squeak also goes down well with most children: go to Formica and strip-lighted cafés, known as 'greasy spoons', throughout London for all-day '**full English Breakfast**', amongst them the cheerfully prosaic **Phoenix** (*441 Coldharbour Lane, SW9* – tea and marmalade toast for under £1 and the full bacon-and-egg works for well under £5). A cheaper option that may tickle children's fancies is to buy polystyrene tubs of **cockles and whelks** from one of the mobile van seafood vendors, which are often stationed outside pubs. Well-behaved children will appreciate and remember for ever **afternoon tea and cucumber sandwiches** at genteel **Fortnum and Mason's** (*181 Piccadilly, W1*).

Department stores tend to have highchairs and do reasonable children's menus, for example **BHS** (British Home Stores) and **Selfridges** on *Oxford Street W1.* Italian, Greek and Indian restaurants tend to be a good bet as places that will give children a friendly welcome, and McDonald's is always a good standby for cheap-ish fast fuel in no-nonsense surroundings which often have special children's areas. It is generally best to go at quiet times with children to cafés and restaurants – say noon for lunch and 6–7 p.m. for dinner – when you'll be treated more civilly. See Eating and Drinking and bear in mind the following especially child-friendly eating places:

MARINE ICES
8 Haverstock Hill, NW3, tel. 071 485 3132, Chalk Farm Underground.

The fifteen types of ice cream, including peanut butter flavour, delight children, and the Knickerbocker Glories and Banana Splits absorb them for quite some time while you enjoy reading the papers with a strong coffee and a coppa ham roll after Regent's Park Zoo or kite-flying on Primrose Hill.

HOLLAND PARK CAFÉ

Holland Park, W8, tel. 071 602 2216, Holland Park Underground.

This café near the toddlers' One O'Clock club and preteens' Playpark serves coffee and cake snacks or meals from light soup to spaghetti Bolognese indoors or outdoors, all good quality and decent prices.

CAFÉ IN THE CRYPT

Crypt of St Martin-in-the-Fields, Duncannon Street, WC2, tel. 071 839 4342. Charing Cross Underground, highchairs and reduced price portions on request.

Another reasonably priced great lunch and snack spot, but this time in a prime Central London location with plenty of healthy choices such as celery soup and avocado and cream cheese puffs.

NEW WORLD

1 Gerrard Place, W1, tel. 071 734 0396, Leicester Square Underground, highchairs.

Of the innumerable good Chinatown restaurants, this one is great for authentic downtown Hong Kong atmosphere with decent prices for lunchtime dim sum and evening meals.

KHANS

13–15 Westbourne Grove, W2, tel. 071 727 5420, Bayswater Underground, highchairs.

With 300 seating capacity and a sky-high vaulted ceiling over the cavernous glittering ground-floor section, this is one of Britain's largest restaurants – loads of room for children to run around in, and a bustling happy atmosphere to make up for the sometimes curt service.

TGI FRIDAY'S

6, Bedford Street, WC2, tel. 071 379 0585, Charing Cross Underground, highchairs, children's menus.

One child-wearied uncle couldn't believe his good fortune when he stumbled into TGI's (short for Thank God It's Friday) – his niece got a free balloon and endless attention from an ebullient Australian waitress as well as a fair-priced burger meal which ended with a massive, deeply unhealthy and irresistible dessert from a menu the size of a book.

SMOLLENSKY'S BALLOON

1 Dover Street, W1, tel. 071 491 1199, Green Park Underground, highchairs, children's menus.

Another winner. As if it's not enough for children to be able to choose through the week from a well-priced good-quality children's menu that features Kid's Koktails so that they don't feel left out while you relax with an impeccably made and highly alcoholic cocktail ... on Saturday and Sunday afternoons there are Punch and Judy shows, magicians and clowns.

CHICAGO PIZZA PIE FACTORY

17 Hanover Square, W1, tel. 071 629 2669, Oxford Circus Underground, highchairs, children's menu.

Of course there are pizzas and burgers and artefacts from and about Chicago all over the walls, but there are also crayons and colouring books to keep your children quiet while you enjoy the early-evening cheap drinks 'happy hour'. An alternative restaurant in the same 'My Kind of Town' group that also has children's menus, highchairs and staff briefed to be child-friendly and, in addition, a magician every Sunday and a model train suspended from the ceiling is the **Chicago Meatpackers** (*96 Charing Cross Road, WC2, tel. 071 379 3277, Tottenham Court Road Underground*).

Shops

If you're in need of fair-priced basic clothes, go to branches of **Gap** or **Marks and Spencer,** and for exclusive English designer wear go to **Liberty's** (see Shops and Markets). Branches of **Mothercare** cover pretty well all your children's clothes and equipment needs from dummies (pacifiers) to cots (cribs); get healthier high Chairs from the Back Shop (see Shops and Markets). For toys and books which 'make learning fun!' go to any branch of the **Early Learning Centre.**

Hamleys

188 Regent Street, W1, tel. 071 734 3161, baby changing facilities.

Five floors of 'the most famous toy shop in the world' whizz with radio-controlled cars and planes, and ecstatic children skidding from magic tricks to model kits and dolls and teddy bears.

Harrods

Knightsbridge, SW1, tel. 071 730 1234.

The fourth-floor toy department is extremely well-respected and much enjoyed by children for its resident magician who is, of course, briefed to sell the store's magic tricks, so expect to come away with a bag full of purchases as well as a happy youngster.

Puffin Bookshop

1 The Market, Covent Garden, WC2, tel. 071 379 6465.

A vast array of titles from children's publishers including Puffin in a pleasant bookshop conveniently near the jugglers and buskers who make Covent Garden a great place to keep children entertained for free.

BUSINESSWOMEN

Many find that London, one of the world's business capitals, is appallingly ill-equipped – photocopy shops shut at 5.30 p.m.; dry cleaners won't deliver – but if you are prepared for the problems and slowed pace, then you can enjoy genteel business meetings and generally civilised working hours that leave you time to take in a tourist attraction at lunchtime or some top-rate theatre and classical concerts in the evening.

While you're packing for your business trip to London, consider some common complaints and adjust the contents of your suitcase accordingly. Some say that even the houses, hotels and office buildings with central heating are too cold in winter, and the scarcity of adequate air-conditioning makes them airless in summer. Thermal underwear allows you to wear a blouse and light jacket from November to April; stockings instead of tights help see you through occasional hot spells July to September. Many businesswomen coming from urban America and Italy are amazed at Britons' dowdy business attire. Although red suits are acceptable, colours are mostly low-key, so to be on the safe side combine navy, grey, dun or Jaeger-style tweed patterned suits with white shirts, black or dark brown translucent stockings/tights and dark court shoes with small heels. Trousers are never worn unless there is no chance at all that you will see a client, and skirts are kept knee-length. Hair doesn't generally go beyond shoulder length (if yours is long you could tie it up sedately) and accessories (scarves, jewellery, etc.) are kept to a minimum. If you wear make-up, go for the *au naturel* look, and don't feel obliged to paint your nails. In the evening, many of the most high-powered British women dress down to go to the theatre (casual slacks and a good-quality sweater), and for dinner it's 'not done' to bare your shoulders (if you're wearing a revealing cocktail dress, add a small jacket). If your itinerary includes an event such as Ascot, Glyndebourne or a society ball and you want to travel light, you could hire a dress on arrival (see Businesswomen's Directory).

If you are in a position to choose your accommodation, bear some pros and cons in mind: large, international hotels can feel lonely and impersonal but they are likely to have, as well as the usual formal restaurant, an informal grill where a woman alone will feel comfortable, and large hotels will sort out everything you can't fit into a frantic schedule, such as dry-cleaning and booking theatre tickets; B&Bs are refreshingly intimate, and individual apartments are more private again, but for both these options you must realise that London does not rate well as a service or twenty-four-hour city, so be prepared to spend your Saturday mornings doing errands, such as picking up dry-cleaning, having your shoes re-heeled, having a haircut, and so on. Remember when planning your dates that business can be slow in August, and London grinds to a halt during the two weeks over Christmas and New Year.

Once in London, if you find you're short of, say, a skirt or jacket, suitable shops for replacements or additions to your wardrobe include Marks and Spencer's for basics like underwear and shirts, Jaeger and Simpson's for traditional suits, Harvey Nichols and Harrods for a mixture of traditional and a wide range of designer wear, and Browns in South Molton Street for top designer wear with quietly attentive service combined with an expensive shopping experience. Read the daily *Financial Times* for news on City and international money markets, the *London Evening Standard* for local news and society gossip, and read monthly women's magazines including *Vanity Fair, Marie Claire, Cosmopolitan, Harpers and Queen* and *Elle* to keep up to date with trends and concerns shared by your British colleagues. In *How to Survive from Nine to Five* (Mandarin), Jilly Cooper offers some not entirely serious advice, such as 'Never drink black coffee at lunch; it will keep you awake in the afternoon' and, she says, 'Meetings ... are rather like cocktail parties. You don't want to go but you're cross not to be asked.'

The classic British reserve often shows itself as deference, but don't equate deference with inefficiency. Once you're accustomed to what you might at first consider excessive politeness, you'll find that members of the British business community can be just as hard-nosed as their counterparts in America, Japan and Germany.

See Eating and Drinking for selective restaurant listings and advice, and keep a copy of the dauntingly comprehensive, annually updated *Time Out Guide to Eating and Drinking in London* (£6.99) in your desk if you want to be *au fait* with currently 'in' and 'out' restaurants, and here are a few suggestions to suit specific situations: famous advertising executives' breakfast-meeting venues include the Connaught and Claridges; for elegant City lunches and snacks try Swithins or Le Poulbot; if you're sick of huge business meals and don't want to eat in your hotel, expense account at the Saint Quentin Grill or the ground-floor Bibendum Oyster Bar; and finally, a perennially safe restaurant choice for a formal dinner is Le Gavroche (see Eating and Drinking for addresses).

Business Directory

Couriers

One of the biggest and best courier firms is **A–Z** (*tel. 071 254 2000, fax 071 254 7965*). A–Z offers twenty-four-hour service with a large fleet of vans, cars and bikes; deliveries cost £4 within the eleven central zones (i.e. the City to the West End); individual customers are welcome, or you can open an account over the phone. For same-day parcel posting nationally and internationally, use the Post Office's **Datapost** (*Datapost Service Centre, 4th Floor, 20–23 Greville Street, EC1N 8SS, freephone Datapost 0800 884422, fax 071 250 2938*); parcels accepted at any main post office.

Dress Hire

You've been invited to a high-powered society event; it seems crazy to buy an outfit you may never wear again; so hire something: **Puttin' on the Glitz** claims London's 'largest selection of ball gowns, cocktail, party dresses and accessories' and has two branches (*Hay's Galleria, Low Level Walkway, London Bridge, Tooley Street, SE1, tel. 071 403 8107; Galen Place, Pied Bull Court, off Bury Place, Holborn, WC1, tel. 071 405 5067*). For special-occasion designer suits try **Andrea Galer** (*4 England's Lane, Belsize Park, NW3, tel. 071 483 3242*). If required, they'll give advice on what's appropriate.

Health and Beauty

If you're after a good haircut, **Vidal Sassoon** is reliable and the Sloane Street branch is renowned for its colourist (*130 Sloane Street, SW1, tel. 071 730 7288*); for highlights, everyone in the know – including, it's said, Princess Diana – goes to **Daniel Galvin** (*42–46 George Street, W1, tel. 071 486 8601*). For a total make-over including well-styled hair, join high-powered executive colleagues at the Harrods or Harvey Nichols beauty salons (Harrods' **Essenelle,** *87 Brompton Road, SW3, tel. 071 584 8881/581 2021* or **Glenby** at Harvey Nichols, *Knightsbridge, SW1, tel. 071 235 5000*). If you're finding the hotel pillow's a nightmare or your office chair's making your spine crooked, go to the **Back Shop**, which is listed in the Shopping section along with relaxation options including the **Sanctuary** and the **Porchester** steam baths. For a one- or two-day beauty, health and fitness binge alongside some of London's top executives, go to the health farm that's lauded but feels rather like an airport complex, **Champneys** (*Chesham Road, Wiggington, Tring, Hertfordshire, HP23 6HY, tel. 0442 873155*). Or, for three or four days at a welcoming and wonder-working health farm, go to Forest Mere (see p.331).

Information

Twenty-eight **Financial Times Citylines** give constantly updated twenty-four-hour recorded information and news on the financial markets (*tel. 0898 123456, and for a list of all lines, 0898 123099*). For a wide range of business reference works, newspaper cuttings and Extel cards (that is, financial data on 700 British and foreign businesses) go to the **City Business Library** (*106 Fenchurch Street, EC3, tel. 071 638 8215, open Mon–Fri 9.30 a.m.–5.30 p.m.*). And for general commercial information and comprehensive coverage of export and international trade, use the **Chamber of Commerce and Industry Reference Library** (*69 Cannon Street, EC4, tel. 071 248 4444, fax 071 489 0391, open Mon–Fri 9.15 a.m.–5.15 p.m.*).

NETWORKING

Film, engineering, banking and many other industries have their own women's networking organisations, and you can find yours through the annually updated *Everywoman's Directory* (£5.95), or you can contact the **UK Federation of Business and Professional Women** (*21 Ansdell Street, Kensington, W8 5BN, tel. 071 938 1729*), which lobbies for all working women on issues such as tax, pensions and childcare, and has clubs nationwide where you can network and meet women aged twenty to seventy from all sorts of levels from a wide variety of jobs – from fire chiefs to secretaries to women in the House of Lords (£28 annual membership for information on the Federation and events held; £50–£80 annual club membership).

SECRETARIAL SERVICES

A wide range of requests, from hiring a temp to having a professional document produced and translated, can be met by **Angela Pike Associates** (*Business Centre, Mezzanine Floor, Le Meridien Hotel, 21 Piccadilly, W1V 9PF, tel. 071 434 4425, Mon–Fri 8 a.m.–8 p.m.; other hours call 081 840 7000 and ask for 485 8693*). If you don't need translation or printing services but you want basic typing/word processing, message-taking and a 'prestige address', use **Typing Overload?** (*170 Sloane Street, SW1, tel. 071 235 6855*).

STATIONERS

Rymans is a decent chain you'll find everywhere (look in the Yellow Pages under Office Stationery, for your local).

THANKYOUS

If you want to send flowers, **Interflora** is a reliable chain (check in the Yellow Pages under Florists), all big department stores offer a delivery service, and if you really want to impress, contact one of these three high-class institutions: wedding and bouquet specialists **Moyses Stevens** (*6 Brouton Street, W1, tel. 071 493 8171, fax 071 493 0618*); **Longmans in the City** (*59–60 Holborn Viaduct, EC1, tel. 071 248 2828, fax 071 236 7495*); or **Pulbrook and Gould** (*127 Sloane Street, SW1, tel. 071 730 0030*). **Liberty's** and the **V&A** shop are good for intimate gifts, and for food go to **Harrods Food Hall, Fortnum and Mason's** and **Harvey Nichols'** fifth floor.

BACKGROUND

RECOMMENDED BOOKS

Books set in London

Martin Amis, *London Fields* (Penguin). Love it or hate it, you won't remain indifferent to this epic rampage through Amis's London, which is a Notting Hill mix of pub-pool-room low life and upper-class high life.

Elizabeth Bowen, *The Death of the Heart* (Penguin) and *The Heat of the Day* (Penguin). In *The Death of the Heart* sixteen-year-old orphan Portia is thrown into a grand coterie of 1930s London society. *The Heat of the Day* is set in the London of World War II. Elizabeth Bowen is thought by some to rival Virginia Woolf for literary greatness.

Anita Brookner: Novels including *A Start in Life, A Friend from England, Latecomers* and *Brief Lives* (Penguin) are set at least largely in London, where Anita Brookner lives and works. 'Anita Brookner has proved herself so fine a novelist that she deserves to be judged always in a class of her own,' wrote Selina Hastings in the *Daily Telegraph*.

Angela Carter, *The Magic Toyshop* (Virago) and *Wise Children* (Vintage). *The Magic Toyshop* is an at once fantastical and grimly real rites-of-passage story of orphaned Melanie, who is sent to live in South London with her aggressive uncle. *Wise Children* is also based in South London, but this time the twin protagonists are in their seventies, looking back on their eccentrically engaging lives treading the boards and gracing the Hollywood screens for some of the first silent movies.

Charles Dickens: Charles Dickens's output of page-turner novels set in nineteenth-century London was prodigious. The following are especially avocative: *Bleak House, David Copperfield, Great Expectations, Dombey and Son, Our Mutual Friend* and *Little Dorrit* (Penguin).

Margaret Drabble, *The Needle's Eye* (Penguin). Middle-class marital trouble. 'Nothing she has written in the past quite prepared me for the depth and richness of *The Needle's Eye*,' said American novelist Joyce Carol Oates.

Esther Freud, *Peerless Flats* (Hamish Hamilton). In the second novel by Esther Freud (who was picked out by Granta as one of Britain's twenty best young novelists), sixteen-year-old Lisa comes to 1970s London and tries to emulate her older sister Ruby, who wears platforms and likes to overdose on drugs.

Ellen Galford, *Moll Cutpurse* (Virago). Through Moll's lifelong friend and lover, Bridget, the apothecary, Ellen Galford's novel tells the 'true' swashbuckling history of London's seventeenth-century pickpocket and upholder of women's rights, Moll Cutpurse.

Doris Lessing, *London Observed* (HarperCollins). Eighteen pen-portraits of Londoners and the city that Zimbabwean-raised novelist Doris Lessing at first found a nightmare and then in 1957: 'one evening, walking across the park, the light welded buildings, trees and scarlet buses into something familiar and beautiful, and I knew myself to be at home.'

Iris Murdoch, *Under the Net* (Penguin). In a plot of tightly controlled chaos, the engaging and only occasionally sober rake hack writer-narrator, Jake Donaghue, rampages through 1950s London in search of a nail-biting firework-maker turned film magnate, and an elusive chanteuse.

Radclyffe Hall, *The Well of Loneliness* (Virago). Celebrated now as the first explicitly lesbian novel, *The Well of Loneliness* was put on trial for obscenity in 1928 and banned, despite declarations of its literary merits by writers such as Virginia Woolf and E.M. Forster. Sir Philip and Lady Gordon long for a male heir, so they name their only daughter Stephen; she grows up in breeches and later falls passionately in love – with another woman. Scenes of Great Malvern, London and Paris.

Michèle Roberts, *The Visitation* (Women's Press). Set in North London, this novel is an exploration of sexuality that charts the growing-up of rebel suburbanite Helen and her relationships with members of her family, and with Beth.

Sheba Collective, *Serious Pleasure: Lesbian Erotic Stories and Poetry* and *More Serious Pleasure* (Sheba). A handful of these stories are set in London; many of the writers are London-based, other contributors include Tyneside's Fiona Cooper and New York's Jewelle Gomez.

Alice Thomas Ellis, *Pillars of Gold* (Penguin). A Camden Town-set comedy of errors in which a bloodstained corpse is pulled out of the canal, yet domestic dramas take priority over informing the police. Wit and an obsession with disaster from the 'doyenne of urbane English comedy' (*TLS*).

Rebecca West, *The Fountain Overflows* (Virago). Family love and feuds and the risk of social disgrace in Edwardian South London. This is West's most acclaimed novel.

Jeanette Winterson, *Sexing the Cherry* (Vintage). Big lesbian following for the writer of this novel, in which the boy Jordan and his massive adoptive mother, the Dog Woman, live on the slimy banks of the River Thames in seventeenth-century London.

Virginia Woolf, *Mrs Dalloway* (Penguin). *Mrs Dalloway* is the best-known of the novels Virginia Woolf set in London. The novel charts one summer's day, at the end of the First World War, in the life of Clarissa Dalloway, the wife of an MP, and Septimus Warren Smith, who is going mad with shell-shock. *The Years* (Penguin) is a satirical analysis of the patriarchal structures of Victorian London. It follows the fortunes of the middle-class Pargiter family.

Poetry

ed. Gerard Benson, Judith Chernaik, Cicely Herbert, *Poems on the Underground* (Cassell). Poems that you see on posters on London Underground trains are gathered together in this collection. International poets featured range from Anon. (1600) to Emily Dickinson (1830–86) to Elizabeth Jennings (b.1926).

Wendy Cope, *Making Cocoa for Kingsley Amis* and *Serious Concerns* (Faber). London landscapes and concerns feature in the poems of Wendy Cope, perhaps Britain's best-known woman poet. There's Brockwell Park (where mankind is 'a wind-tossed ice-cream wrapper'), bottle banks, Tesco's own-brand Beaujolais, the *Evening Standard* horoscope and the literary Casanova of Tulse Hill.

Edith Sitwell, *Collected Poems* (Sinclair-Stevenson). Dame Edith, whose greatest pleasures were listening to music and silence, gained notoriety for her poetry during the 1920s and 1930s, and also numerous honorary degrees from universities.

ed. Hermione Lee, *Stevie Smith: A Selection* (Faber). This selection includes poems from *Not Waving But Drowning*

(1957), perhaps Stevie Smith's best-known collection of poems. It also includes extracts from her novels. The London Smith lived and worked in features in her writing.

Travel/Specific Guides

Beryl Cook's *London* (Penguin). London painted the way Beryl Cook sees it. Her images have been described in *The Sunday Times* as 'witty, ebullient, fleshy evocations of humanity', and art critic Edward Lucie-Smith loves her work 'because it makes me laugh out loud'.

Christopher Hibbert, *The London Encyclopedia* (Papermac). Over a thousand pages are devoted to covering practically every nook and cranny of London and describing those that haven't survived into the 1990s. A range of other entries are on subjects such as 'Riots', 'Population' and the 'Bloomsbury Group'. 'If I had my way this book would be in every cab in London,' wrote the reviewer for the *London Cabbie News* when this encyclopaedia was published.

Gay Eurocity Guide, *The London Scene* (Gay Men's Press). This is written for gay men, but there is a section for lesbians.

Roger Protz, *The Best Pubs in London* (Alma Books). It's true that some pubs can be hangouts of macho beer-swillers, but then there's the other kind of pub: in winter a real fire roars in the grate and hearty shepherd's pie is on the menu; in summer there's a sunny beer garden where children can play. More often than not, this kind of pub sells real ale. Protz describes this book as a celebration of the London pub, and of real ale, which anyone used to mass-produced canned beers will find an entirely different drinking experience. Other Campaign for Real Ale (CAMRA) guides include *The Good Beer Guide, The Best Pubs for Families* and *Good Pub Food*.

Jenny Uglow, *The International Dictionary of Women's Biography* (Macmillan). 'A hoard of heroines,' says the *Times Literary Supplement* of this evocative, entertaining source book of women through history in London and all over the world.

Lindsy Van Gelder and Pamela Robin Brandt, *Are You Two ... Together? A Gay and Lesbian Guide to Europe* (Virago). This is a witty, anecdotal guide by two women who love travelling and want others to enjoy it too. There's a chapter on London, and lots of general advice that's come from personal experience.

Christopher Hibbert, *London: the Biography of a City* (Penguin). Hibbert's biography brings London alive from its Roman beginnings to the twentieth century, with surprising historical facts plus amusing and shocking anecdotes.

The Pelican History of England Series (Penguin). Nine books by different historians cover the history of England from Roman Britain to the Twentieth Century in a worthy and comprehensive, if sometimes dully plodding, series.

Feminism

Olive Banks, *The Biographical Dictionary of British Feminists. Vol. Two: A Supplement, 1900–45* (Harvester Wheatsheaf). Sadly, the fascinating Volume One is out of print and Volume Three has yet to be compiled, but still – this valuable book contains commendably full entries on feminists active during the comparatively quiet period between the fierce fight for suffrage and the emergence of the Women's Liberation Movement in the 1960s and 1970s. Too expensive for a rush buy – this is a marvellous reference book.

ed. **Veronica Beechey and Elizabeth Whitelegg,** *Women in Britain Today* (Open University Press). This book collects essays that analyse women's situation in Britain today, concentrating on four main issues: the family, employment, education and health.

Anna Coote and Beatrix Campbell, *Sweet Freedom: The Struggle for Women's Liberation* (Blackwell). This account of the phase of the women's movement that was a product of the 1960s and peaked in the 1970s has been updated – new material has been added on the Black women's movement. Greenham Common and the peace movement, Women Against Pit Closures and other groups and developments through the 1980s.

ed. **Moira Ferguson,** *First Feminists: British Women Writers 1578–1799* (Indiana University Press). Ferguson has gathered an almost daunting number of essays and articles by sixteenth-to-eighteenth-century British women whose ideas have contributed to the advancement of feminist thought, including Aphra Behn and Mary Wollstonecraft.

ed. **Terry Lovell**, *British Feminist Thought, A Reader* (Blackwell). Read this collection of essays to get an overview of recent British feminist thought from the influence of Marxism to psychoanalysis and featuring historically ground-breaking works by, amongst others, Germaine Greer and Juliet Mitchell.

Mary Wollstonecraft, *A Vindication of the Rights of Woman* (Penguin). Celebrated as Britain's first feminist, eighteenth-century Mary Wollstonecraft was inspired by the start of the French Revolution to put her thoughts on women's position in society in writing.

Children's

Frances Hodgson Burnett, *The Little Princess* (Puffin). This Puffin Classic opens with the loving, imaginative young heroine, Lavinia, in a cab in the yellow fog of Victorian London. She's just arrived from India to go to school, and she appears to have everything – then poverty strikes.

Pat and Laurence Hutchins, *Follow That Bus* (Red Fox). Pre-school children will enjoy this story about a Hampstead school by an author-illustrator couple who live in Flask Walk, Hampstead. A school trip turns into a cops, robbers and class chase when the teacher accidentally swaps her holdall with the bag of some thieves.

E. Nesbit, *The Phoenix and the Carpet* (Puffin). Life in Camden Town just isn't the same after a second-hand carpet arrives in the nursery. An egg rolls out and proceeds to hatch into a phoenix, and a vain one at that – an event that turns out to be only the start of a series of exotic, exciting adventures. Another nineteenth-century classic for young teenage readers.

Beatrix Potter, *The Complete Tales of Beatrix Potter* (Warne). Here, gathered in one volume, are the famous stories of animals and costumes that were inspired by pets in the nursery menagerie of Potter's Kensington home, and by trips to the South Kensington museums, from the tailor of Gloucester to Mrs Tiggywinkle to Jeremy Fisher.

Jill Paton Walsh, *Fireweed* (Puffin). Bill and Julie are runaways, trying to survive during the Blitz in London. A gripping wartime adventure for teenagers.

Nikolaus Pevsner and Bridget Cherry, *London, Volumes One, Two and Three* (Penguin). These books are revered by everyone from architecture scholars to lay readers who love London's heritage. 'The series will be a precious gift to posterity,' wrote A.J.P. Taylor in the *Observer*. They're hefty tomes, in-depth reference books that are to be pored over at leisure, not crammed in your bag while you zip round London. Volume One covers Central London, Volume Two South London and Volume Three North-West London. Volume Four, East London, is due out soon.

Edward Jones and Christopher Woodward, *A Guide to the Architecture of London* (Weidenfeld & Nicolson). Concise, pithy entries on most of the buildings in London you'll want to know about.

INDEX